Beacham's Encyclopedia of Social Change

AMERICA *in the* TWENTIETH CENTURY

Beacham's Encyclopedia of Social Change

America in the Twentieth Century

Edited by Veryan B. Khan

Volume 1: Pages 1–498

Published by
The Beacham Group LLC

Beacham's Encyclopedia of Social Change: America in the Twentieth Century

Veryan B. Khan, Editor
Walton Beacham, Project Director
Deborah Beacham, Production Manager

Distributed worldwide exclusively by The Gale Group

Book Design by Jill Dible

Library of Congress Cataloging-in-Publication Data

Beacham's encyclopedia of social change: America in the twentieth century / edited by Veryan B. Khan.
p. cm.
Includes bibliographical references and index.
Summary: Traces the evolution of social ideas and values in the United States during the twentieth century, using such indicators as advertising, crime and justice, family life, fashion, music, race and class, sex and gender, and work.
ISBN 0-933833-62-8 (set: alk. paper)
ISBN 0-933833-64-4 (v. 1: ak. Paper)
ISBN 0-933833-65-2 (v. 2: alk. paper)
ISBN 0-933833-66-0 (v. 3: alk. paper)
ISBN 0-933833-67-9 (v. 4: alk. paper)

1. United States—Social conditions—20th century—Encyclopedias, Juvenile. [1. United States—Social conditions—20th century—Encyclopedias.] I. Title: Encyclopedia of social change. II. Khan, Veryan B., 1970-

HN59.2 .B43 2001
306'.0973Bdc21 2001043141

Printed in the United States of America
10 9 8 7 6 5 4 3 2 1

Comments and Suggestions are Welcome

The editors invite comments and suggestions from users of *Beacham's Encyclopedia of Social Change: America in the Twentieth Century*. You may contact us by mail at: The Beacham Group LLC, P. O. Box 1810, Nokomis, FL 34274-1810; by telephone at (941) 480-9644 or (800) 466-9644; or by facsimile at (941) 485-5322. Our email address is beachamgroup@aol.com

Photo Acknowledgments

These photos are on the covers of all four volumes of *Beacham's Encyclopedia of Social Change: America in the Twentieth Century*: *U.S.S. Shaw*, Pearl Harbor, Hawaii, December 7, 1941, photograph. National Archives and Records Administration; Dr. Martin Luther King, photograph. The Library of Congress; Children in a parade of suffragettes, May 1913, Long Island, New York, photograph. The Library of Congress, George Grantham Bain Collection; Jim Thorpe, photograph. National Archives and Records Administration; Anti-Vietnam War protest at the Pentagon, Washington, D.C., photograph. National Archives and Records Administration; Dust bowl farm, parts of wagon wheels visible above sand, photograph. National Archives and Records Administration; President Franklin Delano Roosevelt shaking hands with Chief Noal Bad Wound, circa 1936, photograph. Hulton/Archive. Reproduced by permission; Laptop computer, Copyright © 2000 PhotoDisc, Inc. All rights reserved; Hindenberg flying over city, photograph. Archive Photos/Lambert. Reproduced by permission; Dorothy Dandridge, photograph. AP/Wide World Photos. Reproduced by permission; The Beatles wave to a crowd at an airport as they arrive in the U.S. for concerts and television appearances, photograph. Hulton/Archive. Reproduced by permission; Ulysses spacecraft in orbit, illustration. National Aeronautics and Space Administration (NASA). Reproduced by permission. All photos throughout the text are reproduced by permission from Hulton Archive/Getty Images.

Contents

It is a time for reflection as America steps into the twenty-first century, a century which in some ways resembles the transition from the Dark Ages to the Renaissance, a century of excitement and turmoil, of hope and resignation, in which perceptions about humankind's significance was constantly changing through booms, depressions, and wars.

Perhaps as never before, the delineation between two centuries can be seen through the terrorists' attacks on the World Trade Center and the Pentagon on September 11, 2001. Rarely has a single event established such a clear differentiation between centuries; ironically, the Spanish-American War (1898-1902), which marked the end of U.S. territorial imperialism, ushered in a new century that would demand a completely new role for American leadership, just as the terrorists' attacks on September 11 a century later forces new directions for the United States for the twenty-first century in which world interests take precedence over the ambitions of individual countries. As the United States achieved a position of world dominance at the end of the twentieth century, it renewed some of the same social arguments that prevailed during the period of American imperialism a hundred years before.

The evolution of the century provides fascinating insight into the spirit, values, and ingenuity of the American people. From our roots as outcasts and nonconformists, we developed instincts for survival, respect for social order, and a passion for independence and personal freedom. From the bounty of our land we learned the potential of natural resources and the possibility of abusing them. And from our naiveté we blundered into wars that secured our independence, turned our nation against itself, liberated Europe from tyranny, forced generations to reject each other's values, and established the United States as the most powerful nation.

America is the story of slaves, immigrants, Native Americans, and a European ancestry that created paradox and energy. America in the twentieth century has not been so much a "melting pot" as a nuclear reactor. To understand and appreciate the road from Kitty Hawk to Cape Canaveral, from Jamestown to Montgomery, from barley soup to Lean Cuisine®, *Beacham's Encyclopedia of Social Change: America in the Twentieth Century* traces American history through forty-one key indicators of social change. Each of the chapters—"Advertising and Consumerism" to "Work and the Workplace"—explains the progress of American culture each step of the way. Through our journey we see how Americans made their own history.

In a traditional sense, this encyclopedia is a history book with the usual timelines and statistical charts, but we prefer to think of it as a story book in which ordinary people struggle, suffer, strive toward great accomplishment, and change. What does food or fashion, family life or morality tell us about American values? Plenty. In 1909, as the suffragette movement gained strength, designers abandoned the corset and created the freedom of the Gibson Girl look; in the 1920s, when the proliferation of automobiles provided young people with privacy to pursue their own lives, women wore scandalous clothing, only to retreat to practical clothing during the Depression and World War II years. In the prim and proper 50s women wore tailored clothes and pillbox hats, and in their rebellion against their prim and proper mothers, the 70s women burned their bras and adorned baggy, tie-dyed pants. The fitness generation of the 80s wore her Calvins and in the 90s her spandex running shorts. The times they were a-changing, and what people wore tells us something about their times.

Rather than approaching history from a universal perspective, we look at it piece-by-piece, decade-by-decade, from a human perspective. We attempt to place readers *in* the historical moment, not above it looking down. How did American soldiers during World War I spend their countless miserable hours in the trenches? How did World War II women on the home front contribute to the war? What was life like without men? How did African Americans contribute to the war effort? Prisoners? Native Americans? You'll experience immigration through Mary Hagen's first Christmas after leaving Ellis Island twelve hours earlier; you'll discover that Thomas Edison had a dispute with an employee that forever changed the use of electricity; you'll learn that the bikini is named from an atoll in the Pacific Ocean that the Allies used for testing the atomic bomb during World War II. The fascinating facts, the photos, the timelines, and the sidebars help the reader experience life during a different time.

~

How to Use This Encyclopedia • We think of this encyclopedia as comparative history. Each chapter presents a separate key indicator of social change, but they are all interlocked and together complete a picture puzzle of American culture. Fashion alone reflects something about society; when compared to the same timeframes for other key indicators, we begin to see the whole of American society.

To facilitate studying American social history through comparison, we present each key indicator in small units with associated dates. Using the margin date to generally locate a timeframe and the subhead dates to narrow the time period, researchers can compare what was happening across key indicators, and thus see the influence of one on the other. The timeline at the beginning of each key indicator is divided into two parts: the top section list events related to the key indicator while "Milestones" lists other interesting events during the same time period.

Other study features include a composite timeline, which is useful in seeing connections across key indicators, and for generating ideas for research projects. Most of the references in the composite timeline are discussed in the encyclopedia, so that research on any one of them can begin here, then continue through the bibliographies and Internet resources. The comprehensive index provides the gateway for researchers.

The story behind many key indicators begins before the twentieth century opens, and our authors provide the background as far back as necessary to understand the twentieth century. Business and labor practices, for example, established their roots in the 1800s, while modern warfare begins with the Civil War, and modern economy begins with the development of the corporation and industrialization after the Civil War. Other key indicators—modern farming, health care, leisure, and retirement, for example—did not begin until the turn of the century, and thus our story begins there.

Social history is different from the history of great moments. Famous people or intensive events tell only one side of a story—an extreme side. Most people did not fly solo across the Atlantic Ocean or create great wealth by mining gold in California. Most of us who have flown the Atlantic were taking vacations to Europe; most of the miners who rushed to California panned a lifetime without finding an ounce of gold. To identify with these people is to be aware of who Americans are. To appreciate the plights of peoples past is a signpost as to where we might be going. Customs, traditions and behaviors have evolved dramatically in the hundred years of this past century. Following these changes is exciting, fascinating, and fun.

We think that the key indicators provide a personal approach to learning about history and culture. Whether or not readers are concerned about the larger historical picture, they are certainly interested in specific topics: how did Barbie contribute to the women's liberation movement (Sex and Gender); who did the Ku Klux Klan persecute before it turned its wrath on African Americans (Crime and Justice); and most important—a subject that touches on every aspect of American culture—what part have immigrants played in our evolving country (every article).

Usually, social changes occur over a slow, evolutionary process in which history, years later, reveals the gradual development and discernible changes between past and present. However, with a single event, much like the Japanese attack on Pearl Harbor, the twenty-first century has already become unique; we know, without the benefit of history, that America is a different society. Modern-day terrorism, domestic and foreign, began its infancy in the late twentieth century through horrific attacks on American soil and against civilians; the utter destruction of the twin towers in New York City will lead to many changes during the opening years of the twentieth-first century, and the clues to where America will refocus society for a strangely different century are embedded in the key indicators in this encyclopedia.

Veryan B. Khan

Kenneth Adderley
Upper Iowa University

James F. Adomanis
Maryland Center for the Study of History

Cara Anzilotti
Loyola Marymount University

Brian Black
Pennsylvania State University, Altoona

Benita Blessing
Fellow, Institute of European History, Mainz

Stephen Burwood
SUNY, Geneseo

Peter Cole
Western Illinois University

Joel S. Franks
San Jose State University

Richard A. Garcia
California State University, Hayward

Jennifer Hamil-Luker
University of North Carolina, Chapel Hill

R. Steven Jones
Southwestern Adventist University
Keene, Texas

Veryan B. Khan

Judy Kutulas
St. Olaf College

R. A. Lawson
Vanderbilt University
Joan D. Laxson

Christina Lindholm
Virginia Commonwealth University

Mark Malvasi
Randolph-Macon College

Greg Moore
Notre Dame College, South Euclid, Ohio

Marie Marmo Mullaney
Caldwell College, New Jersey

Don Muhm

Michael V. Namorato
University of Mississippi

Karen S. Oakes

Paul Ortiz
University of California, Santa Cruz

Diane N. Palmer

Judith Reynolds

Elizabeth D. Schafer

Peter N. Stearns
George Mason University

Kathleen A. Tobin

Peter Uhlenberg
University of North Carolina, Chapel Hill

Christopher Waldrep
San Francisco State University

James D. Watkinson
Randolph-Macon College

The publisher wishes to thank the contributors for their outstanding contribution to this project.

Walton Beacham

Advertising and Consumerism

~

(circa 1945) Model Marilyn Crane poses with Minute Maid's 'Mechanical Man' made from aluminum cans of orange juice and Hi-C drinks.

TIMELINE

1850-1889 ~ Mass Production Becomes Reality

Mass production of boots and shoes (1850s) / Proliferation of sewing machines (1860s) / First full service advertising agency (1869) / First full page advertisement, placed by Wanamaker in Philadelphia (1879) / Coca Cola created (1886) / Modern electric motor opens way for consumer appliances (1888) / *Printer's Ink* is first advertising trade journal (1888)

MILESTONES: Joseph Lister creates antiseptics for use in surgery in England (1867) • Wyoming is the first state to grant women the vote (1869) • Comstock Law prohibits possessing any obscene book, pamphlet, paper, writing, advertisement, circular, print, picture or drawing of an immoral nature (1873) • The weekly *Independent* is the most influential religious paper in the country, with over 6,000 clergymen on its mailing list (1880)

1890-1909 ~ The Beginning of Mass Consumerism

Illuminated and talking advertisements (1890s-1910s) / National Consumer League founded (1892) / First commercial automobile produced (1892) / Free rural postal delivery proliferates mail order catalogs (1896) / Color photo reproduction provides cheap, eye-catching images for ads (1900) / Hoover vacuum cleaner mass marketed (1908) / Ford introduces the first inexpensive car, the Model T (1908)

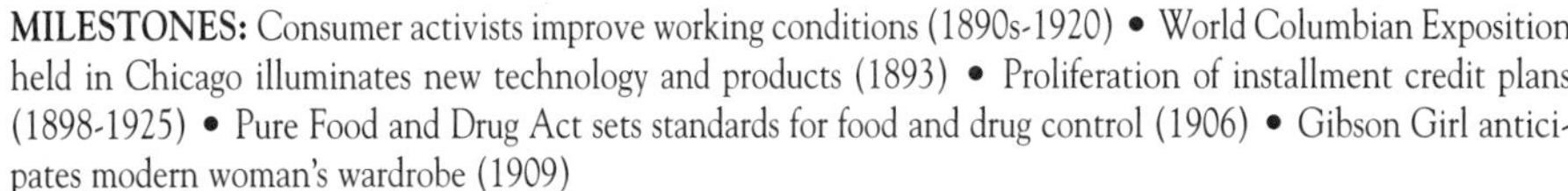

MILESTONES: Consumer activists improve working conditions (1890s-1920) • World Columbian Exposition held in Chicago illuminates new technology and products (1893) • Proliferation of installment credit plans (1898-1925) • Pure Food and Drug Act sets standards for food and drug control (1906) • Gibson Girl anticipates modern woman's wardrobe (1909)

1910-1919 ~ Affordable Products

First publicly advertised maternity wear (1911) / F.W. Woolworth has 600 stores (1912) / Ford perfects assembly line production (1913) / Life Savers first marketed (1913) / First mass advertising campaign to win support for war (1917)

MILESTONES: First voice communication by radio (1914) • Landmark film, *The Birth of a Nation*, about the Civil War, portrays the Ku Klux Klan in a heroic role (1915) • German-language press has a circulation of 1 million, the Polish and Yiddish press each have 1 million subscribers, the Italian American press has 700,000, and the Swedish American press has 500,000 (1914-1920) • 17,000 weeklies, semi-weeklies and tri-weeklies are published (1915)

1920-1929 ~ Brand Names, Drive-ins, and Radio

RCA formed (1920) / Commercial sponsors for radio programs (1920s) / Golden age of brand names (1920s-1930s) / Consumer Research and Consumer Cooperative founded to educate consumers about products (1920s-1930s) / First radio commercials (1922) / Mail order catalogues and magazines bring fashion awareness to every household (1925-1929) / NBC creates first national radio system (1926) / Total advertising budget for the major newspapers rises to $860,000,000 (1929)

MILESTONES: Half of American homes have electricity (1920) • Pig Stand in Dallas is the first drive-in restaurant (1921) • Henry R. Luce and Briton Hadden found *Time* magazine (1923) • George Eastman invents the Kodak color film process (1928) • Coca-Cola is sold in sixty-six countries (1929)

1930-1945 ~ Hard Times and War

The satirical magazine *Ballyhoo,* aimed at advertisers, is launched with enormous success (1931) / Listerine advertising creates fear (don't lose your job) because of bad breath (1932) / Proliferation of African American newspapers (1930s) / World War II restricts production of consumer goods (1941-1945) / Radio is used to sell war bonds (1942-1944) / *Seventeen Magazine* founded (1944) / G.I. Bill provides housing and consumer credit (1944-1950s)

MILESTONES: Experimental broadcasting of television (1929-1935) • Under pressure, the movie industry enacts the Production Code, addressing crime, sex, vulgarity, obscenity, profanity, costumes, dancing and religion (1930) • Proliferation of radio soap operas, detective shows and daytime programming (1930s) • Studies relate fluoride and reduction of tooth decay (1933) • *Reader's Digest* has a circulation of over 1,000,000 readers (1935) • First commercial televisions displayed at New York World's Fair (1939)

1946-1959 ~ Boom Years for Consumerism

First television sets go on sale (1946) / Baby boomers create enormous demand for products (1950s) / Marlboro Man ad introduced to enormous success (1954) / Bank of America introduces credit cards (1959)

MILESTONES: Christian Dior becomes the first designer to license his name for ready-to-wear clothing (1948) • Housing starts reach 1.7 million (1950) • First color television broadcast (1953) • First fully enclosed shopping center opens in Minnesota (1956)

1960-1969 ~ Reforms to Protect Consumers

Hazardous Substances Labeling Act requires warnings on dangerous household products (1960) / Sam Walton establishes the first Wal-Mart (1962) / Consumer activism influences Civil Rights success (1964-1975) / Federal Trade Commission requires cancer warning labels on cigarettes (1964) / Child Protection Act bans toys containing hazardous substances (1966) / Truth in Packaging Act responds to growing public dissatisfaction with deceptive advertising (1966) / Mastercard introduced (1966) / Concerned parents form Action for Children's Television to force networks to provide more programming than advertising (1968)

MILESTONES: Bra burning protests symbolize women's liberation and have tremendous impact on the fit of clothing and the undergarment industry (1963) • *Ms.* magazine reflects a revolution in women's thinking (1960s) • *Woman's Day* adds articles on health and money management to help working women (1966) • Film industry drops the Hays Code, lifting its ban on political and moral content in movies (1968)

1970-2000 ~ Mass Media and Consumerism

Magazine advertisers begin profiling and segmenting readers (1970s) / Consumer Product Safety Commission provides a continuous review of consumer goods for risks (1972) / Supreme Court ruling protects advertising as free speech (1976) / Commercial advertising appears on religious television networks (1980s) / Channel One, targeted at children, inaugurated (1989) / Home shopping network and ATM machines encourage spontaneous buying (1990s) / E-commerce companies vie for Internet consumers (1998-2000)

MILESTONES: Fair Packaging and Labeling Act sets standards for labeling additives to food (1975) •MTV begins (1981) •Supply side economics is designed to increase consumption (1982-1988) •Fashion industry creates Supermodels to conceal the fact that fashion is in a slump (1985-1987) •Trendy teen glossies, *Teen Vogue, Cosmogirl, Teen People, Teen* and *Elle Girl,* publish frank articles about self-empowerment, racism, eating disorders, rape, sexual diseases, pregnancy and depression (1995-2000) •1.3 million households apply for personal bankruptcy (1998)

Introduction

Any understanding of the United States in the twentieth century would be incomplete without taking into account the revolutionary impact of advertising and consumerism. Making America a modern country was a process that required the achievement of mass production to be accompanied by the equally important necessity of mass consumption. America's greatness during the century was founded squarely on its economic power. That economic power was largely founded on the establishment of a huge domestic market to absorb the ever-increasing production of its workplaces. To encourage Americans to consume took billions of dollars in advertising and required a modification of the national ideology. By the end of the century, the United States had become a consumer society like no other in history and consumerism became its popular culture.

~

"In the nature of things, luxuries and the comforts of life belong to the leisure class."

Thorstein Veblen,
The Theory of the Leisure Class. (1899)

"One would not expect that the preoccupations of a poverty-ridden world would be relevant in one where the ordinary individual has access to amenities—foods, entertainment, personal transportation, and plumbing—in which not even the rich rejoiced a century ago. So great has been the change that many of the desires of the individual are no longer even evident to him. They become so only as they are synthesized, elaborated, and nurtured by advertising and salesmanship, and these in turn, have become our most important and talented professions. Few people at the beginning of the nineteenth century needed an adman to tell them what they wanted."

John Kenneth Galbraith,
The Affluent Society. (1958)

"For good or ill, the consumerist society created meaning for Americans far more effectively than politics and civil society."

Gary Cross, *An All Consuming Century: Why Commercialism Won in Modern America.* (2000)

"Commercial speech—advertising—makes up most of what we share as a culture. No one is happy about this, not even the people who make it. They call it clutter, which is rather like a doctor complaining about a frantic patient after he has shot him full of adrenaline. The rest of us call the current glut of advertising by worse names. But, call it what you will, language about products and services has pretty much replaced language about all other subjects."

James B. Twitchell,
Twenty Ads That Shook The World. (2000)

~

Consumerism

The Beginnings of Mass Consumption • 1870s – 1930 ~ As the capitalist and industrial economy grew toward the end of the nineteenth century, extended periods of severe economic downturn accompanied an overall expansion of the economy. The beginnings of mass consumption lay in the realization by some manufacturers and economic analysts that the explanation for the devastating depression of 1873 lay not in faults related to production but to serious problems related to enough people's ability to buy the products offered for sale. The solution, they speculated, lay in manufacturing more goods, cutting their prices to make them more affordable to more people, and therefore to make it possible for consumers to buy everything produced. By this means, control over the production and selling of goods throughout the economy could be achieved and with it steady and ever-expanding affluence for all. Achieving such a state of affairs was much easier said than done. By 1930, strategies to achieve mass consumption had succeeded only partially despite the self-promoting and wishful thinking of advertisers and others.

The Growth of Mass Consumption ~ Mass consumption was incomplete but growing by 1930. Starting with America's middle class of professionals, mass consumption spread slowly into the upper ranks of its working families.

Tables 1 and 2 below show the spread of mass consumption as revealed both overall and in various categories. It should be noted that the tremendous leap forward in consumption between 1914 and 1919 was in large part due to the economic stimulus provided by World War I.

Further measures of the growing consumer market in America can be seen by examining Table 2. Total consumer spending increased by over 50 percent in the ten years between 1909 and 1919. More spectacular are those that document spending on medical care and insurance, items that poorer people simply went without, and on cars, a tribute to the mass production methods that made car ownership affordable by millions of Americans especially after 1914.

Developing the Habit of Mass Consumption ~ Consumption had been a feature of American, European and world cultures for thousands of years. Urban people bought food to survive.

Table 1: Personal Consumption Expenditures by Type of Product, 1909-1919
(rounded to the nearest $100m)

Year	Total Consumption Expenditures	Food & Non-Alcoholic beverages	Alcoholic Beverages	Tobacco Products	Clothing & Related Products Purchases
1909	$28.8bn	$7.4bn	$1.8bn	$0.6bn	$3.7bn
1914	$33.4bn	$9.0bn	$2.0bn	$0.7bn	$4.1bn
1919	$60.6bn	$18.6bn	$2.0bn	$1.4bn	$8.4bn

SOURCE: Ben J. Wattenberg, *The Statistical History of the United States From Colonial Times to the Present.* (New York: Basic Books, 1976)

Increasingly, over the course of the nineteenth century tasks done previously in the home or by the family became commodified, that is they became part of the commercial world. In the 1850s, for example, in the United States, mass production of boots and shoes meant that Americans no longer had to either fashion their own or buy from skilled craftsmen locally. By the 1860s and 1870s, hand sewing at home was made a great deal easier with the invention and marketing of the sewing machine. The late nineteenth century witnessed a huge leap forward, not only in the range of mass production industries, but in the mass production of items useful for tasks previously taking great time at home or requiring great skill or endurance. The advantages in time and sometimes money over traditionally achieved tasks transformed life for middle class Americans by 1910.

Companies spent enormous resources trying to get people to buy their products. No one was free from the pressures to consume. Even the most isolated rural dwellers had access to the consumer market. Mail-Order catalogs from Sears and a host of other companies became widely available after 1896 with the introduction of Rural Free Delivery by the Post Office. Deliveries of their goods became easier with the introduction of parcel post in 1913. In urban areas, the rise of the department stores provided what Susan Porter Benson called "palaces of consumption." From their beginnings in the 1850s by 1890 they had become the leading force in American retailing. They did not just sell goods. As Benson noted, "These giant emporiums told their patrons in myriad ways that shopping was not just purchasing but an agreeable and leisurely diversion in luxurious surroundings, laced with exciting events to relieve daily tedium and newly linked to traditional celebrations such as Christmas." They appealed primarily to women with disposable income, people who could be persuaded to buy a pair of gloves on a whim or an extra pair of expensive underwear.

While working class Americans were left out of the business strategies of department stores and could feel very unwelcome if they had the temerity to wander into one, chain variety stores opened in small towns and urban neighborhoods. F.W. Woolworth, for example, boasted 600 stores by 1912 selling cheap-

Table 2: Personal Consumption Expenditures by Type of Product, 1909-1919

(rounded to the nearest $100m)

Year	Total Consumption Expenditures	Rent or Imputed Rent	Medical Care	Insurance	New Cars & Net Purchases of Used Cars (Private)	Public Transportation
1909	$28.8bn	$5.6bn	$0.8bn	$0.2bn	$0.2bn	$0.8bn
1914	$33.4bn	$6.2bn	$0.9bn	$0.2bn	$0.4bn	$1.0bn
1919	$60.6bn	$8.1bn	$2.0bn	$0.4bn	$1.3bn	$1.4bn

SOURCE: Ben J. Wattenberg, *The Statistical History of the United States From Colonial Times to the Present.* (New York: Basic Books, 1976)

A montage showing four types of equipment used in laundries at the turn of the century. Clockwise from top, left : a mangle, a wringer, an iron and a steamer.

er versions of main street department store merchandise. Department stores (and variety chain stores) were among the first businesses to involve themselves in systematic sales, rapid cycling of goods through the store, developing the art of display and constant advertising. They transformed the advertising industry with the introduction of drawings, photographs and humorous copy. The first full-page advertisement was placed by John Wanamaker in 1879.

GOLDEN AGE OF BRAND NAMES ~ Besides advertising, the period before the Great Depression of the 1930s was, as Richard Tedlow dubbed it, the "Golden Age" of national brand names. First came the elimination of bulk selling by some companies and its replacement by packaging of products. Campbell and Heinz offered pre-cooked soups and vegetables suitable for a single family meal. C.W. Post and W.K. Kellogg provided boxed cereals to replace heavy meat and egg breakfasts. Colgate and Gillette sold toothpaste and safety razors. Life Savers were introduced in 1913, sold especially in saloons and tobacco shops. As technological and organizational improvements influenced business practice just a few manufacturers came to dominate in every industry. Trademarks were invented to make products instantly recognizable and to encourage brand name loyalty. The stereotyped black cook, Aunt Jemima, sold pancake mix, just as the smiling face of the old white man in the old-fashioned hat sold Quaker Oats.

Perhaps the best example of the power of the name brand is found with Coca-Cola. Invented in 1886 in Atlanta, the product became a national drink of choice during the 1890s. Its appeal rested on massive advertising, wide distribution, a simple but striking trademark label and bottle shape and a mystique about its secret ingredient. Aggressive legal battles against trademark infringements during the 1910s and a commitment to producing a uniform product made Coca-Cola the unchallenged industry leader until the advent of Pepsi-Cola in the late 1930s. By 1929, Coca-Cola was sold in 66 countries and had come to symbolize American consumerism.

The pressure on people to buy all these products was obviously limited by consumer disposable income. If people could not afford it they could not buy it. The barrier presented to companies was overcome by the extension of consumer credit in new ways. Between 1898 and 1916, sales of cars, pianos and other big-ticket items nearly doubled because of credit. By 1924, almost 75 percent of new cars were bought on the installment plan whereby customers paid a certain amount up front and the balance each month until the purchase was complete but in the meantime had use of the item desired. In 1925, 70 percent of furniture, 75 percent of radios, 80 percent of phonographs, and 90 percent of pianos were bought by installment.

Consumerism for Social Progress

~ The term "consumerism" as we understand it at the beginning of the twenty-first century does not correspond to the way it was used at the beginning of the twentieth. Today, when we speak of consumerism we usually refer to a culture of consumption, one that many observers argue IS American culture. In the years after 1900, the term referred to a movement of citizens to curb the worst aspects of capitalism by utilizing the purchasing power of the citizen to obtain better treatment for company employees, better quality products, social justice and sometimes better prices. Examples of consumerism in this sense are given below in describing labor boycotts, the union label movement and "Don't Buy Where You Can't Work" campaigns. Among the most striking instances of consumerism was the National Consumer League, an organization influential until after World War I.

The NCL was founded in 1892. It attempted to bring the power of purchasers to bear to get seats for saleswomen in department stores, promote clean, well-ventilated lunchrooms and to improve conditions for women working in sweatshops. Led mainly by middle class women, it produced its White List of stores that treated employees well and issued labels to be attached to items made under sanitary and healthful conditions. Middle Class women's clubs joined the NCL in supporting consumer protection measures such as the licensing of food vendors and inspection of dairies. Under the leadership of Florence Kelley, the NCL agitated for legislation to regulate department store conditions and prescribe sanitary and safety measures on the shop floor. More broadly, it advocated for child labor protection, elimination of potential health hazards and women's suffrage. Perhaps its greatest triumph came in 1908 when the U.S. Supreme Court upheld an Oregon law restricting the hours that could be worked by women.

Mass Consumption and the Middle Class ~ By the end of the nineteenth century, the middle class was in transition. For the most part, it still consisted of the professional classes and business owners. Increasingly, they were joined by a new group of professional managers, engineers and accountants. White collar workers like shop clerks, office workers, telephone operators and teachers were uncertain members of the middle class, far beneath the others in terms of income and status and, in numerous cases, earning less than skilled workers. For those who could afford it, life improved dramatically between 1870 and 1910.

The invention of electricity and more importantly the modern electric motor in 1888 not only transformed transportation. Middle class homes enjoyed the benefits of the electric fan after 1890, electric irons and kettles after 1893. Electric toasters, hotplates and waffle irons came onto the market after 1900 while the Hoover vacuum cleaner hit the markets in 1908. Once homes were re-wired for electricity and the two-prong plug adopted as standard in 1917, such inventions became common. By 1920, about half of all American homes had electricity.

A trend toward the increasing purchase of goods outside the home and away from home production became a stampede as a national market emerged and virtually everything was capable of mass production. In its wake, regionalism and the rural/urban divide were severely weakened. The middle class was able to take advantage of the deflationary trend in prices beginning in the last third of the nineteenth century, the most significant consumer benefit of mass production. Spurred by national advertising through the mass circulation magazines, products in people's homes became standardized, an American domestic aesthetic emerged, and with it, style and fashion for all. By the 1890s, women across America could wear Invigorator corsets, Pompeian massage cream to make them presentable to potential mothers-in-law or wear the latest "New York-style" dresses. Men could wear the same derby hat in Denver, Colorado as in Savannah, Georgia, courtesy of the Sears Roebuck mail order catalog or use Williams shaving soap and a Gillette safety razor that "assists in establishing amicable relations with the world at the beginning of the day."

Testimony to the spread of mass consumption and mass advertising for America's middle class before 1920 was that even houses could be purchased by mail order. Beginning in the 1870s, complete floor plans were made available through mass circulation magazines like *The Ladies Home Journal*. By the turn of the century, companies like the Aladdin Company of Bay City, Michigan, and Sears Roebuck of Chicago shipped prefabricated parts by railroad for assembly by local workmen at the house-owners site.

Consumer Influence on Working Conditions ~ Working people responded to mass production and attempted to influence patterns of consumption. In the late nineteenth century, labor unions fought hard to reduce hours of work in the Eight Hour movement. Indeed, hours of work did decline overall, leaving working people more leisure time. In 1860 the average workweek was sixty-six hours. By 1920 it had been reduced to 47. Workers recognized that

(circa 1900) View of the intersection of Broadway and 42nd Streets, New York City, where billboards advertise theater performances of the day. Pedestrians and horse-drawn carriages use the sidewalks and cobblestone roads.

their purchasing power could supplement action on the job in their increasingly uneven relations with employers. Unions added to their arsenal of resistance the weapons of the boycott, the union label, and demanded a "living wage."

Consumer boycotts of "unfair" employers became powerful levers short of striking to bring employers to the bargaining table, and appeals to union members in all unions as well as to non-union members of the community proved quite effective. Union label campaigns similarly proved effective in some industries and areas. The union label was affixed to all goods produced by union labor. Goods produced in shops without unions did not have such a label. This allowed customers to choose a brand made by companies that dealt fairly with labor unions. In this way, firms that paid fair wages and with improved working conditions could be rewarded and uncooperative firms punished. As one union organization in Philadelphia put it, " You are your brother's keeper to the extent of your purchasing power. Every cent you spend for bread, for instance, can become a potential demand for better conditions for one of the most oppressed class of workers—the bakers." Beyond a political use of consumer power, workers were also concerned with the notion of a "living wage." They wanted to be able to feed, clothe and house their families adequately, and have something left over.

LEISURE ACTIVITIES ~ Mass consumption touched workers' lives most directly in the increased leisure time they had toward the end of the nineteenth century. Baseball and football were professionalized. They attracted a large, mainly male, working class audience. Amusement parks sprung up around most major cities and some less so. Show business developed as workers used their extra leisure time to attend circuses, the theatre for popular drama, vaudeville and burlesque shows, and nickelodeons or movie theatres. By 1910 in New York City alone there were over 600 nickelodeons grossing more than $6 million each year catering to 1.5 million patrons. In his study of early Hollywood films, Steven Ross calculated that 72 percent of the early film audiences were blue-collar workers, 25 percent were clerical workers, and only 3 percent belonged to the "leisure class." Newspapers and magazines similarly developed much larger readerships. The famous "yellow journalism," sensationalist reporting to increase sales was, in part, an attempt by newspaper owners like Joseph Pulitzer and William Randolph Hearst to attract working class readers.

For working women, participation in a consumer society manifested itself in the reading of dime novels, fashion, and especially movie attendance. By 1910, women made up 40 percent of working class movie audiences. Their influence was reflected in the content of films and in long-running movie serials like *Whatever Happened To Mary?* and *The Hazards of Helen*, both of which featured as the central character a young working woman. Fashion gleaned from the movies and by watching richer women became an important part of women's lives. For working women, "Keeping up with the Joneses," an expression first coined in 1910, meant buying cloth and other items from pushcart salesmen or small, local stores and adapting or making up fashionable clothing for themselves.

Mass Consumption and the Americanizing of Immigrants ~ Mass consumption affected American society in numerous ways, one of which was to create an ideal for living. The pressures to participate in the ideal did a great deal, along with more organized efforts before and during World War I, to Americanize the nation's immigrants. Many of the working women were of Jewish or Italian origin working in New York's garment industries. Consumer ideals led to conflict between generations as first-generation immigrants battled with their children over values and proper behavior.

Most historians have assumed that mass culture did its job in standardizing the nation's inhabitants, blurring the divisions between the classes and between immigrants and the native-

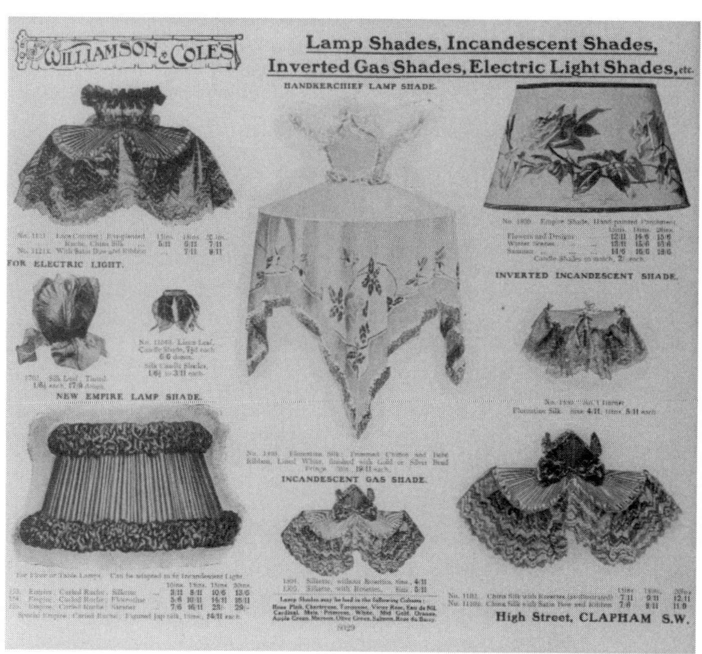

(circa 1906) Soft Furnishings. Spurred by national advertising through the mass circulation magazines, products in people's homes became standardized, an American domestic aesthetic emerged, and with it, style and fashion for all. Seen here, an advertisement for lampshades of various designs from Williamson & Coles as advertised in Home Beautiful *magazine.*

born. However, by 1930 as Lizabeth Cohen has pointed out, the integration of ethnic communities into the consumer mainstream was far from complete. The phonograph was thought to make available to all Americans of whatever background a national taste in music. Cohen points out that in Chicago, the 1910s and 1920s were the heyday of ethnic, foreign language and "race" records. In other words, immigrants and African Americans used the new technology to reinforce rather than eliminate their cultural identities. Ethnic Americans also went in very large numbers to the movies. Rather than attend the magnificent and palatial theatres downtown, they tended to go to movie theatres in their own parts of town. There, local owners, often immigrants themselves, selected movie programs to suit their audiences and reinforced rather than eliminated ethnic identities (as evidenced by local Chicago movie house segregation of blacks and Mexicans to the balcony section). Cultural loyalty similarly kept ethnic consumers from patronizing chain stores. Local ethnic businesses offered the chance to converse in a native tongue, catch up on gossip, not have to repeat oneself to be understood and buy on credit when needed. Cohen concluded that ethnic Americans were consumers by the 1920s but they consumed on their own terms outside the mainstream.

1900-1917 • MASS CONSUMPTION AND RACE ~ For African-Americans before World War I, faced with segregation, disfranchisement and violence, open and implied, the spread of mass consumption offered a space for self-expression and an alternative to open political dissent. As Grace Elizabeth Hale noted, despite the fact that Southern whites wanted as little to do with blacks as possible, blacks did have something they wanted, a few dollars to spend. Complete segregation, especially in the South's stores was to some extent undermined by the fact that individual white businessmen simply could not afford to deny selling items considered "too fine" for black folks. Black purchasing power was potent enough in some places to gain better treatment. In Cleveland, Mississippi, for example, blacks preferred to shop at Chinese-owned markets rather than be treated poorly at the grocery-chain store. In larger cities the reverse often proved true. As one Richmond, Virginia, black professional put it, "Of course none of them want to give you the same service they give white people, but competition for Negro trade is so keen that every store has to make some pretense of fair play." As historians like Hale have put it, however restricted, the contradiction between making money and enforcing racial taboos allowed black Americans to create a site of resistance and a space for individual expression.

Mass consumption on the part of northern African Americans led to quite the opposite effect to that intended, according to Lizabeth Cohen. She argued that "by participating in mainstream commercial life—which black Chicagoans did more than their ethnic co-workers—blacks came to feel more independent and influential as a race, not more integrated into white middle-class society." Mass culture, she concluded offered blacks the ingredients to construct a new, urban black culture. Black Chicagoans patronized chain stores and bought brand-name goods because they felt they were non-discriminatory. By 1930, in Chicago and New York, black consumer boycotts were used to force chain stores to hire African Americans under the slogan "Don't Buy Where You Can't Work."

THE IMPORTANCE OF THE AUTOMOBILE ~ Many historians of consumerism stress how mass consumption created profound changes in the ways Americans viewed themselves and the world around them, that it wrought new values. No example is more illustrative than the effects of the mass ownership of the automobile.

The first American automobile was built in 1892. It was a handcrafted luxury item and continued to be so into the new century. In 1905, while the mean annual income was $450, a new car cost between $600 and $7,500. Cheaper cars had a life expectancy of less than 10,000 miles. Henry Ford changed all that. In 1908, he produced his first automobile to appeal to the solidly middle class at $950. Determined to make his vehicles available to all, Ford introduced assembly-line production in 1913. Standardized models produced quickly, identically and only in black gradually allowed for the price to be reduced to $290 by 1924. In 19 years of production, the Model-T Ford sold to 15.5 million customers. Ford's methods were adopted and adapted by other auto manufacturers. In 1910 only 180,000 cars were produced in the United States. By 1924, over 4 million were rolled out. In 1927, according to Gary Cross, the United States accounted for 85 percent of the world's production of automobiles and by 1929, one in every five Americans owned a car (compared to one in every 43 Britons and one in every 335 Italians).

The solid, dependable and dull Model-T was overwhelmed in the 1920s by Ford rival General Motors. Market share reflected the new individuality available to customers offered by GM. In 1921 Ford sold 55 percent of all cars. By 1927, it sold only 25 percent. Not only were automobile models modified each year, but Ford's competitors offered a full range of models and colors, thus stimulating claims to social status among customers.

The social effects of the automobile were captured well by Robert and Helen Lynd in their class sociological study of a medium-sized Midwestern city in the 1920s they called *Middletown*. Comparing the city and its inhabitants to the situation in 1890, the Lynds reported the complete elimination of the use of horses for transportation. By the end of 1923, there were two cars for every three families in the city. So important had ownership of a car become that the Lynds reported many families mortgaged their house to acquire one. 75 to 90 percent of cars purchased locally were bought on time payment and "a working man earning $35.00 a week frequently plans to use one week's pay each month as payment for his car." The Lynds reported the impact of automobiles on union and other group activities, on Church attendance (all down), on family life, on sexual mores, on leisure activities and on the creation of something new to Middletown, the vacation.

Pleasures were privatized by the automobile. Royce Hailey's Pig Stand in Dallas became the nation's first drive-in restaurant in 1921. Kansas City hosted the first suburban shopping center in 1923. By the mid-1920s New York City department stores built branches in the suburbs to accommodate motorists who had trouble finding city center parking and motels greeted the weary traveler at the end of a tiring day's drive with a room overlooking the parking lot.

ADVERTISING

THE PROFESSIONALIZATION OF ADVERTISING ~ Advertising was one of a number of ways devised to increase consumption of goods produced in America's workplaces. Its rapid expansion can be gauged by considering how much was spent on it. Before the turn of the twentieth century and well after, the bulk of advertising was carried in low-cost, mass-subscription magazines. Between 1890 and 1905 the subscriptions of all magazines rose from 18 million to 64 million. Advertisers used magazines so much to sell their wares that one advertising executive admitted in 1907, "a magazine is simply a device to induce people to read advertising." According to historian Gary Cross, by 1931 advertising constituted between 50 and 65 percent of the content of all general and women's magazines. Advertising revenues for the magazines rose from $542 million in 1900 to $2.94 billion in 1920 to $3.43 billion in 1930.

Between 1870 and 1917, mass consumption was enjoyed by the solidly middle class. America's skilled, semi-skilled and unskilled workers, including most of America's rural folk were largely untouched. For them to enjoy the fruits of mass consumption they needed steady employment without periodic bouts of unemployment, wages that would give them disposable income beyond what was necessary for survival, and the desire for goods they may not previously have considered as necessary. In these years, few workers were able to achieve such preconditions for mass consumption. Until the 1930s, advertisers rarely appealed directly to workers, blacks or ethnic minorities but only to the richer half or two-thirds of the population. If they sold to those groups it was on the basis of the desire of the "outsider" to emulate the outlook and life styles of the "insider."

Between the 1880s and the 1920s, advertising developed into a recognizably modern form. While advertisers had been a feature of the American business world since at least the 1840s theirs was not a respectable profession. Best summed up by P.T. Barnum's famous exclamation "There's a sucker born every minute!" advertisers were regarded as charlatans and tricksters, if not worse. Attempts to professionalize advertising enjoyed some success only in the 1870s and 1880s. George P. Rowell and F.W. Ayer pioneered the effort in 1869 when Rowell began *Rowell's American Newspaper Directory* and Ayer started one of the first full service advertising agencies, N.W. Ayer & Son.

For over half a century Rowell's advertising trade journal, *Printer's Ink*, founded in 1888, was the most influential in the country. Through it he sought to regularize relations between advertisers and publishers, to mediate between advertisers and potential buyers, and to offer advice to advertisers. As Jackson Lears notes "Rowell played a major role in formulating the chief tasks of the modern advertising agency: to serve the interests of its corporate clients by identifying their products with rationality and progress, and to cleanse advertising of its associations with peddlers and other marginal operators." N.W. Ayer & Son conducted the first marketing survey in 1879. In the 1880s and 1890s it increasingly dealt with national corporations rather than local retailers. In 1900, the Copy Department was established to make advertising copy, as opposed to simply placing copy from the client with magazines and other outlets. At a testimonial dinner in Ayer's honor in 1919, former President William Howard Taft, shortly to be nominated Chief Justice of the U.S. Supreme Court summed up the man's career: "We are honoring a man who has made advertising a science, who has made it useful, and who has robbed it of many of its evil tendencies...we owe a debt of gratitude to Mr. Ayer, for having rendered a form of publicity so useful and elevating, which might have been vicious and deplorable." Rowell and Ayer led the way though even by 1900 there were still plenty of advertisers who were less scrupulous.

Developing the "Science" of Advertising ~ By the beginning of the twentieth century, advertisers realized that simply placing information before the public was not enough to sell products. The "science" of advertising took into account what P.T. Barnum had known all along, that people's desires and prejudices could be successfully appealed to in order to shift merchandise. *Printers' Ink* recognized as early as 1898 that women and children sold goods. In discussing the use of photographs in ads it noted; "An advertisement that contains the photograph of a beautiful woman is certain to be attractive, and consequently its success is guaranteed.... But though the photographs of pretty women are only supposed to be attractive to the male sex, the picture of a baby or "cute" child will immediately captivate ninety-nine percent of humanity.... Whatever he or she is supposed to advertise, we feel kindly toward, even if it is only for introducing us to the baby...."

By the early twentieth century, advertisers had come to realize that visual imagery was often more powerful than the written word. Color, form and light were harnessed to induce purchasing. Between 1890 and 1915, posters, signboards, billboards and electrical images spread out across the country. After 1895, colored posters were used for theatres, amusement parks and dry goods stores. In 1913, when the young English poet Rupert Brooke toured the Wanamaker's department store in Philadelphia, he was astonished to learn that leading post-impressionist painters from Paris had been designing store posters for years.

Advertising posters were placed on street transportation, at railroad stations and from the very first in the newly opened subways. Writing of what he saw on the subway, cultural critic Joseph Huneker wrote in 1914, "It was a poster that sent me to Coney Island... I had sworn never to tread [there] again... But that poster! Ah! If these advertising men only knew how their signs and symbols arouse human passions they would be more prudent in giving artists full swing with their suggestion brushes..." In 1901, Emily Fogg-Mead could sum up the evolving science of advertising when she argued, "The successful advertisement is obtrusive. It continually forces itself upon the attention. It may be on signboards, in the streetcar, or on the page of a magazine. Everyone reads it involuntarily. It is a subtle, persistent, unavoidable presence that creeps into the reader's inner consciousness."

By the mid-1890s, electrical advertising with flashing devices came into vogue. After 1900, the medium evolved rapidly, perhaps spurred on by the success of the 45-foot Heinz pickle illuminated by green light bulbs located at Madison Square in New York City. The first "talking signs" appeared along Broadway and in 1912 moving signs known as sky signs allowed copy to move swiftly along the

(1921) Times Square. By 1910, gaslight, arc light, prismatic light, carbon-burning electric light, tungsten filaments, floodlights and spotlights had been invented. Seen here, the view of the traffic and illuminated advertisements in Times Square at night, viewed from 45th Street.

boards from left to right and to change reading matter daily.

Light and color benefited from technological improvements that were used to great effect by advertisers. By 1910, gaslight, arc light, prismatic light, carbon-burning electric light, tungsten filaments, floodlights and spotlights had been invented. The introduction of phototechnology and color lithography by 1900 allowed for the reproduction of all kinds of images cheaply, abundantly and in a more eye-catching way. Commercial artists were given a much broader field of endeavor with these new developments. Perhaps most famous of all was Maxfield Parrish. He designed murals, billboards for automobile companies, advertising panels and magazine illustrations. One of his more famous advertising illustrations in *Collier's* magazine featured a courtier serving Jell-O to a Renaissance king and queen seated on a throne in their purple robes. So popular was he that people clipped his illustrations out of magazines and put them on the walls of their homes.

THE MISSION OF ADVERTISING ~ By 1915, advertisers took their business very seriously and had developed a mission or philosophy of what they were doing. They were apostles of modernity who also appealed to traditional values. They were civilizers. They were Americanizers. They were prophets of what they liked to call the "democracy of desire." If desire for a given product did not exist, it was their task to create it. The importance of their mission (at least for advertisers themselves) can be seen in *The Business of Advertising* written by Earnest Elmo Caulkins and published in 1915. In it he claimed: "Advertising modifies the course of people's daily thoughts, gives them new words, new ideas, new fashions, new prejudices and new customs. In the same way it obliterates old sets of words and phrases, fashions and customs. It may be doubted if any other one force, the school, the church and the press excepted, has so great an influence as advertising." By the 1920s advertisers were using every resource at their command to create a market for every product.

Without the establishment of desire as a drive to be satisfied more widely in society though, advertisers would have had limited success. From the late 1800s into the first decades of the twentieth century, American culture underwent a profound transformation. New religious movements, a new institutional life in America, the government, universities and colleges, the museums and art schools, all collaborated with business, according to historian William R. Leach, in the creation of America's new culture. The new culture allowed for new myths and dreams promising comfort, pleasure and ever-increasing abundance. Pain and suffering could be eradicated through consumption.

Not all observers thought the new culture an unbridled good thing. The distinguished French writer and politician André Siegfried visited America four times in the first two decades of the twentieth century and by 1925 had come to some conclusions. He wrote, "From a *moral point of view* it is obvious that Americans have come to consider their standard of living as a somewhat sacred acquisition, which they will defend at any price. This means that they would be ready to make any intellectual or even moral concession in order to maintain that standard." Similarly, Samuel Strauss identified the new culture as "consumptionism." Writing in the *Atlantic Monthly* in 1924, Strauss lamented the compulsion to buy what was not wanted, the manipulation of public life and the invasion of market values into every aspect of culture. He noted, "Consumptionism is the science of compelling men to use more and more things. Consumptionism is bringing it about that the American citizen's first importance to his country is no longer that of citizen but that of consumer."

LISTERINE AND THE CREATION OF BAD BREATH ~ One example of the advertisers' art (and of "consumptionism") that proved particularly successful was in the promotion of Listerine into an instantly recognized household brand. Listerine was developed in America as a commercial product, after its invention in England by Joseph Lister during the late nineteenth century as an antiseptic for use in surgery. An American, Jordan Wheat Lambert, perfected a less powerful version in liquid form and gained permission from Lister to use his already famous name for the product. Initially, it was

~

"People are like sheep. They cannot judge values, nor can you and I. We judge things largely by others' impressions, by popular favor. We go with the crowd. So the most effective thing I have ever found in advertising is the trend of the crowd."

Claude Hopkins, 1927

~

marketed as a floor cleaner as well as for medical purposes, then as an after-shave, a nasal douche, a cure for dandruff and a cure for gonorrhea. In 1895, it was marketed to the dental profession to kill oral germs. In 1914, it became one of the first prescription products to be sold over the counter. As yet, it was not intended as a mouth deodorant.

Until the 1920s, personal hygiene was not a distinguishing characteristic of Americans. Most Americans bathed only once a week on Saturday night, hair was rarely washed and soap usually smelled worse than body odor. Gerard Lambert, one of Jordan's sons, and his advertising copywriters gave to the nation the concept of halitosis (bad breath). On the strength of bad breath, company earnings rose from $115,000 in 1922 to over $8 million by 1929. The company spent as much in advertising each year as it gained in profits. The point was made endlessly, usually to marriageable-age young women and men, "Could I be happy with him in spite of *that*?" "Halitosis makes you unpopular" and, particularly hard hitting, "Often a bridesmaid but never a bride." In the latter case, the sad face of a beautiful young woman looked downcast at the story of her tragedy printed toward the bottom of the full-page magazine ad. The story began, "Edna's case was a pathetic one. Like every woman, her primary ambition was to marry. Most of the girls of her set were married—or about to be. Yet not one possessed more grace or charm or loveliness than she. And as her birthdays crept gradually toward that tragic thirty-mark, marriage seemed more far from her life than ever. She was often a bridesmaid but never a bride.... That's the insidious thing about halitosis (unpleasant breath). You, yourself, rarely know when you have it. And even your dearest friends won't tell you." Creating an ailment or discontent where none existed before was a brilliant marketing ploy. It has subsequently served America's advertisers and their clients remarkably well. First, supply the ailment, shame the customer who has it, then, at a small price, provide the antidote.

RACE IN ADVERTISING ~ Advertising reflected as well as led consumers. In the effort to create national tastes in a national market, to establish the desirability of products and the happiness they would bring, consumers were always defined as white. In this, advertisers joined with society as a whole in declaring non-whites, particularly African-Americans as undeserving, inferior beings. Stereotyped figures of black Americans helped sell products. Racially explicit brand names helped sell goods like "Niggerhair Chewing Tobacco," the name supposedly describing the texture of the product.

The desirability of products was often underlined in advertisements by the inclusion of pictures showing blacks serving the product to whites. One example from the late nineteenth century, particularly offensive to modern sensibilities was for soap. Kirkman's wonder soap showed a black nanny washing her son. Taking the white bar of soap to his black skin, he was depicted as getting out of the tub, his skin scrubbed clean, his skin white. By the twentieth century, advertisers developed black spokespeople for their products complete with story lines, always as what Grace Elizabeth Hale terms, the "spokeservants" of white people. The implied consumer, the modern American, a person who would appreciate such representations, was always white. In defining consumers as white, advertisers enabled those who had not previously been considered quite white, the immigrants and ethnics, to become truly American. They did so by defining themselves as consumers and thus, not black.

ADVERTISING THE WAR ~ Advertising gained new respectability during and as a result of World War I. The ambiguity felt by many about advertising disappeared as the industry was pressed into service for the war effort. Government, fully aware of how deeply unpopular intervention in World War I was in a country divided by region and ethnicity, mounted an enormous propaganda effort to unite Americans. Propaganda, persuasion and advertising were seen to be nearly the same. The liberal magazine *New Republic* in November 1917 wrote, "A nation is forced to advertise its needs in order to win recruits, just as a manufacturer is forced to advertise his promises in order to gain purchasers."

World War I was the first war to be marketed by the government to the American citizen using commercial techniques of mass persuasion. Three days after the Armistice ending the war, the advertisers' trade journal *Printer's Ink* gloated, "The war has been won by advertising, as well as by soldiers and munitions." And of the Versailles Treaty and America's refusal to ratify it, the journal lamented "the world's greatest advertising failure." More than the industry's self-serving rhetoric, the influence of advertising in national life could be seen in the fact that the Army intelligence tests, supposedly measuring universal, professional knowledge, included knowledge of advertising slogans as part of the norm of "intelligence." Advertising's successful wartime role in creating at least the appearance of consent and consensus and in fostering morale, led Guy Emerson of the National Bank of Commerce in New York to write in *The Nation* in March 1918. He triumphantly declared that it "has proved that the American people is sound at the core, is more truly a unit than we would have dared believe could be molded from the heterogeneous

Table 3: Personal Consumption Expenditures by Type of Product, 1919-1929

(rounded to the nearest $100m)

Year	Total Consumption Expenditures	Food & Non-Alcoholic beverages	Alcoholic Beverages	Tobacco Products	Clothing & Related Products Purchases
1919	$60.6bn	$18.6bn	$2.0bn	$1.4bn	$8.4bn
1921	$55.8bn	$14.0bn	$1.4bn	$1.5bn	$8.2bn
1923	$66.6bn	$16.1bn	$1.5bn	$1.5bn	$9.6bn
1925	$71.8bn	$18.0bn	$1.7bn	$1.5bn	$9.4bn
1927	$74.6bn	$18.3bn	$1.8bn	$1.6bn	$9.9bn
1929	$80.8bn	$19.7bn	$2.0bn	$1.7bn	$9.8bn

SOURCE: Ben J. Wattenberg, *The Statistical History of the United States From Colonial Times to the Present.* (New York: Basic Books, 1976)

Table 4: Personal Consumption Expenditures by Type of Product, 1919-1929

(rounded to the nearest $100m)

Year	Total Consumption Expenditures	Rent or Imputed Rent	Medical Care	Insurance	New Cars & Net Purchases of Used Cars (Private)	Public Transportation
1919	$60.6bn	$8.1bn	$2.0bn	$0.4bn	$1.3bn	$1.4bn
1921	$55.8bn	$9.7bn	$1.5bn	$0.5bn	$1.2bn	$1.7bn
1923	$66.6bn	$10.6bn	$2.1bn	$0.7bn	$2.3bn	$1.8bn
1925	$71.8bn	$11.5bn	$2.4bn	$0.8bn	$2.4bn	$2.0bn
1927	$74.6bn	$11.3bn	$2.6bn	$0.9bn	$2.0bn	$2.1bn
1929	$80.8bn	$11.4bn	$2.9bn	$1.1bn	$2.6bn	$2.2bn

SOURCE: Ben J. Wattenberg, *The Statistical History of the United States From Colonial Times to the Present.* (New York: Basic Books, 1976)

jumble of races that makes up the nation. Through nation-wide publicity, the American people has discovered itself." More briefly, the president of Eastman Kodak declared advertisers to be "the cheerleaders of the nation."

More than just a new respectability with government and the corporate world more generally, advertisers learned a great deal from the experience. During the 1920s, many of the lessons learned were put into practice with quite spectacular results.

Consumption and Prosperity ~

The 1920s have often been described as "the Prosperous Decade." Following a brief but deep post-war economic depression, America embarked on a period of unprecedented prosperity. As shown in the following tables, personal expenditures during the 1920s increased dramatically. In the space of ten years, total consumer spending increased by 30 percent.

It should be noted that the fall in consumption between 1919 and 1921 is accounted for by the severe economic depression of 1919-1921 and the Spanish flu epidemic of 1919. During the 1920s, a period of continuous prosperity (unless you were a farmer, garment worker or worked in mining) displays a steady upward trend that can be seen especially if you look at the growth in expenditures for clothing. Alcohol, however, suffered from the constitutional amendment passed in 1920 making it illegal to produce, distribute, sell and consume. It is testimony to the utter disregard Americans had for this law that sales figures remained so high. The effects of Prohibition were wiped out by 1929 in terms of expenditures.

The effects of prosperity are more apparent if you look at the second table above. Greater disposable income is reflected in the rising levels of medical care expenses and in the purchase of insurance. In these ten years, medical care expenses rose by almost 50 percent as more people sought the aid of doctors while an almost three-fold increase in insurance purchases reflects the luxury of long-term planning by more Americans.

Radio and the Movies ~ The mass appeal of the movies did not diminish during the 1920s. What did happen was that the culture of movie-going changed. The sometimes raucous but always vocal dialogue kept up by audiences in the era of the "Silents" was replaced after 1927 when "Talkies" were introduced. Movie-going became more private and passive.

Just as revolutionary in terms of mass entertainment and the spread of a consumer culture was the widespread appeal of radio. Manufacturers joined together in 1920 to form the Radio Corporation of America (RCA). The first national system of radio stations went on the air in 1926 with the National Broadcasting Company (NBC). A year later it gained a rival in the Columbia Broadcasting System (CBS). As telephones linked transmitters, the radio was able to carry live sports events and concerts. From a few scattered stations in 1920, by 1930 over 300 stations broadcast regular programs and 40 percent of American homes contained a radio, an honored piece of furniture often taking pride of place in the living room. As the national networks grew they tended to overshadow the ethnic and local culture so vital during most of the decade on local radio stations. Radio became a focal activity of family time. It provided a national culture and linked isolated rural dwellers and individual homemakers as passive consumers. As Gary Cross noted, "It

(1925) The radio and subsequent portable radio provided manufacturers with a massive potential audience to hear advertisements.

offered privacy, mobility, choice, and a plethora of sounds and information at the twist of a dial. Most of all, it reconciled privacy with longings for a community of shared information and entertainment." And it brought celebrities into one's own home. From the start, programming was heavily influenced and reinforced with advertising as favorite characters, dramatic productions, music and everything else was commercially sponsored.

CONSUMERISM 1930-1950

FROM CONSUMPTION TO CONSUMERISM ~ By 1930, mass consumption and mass advertising had transformed America. For many scholars, the importance of advertising and mass consumption lay not so much in the products themselves as in their social function. Scholars like Roland Marchand and James B. Twitchell argue that advertising and product purchase acted to reconcile individual Americans with the enormous scale of business and government organization and the increased anonymity of modern living. Their ambiguous response to modernity was mediated and soothed by consumption and by advertising that promised the product would make them individual or successful or satisfied.

Between 1930 and 1980, despite the disruptions of the Great Depression and World War II, mass consumption spread to all sectors of the population and an ideology of consumerism took hold of the United States aided by the most profound economic expansion in American history between 1945 and 1970. An idea of the expansion of mass consumption may be gained from the following tables.

It becomes clear from Table 5 that overall consumer expenditures leaped eight-fold between 1929 and 1970 despite the fact that for more than ten years

Table 5: Personal Consumption Expenditure by Type, 1929-1970

Year	Total Expenditures	Food & Beverage (incl. Tobacco Products)	Clothing & accessories	Housing	Household Operation
1929	$77.2bn	$19.5bn	$11.2bn	$11.5bn	$10.7bn
1933	$45.8bn	$11.5bn	$5.4bn	$7.9bn	$6.5bn
1937	$66.5bn	$20.0bn	$8.1bn	$8.5bn	$9.5bn
1940	$70.8bn	$20.2bn	$8.9bn	$9.5bn	$10.5bn
1945	$119.7bn	$40.7bn	$19.7bn	$12.5bn	$15.5bn
1950	$191.0bn	$53.9bn	$23.7bn	$21.3bn	$29.5bn
1955	$254.4bn	$67.2bn	$28.0bn	$33.7bn	$37.3bn
1960	$325.2bn	$80.5bn	$33.0bn	$46.4bn	$46.9bn
1965	$432.8bn	$98.8bn	$43.3bn	$63.5bn	$61.8bn
1970	$617.6bn	$130.0bn	$62.8bn	$91.0bn	$87.4bn

SOURCE: Ben J. Wattenberg, *The Statistical History of the United States From Colonial Times to the Present.* (New York: Basic Books, 1976)

America was gripped in the throes of the worst economic depression in its history. All indicators show the dramatic decline from 1929 to 1933, a drop in all consumer expenditures of approximately 40 percent in those years followed by a gradual climb so that by 1937 total consumer expenditures had recovered to 86.3 percent of the 1929 level. What is not shown in the figures is the short, sharp Roosevelt Recession of 1938 that slowed recovery. By 1940, total consumer expenditures had reached 92.6 percent of the 1929 level. Beginning in 1940, consumer expenditures leaped forward, especially so in the affluent years from 1945 to 1970.

Table 6 reveals spectacular growth in other areas of personal expenditure in these years.

In the areas of medical care, transportation and recreation personal expenditures shot up between 1929 and 1970 in the order of 2000 percent, 1000 percent and 1000 percent respectively. Increased affluence during these years (particularly after 1945), meant that a large majority of the population was able to gain medical insurance, own not only their own car but a second or even a third, and to spend a great deal more time

(circa 1941) Cigarette manufacturers were notoriously good at advertising. Once seen as a necessity (bought whether the economy was good or not), cigarettes were widely advertised in all mediums.

Table 6: Personal Consumption Expenditure by Type, 1929-1970

Year	Total Expenditures	Medical Care Expenses	Transportation	Recreation
1929	$77.2bn	$2.9bn	$7.6bn	$4.3bn
1933	$45.8bn	$2.0bn	$4.0bn	$2.2bn
1937	$66.5bn	$2.7bn	$6.5bn	$3.4bn
1940	$70.8bn	$3.0bn	$7.1bn	$3.8bn
1945	$119.7bn	$6.2bn	$6.9bn	$6.1bn
1950	$191.0bn	$8.8bn	$24.7bn	$11.1bn
1955	$254.4bn	$12.8bn	$35.6bn	$14.1bn
1960	$325.2bn	$19.1bn	$43.1bn	$18.3bn
1965	$432.8bn	$28.1bn	$58.2bn	$26.3bn
1970	$617.6bn	$47.4bn	$77.8bn	$40.7bn

SOURCE: Ben J. Wattenberg, *The Statistical History of the United States From Colonial Times to the Present.* (New York: Basic Books, 1976)

Table 7: Distribution of Personal Consumption Expenditures by Type, 1929-1970

Type	1929	1933	1940	1950	1960	1970
Food, Beverages, & Tobacco	27.5%	27.9%	31.1%	30.4%	26.9%	23.2%
Clothing, Accessories & Jewelry	14.5%	11.9%	12.5%	12.4%	10.2%	10.0%
Personal Care	1.4%	1.4%	1.5%	1.5%	1.6%	1.7%
Housing	14.9%	17.3%	13.3%	13.3%	14.2%	14.7%
Household Operation	13.9%	14.1%	14.8%	14.8%	14.4%	14.0%
Medical Care Expenses	3.8%	4.3%	4.3%	4.6%	5.9%	7.6%
Personal Business	5.4%	6.2%	4.7%	3.6%	4.6%	5.7%
Transportation	9.9%	8.7%	10.1%	12.9%	13.3%	12.6%
Recreation	5.6%	4.8%	5.3%	5.8%	5.6%	6.5%
Other	3.1%	3.4%	2.4%	2.4%	3.3%	3.9%

SOURCE: Ben J. Wattenberg, *The Statistical History of the United States From Colonial Times to the Present.* (New York: Basic Books, 1976)

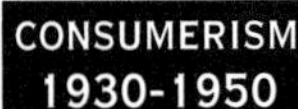

and money on personal leisure activities.

It is thus clear that while the United States was expanding its consumer base before World War II, it was only after 1945 that we can truly describe America as a whole as a consumer society in virtually all things.

Table 7 shows the changes in another way. It displays some alteration in the balance of personal consumer expenditure, but more than anything it shows the consistency of the distribution of personal expenditures over the 41 years. Taken together with tables 5 and 6, it shows quite clearly the large increase in the amount Americans were able to spend on themselves and their families. Americans did not spend proportionally much more on recreation in 1970 than in 1929. They spent virtually the same share of their expenses on their housing and its operation (28.7 percent and 28.8 percent respectively). While they spent significantly less on clothing and accessories, they did spend more on medical expenses and transportation.

Advertising 1930-1950

Effects of the Great Depression on Consumerism and Advertising

~ Between 1929 and 1933, America went from virtually full employment to a situation where 25 percent of the workforce was unemployed. Roughly the same proportion again was on short-time and many more endured pay cuts. In those years, America's Gross National Product was halved. For consumption, some indicators can tell the story of what this meant and the changes it brought. Luxury car sales, for example, stood at 150,000 in 1929. By 1937, they had slumped to 10,000. On the other hand, low-priced cars increased from 52 percent of all car sales in 1926 to 73 percent in 1932. Weekly movie attendance also slumped from 90 million in 1929 to 60 million in 1932, prompting the introduction of the double feature to get people in the doors. In retailing, the lack of customers led to extended hours and the rise of discount stores appealing not to brand name, style or status, but just to price.

The advertising industry was not spared. Companies withdrew advertising from the advertising agencies in order to save money. No contract was safe between agencies and corporations as competitors began sending in speculative copy in an attempt to poach advertising accounts. Agencies found themselves in the same position as industry with declining revenues. They took the same steps to survive. They cut working hours, laid off employees, became utterly ruthless in the pursuit of fewer opportunities, and tried everything they knew to survive. For a business that had appealed to Americans to improve their standard of living by buying products used by the wealthy, the Depression posed a profound challenge. They could not ignore it.

Advertising was forced to change its style. In its trade papers, advertising men denounced the "lazy, band music advertising" of the 1920s and its tasteful use of artistic talent. In its place they proposed what they liked to call "shirt-sleeves advertising." The new style was loud, uncluttered, undignified and direct, according to advertising historian Roland Marchand.

Advertisers attacked what they considered to be a consumers' strike on the part of the public or, as one put it, "consumer constipation." They redoubled their efforts to get Americans out of work, on short wages, or just fearing what might happen to them tomorrow, to part with their money. Gentility went out the window as advertisers sought to elevate their product over the competition with unknown levels of competitive copy, the comparison of one's own product to the detriment of the competition. Radio advertising led the way with ever-greater promotions offering a free premium or promotional contests.

Indeed, the Depression changed radio profoundly. Its key role as a selling medium right in the living rooms of America greatly encouraged its commercialism. Revenue from radio advertising revenue rose 316 percent between 1928 and 1934. In Detroit, radio station WJR provided perhaps the worst example of the trend when it aired 30 commercials in 45 minutes. The gap between programs and ads was blurred as radio stars like comedian Jack Benny and singer Rudy Vallee increasingly endorsed the products of the program sponsors and ads in other media ran cartoons featuring radio celebrities to sell their products.

FEAR TACTICS IN DEPRESSION ADVERTISING ~ Knowing that empathy was a powerful advertising tool, agencies appealed to the public to keep their spirits up. Listerine, for example, in the 1920s advertised that by buying its product for less than you would pay for rival versions you could afford a little extra luxury. By 1932, Listerine's ads changed in recognition of hard times by listing over forty different possible uses for the money saved, from underwear to milk, flour and potatoes. Others more cynically sought to manipulate desperate people by arguing for the necessity of their product. Lifebuoy soap, for example, argued, "Don't risk *your* job by offending with B.O.... Take no chances! When business is slack, employers become more critical. Sometimes very little may turn the scales against us." Surviving the Depression, these ads counseled, depended on first impressions, avoiding bodily odors, bad breath through wearing old or poor quality underwear, or threadbare clothing.

CONSUMER EDUCATION ~ Faced with the ever-more shrill character of

Depression advertising, a reaction set in. In August 1931, a new magazine, *Ballyhoo*, was launched. It was an immediate success. Each issue that year sold out in a few days. By October, all 650,000 copies were sold. Within five months, its circulation topped one and a half million. The magazine was notable for its irreverence. It exploded like a bombshell in the advertising scene. The entire focus of its humor was in lampooning notorious advertisements. A parody of a toothpaste ad had the product named "Blisterine." In a humorous take-off of the real campaign, the spoof ad urged readers; "Buy yourself some false teeth with the money you save on toothpaste." "Lox Toilet Soap" featured a movie star who kept her girlish figure by bathing "every fortnight" with the product. Nine out of ten stars, the magazine's fake ad announced, really "clean up" with the paid "Lox Soap" testimonials.

Even more disturbing to advertisers was the expansion of a small consumers' movement begun at the end of the 1920s. A national organization, Consumers Research reached a membership of 12,000 by 1930 and doubled the following year. A Consumers Cooperative movement expanded by educating the public about the misleading aspects of advertising. Finally, as the New Deal began in 1933, advertisers became increasingly worried about the prospect

(circa 1941) Inventive advertising techniques like turning a car into a roll of Life Savers candy, made Life Savers a household name.

of government regulation of the industry to eliminate false product claims and the more blatant forms of consumer manipulation indulged in by some.

Within the industry, voices were raised denouncing the "bombastic ballyhoo" of the more aggressive advertising campaigns. Self-regulation was urged to avoid worse, and advertisers took it upon themselves to offer encouragement to consumers. The symbol of the clenched fist of resistance to Depression and reinforcement that the courage of regular Americans in the face of calamity was recognized provided a morale-boosting element to advertising in the 1930s. Together with large doses of escapism, advertisers sought to reassure the American public that everything would turn out well in the end.

WORLD WAR II RESTRICTIONS ON CONSUMER GOODS ~ Despite the heroic and quite successful efforts of the New Deal, the Depression was finally lifted when the government prepared for and waged the Second World War. A gauge of what this meant can be had by comparing the size of the federal budget before and at the end of World War II. In 1939, the federal budget stood at $9 billion. By 1945, it was $100 billion. Unemployment was eliminated. The effect of government spending and its war orders was to dramatically increase the Gross National Product. In 1939, GNP stood at $91 billion. By 1945 it had increased to $166 billion.

During the war, consumer spending was severely hampered. The economy was closely directed toward waging a titanic struggle throughout the world against fearsome opponents. The United States made it possible for Great Britain to continue to fight, it equipped the Free French, gave massive amounts of war materials to China, and made considerable Lend-Lease donations to help the massive Russian Red Army take on, hold up, and defeat the bulk of the Nazi forces, as well as providing millions of troops to fight in North Africa, Italy, France and the islands of the Pacific. American industrial production was devoted to the war effort. Consumer production was at a minimum. Auto plants were converted to the production of tanks, armored personnel carriers and the like. The garment industry was revived by orders for military clothing. Cotton factories produced sheets and blankets. The result was that America's home front workers and military personnel had little on which to spend their wages. By the end of 1944, Americans had saved $140 billion.

WAR PROPAGANDA ~ During World War II, the flagging image of advertisers was revived. They gained respect, as they had in the previous world war, from providing effective propaganda for the war effort. The war, according to the advertisers, was to protect the American Way of Life. They shaped public opinion by tackling the question of what Americans were fighting for. As one ad declared, "For years we have fought for a higher standard of living, and now we are fighting to protect it against those who are jealous of our national accomplishments." The image of freedom as a consumer society was underlined in a Nash-Kelvinator ad in 1943. It showed a paratrooper agreeing, "We have so many things, here in America, that belong only to a free people... warm, comfortable homes, automobiles, and radios by the million." By implication, America's enemies wanted to take them away and deny their own people such things.

(late 1940s) Advertisement shows a woman sitting in a hair salon, wearing electric curlers on her head strung from long cords.

CREATING THE POSTWAR MYTH OF PROSPERITY FOR ALL ~ As the tide turned, advertisers prepared Americans for a postwar future of private consumption. Refrigerators would replace tanks on the assembly line. New technologies developed for the war would benefit consumers afterward. Wait just a little more and televisions would be available to all. A "happily ever after" myth was developed and promoted. Kelvinator even spelled it out in one ad. The postwar woman and her family would, of course, have a Kelvinator refrigerator but also, "A bright, sunny house that's a blend of old and new, with a white shuttered door and a picket fence around a world all our own... A garden where you can go while sunshine warms you through and through... And a kitchen... that's *full* of magical things..." A survey of bank depositors revealed that 43 percent of those with bank accounts were eager to spend their money on "future needs." In June 1944, an opinion poll asked Americans about their most desired consumer items. Appliances topped the list. When asked what they hoped to purchase in the postwar years, respondents listed in order: washing machines, electric irons, refrigerators, stoves, toasters, radios, vacuum cleaners, electric fans and hot water heaters.

The government itself became involved with helping people enter the consumer society. Most notable of all was passage of the G.I. Bill of Rights in 1944. Under it, not only were millions of veterans enabled by a grateful nation to go to college or university to enhance their possibilities for careers and income but they were also furnished with low-inter-

Does she... or doesn't she?

~

Hair color so natural only her hairdresser knows for sure! She's as full of fun as a kid—and just as fresh looking! Her hair sparkles with clear, radiant, young color that looks as natural in the bright light of snow as it does in the soft light of a candle. And this is the beautiful difference with Miss Clairol. In every light, Miss Clairol hair color looks natural. It keeps your hair lovely to touch—silky, shiny, in wonderful condition.

Ad for Miss Clairol, 1955

est home mortgage loans so they could buy their own homes. As historian Gary Cross noted, "The promise of the postwar era was a resurrection of the consumerist message of the 1920s—an image of seamless harmony, blending the old and new, the spiritual and material, the private and public. To consume was to be free."

CONSUMERISM 1950-1980

POSTWAR CONSUMERISM AND THE IMAGE OF SUCCESS ~ Freedom after World War II was a precious commodity. As relief at the defeat of fascism gave way to fear of Communism, Americans took comfort in their attachment to consumption as a practical embodiment of their own liberty. Even so, after the deprivations they had endured during the Depression and World War II and fears they harbored of potential economic hard times to come, they did not give way to frivolity and wild spending. Old habits of thinking about conspicuous consumption as a moral negative were overcome by a wave of spending directed, as Americans thought, to strengthening the family. Veterans Administration home loans as allowed through the G. I. Bill and the easing of terms of home mortgage by the Federal Housing Administration (FHA) as well as changes in tax benefits for home owners and government financing for suburban housing tracts led to a surge of house buying and furnishing. Between 1945 and 1950, the amount spent on home furnishings and appliances rose 240 percent. As for housing, in 1945, 98 percent of

(1950s) Demonstrating a vacuum cleaner's effectiveness. New and plentiful appliances introduced in the 1950s revolutionized housework.

American cities reported shortages of houses and over 90 percent reported shortages of apartments. By 1947, 6 million families were doubling up with relatives. With all the incentives and the crisis in housing, housing starts rose from 114,000 in 1944 to an all-time high of 1,692,000 in 1950.

Cold War government policy contributed to new patterns of living. Under the threat of nuclear war, depopulating the large urban centers was characterized as "defense through decentralization." Suburbs were preferred. The government provided 90 percent of the cost of building the interstate highway system after 1956, mainly for its potential military use and for speed of evacuation from key cities in the event of an atomic attack. Similarly, efforts were made to disperse the location of industries into the suburbs. In 1946, partly as a result of these policies, for the first time in the nation's history a majority of the nation's families lived in homes they owned. Between 1950 and 1970, the number of Americans living in suburbs doubled, from 36 million to 74 million. Government policies stimulated these new living arrangements, underwrote the baby boom and fostered traditional gender roles. Few of the beneficiaries were African Americans. Prevailing racial attitudes, not least on the part of mortgage agencies including arms of the government, prevented black Americans from taking advantage of the opportunities to improve the lives of their families in the suburbs.

From 1935 to 1950 income for Americans rose on average 50 percent. National income between 1947 and 1961 increased over 60 percent. The numbers of people with discretionary income (money available to be spent on nonessentials) doubled in the same period. Between 1944 and 1949, Americans bought 21.4 million cars, 20 million refrigerators, 5.5 million new stoves, 11.6 million televisions and moved into new housing units at the rate of over a million each year. Between 1947 and 1961, the number of families increased 28 percent. The middle class led the upward march of American living standards but workers were not excluded. Between 1940 and 1954, the proportion of households with indoor plumbing rose from 65 to 80 percent. Telephones rose from being owned by 36 percent of American families to 80 percent in these years. Refrigerators, a key element in the new standard of comfort rose from 44 to 91 percent. Televisions went from almost none in America's homes to 61 percent. The expectation by the end of the decade was that new goods represented progress and were a measure of the upward march of time.

Consumerism as a Measure of Political Power ~ Debating the Russian leader Nikita Khrushchev in 1959, Vice President Nixon identified the core of American superiority by describing the consumer-oriented suburban home. Triumphantly he declared, "Let us start with some of the things in this exhibit. You will see a house, a car, a television set—each the newest and most modern of its type we produce. But can only the rich in the United States afford such things? If this were the case, we would have to include in our definition of rich the millions of America's wage earners." Driving the point home, he stated that America's 44 million families owned 56 million cars, 50 million television sets, and 143 million radios. He continued that every year each of these families bought on average nine dresses and suits and fourteen pairs of shoes. As with everything else in the Cold War, consumption and living standards were conceived as a race between the two contending political systems. For Nixon as for many other Americans, the material things represented the possibility in America for individualism and upward mobility.

SELF INDULGENCE ~ The boom in consumer spending, tied as it was to the identification of mass consumption with Americanism, was fueled to some extent by advertising. During the 1950s, the advertisers' dream of prewar years came to fruition. Goods were increasingly sold for style, convenience and fashion rather than mere utility. The temporary became permanent. The pace of life quickened. By the late 1950s, 20 percent of Americans moved every year. Even as early as 1949, retailers reported that the average hit record stayed only three weeks on the charts. Cars embodied the temporary nature of fashion perhaps better than any other commodity. Changes in each year's new models helped create demand as they helped create dissatisfaction with older models. In 1957, auto manufacturers indulged in the "battle of the fins," a style war of tail fins. Thomas Hine characterized the era as "Populuxe," popular luxury enjoyed as continuous change. Psychologist Ernest Dichter told advertisers it was their job to teach Americans to enjoy themselves. Ads should offer absolution to consumers who commonly experienced both guilt and pleasure in spending, he told them. He concluded: "America is experiencing a revolution in self-indulgence.... We've learned that one rarely make's one's ultimate goal—so why not enjoy life now?" In his "Kitchen Debate" with Vice President Nixon, Soviet leader Khrushchev showed he did not understand the dynamic of the new consumerism when he complained that American houses were shoddily built and designed to last only twenty years so that contractors could sell more houses.

CHILD AND TEENAGE CONSUMERISM ~ The 1950s saw the flowering of teenage culture and consumerism. *Seventeen Magazine*, founded in 1944 developed new marketing formulas with advice designed for young women to reduce their anxieties about grooming, fashion, diets and friendship. Youth became an ideal. Magazine staff advised clothing manufacturers on clothes design and convinced department stores to stock special lines for teenagers. Young people formed the majority of audiences in the drive-in movie theaters that emerged after World War II. They flocked to the new 3-D movies after 1951. By 1954, rock 'n' roll reached the radio. Cheap table radios, transistor radios (introduced in the late 1950s), and inexpensive record players brought the new music and the latest sounds to almost every teenager. In 1948, the small, lightweight, inexpensive 45 rpm disc was marketed by RCA. Elvis Presley brought black music into the mainstream, frightening parents, but was so popular that Ed Sullivan was forced to book him on his TV show in 1956 with the condition that his image appear above the waist only. His gyrating hips were considered to be dangerously immoral. Rock 'n' roll was the music of youth rebellion marketed in the main by giant corporations.

Childhood became increasingly recognized as a training period for consumption. As David Riesman noted in 1950, "Middle class children have allowances of their own at four or five. The allowances are expected to be spent, whereas in the earlier era they were often used as cudgels of thrift." Through their toys, children were socialized as consumers.

CRITICS OF CONSUMPTION ~ The burst of consumerism in the postwar years did not happen without criticism. In a series of best sellers, Vance Packard wrote *The Hidden Persuaders* (1957), *The Waste Makers* (1960) and *Status Seekers* (1961). He lamented the planned obsolescence of product design, the waste of natural resources in creating artificial demand through changing color, style and material to make products indispensable for one season only, then old news the next. Alarmed, he was dismayed that Americans seemed to be taking their ideas from advertising and the media instead of themselves. The new affluence, he argued did not produce a classless society but an insecure one with individuals trying to define and display themselves through their material possessions. He was not alone.

During the late 1950s, the threat of mass consumer society to creative individuality found expression in the pages of leading magazines. The Beat poets and their novelist counterparts trumpeted rebelliousness as the way to avoid "slow death by conformity." In 1961, David McReynolds saw an emerging middle class rebellion against conformity. In the 1960s, much of this feeling of unease found expression in the youth Counterculture. A 1966 survey of college seniors in *Newsweek* found only 31 percent seriously considering careers in business while 74 percent considered it a "dog eat dog" world. *Fortune* magazine found that money making appealed to few students. Many criticized the conformity and lack of personal fulfillment in business.

Consumer advocacy also re-emerged in the 1950s and 1960s. Packard's *The Hidden Persuaders* revived the idea that business manipulated consumers into buying goods they did not need by using motivational psychology to prey on insecurities like status anxiety and desires for self-indulgence. The following year, 1958, TV quiz show scandals involving sponsors who fed contestants answers to boost ratings capped a growing discontent with hard-sell advertising and commercial manipulation. In the 1960s, Sidney Margolius warned about unnecessary car repairs, home improvement tricks and inflated insurance rates. His attack on the food industry highlighted how inexpensive ingredients were packaged as high-cost processed foods. He noted that prices for heavily advertised breakfast cereals rose twice as fast as those for other foods and were often of little nutritional value. Deceptive and misleading advertising duped customers, he complained.

However, the biggest bombshell for the rising consumerism-critic wave came in 1965 with the publication of Ralph Nader's *Unsafe At Any Speed*. In it, he attacked the very symbol of American consumerism, the automobile. Nader demonstrated the designed-in flaws of American cars and argued that fatalities and injuries resulted not so much from bad driving as from the lack of safety devices in the vehicles. In fact, Nader's critique went much further. He argued that consumers had rights that needed to be protected. Corporate influence over regulatory agencies, monopolistic pricing policies, and deceptive advertising all needed to be stopped. Only in a truly free competitive economy would producers be forced to respond to consumers, he stated.

Private efforts resulted in the formation of a powerful lobby with the formation from 147 groups of the Consumer

~

The emerging consumer movement achieved considerable success. Some examples are instructive:

- The Hazardous Substances Labeling Act (1960) required warnings on dangerous household products.
- The Child Protection Act (1966) banned toys containing hazardous substances
- The Consumer Product Safety Commission (1972) provided a continuous review of consumer goods for risks
- The Federal Trade Commission required warning labels on cigarette packets in light of growing evidence that tobacco caused cancer (1964)
- The Truth in Packaging Act (1966) responded to growing public dissatisfaction with deceptive advertising

~

Federation in 1967. Their efforts and those of sympathetic lawmakers and others resulted in the establishment of the Corporation for Public Broadcasting to provide an alternative to the ad-ridden networks. Similarly, the Federal Trade Commission was encouraged to step up regulation of TV advertising, aided enormously by legislation in 1974 giving it the power to issue regulations applicable to the whole industry. In 1968, concerned parents formed Action for Children's Television to force networks to provide programming that did more than gather children before the TV to see commercials.

CONSUMPTION AND CIVIL RIGHTS ~ Economic power played a significant role in the changes in civil rights for African-Americans in the 1960s. It had played a growing part in resistance to segregation from the 1890s on. After the lynching of three black businessmen in Memphis in 1892, newspaper editor Ida B. Wells called for black Memphians either to leave the city or boycott the new streetcar lines. 2,000 people left and the streetcar line almost went bankrupt. Between 1900 and 1906, in twenty-five southern cities, systematic consumer boycotts were initiated against "Jim Crow" streetcar lines. As an editorial in one black newspaper in 1906 put it, "Let us touch to the quick the white man's pocket. 'Tis there his conscience often lies." In the 1930s, the "Don't Buy Where You Can't Work" campaigns used increasing consumer power to secure jobs for black people in stores heavily patronized by the black community and helped educate black people as to the power they actually possessed. World War II enhanced black consumer activism with its concept of the double victory, abroad and at home. Cultural assaults on blacks by companies were punished by black consumer boycotts. The American Tobacco Company lost black smokers in protest against its marketing of "Niggerhair" tobacco. The Whitman Candy Company was boycotted for its "Pickaninny Chocolate." Black car owners boycotted Shell Oil Company products because its advertising featured a black man eating watermelon. Public apologies by the companies concerned and the removal of the offensive ads and products underscored growing black consumer power.

SIT-INS AND BOYCOTTS ~ The Montgomery Bus Boycott remains the most graphic symbol of black consumer activism in the Civil Rights years. Conducted over thirteen months in 1955-1956, the boycott united the black community and provided a focus for its feelings of oppression. Humiliating treatment, the fact that 70 percent of bus riders were black, and that the company employed no black drivers combined powerfully. Ultimately successful, the Montgomery Bus Boycott stands as the beginning of the Civil Rights Movement in modern accounts. Another tactic of the movement was the sit-in designed to desegregate lunch counters and downtown stores. By 1960, sit-ins and boycotts had become serious. As one Nashville retailer told *Business Week*, "This thing has frightening ramifications. It is more serious than many people realize. It has now become an economic situation affecting the entire community, the whole city, the whole country." After success in desegregating Birmingham, Alabama, in 1963, Dr. Martin Luther King Jr. concluded that organized black economic retribution represented the best strategy for achieving human and civil rights. By 1964, with the passage of the Civil Rights Act, white business support was secure for those sections of the legislation that dealt with issues related to black consumers.

Evidence of the growing power of African-Americans as consumers can be gauged in the following table. *Ebony* magazine established itself in the 1960s as a major magazine. Its advertising revenues suggest that major corporations tripled their spending between 1962 and 1969.

CONSUMERISM TRANSFORMED ~ The emergence of movements in reaction to the growth of consumerism during the 1950s and 1960s posed a profound challenge to both business in general and to the ethic of consumerism in society. Adding weight to the challenge was the slow-down in the long economic boom that followed World War II. While the

Table 8: Advertising Revenue, Ebony Magazine, 1962-1969

Year	Revenue
1962	$3,630,804
1963	$5,129,921
1964	$5,641,895
1965	$5,495,537
1966	$7,020,279
1967	$6,895,379
1968	$8,551,463
1969	$9,965,898

SOURCE: Robert E. Weems Jr., "The Revolution Will Be Marketed: American Corporations and Black Consumers During the 1960s" in *Consumer Society in American History: A Reader*, edited by Lawrence B. Glickman. (Ithaca & London: Cornell University Press, 1999)

The man in the Hathaway shirt

~

American men are beginning to realize that it is ridiculous to buy good suits and then spoil the effect by wearing an ordinary, mass-produced shirt. Hence the growing popularity of HATHAWAY shirts, which are in a class by themselves.

HATHAWAY shirts *wear* infinitely longer—a matter of years. They make you look younger and more distinguished, because of the subtle way HATHAWAY cuts collars. The whole shirt is tailored more *generously*, and is therefore more *comfortable*. The tails are longer, and stay in your trousers. The buttons are mother-of-pearl. Even the stitching has an ante-bellum elegance about it.

Ad for Hathaway shirts, the *New Yorker*, 1951.

real spendable income of an average family of four in the United States rose 20.4 percent between 1947 and 1957, in the next decade it slowed to 13.1 percent. Worse, between 1969 and 1979 it declined by 1.7 percent. The 1970s were a decade characterized by a new economic term—stagflation—a combination of a stagnant economy and inflation. Economic growth was dramatically reduced by a number of factors among which were a recession brought on by the strains of paying for the immensely costly and unpopular war in Vietnam, the growth of foreign competition in foreign and increasingly also in domestic markets, and the Oil Crises of 1973 and 1979. The importance of inflation can be measured by the purchasing power of the dollar. By 1980, what could be bought for $1 in 1967 cost $2.46.

All this posed a significant challenge to American business and advertising. During the 1960s, economic growth was stimulated not so much by investment as by spending. Credit cards, first introduced by the Bank of America in 1959 as Bank Americard—later renamed Visa (Mastercard was introduced in 1966 by rival banks)—had, by the end of the 1960s become far more profitable than bank loans and proved to be a convenient way to shop. By the 1970s, Americans spent four times as many hours shopping than Europeans while retail space, including shopping malls, took up far greater space with almost unlimited parking. Responding to changing patterns of buying, department stores spun off suburban retail chains. In the early 1960s S.S. Kresge established Kmart as a suburban mall superstore. In 1962 in Rogers, Arkansas, Sam Walton established the first Wal-Mart. The mall replaced the downtown department store as the primary location of retail purchasing.

ADVERTISING 1950-1980

THE MARLBORO MAN ~ Perhaps the most notable advertising success in the face of evidence to the contrary came with cigarettes. In the early 1950s widely publicized scientific evidence provided a link between smoking cigarettes and cancer. Cigarette makers attempted to calm fears by introducing filters. Advertising in *Time* magazine in 1953, Kent issued the vague claim that its product "removed seven times more nicotine and tar" (than what it never said), strongly implying that filters made cigarettes safe. Despite tests showing the filter left as much residue of the chemicals as unfiltered Camel cigarettes, advertising neutralized health fears by increasing budgets. Between 1957 and 1962, tobacco companies raised spending for TV commercials from $40 million to $115 million. After a brief downturn in smoking during the 1950s, sales of cigarettes rose from 332, 345 in 1945 to 506,127 million in 1960.

One of the greatest advertising campaigns of the 1950s was the transformation of a faltering women's cigarette into the world's most recognized brand—Marlboro. Its transformation from a sophisticated "tea room smoke" with an optional red beauty tip (filter) whose advertising slogan was "mild as May" into a symbol of manly independence was entirely due to advertising and nothing to do with product change. The image projected after 1954 for the cigarette was the Marlboro man, a cowboy, considered to be the most masculine figure in America at the time. In 1963, models were dispensed with for the real thing. Carl "Big-un" Bradley, their first real cowboy (who later died of lung cancer) was the perfect projection of the American man as free-ranging cowboy. Introduced as another cancer scare from cigarettes took hold, Bradley and the tough, flip-top box containing the Marlboros swept to a position as the leading cigarette brand in America, instantly recognizable around the world. With very little change the ads and image remained constant into the 1990s.

THE TELEVISION AGE ~ The most important domestic consumer product of the 1950s was the television. Although the technology for the television was available earlier, Depression and War delayed its introduction. Once introduced, its success was phenomenal. In 1950, 9 percent of America's households owned a television. By 1960, 90 percent of families had a television in their home and the average viewer watched five hours of programming every day. It replaced movie going and radio listening. Between 1946 and 1953, movie audiences shrank by one half and radio audiences declined at virtually the same rate. Both media survived primarily because young people needed to get away from home or exercise their right to privacy.

Culturally, television had enormous impact. It helped homogenize American culture. Programming did not extend beyond middle class white America. Shows like "Leave it to Beaver" and the "Donna Reed Show" displayed middle class suburban living and child rearing practices for all Americans. By the late 1950s, live drama and serious news programming was dropped in favor of westerns, sit-coms and detective shows. In 1959, there were 32 western series on television. In 1964, the more working class sport of boxing, "The Friday Night Fight," was replaced by the more middle class NFL Football, screened on Sundays. By the end of the 1950s family disputes on which show to watch could be settled by the purchase of a cheap, portable TV.

For advertisers, television was a boon. By 1957, the average viewer watched 420 ads a week taking up more than five hours. In 1964, one station in the course of two hours in the morning showed 50 ads.

Its impact on American life was summarized by historian Gary Cross who concluded; "Television became a nearly perfect expression of suburban life; it celebrated domesticity in sit-coms and warned of urban dangers in action-adventure shows, while enticing viewers through commercials to the "miracle-miles" of fast-food chains and shopping malls. It reinforced the trend (established by radio) of homebound privacy and a national, even global, entertainment culture."

ADVERTISERS TARGET AUDIENCES ~ Advertisers learned to be less manipulative in response to consumer concerns during the 1960s and adapted to the counterculture and youthful rebellion by stressing individualism. From the 1960s into the 1970s, advertisers became more sophisticated in identifying and reaching target audiences. Nielsen ratings for TV shows provided one instrument and sophisticated polling techniques identified who watched what shows according to age groups, gender and ethnic background. The result was that TV advertising rose from $12 billion in 1960 to $54.5 billion in 1980. Saturday morning children's cartoons offered an easily identifiable market for advertisers but societal trends were reflected, for example, in the perfume industry.

In the late 1960s the women's liberation movement gained great headway. Revlon launched Charlie. The name itself was startling. Perfumes had always been given exotic, usually French names. This was a male diminutive. The ad campaign was revolutionary. Charlie was a woman. She often wore a tweed suit complete with trousers. She was younger than the usual model for such promotions. She was pictured during the daytime, not evening; she was active, and she was, obviously enjoying it, in charge. This was the new woman for a new world. Most famous of all was an ad showing the model Charlie walking along a downtown street with a man. She has long, flowing hair and scarf, carrying a briefcase. The man has his head turned toward her in a friendly but deferential manner. She is taller than he. Part of his image is overlain with the image of the perfume bottle. In effect, his form is stamped with the name Charlie. The woman patting the man on the rear, a graphic reversal of what then was commonplace, dramatically reinforces the image. The caption read "She's Very Charlie."

The increased individualism catered to in advertising in the 1960s and 1970s led, under the pressure of stagflation and the aura of crisis, to the beginnings of what people have called "me-ism." A measure of this can be seen in surveys of college students. In 1968, the percentage of students who rated "developing a meaningful philosophy of life" as a very important personal goal stood at 80 percent. By 1986 the same response was shared by only 40 percent. Those rating "being very well off financially" rose from 40 percent in 1968 to 74 percent in 1986. Provided a powerful boost by American reaction to the oil crisis which rejected having to economize and conserve, this trend provided the basis of a new consumerism that characterized the latter decades of the twentieth century.

GOVERNMENT REGULATION OF ADVERTISING ~ By 1976, corporations regrouped sufficiently from the onslaught of environmentalists and consumer advocacy groups to recapture political influence. As business influence in politics grew with greater lobbying and financial contributions to candidates through Political Action Committee (PAC) funds, consumer rights advocates lost ground. An important Supreme Court decision in 1976 defended ads as protected speech. In 1978, business interests defeated a proposal to establish a federal consumer protection agency. Again in 1978, the Federal Trade Commission (FTC) was ridiculed when it tried to protect children from unscrupulous ads. In 1980, Congress banned the FTC from banning "unfair" ads, just those that were openly deceptive. By the late 1970s, businessmen, advertisers and their allies had little difficulty isolating consumer activists and regulators as hair-splitters and tyrants who caused inflation and promoted "big" government.

CONSUMERISM 1980-2000

CONSUMERISM TRIUMPHANT ~ Trends that had been developing for decades came together and were significantly boosted in the last two decades of the twentieth century. Consumerism triumphed finally over alternate ways of viewing oneself and the world. It was a consumerism that was individual and not socially constructed or oriented. The judgment is still out on what it all finally means but there is no shortage of commentators who lament its existence.

RONALD REAGAN, TRADITIONAL VALUES AND CONSUMERISM ~ Ronald Reagan became President of the United States in January 1981. He was elected on a wave of nostalgia for a "golden age" and to restore values many people thought had been sadly neglected. In some senses, Reagan was the perfect embodiment of the advertising craft. More than a man or politician, Reagan was an icon, a symbol. He had spent much of his adulthood as an actor and in ads. As such, he represented the wave of modernity and consumerism that had been gathering force throughout his life. Yet beyond that, Reagan firmly believed in traditional family values. Conservative Republicans, split into a number of tendencies, provided him with political strength. The irony of Reagan as symbol is that he neatly represented each of the tendencies, and they were at odds with one another. On the one hand, traditional family values referred back to a previous time of solid communities, known moral standards and acceptable forms of behavior. For some, they also included deeply held and universally applicable religious views that everyone should embrace.

On the other hand, there were those conservative Republicans whose beliefs were driven more by economic theories than moral ones. They were adamant that the free market economy should be left to itself, that government was too big and intrusive. In his presidency, Reagan articulated both. In his policies, the lasting trend was toward the economic and toward the acceleration of modern consumerism. With Ronald Reagan, the philosophy of government as having direct obligations to its citizens for their social and economic well being as represented by the New Deal and subsequent presidencies, ended.

Reagan promised to stimulate the economy through tax cuts and an attack on excess. His appointments to key positions like Secretary of the Interior, Chairman of the Environmental Protection Agency, Chairman of the FCC and FTC were conservative ideologues whose chief qualifications lay in long-time criticisms of the bodies they were now appointed to head. The result was that enforcement of regulations was cut back, public lands were opened to commercial exploitation, action against pollution was diluted, public service and educational functions mandated for radio and TV were ignored, restrictions on the number of stations a company could purchase were eased, and ad makers were no longer required to back claims made for their products with research.

Lower tax rates meant growing income inequality and were not matched by an increase in charitable giving. Deregulation led to higher bank fees, cable TV rates, insurance premiums and health costs. A "winner-take-all" society emerged as those with talent and access to media and communications attracted ever-higher salaries. Corporate CEOs and sports stars saw their incomes leap. The top one percent of the richest Americans' pretax income went up 107 percent between 1977 and 1989 compared with median income rising only seven percent. Professional sportsmen earned 50 times the average American wage in 1992 compared with eight times that in 1976. A spending spree was ignited. The rich touched off a consumer-driven economic expansion.

ADVERTISING 1980-2000

CREDIT CARD DEBT ~ Despite the expectations of economic conservatives inside and outside the Reagan administration, tax cuts and deregulation led not to an increase in personal savings but to greater spending. While the rate of personal savings dropped from nine percent of annual income in the 1970s to only 2.8 percent in 1986, spending in real terms grew 21 percent between 1980 and 1986, significantly less than the rise in incomes. Personal debt increased to cover the difference. Credit card and installment debt payments rose from 7.3 percent of annual disposable income in 1950 to 15.5 percent in 1980 and 18.8 percent in 1987. Ten years later, consumer debt had reached the staggering level of $1.25 trillion. Spending became an obsession. Consumers in the 1980s increasingly felt they had to buy *something*. One survey found that 80 percent of consumers polled often felt guilty after a buying trip.

More and more people worked in order to spend. Luxuries were redefined as necessities. By the 1990s surveys showed that 27 percent of people earning over $100,000 a year felt they could not afford "the basics." Studies showed that the higher the income, the worse was the level of debt. Victoria Long, quoted in *Investment News* in October 1999, told reporters, "They're making good money, and they're used to having what they want, when they want it."

ATM machines apparently made a difference to many financially threatened couples by making it so easy to spend. Banks eager to give out credit cards offered cheaper initial interest rates. Some people ended up transferring an ever-growing balance from one card to another. In 1998, 1.3 million households filed for personal bankruptcy, eight times greater than in the Great Depression. The Federal Reserve reported in 1999 that customer borrowing had reached an annualized rate of $1.36 trillion, or $143 million per day. Financial planners coined the term "credit junkies."

EXPANDING AND REFINING ADVERTISING ~ For most Americans, participating in the spending spree came at a price. While the trends were already there, the 1980s and 1990s were, for most, a time of increased living standards

> "To succeed, however, the infomercial had to pretend it was something else, because the bane of all television advertising is the remote-control clicker. The infamous 'rule of two-thirds' applies: two-thirds of all viewers surf as a matter of normal viewing, and two-thirds of all the surfers start surfing whenever *any* commercial comes on. In other words, the mere presence of a commercial caused the finger to itch. Surf's up! Programmers estimate that you only have about two to ten seconds to get them to lighten the finger pressure and come to shore."
>
> James B. Twitchell, *20 Ads That Shook the World* (2000)

based on two incomes. With both parents working, weekends no longer remained sacrosanct. To capture the market opportunity, businesses remained open for longer on weekends thus requiring many working people to work and requiring working parents to shop when they could. Work also meant that household chores had to be relegated to weekends. Family time diminished.

Similarly, although television and radio had already "invaded" the home, the 1980s saw the last constraints removed. TV became dramatically more commercialized. By the mid-1990s there were somewhere near 6,000 commercials aired each week. The United States led the world in the cost of per capita TV advertising, 50 percent greater than any other country. Viewers responded after the introduction of remote controls. Advertisers fought back with the introduction of the 15-second commercial designed to capture attention before the viewer had the chance to switch channels. Commercial promotions were also disguised as news for the consumer and health segments of morning TV shows. Infomercials—lengthy commercials designed also to entertain—became increasingly common. The Home Shopping Network developed advertising into a 24-hour entertainment. By 1990, it reached 64 million cable households and impulse buying was elevated into a daily occurrence. All you had to do was pick up the phone. By 1993, revenue from home shopping reached $2.2 billion. MTV also blurred the distinction between entertainment and advertising as performers hawked their recordings 24 hours a day.

TELEVANGELISTS AND TELEMARKETING ~ Even religion was elevated to a sales pitch in the 1980s. By 1977, 92 percent of religious broadcasts were actually paid advertisements. Televangelists in the 1980s occupied niche markets. Traditional, Christian fundamentalism was represented by the Reverend Jerry Falwell. The emotionally well-endowed Jimmy Swaggert carried the revivalist, small-town, rural version of Protestantism. Robert Schuller attracted the comfortable middle class with his crystal cathedral. Jim and Tammy Faye Bakker presented religion as a celebrity talk show and fully mastered the art of fund-raising until they were fabulously rich from their viewers. All became media superstars.

Like so many stars, some fell victim to their own celebrity. In 1987, Jim Bakker's grandiose plans for a Christian version of Disneyland, his obvious inability to distinguish between money donated for the Lord's work and his own and his affair with a church secretary brought his PTL organization down and landed him in jail. Similarly, Jimmy Swaggert's lucrative program was shut down when he was caught with a prostitute. Despite some jail time and on-air repentance during which he announced to the nation that the Lord forgave him, a second offense found his viewers less charitable.

Telemarketing also invaded the home with a vengeance in the 1980s and 1990s. Sophisticated software helped identify potential customers with details such as the income and age of householders. During the early 1990s, revenue increased by 30 percent a year. The advent of the Internet in the 1990s provided yet another opportunity for advertisers and marketing agents to sell to people in their own homes.

CHILDREN AND ADVERTISING ~ Deregulation of children's programming helped turn the young into another market. Cartoon shows became a merchandising vehicle in the 1980s. About 60 percent of all toys sold in the United States in 1987 were based on licensed characters compared to 10 percent in 1980. The movie trilogy *Star Wars* set new heights in merchandising for children. By 1987, 94 figures and 60 accessories had been manufactured by Kenner. While the first two movies grossed $870 million at the box office, by 1983 licensed products added another $2 billion. Disney movies in the 1980s and 1990s were not slow in learning the lesson. Even public television was forced to join in. As its funding was cut year on year, children's favorites like "Sesame Street" and "Arthur" took up merchandising their characters to pay for production costs.

Even in the classroom children could not escape consumerism. In 1989, Chris Whittle launched Channel One. Educational programming came with ads. General Mills sent science teachers a science program about volcanoes that used Fruit Gushers as illustrations. By the mid-1990s, 350 corporations developed similar blends of education and consumerism reaching children 63 million times a year.

According to Gary Cross, children's goods became part of a new era of "fast capitalism." This was the rapid shift from one product line to another on a global scale. No longer did children's toys serve to connect generations or as links between the past and the future. Increasingly, they formed part of a separate fantasy world understood only by children and merchandisers designed to stimulate only the desire for more.

1990S • TARGETED ADVERTISING, FRAGMENTED CULTURE ~ Cable TV, Satellite TV, personal computers and the Internet led critic Joseph Turow to suggest that sophisticated targeting of advertising "will allow, even encourage, individuals to live in their own personally constructed worlds, separated from people and issues they don't care about or don't want to be bothered with." In the 1990s, the Family Channel offering religious and moral programming was just a click away from the teen rebellious chic of MTV; Lifetime, a channel for adult women was a millisecond away from the more macho westerns and action films of TBS. Even for women, by 1985 advertisers had developed eight consumer clusters, double the number in the early 1980s. They discovered roughly forty lifestyle groups. Surveys and purchase records were used to track customer preference.

All this fragmentation, fully developed in the 1980s and 1990s, had social and political effects. Socially, membership in voluntary groups declined. PTA membership dropped from 12 million in 1964 to 7 million in 1993. Jaycees membership dropped 44 percent since 1979. The Red Cross, fraternal lodges, and women's clubs have all suffered significant losses. As reproduced below, Political Scientists Robert Putnam and Steven Yonish found the frequency of many types of community participation declined since 1973, accelerating after 1985.

The new consumerism, according to Gary Cross, "has undermined the coalition building and compromise necessary to formulate clear public policy. Multiple and changing lifestyles may have contributed to political impotence and stalemate." Social problems for some became manageable through purchasing decisions, as seen through the rise of the gated community— suburban developments protected from the outside world by high-tech electronics, private guards and high walls. Thus living environments became packaged.

CONCLUSION

The consumerism that developed during the course of the twentieth century was spearheaded in the United States but was not restricted to it. While the United States in 2000 was the epitome of consumerism, its companies spanned the world, joined by those based in other countries to spread the benefits of mass production and mass consumption. In his 1999 book, *Michael Jordan and the New Global Capitalism*, historian Walter LaFeber tracked the spread of the American consumerist model, the central role of advertising and the growing concentration of economic power in fewer and fewer hands. It is clear that living standards for the majority in the developed world have risen dramatically since the 1950s. It is less clear what the long term effects of our present model of consumerism will bring. Offering no guidance, LaFeber referenced the words of multibillionaire George Soros that we

Table 9: 1973-1994 Declining Community Activities

Served as officer of a club or organization	–42%
Worked for a political party	–42%
Served on a committee for a local organization	–39%
Attended a public meeting on town or school affairs	–35%
Attended a political rally or speech	–34%
Made a speech	–24%
Wrote a congressman or senator	–23%
Signed a petition	–22%
Belonged to a "better government" group	–19%
Held or ran for political office	–16%
Wrote a letter to the paper	–14%
Wrote an article for a magazine or newspaper	–10%
Participated in at least one of these activities	–25%

SOURCE: David G. Myers, *The American Paradox: Spiritual Hunger in an Age of Plenty.* (New Haven: Yale University Press, 2000)

can have a market-driven society but we cannot replace society with the market. If consumerism fragments rather than offers points of common identity then we may be in for a bumpy ride.

Bibliography

Becker, Gary S. and Kevin M. Murphy, "A Simple Theory of Advertising as a Good or Bad." *The Quarterly Journal of Economics*, 108 (November 1993).

Belk, Russell W. and Richard W. Pollay. "Images of Ourselves: The Good Life in Twentieth Century Advertising." *Journal of Consumer Research*, 11 (March 1985).

Boyce, David B. "Coded Desire in 1920's Advertising." *The Gay & Lesbian Review*, 7 (Winter 2000).

Carter, Lendol. *Financing the American Dream: A Cultural History of Consumer Credit*. Princeton: Princeton University Press, 1999.

Comstock, George and Haejung Paik. *Television and the American Child*. San Diego: Academic Press, 1991.

Cross, Gary. *An All-Consuming Century: Why Commercialism Won in Modern America*. New York: Columbia University Press, 2000.

Enstad, Nan. *Ladies of Labor, Girls of Adventure: Working Women, Popular Culture, and Labor Politics at the Turn of the Century*. New York: Columbia University Press, 1999.

Ewen, Stuart. *All Consuming Images: The Politics of Style in Contemporary Culture*. Rev. ed. New York: Basic Books, 1999.

——— and Elizabeth Ewen. *Channels of Desire: Mass Image and the Shaping of American Consciousness*. Minneapolis & London: University of Minnesota Press, 1992.

Frank, Thomas. "The Rise of Market Populism: America's New Secular Religion." *The Nation*, 271 (October 30, 2000).

Galbraith, John Kenneth. *The Affluent Society*. Boston: Houghton Mifflin, 1958.

Glickman, Lawrence B. *A Living Wage: American Workers and the Making of a Consumer Society*. Ithaca & London: Cornell University Press, 1997.

———, ed. *Consumer Society in American History: A Reader*. Ithaca & London: Cornell University Press, 1999.

Hayden, Anders. "Good Work, Less Toil." *Alternatives Journal*, 27 (Winter 2001).

LaFeber, Walter. *Michael Jordan and the New Global Capitalism*. New York: W.W. Norton, 1999.

Leach, William. *Land of Desire: Merchants, Power, and the Rise of a New American Culture*. New York: Pantheon, 1993.

Lears, Jackson. *Fables of Abundance: A Cultural History of Advertising in America*. New York: Basic Books, 1994.

Leiss, William, Stephen Klein, and Sut Jhally. *Social Communication in Advertising: Persons, Products, and Images of Well-Being*. Toronto: Methuen, 1986.

Lynd, Robert S. and Helen Merrell Lynd. *Middletown: A Study in Modern American Culture* 1929. New York: Harcourt Brace Jovanovich, 1956.

Manning, Steven. "Students For Sale: How Corporations Are Buying Their Way Into America's Classrooms." *The Nation* 269 (September 27, 1999).

Marchand, Roland. *Advertising the American Dream: Making Way For Modernity, 1920-1940*. Berkeley: University of California Press, 1986.

McGuire, William J. "Standing on the Shoulders of Ancients: Consumer Research, Persuasion, and Figurative Language." *Journal of Consumer Research*, 27 (June 2000).

Miles, Steven. *Consumerism As A Way of Life*. London: SAGE, 1998.

Moschins, George P. *Acquisition of the Consumer Role by Adolescents*. Research Monograph No. 82. Atlanta: College of Business Administration, Georgia State University, 1978.

Myers, David G. *The American Paradox: Spiritual Hunger in an Age of Plenty*. New Haven & London: Yale University Press, 2000.

Ownby, Ted. *American Dreams in Mississippi: Consumers, Poverty, and Culture, 1830-1998*. Chapel Hill & London: University of North Carolina Press, 1999.

Peiss, Kathy L. "American Women and the Making of Modern Consumer Culture." *The Journal for MultiMedia History*, 1 (Fall 1998). Accessed March 19, 2001. http:www.albany.edu/jmmh/vol1no1/peiss-text.html

———. *Hope in a Jar: The Making of America's Beauty Culture*. New York: Metropolitan Books, 1998.

Pleck, Elizabeth H. *Celebrating the Family: Ethnicity, Consumer Culture, and Family Rituals*. Cambridge, MA: Harvard University Press, 2000.

Pollay, Richard W. "The Distorted Mirror: Reflections on the Unintended Consequences of Advertising." *Journal of Marketing*, 50 (April 1986).

Richins, Marsha L. "Social Comparison and the Idealized Images of Advertising." *Journal of Consumer Research*, 18 (June 1991).

Rutherford, Janice Williams. "A Foot in Each Sphere: Christine Frederick and Early Twentieth-Century Advertising." *The Historian*, 63 (Fall 2000).

Scanlon, Jennifer. *Inarticulate Longings: The Ladies' Home Journal, Gender, and the Promises of Consumer Culture*. New York & London: Routledge, 1995.

Strasser, Susan, Charles McGovern, and Judt Matthias, eds. *Getting and Spending: European and American Consumer Societies in the Twentieth Century*. Washington, DC: Cambridge University Press for the German Historical Society, 1998.

———. *Satisfaction Guaranteed: The Making of the American Mass Market*. New York: Pantheon, 1989.

Twitchell, James B. *20 Ads That Shook The World: The Century's Most Groundbreaking Advertising and How It Changed Us All*. New York: Crown, 2000.

Veblen, Thorstein. *The Theory of the Leisure Class*. New York: Macmillan, 1899.

Weems, Robert E., Jr. *Desegregating the Dollar: African American Consumerism in the Twentieth Century*. New York & London: Columbia University Press, 1998.

Zunz, Olivier. *Why the American Century?* Chicago & London: University of Chicago Press, 1998.

Internet Resources

Advertising Age. On-line version of an industry journal mainstay. Gives news and analysis of the top stories in business and the advertising industry.

http://www.adage.com

American Advertising Federation. The industry organization. The site gives news, advertises its conferences, maintains an Advertising Hall of Fame, shares its club services, has a strong college connection, monitors govern-

ment affairs of interest to the industry, and maintains a section on multiculturalism.
http:// www.aaf.org

Advertising Age- 50 Best Commercials. Exceptionally good for classics of the advertiser's craft. Selections run from the 1940s to the 1990s.
http://www.adage.com/news_and_features/special_reports/commercials/

University of Texas, Department of Advertising. An outstanding site that provides links to large numbers of advertising agencies around the world, particularly those dealing with web advertising. Other pages deal with research in the field, academic courses at the undergraduate and graduate levels, developments in the field around the world and, my personal favorite, great quotes concerning advertising.
http://advertising.utexas.edu/

Adbusters. One of a number of websites devoted to anti-consumerism. Contains details of campaigns, its magazine, spoof ads, and what are called uncommercials.
http://www.adbusters.org/

Supermarketing: Ads From the Comic Books. A very interesting round-up of ads from a specialized medium. Contains classic ads like "Draw any person in one minute. NO TALENT! NO LESSONS!" and "What You Can Do About Pimples" Remember, the YOU that people see first is your face." Part of a much larger commercial site by interactive ad agency Steve Conley that handles accounts for institutions like MTV, World Wide Wrestling Federation, and the World Bank.
http://www.steveconley.com/comindex.htm

American Academy of Advertising. The site of the academic study of advertising. Contains details of membership, a job bank, competitions, fellowships, and awards, and details of upcoming conferences.
http://advertising.utexas.edu/AAA/home.html

"Consumerism" by R. Altschuler & N. Regush. An article excerpted from their book *Open Reality: The Way Out of Mimicking Happiness*. It is a generally hostile analysis of consumerism and its effects on American society.
http://www.bconnex.net/~cspcc/daycare/consume.htm

Ethical Consumerism. Part of the organization OneWorld's efforts to fight consumerism, this site is packed with information. Contains guides to topics like genetic engineering, fair trade, and the World Trade Organisation. Explores issues like full and frank labeling, ethical goods & products, ethical investments.
http://www.oneworld.org/guides/ethcons/front/shtml

Anticonsumerism. If the title is not explicit enough, the site tells that it seeks an end to: Irresponsible Telemarketing, Taxpayer Abuse, Wage Slaves, Multinational Corporations, GATT, the Two-Party System, Career Legislators, 6-Day Work Weeks, Right-Wing Conservatives, Republicans, the Mass Media, Consumer Privacy Abuse, Corporate Welfare, the WTO, False Advertising, Monopolies, "The Company Comes First," Consumer Abuse,

Industry Lobbying, Conservative Judges/ NAFTA, Laissez-Faire Economics, SSN Abuse, Unregulated Credit Bureaus, and Bailouts !!
http://www.consumerzone.org

Consumer.gov. One of a number of federal government web sites that give consumer information. This one provides information, the Consumer Action Handbook, and links to related government sites. Closely related to the Federal Consumer Information Bureau site.
http://www.consumer.gov
and
http://www.info.gov

Food & Drug Administration. Provides a complete listing of products regulated by the FDA, together with safety alerts, press releases, FDA activities, information, research, the FDA Consumer magazine, and FDA Kids.
http://www.fda.gov

Stephen Burwood
SUNY, Geneseo

AMERICAN EXPANSION

~

(1870) A Pullman Locomotive and a line of freight cars at a railroad station in Kankakee, Illinois.

TIMELINE

1785-1860 ~ The New Frontier

Western lands survey procedures set (1785) / Northwest Ordinance (1787) anticipates 3-5 new states / Napoleon Bonaparte threatens to occupy Louisiana (1800) / Northwest Indians side with the British in the War of 1812 / Moses Austin receives 18,000 acres in Texas from Mexico (1820) / U.S. and Britain agree to share Oregon (1827) / Extensive westward migration from the South to claim free land (1830s-1840s) / Mexico forbids American settlers and slaves in Texas territory (1830) / U.S. defeats Mexican army in Texas (1836) / Doctrine of Manifest Destiny begins (1845) / By 1860 half the U.S. population lives in the west / U.S. and Britain settle dispute over Oregon, which they had agreed to share in 1827 (1846) / California and Oregon prohibit slavery (1849)

MILESTONES: Louisiana Purchase doubles the size of the U.S. (1803) • Indian Removal Act forces southern Indian tribes to relocate west of the Mississippi (1830) • Texas Revolution (1835); Texas annexed to U.S. (1845) • After three years of fighting, Mexico cedes California to the U.S. (1848) • Debates rage over slavery in the western territories (1850) • Japan opens doors to the U.S. (1853) • Gadsden Purchase adds southern Arizona and southern New Mexico to U.S. territory (1853) • Colorado gold rush begins (1858)

1860-1900 ~ The West Expands

Homestead Act gives land to settlers (1862) / Indian uprisings cause U.S. military retaliation (1862-1867) / The great cattle drives roll (1865-1870) / Sioux kill Custer's men at Little Bighorn (1876) / Indians massacred at Wounded Knee (1890) / Open Door policy with China begins (1899)

MILESTONES: U.S. purchases Midway Islands (1867) and Alaska (1868) • Britain establishes dominion over Canada (1867) • Panama Canal construction begins (1869; completed 1914) • Capture of Geronimo ends formal warfare between whites and Native Americans (1886) • Pan American Union formed (1889) • Spanish-American war (1898) gives U.S. control of Cuba and the Philippines • Hawaiian Islands (1898) and Samoan Islands (1899) annexed

1900-1945 ~ A Half Century of War

After the Spanish-American War, the U.S. becomes increasingly isolationist (1900-1917) / World War I (1914-1918) forces U.S. into world politics / Puerto Rico becomes U.S. territory (1917) / In the Atlantic Charter (1942), Allies agree not to occupy conquered countries

MILESTONES: U.S. provides war material to Allies (1939-1940) • U.S. freezes Japanese assets (1940) • Japanese bomb Pearl Harbor, forcing the U.S. entry into WWII (1941) • Internment of Japanese Americans (1942-1944) • Allied invasion at Normandy begins the end of WWII (June 6, 1944) • Atomic bombs dropped on Hiroshima and Nagasaki, Japan end the Pacific war (1945)

1946-1969 ~ Fear of Being Conquered

Cold War begins with the Soviet Union demanding control over East Germany (1946) / U.S. deploys military troops at bases throughout the world (1950s) / Proliferation of American culture (fashion, music, sports, entertainment, fast food) throughout the world (1950s-present) / Nikita Kruschev threatens to "bury" America (1957) / Bay of Pigs (1961), Cuban Missile crisis (1962) / President Kennedy commits U.S. to space race (1962) / Americans land on the moon (1969)

MILESTONES: Marshall Plan implemented to rehabilitate Europe (1948) • House Committee on Un-American Activities conducts investigations to find Americans who might be communist (1947) • Korean War (1950-1953) • Alaska and Hawaii become states (1959) • Vietnam War (1964-1975)

1970-2000 ~ Expansion through Commerce

Space exploration continues in full force (1970s) / President Nixon adopts "Détente" policy toward China and the Soviet Union (1971) / President Nixon approves Strategic Arms Limitation Talks to reduce nuclear and conventional weapons (1972) / President Nixon agrees to cooperate with Soviets in space exploration (1972) / Congress eases trade restrictions on China (1972) / Panama Canal scheduled for return to Panamanian control in 1999 (1979) / Fall of the Berlin Wall (1989) / START II treaty further reduces nuclear weapons (1990) / Congress authorizes U.S. troops in Kuwait; Gulf War begins (1991) / North American Free Trade Agreement opens markets between Canada, the U.S. and Mexico (1993) / U.S. commits troops for peace-keeping missions to Africa and the Balkans (1990s)

MILESTONES: Arab Oil Embargo causes energy crisis in the U.S. and accelerates the development of Alaskan oil supplies (1973) • First test-tube baby born in England (1978) • AIDS is recognized as beginning a world-wide epidemic (1981) • First space shuttle, *Columbia*, is launched (April 12, 1981) • Exxon *Valdez* oil spill in Alaska wreaks havoc on the environment (1986) • Dissolution of the Soviet Union ends the Cold War (1991) • Scottish doctors report the cloning of a sheep, "Dolly" (1996)

Introduction

The New World was an unparalleled lure for Europeans because of the belief that it contained vast stores of wealth that were just waiting to be found. The first Europeans who came to the New World were primarily explorers or adventurers seeking gold and glory, both for themselves and the countries they represented. In time, however, the Spanish and Portuguese, who were then followed by the French, Dutch and English, established permanent settlements. Of these settlements, those established by the English in North America would be fated to grow from colonial enterprises into nationhood and then to extend the boundaries of that nation across the continent. The process of national expansion would profoundly shape the character of the American nation.

Englishmen came to the New World in search of wealth, religious freedom, and the chance to start life over again or to own a tract of the apparently infinite amount of land that was available. Many factors fueled the urge for colonial expansion, including population increases, the emergence of new towns in the New England colonies and the growth of the plantation system in Virginia, Maryland and the Carolinas. When the United States gained its independence, expansion not only reflected the continued trend of population growth, but also the attractiveness of the fertile lands of the Mississippi Valley, a sense of national pride and a strategic concern for the safety of the nation. The peace with Great Britain, concluded in 1783, assured American dominance over the eastern part of the continent, opening up access to lands the former colonists had lusted after for decades.

1785 • Land Policy After The Revolution ~ One of the major successes of the new United States of America under the Articles of Confederation was its land policy. The new nation could have treated the "wild west" as a dependency, but chose, instead, to plan for the proper organization and the eventual equality of the western lands. Maryland had insisted that the western lands be pooled for the common good, and this was done. Seven states had claims in the west and finally gave them up, ceding some 150 million acres of land to the United States.

The problem for Congress was how to regulate and dispose of all of this real estate. The answer was provided in the Land Ordinance of 1785. This law called for surveying the western lands before they could be settled, division of the land into rectilinear blocs (for ease of surveying and recording) and the reservation of a section of land for public purposes. These steps would serve to reduce the kind of confusion and litigation that had been common before.

The ideas put forth in the Land Ordinance of 1785 were not new. Surveying, rectilinear division and the public reservation of land were all common practices in New England. The size of individual sections of land—640 acres—was taken from the customs of Virginia and North Carolina.

1787 • Political Organization of the Northwest ~ Once the problem of organizing the western lands had been dealt with the question of the political organization of the northwest arose. The purchase of land by the Ohio and Scioto Companies (in which a number of Congressmen had investments) led to the creation of a territorial government. Congress dealt with this issue when it passed the Northwest Ordinance of 1787.

In this law, Congress decided that the Northwest Territory would eventually be carved up into no less than three and no more than five new states. An "executive government" would administer each of these potential new states until such time as the territory reached a population of five thousand or more free adult males. Then a territorial legislature could be elected and non-voting members could be sent to Congress. Once the population reached sixty thousand or more, a territory could apply for statehood. The Northwest Ordinance also prohibited slavery.

1700s • The Southwest ~ In the Southwest, things were handled differently. All of the land in Kentucky was in private hands when Virginia surrendered her claims there. Additional southern land was not ceded to the United States until after 1790. Land practices in the South proved advantageous to speculators. State governments sold land cheaply, gave away tracts of land to encourage settlement and awarded land as bonuses to veterans. Speculators bought up the rights and held on to them, gambling that they could turn a profit as settlers moved into these lands.

1803 • The Louisiana Purchase ~ Undoubtedly the most significant acquisition of territory in American history was the purchase of Louisiana from France in 1803. This vast territory included the present-day states of Arkansas, Missouri, Iowa, Minnesota, North and South

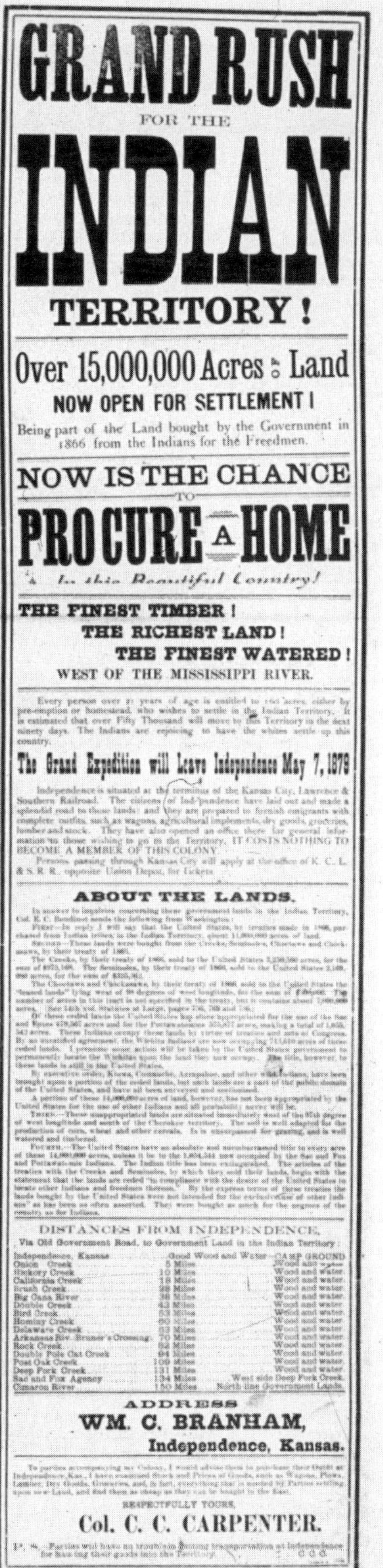

(1879) Rush For Land

Dakota, Nebraska, Oklahoma, most of Kansas, and portions of Montana, Colorado, Wyoming, and Louisiana. It doubled the land size of the United States. After reacquiring Louisiana from Spain, the French Emperor, Napoleon Bonaparte, was dreaming of reviving the French Empire in North America. However, a disastrous slave rebellion in Haiti shattered Napoleon's plan. In addition, Napoleon was planning a new war with England and needed money. To help raise the necessary funds, Napoleon offered Louisiana to the United States. In doing so, Napoleon was playing into American hands.

The presence of France in Louisiana worried the new American president, Thomas Jefferson, who understood the importance of the Mississippi River to the growing number of settlers in the west. Fearing loss of access to the Mississippi, Jefferson and Secretary of State James Madison devised a series of policies that helped convince Napoleon that he would be better off selling Louisiana to the United States.

The United States provided secret support to the slaves rebelling in Haiti in order to undermine French control. In a similar tactic, the government forcibly moved the Indians of the northwest to the regions around the Mississippi to apply additional pressure. Should these strategies prove ineffective, the U.S. prepared plans for an assault on the lower Mississippi.

Napoleon decided to give up France's possessions in North America, and offered Louisiana to the United States for $15 million. Jefferson agreed to the sale. Napoleon would later declare, "This accession of territory affirms forever the

TERRITORIAL EXPANSION OF THE UNITED STATES

(1783–1898)

Date	Territory
1783	The area comprising the 13 original states plus adjacent western territory as agreed to by Great Britain and the United States in the Treaty of Paris.
1803	The Louisiana Purchase (acquired from France)
1810–1813	Annexation of western Florida (taken from Spain as the result of American settlement)
1819	East Florida (acquired from Spain by the Adams-Onis Treaty)
1845	Annexation of Texas (including the Republic of Texas and adjacent territory)
1846	Annexation of Oregon Territory (Oregon Treaty with Great Britain, ending joint occupation of the territory)
1848	Mexican Cession (Treaty of Guadalupe Hidalgo, ending the Mexican War) over Texas
1853	Gadsden Purchase of southern New Mexico and Arizona (from Mexico)
1867	Alaska (purchased from Russia)
1898	Annexation of the Hawaiian Islands
1898	Cession of Puerto Rico and the Philippine Islands (Treaty of Paris with Spain, ending Spanish-American War, ratified February 6, 1899)

power of the United States." He could not have realized just how true his words would prove to be.

The purchase of Louisiana created a constitutional crisis, as nothing in the Constitution specifically authorized this type of acquisition. Jefferson chose to take a liberal interpretation of the Constitution and assumed the nation could acquire and govern large new territories. Congress would authorize the funds and the Louisiana Purchase effectively doubled the size of the United States.

Late-1700s • Attitudes about the Indians ~ Both the laws (1785 and 1787) passed by Congress and the actions of Americans were based on the assumption that they were entitled to the lands of the various Indian nations in the west. Inherent in the process of expansion was the idea that while individuals might settle an area, they would do so with the support of the federal and state governments. This concept would become a cornerstone of American expansion over the next century or more.

From colonial days, the desire of whites for land precipitated conflict with the Native American population. Although the English colonists would concede that the Indians had a right to occupancy—a right of soil—and tried to purchase their lands, the settlers acquired much of the Indian territory through warfare and the seizure of lands by force. The Indians realized the settlers wanted land, and their desire was not compatible with Indian occupancy. The settlers' desire for land ownership was incompatible with traditional Native American attitudes toward shared resources, which does not recognize individual ownership of what belonged to the group. From the first Indian attack on Jamestown in 1622, a series of Indian wars would shatter any hope that white settlers could expand the thirteen colonies without infringing on Indian territory. The new United States would inherit this problem.

Late-1700s • Early Indian Policies ~ The desire of the Founding Fathers for fair treatment of the Indians reflected their sense of rightness of the American Revolution, and their conviction that they were conducting a new and noble experiment. Some of them argued that poor treatment of the Indians would tarnish the national honor and risk comparison with the decadent nations of Europe. These men had to reconcile the national desire for land with the desire for a clear conscience.

At first, the United States pursued a policy of naked power based on the assumption that all the land east of the Mississippi River was American land and the Indians were pawns to be moved at the discretion of the American government. But the expense of a policy of conquest and the moral considerations involved soon ended this approach. Instead, a more elaborate approach was tried. The government returned to the colonial practice of recognizing the Indian's right of soil and tried to purchase it. Additionally, efforts were made to regulate the advance of the frontier. It was hoped that the Indians would be appeased by the purchase of their land and federal controls over expansion.

Despite this policy there was no intention of abandoning national expansion. It was expected that as settlers approached the boundaries of Indian lands, the disappearance of game and their fellow tribesmen would make the Indians agreeable to further purchases and new boundary lines.

(1851) Fort Union was established in 1851 in Watrous, New Mexico to protect the Santa Fe Trail.

Late-1700s • Assimilating the Indians ~ Along with this came the idea of "civilizing" the Indian. Although it was hoped that a policy of purchase and regulated expansion would prevent major Indian wars, it did not solve the problem of a troubled conscience. Continued expansion, even if orderly and controlled, would eventually cause Indian tribes to dwindle in numbers and eventually disappear. The United States might benefit greatly by advancing to the Mississippi, but a nation priding itself on its superiority to the nations of Europe could not allow itself to be placed in a position of exterminating an entire people.

Instead, expansion would be justified by bringing to the Indian the benefits of American civilization. This concept would offer a perfect rationale for the westward advance. Taking lands away from the Indians would ultimately prove to be a blessing for them. American expansion, therefore, would benefit not only the American people but also those who stood in its path.

There were flaws in this thinking. No allowance was made for the desires of the states, the settlers, or the Indians. The states constantly ignored federal endeavors to assure an orderly westward migration and the American frontiersman had no interest in an orderly advance. Faced with the choice of conflict with its citizens or the Indians, the federal government invariably chose the latter.

The fatal flaw in this reasoning was the misjudgment of the Indians themselves, perhaps from a refusal to face reality. The Indians did not want to give up their lands, and were prepared to fight rather than accept repeated requests for sales of land. Every significant white advance brought about bitter resentment and hostilities.

Attempting to "civilize" the Indians failed as well. The white people of this age did not understand that acculturetion was a long and incredibly difficult process. Even when there was limited success, as with the Cherokees, the advancing settlers had no interest in maintaining the good reputation of the United States government. The frontiersman was more interested in getting the Indian to give up his land rather than having him learn to farm it. The result was hostility, hatred and bloodshed all along the frontier.

The policies of the American government foreshadowed later attempts in the 19th century to defend expansion on the basis of a firm moral foundation. Now it was the Indian who would receive the benefits of American civilization. Later it would be Mexicans and the Canadians; still later, Hawaiians, Filipinos and even the Chinese.

1790s • Impact of Expansion on the Eastern Tribes ~ The attempt to develop a policy of peaceful expansion that would satisfy national honor and interests ultimately failed. Instead, the process of expansion forcibly displaced Indian nations or totally wiped them out.

Expansion, for example, completed the breakup of the Iroquois Confederation, begun with their earlier support of the British. War and continued encroachment of whites destroyed the unity of the confederation and any coherent plan for resisting American expansion. Some of the Mohawks decided to move to Canada rather than resist white expansion. While part of the Iroquois chose to move west in the hope of preserving their way of life, those in upstate New York bargained away large tracts of their land in return for guaranteed settlements on reservations. These actions did not prevent social collapse or demoralization, however. In the 1790s a Seneca warrior named Handsome Lake would urge an accommodation with white Americans, calling for the warriors to become farmers, to accept Christian missionaries and to avoid the white evils of alcohol and gambling.

Other Indians resisted American settlers more aggressively. Shawnee resistance in Ohio was broken at the Battle of Fallen Timbers in 1794, leading to the cession of most of the Shawnee lands east of the Mississippi. Before long, what was left was invaded by whites, leaving the Shawnees close to starvation. In response to Shawnee pleas for relief from the United States, federal officials advised the Shawnees to take up farming in place of hunting and to sell off more land to raise cash.

As the federal government extracted more land from the Indians, younger braves rebelled, social disintegration set in and the Indians became more dependent on trade with the whites. Growing frustration led many to alcohol, and the drunkenness, along with random violence, only intensified the sense of shame for many. Family ties broke down, as did other traditional patterns of conduct and behavior.

1800-1840 • The Last Indian Wars in the Northwest ~ In 1808, a spiritual movement that had begun with the Shawnee and spread to other tribes became more openly political. Under the leadership of the Shawnee warrior, Tecumseh, the northwestern tribes again began to resist white incursion. A defeat at Tippecanoe was a major setback, and despite allying themselves with the British during the War of 1812, another defeat by American forces at the Thames River in Canada effectively broke Indian resistance to white settlement of the Old Northwest for nearly twenty years. A last attempt at resistance was the Black Hawk

War of 1832. The Sac and Fox Indians tried to take back their old lands in Illinois after having been removed from them. This led to federal military action and the Sac and Fox were defeated. There were no further attempts at Indian resistance in the Old Northwest.

By the 1830s the United States had acquired most of the Indian lands of the Northwest and the Shawnees and other tribes had been moved further west. In the South, tribes such as the Creeks, Choctaws, Cherokees and others tried various methods to deal with the white invaders. Some tried armed resistance; others voluntarily moved west; still others made the change to an agricultural lifestyle. However, most faced the same result: defeat and forced removal to the west in the 1830s.

Many Americans viewed the Indian as a nuisance or, perhaps more accurately, as an impediment to the growth and prosperity of the West. Even those tribes which conformed to white standards of civilization were not immune to land encroachment. The five "civilized nations" in the South—the Choctaw, Creeks, Cherokees, Chickasaw and Seminoles—controlled some 33 million acres of valuable land, which was coveted by whites. These five tribes had become settled agricultural societies, were politically sophisticated and quite literate. They had conformed to white society and hoped to be left alone. However, their 33 million acres of valuable land made them an impediment to white progress. During the 1820s, the Georgia, Alabama and Mississippi legis-

(circa 1850) Westward! Until the transcontinental railroad line was completed in 1869, wagon trains provided transportation across the frontier.

latures passed legislation overturning federal treaties granting special self-governing status to the Indian lands. This represented a challenge to federal authority as only the federal government had the responsibility for dealing with Indian affairs.

However, the states had the support of President Andrew Jackson. At his urging, Congress passed the Indian Removal Act in 1830, which provided money for the relocation of Indian tribes, by force if necessary. The Choctaws moved west in that same year. However, the Cherokees fought back through the law. In a pair of lawsuits in 1831 and 1832 (*Cherokee Nation v. Georgia,* and *Worcester v. Georgia)*, the Cherokees won a Supreme Court decision stating they could not be forced to give up their land against their will.

President Jackson refused to uphold the court's decision and continued to press for the relocation of the remaining tribes. The removal of the Creeks was completed in 1836, that of the Choctaws in 1837. The Cherokee were also forced to relocate. Escorted by 7,000 federal troops, they were moved to Oklahoma. Thousands of Cherokees died during the journey over what became known as the *"Trail of Tears"*.

1830s-1840s • Westward Migration ~ The westward movement of the 1830s and 1840s was made up mostly of people from the South. These people came from the southern part of the Ohio Valley, the Cumberland and Tennessee Valleys and the valley of the lower Missouri and lower Arkansas. What they found especially attractive were the beautiful farmlands in Texas and the Far West that could be purchased for a relatively cheap price.

1830s-1840s • Western Society ~ The society among those who went west during this time was made up of a variety of unruly characters. They believed in direct action and could quickly become violent. The southern code of honor and dueling was very strong. Duels were often fought with knives, brawls with clubs and shillelaghs were common, and "wars" that sprawled over several counties between outlaws and vigilantes took place on occasion. The rough river towns along the Mississippi attracted keelboat men and flatboat men. These were the men Mark Twain would later describe as "half-horse, half-alligator;" river pirates and outlaw gangs haunted other parts of the river.

The chief rivers of the region—the Ohio, Missouri and Mississippi—kept card sharks, gamblers, outlaws, counterfeiters and thieves in constant circulation. Into St. Louis came the half-wild mountain men, eager to sell their furs and drink. Arkansas and Missouri were the last stops for the coarse traders from Santa Fe; the hill areas of the South contained so-called "poor white trash," and the Indian reservations along the western borders of Missouri and Arkansas attracted those who preyed on the Native Americans.

1607-1916 • Women on the Frontier ~ Although most often associated with the treks across the Great Plains and the years of expansion after the Civil War, women had an essential role in the process of American expansion from the earliest days of the colonial period. The first women to play an important role in American history were those who arrived at Jamestown in 1607, followed by the Pilgrim women who landed in Massachusetts in 1620. The arrival of these women and those who came after them established a basic pattern in the expansion of the colonies and later the United States; as long as there was an American frontier, women worked side by side with men in the exploration and settlement of the North American continent.

Women survived tribulations and conditions equivalent to any that men suffered through. Women, like men, were killed or taken captive by Indians along the frontier, saw their children killed or taken captive, fought alongside men against Indian attacks, and also survived harrowing journeys. Hannah Dustin of Massachusetts is said to have killed and scalped ten Indians in revenge for having been taken captive in 1697. Women were among ten defenders of a cabin that fought off an Indian attack that resulted in the deaths or capture of most of the inhabitants of Deerfield, Massachusetts in 1704. Some women, like Mary Jemison, adopted the culture of those who took them captive. Others, such as Mary Draper Ingles, managed to escape and return to their homes, although often at the cost of leaving their children behind. These conditions were common throughout the colonial period.

Similar dangers were faced by women as the American frontier continued to move west. Women did their part in fighting off Indian attacks, dealing with harsh conditions and often endured near-starvation when game was scarce. Settlements carried their share of dangers, too. Women often spent a great deal of time alone while their men pursued political or military careers, and had to deal with the perils of frontier living by themselves.

Atrocities occurred on both sides of the wars with the Indians, and women were killed just as men were. Often, if women survived an Indian attack, they suffered a much worse fate than those who died during a battle. This was the case of frontier women in Minnesota who were captured and burned alive by the Sioux, or who were kept as slaves and hostages. American soldiers shot Indian women and children at Wounded Knee.

While women proved themselves by suffering through the same frontier ordeals as men, their status was also enhanced by their relative scarcity. Men were so anxious to have women join them in remote parts of the west that they offered economic and political incentives that were not common in urban areas. The ability of a woman to easily find another man if one mistreated her tended to limit male misconduct and led to liberalized rules and legal codes, particularly regarding divorce. Jobs were also available to women in the west that were generally limited to men in the east.

This was especially true in education. Men moving west in search of free or cheap land were not interested in teaching. Women were recruited to fill the void, and thousands moved west to become teachers. Some, such as Carrie Chapman Catt, became the heads of large educational institutions. By the early twentieth century, women were serving as trustees of state universities. Western women also enjoyed greater educational opportunities in the more liberal west.

Thousands of black women moved west. While often employed as domestic servants or professional cooks, they settled the west in significant numbers. In 1870 there were some 8,000 black women in Kansas; by 1910 the number exceeded 26,000. Oklahoma, once reserved only for displaced Native Americans, was also popular with black settlers. According to Ida Wells-Barnett, entire black congregations moved to

Oklahoma in order to escape racial violence, which was common in Memphis in the early 1890s.

The more liberal attitudes of the west benefited women in a number of ways. Women in the Wyoming Territory were the first to become enfranchised, in late 1869. However, the first women actually to exercise the right to vote lived in the Utah Territory and cast ballots for the first time in 1870. The Mormon Church proved to be active in the support of women's suffrage into the first part of the twentieth century.

The west also led the way in establishing a number of other civil rights for women. Wyoming provided for property rights for married women in 1869. Wyoming women could also sue, enter into contracts and serve on juries by 1870. Wyoming even provided for equal pay for women and men in public employment. The west also gave the nation its first female public officials. Again, Wyoming led the way with the election of Esther Morris as a justice of the peace in 1870. Over the next three or four decades, western women won positions in state governments, legislative positions, and in 1924, Wyoming and Texas elected the first women as state governors, Nellie Tayloe Ross and Miriam Ferguson. The first woman elected to Congress, Jeanette Rankin, was elected from Montana in 1916.

1830s-1840s • Economic Motives for Going West ~ Economic troubles in the 1830s and 1840s contributed to the restlessness and social disorder of the time. The Panic of 1837 produced a depression that made American society tense, restless and eager for change. The result was social discontent and movement westward toward California, Oregon and Texas.

Texas was particularly attractive because of an abundance of good, cheap land and sparse settlement. There were only three important outposts of Spanish civilization and no more than three or four thousand settlers. Several efforts were made by Americans to get the area to break away from Spain so that it could be added to the United States but they all failed.

In 1821, Mexico gained its independence from Spain, and, in an effort to increase the settlement of Texas, the Mexican government passed a law in 1823 permitting foreign colonization and offered generous land grants to attract settlers. Colonists were exempt from taxes for six years and would pay half-taxes for six years afterwards. Each family was permitted to bring $2,000 in duty-free goods with them. The only requirements were conversion to Catholicism and citizenship with Mexico after three years of settlement.

1820s • The Austins in Texas ~ A pair of Americans, Moses Austin, and his son, Stephen F. Austin, helped conceive this idea. Moses Austin had settled in Texas in 1820 after receiving a grant of 18,000 acres of land from the Mexican government. However, he died in 1821, and Stephen took over the grant and assisted in writing the final provisions of the 1823 law.

This system was expected to benefit Mexico by developing Texas and other parts of the country as well as enriching the new nation. The new settlements were intended to provide a buffer against the Indian raids from the Great Plains while, at the same time, communities of superior quality would be quickly established. It was assumed that Europeans, Americans and Mexicans would find the opportunity equally attractive. It apparently did not occur to the lawmakers that only Anglo-Americans would settle in Texas.

In fact, only Americans came in substantial numbers. Most Mexicans were either unwilling to run the risks of the frontier, or lacked the means or the enterprise to move north. Those Europeans who came to the Americas usually preferred to settle in the United States.

By 1830, out of a total population of between 25 and 30 thousand people in Texas, only about 4,000 were native Mexicans. The rest were chiefly Americans. The rapid growth of American settlers in Texas alarmed the Mexican government, which feared Texas was becoming an American state. Repeated efforts of the United States to buy Mexico (1825, 1827, 1829) only added to the growing concern.

The Mexican government sent a fact-finding commission to Texas in 1828 to investigate and report on the situation there. The commission took a year to complete its task and its report confirmed what Mexico feared. Americans were clearly in the majority in Texas and they were ignoring the colonization law of 1823. Also, they were bringing slaves into Texas with them.

In 1830, the Mexican Congress passed a law forbidding further American colonization of Texas and the importation of slaves. A greater effort to encourage Mexican colonization was made, but was unsuccessful. Meanwhile Americans continued to come to Texas, increasing friction between Mexico and the United States.

1830s • The Status of Americans in Texas ~ Texas did not have the status of statehood in Mexico. That area had been joined with another region called Coahuila to form a state. Coahuila had a larger population and was able to send more delegates to the Mexican Congress than Texas. But, as the population of Texas grew, the settlers began to demand that Texas be made a separate state.

There were other areas of dissatisfaction for Americans in Texas. They had enjoyed an exemption from tariffs until 1830; once the exemption expired, Americans were paying the same high duties as the Mexican people. These duties were quite high in order to protect Mexican industry, and many Americans simply evaded the tariff issue through wholesale smuggling.

Texans were expected to become Catholics as a condition of receiving land. Few did so. However, Mexican law required all marriages to be performed by Catholic priests and children born into marriages not performed by a priest had no right of inheritance. This was a constant irritant for Americans in Texas.

Mexico did not permit slavery, and this too became a major source of friction. Texans avoided the law by claiming their slaves were indentured servants who would be freed once their value in wages was worked out. The amount of wage value was set high enough, however, that the "indentured servant" could never earn his freedom. While the number of slaves in Texas was small, perhaps no more than a thousand, many Texans planned to create cotton plantations (most were raising cattle then), and they resented Mexican restrictions.

1830s • Efforts to Resolve the Problems ~ The take-over of the Mexican government by General Antonio Lopez de Santa Anna in 1832 led to some efforts to find a solution to these issues. Santa Anna appeared willing to repeal the 1830 law forbidding further American settlement, but he would not give in on the tariff issue or separate statehood for Texas. Over the next few years, Stephen F. Austin attempted to mediate a settlement of these problems, even being imprisoned for eighteen months because of his efforts, but failed to bring the Mexicans and Texans together.

1835-1836 • The Texas Revolution ~ Mexican officials saw the unrest in Texas as a rebellion against their authority. Arrest warrants were issued for all the troublemakers that could be identified and troops were sent to San Antonio. Texans were advised to arm themselves and when the town of Gonzales refused to surrender a cannon to Mexican officials in September 1835, the Texas Revolution was under way.

The Texas Revolution was not the result of a cruel, tyrannical Mexican government. Instead it came about partly because the Mexican government had proved to be weak and indecisive, and because the government was suffering from disorder and corruption. The misperception of the Mexican government as being tyrannical was the result of Texan propaganda. Mexico made the mistake of allowing unruly and aggressive American frontiersmen into her territory—people who proved to be contemptuous of Mexico and Mexican authority—and these frontiersmen promoted the Texas Revolution.

American public opinion completely favored the revolution in Texas. The propaganda of the Texans themselves and the American press were very effective. Santa Anna was portrayed as a tyrant and a butcher who would soon be overthrown, while the Texans were pictured as heroes, especially those who died defending the Alamo. Americans were also led to believe that this was a conflict between Protestants and Catholics, which strengthened support in the United States for the revolt in Texas among a predominantly Protestant constituency. Volunteers rushed to Texas to help in the fight; money and supplies also poured in.

The revolution ended with the *Battle of San Jacinto* on April 21, 1836. Thinking he had the Texan army trapped, Santa Anna allowed his army to rest in the afternoon. Having failed to post sentries, the Mexicans were caught by surprise when the Texans attacked and overwhelmed them. Santa Anna signed a treaty recognizing Texan independence and setting the southern border of Texas at the Rio Grande River. The Mexican Congress, however, rejected the treaty

(1851) A crowd gathering around a man reading the news of American successes in Mexico, which led to the ceding to the United States of California and New Mexico.

1815-1860

and refused to recognize Texan independence. Texas would be annexed by the United States in 1845, but the question of admitting a slave state and other issues would delay the process of annexation.

1815-1860 • Population Growth in the West Before the Civil War ~ Between 1815 and 1860 the West gained a population of about 15,000,000 Americans. By 1860, even California had a population of about 380,000. Out of a population of nearly 31,000,000 Americans in 1860, half lived in the West, occupying territories and states that had not even been settled when George Washington was president.

Americans moved west in large numbers between 1815 and 1860; the motivation for doing so varied among individuals and groups and from region to region.

Personal motives included restlessness or individualism, fleeing the law, running away from debts or escaping an unhappy marriage. Women and children normally traveled west with husbands and parents. The move was often difficult for married women, who left family, friends and

Rapid Growth in Western Cities

STATE/CITY	1840	1850	1860	1870	1880	1890	1900	1910
ARIZONA								
Phoenix				240	1708	3152	5544	11134
Tucson		400	915	3224	7007	5150	7531	13193
CALIFORNIA								
Los Angeles		1610	4395	5728	11183	50395	102479	319918
San Francisco		34870	56802	149473	233959	298997	342782	416912
COLORADO								
Colorado Springs				1480	4226	11140	21085	29078
Denver			4749	4759	35629	106713	133859	213381
KANSAS								
Abilene				800	2360	3547	3507	4118
Wichita				960	4911	23853	24671	52450
MONTANA								
Butte				241	3363	10723	30470	39165
Helena				3106	3624	13834	10770	12515
OKLAHOMA								
Oklahoma City						4151	10037	64205
Tulsa						57	1390	18182
TEXAS								
Amarillo						482	1442	9957
Dallas		250	2000	4500	10358	38067	42638	92104
Houston	1500	2396	4845	9382	16513	27557	44633	78800

SOURCE: Moffat, Riley. *Population History of Western U.S. Cities and Towns 1850-1990*. Lanham MD: The Scarecrow Press, 1996.

familiar things behind, but for single women the West provided a land of opportunity. Their chances of finding a husband improved because of the high ratio of men to women, and because they were not hampered by their previous circumstances of social status.

Economic motives may have been the strongest reason for going west. New England began to turn toward wool production in the 1820s and most arable land was being turned into sheep-grazing areas. This process dislodged many small and tenant farmers who then went west in search of new opportunity. Later on, immigration from New England was spurred by competition from the west due to the influx of cheaper grain and wheat, which was coming in by canal and railroad. New England farmers found it impossible to undersell their western competitors; so many farmers packed up and headed west to join the competition.

At first people in the Mid-Atlantic States had less reason to move west, primarily because the land they were working was better than that of New England. However, by the 1840s even these people

1920	1930	1940	1950	1960	1970	1980	1990
29053	48118	65414	106818	439170	581562	789704	900013
20292	32506	36752	45454	212892	262933	330537	405390
576673	1238048	1504277	1970358	2479015	2811801	2966763	3485398
506676	634394	634536	775357	740316	715674	678974	723959
30105	33237	36789	45472	70194	135517	215150	281140
256491	287861	322412	415786	493887	514678	491396	467710
4895	5658	5671	5775	6746	6661	6572	6242
72217	111110	114966	168279	254698	276554	279272	304011
41611	39532	37081	33251	27877	23368	37205	33336
12037	11803	15056	17581	20227	22730	23938	24569
91295	185389	204424	243504	324253	368164	403213	444719
72075	141258	142517	182740	261685	330350	360919	367302
15494	43132	51686	74246	137969	127010	149230	157615
158976	260475	294734	434462	679684	844401	904078	1006877
138276	292352	384514	596163	938219	1232802	1595138	1630553

were beginning to trek westward, drawn by the pull of new and better lands to work. Meanwhile, in the Old South, the declining fertility of the soil in the Chesapeake region and in South Carolina and Georgia sent people west in the hope of finding better land on which to grow cotton. In addition to individuals moving west, so did entire communities. Most notable were the Mormons, whose journeys took them from New York to Ohio, then to Missouri, back to Illinois and finally to Utah.

1840s • Effects of the Westward Movement on Society ~ American society was deeply affected by the Westward Movement. The historian Frederick Jackson Turner would later argue (the *Turner Thesis*) that this movement had several effects on both individuals and society:

1. The Westward Movement reduced society to its essentials—men and women were forced to rely on their unaided resources in order to survive and prosper.
2. People became more egalitarian—one man was just as good as another, and people came to believe in the worth of the plain or average person.
3. People became more idealistic—many people moved west in search of new ways of living or a better social order.

The pioneers, who were spread out and faced a harsh, primitive environment, had to be extremely self-reliant in order to survive. Western codes included mutual support, often through social activities such as barn raising, fence building, cooperative harvesting, and quilting bees. When medical help was unavailable, neighbors pitched in there as well.

Westerners tended toward brawling and violent behavior, even before the day of the gunfighter. Iowans were famous for knife fighting in the 1840s, for example. Fights in which cutting, eye gouging and nose biting were common ways of settling disputes. Efforts to impose law and order were often carried out by vigilantes, demonstrating a tendency of westerners to take the law into their own hands.

Many people went west in search of independence and wealth, and many were beguiled by "get rich quick" schemes and speculation. The previous table shows the rapid growth in Western cities as a result of people seeking fortune and opportunity.

1844 • Year of Decision ~ America's year of decision regarding the west came in 1844. The concept of Manifest Destiny, which embraced the idea that the borders of the United States should extend all the way to the Pacific shore, was embraced by politicians and the press. Earlier presidents had hesitated to annex Texas, fearing war with Mexico. But now, popular opinion demanded that not only Texas, but California and Oregon be annexed as well. Former statesmen had avoided offending England, as that nation also had claims in the Oregon territory. An overwhelming shift in public opinion was taking place, with American expansion to the Pacific Ocean the inevitable result.

The first expression of this new sentiment took place during the presidential election of 1844. The Whig candidate, Henry Clay, opposed the annexation of Texas. The Democrats chose to meet the issue head on, bypassing the favorite for the party's nomination, Martin Van Buren, who also opposed annexing Texas, for James K. Polk of Tennessee, who was an avowed expansionist.

While the election itself was not a clear mandate for expansion (Polk won 15 of 26 states by an electoral vote of 170-105), the important aspect was the *impression* created by Polk's victory. He had run on a platform in favor of expansion at any cost and he was obligated to carry out his campaign promises.

1840s • American Opinions about Expansion ~ The shift in public opinion can be traced to three basic factors: a persistent westward movement, the fear of other nations, and the emergence of a new spirit that would come to be called "Manifest Destiny".

The relentless advance of the pioneers made expansion almost inevitable. Wherever he went, the frontiersman demanded that America's protective arm be extended over him. The statesmen of the day also believed expansion was inevitable, and that whoever was willing to fight for land should own it. This, for many, was justification enough to add Texas, Oregon and California to the Union.

Many loyal citizens fervently believed that the western territory would be taken by some foreign power if the United States did not act at once. The most dreaded rival was England, which had attempted to reclaim America during the War of 1812. The animosity was revived in the 1840s by British criticisms of the United States as "a nation of swindlers" who had repudiated their debts during the Panic of 1837. Unfavorable characterizations by British travelers such as Charles Dickens, who portrayed Americans as tobacco-spitting, eye-gouging, drunken, brawling, slave-beating semi-barbarians, added to the resentment. Also, the two countries had been bickering since 1837 over American aid to Canadian revolutionaries, and a boundary dispute between Maine and New Brunswick.

Rumors that England was working to prevent the U.S. annexation of Texas only added fuel to the fire. The rumors did have some truth to them. The British would have preferred an independent Texas in the belief it would make a good ally in the event of war with the United States, as an outlet for British capital and manufactures and as a source of supply of cotton for British textile mills. The British may also have believed an independent Texas might help bring a halt to the expansion of American slavery. While it was obvious that if Texas were admitted to the United States it would be as a slave state, there was the possibility that an independent Texas might be persuaded to free her slaves.

American public opinion, especially in the South, was filled with anger. It was believed that England was working to end slavery in the United States now that slavery in the British Empire had been eliminated. A slave rebellion in Cuba that broke out shortly after the visit of a British dignitary seemed to confirm this thinking.

The French were also perceived as a threat, especially in Texas. France also preferred Texan independence rather than lose a profitable market, and feared the annexation of Texas would lead to a war with Mexico. A Mexican defeat would harm the prestige of the Catholic Church and France's ally, Spain. France instructed her minister in the United States to quietly oppose annexation every way he could. Rumors of the French attitude also aroused American indignation and concern about European intervention in North America.

California also seemed to be a target of both England and France, although, in fact, there was little real danger in that regard. Neither nation had much interest in California. Mexican offers to repay her debts with tracts of land in California and the efforts of a few Englishmen to plant colonies there stirred American concerns but the British government was opposed to such schemes. The appearance of a French gunboat off the California coast following an uprising there in 1840, which led to the deaths of a few French nationals, also alarmed Americans who feared California would be lost unless it was annexed immediately.

1840s • Manifest Destiny ~ During the 1840s Americans began to ascribe to the idea that they possessed a God-given destiny in world affairs. They now believed that eventually their "perfect" democratic institutions would spread first throughout North America, and then the world. By the 1840s the idea that the example of the United States would be enough to change institutions elsewhere was no longer sufficient. The rest of the world wasn't changing and some of the "backward" "unenlightened" monarchies appeared to be threatening to halt the march of democracy in America. Positive steps were needed to extend what Andrew Jackson had once called the "area of freedom".

This decision was easy to rationalize. Expansion would allow the United States to fulfill its role as the "mother of liberty," and would elevate and enlighten the millions kept in bondage by the archaic governments of Mexico or England and give them a new spirit of enterprise. It would also solidify the liberties of the American people by creating new states to challenge the authority of the federal government, while leading Americans west where the democratic forces of the new frontier would radiate over the land. The editor of the *New York Morning News*, John L. O'Sullivan, who wrote in December of 1845 of America's "manifest destiny" to possess the entire American continent, provided the slogan. The phrase swept the nation and was caught up by Congressmen and editors, who urged the nation to extend American blessings to the unfortunate. This, they claimed, was America's destiny and the will of God.

Therefore, the continuous advance of the frontier, the fear of England and France and the belief in "Manifest Destiny" all shaped American opinion in the 1840s and fueled the expansionist movement.

1840s • Manifest Destiny and Texas ~ Texas was the first area to be impacted by this new belief. In the past, John Quincy Adams, Andrew Jackson and Martin Van Buren had all resisted the annexation of Texas, fearing war with Mexico and opposition from conservative southern Whigs and radical northern abolitionists. The election of Polk, however, was now seen as a mandate for the annexation of Texas. This led outgoing president, John Tyler, to call for Texas' annexation.

Adding to the drive to bring Texas into the union was a British scheme to guarantee the independence of that state. The British foreign minister offered a proposal calling for a combination of England, France, Mexico and Texas to guarantee Texan independence. This proposal, if accepted by all the parties, would have committed England and France to go to war to keep Texas independent. Once the British understood the depth of American hostility to the proposal, they backed away from it and the matter was dropped.

The harm had been done, however. News of the proposal inflamed Americans, who were convinced England was ready to go to war over Texas. Well, so were they! President Tyler urged Congress to pass a joint resolution of annexation. This was done in January 1845 and Tyler signed the resolution two days before leaving the presidency. The Texas Congress voted unanimously to join the United States in June 1845, and Texas officially joined the union on December 29, 1845.

1840s • Manifest Destiny and Oregon ~ The Oregon territory, comprising the current-day states of Oregon and Washington, was the next ripe plum to fall. The area was claimed by both the United States and England in the Treaty of Joint Occupation of 1827, which had opened the area to settlement. There had been no problems as long as just a few trappers were the only people in the area. By the early 1840s, however, thousands of Americans were pouring into the Willamette Valley of Oregon to settle, and they were demanding a stable government to protect them. The obvious solution was to divide the territory between England and the United States. The question was where to divide it.

The boundaries of the Oregon territory were from the forty-second parallel in the south to the line of fifty-four degrees, forty minutes in the north. The entire area was not in dispute. The British were willing to settle along a line that followed the Columbia River to the sea. This would assure British control of an area dominated by the Hudson's Bay Company. Four times earlier, the United States had offered to extend the forty-ninth parallel boundary to the Pacific. The area of dispute lay between the forty-ninth parallel and the Columbia River.

The Democrats, however, had campaigned on the slogan of "fifty-four, forty or fight", and talked brazenly of "all of Oregon or none" during the campaign of 1844. James K. Polk had been elected with a dangerous promise to keep: he had to get all of Oregon from England, even if it meant war.

The temper of the American people would not allow Polk to delay. Oregon conventions had met regularly out west since 1842. A national convention in Cincinnati indicated war was agreeable if that was what it would take to obtain Oregon. Congress debated fortifying the Oregon Trail, abrogating the Treaty of 1827, and setting up a territorial government. None of these warlike measures was passed, but Polk understood something would have to be done soon.

In his inaugural address, Polk bluntly warned England that the United States had clear title to Oregon and was prepared to defend it. As war rumors flared, Polk advised the British Minister to the United States, Richard Pakenham, that the United States was willing to accept a compromise along the forty-ninth parallel. Pakenham refused the compromise and did not bother to inform his government of the President's offer.

In December 1845, Polk asked Congress to give him the power to abrogate the Treaty of 1827 and to extend the protection of American laws over the settlers in Oregon. Three weeks later, Polk rejected British offers to negotiate. He had public opinion behind him and was willing to risk war if necessary to get what he wanted.

A settlement was eventually made possible by the Hudson's Bay Company, which controlled the area in dispute. The presence of some five thousand American settlers in the Willamette Valley, as

(circa 1850) Gold Prospectors in California

1840s

opposed to a few hundred British in the region, made the Americans a threat that could not be ignored. If the settlers decided to march across the Columbia River and burn Fort Vancouver, there was no stopping them. But, more importantly, so many settlers in the area had already seriously disrupted the fur trade. The Hudson Bay Company, therefore, decided to withdraw from the disputed region and set up its base of operations at Fort Victoria on Vancouver Island.

The British government welcomed this news. Lord Aberdeen, the Foreign Minister, had a low opinion of the Oregon territory to begin with, having referred to it as a "pine swamp", and he believed the United States had a legitimate claim to a port on the Pacific coast. However, Aberdeen delayed accepting a settlement immediately, preferring to wait and make an agreement seem less like a British surrender. Some opposition within the government had to be overcome, but the general support of the British public for a peaceful resolution and the sense that the Empire should not expand any further, allowed Aberdeen to propose a settlement of the dispute at the forty-ninth parallel in June 1846.

Polk was agreeable and a treaty was soon sent to the Senate for ratification. The Senate quickly approved the agreement and within two weeks of the British proposal, the Senate's swift ratification meant another parcel of territory had been added to the expanding American nation.

1840s • Manifest Destiny and California ~ Meanwhile, the same formula was beginning to operate in California. As in the case of Texas, a rich area was held by a weak neighbor, and just barely at that. The United States openly desired California and made futile efforts to buy it from Mexico. As with Texas, the peaceful settlement of Americans in California was followed by a revolution designed to secure the independence of the region, then annexation. Mexico naturally felt the United States was plotting to steal its northern provinces and would come to believe that war was the only way to keep this from happening.

The efforts to acquire California began with Andrew Jackson, whose attempts included trying to bribe the Mexican government to sell the area. President Tyler tried to acquire the San Francisco harbor in 1842, but negotiations fell through after an American naval squadron seized Monterey on an erroneous report that Mexico and the United States had gone to war. Despite American apologies, the damage had been done and further negotiations were impossible.

Fate played into American hands in 1845. After numerous rebellions, California had descended into anarchy. Two governors now claimed to rule California. The appointed governor, Pio Pico, made his capital at Los Angeles, while the military commander of the region, Jose Castro, controlled the old capital at Monterey. Quarrels between the two led to fighting, which caused the government to cease functioning; the machinery of justice collapsed and the small army there degenerated into an uncontrolled mob. The resulting chaos led many respectable Californians, including native-born Mexicans, to believe the time had come to leave Mexico. Many of them preferred to join the United States rather than become an independent state when Polk became president.

Word that the Mexican government was near collapse led Polk to dispatch an agent named John Slidell, of New Orleans, to Mexico with an offer to buy California. Slidell was instructed to avoid antagonizing the Mexicans and to offer $40 million for California and as much of the Southwest as Mexico might wish to sell. Given the situation in California and the tense relations between Mexico and the United States, Slidell's best hope was to complete the transaction before his mission became known. However, word leaked out and the Mexican government refused to receive Slidell and the last hope for the peaceful acquisition of California died.

Polk immediately turned to intrigue. He sent a letter to the American consul in Monterey, Thomas O. Larkin, instructing him to further the designs of those who preferred to separate from Mexico, but not to start a revolution. Larkin was quite skillful and, if left to his own devices, might have won California for the United States.

However, Polk was becoming impatient, and the continued settlement of aggressive American frontiersmen in California led to a violent solution. Alarmed by rumors that Pio Pico was leaning toward England, Polk used his connections with explorer John Charles Fremont and, by doing so, may have brought about a clash. Fremont was the son-in-law of Senator Thomas Hart Benton, and had established a camp near Sutter's Fort in California late in 1845. The presence of Fremont and his sixty well-armed frontiersmen made Californians edgy and suspicious of his motives. The other California "governor", Castro, ordered Fremont and his men to leave in March 1846. Fremont flew into a rage, moved his band to a steep hill called Hawk's Peak, raised the American flag, and defied the Mexicans to make him withdraw. Larkin and others persuaded Fremont to give up his stronghold and go, but his actions had undone much of Larkin's work, leaving behind a legacy of hate and suspicion.

Fremont was on his way to Oregon when a messenger arrived bearing a letter from Senator Benton. The contents of the message are still not known, but they led Fremont to turn back to California. Fremont would later claim he was instructed by the president through Benton to turn back, but he may simply have acted on his own. Fremont's decision was probably influenced by the information the messenger brought about conditions in California; particularly that war appeared imminent between Mexico and the United States. Fremont was unlikely to remain in Oregon while events of such importance were taking place. As tensions increased, many began drifting to Fremont's camp where they awaited the outcome of the growing crisis.

Fighting broke out in June 1846. Rebels, who proclaimed the independence of the Republic of California and raised a flag bearing the image of a grizzly bear, captured the small town of Sonoma. Fremont and his men rushed to Sonoma and joined the forces there. Together, they marched on Monterey. When they arrived they discovered that the United States and Mexico had gone to war in April, and elements of the Pacific fleet, acting on orders from Polk, had already seized the city. American forces had invaded New Mexico in May, and within a short time all of California and New Mexico were held by the United States. The war with Mexico would continue until March 1848, at which time the Treaty of Guadalupe Hidalgo would confirm the acquisition of California and the Southwest for the United States. As part of the peace settlement, the United States paid Mexico $15 million for the land it had taken.

1840-1860 • Settlers of the Far West ~ The movement of settlers to Texas and Oregon was part of an overall movement of Americans to the far western regions of North America between 1840 and 1860. An estimated 300,000 Americans traveled west during these two decades. While Southerners tended to move to Texas, most of those who moved west in search of new opportunities came from the Old Northwest. The

(1893) More than 100,000 hopeful settlers rush onto the Cherokee Strip in Oklahoma on the day that it was opened to colonization after the removal of all Native Americans.

majority of these men and women were white, although some blacks did migrate to the west, and they tended to travel in family groups. The exception to this was the California gold rush, which attracted primarily single men.

Most of these new settlers were fairly prosperous, and a few were wealthy. Poor people generally joined other families or groups as laborers in order to afford the trip west. Groups that were headed for areas where mining or lumber provided the majority of jobs tended to be made up of men, while farmlands attracted families.

The majority of these migrants headed west along the great overland trails, gathering at one of the departure points in Iowa or Missouri such as Independence, where they joined a wagon train. With hired guides to lead them, they traveled in covered wagons as their livestock followed along. The primary route was the 2,000-mile long Oregon Trail. The Oregon Trail began in Independence, crossed the Great Plains and worked its way through the south pass of the Rocky Mountains. Settlers could then move north into Oregon or follow the California trail south to the California coast. Another popular trail was the Santa Fe Trail, a southwestern route to New Mexico, which also originated in Independence.

The westward journey was hard, lasting five or six months, usually from May to November. It was necessary to cross over the Rocky Mountains before winter set in and the passes were blocked by snow. The slow rate of movement, often no more than 15 miles a day, made reaching the Rockies in time difficult. Disease, cholera in particular, was a constant threat as well. Most of the travelers walked for much of the trip to ease the burden on the horses of pulling the wagons. The women worked hard, preparing meals and washing clothes after a hard day's journey.

New States Admitted from Territorial Expansion

Year of Statehood	State(s) Admitted
1792	Kentucky
1796	Tennessee
1803	Ohio
1812	Louisiana
1816	Indiana
1817	Mississippi
1818	Illinois
1819	Alabama
1821	Missouri
1836	Arkansas
1837	Michigan
1845	Texas
	Florida
1846	Iowa
1848	Wisconsin
1850	California
1858	Wisconsin
1859	Oregon
1861	Kansas
1864	Nevada
1867	Nebraska
1876	Colorado
1889	North Dakota
	South Dakota
	Montana
	Washington
1890	Wyoming
	Idaho
1896	Utah
1907	Oklahoma
1912	New Mexico
	Arizona
1959	Alaska
	Hawaii

Indian attacks were relatively rare between 1840 and 1860, with less than 400 people killed in fights with the tribes occupying the lands they crossed. Indians often proved to be helpful to the pioneers, offering their services as guides or by trading with them. Wagon trains obtained fresh food, clothing and even horses by bartering with the Indians they encountered.

The journey west was often a communal experience. Many wagon trains were made up of groups of friends or families or neighbors who had joined together to seek out new opportunities in the western territories. Because there was little or no contact with outsiders, other than Indians, during the arduous journey, the travelers soon learned the value and importance of cooperation if they were to reach their destination.

1846 • Slavery and Expansion ~ Territorial expansion soon led to the question of expanding slavery to the vast new territories obtained from Mexico and became the most explosive sectional conflict since the Missouri Crisis of 1819-1820 when Missouri applied for statehood as a slave state. The free and slave holding states were equally divided, and the free states feared that the slave states would gain control of the Senate if Missouri were admitted to the Union. As the United States expanded its territory in the west during the 1840s, the same struggle for power between free and slave holding states ensued.

The problem was the narrowing gap between the Southern desire to protect and vindicate slavery and the Northern desire to impose limits on the South. Gaining new territory would reactivate all the constitutional issues as well as the political and moral arguments of the Missouri Crisis. Could the South maintain its balance of power in the Senate? What was the precise nature of Congressional power over territories and the creation of new states? Would the government limit the further extension of slavery, or would it pursue a "hands off" policy and extend equal protection to the property Americans took into the new lands, even if that property included slaves? The complexity of the issue guaranteed a political struggle in Congress over slavery in the new territories.

Congress opened the debate with the Wilmot Proviso in 1846, which would have prohibited slavery in any territory acquired in the war with Mexico. Although the Wilmot Proviso failed to pass the Senate, it eventually received support in all but one northern state legislature.

Late-1840s-1850s • Northern Opposition to the Spread of Slavery ~ The Northern determination to limit the spread of slavery came from many sources. Moral convictions against slavery merged with anger over the ability of the Southern Democrats to lower protective tariffs and restrict internal improvements. Additionally, many westerners influenced by New England's business enterprise and sense of moral improvement viewed slavery in the South as the chief barrier to America's progressive modernization. Moreover, many whites in the west were racially prejudiced, and, while they cared little for the fate of Southern slaves, they feared the possibility of competing against slave labor on the frontier. Another issue was that the Far West was growing in population, and the settlers there resented territorial government run by inefficient military or territorial administrations. They sought to elect their own legislatures, draft their own constitutions and apply for statehood

Northern farmers wanted western lands to be kept free for homesteads, and did not want these lands taken over by slave plantations. Many eastern urban workers or small businessmen expected someday to populate towns and cities in the West. Even if the people back east did not expect to go west themselves, they wanted the west kept free for their descendants. Also, eastern residents hoped that immigrants, who viewed the west as a land of opportunity, would choose to settle there, so that there would be less competition for jobs in the east. Free blacks also feared the extension of slavery, for they were concerned that their own freedoms might be threatened if slavery expanded beyond its present borders. These groups did not want to live among slaves or compete with slave labor. The negative view of slavery meant that northerners were unlikely to support the institution of slavery in the new territories.

Anti-slavery sentiment became acute in California in 1849. The discovery of gold and the ensuing gold rush brought tens of thousands of settlers into the territory, and they soon began to agitate for statehood. Some Southerners and slaves were in the mass of people who migrated to California, along with a few free black prospectors. Many whites felt it was unfair to compete with slaves and believed it to be degrading to work alongside free blacks. These sentiments, especially in the mining areas, led the California Constitutional Convention of 1849 to copy the sections of the newly written Iowa state constitution prohibiting slavery. Oregon would also decisively reject slavery, and would approve the exclusion of free blacks from the state. The emergence for a brief time of a third political party, the Free Soil Party, tended to reinforce these sentiments.

By 1850 Southerners tended to view any form of antislavery sentiment as disguised abolitionism. Many Southern leaders had supported an aggressive policy of national expansion. The demand of Northern legislators for passage of the Wilmot Proviso threatened the creation of a permanent barrier to Southern expansion. The South feared that passage of the proviso would turn the federal government against an institution it had, so far, protected. If the South were at once deprived of land and labor for expansion, it would be rolled back from the west and the Gulf of Mexico as well as from the North.

While the Compromise of 1850 resolved some of these problems for a time, the territorial issue continued to remain a major problem for the future. Myths about the "Great American Desert" and the so-called "natural limits" of growing cotton in the wet, sub-tropical south supposedly confined slavery to the Old South. Although Utah and New Mexico would permit slavery in the 1850s, only a handful of black slaves appeared in either territory. Southerners were reluctant to transport valuable human property into a territory where slavery might suddenly be prohibited.

1850 • The Southern Dilemma ~ Few Congressmen believed Congress could prohibit slave states from joining the Union. The Missouri Compromise had reinforced the precedent of excluding slaves from the unorganized territories and the South had, until 1850, favored extending the Missouri Compromise line to the Pacific. But the emergence of Free

Soil sentiment in California and elsewhere led more and more Southerners to take the extreme position that the territories were the common property of all the states. The central problem now became that of delaying decisions by the territorial legislatures regarding slavery while making sure that the territory was safe and attractive to slaveholding emigrants. So, the South would take up the argument that the federal government, as an agent for the states, had to extend protection to slave holding minorities in all territories during the period of territorial government. The ambiguity of the Compromise of 1850 regarding the western territories was deliberate, and, in effect, registered some doubt about the authority of Congress regarding the territories. In effect, if territorial governments infringed upon the property rights of slaveholders, the slave owner was invited to challenge the constitutionality of any restrictions before statehood was established. Southerners accepted this reluctantly for it avoided the stigma of federal exclusion and apparently left the door open for slavery in the west. By failing to resolve the issue of whether or not slavery would be part of the process of settling the west, the Compromise of 1850 narrowed the limits of any further compromise and contributed to the outbreak of the Civil War a decade later.

1850s • The Lure of Overseas Markets in Asia ~ Expansionist fervor was not limited entirely to the North American continent. Opportunities in Asia beckoned as well. Pressure from missionaries and traders in China, as well as the impact of an economic depression from 1837 to 1841, led the United States to acquire most favored nation status and extraterritorial privileges from the Chinese government in 1844. American trade in China increased and the hope of bringing both Christianity and the benefits of American civilization to the Chinese grew as well.

American efforts also opened Japan to trade with the western world in the 1850s. United States warships arrived in Japan in 1853, and the commander of the mission, Matthew C. Perry, was able to coerce the Japanese to accept a trade relationship with the Americans. In 1858, the American consul to Japan, Townshend Harris, successfully negotiated a more comprehensive trade treaty that included most favored nation and extraterritorial privileges.

1850s • Expansion into the Caribbean and Central America ~ Central America and Cuba also attracted the interest of American expansionists. There were a number of abortive efforts to expand into parts of Mexico and Central America, as well as talk of buying Cuba from Spain. Each of these attempts ended in failure and contributed to generations of bad feelings between the United States and some of her southern neighbors. Only an attempt to buy nearly 30,000 square miles of territory from Mexico that would allow the southern states to complete a transcontinental railroad, the Southern Pacific, was successful. Through the Gadsden purchase (1853-1854), the U.S. paid Mexico $10 million for the land that became southern Arizona and southern New Mexico, and served to complete the borders of the continental United States.

1860s • William H. Seward and Expansion ~ The Civil War buried the expansionist fervor of Manifest Destiny, and after the war, the problems of reconstruction and an increasing interest in industrial growth heightened anti-expansionist sentiment in America. Nonetheless, William H. Seward, Secretary of State under President Andrew Johnson, and an avowed expansionist since before the Mexican War, was able to acquire new territory for the country.

The difficulties of the United States Navy during the Civil War in controlling Confederate blockade-runners led Seward to try to obtain a naval base in the Caribbean. Under the cover of a cruise for his health, Seward visited harbors in the Virgin Islands (which belonged to Denmark) and the Dominican Republic. Denmark was willing to sell her islands and a price of $7.5 million was agreed upon. The Senate, however, refused to ratify the treaty. Lack of Congressional and public support meant that efforts to acquire the Dominican Republic would also fail.

The failure of his efforts in the Caribbean did not deter Seward's enthusiasm for expansion, and he would enjoy more success in the Pacific. Seward was able to bring about the annexation of the Midway Islands, roughly a thousand miles northwest of Hawaii in 1867. In that same year Seward would also acquire a far more important possession for the United States with the purchase of Alaska.

The American people were not really interested in Alaska when Russia offered it for sale. Russia considered Alaska a liability, and the Russian-Alaska Company that administered the territory was nearly bankrupt. Additionally, Alaska could not be defended against a strong naval power such as Great Britain. Russia preferred to sell Alaska to the United States in order to make America stronger so she might one day serve as a counterweight to British power.

Baron Edward de Stoeckel was commissioned by the Russian government to negotiate the sale of Alaska to the United States, and was instructed to accept no less than $5 million for the region. This was a generous offer since Russia was aware that there was gold in Alaska.

In Seward, Stoeckel found a willing buyer, and he was able to ask for and get Seward to agree to a price of $7.2 million. The negotiations were so secret that only a handful of people in Washington knew that the U.S. was seriously thinking about purchasing Alaska. News of Seward's treaty with Russia caught the country by surprise. The American public was largely ignorant of Alaska, and newspapers opposed to the sale claimed that Alaska produced only icebergs and polar bears. Opponents of the deal called Alaska "Seward's Folly", "Frigidia", "Walrussia" and "Johnson's Polar Bear Garden".

With the Senate hostile to the treaty, Seward launched a nation-wide campaign to build popular support for the acquisition. He pointed out that Alaska offered natural resources such as fish, furs and lumber, and would be important, commercially and strategically, to the United States in the Pacific. The argument that swayed the Senate, however, was that Russia was anxious to sell the treaty and refusal to ratify the agreement would jeopardize Russian-American friendship, which had been expressed by Russia's support of the Union in the Civil War. The Senate ratified the treaty in April 1867, and the United States took possession of Alaska in October of that year although the House of Representatives did not appropriate the funds for the sale until the summer of 1868.

While popular demand for Russia never truly existed, buying Alaska turned out to be the biggest bargain for the

1860s

United States since the Louisiana Purchase. The resources in Alaska meant that the region provided the United States with far more than the purchase price within a few decades, and the 600,000 square miles the country obtained would prove to be invaluable strategically as well, particularly during the Second World War and the Cold War. Radar bases in Alaska in the Cold War were part of the early warning system designed to alert the American military to a Soviet nuclear missile launch against the United States.

1860s • Interest in Canada ~ A side effect of the Alaskan purchase was the reawakening of old sentiments for annexing Canada. This agitation only strengthened nationalist sentiments in Canada, and did much to give Canadians the final impulse that would lead to the formation of their own nation. Britain responded with the passage in Parliament of the British North American Act of 1867, creating the Dominion of Canada.

(circa 1880) Plains Indians

1860s • Indian Relations after the Civil War ~ While those who traveled west before the Civil War rarely encountered problems with Indians, Native Americans had always been a "problem" for settlers as they occupied the frontier. The Indians, after all, owned and occupied the land and they eventually began to resist white encroachment.

The Indian wars of the 1860s represented something different in the relations between Indians and whites. Although the wars against the Plains Indians were among the most savage and epic in the long history of conflicting cultures in North America, a final phase was under way, for these were the last wars between the Indian and the white man. It was during these years that the Indians finally ran out of space, numbers and time.

The post-Civil War generation inherited two of the most difficult problems ever to face American citizens. The first was that of devising new roles for the freed slaves, the second was fashioning a new policy toward the Native American as armed resistance entered a spectacular, although final, chapter.

At the close of the Civil War, Indians roamed freely over roughly half the continent. The survivors of the major eastern nations occupied reservation lands in Oklahoma, and, along with the shattered tribes in California, were incapable of offering further resistance to white settlement. But roughly a quarter of a million or more Indians of undiminished vigor still occupied their ancestral lands in the west and wandered them without restriction.

Particularly formidable were the buffalo hunting nations of the Great Plains; the Blackfeet of southwestern Canada, the Sioux of Minnesota and the Dakotas, the Cheyenne of Colorado and Wyoming, the Comanche of northern Texas and the fierce Apache in New Mexico, Arizona and northern Mexico. These nations resisted the white advance with considerable resourcefulness, courage, and savagery.

1860s • Early Federal Policy Toward the Plains Indians ~ As early as 1851, the federal government had tried to develop a policy to put an end to increasing friction between Oregon and California bound wagon trains in the Treaty of Fort Laramie. This agreement induced a number of Plains Indian nations, including the Sioux, Arapaho and Cheyenne, to accept separate reservations off the main lines of white advances. In return, the federal government promised food supplies to the hard-pressed Indians, who were already beginning to show signs of suffering from a decline in the buffalo herds. What would become a familiar cycle of events would cause the peace-making efforts to fail.

Agreements between tribal elders and the U.S. government were jeopardized by the fact that they were not universally accepted by all the tribal members. The younger generation of Native Americans, in particular, resisted the confinement of the reservation system and were highly suspicious of government intentions. Their fears proved to be founded as a pattern of broken promises on the part of the government emerged.

While the federal government intended to honor its promises regarding supplies, the agents chosen to distribute them often proved to be unreliable. Food was too often stolen by whites or, if distributed, of inferior quality. The army, meanwhile, was unable to stop the constant white encroachment on reservation lands. As white intrusion onto reservation lands continued, a broad uprising flared up.

The timing of the uprising coincided with the beginning of the Civil War, when troops were diverted from the frontier. For five years, from 1862 to 1867, Indians conducted running warfare throughout the west, raiding isolated settlements and cabins with devastating effect. Whites struck back in kind and carried the war to the "civilian" population of the Indians as well.

In 1864, at the Sand Creek reserve in Colorado, a large number of Arapaho and Cheyenne warriors and their families were trapped by a unit of Colorado militia under the command of Colonel J. M. Chivington. Retaliating for raids on stagecoach lines and settlements, in which some of the warriors at Sand Creek may have taken part, Chivington ordered his men to "kill and scalp all, big and little, nits make lice". In a few hours virtually all of the Indians at Sand Creek were annihilated.

The eastern Sioux in Minnesota also resorted to warfare during the Civil War. Cramped on an inadequate reservation and exploited by Indian agents, they struck out under the leadership of Little Crow. Over 700 whites were killed before federal troops and militia forces subdued the Sioux. Thirty-eight of the Indian leaders were hanged and the nation was exiled to the Dakotas.

After the Civil War, Indian uprisings occurred on several fronts. The most serious and sustained conflict was in Montana, where the army was attempting to build a road, the Bozeman Trail, from Fort Laramie to the new mining areas in the Black Hills. Resentful of the incursion into their buffalo lands, the western Sioux, led by Red Cloud, so harassed the army and construction crew that the road could not be completed.

Late-1860s • The Federal Response ~ Shocked by the Sand Creek massacre, Congress launched an investigation into the Indian situation, and created an Indian peace commission made up of soldiers and civilians to formulate and recommend a permanent Indian policy. The commission was able to negotiate peace treaties in 1867 and 1868 that quieted things for a bit.

After 1870, the broad outlines of a new Indian policy were taking shape. The major nations were concentrated in two large reserves: one in the Dakotas and the other in the Indian territory. Restricted in this manner, the ability of these tribes to make war was seriously impaired. A civilian advisory Board of Indian Commissioners counseled the government to continue the reservation program and to break down the tribal structure with a view toward eventual assimilation of the Indians to white culture. Congress responded to this recommendation in 1871 by abolishing the practice of treating the Indian nations as sovereign, a step designed to undermine the collective nature of Indian life.

1870s • Indian Resistance and Defeat ~ Indian resistance had not ended, however. In 1875, many Sioux, angered by the dealings of crooked Indian agents and alarmed by the entrance of miners into the Black Hills, suddenly left the reservation. Led by Crazy Horse and Sitting Bull, they gathered in Montana. Three army columns were sent to round them up, including the 7th Cavalry, commanded by George Armstrong Custer. At the Little Bighorn, in 1876, Custer and part of his regiment were surprised by a large Indian army, which surrounded and killed them all. While Custer has been accused of acting rashly in approaching the Indian encampment, he and his men ran into something no white man would have believed possible—an Indian army that may have included as many as 2,500 warriors. This was the largest Indian force ever assembled at one time during the frontier wars.

However, lack of political organization soon split the Indians apart and they began drifting off in smaller bands to search for food. The army was able to run them down and return them to the reservation, and the power of the Sioux was broken for good. Accepting defeat, Crazy Horse and Sitting Bull returned to reservation life where reservation police later murdered them both.

The year 1877 saw a dramatic episode in Idaho. Here, the Nez Perce, a small nation, refused to accept confinement to an undersized reservation and were forced into resistance. Fleeing federal troops, their leader, Chief Joseph, tried to escape with his people to Canada. A remarkable chase began, as 200 warriors and 350 women, children and elderly Indians covered nearly 1300 miles in twenty-five days. The flight ended with the capture of Joseph and his followers just south of the Canadian border, and the Nez Perce were shipped to the Indian territory.

The last of the Indian nations to maintain an organized resistance to the whites were the Apache, who fought from the 1860s to the 1880s. Among the ablest leaders of this fierce nation were Mangas Coloradas and Cochise. Mangas was mur-

(1899) United States Army cavalry pursuing two mounted Indians.

dered during the Civil War, while Cochise agreed to a peace treaty and led his people to a reservation in 1872. But other leaders, notably Geronimo and Vittorio, carried on the fight. Vittorio was killed in 1880 and Geronimo surrendered in 1886. The capture of Geronimo ended the formal warfare between whites and Native Americans.

A final, tragic episode took place in 1890. As Indians saw their culture and glories fading, some turned to an emotional religion that emphasized the coming of a messiah and featured a ceremony that included the "ghost dance," which inspired visions. Agents on the Sioux reserve, fearing an outbreak of violence, called in federal troops and some of the Indians fled the reservation and went to the Badlands. They were caught at Wounded Knee, South Dakota, where 40 soldiers and some 200 Indians, including women and children, were killed when fighting broke out. The battle was really a one-sided affair as the soldiers slaughtered the Indians with newly issued machine guns.

While American folklore preserved the memory of the Indian wars in the west as a story of courageous whites ultimately victorious in a good cause, for Native Americans it was an historical moment of indescribable sadness.

"I don't want to settle," one Kiowa chief declared. "I love to roam the prairie. Those soldiers cut down my timber, they kill my buffalo, and when I see that, it feels as if my heart would burst with sorrow". One Oglala Sioux leader summed up Indian-white relations of the

Return of the Natives

~

The 2000 census revealed a remarkable fact about the Great Plains states that are equal in size to the original Louisiana Purchase (which doubled the size of the United States in 1803): it is being returned to Native Americans. Sixty percent of the counties in 900,000 square miles of the Great Plains lost population during the last 10 years, and a large portion is so vacant that it meets the government's criteria of "frontier" with fewer than six people per square mile. But as the all-white counties of the Great Plains are decreasing, Native Americans are moving back in. The Indian population grew by 20 percent in North Dakota, 23 percent in South Dakota, 18 percent in Montana, 20 percent in Nebraska, and 12 percent in Kansas. The Native American population in Shannon County, South Dakota, grew by 94 percent. Conversely, Slope County, North Dakota, which had a booming population of 4,945 white people in 1915 now has 767 residents and feels like a ghost town. The prairie, once converted to grazing and farming, is returning, and the buffalo herds, almost extinct in 1900 with only a few hundred head, now number 300,000. Some social historians are referring to this phenomenon as reverse Manifest Destiny.

nineteenth century: "They made us many promises, more than I can remember, but they never kept but one; they promised to take our land, and they took it".

1860s • Conditions on the Great Plains ~ In 1860, the western edge of settlement of the United States included the western borders of Minnesota, Iowa, Missouri and Arkansas, while jutting out to include eastern Nebraska and Kansas, and cutting across central Texas. West of this line was a huge expanse inhabited primarily by Indians, wild animals and a tiny population of white settlers that continued until the settled districts of California and Oregon were reached.

Once the westward moving pioneers reached the Great Plains, they encountered a strange, even alien environment. Unlike the fertile prairie lands, or the wooded Ohio Valley they had left behind, this area was level in surface, lacked timber and sufficient rainfall. Early explorers had referred to this region as the "Great American Desert," and in the 1840s settlers hurried across the Great Plains on their way to California or Oregon. The forbidding reputation of the area was largely responsible for the 1500-mile gap between settlements along the Mississippi River to the Pacific Coast.

By the 1860s, however, pioneers were heading for the unsettled parts of the west. They were attracted by deposits of gold and silver, short-grass pasture lands for cattle and sheep grazing and the sod of the plains or mountain meadows that seemed suitable for farming.

1860s • The Railroads ~ The great transcontinental railroad lines further encouraged settlement. These railroads and their respective feeder lines moved settlers and supplies into the extensive interior spaces and furnished access to outside markets. This provided the basis for a permanent population and a durable economy. The railroads also directly stimulated settlement by disposing of their lands. Overall, in terms of state and national land grants, the railroads controlled more than 180 million acres.

Some railroad companies tried reserving their lands and selling the acreage at high prices, but most understood that an increased population would mean more revenues from carrying freight and passengers. So they sold land cheaply, for as little as $2.50 an acre, advertised the glories of the west back East and in Europe and transported prospective land buyers at reduced rates.

1860s • The Homestead Act ~ Settlement was also encouraged by the federal government, although its policies were not as effective as they were intended to be. The Homestead Act of 1862 allowed a settler to obtain 160 acres of land for a small fee as long as he occupied and improved the land for at least five years. The essential feature of the Homestead Act was its idealism, for it was intended to be a democratic measure. A full farm was made available to those persons who wanted one, and the act served as a form of government relief that the masses could use to raise their standard of living.

In practice, the act proved to be a disappointment. While some 400,000 homesteaders became landowners, a greater number gave up the attempt to stake out a farm on the windswept plains. The Homestead Act was defective in that it was based on the assumption that the mere possession of land was sufficient to sustain farm life. But the law ignored the rising costs of operation and was based on farm experiences back in the east, which did not apply to the region west of the Mississippi. A plot of 160 acres simply was not enough to sustain the grazing and grass farming that became the basis of agriculture on the Great Plains. Later laws would make it possible to acquire additional lands, so that an individual could acquire as much as 1,280 acres for a low price. Enterprising individuals often obtained more. Fraud was rampant in the administration of the laws. By employing dummy registrants and other tricks, timber, mining and cattle companies were able to buy up millions of acres of the public domain.

1850s • Miners ~ The first settlers in what would become the last frontier were miners since the first portions of the area to be settled were the mineral-rich regions along the mountains and plateaus. The life span of the mining frontier was brief, bursting into being in the 1860s and flourishing until the 1890s before quickly declining. News of a gold or silver strike would start a stampede similar to the California gold rush. The discovery of gold near Pike's Peak in Colorado in 1858 caused 50,000 people to mob the area within a year. Denver and other towns sprang up overnight. A similar experience occurred in the Nevada portion of the Utah Territory with the discovery of the great Comstock lode of silver in 1859. The discovery in 1874 of gold in the Black Hills of South Dakota produced a similar situation.

Life in the mining towns took on a gaudy aspect not found in any other part of the last frontier. A speculative spirit, sense of optimism and a get-rich quick philosophy gripped the community and often dominated every aspect of community activities. The conditions of mine life; the presence of precious minerals, the vagueness of claim boundaries and cargoes of gold and silver being shipped out, tempted outlaws to ply their trade either individually or in

Population Growth of Western States

STATE	1790	1800	1810	1820	1830	1840	1850	1860	1870	1880
Ohio		45,365	230,760	581,434	937,903	1,519,467	1,980,329	2,339,511	2,665,260	3,198,062
Indiana		5,641	24,520	147,178	343,031	685,866	988,416	1,350,428	1,680,637	1,978,301
Illinois			12,282	55,211	157,445	476,183	851,740	1,711,951	2,539,891	3,077,871
Michigan			4,762	8,896	31,639	212,267	397,654	749,113	1,184,059	1,636,937
Wisconsin						30,945	305,391	775,881	1,054,670	1,315,497
Minnesota							6,077	172,023	439,706	780,773
Iowa						43,112	192,214	674,913	1,194,020	1,624,615
Missouri			19,783	66,586	140,455	383,702	682,044	1,182,012	1,721,295	2,168,380
N. Dakota									2,405	36,909
S. Dakota								4,837	11,776	98,268
Nebraska								28,841	122,993	452,404
Kansas								107,206	364,399	996,096
Kentucky	73,677	220,955	406,511	564,317	687,917	779,828	982,405	1,155,684	1,321,011	1,648,690
Tennessee	35,691	105,602	261,727	422,823	681,904	829,210	1,002,717	1,109,801	1,258,520	1,542,359
Alabama		1,250	9,046	127,901	309,527	590,756	771,625	964,201	996,992	1,262,505
Mississippi		7,600	31,306	75,448	136,621	375,651	606,526	791,305	827,922	1,131,597
Arkansas			1,062	14,273	30,388	97,754	209,897	435,450	484,471	802,525
Louisiana			76,566	153,407	215,739	352,411	517,762	708,002	726,915	939,946
Oklahoma										
Texas							212,592	604,215	818,579	1,591,749
Montana									20,595	39,159
Idaho									14,999	32,610
Wyoming									9,118	20,789
Colorado								34,277	39,864	194,327
New Mexico							61,547	93,516	91,874	119,565
Arizona									9,658	40,440
Utah							11,380	40,273	86,786	143,963
Nevada								6,857	42,291	62,266
Washington							1,201	11,594	23,955	75,116
Oregon							12,093	52,465	90,923	174,768
California							92,597	379,994	560,247	864,694
Alaska										33,426
Hawaii										

SOURCE: Donald J. Bogue. *The Population of the United States*. New York: The Free Press, 1985.

1890	1900	1910	1920	1930	1940	1950	1960	1970	1980
3,672,329	4,157,545	4,767,121	5,759,394	6,646,697	6,907,612	7,946,627	9,706,397	10,657,423	10,797,630
2,192,404	2,516,462	2,700,876	2,930,390	3,238,503	3,427,796	3,934,224	4,662,498	5,195,392	5,490,224
3,826,352	4,821,550	5,638,591	6,485,280	7,630,654	7,897,241	8,712,176	10,081,158	11,110,285	11,426,518
2,093,890	2,420,982	2,810,173	3,668,412	4,842,325	5,256,106	6,371,766	7,823,194	8,881,826	9,262,078
1,693,330	2,069,042	2,333,860	2,632,067	2,939,006	3,137,587	3,434,575	3,951,777	4,417,821	4,705,767
1,310,283	1,751,394	2,075,708	2,387,125	2,563,953	2,792,300	2,982,483	3,413,864	3,806,103	4,075,970
1,310,283	1,751,394	2,075,708	2,387,125	2,563,953	2,538,268	2,621,073	2,757,537	2,825,368	2,913,808
2,679,185	3,106,665	3,293,335	3,404,055	3,629,367	3,784,664	3,954,653	4,319,813	4,677,623	4,916,686
190,983	319,146	577,056	646,872	680,845	641,935	619,636	632,446	617,792	652,717
348,600	401,750	583,888	636,547	692,849	642,961	652,740	680,514	666,257	690,768
1,062,656	1,066,300	1,192,214	1,296,372	1,377,963	1,315,834	1,325,510	1,411,330	1,485,333	1,569,825
1,428,108	1,470,495	1,690,949	1,769,257	1,880,999	1,801,028	1,905,299	2,178,611	2,249,071	2,363,679
1,858,635	2,147,174	2,289,905	2,416,630	2,614,589	2,845,627	2,944,806	3,038,156	3,220,711	3,660,777
1,767,518	2,020,616	2,184,789	2,337,885	2,616,556	2,915,841	3,291,718	3,567,089	3,926,018	4,591,120
1,513,401	1,828,697	2,138,093	2,348,174	2,646,248	2,832,961	3,061,743	3,266,740	3,444,354	3,893,888
1,289,600	1,551,270	1,797,114	1,790,618	2,009,821	2,183,796	2,178,914	2,178,141	2,216,994	2,520,638
1,128,211	1,311,564	1,574,449	1,752,204	1,854,482	1,949,387	1,909,511	1,786,272	1,923,322	2,286,435
1,118,588	1,381,625	1,656,388	1,798,509	2,101,593	2,363,880	2,683,516	3,257,022	3,644,637	4,205,900
258,657	790,391	1,657,155	2,028,283	2,396,040	2,336,434	2,233,351	2,328,284	2,599,463	3,025,290
2,235,527	3,048,710	3,896,542	4,663,228	5,824,715	6,414,824	7,711,194	9,579,677	11,198,655	14,229,191
142,924	243,329	376,053	548,889	537,606	559,456	591,024	674,767	694,409	786,690
88,548	161,772	325,594	431,866	445,032	524,873	588,637	667,191	713,015	943,935
62,555	95,531	145,965	194,402	225,565	250,742	290,529	330,066	332,416	469,557
413,219	539,700	799,024	939,629	1,035,791	1,123,296	1,325,089	1,753,947	2,209,596	2,889,964
160,282	195,310	327,301	360,350	423,317	531,818	681,187	951,023	1,017,055	1,302,894
88,243	122,931	204,354	334,162	435,573	499,261	749,587	1,302,161	1,775,399	2,718,215
210,779	276,649	373,351	449,396	507,847	550,310	688,862	890,627	1,059,273	1,461,037
47,355	42,355	81,875	77,407	91,058	110,247	160,083	285,278	488,738	800,973
357,232	518,103	1,141,990	1,356,621	1,563,396	1,736,191	2,378,963	2,853,214	3,413,244	4,132,156
317,704	518,103	672,765	783,389	953,786	1,089,684	1,521,341	1,768,687	2,091,533	2,633,105
1,213,398	1,485,053	2,377,549	3,426,861	5,677,251	6,907,387	10,586,223	15,717,204	19,971,069	23,667,902
32,052	63,592	64,356	55,036	59,278	72,524	128,643	226,167	302,583	401,851
	154,001	191,784	255,881	368,300	422,770	499,794	632,772	769,913	964,691

1860s

groups. Those who were interested in law and order normally established their own laws and established vigilante committees to enforce them. Occasionally criminals would gain control of such a committee, and, sometimes, they continued to operate successfully even after the arrival of formal law enforcement and government services.

1860s • The Cattle Industry ~ Meanwhile, the unclaimed grasslands of the public domain provided a huge area on the Great Plains where cattlemen could graze their herds free of charge, unrestrained by boundaries that would have existed in a farming economy. Railroads gave the cattle industry access to markets and helped to create the industry. However, railroads would also contribute to the eventual destruction of the industry by bringing farmers out to the Great Plains.

The cattle industry originated with Mexicans and Texans. Long before Americans invaded the Southwest, Mexican ranchers and *vaqueros* had developed the techniques and tools that were later employed by American cattlemen and cowboys. Branding of cattle, the roundup, roping and the equipment—the lariat, saddle, leather chaps and spurs—were all taken over by Americans in Texas and transmitted throughout the cattle kingdom.

Texas also contained the largest herds of cattle in the country. These animals were descended from Spanish stock, the famed wiry, hardy longhorn cattle that had been allowed to run wild and semiwild. Here, too, were the horses that allowed cowboys to control the cattle.

(circa 1870) Frontier Town

The small, muscular broncos, or mustangs, which were also descended from Spanish stock, were ideally suited for the requirements of the cow country. By the end of the Civil War, an estimated five million cattle roamed the Texas range and northern markets were offering fat prices for steers no matter what their condition might be.

Early in 1866, a group of Texas cattlemen combined their herds, roughly 260,000 head of cattle, and began driving them north to Sedalia, Missouri along the track bed of the Missouri Pacific Railroad. Traveling through rough country, attacked by outlaws and Indians, the cattle drive sustained heavy losses. Only a fraction of the animals were delivered to the railroad, but a great experiment had been performed. Cattle could be driven to distant markets and successfully pastured along the trail so that they would gain weight on the journey. The first of these "long drives" paved the way for the emergence of the cattle kingdom.

From beginning to end a cattle drive was a spectacular event. It would begin in the spring with the cattle roundup. Cattlemen met with their cowboys at a specified place, all the cattle were rounded up from the open range and the calves were branded with the same mark as their mothers. "Mavericks"—stray calves without identification—were distributed on a *pro rata* basis. Calves and cows were turned loose to pasture and the yearling steers were readied to move north. Then the combined herds, usually 2,500 to 5,000 head apiece, moved out, attended by the cowboys of each outfit.

1870s • Cow Towns ~ Easier routes north were soon established and, located on the Kansas Pacific Railroad, Abilene, Kansas provided special market facilities for cattlemen. For years, Abilene would serve as the primary railhead for the cattle kingdom. Between 1867 and 1871 an estimated 1.5 million cattle were moved along the Chisholm Trail to Abilene. As the frontier moved further west and the supply of animals increased, cattlemen developed other market outlets and trails. Towns that thrived after Abilene, included Dodge City and Wichita, Kansas; Ogallala and Sidney in Nebraska; Cheyenne and Laramie, Wyoming; and Miles City and Glendive in Montana.

The Cowboy

The majority of the cowboys in the early years were veterans of the Confederate Army. Outnumbering all of the others—white northerners, Mexicans and other foreigners—were free blacks, who usually performed the menial jobs of the trail crew. Blacks, however, played a role not only as cowboys, but also as explorers, trappers, miners, outlaws and cavalrymen in the Wild West.

Despite the later glorification of the cowboy, the actual life of cowboys was dull, dirty and somewhat brutish. He was, at best, a hired hand who made little money and kept even less. The big profits went to his boss, the cattleman.

Because the cattleman needed a permanent base of operations, the ranch emerged. This consisted of the employer's house, quarters for his employees and a tract of grazing land. It might be fenced in or open; owned, leased or held by some quasi-legal means, but the ranch was definite and durable. Owning a ranch meant unquestioned access to precious water, and as farmers and sheepmen encroached on the open plains, the ranch replaced the range.

The Myth of the Gunfighter

~

One of the most enduring images of the Old West is that of the gunfighter. From the dime novels of the last part of the nineteenth century to modern films about the Wild West, the icon of the gunfighter remains a central part of western lore. Although most cowboys did very little shooting, professional gunfighters were renegades. Some were outlaws who robbed banks and stagecoaches; others were hired to help resolve "range wars." Still others worked as lawmen. And it was not uncommon for a gunfighter to work on both sides of the law during his lifetime. To some degree, these men were always looking over their shoulders for they never knew when some aspiring gunfighter seeking to make a reputation might make them a target.

While gunfighters might practice the "draw" until it became a conditioned reflex, the reality of gunfights in the old west was that speed was secondary to accuracy. Despite the many portrayals of two men facing each other, hands poised to see who could draw his six-shooter and fire a shot the fastest, in actual fact the primary concern was shooting accurately. Handguns weren't always carried in holsters, either. Gunfighters often carried their pistols in hip pockets, shoved them into waistbands or into a coat pocket. And pistols were not even the preferred weapons. Shotguns or rifles were always favored over handguns.

In a shootout, the first consideration was not simply drawing a gun and shooting first, hitting the opponent first or hitting him in a vital spot. The real concern was just hitting the opponent. In many gunfights the adversaries emptied their pistols at each other without inflicting any injuries at all, or, at best, only minor wounds. The speed of the draw was unimportant. The winner of a gunfight was often the one who had the nerve to draw his pistol and fire accurately at his opponent even if he had not been the fastest draw.

1870s • Risks and Profits in the Cattle Industry ~ Risk and speculation were major elements of the cattle business. Herds could be decimated by diseases, such as "Texas fever," rustlers and Indians. Sheepmen brought their herds in from California and Oregon to compete for grass, resulting in bitter range "wars" and farmers fenced off their claims, blocking trails, breaking up the open range and bringing about more "wars" with the cattlemen. But the profit potential of the cattle business attracted Eastern, British and Scottish capital to the plains. Eventually the structure of the cattle business became corporate in nature. In one year, twenty corporations, representing an investment of $12 million, were operating in Wyoming.

1880s • The End of the Open Range ~ Eventually the range, already shrunken and severed by railroads and farmers, became overstocked. Not enough grass remained to support the overcrowded herds or to sustain long drives. Overstocking caused prices to fall. Nature provided the final blow to the cattle industry with the harsh winters of 1885-1886 and 1886-1887, separated by a scorching summer in between. Hundreds of thousands of cattle perished, streams and grass dried up, and many great ranches and millions of dollars of investments were wiped out in a season. The open-range industry never recovered and the long drives disappeared for good. But the cattle ranches, with fenced in grazing land and stocks of hay for winter feed, not only survived, but recovered, grew and prospered to eventually produce more beef than ever before.

The decline of the cattle and mining industries and the fencing in of the range by farmers and ranchers was the signal of the end of the frontier. When Frederick Jackson Turner delivered his paper on the significance of the frontier in American History in 1893, he concluded by stating that the frontier was gone, and what Jackson called the first period of American history had come to a close.

What was left, however, was a romanticized sense of the West and the frontier that has persisted down to this day. The popular "dime novels" of the time, along with the writings of Mark Twain and Owen Wister, and later on, Louis L'Amour, helped to engrain this sense of romanticism about the frontier. Various "wild west" shows, such as that of "Buffalo" Bill Cody helped popularize the west in the American mind. Artists like Frederic Remington, through sculptures and paintings, portrayed the independence of the cowboy, while the real-life experiences of Theodore Roosevelt and his later history, *The Winning of the West*, also contributed to this romantic view of the spread of American civilization throughout the frontier.

1890s • Overseas Expansion ~ With the exception of the annexation of the Midway Islands and the purchase of Alaska, the geographic expansion of the United States had essentially stopped after the Civil War. By the 1890s at least some Americans were anxious to revive the idea of Manifest Destiny and to begin to expand beyond the American shore. The United States would now join the other industrialized nations in the quest to bring the undeveloped regions of the world under their control.

In the 1880s the United States increased its influence somewhat in the western hemisphere. The primary step in this process was in assisting in the establishment of the Pan American Union in 1889, although efforts to create a hemispheric customs union and arbitration procedures failed. The building of the Suez Canal in 1869 brought about interest in a Central American canal, and the United States negotiated treaty rights for a canal across Panama, but several obstacles kept it from being built.

Americans were attracted to overseas lands for a number of reasons. The perceived closing of the frontier led to fears that America's natural resources would begin to decrease, so that alternative sources would have to be found. The impact of the Panic of 1893 caused businessmen to consider the need for overseas markets. And, well aware of the imperialist drive of the European nations, Americans did not want to be left out of the scramble for new markets and sources of raw materials.

Some justification for imperialism could be found in the ideas of Charles Darwin, which became the foundation for Social Darwinist concepts. This led to the belief that nations, like biological organisms, struggled for their survival, and only the fittest would continue to exist. Therefore, it seemed reasonable to conclude that the strongest or fittest nations should dominate the weaker ones.

A leading advocate for American imperialism was Alfred Thayer Mahan, an officer in the United States Navy.

1898

Mahan argued that sea power was essential to make a nation great and that the great powers in world history had all been significant naval powers. Mahan believed that modern sea powers required colonies and felt the United States should acquire bases in the Caribbean and the Pacific, including the Hawaiian Islands.

1898 • Hawaii and The Philippine Islands ~ Hawaii had been a focal point of American interest since the 1840s, and there had been earlier efforts to bring the island chain under U.S. control. The islands were an important source of sugar and the dependence of Hawaiian sugar planters on the American market helped create an interest in annexing the islands. Hawaii also offered the possibility of a vital naval base at Pearl Harbor. Opposition from domestic sugar producers and other issues prevented the annexation of Hawaii until 1898. By then, fears of growing Japanese influence in the Pacific and the desire for a Pacific empire enabled the McKinley Administration to gain Congressional approval for annexation. In 1899, the United States added part of the strategically important Samoan islands to the growing list of Pacific possessions.

The other main prize in the Pacific was the Philippine Islands. The islands had been captured by the United States during the Spanish-American War. After some consideration, President McKinley determined to annex the islands, rather than return them to Spain. McKinley justified his decision on the basis of his belief that the Philippines were not yet ready for self-government and therefore the only thing left to do was annex the islands, educate the Filipinos and bring Christianity to them, "and by God's grace do the very best we could by them."

Not all Americans shared McKinley's viewpoint. As Congress debated the question of annexation, a strong anti-imperialist movement emerged to challenge the acquisition of the Philippines. Among the leaders of the movement were Mark Twain, Andrew Carnegie and Samuel Gompers. Arguments against annexation included reminders of America's commitment to freedom, fears of cheap labor entering the country and racist opposition to the inclusion of Asians into the population. Supporters argued that possession of the islands would help the United States dominate trade in Asia and that the Filipinos could be treated as dependents rather than extended citizens. Ultimately, the Senate approved annexation early in 1899.

Governing Hawaii and Puerto Rico posed relatively few problems for the United States. The new acquisitions received territorial status relatively quickly, and their residents became American citizens. However, the Philippines would prove to be another matter altogether. The Filipinos had been in rebellion against Spain even before the Spanish-American War. As soon as it became apparent the United States intended to stay, rebellion broke out once again.

For the next three years, more than 100,000 American troops were called upon to put down the insurrection. The bloody conflict would prove to be reminiscent of the Indian Wars in its savagery and brutality. Eventually reports of the brutal war and mounting American casualties turned public opinion against the campaign. By then, however, the rebellion was largely over and the United States had asserted its control over most of the islands. Fighting would continue on and off until 1913, but America had secured the Philippines. The Philippine insurrection remains the least remembered war fought by the United States.

1898 • Puerto Rico and Cuba ~ In the Caribbean, also as a result of the Spanish-American War (1898), the United States gained the island of Puerto Rico. American forces had occupied the island during the Spanish-American War, and Spain turned Puerto Rico over to the United States as part of the peace agreement. In 1900, Congress passed the Foraker Act, which ended military rule there and established a colonial government in its place. In 1917, Congress made Puerto Rico a United States territory and its people became American citizens.

Cuba, which had been the issue that had led the United States into the war with Spain, would remain independent. McKinley opposed annexation on the grounds that too many mixed races would be brought into the Union. Instead he preferred to allow Cuba nominal independence so that the Cubans would have self-government, while remaining under the informal control of the United States. This policy was implemented in the Platt Amendment of 1901, which allowed the United States the right to intervene in Cuban affairs, placed restrictions on the Cuban debt, gave the United States a 99-year lease on the naval base at Guantanamo and established parameters to make Cuba attractive to American investors. In this manner, Cuba became an American protectorate.

(1898) Tampa, Florida. Smiling soldiers bound for Cuba prepare to board a train during the Spanish-American War.

For the most part, American territorial expansion, both on the North American continent and abroad, had come to a conclusion. The United States was now clearly a world power, and her influence and strength would continue to increase in the twentieth century. If the United States would no longer add new territories to its empire, other forms of 1898
expansion would follow. The growth of American power would result in the expansion of American influence around the world in a number of ways.

1898 • Anti-Imperialism ~ The process of American expansion did not take place without criticism. Anti-imperialist sentiment in the United States became especially strong by the middle of 1898 in opposition to President McKinley's foreign policy, particularly in regard to the possible acquisition of the Philippine Islands.

Many Americans felt that acquiring the Philippines without their consent was unconstitutional and a distortion of the crusade to liberate Cuba. Even before McKinley introduced the peace treaty with Spain to the Senate, opponents of expansion had begun a significant debate on the future direction of American for-

1898

eign policy. In Boston, the formation of the Anti-Imperialist League heralded the debate that was to come. Similar groups also appeared throughout the country.

The leaders of the anti-imperialist movement included a number of prominent Americans. Among them were the industrialist Andrew Carnegie, labor activist Samuel Gompers, various university presidents such as Harvard's Charles W. Eliot and David Starr Jordan of Stanford, along with numerous intellectuals and writers, including Mark Twain. Notably, the movement attracted many women, and about half of the audience at the formation of the Anti-Imperialist League in June 1898 was female. It may be that women, who were fighting for the right to vote, identified with peoples such as the Filipinos who would be governed without their consent. African-Americans also were active in the movement, and many prominent black leaders spoke at anti-imperialist meetings and rallies.

One argument made by the anti-imperialists was that expansion into the Pacific might lead the United States into war. Others were concerned that extending the provisions of the Constitution to the peoples of the Philippines, Puerto Rico and Hawaii might bring into the American system races that could prove dangerous to the traditional values of the nation. The argument was made that the Philippines were not yet ready to govern themselves, but if the United States assumed this role it would become an imperialist power and its own democratic values would be destroyed. At a time when as many as 150 black people were lynched each year in the United States, and race riots were occurring regularly, Democratic presidential candidate William Jennings Bryan and others argued that this was not the time to be teaching democracy in the Philippines at bayonet point.

An economic case against imperialism was also offered. Andrew Carnegie feared that free trade with the Philippines would bankrupt American farmers and raw materials manufacturers, yet tariffs on Filipino goods would violate the Constitution and threaten the economy of the islands. And if the Philippine market was made an exclusive American market, the European powers might take offense and an international crisis could result. Another businessman, Edward Atkinson, argued simply that the cost of acquiring markets in Asia and Latin America was not worth the investment. Better to wait until these markets developed to the point where they could buy American manufactured goods in quantity. Until then, Atkinson concluded, it would be best to focus on trade with Canada and the European nations.

Others felt that imperialism would drag the United States deeper into world politics. They argued that this was a violation of the principle of non-entanglement, would require the creation and maintenance of a large navy to defend these possessions and the cost of doing so would undermine the American economy and divert attention away from critical domestic problems that needed resolving.

Morally, the opponents of imperialism declared, it was simply wrong for the United States to force its will on other peoples, such as the Filipinos, who wanted their independence. The anti-imperialist movement also reflected a racist point of view, particularly as opponents of expansion generally shared the expansionist's point of view that the colored races of the world and the undeveloped regions were inferior. However, the anti-imperialists rejected the expansionist argument that they meant to benefit and care for the "backward" peoples of the Caribbean or the Pacific, and argued for the exclusion of these peoples from the American system.

Finally, the historic identity of the United States as the guardian of the ideals of liberty and the notion that the nation should serve as an example of democracy and freedom were held to be inconsistent with a policy of imperialism. Therefore, the United States could not live up to its own ideals if it was denying freedom or the right of self-government to others.

Ultimately, the anti-imperialist movement failed to make its case. American public opinion overwhelmingly favored expansion as the "spoils of war," and powerful political forces led by President McKinley, Theodore Roosevelt and Henry Cabot Lodge opposed the movement. The fact that many of the anti-imperialists had supported the war with Spain tended to undermine their protests against expansion. They were also weakened by having to ask the American people, who were caught up in the excitement of victory, to refuse to accept the material benefits of the war. Inconsistencies in their own positions, such as accepting the annexation of Hawaii, yet condemning the acquisition of the Philippines, further diluted their arguments. And, while acquiring the Philippines, Hawaii and Puerto Rico led to the extension of American interests in Latin America and the Pacific, it did not lead to a long-term policy of territorial expansion. American rule over the new possessions would prove in general to be far more just and restrained in comparison with their previous European colonial governments.

The anti-imperialist movement did raise important issues, and some of their

Theodore Roosevelt and the Spanish American War

According to the traditional story, about two months before hostilities broke out between Spain and the United States, Theodore Roosevelt, then Assistant Secretary of the Navy, became Acting Secretary for a few hours while the Secretary was away. According to the story, Roosevelt supposedly made a crucial decision that influenced the course of history when he cabled the commander of the Asiatic Squadron, Commodore George Dewey, with orders to prepare for an attack on the Philippine Islands. But in fact, Roosevelt's orders merely reflected standard naval policy and Dewey would have acted accordingly even without Roosevelt's orders. Dewey and the fleet sailed from Hong Kong on instructions from President McKinley, not from Roosevelt, and destroyed the Spanish fleet in Manila on April 30, 1898.

Meanwhile, Roosevelt left the Navy Department and rounded up a group of friends, many coming from South Dakota where he had spent time as a cowboy, and organized a unit he called the "Rough Riders." Upon reaching Cuba, Roosevelt nearly got his unit destroyed when he led them up a steep hill called Kettle's Hill in the face of hostile gunfire. Fortunately for Roosevelt and the Rough Riders, the Spanish weapons were too inaccurate to hit even the slow moving Americans. In spite of his near disaster, Roosevelt emerged from the fray as a national hero, an image he reinforced with the publication of his book *The Rough Riders* in 1899.

predictions proved to be accurate. Possession of the Philippines and Hawaii weakened the American military and diplomatic position in the Pacific, especially as they were vulnerable to attack. As many opponents of expansion felt would be the case, the American economy was not significantly improved by the acquisition of colonies in the Caribbean or the Pacific. Most of all the anti-imperialists raised the important questions of morality and justice when they argued that a nation that stands for principles of liberty and freedom could not justify ruling over other peoples without their consent, no matter how benign that rule might be.

1900 • The Open Door and American Economic Expansion ~ While the United States had been extending its influence in the Western Hemisphere and building an empire in the Pacific, events in China threatened nearly a century of American trade and investment in China. China had been divided into spheres of influence by several European powers and Japan, These spheres of influence, which were economic concessions wrested from the Chinese government, alarmed American businessmen who feared they would lose the ability to compete in China. Lobbying by these business interests, along with the belief in the need to develop overseas markets, led the McKinley Administration to call upon the other imperial powers in 1899 to maintain an Open Door in China for commercial and financial activities. A second note in 1900 asked the powers to respect China's territorial integrity.

The other powers offered noncommittal responses, with the exception of Russia, which rejected the Open Door concept. However, despite some trade and investment in East Asia, the United States was not as deeply involved there as the other powers were. A general lack of public support for a more assertive policy in the Far East rendered the Open Door Policy essentially unenforceable by the United States. However, the Open Door became a basic principle of American foreign policy in the twentieth century. The nation's economic interests would now expect the federal government to support their efforts to penetrate the global marketplace. One aspect of American expansion in the new century would be commercial expansion, rather than territorial.

1901-1904 • The Panama Canal ~ The United States had long been interested in the idea of a canal through Central America that would eliminate the long, dangerous voyage around South America. The commercial advantages of a canal were obvious and the Spanish-American War pointed out the strategic value as well, especially with the acquisition of Hawaii and the Philippines.

Following McKinley's assassination in 1901, the new President, Theodore Roosevelt, moved to make the canal a reality. A French company had unsuccessfully tried to build a canal through Panama, which was part of Colombia. The Panama Canal Company was eager to sell its rights to the project, which expired in 1904. Congress authorized Roosevelt to buy the rights, provided Colombia would accept reasonable terms for a strip of land in Panama to build the canal.

Efforts to reach an agreement with Colombia failed in 1903. Roosevelt, in league with a French official of the Panama Canal Company, took advantage of long-term Panamanian discontent with Colombian rule. Backed by American naval forces and directed by officials of the

Panama Canal Company, a revolution broke out in Panama. Colombian troops were unable to deal with the situation since the U.S. Navy prevented them from entering Panama. Panamanian independence was proclaimed and the new nation granted the United States a canal zone for $10 million and an annual lease payment of $250,000. As Panama's independence depended on American support, the new nation was really no more than an American protectorate. The United States took possession of the Canal Zone in 1904, and the Panama Canal was completed ten years later. The actions of the Roosevelt Administration would cause resentment of the United States throughout Latin America for many decades afterward.

(circa 1909) Panama Canal construction

1905 • The Roosevelt Corollary ~ In order to enhance security of the canal, Roosevelt worked to increase the authority of the United States in the Western Hemisphere. Because many Latin American nations had trouble paying their debts to European lenders, inviting intervention to force repayment, Roosevelt announced what would become known as the Roosevelt Corollary to the Monroe Doctrine. Roosevelt stated that the United States would serve as a sort of international policeman to maintain order in the Western Hemisphere. Rather than let Europe intervene in Latin America, the United States would do so instead, in order to restore stability and see to it that debts were paid. American intervention in the Dominican Republic in 1905 proved to be the first exercise of the Roosevelt Corollary. In this way, the United States could assert its authority over the Western Hemisphere and promote American dominance over trade and investment in the region.

1909-1913 • Dollar Diplomacy ~ Through the use of "dollar diplomacy," the administration of William Howard Taft used government action to promote private investment in Latin America to replace European interests there. American commercial expansion in the Western Hemisphere increased dramatically and American banks actually gained financial control of Haiti and the Honduras. Taft also authorized interventions in Nicaragua. Dollar diplomacy would significantly increase American investments in the Western Hemisphere and give the country the lion's share of trade with many nations in the Caribbean and Central America. 1909-1913

Efforts to apply dollar diplomacy in the Far East were less successful. The Taft Administration desired to maintain the Open Door in East Asia for American investments and trade. But China was sinking into revolution, and competition from other powers, notably Japan and Russia, made efforts to increase U.S. investments or market share in East Asia more and more difficult. Taft and Knox's attempts to increase the American commercial presence in East Asia led Japan and Russia, formerly bitter rivals in Asia, to move closer together to resist the United States. American trade suffered setbacks and investment opportunities fell through. Dollar diplomacy would prove to be a failure in the Far East due to the desire of the other powers involved in Asia to protect their own interests and the lack of a strong, stable government in China.

1912-1920 • Wilson and Intervention ~ Under Woodrow Wilson, the United States returned to interventionist policies in Latin America in order to protect American interests there, including commerce and investments. During his administration, Wilson intervened in Cuba, the Dominican Republic, Haiti and Mexico. Wilson was motivated by his belief that the peoples of Latin America were inferior and required guidance from the United States, his determination to transform other cultures and traditions so that they would conform to American principles and goals, a commitment to military force when necessary and a reliance on economic power to dominate the region. His interventionist polices increased Latin American resentment toward the United States.

1920s • Economic Expansion ~ The First World War would end with the United States as the world's dominant economic power. No longer a debtor nation, the United States had made substantial loans to her allies during the war. During the 1920s, the United States made loans to Germany to help that country meet its reparations payments to England and France. Those nations, in return, used that money to repay the loans they had received from the U.S. during the war. A continual flow of money from America was necessary to maintain this system.

During the 1920s the role of the United States in the world economy expanded dramatically. Exports skyrocketed, particularly manufactured goods. By the end of the decade the United States had become the world's largest exporter. American investments around the globe would at least double in this period. This increased involvement in the international market saw many American firms become multinational companies, establishing offices and plants around the world. Some companies would take charge of foreign supply sources, such as oil fields in Latin America. The United Fruit Company had operations in Central America that were so large that it could actually dominate the economies of these nations.

This expansion was supported by the federal government, which worked to develop opportunities for American business in foreign nations, helped them develop markets for trade, prospects for investment and access to raw materials. Bankers and businessmen could get relief from antitrust laws so that they could form combinations in order to develop foreign markets. Interventionist policies continued in the Western Hemisphere as well, as the United States continued to promote its own interests there.

1930s • The Depression Years ~ The search for markets abroad continued during the depression years of the 1930s. President Franklin Delano Roosevelt took the United States off the gold standard, devaluing American dollars and making them more competitive with cheaper currencies. The Export-Import Bank and the Reciprocal Trade Act helped Americans trade with other nations and gave the president additional powers to help develop foreign markets. Both were especially effective in Latin America, and the economies of a number of countries, particularly Cuba and Mexico, became dependent on the United States. Trade in the Western Hemisphere was effectively integrated by trading manufactured goods from the United States for raw materials from her southern neighbors. Roosevelt's "Good Neighbor" policy served to lessen earlier interventionist policies, although the U.S. did not abandon the practice of interfering in the affairs of Latin American states to protect its interests.

1945-1960 • THE POST-WAR WORLD ~ After the Second World War, the United States attempted to combat the spread of Soviet communism through a policy of containment. Part of the strategy of containment emphasized the spread of capitalism through the promotion of free trade and open market policies. In order to carry out this policy, the United States would implement the Truman Doctrine and the Marshall Plan in 1947-1948 and cooperate with more than twenty other nations to create the General Agreement on Tariffs and Trade (GATT). Through the Marshall Plan and GATT, American policymakers were able to construct a sizable new global marketplace. The Marshall Plan eventually provided Europe with $13 billion in economic aid, with the largest amounts spent in Great Britain,

(1949) Shown here is a rocket designed to protect the Western Hemisphere during the era of the "Good Neighbor Policy"

France and Germany. The plan funneled aid to the key industrial nations whose recovery would contribute most to restoring living standards throughout Europe. By providing aid the United States hoped to stave off an economic collapse that could propel Western Europe toward socialism while establishing conditions that would allow the United States to export goods in sufficient quantities to avoid a massive post-war depression. By providing aid to the bankrupt nations of western Europe and promoting economic recovery, the specter of a powerful West Germany may have been perceived by the Soviet Union as a threat to its security. So, in an effort to aid Europe's economic recovery to assure markets for American exports, the United States may have contributed to the origin of the Cold War. GATT furthered the process of promoting free trade by working to keep tariffs low and minimizing government restraints on trade.

In the late 1950s, American investors rushed to take advantage of new investment opportunities in Europe, which came about as a result of the creation of the Common Market. The United States had become wealthy as a result of post-war trade, and overseas investment had increased dramatically during the 1950s. Much of this money, which in the past had flowed into Canada and Latin America, now found its way into the European economy. However, the United States was beginning to run out of money. For over a decade, Americans had not only invested billions of dollars overseas, but were also sending additional billions abroad in the fight against communism. Until 1957, these expenditures had been supported by large trade surpluses. Now these surpluses began to decline, and the U.S. had to tap into its gold reserves and print more currency in order to offset the increasing shortfalls. Trade surpluses would continue through the 1960s, but in 1971, the country began to experience a series of trade deficits that have continued to the present. For the first time in decades, Americans could no longer compete as they wanted to in world markets. Having once flooded other markets with its manufactured goods, the United States now found its own marketplace inundated with goods from Europe, Latin America and Asia.

1950s • The Cold War and Military Expansion ~ The emergence of the United States from one of several major powers in the early twentieth century to global superpower involved more than economic expansion. Out of the destruction of World War II emerged two great powers, the United States and the Soviet Union. Their differing views on the nature of the post-war world brought about a decades long "Cold War" between them.

Throughout its history, the United States had pursued a foreign policy usually referred to as "isolationism". Americans did not withdraw from world affairs, but pursued policies calling for free trade and open markets, a hands-off policy in the Western Hemisphere and the avoidance of "entangling alliances" or involvement in European quarrels. However, the growing power of America began to force the nation to reconsider these traditional policies. Imperialism and the competition for markets began to draw the country more and more into the rivalries of the other powers. The entry into World War I engaged the United States in a European war for the first time since 1812. And the destruction of all the major powers except the Soviet Union in World War II left the United States as one of only two significant military powers left in the world when hostilities came to an end.

The United States expanded its military presence around the world following world war ii as part of an agenda to limit the communist influence of the Soviet Union and its satellites. In the late 1940s and through the 1950s, the United States broke its traditional policy of avoiding alliances and arranged a series of pacts designed to defend the free world. These treaties included collective defense alliances and bi-lateral defense agreements.

This process began with the signing of the Rio Treaty, a military alliance between the United States and the nations of Latin America. This was followed in 1949 with the formation of the North Atlantic Treaty Alliance (NATO) comprised of Belgium, Canada, Denmark, France, West Germany, Greece, Iceland, Italy, Luxembourg, The Netherlands, Norway, Portugal, Turkey, the United Kingdom and the United States. NATO pledged its twelve members to collaborate politically and economically and established the principle that an attack on any member of the alliance was to be considered an attack on all of them. The United States further promised to become involved in any future European wars. The next collective defense organization was ANZUS, a pact between Australia, New Zealand and the United States signed in 1951. The Southeast Asia Treaty Organization (SEATO) followed this in 1954. Additionally, the United States entered into bi-lateral defense agreements with the Philippines in 1951, South Korea in 1953 and Japan in 1960. The United States thereby surrounded the Soviet Union with allies that America was pledged to defend in the case of attack.

1950s • An Expanded Global Military Presence ~ In order to demonstrate its commitment to the defense of its allies, the United States was obliged to expand its physical military presence in the world as well. American forces were scattered throughout the world at hundreds of military and naval bases in Europe, Asia and elsewhere. Missile bases were built around the globe, American naval vessels patrolled the seven seas and submarines armed with nuclear missiles took up station in designated underwater zones, their lethal cargoes aimed at strategic enemy targets.

1950-1991 • Military Conflict ~ Containment and an expanded military presence also meant involvement in a series of undeclared wars between the 1950s and 1990s. The major military actions took place in Korea, Vietnam and Iraq, with only the Persian Gulf War against Iraq resulting in anything approaching a military victory. In the Korean War, three years of fighting produced a stalemate that left North Korea and South Korea divided as they had been before the war began in 1950. The Vietnamese conflict would demonstrate the limitations of even a great military power against a determined foe fighting for its independence. Despite the commitment of more than half a million troops and billions of dollars to the Vietnam War, the United States was unable to prevent the unification of North and South Vietnam by the North Vietnamese. Only in the Gulf War did the United States experience any form of success. Following the invasion and occupation of Kuwait by Iraq, the United States was able to organize an international coalition, including the nations of the Middle East, to bring an end to Iraqi aggression. In a swift campaign, American forces led the way in driving the Iraqis out of Kuwait and destroying much of Iraq's military capability. In the decades following the Second World War, United States troops also took part in other actions throughout the Western Hemisphere to maintain order and protect American interests there. And, most recently, United States forces took part in efforts to restore order to the Balkans where hostilities between Serbian and Croatian nationalists had been escalating.

1961-1969 • Space: The Second New Frontier ~ On July 20, 1969 an American astronaut, Neil Armstrong, became the first human being to set foot on the moon, thereby culminating a goal set eight years earlier by President John Fitzgerald Kennedy. In proclaiming his first step onto the moon as "one giant leap for mankind," Armstrong pointed the way to the future expansion, not only of the United States, but also for all of humankind.

(1958) America's first satellite, Explorer, preparing to launch from Cape Canaveral, Florida. Explorer was fired from the nose cone of a Jupiter C rocket, seen here next to the gantry crane.

The decision to go to the moon had been made by President Kennedy in 1961 largely in order to overtake the Soviet Union in what had become a "space race" between the two superpowers. The space race had begun in October 1957 when the Soviet Union successfully launched a Sputnik satellite into orbit. This was followed by a series of successes that climaxed when a Soviet cosmonaut, Yuri Gagarin, became the first man to orbit the earth on April 12, 1961. John Glenn, the first American to orbit the earth, would not do so until February 1962.

The Kennedy Administration was also smarting from the Bay of Pigs fiasco, an abortive invasion of communist Cuba by CIA-supported Cuban refugees that had failed miserably. After consulting with his science advisers and Vice President Lyndon B. Johnson, Kennedy concluded that, despite the technological challenges, landing a man on the moon by the end of the 1960s was feasible. Anxious to overtake the Soviets in the space race, Kennedy announced his goal on May 25, 1961 in an address to a joint session of Congress. In his speech the President declared: "I believe that this nation should commit itself to achieving the goal, before this decade is out, of landing a man on the moon and returning him safely to the Earth." Kennedy added, in presenting his challenge, that no "single space project will be more impressive to mankind, or more important in the long-range exploration of space; and none will be so difficult or expensive to achieve."

Actually, for most of the twentieth century, and even a bit earlier, the idea of traveling, exploring and even living in space had been gaining the attention of humanity. The speculative works of Jules Verne, for example, had dealt with the possibility of putting a man on the moon and Verne's idea had influenced late nineteenth and early twentieth century space pioneers such as self-taught Russian physicist Konstantin Tsiolkovsky, who worked out the basic principles of rocketry, and American Robert Goddard, who conducted a series of experiments that led to the launching of the world's first liquid-fueled rocket. The German rocket scientist Werner von Braun, whose team developed the V-1 and V-2 rockets used in World War II, and who joined the American space program after the war, also added significant developments. Each of these men, and many others, wrote and thought about space travel and the idea than human beings might live and work on other worlds. Science-fiction writers speculated about the time when humanity might roam outer space freely. By the time that Yuri Gagarin made mankind's first space flight, a substantial number of people had been exposed to the idea of outer space as mankind's final frontier.

It was within the context of the Cold War and the desire of the Kennedy Administration to overtake the Soviets in the space race, however, that the decision to go to the moon was taken. The Soviet Union had dramatized each of its successes and "firsts" in space as proof of the superiority of its system, so that Kennedy had to find a way to achieve a decisive and clear-cut victory in the space race. Congress accepted the president's challenge and ultimately authorized expenditures of some $9 billion for the enterprise. And, although Kennedy would not live to see his goal achieved, the American Mercury, Gemini and Apollo manned space flight missions were all carried out with the ultimate purpose of putting an American on the moon in mind. Despite skeptics who questioned the need for carrying out such a project, most of those who worked on the Apollo moon missions understood the symbolism and that landing on the lunar surface represented a daring and significant step into the future and would demonstrate the technological superiority of the United States.

President Kennedy's bold dream became reality in July of 1969 when the commander of the Apollo 11 moon mission, Neil Armstrong, left mankind's first footsteps on the moon. Over the next three years, ten more American astronauts would stroll the lunar surface, collecting rocks, setting up experimental stations, driving electric cars and even hitting golf balls. By the end of the Apollo mission, astronauts were staying on the moon for three days at a time and working outside for as long as six or seven hours. More significantly, the United States carried out a program that proved to be so expensive and difficult that the Soviet Union could not keep pace. Eventually, the Soviets gave up their plans for putting a cosmonaut on the moon.

With the success of the Apollo flights, some began to talk of a permanent colony on the moon and possibly even a mission to Mars. However, once the United States had achieved a clear victory in the space race, funding and political support for Apollo and future manned lunar programs began to diminish. Kennedy had committed the United States to a program that was so expensive that, while the United States might have taken a giant leap forward, it could not afford to sustain it for very long. It had been the extraordinary political circumstances of the Cold War in the late 1950s and 1960s that had made putting a man on the moon possible. Once the space race had been won, the nation's political leadership concluded that the lunar program was too expensive to continue. In order to beat the Soviet Union to the moon, NASA received all the funding it needed. At its peak in 1965, the Apollo program cost about 0.8 per cent of the nation's gross domestic product. Funding dropped so dramatically after the success of Apollo that NASA was forced to cancel three lunar missions for which the spacecraft had already been built. Today, political and popular support for the space program permits funding that takes about 0.25 per cent of the GDP, which is enough to support a small fleet of space shuttles, a space station and various other programs but not a renewed lunar program.

This does not mean the United States is no longer committed to the exploration of space. During the debate over whether or not to send a man to the moon, many scientists argued that instruments carried by unmanned space vehicles could best carry out the exploration of space. Since the end of the Apollo missions, the United States has launched dozens of space probes that have carried out a wide variety of missions. Robotic vehicles have roamed over the surface of Mars, for example, while other craft orbit most of the planets in the Solar System, or have conducted flybys. Millions of images of these worlds, their satellites and even asteroids have been relayed to Earth for scientific study. Some of these space vehicles will eventually leave the Solar System altogether. Other instruments, like the Hubble Space Telescope, are revealing some of the mysteries of the universe. All of this information will eventually help humans learn how to live and work in space, and may eventually lead to the exploration, colonization and industrialization of our neighboring planets. Even the rocks and other information brought back from the moon over thirty years ago will undoubtedly aid in developing the knowledge needed to return, possibly on a permanent basis.

The commitment to outer space has been maintained for other reasons as well. It has led to the development of new technologies, helps attract young people to the sciences and engineering, and serves as an investment in the long-range expectation that the exploration of space will prove to be economically profitable. Space beckons as the newest, and possibly the final, frontier for man to explore. Without doubt the technologically advanced nations of the world, of which the United States is still the leader, will continue to focus on outer space and its exploration.

It is likely that the United States will continue to lead the way in exploring the solar system and perhaps beyond in the twenty-first century. Each new discovery and technological advance will help begin the eventual and possibly inevitable expansion of humankind into outer space. With sufficient funding and the improvements in technology that have taken place since President Kennedy committed the United States to go to the moon, a permanent lunar base could be established early in this century. And, while the United States may well play a significant role in the exploration of space and the placing of colonies on nearby worlds, the story of American expansion into outer space will not simply be a national history. The future of humankind, and the next significant chapter in its progress may take place

(1971) Singer Diana Ross became so popular abroad that she moved to Germany for some time.

among the stars—but it will take a global effort and the merging of the resources of the planet as a whole to achieve success. As President Kennedy noted: "Space is open to us now; and our eagerness to share its meaning is not governed by the efforts of others. We go into space because whatever mankind must undertake, free men must fully share."

1950-2000 • The Spread of American Culture ~ Great power status also meant the extension of American influence in other ways. Economic and military involvement worldwide contributed to the spread of American culture around the globe. Movies, music, clothing styles and other cultural elements began to grow in popularity in many countries around the world. Through the presence of military personnel, businessmen and tourists abroad, the peoples of other nations were made aware of the many aspects of American culture. Motion pictures, tours by entertainers and sports figures, and television added to the international exposure of the culture of the United States, as did official government policies.

Sports

Some aspects of American culture had become popular in other parts of the world before the United States became a superpower. Baseball, for example, was already popular in many Latin American and Caribbean countries, and in Japan, long before World War II, and have grown in popularity since then. Today, there is a continual flow of baseball players back and forth between the United States and many other countries. American professional leagues today include players from Latin America, the Caribbean, Asia, Australia and Japan. Baseball has become an Olympic sport as well. Teams from as far away as Japan compete in the Little League World Series.

Other sports once popular only in the United States have also spread to other countries. American football is now played professionally in Europe (although primarily by American players), and the National Football League has been playing exhibition games in Mexico and Japan for several years.

Basketball, which was invented in America, is even more prevalent as an international sport. Professional leagues exist throughout Europe, and attract American players each year. Additionally, some of the best European players are being recruited by American colleges, and drafted by the National Basketball Association.

Entertainment

Motion pictures and television programs often prove to be as popular overseas as they are at home. Box office successes often do as well abroad as they do with domestic audiences, and every successful television program is almost certain to find a market in dozens of other countries. Filmmakers overseas have often borrowed traditional American movie themes such as the Western or gangster films. On the other hand, American films and television programs such as these have often given overseas audiences a distorted view of the United States. They also have contributed to a sense of America as a vast place, technologically advanced and wealthy, yet torn apart by various issues such as conflicts within families, racism, gender inequities and poverty that neither democracy nor advanced technologies are able to resolve.

American musicians also have an international audience, and it is not unusual for successful singers and bands to tour not only the United States but also any number of countries around the world. Native American music forms such as jazz, country music and rock 'n' roll have likewise influenced musical trends around the world. American stars such as Elvis Presley directly affected groups like the Beatles, who gained popularity in the United States in the 1960s.

Other Cultural Influences

Another staple of American culture that has gained worldwide acceptance is the fast food restaurant. Popular chains, including McDonalds, Burger King and Kentucky Fried Chicken can be found in most countries around the world. Also competing for customers globally are Coca Cola and Pepsi Cola. Blue jeans, a clothing item that developed on the American frontier, are now worn by people all around the world and are possibly the most popular item of American clothing among those overseas. Automobiles, T-shirts, baseball caps, American books, magazines and newspapers, shopping malls, and even theme parks such as EuroDisney are other examples of the cultural influence of the United States worldwide.

1950-2000 • Promoting American Culture Abroad ~ The popularity of American culture throughout the world may at least in part be attributed to the effort of the United States government to create a positive image of America internationally following the Second World War. The idea was not so much to promote American culture, as it was to create a different perception of America in the minds of those who were familiar with the United States only through contact with American soldiers, diplomats or businessmen. The government launched a series of official information programs that would transmit a positive image of the United States through a full range of cultural elements—books, movies, radio, television and exhibits. In effect, the science of advertising was being applied to create a new image of the United States abroad. An act passed by Congress in 1948, the Smith-Mundt Act, authorized the creation of an information service to promote a better understanding of the United States abroad.

Part of the motivation for an effective information program developed out of the Cold War. President Truman called for a "Campaign of Truth" in 1950. In doing so, Truman emphasized the propaganda campaign carried out by the Soviet Union in support of communist doctrines and pointed out the need to get the "real story" to the people of other nations in order to counter the Soviet dissemination of "distortion and lies." This campaign was taken a step further in the Eisenhower Administration with the creation of the United States Information Agency in 1953 in order to promote both the American image and American policies around the world. The USIA spread information about the United States through the Voice of America, which transmitted daily newscasts in the native language of dozens of nations around the world, through the world's largest library system, with branches in many countries. Regional editions of the news were transmitted daily by teletype throughout Europe, Africa, the Middle East, Latin America and Asia. Hollywood films and documentaries were distributed abroad, more educational exchanges took place, more scholars received opportunities to travel and people worked harder then ever to express an American point of view worldwide.

Those abroad saw images of American farms, skyscrapers, automobiles, factories, suburbs, churches, drugstores, schools and countless other aspects of American life and activities. Even in those places where the literacy rate was low, pictures of life in America were available through films, and, later on, television programs. While it was not always possible to determine how effective American propaganda truly was, it undoubtedly played a significant role in spreading images of life in the United States abroad and helped to spread American culture around the world.

The destruction of the economies of Europe and Asia as a result of the Second War was also a factor in the dissemination of American culture overseas. The role of the United States in rebuilding the economies of the nations of Western Europe along with Japan provided plenty of opportunity for American businessmen to sell American-made products overseas, and by doing so, to spread both images of America and its culture around the world. Along with American products, American ideas, methods and practices were disseminated throughout the globe.

Native foods found themselves competing with hot dogs and hamburgers, canned foods were being consumed more often and even food, soft drink and candy vending machines were appearing in various countries. Popcorn, potato chips and canned drinks grew in popularity in Japan. A growing demand for clothing bearing the label "Made in the USA" could be seen. American fads caught on overseas. As American cars were exported, so was automobile culture, which was marked by the appearance of drive-in movies, parking meters, shopping centers, drive-in restaurants and superhighways.

The influence of the United States was not welcomed by everyone. Some critics regarded American culture as superficial or tasteless. The French protested what they called "Cocacolonialism". Others regarded the prosperity of the United States as the result of a system based not on efficiency but on injustice; or they held that American culture was sentimental and lacking in substance. Some blamed television and other forms of mass communication for lowering cultural standards by reaching out to the masses and making culture vulgar rather than tasteful.

Unquestionably, however, both private and public institutions in the United States had a great deal to do with the extent to which American cultural elements penetrated other nations and both had a significant impact abroad. The variety of ways in which Americans could affect other cultures—through missionary activities, scholarly exchanges, business activities, educational institutions, official missions and delegations, the sharing of technology, mass media and, now, the internet—helped to spread American culture over the globe. New products, ideas and methods may have been distributed around the world by the United States, and, at least at a superficial level, American cultural elements have become part of the cultures of many other nations. This does not mean, however, that American culture has made a permanent imprint on the way of life of other nations. The growing economic interdependency among nations and the continued trend toward greater globalization may mean that the twenty-first century will see American culture as only one of many influential cultural systems in the world, and the peoples of the world will be more selective in what they choose to accept or reject from these systems.

Conclusion

Americans have tended to defend the expansion of their nation, both in the development of the North American continent and spread of American influence around the globe, as part of a national mission. While motivated in part by the desire for profit, Americans have justified the growth of the United States from a small nation to the world's superpower as part of a national quest. The belief that the United States represented something new in the world—that the nation would stand as a beacon of liberty and democracy in a dark, decadent, autocratic world, and that, over time, the freedoms enjoyed by Americans would spread around the world.

American domination of the Western Hemisphere, while profit driven, was also motivated by the desire to prevent the European nations from interfering with the process of democratic development there. Intervention in the affairs of the Caribbean states or the nations of Latin America were often defended on the principle of protecting or encouraging democratic influences there, although, in fact, were usually carried out for the purpose of protecting American interests.

The idea of spreading the benefits of American civilization, especially liberty and democracy, was a central theme of expansion, both across the continent and abroad. Americans expected that the peoples they came in contact with would, in time, recognize the advantages of the American way of life and become part of an ultimate "empire of liberty." The process of expansion was influenced by American perceptions of their nation and its role, or perhaps, more accurately, its mission in the world. But expansion also did much to shape the character of the American people. Conquering a vast continent and extending the influence of the United States throughout the world are central themes of American History, and no understanding of the American nation can be complete without an awareness of the importance of the expansionist impulse and the sense of mission that accompanied it.

BIBLIOGRAPHY

Axtell, James. *Natives and Newcomers*. New York: Oxford University Press. 2001.

Beale, Howard K. *Theodore Roosevelt and the Rise of America to World Power*. Baltimore: Johns Hopkins University Press, 1956.

Brinkley, Alan. *The Unfinished Nation*. 3rd ed. New York: McGraw Hill, 2000.

Compton, William David. *Where No Man Has Gone Before*. (NASA History Series)

Dale, Edward. *The Range Cattle Industry*. Norman: University of Oklahoma Press, 1960.

Drinnon, Richard. *Facing West*. New York: New American Library, 1980.

Farragher, John Mack. *Women and Men on the Overland Trail*. New Haven: Yale University Press, 1979.

Gaddis, John Lewis. *Strategies of Containment*. New York: Oxford University Press, 1982.

Healy, David F. *Drive to Hegemony: The United States in the Caribbean, 1898-1917*. Madison: University of Wisconsin Press, 1988.

Katz, Murrin, Greenberg. *Colonial America*. 5th ed. New York: McGraw Hill, 2001.

LaFeber, Walter. *The American Age*. 2nd ed. New York: Norton, 1994.

———. *The New Empire*. Ithaca, NY: Cornell University Press, 1963.

Limerick, Patricia Nelson. *The Legacy of Conquest: The Unbroken Past of the American West*. New York: Norton, 1987.

May, Ernest. *Imperial Democracy*. New York: Harcourt, Brace & World,1961.

McDonnell, Janet. *The Dispossession of the American Indian*. Bloomington: Indiana University Press, 1991.

McDougall, Walter A. *The Heavens and the Earth: A Political History of the Space Age*. Baltimore: Johns Hopkins University Press, 1997.

McCullough, David. *The Path Between the Seas*. New York: Simon & Schuster, 1977.

Rodman, W. Paul. *Mining Frontiers of the Far West, 1848-1880*. Albuquerque: University of New Mexico Press, 1963.

Rosenberg, Emily S. *Spreading the American Dream: American Economic and Cultural Expansion, 1890-1945*. New York: Hill & Wang, 1982.

Smith, Henry Nash. *Virgin Land*. New York: Random House, 1950.

Turner, Frederick Jackson. *The Frontier in American History*. New York: H. Holt, 1920.

Utley, Robert. *The Indian Frontier of the American West, 1846-1890*. Albuquerque: University of New Mexico Press, 1984.

Weinberg, Julius and Cary, John H. *The Social Fabric*. 3rd ed. Boston: Little, Brown, 1978.

White, Richard. *"It's Your Misfortune and None of My Own": A History of the American West*. Norman: University of Oklahoma Press, 1991.

Williams, William A. *The Roots of the Modern American Empire*. New York: Random House, 1969.

Internet Resources

Link to the 1996 PBS documentary about the American West. Includes resources and lesson plans for educators
www.pbs.org/weta/thewest

The *Making of America* – digital library of primary sources relating to 19th Century American History, particularly from the antebellum period through Reconstruction
http://moa.umdl.umich.edu

Offers assistance to educators in understanding the Lewis & Clark expedition through the use of interdisciplinary resources
www.lewisandclarkeducationcenter.com

Site devoted to the American West with information and images about expansion, Native Americans, cowboys, gunfighters, pioneers and various other topics
www.americanwest.com

The Native American History Archive offers information for students and educators
www.ilt.columbia.edu/k12/naha

Online resource about the Trail of Tears
http://ngeorgia.com/history/nghisttt.html

Links to information about African-American soldiers on the frontier
www.buffalosoldiers.net

U.S. Diplomatic History Resources Index – links to a wide variety of primary resources regarding American Diplomatic History, including American Imperialism and the Cold War
http://faculty.tamu-commerce.edu/sarantakes/stuff.html

Online history of American expansion into Asia, the Pacific and Latin America
www.smplanet.com/imperialism/toc.html

Greg Moore
Notre Dame College, South Euclid, Ohio

AUTOMOBILES AND HIGHWAYS

~

(1880s) A parade on a main street in Belfast, Maine, possibly, a Fourth of July celebration. All participants are in horse drawn carriages and wagons, some wearing costumes and uniforms; American flags and banners fly from buildings on either side of the street.

TIMELINE

1675-1849 ~ Early Powered Carriages

Model steam carriages made in China (1678) / Three-wheel, steam-powered carriages in use in Britain (1786) / Oliver Evans builds the first steam-powered motor vehicle in the U.S. (1805) / Congress authorizes construction of the Cumberland Road (1806) / Steam-powered buses in use in London (1832)

MILESTONES: Richard Arkwright invents the spinning jenny and the power-driven spinner (1700s) • Eli Whitney invents interchangeable parts, making mass production possible (early 1800s) • George Goodyear invents rubber tires (1840s) • Beginning of Manifest Destiny doctrine of acquiring western territory (1845)

1850-1899 ~ Evolving the Automobile

First petroleum well discovered in Pennsylvania by Edwin Drake (1859) / John D. Rockefeller forms Standard Oil of Ohio (1870) / Carl Benz and Gottlieb Daimler create the essential elements of the gasoline automobile, including the spark plug (1870s-1880s) / First experiments with gasoline-powered engine (1876) / First American electric car (1891) / First American gas-powered automobile (1893) / First automobile patent granted to George Selden (1895) / U.S. manufacturers produce 35,000 electric cars between 1896 and 1915 / Henry Ford begins production of the gas-powered automobile (1896) / Stanley Steamer produced (1897)

MILESTONES: Alexander Graham Bell with George Watson invents the telephone (1876) • Using alternating current, Nikola Tesla from Croatia develops dynamos, motors and transformers (1880s) Thomas Edison invents the light bulb (1879) and one horsepower generator (1881) • George Eastman invents celluloid rolls of film for use in Kodak cameras (1888)

1900-1929 ~ The Business of Automobiles

August Otto, in Germany, invents the internal combustion engine (c. 1900) / Formation of the Ford Motor Company (1903) / Construction of The Bronx River Parkway (1906) / Formation of the General Motors Corporation (1908) / Model T released by Ford (1908) / Ford Motor Company begins mass production of the automobile (1913) / Formation of Chrysler Corporation (1925) / Last Model T produced (1927)

MILESTONES: Wright brothers' gasoline engine aircraft successfully flies at Kitty Hawk (1903) • Pennsylvania establishes a highway patrol (1905) • Henry Ford institutes the five-dollar day for his factory workers (1914) • Federal Aid Road Act begins government assistance to construct roads (1916) • First commercial aircraft flights for passengers and cargo begin (1920) • White Castle Hamburger chain begins (1921) • Route 66 beginning in Chicago and ending in Santa Monica, CA is begun; by 1937 it is fully paved, crossing 8 states and 3 time zones (1926)

1930-1959 ~ Inactive Years: Depression and War

30,000 Americans die in car accidents (1930) / First Freeway, Pennsylvania Turnpike, opens (1940) / Automobile manufacturers retool for war machines (1941) / Automobile production resumes (1946) / First self-service gas station (1947) / McDonald's opens (1952) / Interstate Highway Act passed to fund a vast network of high speed roads (1956)

MILESTONES: FBI arrests famous gangsters and solidifies its public image (1930s) • Emergency Banking Act closes, then reopens failing banks (1933) • Germany invades Poland, starting WWII (1939) • Richard M. Hollingshead, Jr. of New Jersey patents the first drive-in movie theater (1933) • Fair Labor Standards Act establishes minimum wages, maximum hours and the abolition of child labor (1938) • Massey-Ferguson introduces the first combine farm machine (1944) • First Levittown suburban development constructed (1947) • First fully enclosed shopping center built in Minnesota (1956)

1960-2000 ~ Safety and Shortages

Number of deaths due to automobile accidents increases 46 percent (1960s) / Federal laws require use of safety belts (1971) / Arab Oil Embargo creates gas crisis in U.S. (1973) / Alaskan Pipeline constructed (1977) / Persian Gulf War (1991) / Clean Air Act requires automobile manufacturers to begin developing alternative fuel vehicles. (1991)

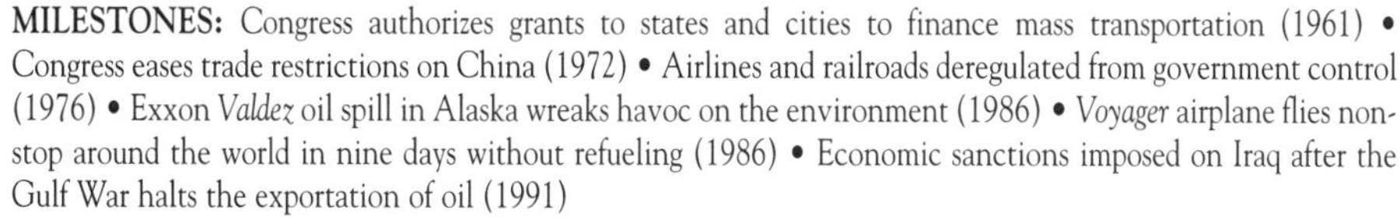

MILESTONES: Congress authorizes grants to states and cities to finance mass transportation (1961) • Congress eases trade restrictions on China (1972) • Airlines and railroads deregulated from government control (1976) • Exxon *Valdez* oil spill in Alaska wreaks havoc on the environment (1986) • *Voyager* airplane flies non-stop around the world in nine days without refueling (1986) • Economic sanctions imposed on Iraq after the Gulf War halts the exportation of oil (1991)

Introduction

(Also see "Automobiles and Highways" in the entry on Transportation)

Soon after automobiles were mass-produced early in the twentieth century, they began to change essential styles of living. Today, the automobile is still causing changes. Easy access by passenger car or truck helps to determine where people build homes, buy food, seek recreation and locate businesses. The immediacy and exactness of travel by car and truck makes a unique form of transportation. They move near the source or destination of farm or manufactured products, unrestricted by the need for rails, runways, or waterways. Automobility, of course, requires roads, which now cover the industrial countries of the world in a vast network. While automobile culture has evolved throughout the twentieth century, some of the most acute changes occurred during in the 1970s, 1980s and early 1990s. Concern with safety and pollution led to design changes and the introduction of new technology. Automobile bodies and engines became smaller and lighter to save gasoline and recently researchers have emphasized alternatives to the gasoline engine.

By the early 1990s more than 50 million automobiles were manufactured worldwide annually. Leading manufacturing areas were Japan, the United States and Western Europe. Today, the automotive industry is so vast that it influences, directly or indirectly, most of the people on Earth. In industrial nations the level of automobile production has become a barometer of the economy and is closely watched by political leaders and business analysts. Changes in auto production directly affect the large steel, aluminum, petroleum and rubber industries and their suppliers and employees.

At the close of the millennium, many local and national politicians admitted what architectural critics and planners had noted for years: the landscape of post-World War II America had been planned around cars more than around people. Reflecting the nation's great enthusiasm for automobility, the twentieth-century landscape integrated this transportation infrastructure and allowed it to be a defining influence. Today, our nation's vernacular landscape is largely defined by terms such as sprawl and the strip.

These aspects of American life are so ingrained in society that many Americans overlook our reliance on the automobile. However, the rapid rise in gas prices during 1999-2000 made our habit obvious to most drivers. Fed-up citizen groups throughout the United States organized "Gas-Out Days," when millions of drivers refused to purchase gasoline in hopes of influencing oil companies' pricing. Undeterred, prices continued to rise and with them went the prices of goods transported using petroleum. The entire situation reveals a basic truth of American life: The U.S. is a chemically dependent nation; it is dependent on fuel. Simply, we love our cars.

1675-1850 • Historical Background ~ Transportation has been part of human culture throughout its history. The automobile is part of the individualization of transport that can be traced as far back as the fifteenth century when the Renaissance genius Leonardo da Vinci considered the concept of a self-propelled vehicle and Robert Valturio planned for a cart powered by windmills geared to its wheels. As early as the sixteenth century, steam propulsion was proposed and in 1678 a Belgian missionary to China, Ferdinand Verbiest, made a model steam carriage based on a principle that suggests the modern turbine. In the seventeenth century the great Dutch physicist Christiaan Huygens built an engine that worked by air pressure developed by exploding a powder charge. Around 1750 French inventor Jacques de Vaucanson demonstrated a carriage propelled by a large clockwork engine.

The first invention to clearly foreshadow the auto was the three-wheeled steam-powered carriage. Steam carriages were produced in England during the late eighteenth and early nineteenth centuries. In 1786 William Murdock built a three-wheeled steam-driven wagon. Richard Trevithick produced several steam carriages in the early 1800s. Steam-driven carriages, built and operated by Goldsworthy Gurney and Walter Hancock, transported passengers in the London area during this same period. Hancock's "steam bus," built in 1832, was in regular service between London and Paddington.

Oliver Evans built the first steam-powered motor vehicle in the United States in 1805. A combination dredge and flatboat, it operated on land and water. Richard Dudgeon's road engine of 1867, which resembled a farm tractor, could carry ten passengers. Steam-driven automobiles were turned out by some 100 manufacturers during the late 1890s and early 1900s. The most famous of these steam-car makers were Francis E. and Freelan O. Stanley of the United States–twin brothers who developed an automobile called the "Stanley Steamer" in 1897. Steam cars burned kerosene to heat water in a tank that was part of the car. The pressure of escaping steam activated the car's driving mechanism. The popularity of the steam car declined at about the time of World War I and production came to an end in 1929.

Several experimental, electrically powered automobiles were built in Europe during the 1880s. William Morrison produced one of the first "electrics" in the United States in 1891. About 54 United States manufacturers turned out almost 35,000 electric cars between 1896 and 1915–the period of

U.S. Personal Travel per Household, Driver and Mode

Characteristics	1969	1977	1983	1990	1995
Vehicles per household	1.16	1.59	1.68	1.77	1.78
Daily vehicle trips	3.83	3.95	4.07	4.66	6
Daily vehicle miles per household	34.01	32.97	32.16	41.37	57
Average vehicle occupancy rate	—	1.9	1.75	1.64	2
Average vehicle trip length	8.9	8.35	7.9	8.85	9
Average distance to work	9.4	9.2	8.54	10.65	12

SOURCE: U.S. Department of Transportation 1997

(1905) Buyers inspecting the floor merchandise at the opening of Smith & Mabley's automobile salesroom and garage at 1765 Broadway, New York City. The showroom featured the #9 Mercedes race car driven in the Vanderbilt Cup Race by Warden, the 1905 Panhard (L), the 1905 Mercedes (C), and the 1905 S & M Simplex (R).

their greatest popularity. The Columbia, the Baker and the Riker were among the more famous models. The electric car ran smoothly and was simple to operate. However, it did not run efficiently at speeds of more than 20 miles per hour and could not travel more than 50 miles without having its batteries recharged. Thus it was limited to city use. In sum, the forerunners of the auto possessed intrinsic differences that prohibited further development. The true revolution in automobility would first require a new source of energy.

1850s-1870s • Creating Petroleum

~ America's dependence on petroleum in the 1990s would have shocked nineteenth century users of "Pennsylvania Rock Oil." Farmers who encountered the oil in the early 1800s considered it a nuisance that threatened crops and water supplies. Petroleum had been a part of human society for thousands of years, but it's value in the U.S. became evident only after European-American immigrants used this natural resource effectively in various commodity-making industries.

Crude oil was found and used in some fashion in various locales throughout the world before the nineteenth century. However, the area in the U.S. that is credited with the first noticeable petroleum reserves is a mountainous area in western Pennsylvania, nearly one hundred miles above Pittsburgh. The oil occurring along Oil Creek was named initially for the Seneca people, who were the native inhabitants of this portion of North America at the time of European settlement. Paleo-Indians of the Woodland period, before 1400, also came to the area to harvest the oil for use in their religious rituals.

Europeans began bottling the loose crude in the 1840s and selling it as a mysterious cure-all. Developers of oil for illumination began experiments with petroleum in the 1850s. In 1857, the Pennsylvania Rock Oil Company of Connecticut sent Edwin Drake to Pennsylvania to attempt to drill the first well intended for oil. The novelty of the project soon wore off for Drake and his assistant Billy Smith. The townspeople irreverently heckled the "lunatic's" endeavor. During the late summer of 1859, Drake ran out of funds and wired to New Haven, Connecticut for more money. He was told that he would be given money only for a trip home; that the Seneca Oil Company, as the group was now called, was finished supporting him in this folly. Drake took out a personal line of credit to continue and a few days later, on August 29, 1859, Drake and his assistant discovered oozing oil.

After the American Civil War, the industry consistently moved toward the streamlined state that would allow it to grow into the world's major source of energy and lubrication during the twentieth century. Oil was a commodity with so much potential that it attracted the eye and interest of one of the most effective businessmen in history, John D. Rockefeller, Sr. Working within the South Improvement Company for much of the late 1860s, Rockefeller laid the groundwork for his effort to control the entire industry at each step in its process. Rockefeller formed the Standard Oil Company of Ohio in 1870. Oil exploration grew from the Oil Creek area of Pennsylvania in the early 1870s and would expand from Pennsylvania to other states and nations during the next decade. By 1879 Standard controlled 90 percent of the U.S. refining capacity, most of the rail lines between urban centers in the northeast and many of the leasing companies at the various sites of oil speculation. Through Rockefeller's efforts and the organization he made possible, petroleum became the primary energy source for the nation and the world.

1860-1900 • Inventors on the Prowl ~ Commodities such as petroleum are culturally constructed: a market must first place a value on them before they are worthwhile. In the earliest years of petroleum, it was refined into kerosene, an illuminant to replace whale oil. After 1900, when electricity became the source of most lighting, petroleum's greatest value derived from transportation, mainly the automobile. Following the various experiments with other power sources for carriages, gasoline-driven automobiles were first developed in Europe. A practical gas engine was designed and built by Ytienne Lenoir of France in 1860. It ran on illuminating gas. In 1862 he built a vehicle powered by one of his engines. Siegfried Marcus of Austria built several four-wheeled gasoline-powered vehicles. By 1876 Nikolaus Otto, a German, was perfecting his four-stroke cycle engine. In 1885, two other Germans, Karl Benz and Gottlieb Daimler, built gasoline cars.

By the early 1900s many inventors in the United States were developing new models of gasoline-powered automobiles. In 1893 J. Frank and Charles E. Duryea produced the first successful gasoline-powered automobile in the United States. They began commercial production of the Duryea car in 1896—the same year in which Henry Ford operated his first successful automobile in Detroit. The first automobile salesroom was opened in New York City in 1899 by

Percy Owen. In 1900 the first automobile show was held—also in New York City.

Combining various developments of independent inventors resulted in mass production in the automobile industry, introduced in 1901 by Ransom E. Olds, a pioneer experimenter since 1886. His company manufactured more than 400 of the now historic curved-dash Oldsmobiles in that first year. Each car sold for only $650. Henry M. Leland and Henry Ford further developed mass production methods during the early 1900s. It remained unclear, though, who actually owned this evolving technology.

1895 • The First Automobile Patent ~ In 1879 George B. Selden, an American attorney, had applied for a patent which covered the general features of a gasoline-powered automobile. He received his patent in 1895. In 1903 the Association of Licensed Vehicle Manufacturers was formed by companies who recognized the Selden patent. They agreed to pay Selden a royalty on each car built. Henry Ford refused to join this association. He sued to break Selden's hold on the industry. After extensive litigation, Ford won. In 1911 a District Court of Appeals held that Selden's patent applied only to a two-stroke cycle engine. Other engines were free for the use of other manufacturers. This decision led to a cross-licensing agreement among most of the American manufacturers, which would be administered by the Automobile Manufacturers Association. Under this agreement, the Ford Motor Company organized in 1903, the General Motors Corporation in 1908 and the Chrysler Corporation in 1925.

1908-1927 • Ford's Mass Production of the Model T ~ Using mass production, the first Model T Ford was made in 1908. More than 15 million would be sold in the next 20 years. The Model T, nicknamed the "flivver" and the "tin lizzie," was probably more responsible for the development of large-scale motoring than was any other car in automotive history. During World War I the manufacture of automobiles for civilian uses was virtually halted as the industry was mobilized to produce vehicles, motors and other war materiel for the armed forces. The automobile assumed a significant new role in the American way of life immediately after World War I.

No longer an extravagant novelty, the motorcar was rapidly becoming a necessity rather than a luxury for many American families as many had moved to the suburbs. By the early 1920s most of the basic mechanical problems of automotive engineering had been solved. Manufacturers then concentrated their efforts on making motorcars safer, more stylish and more comfortable.

In 1929 about 90 percent of all automobiles were drawn from a few original models. By the mid-1920s Henry Ford had decided to abandon the three-pedaled Model T and replace it with the Model A, which was to be equipped with a conventional gearshift. The last Model T was produced in May 1927 and the first Model A

~

There are many resources about autos available through the Henry Ford museum and Greenfield Village, located in Dearborn, Michigan. The online showroom is particularly good (http://www.hfmgv.org/histories/showroom/intro.html). It has photos of various models.

~

rolled off the assembly line in October 1927. An enthusiastic public was soon buying thousands. In 1928 the Chrysler Corporation announced the production of its answer to the Model A—a new low-cost automobile called the Plymouth.

Top Automobile Models of the Twentieth Century

Vehicle

1) Ford Model T
2) Mini (all types)
3) Citroen DS
4) Volkswagen Beetle
5) Porsche 911

SOURCE: Consumer voting collected by Car of the Century, 1999

1800s • Early Roads ~ Inconvenience from a lack of roads and infrastructure as well as a reliance on transportation technologies such as trolleys precluded Americans from rapidly accepting the new "horseless carriage." The manufacturing and marketing efforts of Ford and others changed this attitude by 1913, when there was one motor vehicle to every eight Americans. Mass production ensured that by the 1920s the car had become no longer a luxury but a necessity of American middle class life. The landscape, however, had been designed around other modes of transport—including an urban scene dependent on foot travel. Cars enabled an independence never before possible, if they were supported with the necessary service structure. Massive architectural shifts were necessary to make way for the auto. Most important, of course, were the roads on which the autos would travel.

The first paved road in the world is believed to have been built in about 2500 BC in Egypt as an aid to the construction of the Great Pyramids. The first organized road building was done by the Assyrian empire of western Asia. The most famous road builders, however, were the Romans. From about 300 BC to about AD 200 they built roads for military and trade use throughout Europe and Britain.

In North America, the first roads were constructed by the Spanish along existing Indian trails into New Mexico and California. As colonists poured into the United States from England, wagon trails were carved along the lines of the Indian footpaths. The first major road system in the United States began to take shape in the late eighteenth century, following the American Revolution, when stagecoaches were in general use and there was an increasing demand for surfaced, all-weather roads. In 1806 Congress authorized construction of the Cumberland, or National, Road, which ran from Cumberland, Maryland, to Vandalia, Illinois. The Cumberland Road opened up the American West.

(circa 1910) Brush Motor. The last Model T was produced in May 1927 and the first Model A rolled off the assembly line in October 1927. An enthusiastic public was soon buying thousands. Seen here are Louie and Temple Abernathy in the Brush runabout, one of Ford's competitors.

At this time, many of the roads in the Eastern United States were turnpikes surfaced with tree trunks that were laid across the width of the road to make a so-called corduroy road. Other roads were plank roads, paved with split logs. America's early highway designs were largely the work of Europeans. Two Scottish engineers, John Loudon McAdam and Thomas Telford, pioneered the use of pavements built of broken stone carefully placed in layers and well compacted.

1900-1930 • Better Roads ~ Although the motorcar was the quintessential private instrument, its owners had to operate it over public spaces. Who would pay for these public thoroughfares? After a period of acclimation, Americans viewed highway building as a form of social and economic therapy. They justified public financing for such projects on the theory that roadway improvements would pay for themselves by increasing property-tax revenues along the route. At this time, asphalt, macadam and concrete were each used on different roadways.

By the 1920s, the congested streets of urban areas pressed road building into other areas. Most urban regions soon proposed express streets without stop lights or intersections. These aesthetically conceived roadways, normally following the natural topography of the land, soon took the name "parkways". Long Island and Westchester County, New York used parkways with bridges and tunnels to separate it from local cross traffic. The Bronx River Parkway (1906), for instance, follows a river park and forest; it also is the first roadway to be declared a national historic site. In addition to pleasure driving, such roads stimulated automobile commuting.

The Federal Road Act of 1916 offered funds to states that organized highway departments, designating 200,000 miles of road as primary and thus eligible for federal funds. More importantly, ensuing legislation also created a Bureau of Public Roads to plan a highway network to connect all cities of 50,000 or more inhabitants. Some states adopted gasoline taxes to help finance the new roads. By 1925 the value of highway construction projects exceeded $1 billion. Expansion continued through the Great Depression, with road-building becoming integral to city and town development.

1930-present • Modern Roads ~ Robert Moses of New York defined this new role as road-builder and social planner. Through his work in the Greater New York City area (1928-1960), Moses created a model for a metropolis that included and even emphasized the automobile as opposed to mass transportation. This was a dramatic change in the motivation of design. Historian Clay McShane writes: "...in their headlong search for modernity through mobility, American urbanites made a decision to destroy the living environments of nineteenth-century neighborhoods by converting their gathering places into traffic jams, their playgrounds into motorways and their shopping places into elongated parking lots."

By the year 2000, there were about 120 million miles of roads in the world. The United States has the largest road network: more than 4 million miles of roads and streets. Other modern road networks serve Europe, Asia, South America, Australia and parts of Africa. The smallest national road network is that of Monaco, which has about 29 miles of roads. About half of the roads in the United States have a paved surface. The rest of the country's roads are either surfaced with gravel or stone or remain unsurfaced. Many countries have few paved roads. For example, only about 225 miles of the Central African Republic's 12,600 miles of roads are paved. On the other hand, many European countries, such as Austria, Germany, Denmark, Switzerland, Italy and Great Britain, have few unpaved roads.

1916-1950s • Federally Funded Highways ~ The Federal Road Act of 1916 began a century of road building that some historians have called the "largest construction feat of human history," and the American road system unfolded throughout the early twentieth century. Beginning in the 1920s, legislation created a Bureau of Public Roads to plan a highway network to connect all cities of fifty thousand or more inhabitants. These developments were supplemented in the 1950s when President Dwight D. Eisenhower included a national system of roads in his preparedness plans for nuclear attack. This development cleared the way for the Interstate Highway Act to build a national system of roads unrivaled by any nation.

Most of these developments redefined the local landscape while creating few national thoroughfares, but President Eisenhower changed this in the 1950s. In 1920 he had led troops across the American road system in a military call for new roads. As commander of U.S. forces in Europe during World War II, he had witnessed the spectacle of Hitler's Autobahn first hand and the speed with which traffic could move. When he became President, he worked with automobile manufacturers and others to devise a 1956 plan to connect America's future to the automobile. The Interstate Highway system was the most expensive public works project in human history. The public rationale for this hefty project revolved around fear of nuclear war: such roadways would assist in exiting urban centers in the event of nuclear war. The emphasis, however, was clearly economic expansion. At the cost of many older urban neighborhoods—often occupied by minority groups—the huge wave of concrete was unrolled that linked all the major cities of the nation together.

Federal Highway System, 1999

Type of Roadway	Mileage by system
Interstate	46,317
Other National Highway	113,848
Other Federal-Aid Highways	795,341
All Non-Fed-Aid Highways	2,961,734
TOTAL	3,917,240

SOURCE: U.S. Department of Transportation

Today the Interstate Highway System, used mainly for long-distance travel, comprises about 46,000 miles of the nation's road system. Although interstate highways make up only a little more than one percent of all United States roads, they carry about 20 percent of the country's traffic.

1856-1900 • Development of Suburbs ~ Upper and middle class Americans had begun moving to suburban areas in the late 1800s. The first suburban developments, such as Llewellyn Park, New Jersey (1856), followed train lines or the corridors of other early mass transit. The automobile allowed access to vast areas between and beyond these corridors. Suddenly, the suburban hinterland around every city compounded. As early as 1940, about 13 million people lived in communities beyond the reach of public transportation. Due to these changes, suburbs could be planned for less wealthy Americans. Modeled after the original Gustav Stickley homes, or similar designs from *Ladies Home Journal* and other popular magazines, middle-class suburbs appealed to working and middle-class Americans. The bungalow became one of the most popular house designs in the nation. The construction halt of the Great Depression set the stage for more recent ideas and designs, including the ranch house.

U.S. Population in Urban, Suburban and Rural Areas, 1950-1998

Year	% urban	% suburban	% rural
1950	32.8	23.3	43.9
1960	32.3	30.6	37
1970	31.4	37.2	31.4
1980	30	44.8	25.2
1990	31.6	48.2	20.2
1998	30.2	49.9	19.9

SOURCE: U.S. Department of Commerce

1940s-1970s • Rapid Growth of Suburbs ~ With the national future clearly tied to cars, planners began perfecting ways of further integrating the car into American domestic life. Initially, these tactics were quite literal. In the early twentieth century, many homes of wealthy Americans soon required the ability to store vehicles. Most often these homes had carriage houses or stables that could be converted. Soon, of course, architects devised an appendage to the home and gave it the French name, "garage". From this early point, housing in the U.S. closely followed the integration of the auto and roads into American life.

In the United States roads initiated related social trends that added to Americans' dependence on petroleum. Most important, between 1945 and 1954, nine million people moved to suburbs because of the shortage of housing after World War II. The majority of the suburbs were connected to urban access by only the automobile. Between 1950 and 1976, central city population grew by ten million while suburban growth was 85 million. Housing developments and the shopping/strip mall culture that accompanied decentralization of the population made the automobile a virtual necessity. Shopping malls, suburbs and fast-food restaurants became the American norm through the end of the twentieth century, making American reliance on petroleum complete.

1947-Present • Planned Communities ~ Planners used homestyles such as these to develop one site after another with the automobile linking each one to the outside world. Levittown, the first large-scale planned community constructed in 1947 involved a complete dependence on automobile travel. This shift to suburban living became the hallmark of the late-twentieth century, with over half of the nation residing in suburbs by the 1990s. The planning system that supported this residential world, however, involved much more than roads. The services necessary to support outlying, suburban communities also needed to be integrated by planners.

Instead of the Main Street prototype, the auto suburbs demanded a new form. Initially, planners such as Jesse Clyde Nichols devised shopping areas such as Kansas City's Country Club District that

(1940) Wigwam Motel. The automobile spawned many new industries, one being the motel. Seen here is a Wigwam Motel, Bardstown, Kentucky, approved by the AAA (American Automobile Association).

appeared to be a hybrid of previous forms. Soon, however, the "strip" had evolved as the commercial corridor of the future. These sites quickly became part of suburban development, in order to provide basic services close to home. A shopper rarely arrived without an automobile; therefore, the car needed to be part of the design program. The most obvious architectural development for speed was signage: integrated into the overall site plan would be towering neon aberrations that identified services. Also, parking lots and drive-through windows suggest the integral role of transportation in this new commerce.

1930-1950s • Motor Hotels ~ During the twentieth century, planners and designers gave Americans what they wanted: a life and landscape married to the automobile. Most details of the new, planned landscape reflected this social dynamic. These changes primarily began with utilitarian needs growing out of the use of the automobile for most travel. These changes to the landscape, however, necessitated systematic changes in laws, planning and political power on local and national levels. In addition, the systematic change would play out in the human culture that became increasingly dependent on auto travel.

These changes began in a fairly benign fashion. For instance, while drivers through the 1930s often slept in roadside yards, developers soon took advantage of this opportunity by devising the roadside camp or motel. Independently owned tourist camps graduated from tents to cabins, which were often called Motor Courts. After World War II, the form became a motel in which all the rooms were tied together in one structure. Still independently owned, by 1956 there were 70,000 motels nationwide. Best Western and Holiday Inn soon used ideas of prefabrication to create chains of motels throughout the nation. Holiday Inn defined this new part of the auto landscape by emphasizing uniformity so that travelers felt as if they were in a familiar environment no matter where they traveled. This reliance on uniformity (i.e., locating light switches and bathrooms in standard locations) became part of modern landscape design and twentieth century culture. Some scholars refer to this trend as the "McDonaldization of America."

1930s-Present • Advertising to Motorists ~ In such a world, of course, the driver is a captive audience. As such, the roadside corridor is transformed into an entrepreneurial opportunity. Billboards and advertisements began littering highways and smaller roads almost immediately. Additionally, car radios introduced an entirely new venue from which advertisers could access a national audience as travelers passed in and out of certain regions. Even in the 1990s when communication technology made it possible for drivers to operate an office from their car, radio and billboard advertisements remained profitable. This remains most prevalent in urban areas

(1942) Gas Stations used to be very personalized. Shown here, a gas station in Shannon County, Missouri.

that experience high rates of traffic. Radio remains a primary mode for reporting traffic patterns and thereby creating another platform for potential advertisers.

1920s-1930s • Roadside Facilities ~ The auto landscape, of course, needed to effectively incorporate its essential raw material—petroleum. The gas station, which originally existed as little more than a roadside shack, mirrors the evolution of the automobile-related architecture in general. By the 1920s filling stations had integrated garages and service facilities. These facilities were privately owned and uniquely constructed. By the mid-1930s, oil giants such as Shell and Texaco developed a range of prototype gas stations that would recreate the site as a showroom for tires, motor oil or other services. George Urich introduced the nation's first self-service gas station in California in 1947. By the end of the 1900s, the gas station had been further streamlined to include convenience stores and the opportunity to pay-at-the-pump. The gas station experience steadily became less personalized.

As cars became more familiar in everyday Americans' lives, planners and developers formalized refueling stations for the human drivers, as well. Food stands informally provided refreshment during these early days, but soon restaurants were developed that utilized marketing strategies from the motel and petroleum industries. Diners and family restaurants sought prime locations along frequently traveled roads; however, these forms did not alter dining patterns significantly. In 1921 White Castle hamburgers combined the food stand with the restaurant to create a restaurant that could be put almost anywhere. Drive-in restaurants would evolve around the idea of quick service, often allowing drivers to remain in their automobile. Fast food as a concept, of course, derives specifically from Ray Kroc and the McDonald's concept that he marketed out of California beginning in 1952. Clearly the idea of providing service to automobile drivers had created an entire offshoot of the restaurant industry.

Growth of McDonald's Annual Sales

	Annual sales
1955	$193,772
1957	$3,841,327
1958	$10,896,163
1960	$37,579,828
1966	$200 million
1976	$3 billion
1986	$12 billion
1999	$38.5 billion

SOURCE: McDonald's Corporation

While most roadside building types evolved gradually, the drive-in theater was deliberately invented. Richard M. Hollingshead, Jr. of New Jersey believed that entertainment needed to incorporate the automobile. Hollingshead patented the first drive-in in 1933, but the invention would not proliferate until the 1950s. Viewing outdoor films in one's car has become a symbol of the culture of consumption that overtook the American middle class during the post-war era.

1900-Present • Cars as Extensions of Self ~ The social and cultural impact of the automobile follows a variety of trends. The drive-in symbolizes a crucial aspect of this as the auto came to function as a portable, private oasis.

The back-seat antics of youth at drive-ins defined a new era in courtship and outward expressions of sexuality. Many scholars tie the beginnings of the sexual revolution of the 1960s directly to the experimentation of young lovers in "parking" in secluded areas or drive-ins. In films such as *American Graffiti* or the television program "Happy Days" the growing youth culture of sex and road racing grew into an American icon. While the automobile enabled young people to travel to school and work with new independence, it also afforded young drivers new access to experiments with drugs and alcohol.

The icon of the "open road" became part of an American right of passage in youthful experiences such as "Route 66;" however, the same freedom was accessible to any driver. Car vacations became another portion of the American identity after 1950, as family cross-country treks took on a slow, plodding pattern. The same freedom, however, could easily be tied to speed. From the early days of stock-car racing when southern moonshine was illegally transported via fast cars, Americans were enamored with the image of speed. Of course, this obsession has grown into a major sport today with the interest in NASCAR racing.

Regardless of the speed with which one traveled, the car became an emblem of economic status and personal individuality. From the days of the first automobiles, which only the affluent could afford, to custom sports cars in the 1920s, to luxury imports today, automobiles have reflected personal wealth and taste. This is most obvious in the sports car infatuation that becomes most prominent after 1950. Personal statements, however, are not exclusive to the iconic red convertible. Today, the popular SUVs (sport utility vehicles) are emblematic of a rugged preparedness. While most four-wheel-drive vehicles will never venture off-road, they make a statement about their owner. Mini-vans, developed by Chrysler in the 1970s, also have become an icon of family living. In each case, style and functionality are prioritized over efficiency. The infusion of small imported vehicles in the 1970s presented the opportunity for a separate paradigm: one that allowed drivers to demonstrate that their priority was fuel efficiency. In every case, the auto says a great deal about who is behind the wheel.

1950s-1970s • Controlling Sprawl

~ The automobile reorganized American society after 1950. Certain aspects of this structure are undeniable: license plates, driver's licenses, parking meters and lots, just to name a few. Clearly the development of the auto landscape culminated in the shopping mall, which quickly became a necessary portion of strip-planning. By the 1970s, developers' initiative clearly included regional economic development for a newly evolving service and retail world. Incorporating suburbs into such development plans, designs for these pseudo-communities were held together by the automobile. The marketplace for this culture quickly became the shopping mall. Strip malls, which open onto roadways and parking lots, were installed near residential areas as suburbs extended further from the city center. Developers then perfected the self-sustained, enclosed shopping mall.

Try as they might, such artificial environments could never recreate the culture of local communities. Beginning in the 1960s, Ralph Nader and other critics began to ask hard questions of the auto's

Journey-to-Work Mode for U.S. Working Population, 1960-1990

Mode of Transportation	(percent of American workforce)			
	1960	1970	1980	1990
Private vehicle	69.48	80.63	85.92	88.02
Public transit	12.62	8.48	6.22	5.12
Walked to work	10.37	7.4	5.6	3.9
Worked at home	7.54	3.49	2.26	2.96

SOURCE: U.S. Department of Commerce

restructuring of American society. Shopping malls became the symbol of a culture of conspicuous consumption that many Americans began to criticize during the 1990s.

Critics such as Jane Jacobs and Jim Kunstler identified an intrinsic bias on the American landscape in the 1970s. Kunstler writes, "Americans have been living car-centered lives for so long that the collective memory of what used to make a landscape or a townscape or even a suburb humanly rewarding has nearly been erased." The 1990s closed with the unfolding of the new politics of urban sprawl. "I've come to the conclusion," explained Vice President Al Gore on the campaign trail in 1999, "that what we really are faced with here is a systematic change from a pattern of uncontrolled sprawl toward a brand new path that makes quality of life the goal of all our urban, suburban and farmland policies."

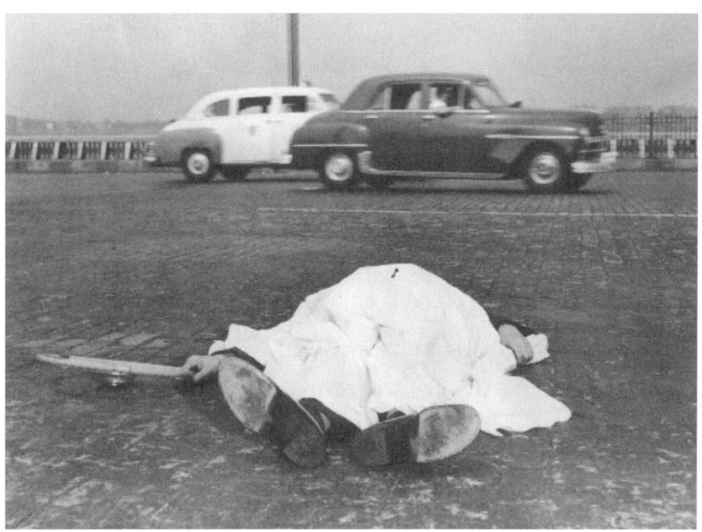

(1939) The victim of a motor accident lies by the side of the West Side Highway in New York.

1960s-1970s • Auto Safety ~ Once auto reliance was fully ingrained in society, basic issues needed to be confronted. Traffic fatalities and auto safety, particularly drunk driving, have played a primary role in efforts to make the auto era less of a fatal attraction. The work of Ralph Nader and others in the 1970s generated increased interest in auto safety. By the late 1960s, most automobiles came equipped with seat belts, but legislation did not require that they be used until 1971. Crash tests and other consumer information became more and more available as public awareness grew.

In the 1970s, federal safety and fuel conservation measures included a national speed limit of 55 miles per hour. Today, consumers have led states to loosen such restrictions; however, concern over fuel conservation continues.

Maximum Speed Limits by State

Maximum Car Limit	# of States
55 mph	1
65 mph	20
70 mph	18
75 mph	11

U.S. Department of Transportation, 1999

1950s-present • Dependence on Oil Supplies ~ During the late twentieth century, American reliance on automobility compounded the political importance of petroleum. Between 1948 and 1972, consumption in the U.S. grew from 5.8 million barrels per day to 16.4. This three-fold increase was surpassed by other parts of the world: Western Europe's use of petroleum increased by sixteen times and Japan by 137 times. Throughout the world, this growth was tied to the automobile: worldwide, automobile ownership rose from 18.9 million in 1949 to 161 million in 1972; the U.S. portion of this growth was significant, from 45 million to 119 million. New technologies enabled some refiners to increase the yields of gasoline, diesel and jet fuel and heating oil from a barrel of petroleum, but the needs remained unlike anything the world had ever seen.

By the late 1960s it had become clear that domestic production, even with quotas, could not keep up with the American needs. Dropping import barriers satiated American needs for petroleum, but also made the nation susceptible to new threats. By the summer of 1973, American imports of petroleum had doubled. As prices began to rise, OPEC (Organization of Petroleum Exporting Countries) realized that the companies were reaping huge profits. Anwar Sadat, president of Egypt, proposed a simple idea to the other ministers of OPEC in October: an embargo of shipments of crude oil to unfriendly states, including the U.S. As approved, the plan reduced shipments by five percent each month. In the U.S., the embargo came as an almost complete surprise. Petroleum had become a tool of diplomacy. The "Arab Oil Embargo" fed national panic, which contributed to gas prices rising by 40 percent. Gas lines and stations with empty tanks became common sights. "Sorry, No Gas Today" read signs in front of many stations. The gas crisis required rationing and cultural changes from the American public.

The Embargo became a resounding lesson of "living within limits" for many Americans. This lesson would be demonstrated again in 1990 when the nation went to war against Iraq largely to maintain control of oil supplies. Additional concerns came with an increasing awareness of the effects of air pollution and particularly auto emissions' relationship to Global Warming. The Clean Air Act of 1991 began a process requiring automobile makers to prioritize increased mileage and also to investigate alternative fuels.

U.S. Emissions of Carbon Monoxide by Sector (in million tons)

Year	Industrial Processing	On-road Vehicles
1940	10.905	30.121
1950	16.353	45.196
1960	15.873	64.266
1970	16.899	88.034
1980	9.25	78.049
1990	5.852	57.848
1998	4.86	50.383

SOURCE: U.S. Department of Commerce

Conclusion

As American culture fueled the popularity of SUVs in the late 1990s, rising gas prices also forced consumers to consider the benefits of smaller, more fuel efficient vehicles. While prices in 2000-2001 will probably set records in purely numerical terms, they will still be roughly 40 percent lower when adjusted for inflation than they were at their record in March 1981. International companies also stepped up efforts to develop new supplies. Most observers believe that nations in the former Soviet Union may hold the most promise. The construction of pipelines around the Caspian Sea promises to unlock new supplies of crude oil to the world over the next ten years. While such oil booms are not open to individual speculation, as were the early oil fields in Pennsylvania, Texas and elsewhere, they will dramatically alter lives in nations such as Azerbaijan and Armenia, as well as many African nations.

Regardless of the location of future supplies, the fact remains that petroleum is a finite resource. The petroleum age, agree most scientists, will near its end by 2050. Modern technology, unfortunately, allows us to account rather exactly for this certain demise: We have guzzled 800 billion barrels during the petroleum era; we know the location of 850 billion barrels more, which are termed "reserves;" and we expect that 150 billion barrels more remain undiscovered. Simply, there is an end in sight. New energy sources will need to be found if we wish to continue our love affair with the automobile.

Bibliography

Belasco, James. *Americans on the Road.* Cambridge: MIT Press, 1979.

Calthorpe, Peter. *The Next American Metropolis*. New York: Princeton Architectural Press, 1993.

Clark, Jr., Cifford Edward. *The American Family Home*. Chapel Hill: University of North Carolina Press, 1986.

Flink, James J. *The Automobile Age*. Cambridge: MIT Press, 1990.

Hart, John Fraser, ed. *Our Changing Cities*. Baltimore: Johns Hopkins University Press, 1991.

Jackson, Kenneth T. *Crabgrass Frontier.* New York: Oxford University Press, 1985.

Jacobs, Jane. *The Death and Life of Great American Cities*. New York: Vintage Books, 1961.

Kay, Jane Holtz. *Asphalt Nation*. Berkeley: University of California Press, 1997.

Kunstler, James H. *The Geography of Nowhere*. New York: Touchstone Books, 1993.

Lewis, Tom. *Divided Highways*. New York: Penguin Books, 1997.

Liebs, Chester H. *Main Street to Miracle Mile*. Baltimore: Johns Hopkins University Press, 1995.

McShane, Clay. *Down the Asphalt Path.* New York: Columbia University Press, 1994.

Relph, Edward. *The Modern Urban Landscape*. Baltimore: Johns Hopkins University Press, 1987.

Scharff, Virginia. *Taking the Wheel: Women and the Coming of the Motor Age*. New York: Free Press; Toronto: Collier Macmillan Canada, 1991.

Schiffer, Michael B., Tamara C. Butts and Kimberly K. Grimm. *Taking Charge: the Electric Automobile in America.* Washington, DC: Smithsonian Institution Press, 1994.

Vieyra, Daniel I. *Fill 'Er Up: An Architectural History of America's Gas Stations*. New York: Macmillan, 1979.

Wright, Gwendolyn. *Building the Dream.* Cambridge: MIT Press, 1992.

Internet Resources

United States Department of Transportation
http://www.dot.gov

National Transportation Library
http://www.bts.gov/ntl/

National Transportation Safety Board (NTSB)
http://www.ntsb.gov/

National Highway Traffic Safety Administration (NHTSA)
http://www.nhtsa.dot.gov/

AAA Foundation for Traffic Safety (AAAFTS)
http://www.aaafts.org/

Fuel Economy Site
http://www.fueleconomy.gov/

Insurance Institute for Highway Safety
http://www.highwaysafety.org/

Truckers/Transportation Homepage
http://www.uky.edu/Subject/transport.html

Web links related to all forms of Transportation
http://www.multcolib.org/homework/trans.html

An interesting account of the invention of the automobile
http://www.ideafinder.com/history/inventions/story054.htm

The Automobile Museum. A full history of the automobile and America's fascination with it.
http://www.themuseumofautomobilehistory.com/

The Packard Club of America. Lots of information and history on the Packard
http://www.packardclub.org/

Website of the Society of Automotive Historians
http://www.autohistory.org/

History of the U.S. highway system from dirt paths to superhighways
http://gbcnet.com/ushighways/history/history_main.html

A history of gas stations on Highway 99
http://www.livinggoldpress.com/rich.htm

Brian Black
Penn State University, Altoona

BUSINESS AND LABOR

(1918) A propaganda poster shows a female factory worker holding a plane in one hand and a shell in the other. The stability of the labor force was an important contribution to U.S. soldiers in World War I.

TIMELINE

1619-1860 ~ Slaves and Immigrants

Slaves imported into the colonies (1619-1808) / Apprenticeship or formal education is required for professional training (1600s-1820s) / Factories employ entire families of immigrants (1820s-1830s) / Census shows great increase in the types of occupations (1850) / Three million slaves live in southern states (1860)

MILESTONES: Early American cities established: Jamestown (1607), Santa Fe (1610), Boston (1630) • Model steam carriage made in China (1678) • Richard Arkwright invents the spinning jenny and the power-driven spinner (1700s) • Boston Tea Party protests taxation (1775) • Economic Crisis brings high unemployment, bread riots, and rent strikes (1837)

1861-1899 ~ The New South and Labor

First labor union, Knights of Labor, formed in the U.S. (1866) / Freed slaves elect sharecropping over paid wages (1867-1868) / Seven out of ten working women hold jobs as domestic servants (1870) / State courts rule that labor reform laws violate the rights of employers to enjoy the freedom to operate their businesses (1881-1900) / Chinese Exclusion Act limits Chinese immigrant labor (1882) / Knights of Labor call a strike against the railroads (1886)

MILESTONES: One-fifth of the American population is killed in the Civil War (1861-1865) • Homestead Act promises land to pioneer settlers (1862) • Indian Appropriation Act permits railroads to lay tracks across Indian lands (1871) • President Hayes removes all federal troops from southern states, ending Reconstruction (1877) • Henry Grady delivers his New South speech in New York (1886) • Alaskan gold rush begins after the discovery of gold in the Klondike (1897)

1900-1919 ~ Labor and the War Effort

Non-whites excluded from most union membership (1900) / Mexicans strike against the Pacific Electric Railway company for equal wages and parity (1903) / Supreme Courts rules against unions (1903 and 1907) / Seven thousand Japanese plantation workers in Hawaii stage a four month long strike (1909) / President Wilson enacts laws to support unions and workers (1913-1917) / National War Labor Board created to settle industrial disputes (1918) / AFL demands and receives better wages for workers (1917-1918) / Unions fall into government and public disfavor (1919-1920)

MILESTONES: Chinese immigration banned except for diplomats, students, and merchants (1900) • NYC Tenement House Act requires that no new tenement could occupy more than 70 percent of its lot (1901) • Oregon hires the first policewoman in America (1905) • Blouses are mass produced in sweatshops (1910s) • Standardized tests developed to determine racial intelligence (1910s) • Ford Model T costs $290, down from $950 in 1908 (1915)

1920-1929 ~ Welfare Capitalism

Welfare capitalism by businesses reduces the power of unions over workers (1920s) / One out of every eight American worker is employed in automobile-related industries, including rubber, steel, and petroleum (1920s) / Union strike in Elizabethtown, Tennessee turns violent (1929) / Collective bargaining laws strengthened (1928 and 1932) / President Hoover presides over an economy he doesn't understand (1928-1932)

MILESTONES: For the first time more Americans live in urban than in rural areas (1920) • Tariffs close foreign markets to farmers (1921) • Federal Trade Commission officially recognizes manmade textile filaments (1925) • Collective bargaining laws strengthened (1928 and 1932) • Over 350 companies give pensions; plant safety and working conditions improve; medical care provided for workers and their families; sports and education for workers subsidized by companies (1929)

1930-1945 ~ The Depression, The War, and Labor Reform

Hoover's programs fail and the American banking system is on the verge of total collapse (1932) / Worker security increased by the Social Security and the National Labor Relations Acts (1935) / United Mine Workers of America (UMW), one of the nation's few interracial organizations, provides the organizational foundation for the emergence of industrial unionism (1935-1939) / Fair Labor Standards Act establishes minimum wages, maximum hours, and the abolition of child labor (1938) / Women, blacks and immigrants increase the work force from 46 million in 1940 to 60 million in 1945

MILESTONES: Working wives publicly criticized as selfish and "a menace to society" (1930) • Women dominate the professions of teaching, nursing, and social work (1930) • Economy Act stipulates that married women be discharged from their jobs (1932) • Civilian Conservation Corps. provides jobs to millions of Americans (1933) • 50,000 coal miners strike in Birmingham, Alabama against exploitation (1934) • President Roosevelt forced to end racial discrimination in war production facilities (1941)

1946-1969 ~ Moving toward Equality

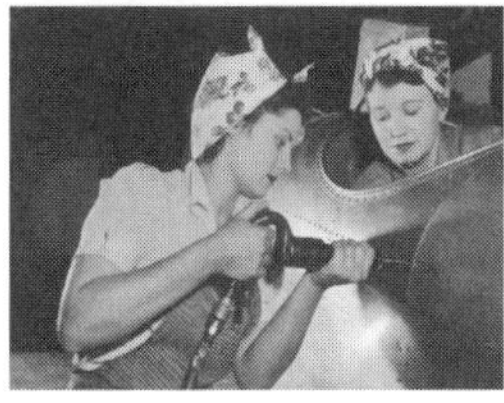

Jackie Robinson becomes the first black to join major league baseball (1947) / United Auto Workers (UAW) signs a national union contract with General Motors that includes seniority provisions, a pension plan, cost-of-living allowances, and wage increases (1950) / 37 percent of the workforce is white-collar (1950) / Union influence declines (1946-1960) / Union contracts include paid vacations of up to four weeks for long-term workers (1960) / Civil Rights Act declares that American citizens cannot be segregated in public accommodations or discriminated against in employment (1964)

MILESTONES: Housing Act provides for slum clearance and community redevelopment (1949) • 10 billion cans of foods are produced each year in the U.S. (1950) • Military spending grows exponentially (1950s) • Montgomery Bus Boycott propels Martin Luther King, Jr. into national prominence (1955) • Boston Celtics draft center Bill Russell, whose rebounding, defensive, and passing skills foster a new style of play that revolutionizes professional basketball (1956) • Betty Friedan's *The Feminine Mystique* attributes women's problems to a sex-based society and not the personal failure of women, starting the women's liberation movement (1963) • Formation of the American Basketball Association (ABA) (1967)

1970-1979 ~ Easing Restrictions

United Farm Workers' five-year grape boycott succeeds (1970) / Women make up 40 percent of the overall labor force and represent a substantial increase in married women who work (1970) / Occupational Safety and Health Act sets safety standards in the workplace (1970)

MILESTONES: Vietnam refugee immigration permitted (1970-1975) • Supreme Court vindicates Muhammad Ali, ruling that the government violated his constitutional rights, clearing the way for his return to boxing (1970) • Congress eases trade restrictions on China (1972) • Airlines and railroads deregulated from government control, making these industries more competitive (1976) • Alaskan Pipeline constructed (1977)

1980-2000 ~ Reconfiguring Business

Recession forces companies to "downsize," laying off many workers (1980s) / Number of temporary workers more than doubles and the number of part-time workers increases by 40 percent (1980-1989) / President Reagan disbands the Air Traffic Controllers union (1981) / North American Free Trade Agreement opens borders to Mexico and Canada (1993) / Albertson's supermarkets pays over $29.4 million in a discrimination case involving women and Hispanics (1996)

MILESTONES: Amnesty granted to illegal immigrants in the U.S. (1986) • National Opinion Research Report finds that a majority of whites believe that African Americans are "innately lazy and less intelligent and patriotic than whites," and prefer welfare to work (1990) • U.S. increases efforts to stop illegal Mexican immigration (1990s) • Number of farm workers declines from 13.6 million in 1915 to 2.85 million in 1995

"Come to me all ye who labor and are heavy laden and I will give you rest."
Matthew 11:28

Introduction

Although Jesus was talking to those who would follow Him, the idea of those working and being heavy laden can be applied to workers throughout American history. Workers from all over the world have consistently come to the shores of the United States to find employment, a better life, and ultimately, peace and rest. In the nineteenth and twentieth centuries, moreover, American workers found an environment that was constantly in flux, not particularly friendly, needing adjustments, and always fast-paced. While these workers may have sought rest, they often found that peace can be and often is a fleeting intangible. How all this has happened provides an intriguing story.

1607-1775

1607-1775 • Colonial America ~ The English colonies were founded primarily as profit-making ventures. Whether the colony started out as a business colony established by joint-stock companies or a proprietary colony headed by an alleged altruist or a royal colony, the goal was always the same – make money for the investors. Given the large amounts of capital investment needed to sustain a colony until it could become established, investors were not patient in waiting for returns. When the gold and silver did not materialize, the colony reverted back to the King. To complicate matters, England practiced mercantilism so as to enhance her world position. According to this theory, the colony existed for the benefit of the mother country, or at least that is what England wanted. The colonies saw things differently and often acted in their own self-interest. Those who came to the colonies, moreover, had a variety of reasons for their new settlements, be it starting a new life, seeking religious freedom, or simply being told to leave England or remain in jail. These were the people who became the core of America's workforce.

Throughout the eighteenth and early nineteenth-centuries, most Americans were rural in character and occupation. There did exist a craft system that depended on the master taking on journeymen who, in turn, would eventually become masters. For those Americans living in cities like New York or Baltimore, indentured servants were common. Generally, these individuals signed articles of indenture binding them to a period of service anywhere from two to seven years in exchange for passage to America and the certainty of work. Often, these contracts were sold to merchants or planters who had their servants work off their contract in order to receive their freedom dues. In the end, the individual was free, which was not the case with the slave as a laborer.

In addition to the free labor system, America also had a coercive labor system – slavery. Up to 1808, slaves could be imported into America. After that time, the slave population had to reproduce itself. Generally, the life of these slaves was not enviable, despite the material conditions the masters provided. Bear in mind too that slaves were not only Africans, but Native American as well. By the time of the American Revolution, America's labor force, free and slave, was growing.

1776-1860 • Colonial and Antebellum America ~ Although America was still an agricultural nation before the outbreak of the Civil War, the foundations for industrialism had been laid and America was transforming rapidly into a powerful industrial giant. Significant changes occurred in every area of American economic life – international trade, transportation, corporate organization, agriculture, and industry. Labor became a particularly vexing problem as American factories slowly began to appear on America's landscape. To fulfill their needs for a workforce, factory owners, such as Francis Cabot Lowell, devised systems of recruitment for labor. Bearing in mind that the factory had to be built near waterfalls for power purposes, this meant that the factory owner had to provide housing for his workers as well since most factories were located outside of a city. To fulfill his labor needs during a time when America was still sparsely populated, American factory owners recruited female and child labor. Two unique labor recruitment devices were the Rhode Island and Lowell systems. Under the Rhode Island system, factory owners employed entire families for their plants, putting each member (father, mother, and children) to tasks appropriate to their physical and mental capabilities. Many of these families were immigrants who arrived in the United States during the 1820s and 1830s.

Under the Lowell system, factory owners employed female farm girls to work in the factories. Very paternalistic in nature, the system provided everyone with what they wanted – the farmer had his daughter employed, the teen-age girl had a job to build a dowry so that she could more easily find a husband, and the factory owner had his workers. Where used, especially in New England, the Rhode Island and Lowell systems worked well.

1820-1860 • Working Conditions ~ Before 1860, the American worker earned more money than his English counterpart (roughly about one-third to a half more). As immigration increased, the differential declined. Once the factory system was able to overcome the problems of the craft system, the need for power, and technology, it grew rapidly and was less dependent on skilled labor. Typically, the American worker worked long hours and received low wages when compared to today's standards. His life was monotonous and the conditions under which he worked dangerous. Job security was almost non-existent, especially in light of the boom-bust cycles of the American economy. To make matters worse, workers had no one to protect them. Unions were ineffective before 1860. Craft guilds did exist and local organizations of skilled artisans appeared regularly in American cities, but they were more concerned with protecting the rights of their crafts than with helping the workingman.

By 1860, American industrialism was taking off, technology was growing, American factories were being established, but American workers were not faring well. Low wages, female and child labor, dangerous working conditions, hostile courts, and weak, ineffective unions were the standard fare American

Slave Population by State 1850 Census Data

State	Total Number (in thousands)
Alabama	342,844
Arkansas	47,100
Delaware	2,290
Florida	39,310
Georgia	381,682
Kentucky	210,981
Louisiana	244,809
Maryland	90,368
Mississippi	309,878
Missouri	87,422
New Jersey	236
North Carolina	288,548
South Carolina	384,984
Tennessee	239,459
Texas	58,161
Virginia	472,528
Total:	3,200,600

SOURCE: U.S. Census Bureau, 1850

workers faced. These were the conditions for free workers; slaves had it even worse. When modern unions, designed to protect the worker from arbitrary dismissal, began to appear after 1860, the courts were hostile toward them. Typically, the courts considered unions to be conspiracies and sought to regulate their actions, be it strikes or boycotts.

1820-1860 • SOUTHERN PLANTATION SYSTEM ~ The southern plantation system was a highly efficient business organization. The master had all the authority, but he tended to rely on others for administering his business, specifically factors who helped him market and

(circa 1900) Stereoscope image of African-American workers loading cotton bales onto a train car on a levee in Texas.

finance his crops, white overseers or black slave drivers who supervised the slaves, and, on bottom, the slave himself who did all the work. There is general agreement among scholars today that slavery was a highly profitable labor system and southern plantations did quite well during the antebellum period. As for the conditions under which slaves lived, there is also more agreement now that the master tended to act as a rational businessman seeking to maximize the profit on his slave investments. 1820-1860

It was in the financial interest of the plantation to treat slaves well, providing them with food, shelter, medical care, and clothing. Studies have also shown that the master generally promoted the slave family, especially after 1808 when slave importation was no longer permissible. If nothing else, statistics (see table) on southern slavery show that in 1860 there were approximately 3 million slaves, demonstrating that the southern slave system was reproducing itself. The

1861-1865

plantation system not only continued to grow but it prospered as well. Certainly, such findings have a profound effect on analyzing the causes of the Civil War.

1861-1865 • American Civil War

~ While historians and economists argue over the causes of the Civil War and its long-term impact, there is general agreement on two specific conclusions. First, the Civil War was very costly in financial and human terms. Second, the Civil War had a definite impact on the American labor force resulting in the South losing its economic system and labor components. Statistics on the impact of the Civil War are staggering. Six hundred thousand men died out of a total population of 32 million Americans; 500,000 men were maimed or wounded. There was the total destruction of the southern economic system. Enormous physical damage was done throughout many of the southern states, as evidenced by General Sherman's march to the sea. The Civil War wreaked financial havoc on the United States as witnessed by the post-war problems of recovery.

Still, the question remains how much did the war cost? Using an ingenious counterfactual argument, Claudia Goldin and Frank Lewis calculated the financial figures in 1975. According to their findings, the Civil War's direct cost was $6.6 billion or $206 for every American living in 1861. Had that amount been invested in productive resources at a safe six percent return, it would have provided every American living in 1861 an annual bonus equal to about ten percent of 1860 consumption expenditures. Putting this another way, the $6.6 billion would have been enough to buy the freedom of all the slaves at 1860 prices, give each slave family a 40-acre farm and a mule, and still leave about $3 billion for other expenses. Of the $6.6 billion, the South lost $3.3 billion even though its population was two-and-a-half

Comparison Balance Sheet of North and South, 1861

	North	South
Number of States	23	11
Population (in millions)	23	9 including 3 million slaves
Primary Economy	Industrial 90% Industry 80% Railroads	Agricultural
Military	Established Army & Navy	Unproven Army
Total Military Strength	Approx. 2 Million	Approx. 900,000

SOURCE: *The Economic Cost of the American Civil War: Estimates and Implications* by Goldin and Lewis, 1975.

times less than the North's. Some economists and historians argue that this figure was so significant that the South played catch-up with the rest of the American economy well into the twentieth-century.

Once the Civil War ended, there was a new problem to confront. During the long four-year war, both northern and southern factories worked at full capacity. When the war ended, the North simply had to readjust to the industrial process to civilian goods whereas the South had to invent a new economic system and rebuild all its destroyed factories. We will see shortly just what the North did as industrialization intensified. For the South, on the other hand, Reconstruction took on a distinct economic tone.

Although Abraham Lincoln and his successor Andrew Johnson sought a conciliatory approach to rebuilding the United States, the radical Republican Congress saw the situation differently. Led by those who harbored deep hatred for the South, such as Thaddeus Stevens and Charles Sumner, Congress in 1867 passed the Military Acts which essentially placed the southern states under federal martial law. Union troops now occupied the South and for twenty years Southerners had no choice but to do as they were told. Northern businessmen and thieves who came to the South and were protected by Union soldiers effectively retarded the reconstruction of the southern economy.

Although the former masters still owned land, they had little or no capital for investment. Nor did they have a workforce since all slaves had been freed. Borrowing money from merchants and employing former slaves to work their lands, these landowners initially tried to use a wage payment system, all to no avail. Given the psychological importance of owning one's land and relishing their freedom to choose who in their families would work and how much they would work, the freed blacks decided upon sharecropping rather than wage labor.

1866 • SHARECROPPING ~ Sharecropping gave the freed balcks a sense of owning their own parcel of land. They could have their wives work at home and

(circa 1910) Child employees at a cotton mill in Georgia, standing in front of the brick mill building.

take care of the children while the head of the family tended the fields. And, what they produced would be their own. Or, at least that is the way black sharecroppers perceived the system. Unfortunately, that was not the reality. As landowners sought to make money and as merchants indebted landowners and sharecroppers more and more, a lock-in system was developed whereby the merchant took control of the land and sharecroppers became indebted for life. Perhaps best described by novelist William Faulkner in his famous trilogy of the Snopes family, Will Varner was an accurate depiction of the monopolistic position these small-town merchants had by 1900 in the redeemed Southern states.

1880s • Envisioning a New South ~ Yet, even in this situation where adequate financial intermediation did not develop, there were those Southerners who saw hope and a future for the South – the New South prophets. Leading the way were people like Atlanta newspaper editor Henry Grady who told the South to shed its old vestiges of slave plantations and look to building a new industrial South that would compete with the rest of the world. In his New South speech delivered in New York in 1886, Grady won the respect of businessmen who understood the resources of the struggling southern states.

As the twentieth century dawned, these New South prophets gained more and more of a following until southern industry developed. By the 1960s, the culmination of their hopes was apparent as the "Sunbelt" lured Frostbelt (North/Midwest) industry to the South because of abundant resources, low taxes, and lack of unions. The Sunbelt states prospered until the South itself suffered the same fate, as countries like Mexico began to attract industries for the very same reasons the Sunbelt had undermined the Northern industrial system.

1870-1920 • American Industrialization ~ With the resolution of the disputed election of 1876 and the Compromise of 1877, Rutherford B. Hayes kept his promise to the South and removed all federal troops stationed there. In so doing, Hayes officially ended Reconstruction. For the United States, this was a very significant event in that the Compromise of 1877 allowed the nation to concentrate on its industrial process. Between 1877 and the end of World War I, the United States rapidly underwent intense industrial growth. Every area of American economic life was impacted. America's infrastructure, the railroads, grew greatly as the transcontinentals were completed and the national railroad system was implemented. A communications revolution occurred as the telephone and telegraph were deployed throughout the country. Edison's work on the incandescent light revolutionized almost every facet of industry. New indus-

~

In his famous speech describing a Southerner who had died, but who had been buried with articles from everywhere else in the United States, Henry Grady said that, "The South didn't furnish a thing on earth for that funeral but the corpse and the hole in the ground. There they put him away...in a New York coat and a Boston pair of shoes and a pair of breeches from Chicago and a shirt from Cincinnati, leaving nothing to carry into the next world with him to remind him of the country in which he lived...."

~

tries appeared, such as the electrical and automobile, while older industries revived as in the case of coal, petroleum, and iron and steel. New corporate forms with trusts and holding companies were developed by American entrepreneurs. And, America's future as a great military and industrial power seemed limitless.

In the late nineteenth and early twentieth centuries, America provided an ideal environment for business. Productivity was considered a key component to social progress. Businessmen were regarded as society leaders whose decisions impacted all Americans through a trickle-down theory. Every American, moreover, could model himself/herself on an Andrew Carnegie or John D. Rockefeller. Hard work, in their minds, would lead to success which, in turn, was measured by material goods. People knew just how successful and virtuous you were if you showed your wealth through what Thorstein Veblen called "conspicuous consumption."

If this America embraced business, it did not show the same affection for American workers. Immigration, poor and dangerous working conditions, female and child labor, industrial accidents and deaths were the unfortunate aspects of the American environment that the working man encountered. As the industrial process boomed, the factory owner sought to secure a cheap, unskilled and pliable labor force. To do that, he relied on immigrants and female and child workers. In some industries, such as coal, steel, iron, textiles and railroads, the system of contract labor was used to fill the work force. Immigrant's passage to America was paid for and the new worker was bound to that company for a number of years. The railroads so exploited the Chinese that the federal government stepped in and passed

(1903) Steel And Smoke. Working conditions for these American steel workers were horrible. Workers typically worked 11-12 hour days, six days a week for relatively low wages. Shown here, a group of boys overlooking the Homestead steel plant in Pittsburgh.

the Chinese Exclusion Act (1882) limiting how many Chinese would enter the United States.

Working conditions for these American workers were horrible. Workers typically worked 11-12 hour days, six days a week for relatively low wages, and their jobs often were dangerous. According to government statistics available for 1907, there were approximately 3, 232 accidental deaths in the coal mining industry alone. In railroads, there were 4,534. By 1913, the federal government was estimating that there were 25,000 worker deaths on the job each year with about 700,000 disabled. To make the situation more intolerable, there was no workman's compensation because the courts had ruled that a worker who accepted employment also accepted the risk associated with the job.

1860s-1880s • The Beginning of Labor Unions ~ Given these circumstances, it is not surprising that workers responded by turning to unions. In 1866, 77 delegates representing a variety of labor interests met in Baltimore and formed the National Labor Union. Well-intentioned, the NLU did not last very long as the Panic of 1873 saw its membership dwindle appreciably. In the 1870s, conditions in the railroad and coal industries were so deplorable that another group appeared – the Molly Maguires. Protesting labor's conditions, they relied on violence to secure their objectives, and by 1877, their leaders were tried and convicted, causing the collapse of the union.

In 1869, Uriah Stephens set up a rather idealistic labor lodge known as the Knights of Labor. As the ceremonial aspects of the group disappeared, the Knights turned into a modern day union. Under the capable leadership of individuals like Terence V. Powderly, the Knights sought to organize all workers – skilled, unskilled, male, female, white, and black. It formulated a program that called for an eight-hour work day, the establishment of cooperatives, arbitration, and the eventual abolition of the wage system. In the 1870s and early 1880s, the Knights participated in strikes that tended to be successful, thereby helping its membership to grow to 700,000 by 1886. But, 1886 was also a significant year for other reasons. In that year, the Knights participated in the famous Haymarket Square riot and a new labor union broke off from its ranks.

A general strike was called for May 1, 1886 in support of the eight-hour day in the railroad industry. All in all, the strike was going well until an incident occurred in Chicago. A few anarchist leaders addressed a group of workers, a bomb was thrown, and police sought to break up the assembly. Rioting followed and troops were sent in. The significance of the incident is that the Knights were identified with violence.

In that same year, Samuel Gompers, a cigarmaker, decided that the Knights were too idealistic. Instead of trying to organize everyone and abolish the wage system, Gompers believed that workers had more concrete concerns. Leading a group of locals, he broke off from the Knights and established the American Federation of Labor (AFL). Exclusive in membership, the AFL concentrated on organizing only skilled workers, sought to improve the worker's position by focusing on bread and butter issues like wages and working conditions, and avoided any political involvement whatsoever. It would be just such policies that allowed the AFL to survive the 1890s.

Presidential Election of 1896

Candidate	Party	Electoral Vote	Popular Vote	Number of States Won
William McKinley	Republican	271	7,104,779	23
William Jennings Bryan	Democrat	176	6,502,925	22

SOURCE: U.S. Bureau of the Census. *Historical Statistics of the United States, Colonial Times to 1970*. Washington, D.C., 1975.

By the 1890s, the Knights of Labor were embroiled in another movement that occupied America's attention. Populism, or the farmer's attempt to adjust to the industrial process, gained significant support throughout the Midwest and South. With its Omaha platform calling for political and economic reforms and with its motto of the "unlimited coinage of silver," the People's Party ran candidates in 1892, 1894, and 1896. The culmination came with William J. Bryan's run for the presidency as a Populist Democrat against Republican William McKinley in 1896. Bryan and the Populists lost, and so too did the Knights who supported them.

1892-1902 • Labor Union Violence

~ Labor was hurt by other events too. The 1892 Homestead strike involved the Carnegie steel plants at Homestead, Pennsylvania. Henry Frick managed the plant, reduced wages, and hired Pinkerton's security company to fight the union, the Amalgamated Union of Iron, Steel and Tin. Violence erupted during the strike and the unions lost. So too did the American Railway Union lose its Pullman strike in 1894. Here, the railroad brotherhoods sought to prevent George Pullman from cutting wages and maintaining high rents in his company town. A strike took place, led by Eugene Debs in which violence erupted, and President Cleveland sent in federal troops. In the end, the defeat at Pullman and Homestead hurt unions in that an image was being projected of associating unions with violence. By 1900, workers and unions were barely holding their own.

Labor's situation continued to worsen as the new century unfolded. Labor, both the workingmen and women in the factory as well as the union and its leadership, needed help, especially from the federal government. Unfortunately for the union, that assistance was not immediately forthcoming, although there were a few bright spots in the offing.

(1935) Crowds of striking miners gathered outside Nine Mile Port Colliery, where non-Union workers continued to labor, under heavy police protection.

1892-1902

In 1902, the anthracite coal strike, supported by the AFL, called for a wage increase and recognition of the union. Ordinarily, whenever strikes occurred, the government on all levels tended to side with business, but in this case President Theodore Roosevelt, although not an avid supporter or believer in unions, sided with the workers and told the coal mine operators to grant the wage increase. While the union issue was not resolved, the precedent was established for the government to intervene in strikes on the side of labor.

1903-1907

1903-1907 • SUPREME COURT INTERVENTION ~ On a more negative note, however, another branch of the government was not very friendly either to workers or unions. The courts, especially the Supreme Court, consistently ruled against their interests. Two cases of note stand out: Danbury hatters (1903) and the Bucks Stove (1907) cases. In the Danbury hatters case, a hat manufacturer from Danbury, Connecticut brought suit against 197 members of the United Hatters union. Arguing that the boycott waged by the unions was a conspiracy restraining interstate commerce, the hat company sought triple damages under the terms of the Sherman Anti-Trust Act. After reviewing the case, the Supreme Court ruled in favor of the company, thereby making the Sherman Act, a law designed to regulate big business, a weapon that employers could use against unions.

In *Bucks Stove and Range Co. vs. the AFL,* the American Federation of Labor placed this company on its boycott list. The company sought an injunction on the grounds that the boycott was doing irreparable damage to its business. Again, the court agreed. In both cases the Court was defining the weapons of employers and employees. Unions could strike on hour and wage questions and could carry out a primary boycott, but they could not strike for a closed shop, in which only union members could work, or use a secondary boycott, in which sympathetic workers from another company would strike to support the brotherhood. Similarly, the courts had acted to give employers other weapons too – the yellow dog contract (a worker had to agree not to join a union as a condition of employment), company unions, and the use of Pinkertons as an industrial army.

In spite of these setbacks, workingmen and unions still had the possibility of gaining momentum. All each needed was a political administration more favorable to their plight. A new reform movement was well underway which could favorably impact them – Progressivism. Led by a broad middle class, the progressives sought to reform the United States politically, economically, and socially. On the local and state level, progressives favored legislation to help the workingman and woman improve their economic conditions. They also favored the abolition of child labor and wanted the government to act on behalf of its citizens. The progressive presidents (Theodore Roosevelt, William Taft, and Woodrow Wilson) all acted on the progressives' demands. Of the three, though, it was

Presidential Election of 1912

Candidate	Party	Electoral Vote	Popular Vote	Number of States Won
Woodrow Wilson	Democrat	435	6,293,454	40
Theodore Roosevelt	Prg/Bull Moose	88	4,119,538	6
William H. Taft	Republican	8	3,484,980	2

SOURCE: U.S. Bureau of the Census. *Historical Statistics of the United States, Colonial Times to 1970.* Washington, D.C., 1975.

the election of Woodrow Wilson that would have the most beneficial effect on labor's role in the United States.

1913-1920 • Union Support from the President ~ Unlike his progressive predecessors, Theodore Roosevelt and William Taft, Wilson was more inclined to be sympathetic to workers as well as the need for unions. Also, Wilson was a minority president (winning fewer votes than his two opponents combined) who depended on workers for re-election in 1916. Between 1913 and 1920, Wilson acted in ways that were far more friendly to workers and unions. He appointed labor leaders to his cabinet; he invited Samuel Gompers to visit the White House; and he supported a provision in the Clayton Anti-Trust Act which said that unions had the legal right to exist. Legislatively, Wilson endorsed the LaFollette Seaman's Act providing for minimum safety standards for seaman on board ships. He supported the Keating-Owens Act, which outlawed the transportation of products made by children across state lines. He endorsed a workman's compensation bill. More importantly, as the United States entered World War I, Wilson took steps to insure that labor's interests would be protected.

Essentially, Wilson established the War Labor Board. The WLB was formed to settle strikes and/or prevent them in industries considered vital to America's defense. Although it had little or no enforcement powers, the WLB was placed directly under Wilson's jurisdiction. In effect, what the president was telling businessmen was to work with workers and unions, at least for the duration of the war, or answer directly to the president.

Realizing the opportunities that World War I offered, the AFL capitalized on labor's new position and fought hard for better wages and working conditions for its members. For their part, businessmen reacted favorably to what Wilson wanted and what workers and unions demanded during the war. As immigration declined and as military work orders increased, businessmen were much more willing to cooperate with employees in order to meet their production and profit goals. It was a situation in which everyone seemed to benefit.

1905-1918 • Industrial Workers of the World ~ While the AFL supported American participation in World War I, there was another union in the United States that expressed a different view. Organized in 1905 by radical socialists and the Western Federation of Miners, the Industrial Workers of the World (IWW or Wobblies) were quite different in the workers they appealed to and the goals they strove for. Unlike the AFL, the Wobblies appealed to migrant workers, the unskilled, and foreigners. In the western United States, they recruited workers in the mines, oil fields, and lumber. In 1912, the union scored a significant victory in a textile strike in Lawrence, Massachusetts. From then on, their membership increased until 1917.

Once the United States announced its intention to enter the war, the Wobblies condemned President Wilson as being imperialistic. Openly opposing the war, the Wobblies became a target for the government. Using a series of laws such as the Espionage and Sedition Acts (1917-18) designed to protect America from subversive activity, the federal government went all out to destroy the IWW. Wobblies' leaders were thrown in jail and its organization was ruthlessly suppressed during and after the war.

Although the AFL did not support the Wobblies nor did they have any association with them, the average American did not make such a fine distinction, often lumping all labor unions into one monolithic movement.

1918-1920 • Red Scare and the Decline of Unions ~ Once the War ended, labor's position, especially unions, worsened. As the ideals that sparked the Bolshevik revolution (1917) spread throughout the world, American fears of communism began to intensify. In 1918-1919, as the American economy underwent a natural reconversion from a wartime economy to a peacetime one, strikes occurred throughout the nation. Unions wanted to secure the gains they had made during the war while businessmen saw an opportunity to attack the vulnerable unions. Claiming that these strikes led to higher prices because of the higher wage demands, and alleging that the unions involved in strikes were not patriotically American, businessmen laid the groundwork for an irrational response to a fear that was growing more and more real in Americans' minds. By 1919, the "Red Scare" had established itself in America. With President Wilson suffering from a serious stroke, the government allowed itself to be led by those willing to take charge. One such individual was A. Mitchell Palmer. Vehemently anti-Communist, Palmer, along with his subordinate J. Edgar Hoover, started the famous Palmer raids of rounding up suspected Americans, throwing them in jail, and eventually deporting them to the Soviet Union. Although the Red Scare and Palmer's tenure were short-lived, the long-term consequences were serious. By 1920, working men and women were still trying to improve their economic lot in an environment very favorable to business interests while unions now had to face charges of being unpatriotic and perhaps even fifth columns of the Soviet Communist movement.

1920-1940 • Boom and Bust for Business and Labor ~ Undoubtedly, the 1920s in the United States was one of the most exciting, and at the same time, the most disastrous decades in the nation's history. Perhaps the best way to characterize it is to say that it was a time of hysterical dreaming, a time of unreality when people felt all was well with society and the economy even though that was not the case. It was a time of rapid economic growth, unprecedented prosperity (at least on the surface), and intense nativism. "Get-rich-quick" was its philosophy while materialism was its religion.

In such a situation, it was inevitable that business would play a major role. In no other decade in American history did the businessman dominate society so much. It was business, not the worker or the farmer or the consumer who was all-important and all-powerful. The results of that domination would be disastrous as labor unions were attacked, the farmer fell deeper and deeper into economic depression, and the American economy began to disintegrate. In hindsight, the obvious question is why did business dominate so much? The best answer is that the American people were ready for isolationism after fighting World War I that President Wilson had promised would "save the world for democracy." They were tired of Wilson's political moralism. They were more interested in their own safety and prosperity, enjoying life, and withdrawing from the world arena. To a large degree, it was this attitude that explained why Americans became obsessed with crime, scandals, and radicals; why the famous Scopes ("monkey trial") trial took place; why the Sacco-Vanzetti case took place, ending in the execution of two Italian immigrants for murder and robbery based not so much on the evidence in the trial as on their association with anarchism; why immigration was restricted with a national quota system; why the KKK grew again to terrorize blacks, Catholics and Jews; and why America experienced a wholesale cultural revolution.

The extent of that cultural revolution affected all of American society. Women demanded their basic rights as symbolized by the "flapper"; American morals changed as automobiles allowed young people to discover one another without their parents' watching; young people experimented with new forms of music, especially jazz; and American pastimes reached an unusually high pinnacle of oddity with people sitting on flagpoles while others danced marathons. However, in all of this ballyhoo, there were some very undesirable things going on – Americans may have liked wealth, but they showed no concern as to how one got it. Americans might have talked about their commitment to freedom and equality, but they also told foreigners to stay out. And, Americans spoke of the high caliber of their heroes, but they also idolized the likes of Al Capone while simultaneously admiring Charles Lindbergh. Contradictions, paradox, disjointed ideas characterized the 1920s.

1920s • The Rising Influence of Business ~ It was in this context that business was supreme. Businessmen were so accepted as societal leaders that Bruce Barton published a book entitled, *The Man Nobody Knows*. What was so

Immigration to the United States 1900-1990

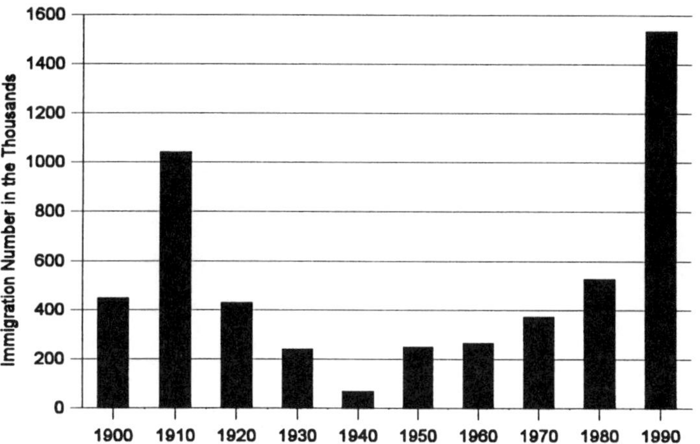

SOURCE: U.S. Immigration and Naturalization Service, Statistical Yearbook, 1995.

1920s

distinctive about this work is that Barton discussed Jesus Christ as a businessman. Barton said that in actuality Jesus Christ was a successful businessman who sold his product (the kingdom of God) to everyone. And, he did it quite well! Combine this approach with a federal government under the presidencies of Warren Harding and Calvin Coolidge who were very favorable to the business ideal and the result is domination. It was Calvin Coolidge who said that a man who builds a factory is actually building a temple. It was also Silent Cal who said that the business of America is business.

Realizing just how influential they were, businessmen openly flouted the anti-trust laws. Always disliking competition for its waste and loss of profit, businessmen felt that the government's anti-trust policy was too unstable and vague to be of any help to them. They wanted to know what they could do before they had done it and they aspired to enlarge the permissive area as much as possible. To do this, they adopted the trade association movement.

These open-price trade associations between producers openly exchanged information about output, inventories, plans, and prices. Many associations confined themselves to promotional or advertising endeavors while others anticipated and hoped such price information would lead to rational and cooperative action on the part of its members. In reality, the trade association became a form of "monopoly" or industrial self-government with businesses cooperating and fixing prices. Trade associations could only exist if the federal government did not enforce the anti-trust laws, something that neither the Federal Trade Commission nor the Department of Justice were willing to do.

Trade associationism, however, was not the end of business' aggressive tactics. During the 1920s, American businessmen became so confident that they decided to attack what they considered to be their most potent enemy – the independent trade union. The rationale behind the attack was simple. By the 1920s, a new American entrepreneur had appeared. He was the professional manager who was concerned with his own position within the corporation and who was very image conscious. These highly educated businessmen decided that the American people needed to realize that the days of the Andrew Carnegie's and Henry Ford's were over. These 1920s entrepreneurs saw themselves as far more sophisticated than their earlier predecessors. They believed that they could improve their image and address the issue of the union by learning a distinct lesson from World War I. Although workers had gone on strike during the war, these businessmen noted that workers often worked hard, for long hours, and without complaint. Divining an answer as to why, they decided that the worker was basically being loyal to his country. If workers could be loyal to the United States, could they not also be loyal to their company? And, if they were, would not these workers be less liable to join unions?

1920s • Welfare Capitalism: Courting Worker Loyalty ~ To foster their new image as educated and caring businessmen as well as to undermine the very reason for workers to join a union, these entrepreneurs introduced "welfare capitalism." Basing their plans on psychological profiles of workers and set up in labor relations departments throughout major corporations, businessmen offered their workers a number of opportunities. They could participate in a home buying plan where the company purchased the home for the worker and allowed the worker to pay the mortgage to the company. Or, workers could participate in a stock-purchasing plan where they could, through payroll deduction, buy stocks. Typically, the stock purchased was the workers' company. Or, large companies would offer medical insurance, health care, and even pensions to workers who participated in these welfare plans designed and implemented by their company. Finally, workers might even be able to join a company union and express their views on a variety of issues to the management. All the plans seemed so well-intentioned, appealing to the workers' needs for security, getting rich, or wanting respect. Where the plans were used, such as in General Electric, workers participated. But, what was the price?

Welfare capitalism was based on a power system in which management had full control over its workers. It also gave business its most powerful weapon against unions – worker contentment and loyalty. Did it work? Based on a cursory glance of union membership in the 1920s, the answer is yes. Union membership declined throughout the decade for a number of reasons. Strikes were unsuccessful, unions suffered from the Red Scare identification with communism, and unions themselves were rather rigid in their ideology and desire to organize all workers. Yet, no one can or would deny that one of the most important reasons for the unions' decline in the 1920s was welfare capitalism.

By the end of the 1920s, welfare capitalism began to wane for a number of reasons. It remained a minority phenomenon throughout the 1920s, limited only to those corporations that could afford the plans. As a result, the welfare plans touched only a minority of the workforce. Another reason for its failure was that, in spite of business' rhetoric, the plans never discussed what was most important to workers – wages and working conditions. Welfare capitalism gave the employer too much power over the worker. And, ultimately, welfare capitalism was based on a promise that business would take care of its workers at all times. That might have been business' intention but, once the Great Depression started, one of the first things to be cutback were the welfare plans. Workers came to realize this and, eventually, they returned to the union movement in the 1930s. There is no question that welfare capitalism had made a serious effort to undermine the independent trade union movement. Where the plans were used, workers did choose them over union membership.

1920s-1930s • Unions in the South

~ American workers were part of a national economic system, not just a northern or midwestern one. In the South, workers had problems too. World War I had brought prosperity to the South. Southern workers, in agriculture and industry, got a taste of the better life and wanted to keep it. Unions realized this and attempted to capitalize on the ambitions of workers. In 1927-1928, textile mill owners introduced the "stretch-out system," whereby workers were made responsible for more spindles in the mills. The National Textile Workers Union entered the southern mills along with the AFL. Some success did follow, albeit briefly. In 1929, the southern situation changed at a mill in Elizabethtown, Tennessee. Workers demanded higher wages and better working conditions. Mill owners refused, a strike followed, and violence erupted. Troops were brought in to quash the strike.

Perhaps, the most famous of the southern strikes occurred in Gastonia, North Carolina. Workers there demanded an eight-hour day, a five-day week, and a minimum wage of $20 a week. Mill owners refused and a strike followed. Like earlier strikes at the Fulton Cotton Bag Company in Atlanta, violence broke out and several people were actually killed. Troops again were brought in and the strike was broken. In the 1930s, tenants farmers organized into the Southern Tenant Farmers Union, especially in Mississippi and Arkansas. Violence typically characterized these strikes and southern hostility towards unions grew even deeper.

1926-1932 • Collective Bargaining

~ Workers and unions had a difficult time in the 1920s. Wages in the 1920s did not keep pace with prices, and although employment seemed to be adequate nationally, job security was not a certainty. Still, it was in the midst of all these dire times that labor gained two very significant pieces of legislation that would have a major long-term impact on workers and union development – the

Railway Labor Act (1926) and the Norris-LaGuardia Act (1932).

The Railway Labor Act, written by the prominent 1920s labor lawyer Donald Richberg, established the principle of collective bargaining in the railroad industry. It also allowed unions to be set up for the different types of workmen in the railroads. And, it established a rather complicated procedure for mediation and arbitration in an industrial-labor dispute. In effect, the Railway Labor Act gave formal recognition to unions in the railroad industry and, in so doing, established a precedent.

The Norris-LaGuardia Act, on the other hand, prohibited the courts from issuing injunctions in ordinary collective bargaining situations. It also said that yellow dog contracts were illegal. Again, the significance of the law is that it not only helped to protect unions from the courts, but it established a precedent.

1929-1931 • Reasons for the Great Depression ~ The 1920s began as a roaring decade, and ended in the most catastrophic economic collapse in American history. The Depression of 1929 was so devastating that it would take the United States until 1942 to recover from it. Even after recovery came, President Truman thought that the Depression would start once again after World War II ended.

Since 1929, historians and economists have analyzed what caused the Depression. The statistics on the 1920s, especially for the number of manufacturing establishments, the value of products, and the production of automobiles seemed to indicate that the American economy had adequate employment, abundant resources, and an American public confident that prosperity would continue. Yet, within the seeming good times, there were fundamental weaknesses in the American economy that ultimately caused it to collapse. The bull stock market of the 1920s was more of a catalyst to the Great Depression, speeding up an event that was going to take place anyway. A convergence of factors occurred which led to the economic disintegration. Essentially, the American economy was in a state of "disequilibrium" of the highest order with costs, prices, wages, and profits totally out of sync with each other.

Aggravating this delicate situation was a mal-distribution of income, a regressive tax structure, and a failure on the part of Europe to pay off its war debts to the United States. Structurally, moreover, the American economy suffered in its corporate organizations and lack of central supervision of many banks, despite the existence of the Federal Reserve System. Finally, the economists of the 1920s failed to watch for the danger signs indicating that something was wrong – farmers in depression, wages not keeping pace with prices, and purchasing power consistently declining. The end result was disaster.

Between 1929 and 1933, the GNP went from \$104 billion to \$74 billion; national income dropped from \$87 billion to \$40 billion; labor income fell from \$51 billion to \$29 billion. Business failures were one-third more numerous in 1933 than 1929; farm prices dropped 61 percent; and unemployment increased dramatically from approximately 1.5 million to over 12,600,000. What these statistics meant in human terms was clear. People lost their jobs, their homes, their cars. Many Americans went to soup kitchens to eat, sponsored by private charities, the American Red Cross, and even Al Capone. It meant that men started selling apples on street corners to earn some money. It meant farmers in Arkansas threatened to take over the country stores if their Red Cross allotments were not given to their families. And, it meant that Americans wondered about their own self-worth and what they had done to deserve such a disaster. No one really understood what had caused the economy's decline with the corresponding corollary that no one knew what to do about it. Most unfortunately, the burden of initially addressing how to confront the economic crisis fell into the lap of Herbert Clark Hoover.

> One of the myths that arose surrounding the Great Depression involved American stockbrokers. Hollywood in its portrayal of the stock market crash had stockbrokers at the New York Stock Exchange jumping out of windows committing suicide. No such thing occurred. Suicide rates, especially among stockbrokers, did not rise because of the market crash.

1928-1932 • The Failed Presidency of Herbert Hoover ~ Had Hoover been elected in 1916 or even 1929, Americans today might be looking back at his presidency as among the best in our history. But, that was not to be. He was the wrong man at the wrong place and time. A Horatio Alger story, Hoover believed in individualism and limited federal intervention in the American economy. While both of these ideals might be lauded at other times in American history, they were not what was needed in 1929-1933. Instead, the United States needed a president who was willing to break with tradition, intervene dramatically in the economy, and pump money into the American system as quickly as possible.

Instead, Hoover's response to the Great Depression was to define specific programs for specific groups in the American economic decision-making process. For farmers, he supported the Grain Stabilization Corporation to buy some of the farm surplus and dump it abroad. When that failed, he supported the Hawley-Smoot tariff to protect the American market for American farmers. When that failed, he did nothing else with the result that American farmers not only blamed Hoover for their economic distress, but they became quite vocal and violent in expressing their frustrations.

1928-1932

For the American worker, Hoover asked businessmen not to lay their workers off and unions not to go on strike. A feeble effort at best, these amelioratives helped no one. Hoover next turned to public works, a good idea. But, his public works programs were so small and limited that they had practically no impact. Once this failed, there was not much else Hoover felt he could do.

The same held for relief. Seeing relief as a private affair, Hoover expected churches,

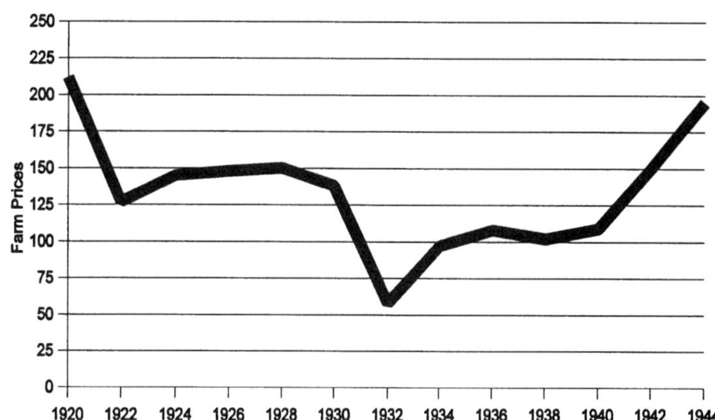

SOURCE: U.S. Bureau of the Census. *Historical Statistics of the United States, Colonial Times to 1970*. Washington, D.C., 1975.

private charities, and the American Red Cross to help destitute people, but with so many people out of work, these altruistic endeavors could not meet the demand. Hoover did relent somewhat by allowing Congress to lend money to states for relief purposes. However, the requirements for the loans were so strict that few, if any, states could even qualify.

His final attempt came with the Reconstruction Finance Corporation. The RFC would loan money to those businesses in danger of collapse, such as banks, insurance companies, and railroads. The trickle-down theory would then take effect and recovery would follow. In reality, no such thing happened. Reaction on the part of American farmers was violent while American veterans of World War I marched on Washington, only to have Hoover send General Douglas MacArthur to disperse the marchers with tanks, cavalry, and bayonets. By 1932, Hoover had failed and Americans went to the polls wanting something and someone new. They got that in Franklin D. Roosevelt and the New Deal.

(1938) American President Franklin Delano Roosevelt (1882 - 1945) interfering in the struggle between the leader of the American Federation of Labor (AFL) William Green (1873 - 1952) and John L Lewis (1880 - 1969), the leader of the breakaway Congress of Industrial Organizations (CIO).

Nineteen thirty-two was an important year in American history. The American economy continued its downward spiral and a presidential election took place. Hoover ran on his record while New York Governor Franklin D. Roosevelt called for a New Deal for the American people. What this New Deal entailed was hard to say. Roosevelt was never one for specific details, but Americans did not even care. They wanted someone to do something and Franklin Roosevelt said he was the one who would act. Americans believed in him and voted him into the presidency, even though the new president and his advisers really had few ideas about how to achieve recovery for the economy.

1933-1939 • A Chicken in Every Pot: Franklin D. Roosevelt's New Deal

~ In March, 1933, the newly elected president took office. In his inaugural address, Roosevelt told Americans that he and they were fighting a war and that the best way to win it was to overcome fear and fight. He said that he would go after the "money changers," implement a new farm program, concentrate on American economic recovery instead of world relief, and use extraordinary presidential powers if necessary to secure victory. Between 1933 and 1941, Roosevelt carried out, however haphazardly, his New Deal. It was a complicated program involving reforms of banking, the stock market, the money supply, budgets, and numerous other areas of American life. For the American working man and woman,

Roosevelt offered relief programs and a host of New Deal legislation that had a profound impact on the future of workers in general and unions in particular.

Affectionately known as the alphabetical agencies, Roosevelt's relief programs were designed to address the immediate problem of unemployment and stimulating the economic pump for recovery. Among the first and the most popular programs was the Civilian Conservation Corps (CCC), designed for young men on relief families. They were placed under the jurisdiction of the War Department, lived in camps in a military-style environment, and worked on reforestation projects. Headed by Robert Fechner, the CCC was so popular that it remained in existence until 1942. Another important relief agency was the Federal Emergency Relief Administration (FERA). Directed by Harry Hopkins, FERA provided relief monies to states on a matching principle of three state dollars to one federal dollar. Two other important projects were the Public Works Administration (PWA), headed by Harold Ickes and the Civil Works Administration (CWA), headed by Harry Hopkins. The former was concerned with long-term building projects like highways and schools while the latter was designed to give money to people as quickly as possible.

Some critics argued that CWA was a "make-work" program offering little or no substantive projects for the general welfare. And there were other worker programs – Federal Writers Projects for white-collar workers like professors, artists, musicians, and actors/actresses and the Works Progress Administration (WPA), which was the largest and most ambitious of all the New Deal relief programs, putting millions of Americans to work building monumental projects. On the surface at least, the New Deal relief programs seemed impressive. Unfortunately, in reality, they did not solve the unemployment problem nor did they stimulate the economic recovery Roosevelt and his advisors hoped for.

1933 • Reforms in Business and Agricultural Practices ~ Realizing that more had to be done, the president turned his attention to two very important programs in 1933 – the National Recovery Administration (NRA) and the Agricultural Adjustment Administration (AAA). Both acts were passed during the famous "100 Days" of Roosevelt's first term in office. The NRA and AAA were seen as complementary programs which, if successful, would restore the American economy to a recovery status. The NRA was established through the passage of the National Industrial Recovery Act. Based on the principle of short-term industrial recovery, the NIRA called for the creation of codes of fair competition written by business and licensed by the president. To protect the rights of the American worker, each code of fair competition included section 7(a), which was designed to provide minimum wages, maximum hours, and a promise of collective bargaining in the industry for which the code had been written. To carry out the codes and make sure the NIRA was working properly, the NIRA set up the NRA, headed by former General Hugh Johnson. Launched with fanfare and parades, the NRA even had its symbol – the famous Blue Eagle decrying to everyone that the business which displayed it was doing its part to overcome the Depression.

While Roosevelt and the American people had high hopes for NRA, its failure became apparent within one year of its creation. There were too many codes,

1934-1938

businesses used the codes to effectively undermine their competition, section 7(a) was ignored with impunity, and the administrators of the NRA disagreed too much. In May, 1935, the United States Supreme Court heard the *Schechter* case (better known as the sick chicken case) in which the poultry code was challenged. Hearing the arguments, the Court ruled that the NIRA was unconstitutional since the president had assumed too much power in licensing the codes. With one fell swoop, the Court made the NRA disappear.

Roosevelt's agricultural supplemental program did not fare any better. Designed to control farm production by paying farmers not to plant all their fields, the AAA got off to a bad start. Surplus farm production was destroyed and farmers immediately violated their domestic allotment agreements by planting their fields with impunity. Again, the Court entered the fray and declared the AAA as unconstitutional. From the tenant farmers' perspective, the legal section of the AAA actually tried to help them by forcing southern landlords to hire the same tenants each year. This too was undone when those favoring the provision were fired by the AAA administrator, Chester Davis.

Labor Union Membership, AFL vs. CIO 1940–1950

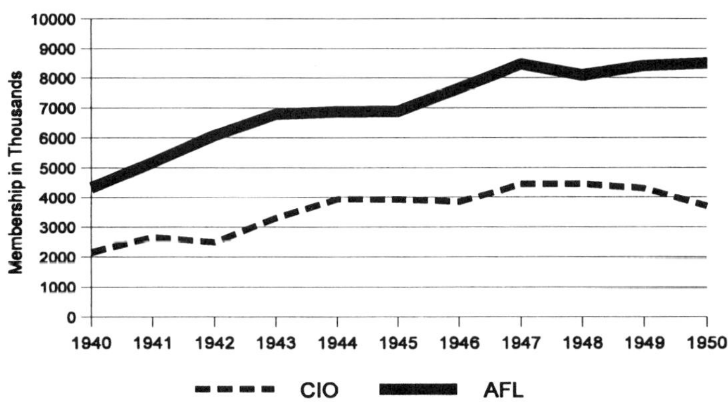

SOURCE: U.S. Bureau of the Census. *Historical Statistics of the United States, Colonial Times to 1970*. Washington, D.C., 1975; *Statistical Abstract of the U.S.*, 1999; AFL-CIO, *Report of AFL-CIO Executive Council*, 1995.

1934-1938 • SOCIAL SECURITY ~ As NRA and AAA failed, opposition to the New Deal became vocal. Francis Townsend attempted to appeal to those over sixty years of age by calling for a program in which he would give all older Americans $200 per month. Huey Long, the Louisiana Kingfish, offered his "Share Our Wealth" program, promising Americans a homestead and money once he became president. And, Father Charles Coughlin told Americans that the real problem in the United States were the Jews! As astute a politician as Roosevelt was, the president listened and reacted. By 1935, as his first New Deal programs failed, he turned to a second New Deal. Concerned more with long-term social welfare, the 1935 New Deal included major legislation reforming banking, relief, and taxes. But, among the most significant laws to be passed affecting American workers generally were the Social Security Act (1935), the National Labor Relations Act (1935), and the Fair Labor Standards Act (1938).

1938 • FEDERAL SUPPORT OF UNIONS ~ Social Security established the principles of unemployment compensation and pensions for American workers. The programs were to be paid jointly by workers and employers through payroll taxes and administrated by state governments (unemployment compensation) and the federal government (retirement pensions). The National Labor Relations Act, on the other hand, also known as the Wagner Act, established the National Labor Relations Board (NLRB) whose purpose was to conduct elections on the issue of unions. The law also outlawed the company union as an unfair business practice. Finally, it was the Fair Labor Standards Act of 1938 that established the principles of minimum wages, maximum hours, and the abolition of child labor by the federal government. When taken together, all of these New Deal laws not only placed the federal government behind the rights of workers but it also demonstrated clearly that the political environment of the New Deal in the 1930s was pro-union.

1930s • Dissent among Union Leaders ~ Unions responded to this favorable environment in a rather strange fashion. The AFL, the primary labor union in the 1930s, saw a schism within its ranks take place. The immediate issue leading to the split was craft unionism versus industrial unionism. The former called for the unionization of skilled workers only, while the latter wanted to organize skilled and unskilled labor into one union. Throughout the early 1930s, the AFL, at its conventions, paid lip service to the proponents of industrial unions, especially John L. Lewis of the United Mine Workers. Finally, Lewis and his followers walked out of the union when the 1935 AFL convention refused to endorse his resolution to organize the basic industries.

Lewis and his followers bolted the convention and, within the year, established a rival labor organization – the Committee (later Congress of) for Industrial Organization. The CIO was more defiant and aggressive in its tone and objectives than the AFL. By 1936, the CIO launched its campaign to organize the steel industry. Before this even got off the ground, the autoworkers in the CIO started their campaign to organize their industry. The result was major strikes at Fisher Body in Cleveland, then Chrysler, and then Ford Motor Company. Using a new weapon, the sit-down strike, the CIO strikers got the sympathy of the American people as newspapers covering the strikes showed the police using tear gas on the peaceful workers sitting at their machines. The strikes proved to be so successful that, by 1941, the CIO had nearly five million members. More importantly, the success of the CIO impacted the AFL to do more in terms of organizing. By the time of American entry into World War II, the AFL and CIO were growing in membership and power as the favorable New Deal environment fostered their growth.

Roosevelt was the beneficiary of all this labor activity. In his 1936 re-election, he won overwhelmingly against the Republican Alf Landon with the full support of organized labor. Nevertheless, Roosevelt had other problems—his failure to "pack" the Supreme Court and the recession of 1937-1938. By 1940-1941, the New Deal was, for all practical purposes, over. The New Deal did not bring economic recovery from the Great Depression, but it did reform the American economy so as to strengthen it against the possibility of another economic collapse. Also, by the time of Pearl Harbor, Roosevelt's attention had turned to other pressing concerns—specifically the outbreak of war in Europe and America's increasing tensions with the Imperial Empire of Japan.

1941-1945 • World War II Rejuvenates the Economy ~ Few events in American history have had the impact on the American economy the way the Second World War did. World War II was responsible for the enormous increases in production, prices, and standard of living. Also, it was World War II that was responsible for the gains that the American workingman and unions made then and later. From 1941, the federal government assumed the authority to organize and run the American economic system. It was the federal government which mobilized manpower for the armed services through the draft as well as recruiting workers for the American factory system. All in all, about 31 million men and women registered for the draft, of which approximately 10 million were inducted. What is so significant about these numbers is the effect it had on the American workforce.

1940-1945 • The War Time Work Force ~ Industry needed an immense workforce to meet its objectives for wartime production. In 1940, there were about 46 million workers available. By 1945, that number had increased to 60 million. The increased number of workers came from a variety of different segments in the American population. About seven million came directly off the relief rolls. Four million more came from teenagers who dropped out of high school to work for the war effort. Another one million retirees returned to the workforce. And, finally and most importantly, it was the American woman who entered the workforce. Between 1940 and 1945, about three million women left home and went to the war factories. Symbolized by "Rosie the Riveter," American women did an excellent job in performing all the necessary tasks assigned to them for wartime purposes. Socially, too, her role in World War II served as a basis for the later 1960s woman's movement in that, after she returned home in 1945, these very women taught their daughters that they could do and be whatever they wanted to.

(1943) One American female worker drives rivets into an aircraft while another sits in the cockpit on the U.S. home front during World War II. They wear aprons and their hair tucked into scarves. Women who went to work in industries to aid the war effort became known under the moniker 'Rosie the Riveter.'

Interestingly, although women and other segments of the population sought to fill the labor force for the war effort, problems still existed. Job-hopping, or workers going from one war factory to another to get higher wages, actually endangered America's production needs. The situation became so serious that President Roosevelt had Paul McNutt of the War Manpower Board even consider the possibility of a national labor service that would assign workers to job positions. Fortunately, military victories, especially at the Battle of the Bulge, negated the need for such drastic measures.

1942-1944 • Unions during the War ~ Like World War I, World War II saw the federal government also attempt to address the issue of strikes in critical industries. The National War Labor Board was set up to prevent strikes occurring in vital industries. Composed of representatives of labor, business, and the general public, the Board was to enter into any dispute between labor and management that could upset production. Businessmen generally were not enamored of the Board while unions saw it as an opportunity to secure more recognition and gains.

Unions, moreover, saw the war as a unique opportunity to foster their growth in membership and influence. Strikes did occur throughout the war, wages did increase, and unions did gain members and influence. One of the most important incidents occurred in 1942 when John L. Lewis and Harold Ickes (Secretary of Interior) clashed over the issue of wage increases for miners. As the cost of living increased in 1942, organized labor demanded a dollar a day raise to offset the increasing costs of living. The War Labor Board granted an increase of $.44 cents per day. The Board then sought to make this a universal wartime formula for wage increases. Wages would thereby increase at the rate of 15 percent a year. Lewis and his mine workers refused to accept the offer and demanded even more. The result was a strike in which Lewis and Ickes eventually agreed on the "Little Steel" formula of 15 percent plus a new concept – fringe benefits. Undoubtedly, this was a major victory for organized labor in that the federal government now had to accept its own legislation and accept the union and collective bargaining. At least in the long-run, the Lewis-Ickes dispute was a labor victory. But, in the immediate postwar period, the dispute would be used by anti-union forces to point out the alleged "unpatriotic" spirit that American unions demonstrated throughout World War II.

World War II caused other developments too. Businessmen gained fairly substantially from government largesse during the war years. American farmers came roaring out of their long depression to such a degree that the federal government even had to control their prices. And, the federal debt began to enlarge again as America carried her allies throughout the war years. But, of all the long-term developments that appeared during 1941-1945, one of the most significant was the outbreak of the Cold War.

During the war years, the Grand Alliance of the United States, England and the Soviet Union showed serious strains in their relationships. The opening of the second front against Vichy, France, the issue of the postwar Polish government, the dropping of the atomic bombs on Japan, and the question of America's identifying loans for Soviet reconstruction after the war with free elections throughout Eastern Europe eventually took their toll. By 1945-1946, the Cold War was a reality and a fact of life that dominated world events from then until the Soviet Union collapsed in 1991.

1945-1960 • Economic Prosperity ~ The United States in the post-World War II world was quite different than it was before 1941. Change permeated every area of American life from its social-cultural milieu to the political environment that Americans confronted. As the Cold War became the reality of everyday life for the world's peoples, increased military spending on atomic bombs, testing, increased military personnel, and conventional military weapons occurred. As technology grew more and more sophisticated, there were no limits to what humans apparently could do. When the Soviets launched the space satellite Sputnik I in 1957, it had an immense impact, not only on the Cold War but also on how Americans perceived their world. Space exploration became a reality, space weaponry was envisioned, and most important, it was clear that the

Soviets could use the rocket that launched Sputnik to deliver atomic warheads to U.S. targets.

1950s • Growth through Military Spending ~ How did all of this affect the United States and the American working population? The answer is quite simple and the effects were quite clear. The United States increased its military spending throughout the Cold War so much so that a fundamental change appeared within the American capitalist system. President Dwight Eisenhower was the first to notice it when he coined the phrase—the "military-industrial complex" (MIC) or, as it was later called, Pentagon Capitalism.

The MIC gave birth to a new form of business—the military-industrial firm. This company, although it appeared to resemble American corporations, was really quite distinct. It did not participate in the normal competitive market that businesses typically faced; nor did it sell its products to everyone; nor did it concern itself with cost overruns. Rather, the military-industrial firm sold its missile systems, new aircraft, new atomic submarines, and whatever other atomic bombs and weapons it developed to the Department of Defense only. As for cost overruns, it merely added those to the final bill for the American people to pay.

With so much military spending, it is not surprising that the American economy experienced economic growth. Throughout the 1945-1960 period, the economy did well as production increased, employment grew, and per capita income went up. This did not mean that recessions were non-existent. Recessions did occur, as in 1953 and 1957. But, the federal government, having learned its lessons in Keynesian economics, immediately reverted to looser credit policies and more spending to revive the economic doldrums. Even unemployment remained fairly steady at around seven percent throughout a good part of the post-war period until Jimmy Carter became president in 1976.

Business was impacted too by all of this economic development. Billion dollar corporations appeared and a new merger wave took place in 1954-1957. Anti-trust laws, such as the Sherman and Clayton Acts, were still on the books, but they were used sparingly. It wasn't until the 1980s when Ronald Reagan's administration broke up AT&T and Bill Clinton's administration examined Microsoft during the late 1990s that these business regulatory laws were re-invigorated.

United States Defense Expenditures 1940–1990

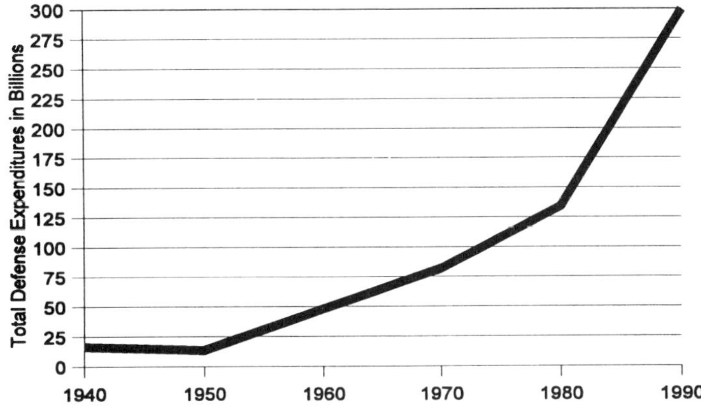

SOURCE: *Statistical Abstract of the U.S.*, 1999

1946-1960 • Post-war Union Decline ~ In all of these changes, labor had a role. In the immediate post-war years, labor unions sought to solidify the gains that they had made during World War II by going on strike. Despite the favorable political environment that the Fair Deal created for unions, Harry Truman had his limits, as witnessed by the railroad strike (1946) and the steel strike (1952). Congress had even less toleration for union activity and decided the time was ripe for action. In 1947, Congress passed the Taft-Hartley Act, a law that organized labor still considers to be among the worst in American history. The law prohibited the closed shop (only union members could be hired), encouraged states to pass "right to work" laws which undermined the union shop principle, and established the "cooling off" period before a strike took place. Although Truman vetoed the legislation, Congress passed Taft-Hartley anyway.

To make matters worse, McCarthyism began to sweep across the United States by 1950. Fueled by the ruthless junior senator from Wisconsin, McCarthyism targeted anyone who was different or might be suspected of Communist sympathy. "Guilt by association" became the order of the day and "fifth amendment Communists" were charges that McCarthy frequently made against those appearing before his inquisitional-type committee hearings. Labor, of course, was center stage in this movement. McCarthy and his followers frequently lambasted unions as "fifth columns" and forerunners of communism in America. Although the senator from Wisconsin was finally censored after the Army-McCarthy hearings of 1954, the atmosphere he created still remained. Congress again decided to look into the union movement. This time, its efforts resulted in the McClellan committee hearings of 1957.

Led by Senator John McClellan of Arkansas and assisted by Robert F. Kennedy, the committee looked carefully at union activities, especially regarding the union leadership's handling of pension funds. Investigating the Teamsters, the committee found that David Beck had misused the pension fund. He was soon replaced by Jimmy Hoffa who would become the target of Robert Kennedy's ire from that point on. The inevitable result of the Congressional inquiry was the 1959 Labor Reform Act, which placed significant controls over how unions expended pension funds. The Teamsters suffered too in that the AFL-CIO actually expelled them.

As labor unions fought for better wages, working conditions, and fringe benefits, their leadership realized that the unions themselves needed to cooperate. In 1955, the AFL and CIO merged into the new AFL-CIO with George Meany as president and Walter Reuther of the CIO as president of the industrial department. In many ways, this was a good move because the unions were beginning to decline in membership and their influence was stagnant. One good example of the limited success the unions were having came in Operation Dixie. Launched after World War II, Operation Dixie targeted the South for unionization. Despite a large war chest of money and a committed effort on the part of unions, the operation failed dismally. The South, perhaps the most recalcitrant in its anti-union attitude, remained a haven for non-union seeking industries and businesses.

1960-1976 • America Unnerved ~

There is no question that the 1960s was one of the most disturbing decades in the history of the United States. Violence erupted on America's streets, universities became the centers of radical unrest, civil rights leaders led their marches into the most brutal areas of America where segregation and racism prevailed, and American leaders were shot down in cold blood. The presidents of the 1960s-early 1970s, John F. Kennedy, Lyndon B. Johnson, and Richard Nixon all had to face some of the most difficult challenges any American leader had ever confronted.

1976-2000

From the perspective of American labor, Kennedy's New Frontier and Johnson's Great Society were more acceptable than Nixon's conservatism. Although the union movement only reluctantly supported Kennedy in 1960, labor did hope the new president would encourage Congress to pass legislation helping workers generally. Although Kennedy introduced civil rights legislation in 1962, it was his successor, Lyndon Johnson, who picked up the gauntlet and went forward. Together, Kennedy and Johnson had Congress pass legislation to help American workers in terms of occupational and job training programs; eliminating discrimination in employment; and providing funding for medical care.

Richard Nixon, on the other hand, saw the American economy in a different light and with different problems. Focusing more on inflation than growth, Nixon was not very favorable either to working men and women nor to unions. He did not support union demands for higher wages, fringe benefits, or better working conditions. The result was that workers went on strike, even in professions that had, seldom if ever, considered striking, such as teachers. After Nixon resigned in 1974 over the Watergate scandal, his successor, Gerald Ford refused to support labor's demands, which eventually cost him the presidency in 1976. With the economy declining and inflation gaining ground, more and more Americans were ready for a change, even if it meant voting for an unknown southern governor, Jimmy Carter.

1976-2000 • America Regains Its Composure ~ Jimmy Carter, a South-

(1970) Robotic welding equipment on the General Motors, Vega production line in action. The automatic welding equipment places 95 percent of the 3,900 welds on each Vega body.

ern Baptist and Georgia governor, took over the reins of government at a time when America needed to reassert herself. Although a highly gifted and intelligent individual, Carter's lack of experience in national politics and his naive expectations in relating to Congress cost him dearly. Plagued by problems of inflation and high unemployment, Carter employed traditional Keynesian methods to handle economic problems. Unfortunately, those remedies did not work, resulting instead in what economists called "stagflation." Organized labor, while it did not particularly benefit under Carter's leadership, still supported him in his re-election bid in 1979-1980 with newly-elected president of the AFL-CIO, Lane Kirkland, endorsing Carter. Stagflation, the Iran-hostage crisis, and Carter's consistent appearance of being "co-opted" placed him in a rather difficult position in 1980 as former actor and political activist Ronald Reagan ran against him. When the results came in, Reagan's victory was overwhelming!

1980-1988 • The Reagan-Bush Years ~ If nothing else, Ronald Reagan's presidency will be remembered for his implementing "Supply-Side" economics. Emphasizing the need for tax cuts, balanced budgets, and restoring business confidence, Reagan did all he could to enhance business' position within the American economy as he spent billions of dollars on rebuilding America's military defense systems. For Reagan and his conservative supporters, helping working-class men and women, and their unions, was not a priority. Rather, he took the position that the federal government should set an example by taking firm stands against unions. No better illustration could have been seen than Reagan's handling of the air traffic controllers strike. Citing reasons of national security, not only did Reagan refuse to bargain collectively with the Professional Air Traffic Controllers Association, but he actually fired them all and replaced them with military personnel. The union itself was eventually "decertified." Inevitably, other strikes followed in this political environment, even in professions that no one ever thought would strike – professional football and baseball players.

Reaganomics seemed to give the impression of a strong economy, a strong defense, and a strong world position for America. Yet, underneath this seemingly strong exterior was an economy delving deeper and deeper into debt. Even Reagan's vice president and successor, George Bush, had once referred to Reagan's economic plans as "voodoo economics." Despite the popularity of "Desert Storm," Stormin' Norman, and Colin Powell, Bush's handling of the American economy was disastrous. Recession set in and eventually caused him to lose re-election. He had promised the American people "read my lips – no new taxes!" a promise he couldn't keep and a costly mistake.

1992-2000 • The Clinton Years ~ With the election of Bill Clinton in 1992, working men and women and unions fared better, for the most part than under previous administrations. Clinton had consistently supported increasing the minimum wage, improving worker benefits, and providing government-sponsored health care. For America's workers, the problem in making advances was not so much Clinton-Gore but the changing character of international economics. By the 1990s, the world had reached a level of international or global interdependence. No longer could any country, especially the United States, operate in a vacuum. What happened in Far Eastern stock markets impacted what happened on Wall Street and labor conditions in Eastern Europe or China affected American imports and thus the American worker.

Globalization had led the United States to favor more internationally-oriented trade policies such as the General Agreement on Tariffs and Trade (GATT) and the North American Free Trade Agreement (NAFTA). Not surprisingly, American labor, especially in its union organizations and leadership, have been outspoken in their opposition to such treaties. Instead, what labor unions want and demand is that the United States force other countries to agree to improving foreign workers' salaries and working conditions before any such trade agreements are reached. In doing so, American unions argue that these agreements would protect the American workers' standard of living while improving the circumstances of foreign workers. Although union membership has gone down since the 1940s and although union influence has waned somewhat, there seems to have been a definite revival in the unions' activity and power base as the 2000 presidential election demonstrated. Union support for Democrat Al Gore was so strong that even political strategists wondered if the union power base is once again beginning to grow.

Total Employment: White Collar vs. Blue Collar 1958–1982

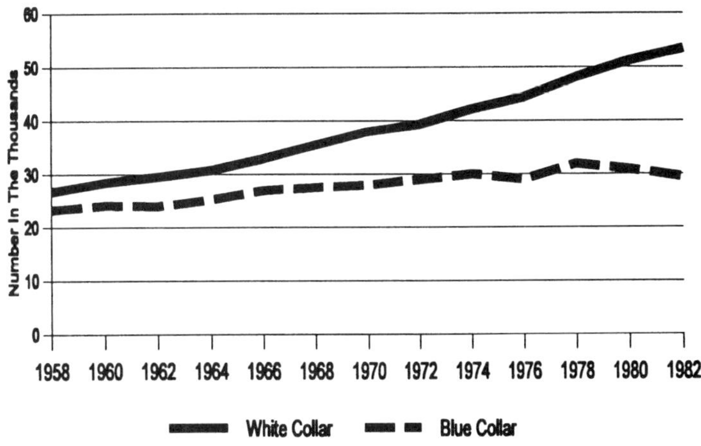

SOURCE: Statistical Abstract of the U.S., 1999; AFL-CIO, *Report of AFL-CIO Executive Council*, 1995.

Conclusion

In assessing American labor and its development in the post-war world, it seems clear that there are a number of problems and challenges that labor has had to face. One of the most significant is technology. Whether it is in the automotive industry or in the changing base of America's economy from steel to "dot.coms," robotics has been an increasing threat to job security. Negative public opinion is also a problem, going back to the 1950s as Congressional investigations uncovered corruption and organized crime within the ranks of the union structure. Unions have not helped themselves either by the internal dissension that existed and still goes on within the AFL-CIO. Foreign competition has increased consistently in the post-war period. American products, union-made or not, now have to compete in a global environment where workers in foreign countries work for far less pay and far more hours. Immigration has not helped America labor either in that immigrants have generally tended to avoid unions and opt for job security through low wages. The changing character of America's workforce is still another issue that American labor has had to confront. Not only have women been enter-

Percentage of Union Membership in the Labor Force

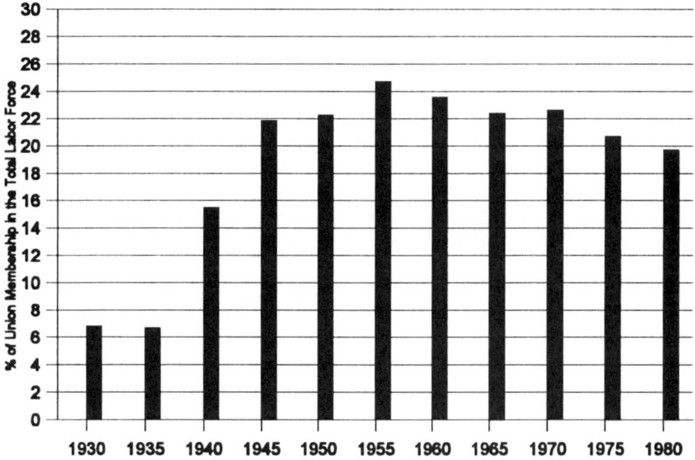

SOURCE: AFL-CIO, *Report of AFL-CIO Executive Council*, 1995.

ing the workforce in greater numbers and demanding equal pay for equal work, but the very character of that workforce is different today. Blue collar workers, however the federal government defines them, have declined in number as white collar workers have increased. This in itself shows just how much America's global role is having a bearing on what happens in its own economic system.

Finally, the decline in union membership has definitely impacted labor's influence on the American political environment. Despite efforts on the part of union leaders to organize workers who had not been unionized before as, for example, Cesar Chavez and the California migrant workers, the percentage of American workers in American unions is still small and has shown continual declines for quite a number of years.

What all this adds up to is that American working men and women and their unions had to confront the changing conditions of the American and global economy and make changes in their own outlooks, attitudes, and objectives. While all of the above may seem like insurmountable problems, the reality is that these problems can also be seen as challenges which, if answered creatively, could lead to a better life for all American workers.

But unions still have to confront their image problem. Since the 1920s, American labor unions have been identified with organized crime and the violence normally associated with it. The McClellan hearings during the 1950s showed that union leaders, especially David Beck of the Teamsters had fraudulently used the enormous union pension funds. The Teamsters did not help themselves either when Jimmy Hoffa took control and ran head on into the Kennedy brothers. Murders of union leaders and members, violence against scabs and strike breakers, violence on picket lines, and union corruption linking it to organized crime still exist and pose a problem that unions will have to resolve if they are to contribute meaningfully to the growth of industry and the economy.

Bibliography

Bernstein, Irving. *The Lean Years*. Boston: Houghton Mifflin, 1960.

———. *The Turbulent Years*. Boston: Houghton Mifflin, 1960.

Chandler, Alfred. *The Visible Hand: The Managerial Revolution in American Business*. Cambridge, MA: Harvard University Press, 1977.

Engerman, Stanley. "The Economic Impact of the Civil War," *Explorations in Economic History* (1966).

Fogel, Robert. *Without Consent or Contract: The Rise and Fall of American Slavery*. New York: W.W. Norton, 1989.

Freidel, Frank. *Rendezvous With Destiny: Franklin Roosevelt and the New Deal.* Boston: Little, Brown, 1990.

Galbraith, John K. *The Great Crash, 1929*. Boston: Houghton Mifflin, 1954.

Gaston, Paul. *The New South Creed*. Baton Rouge: LSU Press, 1983.

Goldin, Claudia and Frank Lewis. "The Economic Cost of the American Civil War: Estimates and Implications." *Journal of Economic History* (1975).

Hawley, Ellis. *The New Deal and the Problem of Monopoly*. Princeton: Princeton University Press, 1966.

Hofstadter, Richard. *Age of Reform*. New York: Vintage, 1955.

Karson, Marc. *American Labor Unions and Politics*. Boston: Beacon Press, 1958.

Lebergott, Stanley. *The American Economy: Income, Wealth and Want*. Princeton: Princeton University Press, 1976.

Livesay, Harold. *Samuel Gompers and Organized Labor in America*. Boston: Little, Brown, 1978.

McCullough, David. *Truman*. New York: Simon and Schuster, 1992.

Namorato, Michael V. *Rexford G. Tugwell: A Biography*. New York: Praeger, 1988.

Pelling, Henry. *American Labor*. Chicago: University of Chicago Press, 1960.

Polenberg, Richard. *War and Society: The United States in World War II*. New York: J. B. Lippincott, 1972.

Ransom, Roger and Richard Sutch. *One Kind of Freedom*. Cambridge: Cambridge University Press, 1977.

Rayback, Joseph. *A History of American Labor*. New York: Free Press, 1959.

Wiebe, Robert. *The Search for Order*. New York: Hill and Wang, 1971.

Wright, Gavin. *Old South, New South*. New York: Basic Books, 1986.

Internet Resources

Information on labor and labor history in the Puget Sound, including the Seattle General Strike of 1919 and the Maritime Strikes of 1934.
http://www.lib.washington.edu/exhibits/STRIKES!/index.html

Information on labor history and strikes in Texas.
http://www.rice.edu/armadillo/Texas/Sharedpast/strike.html

Account of the Haymarket Square Riot in Chicago.
http://www.prairieghosts.com/haymarket.html

In-depth look at the Pullman Strike including causes, events, and consequences.
http://1912.history.ohio-state.edu/pullman. htm

Autobiographical excerpt from Emma Goldman, who attempted to assassinate the chairman of the Carnegie Steel Company during the Homestead Strike in 1892.
http://www.historymatters.gmu.edu/text/1847a-goldman.html

Three different accounts of the Homestead Strike and the attempted assassination of the chairman of Carnegie Steel Company.
http://www.geocities.com/pract_history/homestead.html

Website of the Samuel Gompers Papers including biography, documents, photos, and more on the influential labor leader.
http://www.inform.umd.edu/EdRes/Colleges/ARHU/Depts/History/Gompers/web1.html

Homepage for the AFL-CIO.
http://www.aflcio.org/home.htm

Homepage for the Teamsters.
http://www.teamster.org

Homepage for the Industrial Workers of the World.
http://iww.org

Information on the Pullman Strike in Chicago in 1894.
http://www.cc.ukans.edu/kansas/pullman/index.html

An online study guide for American Labor History.
http://www.geocities.com/CollegePark/Quad/6460/AmLabHist/index.html

Biography of Eugene V. Debs, including labor quotes from Debs.
http://www.cc.ukans.edu/kansas/pullman/texts/debs.html

Site providing information on business and labor history from the World Wide Web Virtual Library.
http://www.iisg.nl/~w3vl/

Michael V. Namorato
University of Mississippi

CITIES

(circa 1935) Pittsburgh. Because of an abundance of coal in Pennsylvania which supplied energy to run the steel mills, Pittsburgh became very industrialized early in the twentieth century.

TIMELINE

1500-1799 ~ The First Cities

First American city, St. Augustine, Florida settled by the Spanish (1565) / Other early cities established: Jamestown (1607), Santa Fe (1610), Boston (1630) / First Indian attack on Jamestown (1622) / Philadelphia becomes the largest city (1799)

MILESTONES: First African slaves arrive in Jamestown (1619) • Boston Tea Party (1775) • Revolutionary War (1776) • Constitutional Convention (1787)

1800-1899 ~ Small, Contained Cities

Boston (1838) and New York (1844) form police departments / New York grows to the largest city by 1860 / First labor union formed in the United States (1866) / Introduction of electricity for streetlights (1870-1900) / First commercial automobile produced (1892) / First U.S. subway completed in Boston (1897) / Police training school established in New York (1897)

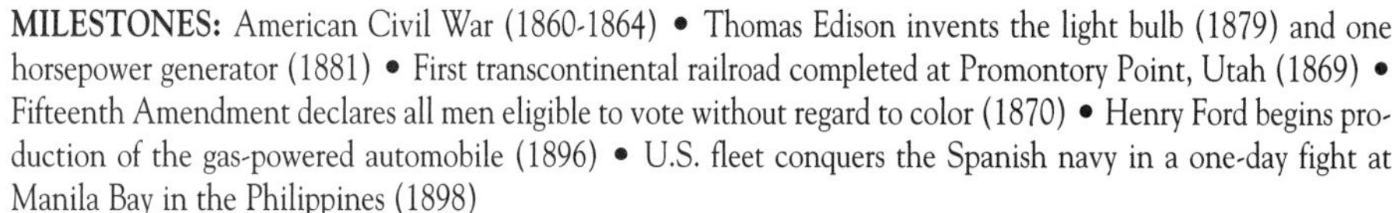

MILESTONES: American Civil War (1860-1864) • Thomas Edison invents the light bulb (1879) and one horsepower generator (1881) • First transcontinental railroad completed at Promontory Point, Utah (1869) • Fifteenth Amendment declares all men eligible to vote without regard to color (1870) • Henry Ford begins production of the gas-powered automobile (1896) • U.S. fleet conquers the Spanish navy in a one-day fight at Manila Bay in the Philippines (1898)

1900-1919 ~ The Growth of Cities

Populations in New York, Chicago and Philadelphia surpass 1,000,000 (1900) / New York introduces first law governing speed in the city (1901) / Oregon hires the first policewoman in America (1905) / New York (1904) and Philadelphia (1907) subways open / Garrett Morgan invents the gas mask to keep firefighters from being overcome by smoke (1912)

MILESTONES: Wright brothers' gasoline engine aircraft Flyer successfully flies at Kitty Hawk (1903) • Lee De Forest invents the vacuum tube, essential to the development of electronics (1906) • Pasteurization of milk begins in large cities (1914) • First transcontinental phone line is established between New York City and San Francisco (1915) • Child labor abuse made a federal crime (1916)

1920-1929 ~ City Services and Skyscrapers

For the first time in U.S. history, more Americans live in urban than in rural areas (1920) / Traffic signal technology developed by African American Garrett Morgan (1920s) / Standardization of building and housing codes (1920s) / Zoning laws enacted (1920s) / Construction of New York skyscrapers (1920s-1930s) / Permanent immigration quotas imposed (1921) / Uniform classification of crimes issued by Chiefs of Police (1929) / First public parking garage is built in Detroit (1929)

MILESTONES: First transcontinental airmail route established between New York City and San Francisco (1920) • Insulin used to treat diabetes (1922) • First motel is built in San Luis Obispo, California (1925) • Sixty-three percent of Americans live in homes with electric lights (1927) • Walt Disney creates the first animated motion picture, *Steamboat Willie* (1929)

1930-1945 ~ Urban Poverty and the New Deal

Rampant urban poverty caused by the Great Depression's economic downturn and massive unemployment (1930s) / U.S. Conference of Mayors formed (1930) / The Home Owners Loan Corporation (HOLC) established to stabilize the home mortgage market in metropolitan areas (1932) / New Deal public works programs benefit cities by building infrastructure, providing jobs (1932-1936) / City slums, a result of middle class suburbanization, are cleared to provide public housing for the poor, but opposition prevents its completion / Federal Housing Administration federally insures long-term mortgages to encourage lending institutions to make loans in a difficult market (1934) / Chicago subway opens (1943)

MILESTONES: 30,000 Americans die in car accidents (1930) • Labor unions gain foothold among semiskilled workers (1930s) • Economy Act stipulates that married women be discharged from their jobs (1932) • Twin engine Boeing 247, the first modern commercial aircraft, is put into service (1933) • Nazis banish Jews to ghettos (1936) • First atomic explosion occurs in Los Alamos, New Mexico (1943)

1946-1959 ~ Rapid Growth

Housing boom begins (1946) / Levittown, on Long Island, is built using mass production to build cheap houses quickly, fueling housing boom (1947) / Federal home loan programs discriminate against minorities (1950s-1960s) / Housing and Rent Act controls rents and provides subsidies for garden apartments (1947) / City beltway construction begins (1956) / Interstate Highway Act passed to fund a vast network of high-speed roads (1956)

MILESTONES: Mao Zedong's communist party seizes power in China (1949) • Sickle-cell anemia described as molecular disease (1949) • North Korean troops invade South Korea, starting the Korean War (1950) • President Truman ends racial discrimination in government (1953) • Ultrasound examines fetuses in the womb (1958)

1960-1969 ~ Decline of Urban America

Union contracts include paid vacations of up to four weeks for long-term workers (1960) / Industrial jobs move to the Sunbelt / Department of Housing and Urban Development (HUD) established to oversee federal projects in cities (1965) / Housing Act authorizes rent supplement subsidy to low-income families (1965) / Model Cities Act authorizes construction of turnkey projects for low-rent housing (1966) / National Historic Preservation Act makes the protection of historic buildings a national policy (1966) / Race riots across America, destroying many inner-city areas, start with Martin Luther King's assassination (1968)

MILESTONES: Telstar satellite makes worldwide transmission possible (1962) • Civil Rights Act prohibits racial discrimination in public accommodations (1964) • Wilderness Act sets aside huge tracts of land for wilderness (1964) • Fierce race riots occur in Los Angeles, Cleveland and New York (1965) • Miranda decision forces police to read a suspect his rights (1966) • *Sesame Street* premieres (1969)

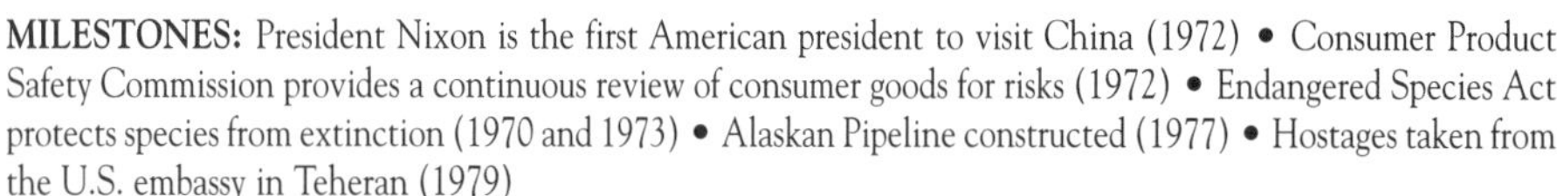

1970-1979 ~ Cities in Retreat

Clean Air Act attempts to minimize vehicle produced pollution (1970) / Occupational Safety and Health Act sets safety standards in the workplace (1970) / Public housing in St. Louis demolished (1972) / Northern and Midwestern cities fall into financial ruin / City schools remain segregated in spite of *Brown v. Board of Education* (1954) / Mass transit systems promoted in cities as a solution to air pollution and traffic congestion (1970s)

MILESTONES: President Nixon is the first American president to visit China (1972) • Consumer Product Safety Commission provides a continuous review of consumer goods for risks (1972) • Endangered Species Act protects species from extinction (1970 and 1973) • Alaskan Pipeline constructed (1977) • Hostages taken from the U.S. embassy in Teheran (1979)

1980-2000 ~ Urban Renewal and Recovery

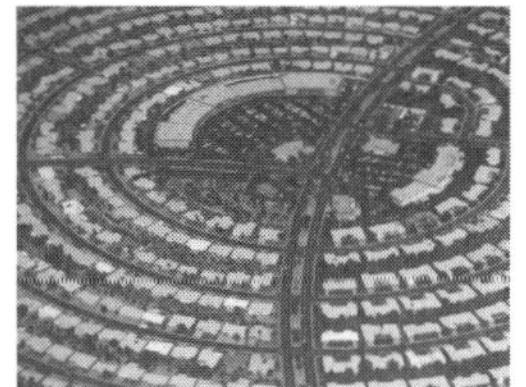

Housing and Urban-Rural Recovery Act provides funds for housing for the elderly, handicapped, and homeless (1983) / Congress considers but rejects most gun control legislation (1985-2000) / Housing and Community Act establishes a housing voucher program (1987) / Indian Housing Act assists Native Americans and Alaska Natives in securing housing (1988) / Warehouses turned into apartments in old industrial cities (1980s) / Northeast and Midwest lose 1.5 million manufacturing jobs, mostly in cities, while the South and West gain 450,000 jobs (1980-1990) / First major Housing Act since 1974 provides matching funds for new construction and rehabilitation of renter-occupied and owner-occupied housing, and for privatizing public housing and multi-family properties owned or financed by federal agencies (1990)

MILESTONES: Number of temporary workers more than doubles and the number of part-time workers increases by 40 percent (1980-1989) • Immigration Reform Act makes it illegal for employers to hire undocumented workers (1987) • Globalization of environmental concerns, especially global warming (1990) • United States increases efforts to stop illegal Mexican immigration (1990s) • Dissolution of the Soviet Union ends the Cold War (1991) • GM introduces the first mass-marketed electric car, the Saturn EV1 (1990)

Introduction

The history of twentieth-century cities in the United States is a microcosm of the history of the United States. Embedded in the history of its cities is the saga of America. During the one hundred years of the twentieth century, the United States has transformed itself from a rural agrarian society to an urban society to a society in which the majority of Americans live in metropolitan suburbs.

To understand the rise of the United States to economic supremacy, urban America's central role in industrialization must be acknowledged. A related theme—that of advances in transportation technology, most notably the automobile—is fundamental to any understanding of American cities, as well. The idea and ideal of America as home to diverse peoples also must focus on cities, as both foreign immigration to the United States and migration of U.S. citizens from rural to urban to suburban areas, revolutionized the demographic make-up of the nation. Of course, central to all of these discussions is the theme of race in U.S. history. As the twenty-first century dawns and America becomes even more ethnically and racially diverse, examining the history of U.S. cities provides insight as to why diversity continues to divide rather than uplift many Americans.

What Is a City?

Across time and place most human cultures have felt the need to establish permanent settlements that evolved over time into cities. A city performs many functions for humans. It is a sacred space, where people erect shrines to honor the dead and the divine. It is a stronghold where people can defend themselves against the elements, rival humans, and dangerous animals. It is a marketplace for people to trade their goods. It is a village where people can come together to socialize and enjoy each other's company and culture. The development of agriculture often provides the impetus for the formation of cities as the hunter-gatherer society gives way to an agrarian society where humans cluster to tend and trade crops and material goods.

1600s • America's First Cities ~ It has been argued that the city is the ideal human community and the European settlement of North America supports this vision of cities. When the Puritans sailed to Massachusetts Bay Colony in 1630, John Winthrop proclaimed that his followers should establish a "city upon a hill," in order to serve as a role model for his home country of England. First settled by Swedes in the 1640s, Philadelphia was the first planned city in British North America and was the most populous and influential city of colonial and early national America after King Charles II granted the land to the Quaker William Penn in 1681. Meanwhile, Spaniards had established the first European cities in what is now the United States by founding Saint Augustine in Florida (1565) and Santa Fe in New Mexico (1610). Most important cities in what became the United States were port cities, of which Jamestown, Virginia (1607) and Boston, Massachusetts (1630) were two early examples. The first African slaves were brought to Jamestown in 1619.

1700s-1800s

1700s • Importance of Cities ~ Even when still overwhelmingly an agrarian and rural nation, cities played an important role in U.S. history. During the American Revolution, when urban dwellers still made up less than five percent of the total population (Philadelphia having the largest population, with only 25,000), they played an instrumental role. Events in Boston (e.g. Boston Massacre and Tea Party) and Philadelphia (site of the Continental Congresses and Declaration of Independence, as well as the Constitutional Convention in 1787) proved decisive in convincing many colonists to join the side of the patriots. Ironically, though, it was America's rural character that made it very hard for the superior British Army to defeat the rebellion. European armies at this time waged war through face-to-face combat; rural Americans took advantage of the countryside using strike and hide tactics.

1860s • Growth of Cities ~ In the decades leading up to the Civil War, most Americans still lived very rural and isolated lives, but cities had started to grow quite rapidly. The Atlantic coast city of New York had grown to more than 800,000 by 1860 (in part, thanks to the Erie Canal, which tied the enormous Great Lakes hinterland to the port of New York) and Philadelphia also surpassed the half million mark. As Americans moved West, so, too, did their cities; interior cities such as Pittsburgh, Cincinnati, and St. Louis all grew phenomenally to service the needs of frontier settlement. Generally, the South remained more rural than the rest of the nation, as its economy depended so heavily upon agriculture for export.

1800s • Walking in Early Cities ~ No matter what size colonial and antebellum cities were, though, many of them shared one characteristic with cities the world over: they were compact walking cities. Since almost all people traveled by foot, cities simply could not be very large. Rather, they were quite densely populated, be it Newport, Rhode Island or Charleston, South Carolina. The typical urban dweller had to live very close to where s/he worked, prayed, and shopped. The rich, the poor, and the middling all lived in very close proximity to each other. No American city extended for more than a few miles out from its center—one could generally walk across a city in the space of an hour. Also significant, even as populations grew, there remained no distinction between residential, commercial, and manufacturing districts; that is, urban life was mixed and diverse.

1900-1915 • Rapid Growth of Cities ~ In the twentieth century the United States became an urban nation. In 1900 a majority of Americans still lived in rural areas and small towns. Nevertheless, the seeds of change had been planted with the beginning of the industrial revolution in the late nineteenth century and this century witnessed the unfolding of this process. In the early twentieth century, a handful of American cities would surpass the million population mark and a dozen other cities would exceed 250,000. Indeed, although the nation grew rapidly in the first fifteen years of the twentieth century (prior to World War I), cities grew twice as fast. Whereas in 1890 only one-in-three Americans lived in cities, by 1920 a majority of Americans were urbanites. The urbanization of the United States is inextricably linked to the two other dominant trends in turn-of-the-century America: industrialization and immigration.

1900 • Industrialization ~ Why did Americans move to cities in ever increasing numbers in the late nineteenth and early twentieth-centuries? No single factor is more important than the economic boom that was taking place in urban America. Industrialization was an almost entirely urban phenomenon at this time. By 1900, 90 percent of the nation's manufacturing occurred in cities. Although this process had begun during the Civil War era and developed quite rapidly during the Gilded Age (1870-1890), the full effects of industrialization would not be felt until the twentieth century. As the urban economy grew, so, too, did its population, although in 1900 a majority of Americans still lived in rural areas (one-in-three Americans still were farmers). The growth of urban-based industrialization would catapult the United States into the realm of the "great powers" decades before its military would catch up.

Industrialization is a complex process that, actually, can be understood quite simply. In human history prior to industrialization, all production, including agricultural, was done through human or animal labor with the assistance of hand tools.

With industrialization new machinery and techniques were introduced that facilitated the mass production of an enormous variety of goods. The harnessing of new methods like continuous production assembly lines, and technologies (first fueled by water power, later coal and oil) resulted in an explosion in the nation's economy and literally remade the lives of every American. While producing amounts and varieties of goods and wealth previously unimaginable, industrialization also dramatically increased economic inequality. Further, industrialization created employment for the working (wage-earning) class where before, most

Ten Largest Cities in 1900

City—1900	Total Population	Native-born Population	Foreign-born population	Percent Foreign-born
New York City	3,437,202	2,167,122	1,270,080	37.0
Chicago	1,698,575	1,111,463	587,112	34.6
Philadelphia	1,293,697	998,357	295,340	22.8
St. Louis	575,238	463,882	111,356	19.4
Boston	560,892	363,763	197,129	35.1
Baltimore	508,957	440,357	68,600	13.5
Cleveland	381,768	257,137	124,631	32.6
Buffalo	352,387	248,135	104,252	29.6
San Francisco	325,902	267,941	57,961	17.8
Cincinnati	321,616	236,738	84,878	26.4

SOURCE: U.S. Bureau of the Census

1890-1915

Americans, both in agriculture and craft production, had worked for themselves or hoped to someday, mostly outside of a cash economy.

With this revolution, millions of workers found themselves with jobs in which they were just one part of a much larger process; this work often was unrelenting, dangerous, and paid poorly. As industrialization evolved, artisans who had produced a complete product by hand now found themselves repetitively completing a single task that was just one part of the larger process of production. Perhaps most importantly, the de-skillization that occurred left workers with less control over their own labor, while simultaneously creating many more and much cheaper goods.

(1909) Chinatown NYC. New Year celebrations in Chinatown in New York City. New York, renowned for having a multi-lingual environment, has many multi-cultural celebrations.

1890-1915 • IMMIGRATION ~
Industrialization produced an enormous demand for workers—a demand that could not be fulfilled by the migration of Americans from rural farms to urban factories. Thus, the American economy pulled its workers from the economically depressed and politically oppressed hinterlands—mostly of southern and eastern Europe. (In contrast, more recently, U.S. corporations moved their production facilities directly to the multitudes of poor workers in the still-developing parts of the world, generally in the southern hemisphere.) While the first waves of European settlers/immigrants primarily hailed from the British Isles, Ireland, and Germany, these "new" immigrants (as they were called at the time) were overwhelmingly Catholics and Jews from countries such as Italy, Greece, Poland, Russia, and the Austro-Hungarian empire (smaller numbers arrived from Mexico and Asia). From 1890 to 1915, twenty million people arrived in the United States, the largest population movement in world history until that time. Like previous immigration waves, the bulk of immigrants were male, with women and children following closely behind.

1900-1915 • ETHNIC ENCLAVES ~
Immigrants transformed American cities, especially the industrial centers, in the early twentieth-century. In places such as Chicago, Detroit, Cleveland, and New York City, huge majorities of the residents were immigrants or the children of immigrants. Usually, these "white ethnics" clustered together in enclaves in the older, less-expensive parts of cities, close to their industrial jobs. These ethnic neighborhoods also allowed immigrants to be near each other, so that they could receive comfort and protection from people with

shared experience, religion, language, and food. Visitors were as likely to hear Italian or Yiddish as they were to hear English. Increasingly, in the eyes of native-born Protestant Americans, originally immigrants themselves, "the city" came to be seen as a "foreign" place, quite literally.

1900-1920 • Population Growth ~ Of course, the growth of cities was not solely a result of immigration. American population increased overall due to improved health care that allowed women to live longer and therefore have more children as well as lower infant mortality rates allowing more children to reach adulthood. Migration within the United States from rural areas to cities also took place. Native born Americans of European and African descent were drawn to cities for the same reasons that immigrants who arrived in the United States settled in cities. As agriculture was transformed from subsistence to commerce, millions of Americans pushed off the land (in the Midwest, South, and Appalachia) and took jobs in cities. Just as with their immigrant counterparts, these migrants often were the first factory wage-earners in their families and were unaccustomed to the discipline of impersonal industrial workplaces. Other motivations, especially for women [such as novelist Theodore Dreiser's *Sister Carrie* (1900)], included increased opportunities for independence.

1900-1920 • Migration of African Americans ~ There were a variety of factors that specifically affected African American migration patterns. In 1900 more than 75 percent of blacks still lived in the rural South. There were, though, numerous reasons for blacks to want to change this situation. Most notably, the brutal oppression of Jim Crow segregation guaranteed that blacks would be second-class citizens without legal protections, voting rights, educational opportunities, or prospects for economic prosperity (a majority being landless agricultural workers, called sharecroppers). Moreover, lynchings of blacks occurred frequently. Many black people who desired equality chose to flee the rural South or else face the real risk of murder and, for women, rape.

What African Americans needed were economic opportunities to pull them out of the South, but jobs were not readily available, especially for men, until the World War I era. It was the cessation of large-scale European immigration during the war that created the conditions that blacks, as well as Mexicans, Mexican Americans, and women, generally needed to succeed. With the labor shortage during the war, employers started hiring large numbers of black men. Once jobs became available, hundreds of thousands of blacks fled the rural South. However, when blacks arrived in Northern and Midwestern cities, they experienced intense racism there, too. Nowhere was this discrimination more visible than in the residential sector, as African Americans were denied access to housing in most parts of cities. As a result of this racism, black-only enclaves, often referred to as ghettoes, formed (Roxbury in Boston, Harlem in New York City, the South side of Chicago, the Filmore in San Francisco are all examples of such ghetto areas). This "Great Migration," which slowed for a while after the war, picked up again during and after World War II, and reshaped both the African American and the urban American experience.

1900-1920 • City Housing ~ As cities grew in diversity, population, and size, they also became more specialized. American cities could not possibly meet the housing needs demanded by the enormous population increases that occurred in this era. Since the U.S government—at the federal level and local/state level—rarely has planned development and usually takes a quite limited role in shaping the private sector, it should come as no surprise that the nation was thoroughly unprepared for the dramatic growth in the early 1900s (even though America's open immigration policy of that era clearly encouraged the process). Thus, more and more city dwellers found themselves living in overcrowded, unregulated apartment houses. Indeed, the highest population density the world had ever seen was in the Lower East Side of Manhattan in this era. Generally, ethnic groups congregated together in distinct residential neighborhoods. In New York City, for example, Chinese lived in Chinatown, Italians in Little Italy, and Eastern European Jews on the Lower East Side. Of course, these boundaries were not entirely rigid, but ethnic enclaves clearly existed.

1910s • Rise of Suburbs ~ Simultaneously, increasing numbers of upper-middle and upper class urbanites moved to the peripheries of cities or outside of cities altogether for a variety of reasons. In the Gilded Age and the Progressive Era the process of suburbanization first took root. In the suburbs, these peoples, overwhelmingly white and wealthy, could own their own homes, far away from the noise, overcrowding, and squalor of ethnically diverse Progressive Era cities.

Prior to the Civil War, the most desirable locations to live were inside of cities. In fact, the United States simply was following the European model of urban development, for in every major European city, the core was where the affluent lived. In contrast, while Europe's wealthy remained committed to urban living, it was the elite in America who led the exodus out of cities.

Clearly, the real public health risks (diseases spread by poor quality air and water) associated with dense populations of people, combined with industrial production in cities, and overburdened services all were major incentives to leave cities. This was only possible, of course, for those who could afford the land, a house, and significantly higher transportation costs. However, the desire on the part of wealthy white families to live in homogeneous communities, both in terms of ethnicity and race as well as class, was an important factor, too. Undeniably, what facilitated this process of increased decentralization and segregation were new transportation technologies.

1900-1920 • City Transportation ~ Slowly, the contained walking city expanded as the city population grew. In order to accommodate ever growing urban populations, new forms of transportation were developed. Although other means were tried (e.g. the horse-drawn buggy), through World War II the dominant form of transportation in American cities came to be the electric streetcar, also called the trolley. Few cities in America were without numerous street car lines. Major cities literally were criss-crossed with hundreds of miles of track, on which the trolleys traveled; generally, trolley services were privately owned but had been granted exclusive franchises on a particular road by the city government. Trolleys were cheap (the fare, generally, was five cents), efficient, and fast; because there was such a high level of ridership, trolleys also ran very frequently. One of the many benefits of trolleys was the elimination of hundreds of thousands of horse-drawn wagons and cars from America's streets. In addition to being faster and able to carry more passengers, trolleys eliminated the millions of tons of horse manure that had proven to be an enormous health hazard as well as being quite unseemly.

Other forms of transportation contributed to the changing city, too. Railroads began to add stops just outside city limits (and in some cases inside), so that a train connecting, for instance, Chicago and Milwaukee, stopped just a few miles north of Chicago in Evanston, Illinois. These railroad suburbs, outside of major cities (especially in Westchester County, just north of New York City) quickly grew into havens for the elite. Also, for a few but growing number of people, the automobile, most popularly, the affordable and dependable Ford Model T, also contributed to the ongoing decentralization of American cities.

One major result of the trolley, commuter railroad, and automobile was that people could start to move further away from their places of work, while still spending the same amount of time (if more money) commuting as they had walking. And, by opening up more land for development, the cost of housing decreased. Before World War II, though, most working and middle class Americans still walked to work or took the trolley. The more distant suburbs, opened up by trolleys and especially commuter railroads and automobiles, remained the exclusive domain of the upper-middle and upper class—those that could afford the additional commuter costs and had more time to travel to work, or who did not have to "punch a clock" and show up for work at a specific time every day. With the expansion of residences came the growth of the city itself. Many cities rapidly expanded their political boundaries and with them, much needed services, into outlying districts.

1910s • City Services ~ In an effort to support the unprecedented numbers of urban and suburban residents, local governments were forced to expand the services they provided. Again, though these processes began in the nineteenth century, cities in the Progressive era were forced to increase and improve various city services. Cities had to provide a wide and increasing assortment of services: fire and police protection, education, adequate and clean drinking water, garbage disposal, creation and maintenance of sewage systems, open space management (Manhattan's Central Park being most famous), street construction, lighting, maintenance, and cleaning. These functions came to be seen as the appropriate domain of local governments in order to protect the public health of its citizens.

1920s • Zoning Restrictions ~ One important part of this increase in government power that deserves special mention was the development of zoning practices. Increasingly, local governments had the power to restrict the uses to which property owners could put their land (upheld by the U.S. Supreme Court in *Euclid, Ohio v. Ambler Realty Co.* in 1926). For instance, a city could forbid the operation of a slaughterhouse, factory, or horse stable from particular parts of the city because these businesses were seen as unattractive to neighbors.

This power could also be used for less benevolent purposes. In subtle ways, poor people could be zoned out of a neighborhood by a zoning law that mandated a minimum lot size for a house, thus segregating an area by wealth. Or, as happened in San Francisco, a local ordinance forbade laundries in many neighborhoods; since Chinese people dominated the industry and lived in the same buildings as they worked, barring laundries essentially removed Chinese from many San Francisco neighborhoods. Similarly, private citizens could consciously segregate their own communities through the use of "restrictive covenants," which specifically denied certain groups, for example African Americans, Mexicans, and Jews, the right to buy a home—even if they could afford it. The U.S. Supreme Court would not strike down these covenants until 1948 in *Shelley v. Kraemer*.

1895-1915 • Political Machines ~ With the expansion of urban populations and services came the transformation of the city governments themselves. Once again, beginning in the nineteenth century but perfected in many places in the twentieth century, many cities came to be controlled by political "machines." In the nineteenth century and before, local governments were fragmented and weak. However, in the Gilded Age new types of political leaders emerged, career politicians whose power was based upon party organizations and partisan loyalties.

These new machines' power absolutely depended upon getting loyal residents of their local wards out to vote for the political party already in power (machines could be either Democratic or Republican, with similar results). As the majority of urban citizens were immigrants or children of immigrants, and adult men, either naturalized or born in America, they had the right to vote. These "new" immigrants found themselves with significant power to affect local elections if they voted as a bloc along ethnic lines, which they usually did. These new machine politicians came from the same working-class, white, ethnic neighborhoods as their constituents. In exchange for votes, machine politicians delivered favors, patronage jobs, and/or needed city services to their constituents. To ensure their own power, which was both political and economic—much money could be made in distribution of road building contracts, for instance, machine politicians also resorted to illegal means, such as ballot box stuffing, bribery, and physical intimidation of opponents and voters.

Thus, local urban politics across the nation developed into "machines" or "organizations," usually dominated by a single ethnic group, often, but not limited to, Irish Americans. Machines flourished because they successfully bartered among cities' diverse groups by centralizing power and material resources and then distributing them on local/ward levels.

In the Progressive era, machine politics came under increasing attack, especially from reformers. Machines were accused of being fronts for organized crime and machine bosses as anti-democratic despots. These critiques were true but only partially, as many machines were, in fact, legitimate political coalitions of different ethnicities/wards.

However, not all ethnic groups in the city were equally represented by the machine. Most notably under-represented were African Americans (although there were exceptions, as in Chicago). As women became more active in local politics as "municipal housekeepers," especially those involved in the burgeoning Progressive settlement house movement, machines were accused of hurting the very people whom they claimed they represented—the working class white ethnics of the city. Truly, most people who supported the machine did not get a job with the city and did live in neighborhoods that lacked needed city services, while wealthier parts of the city received cleaner water, better and more paved streets, and better schools.

1920s • Emergence of the Metropolis ~ 1920 marked a milestone in American history. The federal census revealed that, for the first time, a majority of America's population resided in cities. Of course, some states, especially those in New England, had been urban for decades, while others (in the Mountain West and West) remained predominantly rural. This process was a long time in developing, although the industrial growth of the World War I era and agricultural depression of the post-World War I era were immediate causes. What was different about urban growth from 1915 forward was that it would not be fueled by immigrants (who had stopped coming during the war and were, essentially, denied further access as a result of immigration restrictions passed by Congress in 1924). Rather, increases in city and suburban populations could be attributed to native-born rural Americans (black and white) migrating in ever-larger numbers.

The one exception to the falling numbers of immigrants were Mexicans, who became the leading immigrant group in the 1920s and beyond; most Mexicans joined the already existing, and quite established, Mexican American communities (barrios) in Southwestern cities such as El Paso, San Antonio, Tucson, and Los Angeles, although some made their way to the industrial cities of the Midwest. The plunging of the nation's economy into the Great Depression in the 1930s accelerated this trend from rural to urban, as dropping crop prices and drought led to farm foreclosures. The music of Woody Guthrie defined this movement in songs such as "Do-re-mi," which described the hostility that rural migrants, all derogatorily called "Okies," faced when they tried to moved to the golden city of Los Angeles in the 1930s.

1920s • Los Angeles: The First Twentieth Century City ~ The growth of Los Angeles is worth examining, as its trajectory often predicts the path of other American metropolises. Whereas the large eastern and midwestern cities were mostly products of earlier eras, Los Angeles is truly a twentieth-century metropolis. No American city's development is more closely linked to the automobile than Los Angeles, although other cities increasingly saw their growth shaped by the car, too.

In the 1920s, the population of Los Angeles more than doubled to 1,200,000, while cars increased fivefold to almost 800,000. In the 1920s the business and political elite in Los Angeles made a fateful decision: rather than copying the models of New York City or Philadelphia or

(1914) Mr. Bert Dingley driving a car along a section of the immense aqueduct of Los Angeles in California.

Chicago and investing in a mass transit system of trolleys, Los Angeles would commit itself completely to private cars for all of its transportation needs. Following the successful suburban parkway models pioneered in the New York City suburbs of Westchester County and Long Island, Los Angeles began building its fabled freeway system. Appropriately, the Arroyo Seco Freeway (now Pasadena Freeway) connected Los Angeles' central business district with the outer edges of the city and beyond to the (then) sparsely populated "suburbs" of the San Fernando Valley, which technically are part of the city but truly define suburban living.

Spreading to the Desert

Thus, Los Angeles embarked on a journey to become a centerless city. Los Angeles' downtown became increasingly irrelevant as the population spread out into the cheap, arid desert lands of southern California. In response to suburban growth, the city of Los Angeles annexed lands whenever possible; in the case of the San Fernando Valley, Los Angeles annexed the land and then acquired the requisite water supply which would facilitate expansion. Just as with Philadelphia, Cleveland, and most other American cities, the key to survival for the city of Los Angeles was to continue to expand its boundaries to recapture people who moved to its periphery. But one of the important changes as the twentieth-century progressed in Los Angeles and elsewhere was that suburbs increasingly were able to resist annexation and maintain independent political status.

So, Los Angeles and then other cities became more, ultimately almost totally, dependent on the automobile. Both on roads and in ever growing parking lots, citizens and planners simultaneously discovered that unlike mass transit (trolley, trains, buses), cars require incredible amounts of space; that is, as car use increases so does decentralization of communities. Another of the important results of the conscious decision of Los Angeles' leaders to deviate from the "normal" path of urban development, ostensibly to prevent overcrowding in the urban core, was the traffic jam. Thus, the Los Angeles experience of the 1920s and 1930s foreshadowed much of the rest of the country's post-World War II building boom and subsequent sprawl.

1920-1940 • Los Angeles' Environmental Problems ~ In yet another way did Los Angeles' rapid development in the interwar period reveal some of the integral issues of twentieth century urban development—the effects of metropolitan growth on the environment, especially water. The central fact that all humans must face both in Los Angeles and throughout the American southwest is that water is a scarce commodity. As hundreds of thousands and later millions of people moved to arid southern California, new sources of water had to be found. Since none existed nearby, the city and county of Los Angeles first started tapping into the Owens River of southeastern California, 220 miles to the north and east of Los Angeles, and later the Colorado River as well as the plentiful waters of northern California.

Again, the lack of a tradition of long-term planning would result in dramatic clashes between rural and urban Americans, as well as the depletion and degradation of finite resources. The city of Los Angeles rolled over the small farmers of the Owens River Valley and literally sucked it dry, just as the growing population of the San Francisco Bay area would force the damming of wild Tuolumne River and the flooding of the renowned Hetch Hetchy Valley in Yosemite National Park. As with many such issues, America is still confronted with the crucial issue of growing population and consumption combined with dwindling natural resources, including water and power.

1920s • Urban Entertainment ~ The 1920s, characterized by economic prosperity for many, if not all (notably, farmers and blacks) allowed for a major boost in consumption, again centered in cities. Despite the beginnings of suburbanization in this era, cities remained the centers of culture and leisure activities for most Americans. Every city had a main department store located "downtown," in the central business district, that had become a "palace of consumption," celebrating the new and varied products created by industrialization. Department stores such as Macy's and Bloomingdale's in New York, Marshall Field's in Chicago, Wanamaker's in Philadelphia, and Hudson's in Detroit, consolidated, under one roof, most of the items American consumers needed—and many they did not. This era also saw the creation of the first suburban shopping center in Kansas City's swank Country Club district as well as the rise of chain stores such as Woolworth's and A & P.

The 1920s witnessed a massive increase in attendance at spectator sports such as baseball (300,000 attended the "subway series" between the New York Yankees and the Giants in 1923) and boxing (the first Jack Dempsey-Gene Tunney fight in 1926 was watched by 130,000 in Philadelphia). Musicals, comedies, cabarets, vaudeville shows, and nightclubs were packed with audiences, including wealthy whites who went "slumming" in the jazz clubs of black-dominated Harlem. Most notably, the twenties saw an explosion in attendance at the movies, even before the first "talkie," *The Jazz Singer* (1927). In the average week in the late 1920s, more than 110 million movie tickets were sold.

1920s • The Booming Suburbs ~ Nothing was more important to the transformation of the city into the metropolis (city ringed by suburbs) than the automobile. In the 1920s the number of registered automobiles exploded from eight million to twenty-three million. Simply put, what cars did was allow Americans to live further from their workplaces. With the flexibility, independence and speed offered by cars (sometimes called "automobility" in the 1920s), Americans who could afford a car—and increasingly, thanks to the Ford Model T, they could—also could buy their own home. An enormous amount of land, mostly farmland, was available for purchase at much cheaper prices than real estate within the urban core. This cheap land, combined with affordable automobiles allowed middle and upper class white Americans who desired it, the ability to own a detached home surrounded by a grass lawn in the suburbs.

There were various reasons for wanting to move: home ownership and greater privacy in a semi-rural setting, leaving behind the overcrowding and pollution of cities, as well as racism and fear of African American migrants and European immigrants. Thus, as fast as cities grew, suburbs grew even faster. For instance, the suburbs of Cleveland, Chicago, and Los Angeles all grew by more than 500 percent in the 1920s.

(circa 1900) The Bowery, an Eastside thoroughfare in New York, haunt of tough guys and thugs.

1930s

1930s • Urban Poverty ~ Further incentives for white Americans to move to the suburbs came, from the 1930s onward, from the federal government. One of the most dramatic and long-lasting changes wrought by the Great Depression was the increasing presence of the federal government in the lives of Americans. Just as the economic prosperity of the 1920s was most visible in cities, so too it was with the Great Depression, the worst economic downturn in U.S. history; the largest concentration of poverty existed in America's cities. The massive unemployment (at its worst, upwards of twenty million were without any work) and underemployment caused many Americans to lose their homes or be evicted from their apartments.

Before the 1930s, responsibility for helping the poor, hungry, unemployed, and homeless rested with private charities and local governments. However, these public and private agencies were overwhelmed by the many millions of Americans in need during the Depression. In particular, cities were caught in the financial trap of needing to dramatically increase expenditures at the same moment that revenues plummeted due to massive property tax delinquency. Quickly, Americans, mostly in cities, organized in order to demand federal relief; for instance, on March 6, 1930, hundreds of thousands of urban Americans coordinated their protests. As a result of this pressure, more than twenty mayors met in Detroit and formed the U.S. Conference of Mayors, which also called for federal public works projects to hire the unemployed. However, these efforts met with little success during the administration of Republican President Herbert

Hoover. With the election of Franklin D. Roosevelt in 1932, though, the Democratic president ushered in a "New Deal," that embraced federal involvement in the economy and society to uplift those suffering.

1932-1936 • New Deal Assistance ~ Of course, the New Deal encompassed many programs, but there was a tremendous focus on helping out in the places most in need, the cities. Many of the new public works projects—including roads, bridges, airports, schools, libraries, post offices, stadiums, parks, swimming pools, sewer lines, and water supply and treatment systems—were built in urban areas. The U.S. Council of Mayors, led by New York City's Fiorello La Guardia, lobbied strongly for programs and had significant influence in FDR's Washington, D.C. The ornate marble post office in Oak Park, Illinois (just outside of Chicago), the building housing the teacher education program at Western Illinois University in tiny Macomb, Illinois, and the major bridge crossing the Boise River in Boise, Idaho all were New Deal public works projects.

1930s • Depression Era Urban Housing ~ Yet perhaps the single most important way in which the federal government became involved in cities was through its housing policies. In the early 1930s, between one-third and one-half of all Americans lived in substandard housing. Millions of Americans faced evictions from their homes and apartments for failure to pay their mortgages and rents. Local communities organized themselves into tenant unions in order to protect themselves from evictions, but these efforts were insufficient, so federal involvement was necessary.

The New Deal attempted to stabilize financial conditions for both homeowners and mortgage lenders as well as build more housing for the poor, while simultaneously employing hundreds of thousands of unemployed construction workers. These programs made possible a new and much larger wave of suburbanization after World War II and brought the federal government directly into urban housing issues.

1932-1936 • Federal Assistance to Homeowners ~ The Home Owners Loan Corporation (HOLC) was created to bail out home owners who were at risk of defaulting on their mortgages, thereby stabilizing the home mortgage market in metropolitan areas (rural and farm mortgages were dealt with in a separate agency). The HOLC refinanced private loans with government money at the very reasonable rate of five percent annual interest, which the borrower did not have to repay for fifteen years. This refinancing allowed homeowners to escape foreclosure, pay taxes, and make needed repairs. The HOLC did not pay anyone's loans—the same amount of debt still existed—but it did save millions of Americans from defaulting on their loans. From 1933 to 1936 alone, the HOLC granted more than three billion dollars in loans (to fully 20 percent of the non-farm households in the nation) and controlled almost 20 percent of all urban home mortgage debt.

Cheap Loans for Middle-class Whites

Along with its companion program, the Federal Housing Authority (FHA), insured loans made by private lenders to families who wanted to buy or renovate homes. Thus, by guaranteeing that private lenders would be repaid, the FHA contributed to a major lowering of interest rates (to as low as 4 percent annually) as well as the stretching out of loans over a twenty-five to thirty year period (full amortization)—compared to previous interest rates of 6-12 percent that had to be refinanced (with no guarantees) over a five to seven year period.

In particular, this housing boom would be focused in suburbs because the programs were designed for new, low-density, detached, owner-occupied, single-family housing at the exclusion of all other types of dwellings on the periphery and discouraged renovating or filling-in housing in the urban core. Thus, the federal government encouraged the further decay of urban neighborhoods and decentralization on the fringe by making it easier and cheaper to buy new houses in the suburbs than to build or rebuild houses or apartments in cities. These programs led to an explosion in the housing market after World War II, when American families had much more income than they did during the Depression.

1930s • Government Programs Increase Segregation ~ Furthermore, the HOLC and FHA significantly contributed to heightened residential segregation. The maps generated by HOLC officials designated four types of neighborhoods, with non-white and/or ethnically diverse communities as well as older housing stock rated the worst, represented by the color red. The FHA and private lenders, who had easy access to the HOLC maps, refused to grant or

(1937) D.C. A slum in the shadow of the Capitol building in Washington, D.C. Throughout American history, local governments generally ignored the poor and their neighborhoods, which receive much lower levels of government-funded maintenance. As seen here, even the nation's capitol has its ghetto problems.

guarantee loans to lower rated neighborhoods. Called "redlining" by lenders, the federal government first devalued all non-white neighborhoods and then it refused and/or encouraged private lenders to refuse to grant loans in these communities, which might have resulted in ethnically mixed urban areas. Plus, these programs provided monies for white families to move out of diverse areas provided they moved into all-white ones. So, while non-white and poor white families were denied access by the federal government to the opportunities to buy single-family homes in the suburbs, middle and upper class whites received billions of dollars in subsidies to do just that. Hence, urban areas became increasingly poor and non-white, while suburbs became more affluent and exclusively white.

1930s • Clearing the Slums ~ For the one-third of Americans who suffered the most during the depression, the federal government created a separate program that would begin the noble but decidedly mixed chapter of urban public housing. Throughout American history, local governments generally had ignored the poor, as had their neighborhoods which received much lower levels of government-funded maintenance. With the New Deal came a new federal commitment to fight poverty, armed with the theory that investments made in the present saved money in the long run (just as by helping home owners avoid foreclosure, society would be stronger). One of the first programs created was to clear substandard slum housing and rebuild low-cost modern housing.

However, once slums were cleared, public housing immediately found opposition from the construction industry, which feared direct competition from the federal government, as well as more conservative citizens and politicians, who equated government housing with socialism—even though these same politicians, industries, and citizens seemed to have little problem with accepting massive federal assistance for their own needs (e.g. FHA and HOLC). Eventually, the U.S. Housing Authority was created to build tens of thousands of units for low-income Americans, but the demand far outstripped the number built.

Finally, the New Deal more closely tied cities to the federal government. Considering that two-thirds of the nation's population and wealth was in urban areas, it made sense for the federal government to pay greater attention to urban needs, eventually leading to the creation of the federal Housing and Urban Development agency. To date, cities still receive billions less from the federal government than they pay in taxes.

1946-1955 • Post World War II Suburbia ~ In the aftermath of World War II, cities—the dominant mode of living for two generations—entered a period of decline, as suburbs arose. During the war, the economy finally pulled out of the Great Depression and started to expand—thanks to a truly massive infusion of federal monies for fighting the war. The Keynesian fiscal policies of the New Deal had been correct: what the American economy needed to end the Depression was massive federal spending, but in the 1930s the billions spent were insufficient.

By contrast, spending in World War II was on the order of hundreds of billions of dollars. During the war, all energies were focused upon the war effort, thus, housing starts were restricted by the federal government, and a major housing shortage became a reality. Finally, after fifteen years of economic austerity due to economic depression and war, Americans finally had both the desire and the means to invest in housing. The late 1940s and 1950s witnessed the largest housing boom in American history, with over fifteen million new houses built.

1950s • Housing for the Baby Boom ~ Almost all of these homes were built in suburbs and allowed Americans to live out the ever-more popular ideal that suburbs could serve as sanctuaries from dangerous cities. A great many of these new homes were suburbs modeled along Levittown, New York. Located twenty-five miles outside of New York City on Long Island, Levittown (named after the developer) applied mass production techniques to house construction in order to build enormous numbers of homes at cheap prices and record speeds. Eventually, 17,000 nearly-identical Cape Cod style homes were built in the space of a few years, sold mostly to young, white, married couples looking to start families—part of the famous Baby Boom generation.

1950 • Subsidizing the Suburbs ~ As had been the case in the 1920s, America's celebrated love affair with the automobile made suburbs increasingly accessible to middle class and working class (especially unionized) white Americans. With a personal automobile, more and cheaper land for development was opened up for Americans, meaning they could move further away from their jobs. In several ways, the federal government facilitated this trend. First, home owners were entitled to deduct the interest payments on home mortgages from their personal income taxes, which essentially translates into a fifty billion dollar a year subsidy for those who can afford to buy a home; by contrast, renters, who are generally poorer and younger, do not receive any tax break for their housing expenses.

Ten Largest Cities in 1950

City—1950	Total Population	Native-born Population	Foreign-born population	Percent Foreign-born
New York City	7,887,380	6,026,450	1,860,930	23.6
Chicago	3,611,580	3,078,610	532,970	14.8
Philadelphia	2,068,095	1,830,300	237,795	11.5
Los Angeles	1,965,150	1,702,210	262,940	13.4
Detroit	1,846,660	1,568,400	278,260	15.1
Baltimore	945,940	893,295	52,645	5.6
Cleveland	912,840	779,960	132,880	14.6
St. Louis	853,490	811,435	42,055	4.9
Washington, DC	800,830	758,090	42,740	5.3
Boston	800,590	651,590	149,000	18.6

SOURCE: U.S. Bureau of the Census

Second, the Interstate Highway Act of 1956 provided tens of billions of dollars of federal money to build a network of highways that, although ostensibly built for Cold War purposes, also allowed Americans to live much further from their jobs. Later, the federal Department of Transportation, with the eager assistance of local and state governments, built dozens of "beltways," highways that circled cities. The beltways allowed suburbanites to live and increasingly work nearby but always outside of inner cities, further diminishing the economic prosperity of urban cores by drawing retail and manufacturing businesses away from the center. These same policies also contributed to the shifting of America's population into the Sunbelt centers in the Southeast and Southwest.

1950s • Segregation ~ While suburbs did provide opportunities for many Americans finally to own their own homes, suburbs also further heightened ongoing divisions in American society. Suburbs contributed to increasing segregation in America. The most apparent form of segregation was racial; African Americans and other non-white Americans found themselves concentrated in inner cities, as white Americans "fled" to the suburbs. The programs established in the 1930s under the HOLC and FHA were extended by the Veterans' Administration, through the popular "GI Bill," that provided home loan guarantees to millions of white veterans of World War II and the Korean War while denying non-white veterans.

These federal programs followed in the footsteps of the real estate and banking industries who traditionally had denied non-white Americans the opportunity to buy houses and apartments in white areas. As a result of public and private racism, even Jackie Robinson, who famously had desegregated major league baseball in 1947 by joining the Brooklyn Dodgers (actually named after someone who avoids an oncoming trolley), could not buy a house in Levittown, or any other suburb for that matter.

1950s • Confinement of Housewives ~ But residential segregation was not only confined to race. In keeping with the gender divisions of America, male breadwinners generally took the "family car" (most American families did not have two automobiles until after 1970), thereby leaving wives in the suburbs, often far removed from their extended families. Housewives, the ideal that all American women supposedly were to aspire to, felt increasingly isolated, as documented so vividly in Betty Friedan's groundbreaking 1963 book *The Feminine*

(1950) American steelworker Charlie Grapentine drives his Dodge car to work. He earns $320 per month for a 40 hour week at the United States Steel Corporation works in Youngstown, Ohio. His salary supports his wife Josephine and their two children Charles and Nancy.

Mystique; Friedan, herself a college-educated suburban housewife, diagnosed "the problem with no name," the alienation felt by many suburban housewives.

Unlike urban or rural communities, suburbs were more homogeneous along not only ethnic and racial but also age and socio-economic status. Despite these problems, though, more and more white Americans (as well as a small but growing number of middle class non-whites) would continue to move to suburbs.

Urban Decline and Renewal

1940s-1960s • Minority Majorities Populate Cities ~ Not entirely coincidentally, at the same moment that millions of white working and middle-class Americans found new opportunities to move to the suburbs, millions of African Americans and Latin Americans (especially from Mexico) found their way into cities. African Americans, Latinos, and working-class whites from the South and Appalachia moved to cities because they offered economic opportunities. During World War II alone, more than one million African Americans moved to cities for war work. As mechanization reached the cotton industry, four million more blacks (and millions of whites) would leave the Southern countryside. Chicago's black population went from 8 percent to 23 percent from 1940 to 1960. Cleveland and St. Louis became one-third black. Washington, D.C., the nation's capital, became the first major American city with a black majority; Detroit and Newark followed close behind.

In addition, Mexican Americans (Chicanos) had been a majority in El Paso, Texas since the 1930s, and San Antonio, Tucson, San Diego, and Los Angeles all experienced skyrocketing Chicano populations. New York City saw growing numbers of Puerto Ricans and Miami would, from the 1960s forward, see its Cuban and other Latino populations soar. After immigration policies were eased under President Lyndon Baines Johnson, Asians increased significantly in West Coast cities such as Seattle, San Francisco, and Los Angeles.

White Urban Residents

The only white urban residents who remained in cities were the elderly, poor, and Catholics who remained committed to their local parishes, while white Protestants took their churches with them to the suburbs. These "white ethnics," named so because most of them were second or third generation Catholics from southern and eastern Europe, were unwilling or unable to move to the suburbs. And they fiercely resisted the encroachment of African Americans out of the old "black ghettoes." Struggles over available housing escalated as anxiety in white communities rose to new heights at the fear of living in interracial neighborhoods. The rhetoric of World War II and economic prosperity heightened African American expectations for equality, better jobs, and improved housing, ultimately culminating in the modern civil rights movement. Meanwhile, remaining enclaves of white ethnics feared that their hard-won gains of home ownership and community stability were under attack.

1960s • Flight to the Sun Belt ~ But, at the same moment that large numbers of minorities found their ways to cities, well-paying industrial jobs were departing Northern and Midwestern cities for the anti-union policies and cheaper labor supplies of the rural Midwest, South, and Southwest and later, Mexico, Central America, and Asia. Thus, the opportunities that working class whites and non-whites hoped to find in northern and mid-western cities in the 1950s and 1960s were fast disappearing. In short, blacks and Hispanics unfortunately moved to cities just when these places were losing millions of jobs.

1960s • Urban Renewal ~ In the midst of these dramatic changes, cities tried to reshape themselves and called for "urban renewal." Part of these plans involved clearing "blighted" areas and replacing them with new housing, office buildings, retail complexes, and manufacturing. Coalitions of city and federal officials, downtown business leaders, and urban residents, attempted to stimulate downtown investment. Urban renewal aimed to end urban poverty, housing shortages, and downtown decline.

Perhaps the most important component of this renewal was a commitment to significantly increase the amount of federal-built public housing. As more middle and working class white Americans found homes in the suburbs, more poor and non-white Americans became dependent on federally built public housing. Although there was strong bipartisan support in Congress for public housing, a powerful coalition of conservative politicians, banking and real estate interests, and the U.S. Chamber of Commerce opposed any public housing.

In the issue of public housing, as with many others, race was an integral factor, too. Further, suburbanites fiercely resisted locating any public housing in suburbs, for fear of association with both black and poor people. So a number of compromises were made in order to have any housing constructed at all. First, the government subsidized private redevelopment of "blighted" (i.e. unprofitable) portions of inner cities. Then, opponents agreed to some housing but only if private interests could control the downtown redevelopment. Plus, all public housing had to be located in central cities; since real estate values were far higher in cities, housing authorities were forced to build high-rise apartment houses. The end result were very densely-populated poor and almost exclusively non-white public housing projects located in inner cities, which contributed to the stereotypes that white suburbanites already had about the cities they had left.

Generally speaking, these projects did not alleviate urban poverty, but they did benefit large downtown business developers. Over time, building enormous apartment complexes—rather than single-family homes or small apartments throughout metropolitan areas, including suburbs, concentrated poor people in residentially segregated inner-city neighborhoods and only intensified many of the problems.

1950s • Urban Renewal Fiasco ~ After World War II, as suburbanization exploded, cities tried to reshape themselves to prevent further decline. Often these efforts were called "urban renewal" and were intended to attack "urban blight," in particular by attempting to solve urban poverty, housing shortages, and downtown decline through stimulating downtown investment and building public housing. Major opposition came from conservatives in Congress (who limited appropriations) as well as a powerful coalition including the National Association of Real Estate Boards, U.S.

Chamber of Commerce, and U.S. Building and Loan League, all of whom opposed all public housing. Instead, these groups supported government subsidies of private redevelopment of "blighted" (unprofitable) portions of inner cities.

One of the more noteworthy failures of redevelopment plans came in Los Angeles in the 1950s. Mayor Fletcher Brown and the city council proposed building 10,000 units of public housing, one of the largest, at Chavez Ravine, a 315-acre parcel near downtown where many Chicanos and some Chinese people lived. The residents were moved out, their housing demolished and community destroyed to make way. Then, a powerful coalition of real estate agents, home builders, chamber of commerce, and the *Los Angeles Times* denounced the program as socialist (the 1950s being the height of the Cold War).

The mayor, backed by unions, the League of Women Voters, as well as religious, citizens, and veterans groups supported the project. The California Senate's Un-American Activities Committee investigated the California Housing Authority. As a result of the threat of an investigation, a majority of city council members switched their position. Ultimately, an anti-housing referenda won in the county, several lawsuits were filed, the mayor was voted out, and the housing plans were scrapped. Finally, the federal government resold the land to the city, which gave the land and two million dollars to Walter O'Malley, who built Dodgers Stadium on the site. In short, massive struggles occurred over public housing in this era and redevelopment generally failed.

1960s • Civil Rights in Cities ~ Cities often have been the sites of important social movements, none more dramatic than the modern civil rights movement of African Americans. In the spring of 1963, the push to desegregate the Jim Crow South again made national and international news. Birmingham, Alabama would be a test case for the strategy of nonviolent civil disobedience as practiced and preached by Dr. Martin Luther King, Jr. Civil rights activists chose Birmingham because it was the most segregated large city in America. Segregation was violently enforced, hence its nicknames, "Bombingham" and "America's Johannesburg." The most famous episode of violence occurred when four black girls were killed when the Sixteenth Street Baptist Church was bombed by white racists.

Using the Student Nonviolent Coordinating Committee (SNCC) model of organization, King's Southern Christian Leadership Conference (SCLC) and Birmingham blacks planned their strategy. Activists were determined to provoke a violent confrontation that would expose the extremism of southern white racism and force the nation to act. The movement counted on Police Chief Eugene "Bull" Connor to use violence and create a new crisis.

For sixty-five straight nights, mass meetings were held, often followed by marches downtown, where there would be police attacks and arrests. King and the Reverend Ralph Abernathy were arrested on Good Friday. It was after his arrest that King wrote his famous "Letter from Birmingham Jail" summing up his view of the struggle. King wrote of black frustration with white Americans, especially in liberal churches, who claimed they supported equality but opposed breaking (immoral) laws.

Thousands of students, some even from elementary schools, joined in the protests, along with hundreds of black industrial workers from the city's steel mills and coke factories. The Birmingham police used fire hoses, electric cattle prods, and police dogs to break up marches—all of which appeared in national and international print and television news stories.

The city's elite decided that segregation was too costly and agreed to desegregate municipal facilities and downtown businesses. Birmingham transformed the movement from simple desegregation to a mass movement demanding more thorough social and economic change. Plus Birmingham helped the movement reach out to Northern urban whites. Civil rights activists seized the moment and pointed out that racism was a nationwide problem. In San Francisco, New York, Detroit, and other cities hundreds of thousands of blacks and whites marched. Finally, President Kennedy was forced to respond and he proposed a comprehensive Civil Rights bill in June 1963.

(1967) Black Power. Many urban blacks, especially outside of the South, believed that the Civil Rights movement had not addressed their needs for better job prospects and housing, more political representation, and more respect from white-dominated police departments. Shown here, supporters of Adam Clayton Powell, the Harlem congressman who was denied his seat in the House of Representatives, demonstrate on the House of Representatives steps, shouting black power slogans.

1960s • Race Riots ~ Nothing better demonstrated the intense problems of urban America in the mid and late 1960s than the incredible wave of violence as several hundred cities exploded in rage. Civil unrest of this sort had not been seen in America since 1919, and just as with those eruptions, the riots can be attributed to serious economic and racial inequality. The first large conflagration began in the Watts section of Los Angeles in August 1964, when white police killed a black resident. A week of rioting in Watts occurred that left dozens dead, thousands arrested, and millions of dollars in property destroyed. Over the next four years, a series of enormous disturbances occurred in cities across the nation, including Detroit and Newark, that often are referred to as the "long, hot summers." Ironically, considering his well-known support for non-violence, the largest wave of riots was touched off by the murder of Dr. Martin Luther King, Jr. in April 1968. Why did these riots occur in the aftermath of successful political gains won in the Civil Rights Act of 1964 and Voting Rights Act of 1965? Many urban blacks, especially outside of the South, believed that the civil rights movement had not addressed their needs for better job prospects and housing, more political representation, and more respect from white-dominated police departments.

1970s • Bankrupt Cities ~ Undoubtedly, the ongoing rise of suburbs was linked to the decline and violence of central cities. Just as suburbs of cities such as Chicago, New York, Washington, St. Louis, and others were increasing by two and three hundred percent, central cities were losing population. The loss of tax base, jobs, and people led to the fiscal crises that many cities experienced in the 1970s; Cleveland and New York City faced bankruptcy. Although the suburbs' very existence depended upon their proximity to cities, America seemingly evolved two separate worlds: wealthy, white suburbs and poor, non-white cities. George Clinton, the leader of the 1970s funk music groups Parliament and Funkadelic, aptly described this phenomenon in his classic song, "Chocolate Cities (Vanilla Suburbs)."

1970s • School Segregation ~ One other issue worth highlighting is how the increasing racial divide between white suburbs and non-white cities affected public education. After the civil rights gains of the 1960s, the next struggle for equal rights focused on open housing (i.e. attacking residential segregation) and education. However, the failure to overturn the overt and subtle causes of residential segregation—best represented by the inability of Dr. King to prod white Chicagoans to integrate their neighborhoods in 1967—had profound effects on public schools.

Simply put, most American children attended schools in their own neighborhoods. Thus, the preservation of residential segregation guaranteed the maintenance of segregated schools, despite the fact that the famous *Brown v. Board of Education* (1954) decision specifically outlawed segregation in public schools as unconstitutional. However, when an increasingly conservative Supreme Court ruled in *Milliken v. Bradley* (1974) that Detroit, an overwhelmingly black city, could not bus black students to the mostly white suburbs, the court ensured that integrated schools could not become a reality. The failure to implement a metropolitan (urban-suburban) approach to education stood in stark contrast to existing metropolitan expenditures for transportation, parks and recreation, and water and sewage treatment.

The final chapter of the struggle for integrated schools, therefore, was fought between poor and working class urban whites who violently resisted busing poor and working class blacks within the city limits of Boston and New York City in the mid 1970s. That is, white parents fiercely resisted any effort to bus black students into all-white public schools.

1980s • New Urbanism ~ In response to the dramatic changes that occurred in the last half-century, groups of concerned citizens, urban planners, architects, government officials, and academics have attempted to make cities, once again, the center of American life. These people, sometimes referred to as new urbanists or advocates of "smart growth," are worried that ongoing suburbanization threatens American society. They have argued that increased dependence on automobiles and suburban sprawl has sacrificed too much quality of life for too many Americans.

In particular, new urbanism challenges the dramatic impact of cars on America. America makes up 5 percent of the world's population but uses 25 percent of the world's oil and produces more than 33 percent of the world's pollution. More than 80 percent of all trips that

Americans take from their homes are in cars, while in no other nation are more than 50 percent of its trips taken by car. The costs of driving in America amount to more than one trillion dollars annually. Cars have allowed Americans to spread out—to sprawl, as some would argue—so that the average American spends close to an hour each work day commuting, with significantly longer commutes in large metropolitan areas. Traffic congestion is expected to more than double within the next twenty years.

As decentralization continues, some suburbs have, in effect, become cities in themselves, in some cases larger than the original central cities; for example, the population of suburban Fairfax County, Virginia is almost double the population of Washington, D.C. In effect, metropolitan America in the twenty-first century probably will look like Los Angeles in the twentieth century.

Perhaps the greatest cost, though, is in lives as more than 50,000 Americans die annually in car accidents—roughly equal to the number of American soldiers killed in the entire Vietnam War. America's incredible wealth has created a nation of families who own their own homes and multiple cars but also has produced a numbingly homogeneous and sprawling lifestyle, which many find not livable.

Working Where You Live

To these critics, older cities and towns, built prior to America's total dependence on automobiles, offer insights into better ways to live. First and foremost, Americans should live closer to where they work, ideally close enough to walk or bike because driving, generally alone as most American commuters do, does not foster community. If people lived, shopped, prayed, and worked in the same communities, they would not be forced to use their cars so much. Plus, the many Americans who do not or cannot drive cars, such as the young, elderly, poor, and disabled would be able to live more full lives in more tight-knit communities.

1990s • Smart Growth ~ The theory behind promoting walking is that it contributes to better health and greater civic responsibility because people are more connected with each other. Another core value of new urbanism is diversity, broadly defined to include ethnicity and race, socio-economic class, age, and sexual orientation. Diversity actually increases the value, economic and otherwise, of a community. Everyone benefits, especially children, from living around people of different ages, backgrounds, and beliefs; in contrast, most suburbs are quite homogeneous, not just in terms of race but also wealth and age.

There are many ways that the built environment can influence how Americans live and the issues are quite complex, but encouraging a reassessment of how Americans live is fundamental to such a "smart growth" approach. Portland, Oregon often is pointed to as a model of how to discourage excessive decentralization by limiting growth on the periphery and focusing development in the core. More and more communities have become interested in "smart growth" and are looking to places like Portland to see how to contain sprawl. For instance, in the 2000 elections, more than one hundred communities had initiatives on the ballot to limit certain kinds of development to prevent sprawl.

Ten Largest Cities in 1990

City—1950	Total Population	Native-born Population	Foreign-born population	Percent Foreign-born
New York City	7,322,564	5,239,633	2,082,931	28.4
Los Angeles	3,485,398	2,148,733	1,336,665	38.4
Chicago	2,783,726	2,314,539	469,187	16.9
Houston	1,630,672	1,340,298	290,374	17.8
Philadelphia	1,585,577	1,480,763	104,814	6.6
San Diego	1,110,549	878,411	232,138	20.9
Detroit	1,027,974	993,484	34,490	3.4
Dallas	1,006,831	880,969	125,862	12.5
Phoenix	983,403	898,731	84,672	8.6
San Antonio	935,927	848,378	87,549	9.4

SOURCE: U.S. Bureau of the Census

2000 • Census ~ The 2000 census revealed that the largest cities grew nearly twice as fast in the 1990s as the 1980s, with three out of every four urban areas gaining population. Chicago grew by 112,000 and New York topped eight million for the first time in its history. But cities with a majority of minorities and poor, such as Philadelphia, Detroit, Cleveland, Pittsburgh, Hartford, Baltimore, and St. Louis, declined as jobs decreased and people migrated elsewhere. Cities with highly educated residents, such as the university cities of Madison, Wisconsin and Columbus, Ohio gained populations.

Although the population in some cities declined, the quality of inner city life improved. Downtown Cleveland, with its two new stadiums, Rock and Roll Hall of Fame, and chic restaurants in converted warehouses, is the symbol of revival. Crime rates plummeted in Cleveland, and on the edge of the Hough neighborhood where riots broke out in 1966, gentrification has occurred.

Parking and Traffic in the 21st Century Metropolis

Perhaps no issue galvanizes more people than that of parking and traffic; traffic has replaced the weather as the typical conversation of metropolitan Americans. The core of the problem is that the overwhelming majority of Americans are entirely dependent on their cars and trucks for transportation, so the results are not surprising. Traffic has become a painful fact of life. Drivers often spend long periods of time looking for a space and/or paying high fees to park in a garage. In fact, these issues are worsening. In large metropolitan areas, the average work commute takes the better part of an hour, as people increasingly measure travel in time rather than distance. And as more Americans buy sport utility vehicles and minivans, accidents—the inevitable result of more driving—are ever more frequent, deadly, and polluting, along with worsening public health problems and environmental destruction.

And what to do when you get to your destination? Cities founded prior to automobiles were not constructed to accommodate the huge amount of cars and trucks now driven. There is little possibility of creating large parking lots in urban cores where all of the land already has been developed; of course, this factor was one of the reasons suburbs grew in the first place. Further, as Americans in the 1990s have ignored the environmental consequences of their purchases (i.e. ignoring fuel efficiency) and bought ever larger vehicles, finding parking places is that much harder. Finally, suburbanites have become accustomed to free parking (even though it is not; the government allows businesses to deduct $1,000 from their corporate taxes for each parking space provided). Thus, the sight of people driving endlessly around neighborhoods looking for "free" parking spaces in order to avoid paying at a garage has become common.

Conclusion: Urban America in 2000

Truly, to understand American cities at the dawn of the twenty-first century, we must conceive of the city in the broader term of metropolis—for more Americans live in suburbs than in urban cores. In the span of just one hundred years, American cities have been transformed. In 1900 the U.S. population still lived, mostly, in rural areas. In the year 2000 more than 75 percent of all Americans live in metropolitan areas and two-thirds of these people live in suburbs; more than half of all Americans now live in suburbs. In the New York City metropolitan area, still the largest population center in the nation, 92 percent of the residents do not live in Manhattan. Incredibly, in every major metropolitan area in America, the majority of the population lives in the suburbs, not the actual city. Far more Americans live in areas that look like southern California than New York City. In fact, the twenty million people who live across southern California from Los Angeles to San Diego are, essentially, one "city" spread over thousands of square miles.

The American Revolution was fought based upon the Jeffersonian ideal of an agrarian, rural citizenry who were self-sufficient, which required a nation of family farmers. But between the end of the American Revolution and the turn of the century, cities began to swell so that by 1800 Philadelphia was the largest city, with a population of 100,000. Jefferson's idyllic vision was soon to vanish as the first wave of immigrants flooded the cities to serve the demands of the Industrial Revolution.

(circa 1930) High-angle view of Public Square at Euclid Avenue and the Soldiers and Sailors Monument in Cleveland, Ohio. Pedestrians, automobiles, trolley cars and streetcars are visible.

Bibliography

Chudacoff, Howard P. and Judith E. Smith. *The Evolution of American Urban Society*, 3rd ed. Englewood Cliffs, NJ: Prentice Hall, 1988.

Garreau, Joel. *Edge City: Life on the New Frontier*. New York: Anchor Books, 1992.

Hirsch, Arnold R. *Mata'ng the Second Ghetto: Race & Housing in Chicago 1940-1960*, with a new forward. Chicago: University of Chicago Press, 1998.

Jackson, Kenneth. *Crabgrass Frontier: The Suburbanization of the United States*. New York: Oxford University Press, 1985.

Kunstler, James Howard. "Home From Nowhere," *Atlantic Monthly* (September 1996): 43-66.

Langdon, Philip. *A Better Place to Live: Reshaping the American Suburb*. New York: HarperPerennial, 1995.

Mumford, Lewis. *The City in History: Its Origins, Its Transformations, and Its Prospects*. San Diego: Harvest/HBJ, 1961.

Orfield, Gary and Susan E. Eaton. *Dismantling Desegregation: The Quiet Reversal of Brown v. Board of Education*. New York: The New Press, 1996.

Peiss, Kathy. *Cheap Amusements: Worta'ng Women and Leisure in Turn-of-the-Century* New York. Philadelphia: Temple University Press, 1986.

Sugrue, Thomas. *The Origins of the Urban Crisis: Race and Inequality in Postwar Detroit*. Princeton: Princeton University Press, 1996.

Internet Resources

Cities and Urban Geography
Discover the fascinating subject of urban geography and learn all about the cities of the world and their development, growth, and distribution.
http://geography.about.com/cs/citiesurbangeo/index.htm

Cities, Urban Geography, & Transportation Geography
Urban and transportation geography examine the places we live, how we move ourselves and our goods, the structure of our cities, and the pattern of cities on the landscape.
http://geography.about.com/cs/citiestransport/index.htm

Largest Cities Through History
The largest city of the world throughout the last five thousand years.
http://geography.about.com/library/weekly/aa011201a.htm

The National League of Cities
http://www.nlc.org/

Sister Cities International
Nonprofit citizen diplomacy network posts a directory of sister cities throughout the world.
http://www.sister-cities.org/

U.S. Department of Energy - Clean Cities
Initiative of this federal agency looks at ways to promote use of electric cars and other forms of transportation that produce less pollution.
http://www.ccities.doe.gov/

Many larger cities have websites about their history and current profile. The following are examples.

A history of Kansas City
http://www.sky.net/~bfinch/webpage2.htm

A history of Pittsburgh
http://www.library.cmu.edu/SAA-PghHostCmte/articles/PittsburghHistory.html

On line documentary film about New York City's History
http://www.pbs.org/wnet/newyork/

A history and cultural explanation of New Orleans
http://www.yatcom.com/neworl/vno.html

A history of Indianapolis
http://www.indy.org/history.htm

Peter Cole
Western Illinois University

CRIME AND JUSTICE

(circa 1910) An aerial view of Sing Sing Prison, near New York.

TIMELINE

1810-1899 ~ State Jurisdiction of Justice

New Orleans forms police force to control slavery (early 1800s) / Boston (1838) and New York (1844) form police departments / Michigan abolishes capital punishment (1847) / States enact statutory rape laws (1890s) / First federal prison (1891) / Scotland Yard demonstrates fingerprinting at the St. Louis Worlds Fair (1904) / Labor violence (1877-1907)

MILESTONES: Oregon is established as a white homeland, forcing blacks to leave (1844) • Fugitive Slave Law requires whites to return runaway slaves (1850) • Women in Montana gain the right to sue, enter into contracts, and serve on juries (1870) • Fifteenth Amendment declares all men eligible to vote without regard to color (1870) • Sioux Indians slaughter Custer's men at Little Bighorn (1876)

1900-1919 ~ Federalizing Crime

Nine states abolish or sharply limited the death penalty (1907-1917) / Federal Bureau of Investigation established (1908) / Photos used to catch speeders in N.Y. City (1909) / Mann Act makes it a federal crime to transport women across state lines for immoral purposes (1911) / Ku Klux Klan revives (1915) / Child labor abuse made a federal crime (1916) / Espionage Act prohibits criticizing the government (1917) / Car theft made a federal crime (1919)

MILESTONES: Mexicans strike against the Pacific Electric Railway company for equal wages and parity (1903) • Oregon hires the first policewoman in America (1905) • Pennsylvania establishes a highway patrol (1905) • Race riots erupt in St. Louis (1917), Chicago (1919), and Tulsa, Oklahoma (1921) • Cincinnati police strike for better wages (1918) • Chicago Crime Commission formed to oversee police corruption (1919)

1920-1929 ~ Organized Crime and Prohibition

Cleveland establishes first police radio band (1920s) / Prohibition makes possession of alcohol a federal crime (1920) / Organized crime increases to meet the demand for illegal alcohol / Immigrants Sacco and Vanzetti convicted of robbery and murder but are really suspected of treason (1920) / First modern lie detector invented (1921) / Wickersham Commission investigates police work and crime (1929)

MILESTONES: Traffic signal technology developed by Garrett Morgan, an African American (1920s) • Hays Code restricts filmmakers from ridiculing the law (1920s) • KDKA in Pittsburgh, the first public radio station in the U.S., begins broadcasting on November 2, 1921 • Route 66 beginning in Chicago and ending in Santa Monica, CA is begun; by 1937 it is fully paved, crossing 8 states and 3 time zones (1926)

1930-1945 ~ Depression Era Crime

Police establish fingerprint data banks (1930s) / FBI arrests famous gangsters and solidifies its public image (1930s) / Organized crime reaches its pinnacle (1930-1932) / Lindbergh baby kidnapped (1932) / Supreme Court rules for due process in the Scottsboro Boys case (1932) / Prohibition repealed (1933) / J. Edgar Hoover becomes director of the F.B.I. (1933)

MILESTONES: Supreme Court rules that "malicious, scandalous, and defamatory" journalism can be suppressed (1931) • First FM stations licensed (1935) • First successful treatment of bacterial infection with sulfanilamide (1937) • Rise in the number of labor unions (1937) • French ship, *Normandie* burns in New York City harbor as it is being converted from a luxury liner to a U.S. troop carrier (1942) • Edward R. Murrow pioneers live war reportage (1943)

1946-1969 ~ Civil Rights and Civil Disobedience

Civil Rights Act protects voters against violence (1957) / Civil Rights Act makes it a federal crime to transport explosives across state lines (1960) / Supreme Court applies the Bill of Rights to the states (1960s) / Evidence seized in illegal searches cannot be used in state court trials (1961) / Model criminal code standardizes sentencing (1962) / Boston Strangler murders 13 women (1962-1964) / Supreme Court expands the availability of habeas corpus to state prisoners (1963) / Civil Rights Act rules that American citizens cannot be segregated in public accommodations (1964) / Suspects must be told they have a right to an attorney and the right to remain silent (1966)

MILESTONES: War crime trials for German and Japanese atrocities (1946-1949) • Rosa Parks arrested, starting the Bus Boycott in Montgomery, Alabama (1955) • Race riots occur throughout American cities (1960s) • FBI's authority dramatically expanded (1960s) • Assassinations of John F. Kennedy (1963), Martin Luther King, Jr. (1968), and Robert Kennedy (1968) • Militant Black Power movement begins (1966)

1970-2000 ~ Cracking Down on Crime

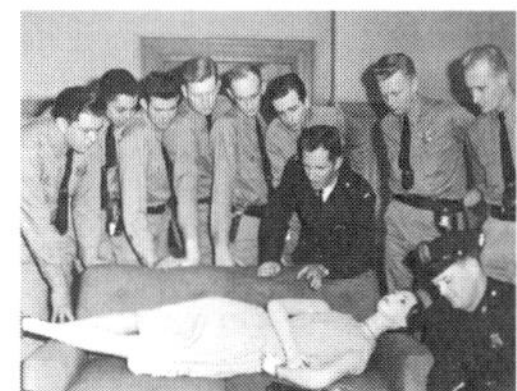

Renewed support for the death penalty (1970s) / Comprehensive Drug Abuse Prevention and Control Act cracks down on drug trafficking (1970) / District court ruling limits police use of force (1975) / Supreme Court limits strip searches (1979) / Hate crime legislation passed in every state (1980-1997) / Attempted assassination of President Reagan (1981) / Congress considers but rejects most gun control legislation (1985-2000) / Brady Bill passed for control of handguns (1994) / Rampage killing in schools (1990s)

MILESTONES: Four students killed by National Guard at Kent State University (1970) • Federal laws require use of safety belts (1971) • Supreme Court ruling protects advertising as free speech (1976) • War on drugs targets minorities (1980s) • Immigration Reform Act makes it illegal for employers to hire undocumented workers (1987) • Smoking banned on all U.S. domestic flights of less than 6 hours (1990)

INTRODUCTION

Society must punish crime and maintain order to protect itself and its citizens from violent predators. But law enforcement does more than merely punish the offenders. The public punishment of law violators is a process where all citizens work out what behavior society will not tolerate.

Fighting crime is politically popular. In the United States, where the power to punish crime is divided between the states and the federal government, political forces compete to control crime. Crime control in the twentieth century is essentially a story of increasing federal power. In 1900, Americans saw policing crime as almost exclusively a job for the states. Thereafter, improvements in transportation technology made it increasingly easier for law violators to operate across state lines. At the same time, national political leaders found it advantageous to position themselves as champions of law and order. By the close of the century, while the states continued to do most of the police work, Americans had become habituated to the notion that the federal government played a big role in crime control.

1850-1920

1850-1920 • LAW AND ORDER IN STATES AND COMMUNITIES ~ Through the nineteenth century, and into the twentieth, states and localities maintained order with little oversight from the federal government. They did so under a constitutional practice called the police power doctrine. Under this rule, the states, and not the federal government, had responsibility for looking after the health, welfare and the safety of their citizens.

Judges and lawyers understood that the Bill of Rights limited the federal government and not the states at all. Persons accused of crimes could expect no protections from the Bill of Rights in the United States Constitution. The states had a free hand to investigate and punish law violators as they wished. Police rounded up suspects on vague charges, often releasing them after a period of time in jail when they realized they had arrested the wrong persons. Police tortured suspects into confessing, calling their torture "the third degree." Legislatures passed laws allowing for "indeterminate sentencing," which gave local judges a free hand in punishing convicted defendants. State courts played fast and loose with defendants' due process rights. Convicted defendants sent to state prisons found overcrowded and filthy cells policed by sometimes sadistic guards. Prisoners in the South faced especially grim prospects, encountering the chain gang and racial barbarism.

1900-1920 • CRIME PREVENTION TECHNIQUES ~ The states improved their policing through the twentieth century. Cities began putting their police departments under civil service, which prevented politicians from simply rewarding valued constituents with police jobs. By 1915, 122 of the 204 largest police departments were under civil service. The technical art of crime detection became more professional as well. A detective from Scotland Yard demonstrated fingerprinting at the St. Louis World's Fair in 1904. Thereafter, St. Louis instituted the first fingerprint bureau in America. The University of California at Berkeley established the first academic law-enforcement program in 1916.

Despite these advances, persons charged with crimes in state courts still went through criminal justice systems that often showed a shocking disregard for due process. One study of wrongly convicted persons concluded that nearly one quarter of such cases resulted from "police error," usually coerced confessions. Almost as many false convictions came from overzealous prosecutors' misconduct.

1800s-1960 • Lynching ~ Throughout the nineteenth century American localities and neighborhoods tolerated and even promoted mob violence: the punishment of individuals by the community outside the law. Journalists most often associated this violence with the brutalization of African Americans by white southerners, but northerners and westerners engaged in extralegal community punishment of miscreants as well.

In the first decades of the twentieth century, white southerners justified this violence as made necessary by the tendency of black males to rape white women. Ida B. Wells, a black journalist, attacked this contention with statistics, showing that only a minority of whites' victims had even been accused of rape. Wells went on to argue that even when the mob did accuse their victims of rape, the charges could often be easily disproved.

This violence continued well into the twentieth century. The National Association for the Advancement of Colored People campaigned against lynching, urging Congress to pass a law against the practice. Congress never passed such a law, largely because southern congressmen mounted stubborn resistance. The Association of Southern Women for the Prevention of Lynching, led by Jessie Daniel Ames, also worked against lynching, as did the Tuskegee Institute in Alabama.

(1907) Vigilante Justice. The lynching of Louis Higgins in Texas. Throughout the nineteenth century American localities and neighborhoods tolerated and even promoted mob violence: the punishment of individuals by the community outside the law.

1800s-1960

After 1950 lynching faded as a daily or weekly occurrence, only to flare up again with well-publicized incidents that attracted national attention. In 1956, two or more Mississippi white men murdered Emmett Till after the youth allegedly whistled at a white woman. In 1959, Mississippi whites killed Mack Charles Parker after he raped a white woman. Members of the Alabama Ku Klux Klan hanged Michael Donald in 1981. Three white Texans dismembered James Byrd, Jr., in 1998 by dragging his still-living body behind their truck.

1877-1907 • Labor Violence ~ By the end of the nineteenth century labor strife had come to characterize American rioting. The most famous instance of this came in 1877 after railroad companies cut the wages of their employees. No union coordinated the workers' response. Instead, violence percolated up from the grassroots. Though not centrally organized, striking and violence spread like a contagion across the country. A mob seized control of Pittsburgh, destroying millions of dollars of railroad property. U.S. Army troops restored order. Violence erupted in Homestead, Pennsylvania when steel magnate Henry Clay Frick tried to break a union by locking out his employees. In 1894 Pullman train car workers confronted Illinois national guardsmen in a battle that killed 25 and paralyzed the railroads in 27 states.

Organizing in 1905, the Industrial Workers of the World or "Wobblies" tended to prompt violent reactions from authorities. Believing the Wobblies represented a foreign threat to the American way of life, one Arizona sheriff organized two thousand vigilantes to put down a copper miners' strike.

In 1905 a dynamite bomb took the life of former Idaho governor Frank Steunenberg. The Pinkerton Detective Agency investigated the case, dispatching its famed operative James McParland to Idaho. McParland extracted a confession from Harry Orchard, who implicated "Big Bill" Haywood of the Western Federation of Miners. As governor, Steunenberg had harshly suppressed a miners' strike six years before. Since Haywood was in Denver, Colorado, McParland kidnapped him, shipping him to Idaho in a special train. The Supreme Court found nothing to object to in McParland's methods. Haywood went on trial in 1907, defended by Clarence Darrow. A jury acquitted him.

1891-1919 • Federal Police Power ~ Even in the nineteenth century, the federal authority had some crime control responsibilities. Federal officers prosecuted counterfeiting, piracy, military crimes and treason. A sign that the federal government would go beyond those four categories came in 1891, when Congress authorized construction of the first federal prison. Another indication of intensified federal interest in crime control came when the Federal Bureau of Investigation began life as the Bureau of Investigation in 1908.

Congress began adding to its list of federal crimes early in the century. In 1911 Congress passed the so-called Mann Act or the White Slave Act, making it a federal crime to transport women across state lines for immoral purposes. In 1919 Congress made it a federal crime to steal a car and drive it across state lines. Congress passed laws designed to punish employers of child labor in 1916 and 1919.

1920 • Prohibition ~ In 1920, drinking alcohol became the most notorious federal crime. The prohibition amendment to the Constitution marked the triumph of a lengthy campaign against liquor by progressive reformers. At least in part, these reformers reacted to the industrial revolution of the late nineteenth century. Industrialization had made possible a mobility that freed individuals from constraints traditionally imposed by families and neighborhoods. With improved transportation, men could drift from community to community with none of the traditional restraints on their behavior imposed by watchful neighbors. The railroads allowed easier

(circa 1935) Bootleggers guarding their private beer brewing hide-out during prohibition.

access to the bar room and the brothel, attracting travelers and more permanently dislocated people. Venereal disease seemed to increase as a direct result. Reformers pressed for a constitutional amendment prohibiting liquor traffic as a way of guarding the family from the threat posed by industrialization.

Organized crime took advantage of the opportunities prohibition provided, but it is a myth to say that the Mafia began in the prohibition era. In Chicago, the crime family that Al Capone came to dominate had been active for a generation before prohibition took effect. Not unlike legitimate business, the crime business consolidated after the turn of the century, with power collected in fewer hands.

Nor is it true that efforts to enforce prohibition failed. It would be more accurate to say that no serious effort was made to enforce the new law. Congress appropriated only six million dollars to enforce liquor laws across the United States. Just eighteen agents tried to prevent illegal drinking in all of Oklahoma. The states proved no less miserly than Congress in appropriating adequate funds to enforce laws against alcohol. Some states, in fact, refused to spend any money at all to halt alcohol consumption.

By 1930, prohibition had become increasingly unpopular. Many conditions account for the public's change of attitude. In their campaign to bring it down, critics of prohibition successfully associated it with the rise of the Mafia. The movie industry and popular writers promoted a stylish devil-may-care attitude that included drinking. Stories of police on the take became legendary. For these reasons, the public turned against prohibition. They did not turn toward drinking, which continued at a lowered rate for some years even after prohibition came to an end.

In 1933, Congress proposed and the states ratified a new amendment to the Constitution, one that repealed the prohibition amendment.

1880-1920 • Outsiders as Criminals ~ Large-scale immigration changed popular conceptions of criminality. Twenty-two million immigrants came to America Between 1882 and 1930. This new wave of immigration included many Southern and Eastern Europeans, peoples who had played no significant role in earlier immigrations. These so-called new immigrants seemed to some to represent a criminal class and triggered anti-foreignism and fears that these strangers somehow threatened American values.

World War I seemed to legitimize such assaults on "radicals." The government promoted suspicion of outsiders as a way of fostering the unanimity President Woodrow Wilson thought necessary to win the war against Germany. Congress passed an espionage act in 1917 and enlarged it in 1918 to include anyone criticizing the government. In 1919 the Supreme Court endorsed this sedition law, finding that socialist Charles Schenck should be in prison for distributing antidraft circulars to men called to service. Oliver Wendell Holmes, Jr., wrote the opinion, finding that every act depends on its circumstances. Congress had a right to punish acts that posed a clear and present danger to the United States.

After the end of World War I, federal and state governments continued their campaigns against radicals, merely shifting their attention from Germans to Bolshevists. The Justice Department acted with local police departments to round up thousands of Communists and unionists across the country. Many states passed laws against "criminal syndicalism" so they could more easily arrest and jail Bolshevists and anarchists.

1915-1925 • The Ku Klux Klan ~ Originally organized after the Civil War, the Ku Klux Klan revived in 1915, its popularity accelerating rapidly in the 1920s, when it attracted three million members. While the 1920s Klan followed the post-Civil War Klan in its attacks on black people, the new Klan also went after violators of morality and immigrants, anyone not "100 percent American." The Klan whipped, tortured and, on occasion, murdered its victims. In Indiana, a Klan organization controlled by David C. Stephenson wielded powerful political influence. Observers compared the 1924 Republican state convention to a Klan rally, with Stephenson at the center of every important decision. Newspaper exposés of Klan crime brought that organization down in Indiana. Stephenson went to jail for kidnapping and abusing Madge Oberholzer, a minor state official. Humiliated by Stephenson's sexual abuse, Oberholzer took poison and died. From his prison cell, Stephenson threatened to embarrass Republican officials by releasing documents connecting them to the Klan. In 1927, Stephenson did release his documents, sparking a statewide scandal. The Indianapolis *Times* won a Pulitzer prize for its investigation of Republican state officials, some of whom joined Stephenson in prison.

Nationally, the Klan supported William McAdoo at the 1924 Democratic national convention. Only after 103 ballots did the Democrats nominate John W. Davis. The convention failed to pass a resolution denouncing the Klan, but came within one vote of doing so. The Klan had come to the convention confident no one would dare challenge their power; instead they had been forced into the open and into a bitter floor fight.

Women became a powerful force in the 1920s Klan, seeing in the Klan an opportunity to exercise political power. Women perceived the Klan as a vehicle to fight moral decay and defend their children, their families, and their homes from crime. Women sometimes directed male Klansmen to punish abusive or unfaithful husbands.

1920s-1930s • Famous Murder Trials ~ In this period, a series of sensational murder trials confirmed public prejudice against the foreign element, against "outsiders." In 1920, Massachusetts authorities convicted and executed Nicola Sacco and Bartolomeo Vanzetti for robbery and murder. Sacco and Vanzetti seemed all the more dangerous, and not fully American, for belonging to a group of Italian anarchists.

In Chicago, authorities tried to execute two teenagers, Nathan Leopold and Richard Loeb for the murder of another teenager, Bobby Franks. Though Leopold and Loeb were both Americans, the press pounced on the pair as Jewish, homosexual and rich. They were highly intelligent, perhaps even at the genius level, and yet strangely deficient morally. Clarence Darrow persuaded a judge to sentence the pair to life in prison rather than to death.

In 1932, the son of famed aviator Charles A. Lindbergh disappeared from his baby bed. Authorities in New Jersey

(1924) American criminals Nathan Leopold Jr. (left) and Richard Loeb sit together in an office. The two men were convicted for the kidnapping and murder of Loeb's cousin, 14-year-old Bobby Franks. They were sentenced to life in prison.

located the dead child in a shallow grave and then arrested and convicted a German immigrant named Bruno Hauptman for the crime. Hauptman had been caught with some of the ransom money. A wood expert testified at Hauptman's trial that the crude ladder used in the abduction had been constructed with wood that matched the wood in Hauptman's attic. New Jersey electrocuted Hauptman and Congress passed a federal law against kidnapping across state lines.

In the 1920s and early 1930s, American values and life seemed under attack by foreign influences. For many Americans, this criminal threat amounted to a terrible crime wave.

1917-1921 • Race Rioting ~ Americans have always rioted. Colonials took to the streets as communities in violence that tended to draw neighborhoods together, reinforcing insular feelings. In the nineteenth century, rioting became bloodier and more factionalized as ethnic groups began attacking each other within neighborhoods. Race characterizes twentieth century rioting, but race as an issue was hardly unknown in the nineteenth century. The 1863 New York City draft riot saw white rioters brutally attack blacks. At the end of World War I, dozens of race riots erupted. The most famous of these riots occurred in East St. Louis (July 1-2, 1917) and in Chicago (1919). In these tumults, police and militia sometimes joined the rioters in attacking blacks. In Chicago, thirty-one persons perished in rioting that lasted five days. Whites roamed black neighborhoods, killing at random, while blacks fired back. In Tulsa, Oklahoma, (May 30-June 2, 1921) whites rampaged through black neighborhoods with machine guns. According to some reports, the attacking whites even strafed blacks from an aircraft. Perhaps two hundred blacks died in the fighting, though the exact figure remains unknown.

1903-1945 • Federal Intervention and Due Process ~ Early in the twentieth century, the United States Supreme Court showed little interest in state criminal trials. In 1903, one justice even proposed doing away with criminal appeals altogether, to make the proceedings more "summary." He hoped to make lynch mobs less necessary by reducing legal "red tape."

Thus, when Georgia convicted Atlanta businessman Leo Frank for the murder of Mary Phagan, a crime he did not commit, the Supreme Court refused to set aside the verdict. In *Frank v. Mangum* (1915), the Court refused to act, even though the Georgia trial had taken place amid headlines screaming for Frank's scalp in a court room demonstrably hostile to the defendant. A Georgia mob kidnapped Frank from prison and hanged him from a tree.

When the Court decided not to intervene in the Leo Frank case, Oliver Wendell Holmes dissented, holding that mob law cannot become due process simply because a frightened jury delivers a verdict pleasing to the crowd outside court. Less than ten years after the Leo Frank case, the Court decided in favor of the due process standards Holmes had urged. Still on the Court, Holmes wrote for the majority in a landmark case, *Moore v. Dempsey* (1923) that established federal due process protections for defendants on trial in state courts.

This case arose out of rioting in Arkansas. The state courts had convicted five black men for murdering a white man in a mob-dominated trial. The Supreme Court ruled that state trials had to provide actual due process protections for defendants and not merely the forms of due process. The convictions were overturned and the era of untrammeled state autonomy in the field of criminal prosecutions came to an end.

In 1932, in its famous Scottsboro Boys case, the Supreme Court further hardened its insistence on true due process for defendants in state trials. This case, called *Powell v. Alabama*, arose in Scottsboro, Alabama, after two white women accused nine black males of rape. State authorities convened hasty trials and swiftly condemned the defendants to death. The Supreme Court found that the trial judge had allowed the defendants only a pretense of true representation. Due process required that they be represented by truly qualified lawyers and that those lawyers be allowed time to prepare a serious defense.

The Supreme Court's determination to protect black Americans from abuse by state authorities was not unwavering, however, In 1945, Claude Screws beat to death a black man in Baker County, Georgia. Screws was the county sheriff and federal officials indicted him in federal court for violating his victim's civil rights. The Supreme Court threw out the conviction on the grounds that prosecutors must prove that defendants in such cases really intended to violate their victims' civil rights. This proved a nearly impossible standard to meet and discouraged federal involvement in state abuses of blacks.

1962 • The Model Penal Code ~ There were efforts to standardize criminal law enforcement in the nineteenth century, most notably David Dudley Field's effort to codify the entire law of the United States. New western states and New York adopted Field's code. Nonetheless, well into the twentieth century, indeterminate sentencing laws resulted in a criminal law that was inconsistent and unfair.

In the 1930s, the American Law Institute approved preparation of a model criminal code. The Great Depression and World War II delayed the enterprise and the institute did not complete its model criminal code until 1962. Assisted by social scientists and legal scholars, the code sought to relate rules and principles to the nation's fundamental moral assumptions that persons convicted of similar crimes should received similar punishments. Within twenty years, two thirds of state legislatures had used the model penal code as the basis for rewriting their criminal codes, introducing greater uniformity in the punishment of criminals. This naturally resulted in a loss of autonomy for local judges as they sentenced convicted felons.

1960s • The Warren Court ~ In the last half of the twentieth century, the Supreme Court became far more attentive to defendants' due process rights. Under the leadership of Chief Justice Earl Warren, the Supreme Court in the 1960s applied the Bill of Rights to the states. Warren and his Court showed new interest in the rights of defendants on trial in state courts, striking down police procedures and state trial practices that had long been accepted.

In 1961 the Supreme Court applied the exclusionary rule to the states, finding that evidence seized by the police in illegal searches cannot be used in state court trials. Two years later, the Court instructed state courts that they must supply lawyers for indigent defendants. In

1966, the Supreme Court ruled that suspects must be told they have a right to an attorney and the right to remain silent during a police interrogation (the Miranda Warning). Warren wanted to end police officers' "third degree" tactics.

In 1963, the Supreme Court expanded the availability of habeas corpus to state prisoners. The federal writ of habeas corpus allowed prisoners to ask a federal court to review their state convictions, looking for due process errors.

1989-1996 • Reversing Some Warren Court Decisions ~ This innovation by the Warren Court did not prove irreversible. In 1989, the Supreme Court sharply limited the availability of federal habeas corpus relief, finding that federal review of state convictions must be based on standards established by the United States Constitution. In 1990, the Court went even further, finding that when state courts acted in good faith, even if they violated federal law, their convictions should not be reviewed through the habeas corpus procedure. In 1996, Congress reduced state prisoners' access to the writ of habeas corpus, passing the "Antiterrorism and Effective Death Penalty Act." Limiting the writ of habeas corpus had the effect of making it easier for the states to execute their prisoners.

1847-1960s • Death Penalty ~ Throughout the nineteenth century, critics increasingly called for an end to the death penalty. In 1847, Michigan abolished capital punishment after it became widely known that the state had executed an innocent man. When Michigan ended the death penalty, it became the first English-speaking jurisdiction in the world to do so. Thereafter Rhode Island halted executions (1852), as did Maine (1876). Between 1907 and 1917 nine more states abolished or sharply limited

SOURCE: *Statistical Abstract of the U.S.*, 2000.

the death penalty. World War I prompted a resurgence of popular support for capital punishment; perhaps the brutalities of trench warfare coarsened public opinion. Some critics pointed out that the states increased their executions at precisely the same time as mob violence declined. To some it seemed as though state governments had rushed in to substitute legal executions for the illegal kind. In the 1930s and 1940s more than one hundred prisoners were executed in the U.S. each year.

In the 1950s, public support for capital punishment declined and the numbers of executions decreased as well. Between 1965 and 1967, states executed only nine prisoners. When the Supreme Court deliberated the death penalty in 1972, there had been no executions since 1967.

1970-Present • Renewed Support for the Death Penalty ~ In the 1972 case the Supreme Court condemned the Georgia death penalty system as too arbitrary. Justice Potter Stewart called the sentences as random as lightening and a violation of the Constitution's prohibition of cruel and unusual punishments for being so arbitrary. Justice Byron White reported that he could not distinguish the circumstances that sent a few prisoners to death from the great mass of cases where the defendant did not get death. Only two of the justices thought the death penalty was inherently unconstitutional, William Brennan and Thurgood Marshall. Marshall asked what purpose the death penalty served other than satisfying a public bloodlust.

The Supreme Court acted at a time when popular support for the death penalty hovered around 50 percent. After 1972, that support rebounded. States quickly passed new capital punishment laws. Georgia passed its new death penalty law in 1973, trying to make the death penalty less arbitrary. That same year Georgia authorities tried and sentenced Troy Gregg to death. In 1976, the Supreme Court returned to the death penalty issue, this time finding the revised law rational. This decision validated the new laws, but did not immediately unleash a flood of executions. Not until 1979 did the states execute a prisoner unwilling to be executed.

As executions resumed, some critics charged that race determined which prisoners state courts condemned to death. In 1987, the Supreme Court heard another Georgia case, involving a prisoner named Warren McCleskey. McCleskey's attorneys produced statistical evidence proving that Georgia discriminated racially in death penalty cases. McCleskey's attorneys alleged that Georgia discriminated in favor of white victims, showing that prosecutors and juries condemned to death the killers of white victims far more readily than the killers of black victims. Justice Antonin Scalia conceded the validity of the statistical evidence, but urged his fellow justices to accept jurors' prejudice as inevitable. The Court thus accepted McCleskey's statistical evidence but did not overturn his death sentence. The Courts, finding that racial prejudice did not matter, argued further that racism-colored death penalty cases were irrelevant.

The numbers of persons executed has been on the increase since 1980. Shocking revelations of innocent persons condemned to death row have led some reformers to demand a moratorium, and Illinois has called a halt to executions in that state. Most of the states, however, have proceeded with the death penalty unabated.

Anyone Hungry?

~

Since December 1982, the Texas Department of Criminal Justice has documented executed prisoner's requests for last meals. One may imagine all types of unusual and exotic types of food that prisoners might request but the overwhelming majority of the last 247 people executed asked for hamburgers, more specifically cheeseburgers. The next most requested meal was steak at 32 people. Fried chicken and some form of breakfast were equally requested at 18 each. Five prisoners requested only a salad. Many people asked for side salad with Italian dressing. Only one prisoner, Pedro Muniz, was not able to get what he wanted (shrimp) and was given a cheeseburger instead. Forty-three people declined a last meal. One prisoner, Delbert Tegue Jr., declined a last meal but ate a cheeseburger at the last minute because his mother insisted that he not die hungry. The following lists some of the more unique requests.

Number	Last Name	First Name	Date Executed	Last Meal Request
223	San Miguel	Jessy	6/29/2000	Pizza (beef, bacon bits, and multiple types of cheese), 10 quesadillas (5 mozzarella cheese, 5 cheddar cheese), 5 strips of open-flame grilled beef, 5 strips of stir-fried beef, chocolate peanut butter ice cream, sweet tea, double fudge chocolate cake, broccoli, and grapes
235	Lawton	Stacy	11/14/2000	1 jar of dill pickles
179	Tuttle	Charles	7/1/1999	Four fried eggs sunny side up, four sausage patties, one chicken fried steak patty, one bowl of white country gravy, five pieces of white toast, five tacos with meat and cheese only, four Dr. Peppers with ice on the side and five mint sticks.
177	Little	William	6/1/1999	Fifteen slices of cheese, three fried eggs, three buttered toasts, two hamburger patties with cheese, 2 tomatoes sliced, one sliced onion, french fries with salad dressing, 2 lb. of crispy fried bacon, one quart chocolate milk and one pint of fresh strawberries
176	Coleman	Clydell	5/5/1999	Salmon Croquettes, scrambled eggs, french fries and biscuits
158	Castillo	David	8/23/1998	Twenty-four soft shell tacos, six enchiladas, six tostados, two whole onions, five jalapenos, two cheeseburgers, one chocolate shake, one quart of milk and one package of Marlboro cigarettes. (Prohibited by TDCJ policy)

150	McFarland	Frank	4/29/1998	Heaping portion of lettuce, a sliced tomato, a sliced cucumber, four celery stalks, four sticks of American or Cheddar cheese, two bananas and two cold half pints of milk. Asked that all vegetables be washed prior to serving. Also asked that the cheese sticks be clean.
123	Madden	Robert	5/28/1997	Asked that final meal be provided to a homeless person
98	Sattiewhite	Vernon	8/15/1995	Six scrambled eggs with cheese, seven pieces of buttered white toast, fifteen pieces of bacon, three hash browns, a bowl of grits with butter, jelly and orange juice
88	Russell, Jr.	Clifton	1/31/1995	No preference. Asked for whatever was on the menu (chili dogs, baked beans, corn and peanut butter cookies)
65	Kelly	Carl	8/20/1993	Wild game or whatever is on the menu and cold lemonade. Served cheeseburger and french fries, declined last meal
45	Clark	David	2/28/1992	Told officials he wanted to fast
37	Derrick	Mikel	7/18/1990	Ribeye steak, tossed green salad with blue cheese dressing, baked potato with sour cream (refused last meal)
12	Barney	Jeffery	4/16/1986	Two boxes of frosted flakes and a pint of milk
11	Bass	Charles	3/12/1986	Plain cheese sandwich

Interesting Facts About Texas Executions

Since 1982, Texas has executed 227 offenders, two of which have been women. One of those, Betty Beets, was convicted in Henderson County (Athens,TX). Beets, 62, was also one of the oldest inmates to be executed in Texas.

Shortest time on Death Row: 252 days.

Longest time on Death Row: 8,982 days (24 years).

Average Time on Death Row prior to Execution: 10.39 years.

Youngest offender executed was Jay Pinkerton, 24 years old.

Oldest inmates executed were Clydell Coleman and Betty Beets, both 62 years old.

Hanging was means of execution between 1819 and 1923.

Executions

1960	56	1970	0	1981	1	1991	14
1961	42	1976	0	1982	2	1992	31
1962	47	1977	1	1983	5	1993	27
1963	21	1978	0	1984	21	1994	31
1964	15	1979	2	1985	18	1995	56
1965	7	1980	0	1986	18	1996	45
1966	1			1987	25	1997	74
1967	2			1988	11	1998	8
1968	0			1989	16	1999	8
1969	0			1990	23		

SOURCE: *Statistical Abstracts of the U.S.*, 2000.

1960s

1960s • Assassination ~ The 1960s fostered a season of assassinations, beginning with the murder of civil rights leader Medgar Evers, followed by the deaths of John F. Kennedy, Robert Kennedy, Martin Luther King, Jr. and an attempt on the life of George Wallace.

In fact, assassination has long been a part of the American experience. Richard Lawrence attempted to assassinate Andrew Jackson in 1835. John Wilkes Booth successfully assassinated Abraham Lincoln at the end of the Civil War. Charles Guiteau shot and killed James A. Garfield in 1880. In 1901, Leon Czolgosz assassinated President William McKinley in Buffalo, New York. John Schrank shot Theodore Roosevelt in 1912, but the bullet struck a fifty-page speech folded in half in the president's pocket. Roosevelt survived the attack, and, in fact, delivered the speech. In 1933 Giuseppe Zangara tried to assassinate Franklin D. Roosevelt in Miami, Florida. Zangara's bullet struck the mayor of Miami, missing Roosevelt entirely. In 1935 Dr. Carl Austin Weiss murdered

(circa 1900) Caucasian priest leads African-American man to electric chair, Sing Sing prison, Ossining, New York.

"Are you in favor of the death penalty for a person convicted of murder?"

	Yes	No	No opinion
1953	68%	25%	7%
1956	53	34	13
1957	47	34	18
1960	53	36	11
1965	45	43	12
1966	42	47	11
1967	54	38	8
1969	51	40	9
1971	49	40	11
1976	66	26	8
1978	62	27	11
1981	66	25	9
1985	72	20	8
1988	79	16	5
1991	76	18	6
1994	80	16	4
1995	77	13	10
1999	71	22	7

SOURCE: *Sourcebook of Criminal Justice Statistics*, 1998.

Governor Huey Long of Louisiana. In 1950, Puerto Rican nationalists Oscar Collazo and Griselio Torresola attempted to assassinate Harry Truman by firing on Blair House. They succeeded only in killing a guard before being gunned down. Collazo survived to be released from prison in 1979. He returned to Puerto Rico. Lee Harvey Oswald shot John F. Kennedy in 1963, Sirhan B. Sirhan murdered Robert Kennedy and Arthur Bremer shot George Wallace in 1968. Lynnett Alice Fromme and Jane Moore both tried to shoot President Gerald Ford in 1975. In 1981 John W. Hinckley, Jr. shot President Ronald Reagan.

In 1998 the Secret Service concluded after a study of assassinations that most of the killers were not deranged madmen. The Secret Service urged law enforcers to look at the behavior of suspects and not assume that potential assassins can be identified by particular personality traits. The history of assassination reveals a strange mix of motives driving the assassins. Richard Lawrence clearly was insane, imagining he was the king of England and America. Anarchism apparently motivated Czolgosz. Guiteau had sent letters to Garfield demanding jobs. Weiss feared that Huey Long planned to spread a rumor that his family included blacks. Collazo blamed Truman for the United States domination of Puerto Rico. Sirhan Sirhan hated Israel and saw Robert Kennedy as seeking Jewish votes. A perverse loner, Arthur Bremer seemed determined to kill some political figure. He had stalked Nixon before turning to Wallace.

1900-1940 • Morality and Crime ~ Interest in morals offenses declined through the twentieth century, with far more interest in sex crimes and gambling in the first three decades of the century than in the last. Reports of sexual bondage, women forced into prostitution and exotic sex acts, prompted Congress to pass the Mann Act, outlawing "white slavery" in 1910. Moralists led protest marches into the so-called red-light districts. Commissions investigated, publishing sensational reports of their findings. Police tried to close many red-light districts, sometimes jailing hundreds. Generally such tactics were not effective as the purveyors of vice simply relocated after police raids.

At the end of the nineteenth century, the states created a new category of crime when they raised the age at which

1950s-1970s

women could legally consent to sex. Sex with a willing, but underage female, was "statutory rape." Each state made its own determination on the question of consent, but only Tennessee went so far as to set the age of consent at 21. California, Arizona, Colorado, Florida and New York set the age of consent at eighteen.

1960s-1970s • "Victimless" Crime ~ In the second half of the twentieth century, states began a retreat from their earlier attack on morals. Nevada decriminalized gambling first, acting finally in 1931, after earlier experiments. Connecticut repealed its fornication law in 1967. Sodomy laws came under attack, but when the Supreme Court had the opportunity to declare them all unconstitutional (in 1986), the justices refused to do so. Some state courts did strike down such laws.

The Supreme Court legalized abortions in 1973, striking down all state laws that made abortion a crime. This proved to be one of the Court's most controversial decisions of the twentieth century. Opponents of abortion took to the streets. Some turned to crime themselves, assaulting and even murdering doctors that had performed abortions. In the 1980s the Supreme Court handed down decisions that allowed the states to restrict abortions but not outlaw them. This retreated a bit from its 1973 decision without abandoning it entirely.

1950s-1960s • Crime in the Civil Rights Era ~ The May 17, 1954, Supreme Court decision declaring segregated public schools unconstitutional sparked a wave of crime and violence. Within months of the decision, an Atlanta factory worker organized the Knights of the Ku Klux Klan, Inc. a new division of the already established Ku Klux Klan. Klansmen and other white racists launched a terror campaign designed to preserve segregation. Violent segregationists bombed six schools, seven churches, seven Jewish temples, a YWCA and an auditorium. When Autherine Lucy tried to desegregate the University of Alabama in 1956, whites attacked cars, burned crosses and waved Confederate flags in Tuscaloosa.

Southern law enforcement officers generally did little to control this violence, and were often implicated in it. As white rioters pelted Autherine Lucy with rocks and tomatoes, Alabama Governor James Folsom was away in Florida, drunk. Folsom's alcoholism suggests indifference, but "Big Jim" was actually a moderate on racial issues. Earlier governors hardly concealed their support for racial violence. Bibb Graves, elected governor of Alabama in 1926, did not hide his membership in the Ku Klux Klan and officially tolerated Klan violence. Some of Folsom's contemporaries espoused racial demagoguery, which "Big Jim" eschewed. In 1957, Arkansas Governor Orval Faubus used the National Guard to thwart integration of a Little Rock high school, which had the effect of encouraging racist mobs. Folsom's one-time protégé, George Wallace, never openly endorsed extralegal violence, but his heated attacks on the legitimacy of federal civil rights efforts seemed to sanction violent racist resistance to civil rights.

In response, Congress passed the Civil Rights Act of 1957. This limited measure protected only persons attempting to exercise the right to vote for candidates in federal elections from physical abuse. Such a weak law did little to staunch the flood of violence and the Congress felt compelled to act again. The Civil Rights

Act of 1960 made it a federal crime to transport explosives across state lines to destroy buildings used for religious, educational or other purposes.

Even the 1960 law had little effect. More violence ensued. In 1961, Birmingham City Police looked the other way as white racists attacked and beat civil rights protesters riding interstate busses through the state. A year later bloody rioting erupted in Mississippi when a black student named James Meredith attempted to desegregate the University of Mississippi. In 1963 Klansmen dynamited Birmingham's Sixteenth Street Baptist Church, killing four children. In 1964 white college students traveled to Mississippi in a scheme to provoke a confrontation with violent racists. In a sensational incident, the Klan kidnapped and murdered three of these civil rights workers.

Congress passed the landmark Civil Rights Act of 1964 in response to President Lyndon Johnson's demand that the government's authority against civil rights violence be made clear. The 1964 law declared that American citizens could not be segregated in such public accommodations as restaurants, theaters, hotels, and public conveyances.

Even with national determination to oppose crimes against American citizens exercising their civil rights, southern officials continued to condone violence. In 1965 Governor George Wallace of Alabama dispatched state troopers to join with local lawmen to brutalize peaceful protesters seeking the right to vote in Selma, Alabama. The 1965 Voting Rights Act did away with such state schemes to prevent black voting as literacy tests. The law also made it a federal crime to intimidate or coerce American citizens attempting to vote.

In the end none of the federal laws had much effect on southern violence. In the mid-1960s white southerners withdrew their support for such violence-prone organizations as the Ku Klux Klan. State juries began to convict white defendants charged with crimes against blacks. State politicians cleaned up police departments and highway patrols. Polls suggest that a fear of disorder, rather than changes in racial attitude, account for this cultural change.

1960s • Rioting in the Era of Civil Rights ~ In the 1960s, Los Angeles erupted in rioting (August 11-16, 1965), as did Newark (July 12-17, 1967) and Detroit (July 23-30, 1967). These three riots were only the most famous of the more than two hundred that occurred during the "long hot summers" of the 1960s. The Commission on the Causes and Prevention of Violence found 239 riots between 1963 and 1968, violence that took the lives of 190 persons and injured 8,000. Riots had occurred before, but these incidents seemed different to some observers. Looting had occurred in the 1930s and 1940s, but had been directed against private homes. In the consumer-oriented culture of the 1960s, rioters went after stores. In the 1960s, rioters rarely turned their violence against people, as had often been the case before. Most of the deaths occurred among the rioters themselves.

Although these disorders never seriously threatened the government, federal authorities moved to restore order with military force. Between 1963 and 1968 the government arrested and detained 50,000 persons engaged in urban rioting. Thousands of troops took to the streets to restore order.

1895-PRESENT • SERIAL KILLERS ~ Herman Webster Mudgett may be the prototype for the twentieth century "serial killer." Arrested in 1895, authorities originally accused Mudgett with a complex murder-for-insurance scam. He had persuaded Benjamin Pitezel to fake his death for insurance money and then killed Pitezel and his three children. Further investigation revealed that Mudgett had lived for some years as "Dr. H.H. Holmes," in Chicago. As Holmes, he killed an unknown number of persons. He claimed to have killed 27, and investigators found that 17 persons associated with "Dr. Holmes" had mysteriously disappeared.

The twentieth-century serial killer, often moving anonymously and acting randomly from jurisdiction to jurisdiction, made detection by police frustrating. Between 1962 and 1964, "the Boston Strangler" raped and murdered 13 females. Panic swept across eastern Massachusetts and women living alone were especially fearful. Authorities accused Albert De Salvo, but never actually tried him for any of the Boston Strangler crimes. Even now, some claim that the Boston Strangler case remains unsolved. Ted Bundy may have killed as many as 18 young women between 1974 and his arrest in 1979. Jeffrey Dahmer allegedly killed 17 young men before his arrest in

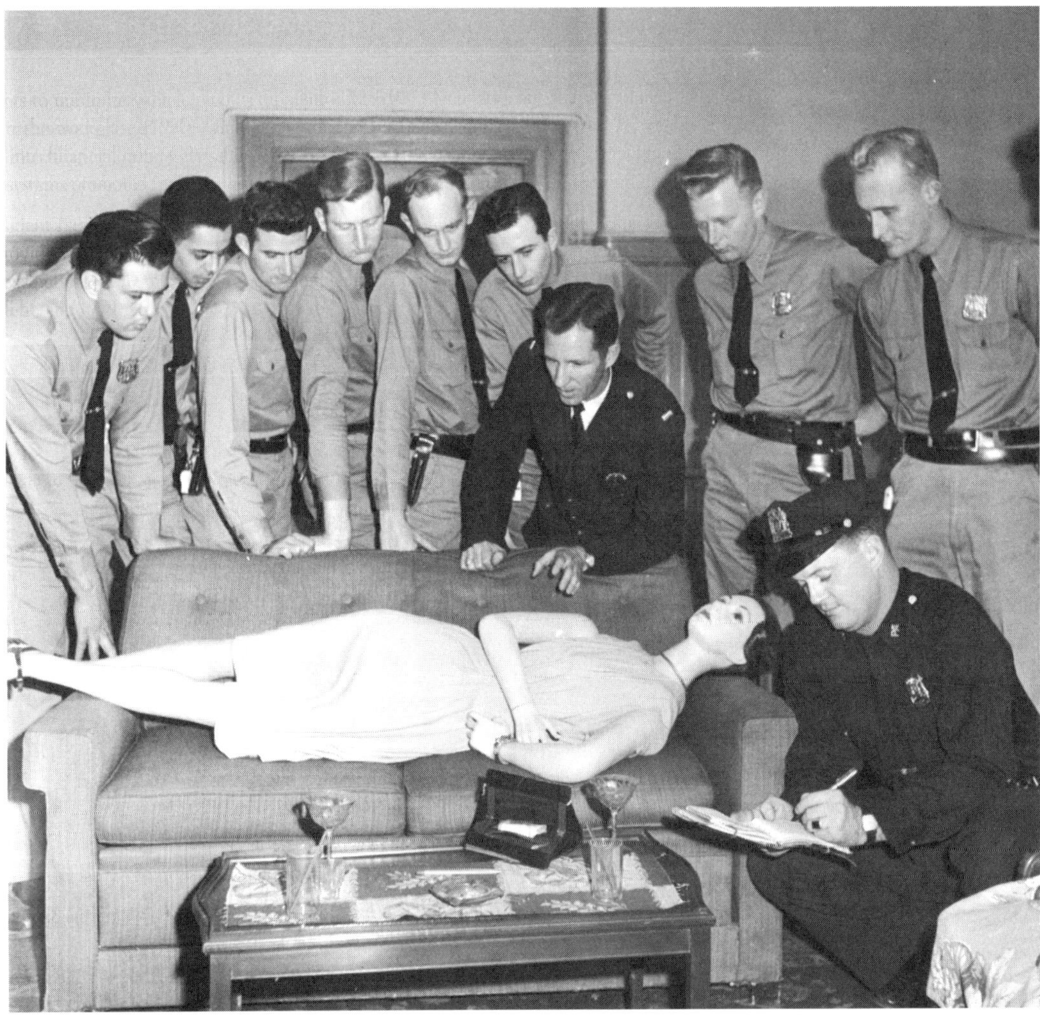

(circa 1954) A murder scene is staged with a room full of clues. American police cadets listen closely as a lieutenant lectures on the correct procedure in investigating a murder scene.

1991. Between 1978 and 1996 the FBI searched desperately for a suspect it called the Unabomber. Theodore Kaczinski had for years mailed explosive devices to persons he associated with high technology. In 1995, Kaczinski forced the *New York Times* and the *Washington Post* to publish his lengthy manifesto. Federal agents finally arrested Kaczinski after his younger brother recognized the manifesto as his brother's writing.

Homicides

~

Guns and violence have come to characterize traffic in drugs. Between 1984 and 1993, gun homicides tripled for persons aged 15 to 19. That rate doubled for persons aged 20 to 24. Criminologists attribute much of this increase to intensified competition among drug marketers.

~

1890s-1920s • Drugs and Crime ~ Opiate addiction increased throughout the nineteenth century, reaching a peak in the 1890s. In this era, middle- or upper-class women composed the bulk of the addict population. Most of these addicts became addicted through the use of physician-prescribed drugs. Prior to 1900 doctors readily prescribed opium and morphine to relieve pain. In the twentieth century, doctors became reluctant to prescribe such addictive drugs to all but the incurably ill. In part, this shift in attitude can be attributed to a campaign by government officials to criminalize addictive drugs. Government reports, such as Hamilton Wright's *Report on the International Opium Commission* for the United States Senate, published in 1910, manipulated statistics to present an exaggerated and sensationalized portrait of American drug use. After 1914, government prosecutors harassed doctors maintaining addicts.

The result of this change in government policy was dramatic. While the typical nineteenth-century addict was a middle-class housewife, the typical twentieth-century addict became the young urban male. The term "junkie" came into vogue in the 1920s when young men collected and sold scrap metal to support their drug habits. Drug use became closely associated with the criminal underworld.

1960s-Present • Heroine and Cocaine ~ After the 1940s, various types of drug abuse predominated in the American urban underworld, with each drug economy bringing with it a distinct paradigm of violence. From 1966 through 1973, many teenagers became regular injectors of heroin in "shooting galleries" using shared needles. Between 1973 and 1983, drug abusers increasingly turned to cocaine powder which could be snorted or smoked.

Crack cocaine, distributed in vials meant to hold perfume samples, made it easier for more people to inhale potent fumes smoked only with some difficulty before. Highly competitive drug markets led to a sharp increase in violence, particularly among black male youth in large cities. In the 1990s, as the crack epidemic subsided, violence declined as well.

1970 • War on Drugs ~ In 1970 Congress passed a law entitled the Comprehensive Drug Abuse Prevention and Control Act. Since passage of this law, the federal government has devoted a major portion of its resources to crimes involving drug use. In the past 50 years the number of drug cases prosecuted in federal court increased 1,085 percent. Critics complain that the war on drugs

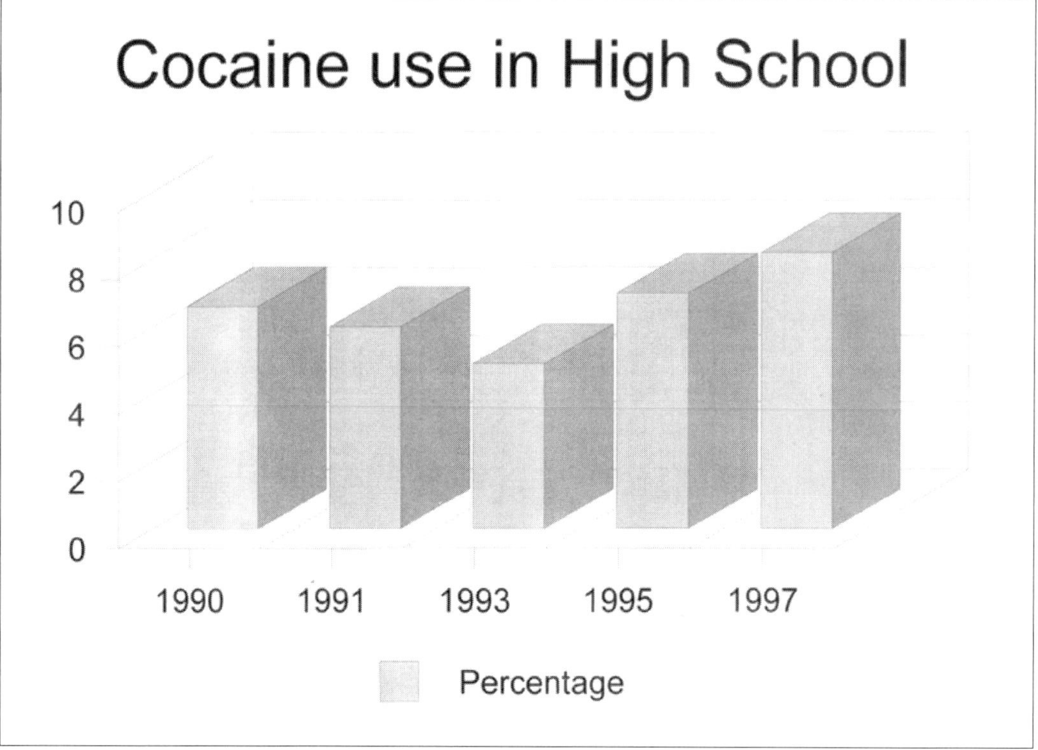

Cocaine Use in High School, 1990-1997, selected years; graphic shows the percentage of high school students who have ever used cocaine in their lives.

SOURCE: *The National Drug Control Strategy: 2000 Annual Report.*

costs too much and has accomplished little while tending to target minorities. The effect of the war on drugs has been to involve federal agents in ordinary street crime, a type of crime control traditionally left to the states and cities.

There are signs that public opinion may be shifting against the war on drugs. At the end of the twentieth century, voters in California, Arizona, Alaska, Colorado, Nevada, Oregon, Washington, Maine and Washington, D.C. passed ballot initiatives legalizing marijuana use for medical purposes. These state initiatives challenge the federal war on drugs. Recent decisions by the Supreme Court protecting state powers suggest that federal supremacy in such cases may no longer be certain.

1970s-Present • Women and Crime

~ Women have always been the minority of crime victims and perpetrators. In the nineteenth century, women often made up less than five percent of persons charged with crimes. At the end of the twentieth century women made up about a quarter of persons charged with such serious crimes as homicide, robbery, assault and arson. Women are also less likely to be the victims of crime. In 1997 men's overall rate of victimization was 45.8 per 1000 population aged twelve or older. The rate for women was thirty-three.

Feminists began studying the political significance of woman as victim in the 1970s. Susan Brownmiller's work on rape as an instrument of patriarchy appeared in 1975. Since radical criminologists generally saw crime as a tool of resistance to an unjust system, feminist scholarship on women as the victims of such crime caught them unawares. Research by feminists has forced some criminologists to shift their focus from the rogue male as social rebel to women's victimization.

Sexual harassment of women in the workplace did not become an issue for most Americans until 1991, when Anita Hill charged that a nominee for the Supreme Court, Clarence Thomas, had sexually harassed her on the job. Thereafter, sexual harassment became a more visible crime. The Equal Employment Opportunity Commission investigated over 15,000 complaints of sexual harassment in 1998 alone. All but 12.9 percent of these complaints were filed by women.

At the end of the twentieth century women began entering criminal justice occupations in large numbers for the first time. Between 1983 and 1995, the portion of women in correctional occupations increased 372 percent. By 1998, 12 percent of all police officers were women, 24 percent of correctional officers and 34 percent of lawyers.

1980s-1990s • Hate Crime ~ Between 1980 and 1997 virtually every state and the Congress passed so-called hate crime laws. These laws either mandated stiffer sentences for crimes motivated by race or religion, or required that records be kept of hate crimes. Congress commenced its debate in 1985, passing a bill in 1990 entitled the "Crime Statistics Act," a law requiring that hate crimes be recorded and published by the Justice Department. In 1994 Congress passed a law directing the United States Sentencing Commission to increase penalties for crimes motivated by prejudice.

The proponents of laws against hate crimes hope to use the power of the government to engineer a more harmonious society. Supporters frankly hoped the new laws would assert the notion of equal rights rather than defend already existing rights. Those in favor of hate crime laws often worry that the number of such crimes is on the increase and urge more laws and more enforcement of existing laws to bring a serious problem under control. In fact, passage of laws against hate crimes had made it seem as if more such crimes have been occurring. Debates over the proposed laws created the appearance of increased racial violence. The number of articles in the major newspapers reporting "hate crimes" or discussing the phenomenon quadrupled between 1989 and 1991.

Critics of hate crime legislation doubt the government has the power to reform behavior. Some have insisted that the criminal justice system should respond to hate-motivated crime with the same laws it uses against all other "ordinary crime." Critics have worried that calling attention to the racial, sexual or ethnic differences between the parties of a crime will worsen social conditions rather than make them better.

Hate crime laws have been tested before the United States Supreme Court and received a mixed reception. In a 1992 case entitled *R.A.V. v. City of St. Paul*, the Court ruled a Minnesota hate crime law an unconstitutional violation of free speech. Lawmakers, the Court decided, cannot discriminate against particular speech on the basis of its content.

In that case the Supreme Court embraced a view put forward by opponents of hate crime laws: such laws punish speech or thought. A year later, in a case entitled *Wisconsin v. Mitchell*, the Supreme Court rejected the free speech argument. Todd Mitchell led a group of black youths in an attack on a young white boy, leaving their victim in a coma that lasted for four days. Mitchell's crime, in addition to assault, was that he had called to his fellows "to move on some white people." For saying that, Wisconsin punished Mitchell with a longer sentence than he would have received for simple assault. Mitchell's lawyer charged that his client's free speech rights had been violated.

The Supreme Court rejected this argument and upheld the longer sentence. Chief Justice William Rehnquist agreed with the state that some persons pose more of a threat to society than others and those persons should be punished more severely than "ordinary" defendants; Rehnquist pointed out that the courts had been distinguishing the more dangerous from the less dangerous for centuries.

1990s • Drop in the Crime Rate ~ In the 1990s the crime rate declined significantly. This marked a dramatic

The Buddy Boys

~

In the mid-1980s the New York City Police Department was rocked with a scandal involving the so-called "Buddy Boys" operating out of the 77th Precinct. Ultimately the department disciplined 38 officers for drug use, burglary and selling drugs.

In the 77th Precinct officers smoked marijuana in their patrol cars. Officers snorted cocaine in the station house. Officers commonly lied on their arrest reports and perjured themselves in court. Several officers took bribes from drug dealers. Officers seized, but did not report, money at crime scenes. Officers also identified drug dealers' apartments while on patrol and, speaking in code over police radios, called on fellow officers to converge. Officers burglarized the apartments, taking money, drugs and electronic equipment. In some cases the officers broke down doors; in other instances they rappelled down the sides of buildings to crash through windows.

At first, police officers intended to loot the drug dealers' homes for money. They destroyed the drugs they found. In time, officers began selling the drugs. Some officers sold on the street. More often, the officers sold the drugs to dealers they knew through their policing.

Officers in the 77th Precinct began to suspect that the department's Internal Affairs Division might be investigating their criminality. The IAD broke up the Buddy Boys drug ring after arresting Benny Burwell for possession of cocaine. Burwell claimed he had been paying off 77th Precinct officers for years. Burwell agreed to work with IAD investigators. IAD investigators videotaped officers Henry Winter and Tony Magno paying Burwell protection money.

IAD officers persuaded Winter and Magno to turn against their fellow officers. IAD fitted Winter and Magno with hidden microphones. In police parlance they "wore a wire" while working with their fellow officers in the 77th Precinct. IAD investigators collected evidence against the corrupt police that allowed them to suspend 13 officers and discipline another 25. One officer, Brian O'Regan, committed suicide rather than surrender.

Sources: Victor E. Kappeler, Richard D. Sluder, Geoggrey P. Alpert, *Forces of Deviance: Understanding the Dark Side of Policing* (Prospect Heights: Waveland Press, 1998).

Michael McAlary, *Buddy Boys: When Good Cops Turn Bad* (New York: Putnam, 1987).

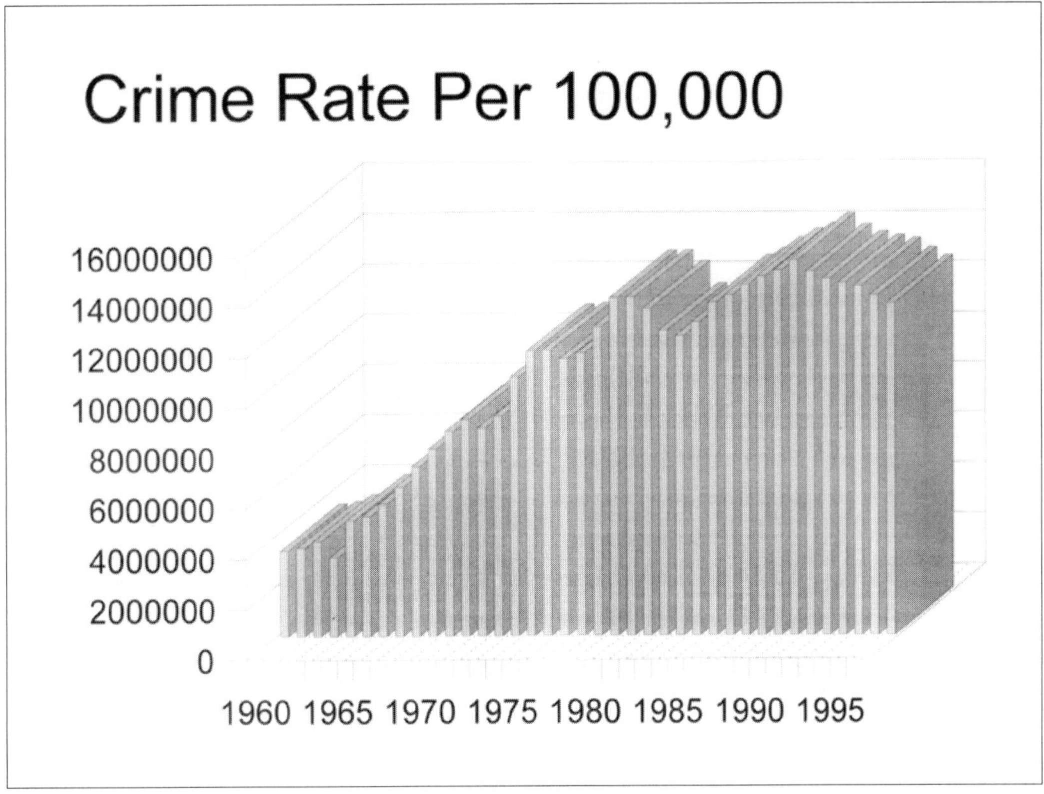

SOURCE: *Sourcebook of Criminal Justice Statistics*, 1998.

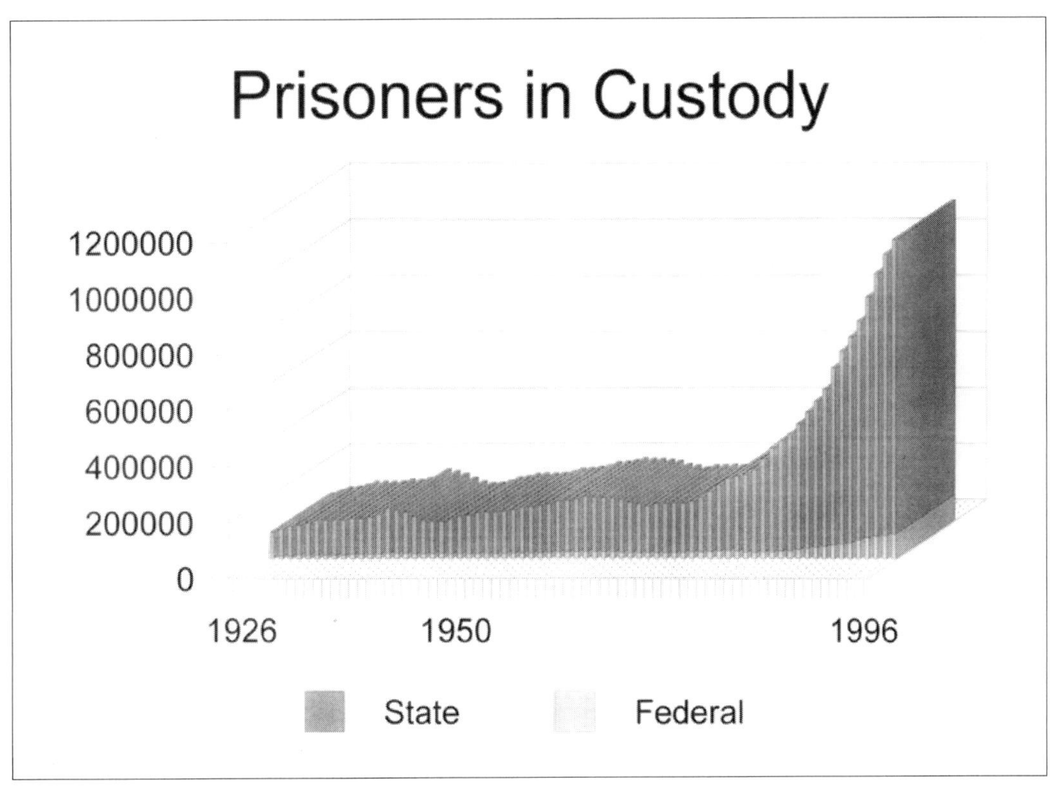

SOURCE: *Sourcebook of Criminal Justice Statistics*, 1998.

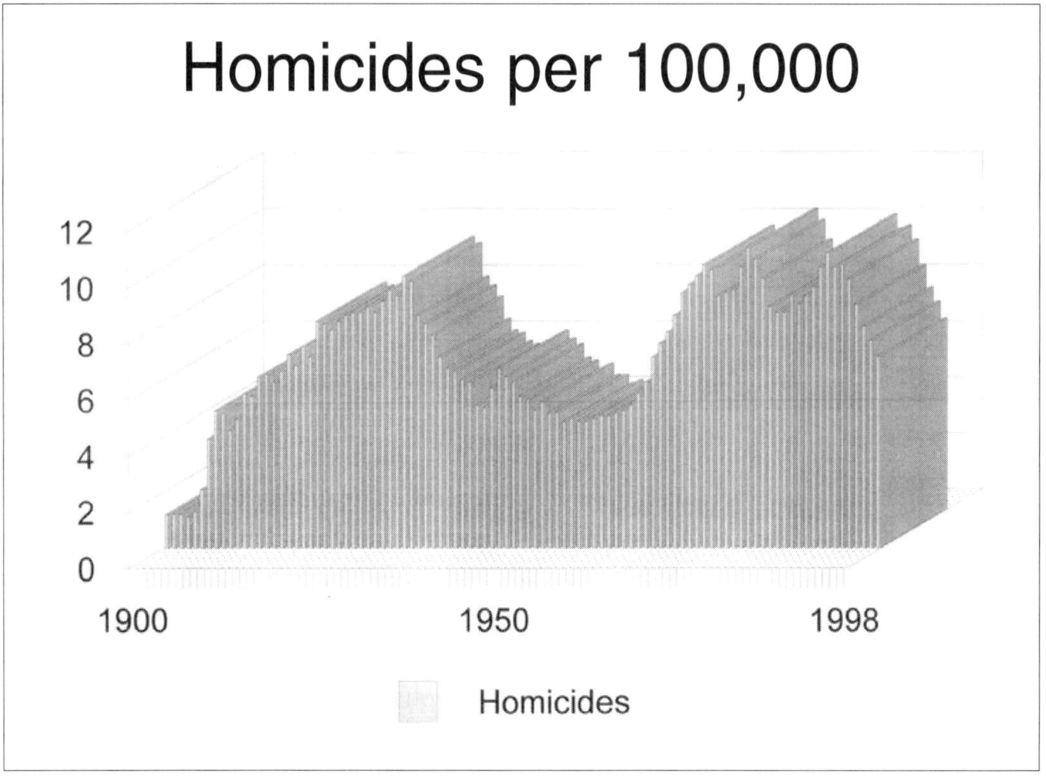

SOURCE: *FBI Uniform Crime Reports* and *Sourcebook of Criminal Justice Statistics*, 1998.

reversal of previous trends. From the mid-1960s to the late 1970s, the homicide rate doubled. It reached a peak of 10.2 per 100,000 in 1980. Thereafter it dropped a bit, climbing again in the late 1980s and early 1990s. In 1991 it peaked again at 9.8 per 100,000. Through the 1990s it dropped, reaching 6.3 per 100,000 in 1998.

Some criminologists pointed to huge increases in the number of persons incarcerated as an explanation for the drop in crime. The number of prisoners in custody increased from 304,692 in 1980 to over a million in 1997. Critics of this view point out that states like Texas, with the largest increases in persons jailed, had smaller drops in the crime rate than the nation as a whole. Others point to a break in the crack epidemic or better gun control or new police tactics or improvements in the job market. Some crime experts claim that the American culture has shifted, with people becoming less tolerant of crime and violence, particularly domestic abuse.

(circa 1970) A bumper sticker supporting the Firearms Owners Protection Act, an amendment to the Gun Control Act of 1968.

All crime did not decline in the 1990s. At the same time the overall crime rate fell, teen drug use increased. The percentage of high school students reporting that they had ever used marijuana increased from 31 percent in 1990 to 47 percent in 1997. Over the same time span, the percentage of high school students admitting they had ever used cocaine jumped from 6.6 percent in 1990 to 8 percent in 1997.

Crime Rate Per 100,000

1990	5,280.3
1991	5,897.8
1992	5,660.2
1993	5,484.4
1994	5,373.5
1995	5,275.9
1996	5,086.6
1997	4,922.7
1998	4,615.5
1999	4,266.8

SOURCE: *FBI Uniform Crime Reports*, 1998.

1960s-Present • Rampage Killers

~ At the end of the twentieth century Americans seemed to confront a new, and terribly frightening, species of crime. Journalists began calling mass murderers acting in schools, workplaces, stores and other public places "rampage killers."

Mass murder did not begin at the end of the twentieth century. In 1966 Charles Whitman shot 45 people, killing 14, from his sniper's perch atop a tower at the University of Texas. Whitman's killings attracted national attention. Also in 1966 Richard Speck murdered eight student nurses in Chicago. Whitman and Speck committed crimes that made national headlines. When Robert Benjamin Smith killed five at a beauty school that same year, he attracted little national attention. Nor did Sylvia Seegrist when she went on a shooting spree in a suburban shopping mall outside Philadelphia in 1985. She killed three and injured seven. In 1995, Jamie Rouse shot two teachers in their heads, killing one, before murdering a fellow student in rural Tennessee. In 1996, fourteen-year-old Barry Loukaitis attacked a middle school algebra class in Moses Lake, Washington. He killed three and wounded one before capture. In February 1997, Evan Ramsey killed a student and a principal in Bethel, Alaska.

Despite such incidents, for many Americans, perceptions that rampage killing had become a national problem did not begin until a school shooting in Pearl, Mississippi. On October 1, 1997 Luke Woodham killed his mother before going to school and shooting nine students, two fatally. The Pearl, Mississippi, shooting proved not to be an isolated event. In December of the same year, Michael Carneal killed three people at his Paducah, Kentucky, high school. In 1998, an eleven-year-old and a thirteen-year-old ambushed students and teachers outside of a Jonesboro, Arkansas middle school. Four girls and a teacher died. Despite earlier incidents in Washington and Alaska, some commentators suggested that the South's violent culture explained the school shooting phenomenon.

Concern that the problem might not be confined to the South or the product of a peculiar southern tendency toward violence developed when Kipland P. Kinkel shot 24 people in his school cafeteria in Springfield, Oregon. In 1999, Eric Harris and Dylan Klebold killed 12 students and a teacher before killing themselves in Littleton, Colorado.

Schools all over America tightened security, installed metal detectors, searched backpacks and began holding duck-and-cover drills. Schools practiced responding to rampage killers just as they held fire drills. Parents demanded that schools hire additional staff to better identify and counsel troubled youth.

In the wake of so many school shootings, Americans launched a national debate over what caused so much bloodshed. Like many others, President Bill Clinton blamed an overly violent popular culture, easy access to guns and lax supervision. Reports that the killers had immersed themselves in particularly violent video games and easily obtained their guns seemed to confirm such theories. Journalists and other observers also noted that the killers had issued numerous warning signs before going on their deadly rampages.

At the same time the country debated how to respond to the crisis. Some pointed out that despite the spectacular series of shootings that grabbed national headlines starting in 1997, school shootings had actually declined throughout most of the 1990s. The peak had come and passed in the 1992-93 school year, when fifty people died in school-related violence.

Although mass murder has long been a problem in America, it seemed not to become a subject of national debate until the fall of 1997. The specter of children killing children generated deep anxiety, though the 1995 shootings by Jamie Rouseor and even the 1997 Bethel, Alaska shootings did not attract the same level of journalistic attention as did school shootings in mid-1997 and later.

1990s • Federal Police Power ~ Members of Congress discovered that passing new laws designed to control or reduce crime was a very popular thing to do. By the end of the twentieth century, Congress could hardly resist passing laws against crime. In its 1997-98 session, Congress considered about one thousand bills dealing with crime.

Even with these new laws, federal prisons and a federal investigative service, federal prosecution of crime remained a tiny percentage of the total number of prosecutions throughout the twentieth century. Today, federal prosecutions make up only about five percent of the total number of prosecutions in the United States. The states remain preeminent in the field of law enforcement.

At the end of the twentieth century the Supreme Court began to more critically review Congressional acts designed to control crime. The Supreme Court declared the 1990 Gun-Free School Zones Act unconstitutional in 1995. Five years later, the Court struck down the 1994 Violence Against Women Act. In both cases the Congress had justified its power to pass criminal laws on the Commerce Clause, that portion of the Constitution giving the federal government expansive power to regulate commerce. Guns in schools and violence against women, the Court found, were not commerce. In the past, the Court had not often questioned laws based on the Commerce Clause. These decisions stand as the only instances where the Supreme Court has invalidated federal anti-crime laws since 1936. The decisions suggest that at the end of the twentieth century the Court wants to protect the powers of the states to control crime.

Conclusion

At the end of the twentieth century, state and local governments remained responsible for most law enforcement, just as they had been at the beginning of the century. Nonetheless, much had changed. Through the twentieth century, more people saw crime as a national rather than a local problem. The emergence of the "rampage killer" illustrates the change. This new kind of outlaw became a subject for national concern, though the first rampage killers attracted only local attention and the first national stories tried to paint rampage killers as a regional problem, characteristic of the South. Most people concluded that rampage killers posed a frightening threat not because of perceptions or judgments made by some local authority but from reporting by national news organizations. Through the twentieth century, localities lost their autonomy. Neighborhood-sanctioned violence against malefactors, sometimes called lynching, declined. Instead, racial violence came to be defined as a "hate crime" or the act of a malevolent individual, to be tracked by the Federal Bureau of Investigation and national news media outlets. Serial killers traveled from jurisdiction to jurisdiction, making old, localized crime detection procedures obsolete. The national government experimented with making alcohol consumption a federal crime and permanently redefined the use of narcotics from a medical activity to street crime. Thus, even local street crime came to be seen as part of an international web of crime.

Even though most policing remained the task of local departments, those departments followed procedures that became more uniform as the century progressed. The science of crime detection made this a necessity. And, at the same time, the United States Supreme Court established standards all police departments had to follow. National policies inspired foreign terrorists to travel to America and domestic terrorists to move across state lines to attack symbols of America as a nation.

Crime and crime control will no doubt continue as a controversial topic in the future. In a system that divides sovereignty between the states and the federal government, there will always be tensions over which governmental agency should control crimes. Those confident in the power of government to reform society through law enforcement will continue to clash with those that see crime control as entirely a matter of punishing particular individuals.

Bibliography

Belknap, Michal R. *Federal Law and Southern Order: Racial Violence and Constitutional Conflict in the Post-Brown South.* Athens: University of Georgia Press, 1987.

Bellesiles, Michael A. *Arming America: The Origins of a National Gun Culture.* New York: Knopf, 2000.

Blee, Kathleen. *Women of the Klan: Racism and Gender in the 1920s.* Berkeley: University of California Press, 1991.

Blumstein, Alfred and Joel Wallman. *The Crime Drop in America.* Cambridge: Cambridge University Press, 2000.

Brewer, David J. "Plain Words of the Crime of Lynching." Leslie's Weekly 97 (August 30, 1903): 182.

Brownmiller, Susan. *Against Our Will: Men, Women, and Rape.* New York: Simon and Schuster, 1975.

Brundage, W. Fitzhugh. *Lynching in the New South: Georgia and Virginia, 1880-1930.* Urbana: University of Illinois Press, 1993.

Chalmers, David M. *Hooded Americanism: The History of the Ku Klux Klan*. New York: F. Watts, 1981.

Cortner, Richard C. *A "Scottsboro" Case in Mississippi: The Supreme Court and Brown v. Mississippi*. Jackson: University Press of Mississippi, 1986.

Courtwright, David. *Dark Paradise: Opiate Addiction in America before 1940*. Cambridge: Harvard University Press, 1982.

Curtis, Lynn A., ed. *American Violence and Public Policy: An Update of the National Commission on the Causes and Prevention of Violence*. New Haven: Yale University Press, 1985.

Frank, Gerold. *The Boston Stangler*. New York: New American Library, 1966.

Friedman, Lawrence M. *Crime and Punishment in American History*. New York: Basic Books, 1993.

Gilje, Paul A. *Rioting in America*. Bloomington: Indiana University Press, 1996.

Kadish, Sanford H. "Fifty Years of Criminal Law: An Opinionated Review." *Columbia Law Review* 87 (July 1999): 943-982.

Lane, Roger. *Murder in America: A History*. Columbus: Ohio State University Press, 1997.

Lukas, J. Anthony. *Big Trouble: A Murder in a Small Western Town Sets off a Struggle for the Soul of America*. New York: Simon and Schuster, 1997.

Maclean, Nancy. *Behind the Mask of Chivalry: The Making of the Second Ku Klux Klan*. New York: Oxford University Press, 1994.

Monkkonen, Eric. *Murder in New York City*. Berkeley: University of California Press, 2001.

United States National Commission on the Causes and Prevention of Violence. *To Establish Justice, to Insure Domestic Tranquility: Final Report*. Washington: United States Government Printing Office, 1969.

Walker, Samuel. *Popular Justice: A History of American Criminal Justice*. New York: Oxford University Press, 1980.

Internet Resources

U.S. Marshals
Official site of the USM, the first accredited federal law enforcement agency. Gives history, top 15 wanted fugitives, new releases, and other data
http://www.usdoj.gov/marshals

Federal Bureau of Investigation
Official website of the FBI with recent news, uniform crime reports, various documents, and the list of "most wanted" criminal.
http://www.FBI.gov

Bureau of Justice Statistics
U.S. Department of Justice Bureau of Justice Statistics official site. Contain statistics about crimes and victims, drugs and crime, criminal offenders, and law enforcement
http://www.ojp.usdoj.gov/bjs

National Criminal Justice Reference Service
Part of the Department of Justice website. Contains data on corrections, courts, law enforcement, and juvenile justice
http://www.ncjrs.org/statwww.html

American Correctional Association
Correction links to federal, state, and international associations
http://www.corrections.com

Bureau of Alcohol, Tobacco and Firearms
Good source for information about the Brady law
http://www.atf.treas.gov

Crime homepage links to 700 crime-related websites
http://lawenforcement.about.com/index.htm

Organized Crime Site
From the Godfather to the Sopranos, Meyer Lansky to Lucky Luciano.
http://organizedcrime.about.com/index.htm

Crime and Law Enforcement Mapping crime and crime statistics is a recent advancement in police technology.
http://geography.about.com/cs/crimeandlawenfo/index.htm

Crime Families - Fictional and Real Links to web sites focusing on North American crime families, both fictional and real.
http://organizedcrime.about.com/cs/crimefamilies1/index.htm

National Crime Prevention Council NCPC is a national nonprofit organization whose mission is to help America prevent crime and build safer, stronger communities.
http://mentalhealth.about.com/library/h/orgs/bl2939.htm

Just For Parents
Crime links for parents
http://crime.about.com/cs/justforparents/index.htm

For Kids and Parents
Crime sites appropriate for children, and of interest to parents.
http://crime.about.com/cs/familylinks/index.htm

Safe Kids
Keeping your children safe
http://crime.about.com/library/blfiles/blsafekids.htm

Rape Prevention & Education What should you do if you've been raped? How can you avoid being raped? Advice about how to arm against rapist and other criminals.
http://littlerock.about.com/library/weekly/aa021201a.htm

Criminal Justice & Law Enforcement
Articles, directories, statistics and all manner of commentary on criminal justice issues.
http://law.about.com/cs/criminaljustice/index.htm

Radio and television networks virtually all have web pages of their own these days that can be found through any reliable search engine. Some examples include
www.cbs.com (CBS television)
www.mtv.org (MTV)
www.pbs.org (PBS)
www.npr.org (National Public Radio)

The Museum of Television and Radio
www.mtr.org

The Academy of Television Arts and Sciences maintains a web site focused on the Emmy awards
www.emmys.org

Information about old radio programs
www.old-time.com

A good source of information about old television programs, which links to the Nickelodeon Network
www.tvland.com

MARKETING VIOLENT ENTERTAINMENT TO CHILDREN
The Federal Trade Commission's report released September 11, 2000, regarding the marketing of violent materials to children by the industries of motion picture, recording, and electronic games. Requires Adobe Acrobat Reader. Subjects: Mass media and children; Violence in mass media; Children and violence
http://www.ftc.gov/opa/2000/09/youthviol.htm

TELEVISION VIOLENCE MONITORING REPORTS
These three reports covering 1994 to 1997 from the UCLA Center for Communication Policy contain historical background, methodology and the findings of the studies for network TV, local, public and cable TV, and home video and video games. Subjects: Violence on television; Violence in mass media
http://ccp.ucla.edu/pages/VReports.asp

MEDIA STATISTICS
This Canadian site includes American and international statistics as well. They cover "television, video and computer games, the Internet, film and video, and the print media." There are sections on media usage, content, industries, and issues. Media issues, for example, contains subheadings for Media Violence, Gender and Minority Representation, and Internet Issues, among others. Subjects: Mass media; Statistics; Internet; Statistics
http://www.media-awareness.ca/eng/issues/stats/index.htm

Christopher Waldrep
San Francisco State University

DEATH

(1963) Jackie Kennedy (1929 - 1994) and her children John and Caroline, walking down steps past a guard of honour at the funeral of President John F. Kennedy. Robert Kennedy is following them.

TIMELINE

1870-1899 ~ Beginning of the Funeral Industry

Stein Manufacturing Company of Rochester, New York, mass produces caskets in many styles, colors, and grades (early 1870s) / First funeral chapel built in the U.S. (1885) / U.S. College of Embalming opens (1887) / Embalming replaces ice as the main method of preserving the appearance of dead bodies (1890)

MILESTONES:
Sioux Indians slaughter Custer's men at Little Bighorn (1876) • The weekly *Independent* is the most influential religious paper in the country, with over 6,000 clergymen on its mailing list (1880) • Russell Conwell becomes famous for his sermons on the virtues of wealth, which he preaches 6,000 times (1880-1900) • American Red Cross founded (1881) • German physician Robert Koch discovers tuberculosis bacterium (1882)

1900-1909 ~ The Decline of Death Rates

Epidemics of yellow fever, malaria, cholera, and smallpox decline (1910) / About 20 percent of Americans die before reaching age 5; less than half survive to age 60 (1900) / Only effective drugs available for treating disease are digitalis, quinine, and opium (1900) / Public health programs begin to be effective (1910)

MILESTONES: U.S. Army Yellow Fever Commission confirms mosquitoes as the disease carrier of malaria (1900) • U.S. Public Health Service identifies the hookworm parasite devastating the South (1902) • Pure Food and Drug Act sets standards for food and drug control (1906)

1910-1919 ~ World War I and the Great Flu Epidemic

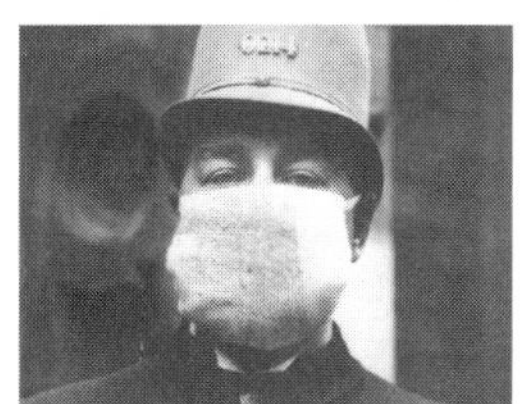

Cremation Society of America founded (1913) / Great Flu Epidemic kills far more civilians than World War I military fatalities (1918) / 53,000 American soldiers die in battle; most soldiers die of influenza (1917-1918)

MILESTONES: Mammography developed to detect breast cancer (1913) • Margaret Sanger risks arrest by opening up birth control clinics and importing and distributing contraceptives illegally (1914) • Chemical warfare and airplanes introduced as new weapons of war (1914-1918)

1920-1929 ~ Steady Advances in Reducing Death Rates

Infant death rates fall by 20 percent (1920) / Penicillin discovered (1928) / Automobile deaths dramatically increase (1920s), rising to 30,000 a year by 1930

MILESTONES: Proliferation of organized crime results in much killing (1920s) • Iron is discovered as a major factor in the formation of red blood cells (1925) • Discovery of vitamin C (1928)

1930-1939 ~ Improvement in Public Services and Hygiene

Infant mortality rates decline by 25 percent (1930-1939) / Heart disease, cancer, and stroke replace contagious diseases as leading causes of death (1939) / On average women outlive men by four years (1940) / Euthanasia Society of America established (1938)

MILESTONES: National Institute of Health established (1930) • 30,000 Americans die in car accidents (1930) • Ernest O. Lawrence uses a cyclotron to accelerate nuclear particles to smash atoms and release energy from matter (1930) • Common cold virus is discovered (1930) • Adolf Hitler rises to power in Germany (1933)

1940-1949 ~ Wonder Drugs

Development of penicillin, erythromycin, tetracycline, and other antibiotics (1940s) / 300,000 Americans die in battle in World War II, and another 115,000 die of non-combat accidents and diseases (1942-1945) / New vaccines developed against typhus and tetanus (1940s) / Chemical sprays developed to control diseases spread by insects (1940s) / Hill-Burton Act restricts certain medical practices to hospitals (1946)

MILESTONES: First treatment of pneumonia with sulfanilamide (1941) • Penicillin and blood plasma become available for battlefield use (1941) • Availability of the new drug penicillin to prevent venereal disease changes attitudes and caution about sexual intercourse (1943) • Atomic bombs dropped on Hiroshima and Nagasaki, Japan (1945)

1950-1959 ~ Fight against Death Declines

33,600 American combat deaths and 20,600 non-combat deaths in Korean War (1950–1953) / 70,000 civilian American males aged 15–34 die from accidents and homicide (1950s) / Polio rate at all-time high (1952) / Federal Food, Drug and Cosmetic Act prohibits cancer causing additives (1958)

MILESTONES: Ben Hogan returns to win the U.S. Open only months after a devastating automobile accident where doctors told him he might never walk again (1950) • First heart attack patient to be revived by electric shock (1952) • President Truman refuses to use atomic weapons against China (1952) • Julius and Ethel Rosenberg, avowed Communists, are executed for transmitting atomic secrets to the Soviets (1953) • Combined vaccine for whooping cough, diphtheria, and polio released (1959)

1960-1969 ~ Low Point in Combating Death

131,000 Americans die of homicide; 50,000 die in the Vietnam War (1966-1973) / Annual number of deaths due to homicide doubles over the decade (1960s) / Number of deaths due to automobile accidents increases 46 percent (1960s) / Enactment of Medicare and Medicaid reduce death in the elderly (1965) / Louis Ketner proposes the living will (1969)

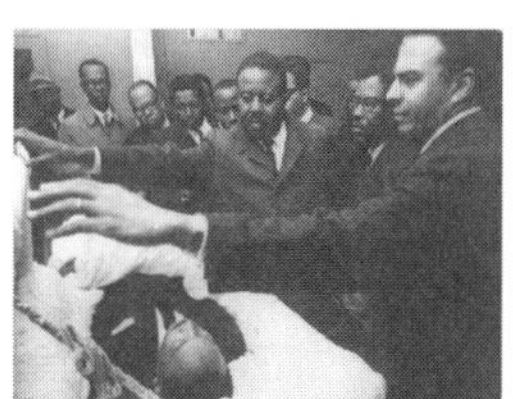

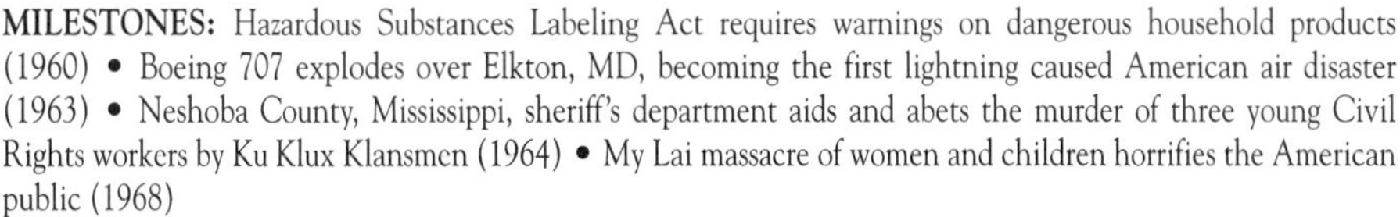

MILESTONES: Hazardous Substances Labeling Act requires warnings on dangerous household products (1960) • Boeing 707 explodes over Elkton, MD, becoming the first lightning caused American air disaster (1963) • Neshoba County, Mississippi, sheriff's department aids and abets the murder of three young Civil Rights workers by Ku Klux Klansmen (1964) • My Lai massacre of women and children horrifies the American public (1968)

1970-1979 ~ Debates over Causes of Death

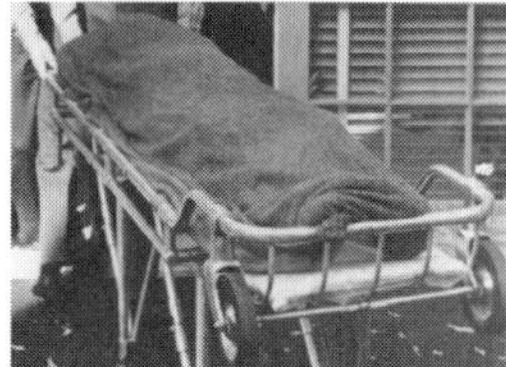

Public health campaigns encourage people not to smoke, to eat less animal fats, and to exercise more (1970s) / New drugs help control hypertension and irregular heartbeat (1970s) / Lung cancer increases more than 30 percent (1970-1979) / Homicide rate doubles (1970-1979) / First hospice in the U.S. opens in New Haven, Connecticut (1974) / Karen Quinlan's parents sue to have her life supports removed (1976)

MILESTONES: Four student protesters are killed by National Guard at Kent State University (1970) • Clean Air Act attempts to minimize vehicle-produced pollution (1970) • Endangered Species Act protects species from extinction (1970 and 1973) • District court rules that deadly force can be used by police only when life itself is endangered or great bodily harm is threatened (1975) • Vegetarian movement advocates eliminating meat products from the diet (1976) • Residents along the Love Canal re-located because of toxic pollution (late 1970s)

1980-1989 ~ Cancer and AIDS Increase

AIDS recognized as responsible for a worldwide death toll and first diagnosed in the U.S. (1981) / Cardio-vascular disease falls 30 percent (1980-1989) / 400,000 Americans die of AIDS (1987-1999) / AIDS becomes the second leading cause of death (following accidents) among men aged 25-34 (1989)

MILESTONES: Exxon *Valdez* oil spill in Alaska wreaks havoc on the environment, killing many animals (1986) • Brady Bill passed for control of handguns (1994)

1990-1999 ~ Progress on Many Fronts

Heart disease, cancer, and stroke remain the leading causes of death, accounting for 60 percent of all deaths (1999) / Death by cancer decreases 8 percent (1990-1999) / Fewer men and more women smoke cigarettes (1999) / Homicide rate decreases by 33 percent (1990-1999) / U.S. Supreme Court upholds states' rights to outlaw physician-assisted suicide (1997)

MILESTONES: Iraqi troops invade Kuwait, starting the Gulf War (1990) • First gene therapy performed on a human to treat an immune deficiency (1990) • Globalization of environmental concerns, especially global warming (1990) • Basketball superstar "Magic" Johnson announces he has AIDS and retires from professional basketball (1991) • EPA labels second-hand smoke a carcinogen (1993) • A pipe bomb explodes in Centennial Olympic Park, Atlanta, during the summer Olympic games, killing two persons (1996)

Introduction

A profound decline in death rates occurred over the twentieth century. One way for a person living at the beginning of the twenty-first century to appreciate the magnitude of this change is to consider the answer to this hypothetical question: What are the chances that you would be alive today if death rates had not changed since 1900? A careful analysis of data by two demographers, Kevin White and Samuel Preston, concludes that the answer is very close to 50 percent. That is, half of the people living in the United States today owe their existence to the improvements in mortality that occurred over the past century. Without this mortality improvement, one-fourth of those living today would never have been born (because one of their ancestors would have died before giving birth to them or their progenitors), and another fourth would have been born but would already have died. Along with the dramatic change in the level of mortality, there have been significant changes in the ages at which people die, the places in which they die, the ways in which death is viewed, the ways of caring for dying people, and the ways of dealing with deceased people. This article discusses changes in these various facets of death in the twentieth century.

Demography of Death

Demographers who study death analyze basic mortality statistics. The primary sources of these statistics are the death certificates that are filled out for individuals who die. Death certificates include such information as age, sex, marital status, and race of the deceased, as well as the cause of death and place of death. Each state collects death certificates for those who die in the state, and then forwards the information from these certificates to the National Center for Health Statistics (NCHS). The NCHS compiles statistics on deaths for the entire United States and reports these statistics in various publications. Although some states did not cooperate with this death registration system in the early 1900s, we have reasonably good estimates of death statistics for the United States for the twentieth century.

A useful statistic for summarizing the overall level of mortality in a population at a particular time is "expectation of life" at birth, or average number of years that a newborn in the population would live under mortality conditions existing at that time. The trend in average years lived over the twentieth century in the United States is shown in Figure 1. From this figure one can see that under mortality conditions existing in 1900, a newborn would on average live about 47 years. There was, of course, a lot of variation around this average. Many of the babies born in 1900 died in their first year of life, while others were still alive in 2000. But comparing the expectation of life at the beginning of each decade provides a simple way to describe changes occurring in the level of mortality.

Over the entire twentieth century, life expectancy increased by nearly 30 years (from 47.3 in 1900 to 76.7 in 1998). This is a far larger increase than that occurring for the population of the world from the beginning of human existence up to the twentieth century. In other words, the revolution in death rates occurring between 1900 and 2000 was unprecedented in the

Death Rates for Selected Ages
(Number of Deaths Per 10,000 in Age Category)

	1900	1910	1920	1930	1940	1950	1960	1970	1980	1990	2000
Under 1	1624	1318	923	690	549	330	270	214	129	97	75
35 - 44	102	90	81	68	52	36	30	31	23	22	21
75 - 84	1233	1222	1189	1127	1120	933	875	800	669	601	574

SOURCE: *Sickness and Health in America* by Leavitt and Numbers, eds., 1997.

history of the world. The most dramatic change of all occurred among infants. In 1900 about 150 out of every 1,000 newborns died before they could experience their first birthday. By the end of the century this tragic experience occurred to only seven of every 1,000 babies. By tracking changes over each decade we can gain an understanding of how this momentous transformation came about.

1900-1909 • Beginning the Decline of Death Rates ~ By the time the nineteenth century came to a close, some significant changes were occurring in the historical patterns of death in the United States. Intermittent epidemics of yellow fever, malaria, cholera, and smallpox that generated such fear of mortality in American cities in the nineteenth century were largely past. Death rates in urban areas, although still higher than in rural areas, were clearly declining. Infant death rates were lower than they had been a hundred years earlier. Nevertheless, by contemporary standards, death rates were

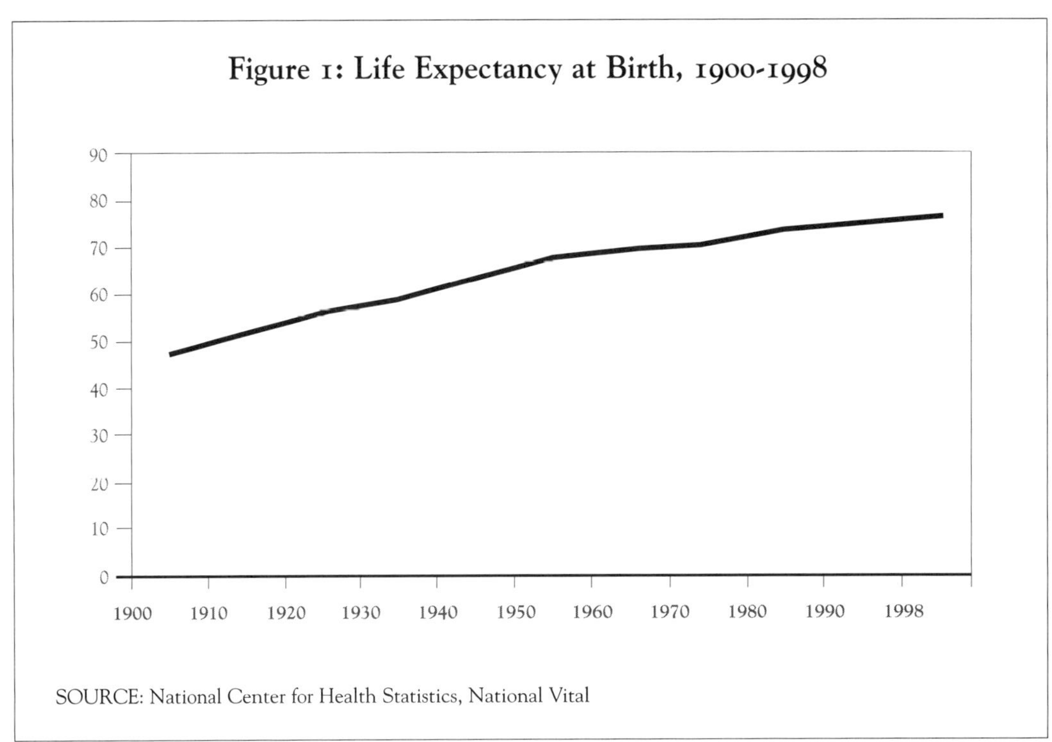

Figure 1: Life Expectancy at Birth, 1900-1998

SOURCE: National Center for Health Statistics, National Vital appallingly high. About 20 percent of all children died before reaching age five, and less than half of all newborns survived to age sixty. In contrast, more than 80 percent of babies born in 2000 are expected to survive to age sixty-five. Why were death rates so high in 1900 and what changes were responsible for the major improvements?

Three possible explanations for the improving mortality conditions up to 1900 have been examined: advances in medical practice, improvement in standards of living, and expansion of public health efforts. The least important of these three factors clearly was contributions from the medical doctors. While important scientific advances in understanding the nature of infectious diseases occurred in the late nineteenth century, these discoveries had little impact on medical practice at that time. Many physicians in 1900 still did not accept the germ theory, and the only effective drugs available to them for treating disease were digitalis, quinine, and opium. Lacking the ability to prevent or cure most diseases, the medical profession was not able to save many lives and, not surprisingly, medicine was not a particularly high prestige occupation.

Medical historians generally agree that advances in public health were primarily responsible for the improvement in mortality conditions before 1900. Improvements in nutrition, housing, and personal hygiene also may have contributed to declining death rates by 1900, although historical data to document this are scarce. But evidence for the contributions of public health efforts is abundant. Even without a sophisticated understanding of how communicable diseases spread, the need for vigorous sanitation campaigns in the burgeoning American cities of the late nineteenth century was obvious. Leavitt and Numbers describe the conditions in their *Sickness and Health in America* (1997).

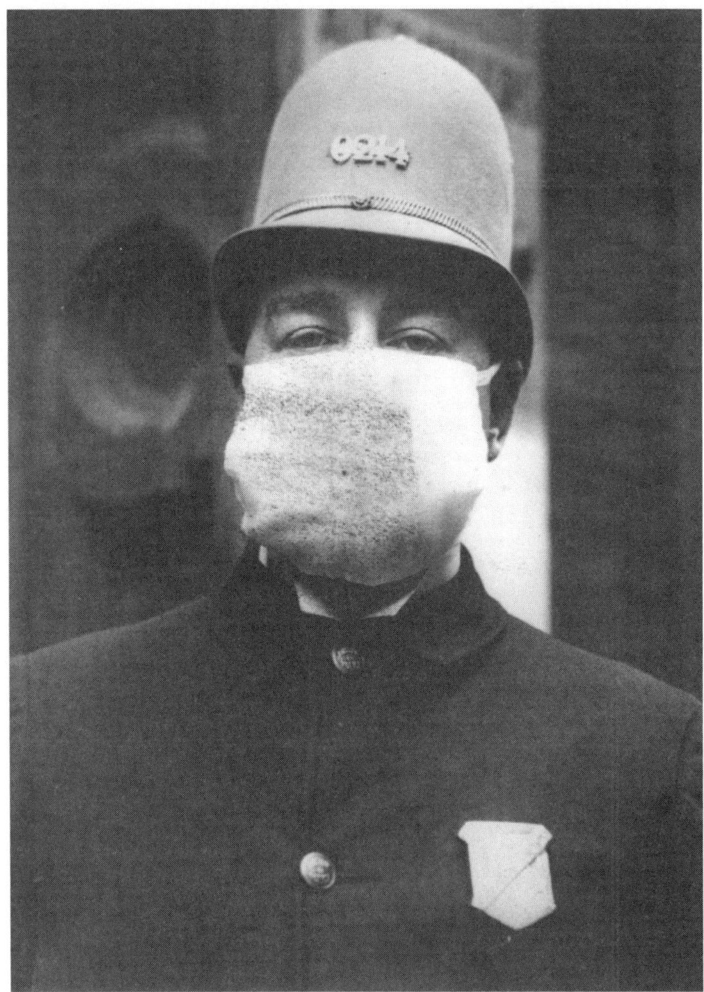

(1918) An American policeman wearing a 'Flu Mask' to protect himself from the outbreak of Spanish flu following World War I.

> Festering piles of garbage littered urban streets, dead animals lay where they fell, privies and cesspools overran into drainless, unpaved streets. Horses defecated indiscriminately. . . . [I]t was [not] possible to walk down the street without dragging one's skirt in the filth or having to hold a handkerchief over one's nose.

Cities and states began to organize health departments with the goal of cleaning up the physical environment, and consequently, mortality from infectious diseases began to decline. Many of the most important contributions from public health efforts occurred in the twentieth century, but attention to problems of urban garbage collection, water supplies, sewage systems, and quality of the milk supply was already beginning to have a positive impact by 1900.

At the beginning of the twentieth century the three leading causes of death—influenza and pneumonia, tuberculosis, and infections of the gastrointestinal tract—accounted for about one-third of all deaths in the United States. By the end of the first decade, the death rate from these causes had declined by 20 percent, and heart disease had become the leading cause of death. This was the beginning of a trend that would continue throughout most of the century, as infectious diseases declined in significance and degenerative diseases (heart disease, cancer, stroke) assumed the role of leading causes of death. The average life span of Americans increased by two years between 1900-1910. All of this gain is explained by decreasing death rates for children and young adults. Death rates for people over age 35 had not yet begun to decline.

In earlier times, high death rates produced a generally fatalistic view of death in the population; death seemed to be something that could not be controlled. By the early twentieth century, however, this clearly was no longer the accepted way to view death. Various sectors of the population were making concerted efforts to prevent unnecessary deaths. Women's groups and mothers' associations made infant mortality a highly visible public issue. The problem of industrial working conditions that caused widespread deaths because of accidents, injuries, and illness became a public issue as various reports on occupational health gained attention. And, above all, there was a determined effort to reduce deaths from tuberculosis. The National Association for the Study and Prevention of Tuberculosis was formed in 1904, and physicians, social workers, and highly motivated citizens worked together on a crusade to defeat TB. Their efforts involved both isolating infected persons to prevent the spread of the disease by treating them in sanatoriums and improving public and personal hygiene. These varied intentional efforts to eradicate communicable diseases and preventable deaths significantly affected the lives of those who would subsequently be born in the United States.

1910-1919 • World War I and the Great Flu Epidemic ~ The efforts to reduce deaths continued in the second decade of the twentieth century, and infant death rates and deaths due to tuberculosis continued to decline. But two unanticipated disasters toward the end of the decade upset the expectation that progress would lead to an uninterrupted decline in death rates. One of these events was World War I. The other event, the Great Flu Epidemic of 1918, was far more deadly than the war.

During the 20 months that the United States was involved in World War I (April 1917 to November 1918), about 53,000 American soldiers died in battle. Understandably, these combat deaths received a lot of publicity and were viewed as a great tragedy. It should be noted, however, that battle-related deaths in World War I comprised less than two percent of all the deaths to Americans during the 20 months that we were involved in the war. It should also be noted that, as in all previous wars, more soldiers died of illness and accidents unrelated to battle than died in combat. During World War I, as many soldiers died from influenza as from battle.

As American soldiers were heading to Europe to fight in the war, an influenza epidemic hit the country with a virulence unprecedented in American history. Before it burned itself out a year later, it is estimated that more than half a million Americans had died from the flu. Near the peak of the epidemic, officials in the *American Journal of Public Health* were asked what a local community could do to fight it. Their answer, reported in the American Journal of Public Health in 1917, reflects the total helplessness of the medical profession to do anything about it:

> Hunt up your wood workers and cabinetmakers and set them to making coffins. Then take your street laborers and set them to digging graves. If you do this you will not have your dead accumulating faster than you can dispose of them.

The 1918 influenza epidemic was the last epidemic disaster of the twentieth century in the United States, until HIV infection and the AIDS epidemic appeared in the 1980s.

1920-1929 • Steady Advances in Reducing Death Rates ~ The 1920s can be characterized as a time of steady advances in reducing death rates. Infant death rates fell by 20 percent over the decade, and expectation of life at birth increased by about three years. The mortality improvements were not the result of any new medical breakthroughs. Although penicillin was fortuitously discovered in 1928, it was not developed for medical use until the 1940s. As in the preceding decades, progress came from improved standards of living and improved sanitation related to public health efforts. But some changes associated with growing affluence created new risks. As use of automobiles increased, the death rate caused by motor-vehicle accidents jumped from less than two per 100,000 in 1910 to over 26 by 1929. Fortunately, the number of deaths per million vehicle miles traveled decreased after the 1920s, and was 90 percent lower in 1997 than it was in 1925.

1930-1939 • Improvement in Public Services and Hygiene ~ The economic prosperity of the 1920s ended with the stock market crash in October 1929. The Great Depression that followed lasted throughout the 1930s. This decade is remembered as a time of high unemployment, widespread poverty, and general

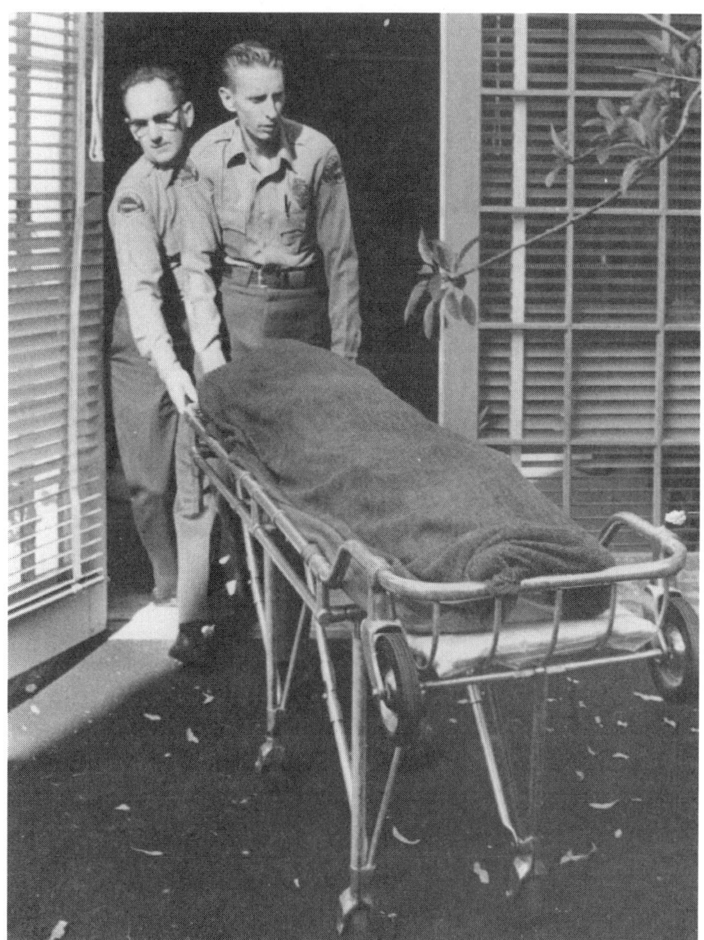

(1962) Medical attendants removing the body of Marilyn Monroe (Norma Jean Mortenson or Norma Jean Baker, 1926 - 1962) from her home.

economic decline. A lasting image of this era is that of devastated business executives committing suicide. The death rate from suicide did increase with the onset of the depression; the average annual number of suicides per 100,000 in the population was 15.4 during the 1930s, compared to 12.3 in the preceding decade. But suicides were responsible for only about one percent of all deaths, and changes in other causes of death over the 1930s were far more consequential.

Despite the economic difficulties, death rates declined during the Great Depression. Infant mortality rates declined by 25 percent between 1930 and 1939, and expectation of life increased by four years. Once again the changes leading to this progress were concentrated in the area of public health—improving sewage disposal, water treatment, food safety, solid waste disposal—and public education about personal hygiene. But improvements in hospital sanitation and health care were also having some impact. A particularly important change beginning in the 1930s involved the risk of death related to childbearing. In 1930, 670 of every 100,000 women giving birth died from complications of pregnancy (e.g. toxemia), complications of childbirth (e.g. hemorrhage), or infection (sepsis) causing death after childbirth. This level of maternal mortality, which had not changed much since 1900, fell to 400 per 100,000 by the end of the decade. Even larger declines in the maternal mortality rate occurred after 1940, so that by 1950 it was down to 83 and by 2000 it was at just one per 100,000.

Infectious and contagious diseases continued to decline as significant causes of death in the 1930s, and by the end of the decade the three leading causes of death were heart disease, cancer, and stroke. Ever since that time these have maintained their positions at the top of the list of the major killers of Americans. In 1940 these three causes were responsible for nearly half of all deaths; by 2000 they accounted for 61 percent of all deaths. One consequence of the shift in the leading cause of death from infectious diseases to degenerative diseases was an increasing advantage of women over men in expectation of life. On average, women were outliving men by four years in 1940, compared to just two years in 1900. This gender gap would continue to increase until it reached 7.8 years in 1975, after which it began to decrease. By 1998 the female life expectancy advantage over males was down to 5.7 years.

1940-1949 • Wonder Drugs

Expectation of life increased by 5.1 years between 1940 and 1949, the largest jump in any single decade of the twentieth century. The infant death rate declined by 35 percent over the decade, and by 1949 half of all newborns could be expected to survive past age 70. The most important breakthrough affecting deaths in the 1940s was the development of penicillin and other antibiotics (erythromycin, tetracycline, etc.) that were found to be effective in treating a host of infectious diseases. After the mid-1940s, when use of antibiotics to treat infections became widespread, death rates from pneumonia, tuberculosis, syphilis, rheumatic fever, and various other infectious diseases plummeted. The potentially life changing effect that these "wonder drugs" could have is illustrated by the first American civilian whose life was saved by penicillin.

It was not lives saved by antibiotics that received newspaper headlines in the 1940s, but rather lives lost at war. On December 7, 1941, the bombing of Pearl

Harbor killed 2,000 Americans. The next day the United States entered World War II, and between then and the end of the war in September 1945, over 15 million Americans served in the military. Almost 300,000 Americans died in battle in World War II, and another 115,000 died of non-combat accidents and diseases. As in World War I, combat deaths did not comprise a very large proportion of all deaths occurring to Americans during the war years (they were less than six percent of all deaths). But in contrast to all previous wars, the number of soldiers dying from combat injuries exceeded the number dying from other causes. This reflects a growing ability to protect people against infectious diseases.

The government was able to mobilize the pharmaceutical industry to rapidly expand the production of penicillin for soldiers. It also invested in major wartime research efforts to develop new vaccines against typhus and tetanus and to develop chemical sprays to control diseases spread by insects. Further, the wartime research led to advances in the use of blood and blood derivatives and in the treatment of shock. Thus, out of the war came valuable new weapons for fighting death in the population at large.

1950-1959 • Fight Against Death Declines ~ The marked decline in death rates that characterized the preceding decade continued for the first several years of the 1950s. Life expectancy increased by 1.4 years between 1950 and 1954, and the infant death rate declined by more than ten percent. But then the progress that had persisted with few interruptions since 1900 seemed to come to an end. Life expectancy at the end of the 1950s had hardly changed from where it was in 1954, increasing only from 69.6 to 69.9 years. A number of experts concluded that the era of declining mortality probably had come to an end. A report from the National Center for Health Statistics asserted that, "the death rate for the United States has reached the point where further decreases as experienced in the past cannot be anticipated." The reasoning behind this pessimistic conclusion was that success in reducing deaths caused by infectious diseases meant that cardiovascular diseases and cancer now caused a majority of deaths. Because there was no

~

The first U.S. civilian whose life was saved by penicillin died in June 1999 at the age of 90 years. In March 1942, a 33-year-old woman was hospitalized for a month with a life-threatening streptococcal infection at a New Haven, Connecticut, hospital. She was delirious, and her temperature reached almost 107° F (41.6° C). Treatments with sulfa drugs, blood transfusions, and surgery had no effect. As a last resort, her doctors injected her with a tiny amount of an obscure experimental drug called penicillin. Her hospital chart, now at the Smithsonian Institution, indicates a sharp overnight drop in temperature; by the next day she was no longer delirious. She survived to marry, raise a family, and meet Sir Alexander Fleming, the scientist who discovered penicillin.

~

historical evidence that we could significantly reduce deaths from these degenerative diseases, it was assumed that future progress in reducing deaths would be slow.

It should be noted that the United States was engaged in another war in the 1950s, the Korean Conflict that lasted from mid-1950 through mid-1953. Although it was an undeclared war, over 50,000 American soldiers lost their lives (33,600 combat deaths and 20,600 non-combat deaths). By comparison, during the Korean War, 70,000 civilian American males aged 15–34 died from accidents and homicide.

1900-1959 • Great Strides in Combating Death ~ From the perspective of 1959, it was possible to look back and observe a number of interesting changes in mortality since the beginning of the century. Most striking, of course, was the overall increase in life expectancy from 47 years to 70 years. But the mortality gains were not spread evenly across the population. Mortality improvements had affected the young far more than the old. The chances of a newborn dying before reaching adulthood had fallen by 83 percent, but the chances of someone aged 65 dying before reaching age 80 had fallen by only 15 percent. Also, gains in longevity had been much greater for women than men. The female advantage in life expectancy more than tripled between 1900 and 1959, going from 2.0 years to 6.4. Finally, gains in life expectancy were greater for black Americans than for whites. Figure 2 depicts the years of added life expectancy by sex and race. Between 1900 and 1959, the racial difference in average years lived fell from 14.6 years to 6.8 years. Despite this gain in closing the racial gap, it should be noted that life expectancy for blacks in 1959 was about the same as it had been for whites 30 years earlier, as shown in Figure 3. Comparing infant death rates in 1959 also indicates the size of the racial disparity—44 of every 1,000 black babies died in the first year of life compared with 23 of every 1,000 white babies.

Figure 2: Gains in Life Expectancy by Sex and Race, 1900-1960

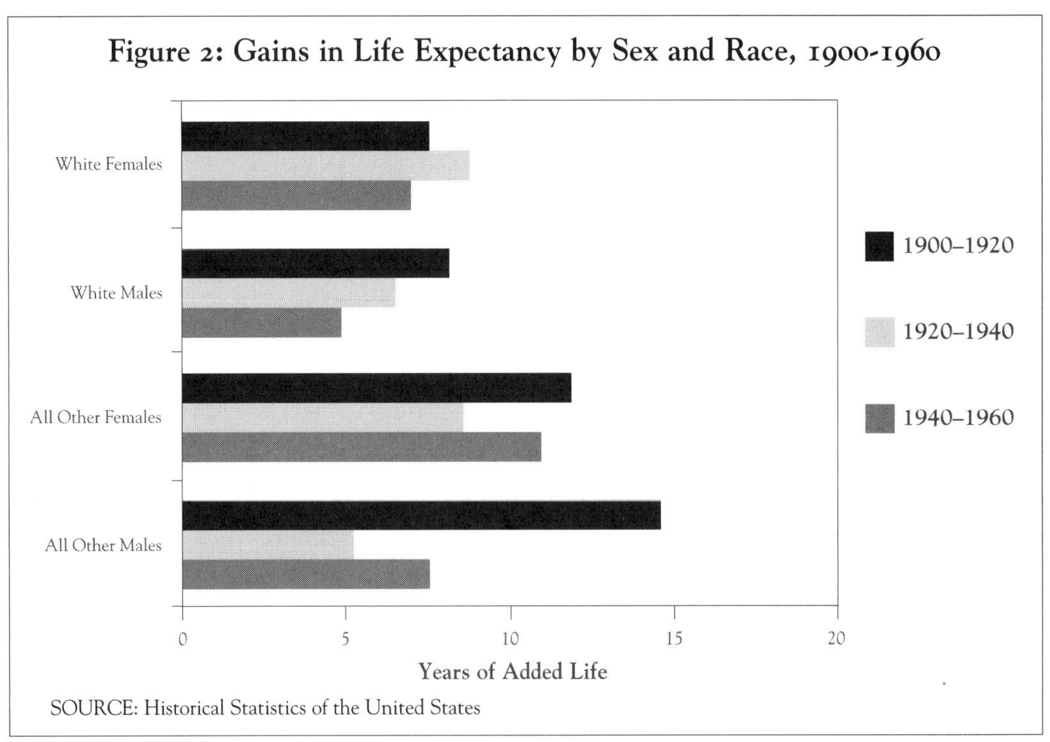

SOURCE: Historical Statistics of the United States

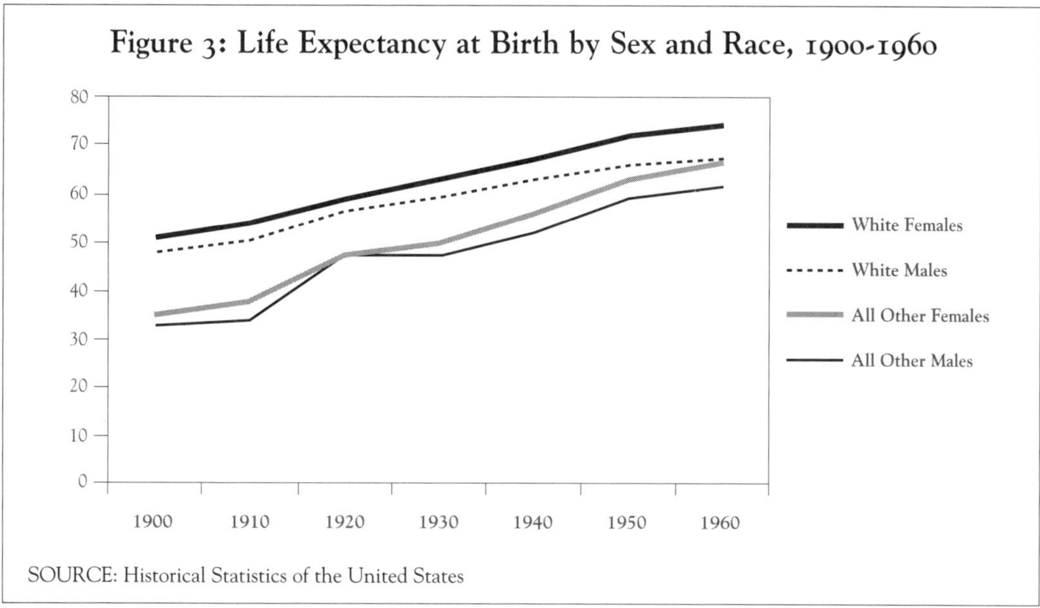

1960-1969 • Low Point in Combating Death ~ Mortality in the 1960s tended to follow the pattern that experts had predicted; there was not much change. Expectation of life in 1968 was 70.2 years, exactly the same as it had been in 1961. The Vietnam War (the second longest war in United States history, lasting from August 1964 through June 1973) had almost no perceptible effect on overall death rates during this time. The 58,000 deaths to soldiers during the Vietnam War amounted to only 0.3 percent of all deaths to Americans. Because of increasing violence in our cities during this era, twice as many (131,000) Americans died of homicide in the United States as died of war related causes.

The 1960s can be viewed as the low point of the twentieth century in America's attempt to lower death rates. Death rates from the leading causes of death (heart disease, cancer, stroke) were at the same level at the end of the decade as at the beginning. The annual number of deaths due to homicide nearly doubled over the decade, and the number of deaths due to automobile accidents increased 46 percent. Because car accidents and shootings disproportionately affect adolescents and young adults, the death rate for the 15–34 age category actually increased over the decade. But there were two hopeful signs as the 1960s came to an end. First, death rates did decline between 1968 and 1969. Second, because of the enactment of Medicare and Medicaid in 1965, older people and poor people had greater access to health care than in the past.

1970-1979 • Heart Disease Deaths Decline ~ To the surprise of many experts, the progress in reducing death rates that had been stalled since the early 1950s, resumed after 1970. Expectation of life at birth increased by 3.1 years over the decade. The most important reason for this advance was a 30 percent decline in the leading cause of death, heart disease. Both changes in lifestyle and advances in medical care are given credit for the significant downturn in the death rate from heart disease.

Based on findings from research conducted in the 1960s, public health campaigns encouraged people not to smoke, to eat less animal fats, and to exercise more. There is evidence that changes in

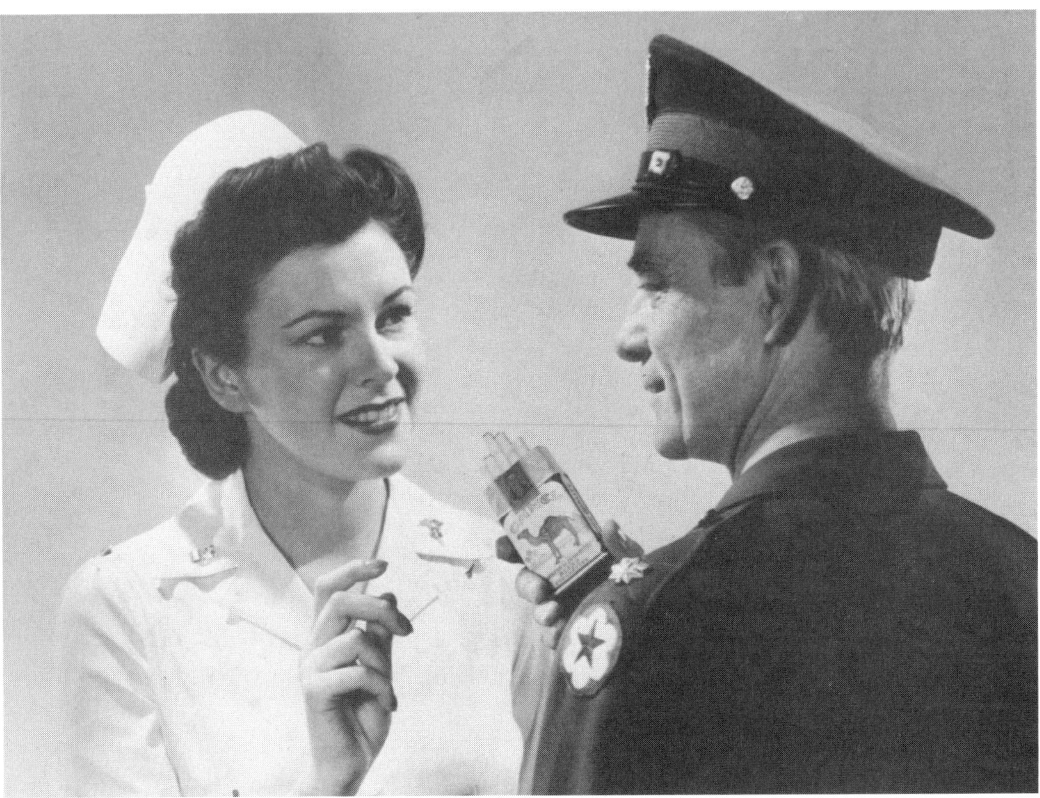

(circa 1945) Advertisement shows a uniformed man offering a Camel cigarette to a nurse, whose smile suggests approval of this cancer-causing substance.

all of these areas occurred in the 1970s, with clearly beneficial health consequences. On the medical front, advances were made in emergency care and diagnosing coronary artery disease. New drugs helped control hypertension and irregular heartbeat. Coronary bypass surgery also gained in popularity. Perhaps as important as the new technology was the increased availability of health care to the poor and the elderly.

Despite the generally good news of overall decreasing death rates, the increasing death rate from two particular causes created a great deal of concern. One of these causes was murder. Figure 4 shows the trend in the U.S. murder rate, or number of murders for every 100,000 citizens between 1900 and 1995. As depicted, the murder rate in the United States started increasing in the mid-1960s, and by 1974 it was twice what it had been a decade earlier. The death rate due to murder fluctuated around this new high level for the next 20 years. The odds of being a murder victim varied drastically by race and sex. Using 1978 murder rates, it was calculated that one out of every 29 black males could expect to be murdered during the course of a lifetime, compared to one out of every 186 white males and one out of every 606 white females.

The other cause of death that was increasing was cancer. Most disturbing was the change in the death rate from lung cancer, which increased by more than 30 percent over the decade. Concern over deaths from lung cancer would generate a major public health effort to reduce cigarette smoking.

1980-1989 • Cancer and AIDS Increase ~ The good news of the renewed decline in death rates that began in the preceding decade continued through the 1980s. The age-adjusted death rate from cardio-vascular disease fell 30 percent over the decade, and 1.4 years were added to the expectation of life at birth. However, no progress was made in reducing deaths caused by cancer. In addition, a new disease was first diagnosed in the United States in 1981. Although hardly noticed at the time, acquired immune deficiency syndrome (AIDS) gained an enormous amount of attention in coming years. By 1989, AIDS was the eleventh leading cause of death in the United States, and the second leading cause of death (following accidents) among men aged twenty-five to thirty-four.

1990-1999 • Progress on Many Fronts ~ After the tremendous reduction in deaths from infectious diseases over the twentieth century and the apparent end of epidemics, it was a shock for a new epidemic to capture headlines through much of the 1990s. From 1987, the first year that AIDS was classified as an official cause of death, through 1999, over 400,000 Americans died of AIDS. The peak year was 1995, when 50,610 deaths were attributed to AIDS and it was the eighth leading cause of death in the country. With the advent of more effective therapy to slow the progression of HIV disease, and some success in reducing risk of acquiring the human immunodeficiency virus (HIV), deaths caused by AIDS tumbled for the rest of the 1990s. By 1999, slightly more than 16,000 people died of AIDS in the United States, and this was no longer one of the 15 leading causes of death.

Heart disease, cancer, and stroke remained the three leading causes of death and accounted for about 60 percent of all deaths in the late 1990s. However, important changes in these leading causes of death occurred over the decade. Although not as rapidly as in the preceding decade, the age-adjusted death rate from cardiovascular diseases (heart disease and stroke) continued to decline throughout the 1990s. In 1998 the risk of dying from heart disease or stroke was only 38 percent of what it had been in 1950. More interesting, perhaps, was the decline in the age-adjusted cancer death rate that occurred

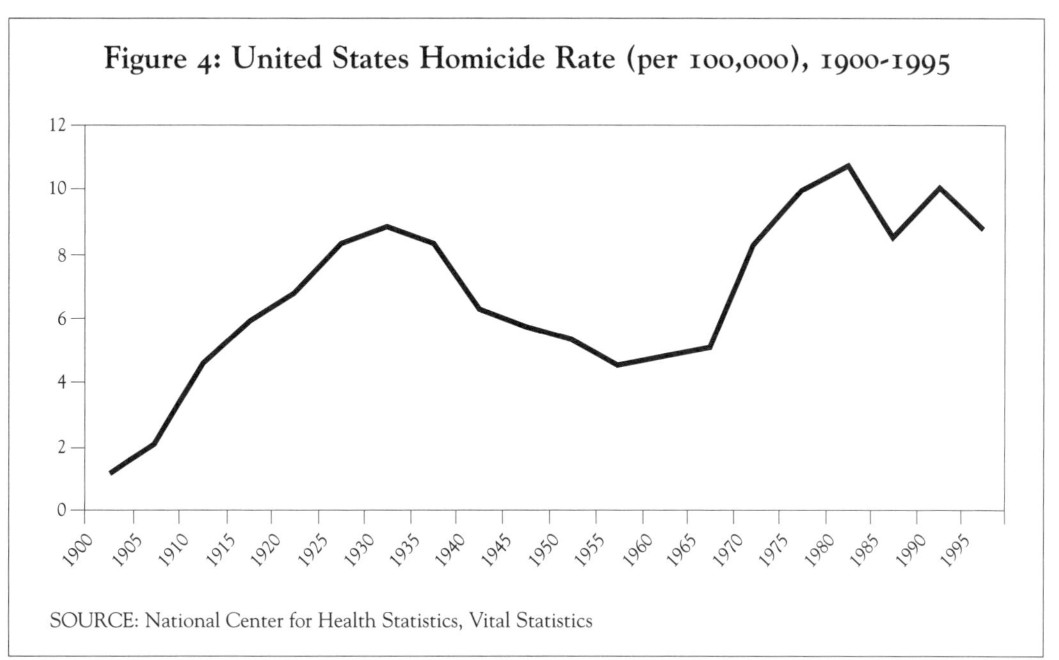

Figure 4: United States Homicide Rate (per 100,000), 1900-1995

SOURCE: National Center for Health Statistics, Vital Statistics in the 1990s. The cancer death rate, which had steadily increased since 1950, fell by eight percent between 1990 and 1998 (the last year for which statistics are available). The significant decline in lung cancer—the leading cause of cancer mortality—was particularly encouraging. This was attributed to the decreasing prevalence of cigarette smoking after the 1960s among males. Indeed, the entire decline in deaths from lung cancer in the 1990s is accounted for by the decline in smoking among men. Among women, who had not decreased smoking as much as men, lung cancer death rates actually increased slightly throughout the 1990s.

Several other encouraging changes in mortality occurred during the last decade of the twentieth century. The homicide rate, which caused great anxiety through the 1970s and 1980s, declined by 33 percent between 1990 and 1998, to a level not seen since 1967. Credit for this decline is given to a number of factors: changes in the illegal drug markets, economic expansion, fewer guns on the street, and increases in the prison population. Death rates from car accidents and from suicide declined over the 1990s. The infant death rate declined by 26 percent, reaching an historic low of 6.8 percent per 1,000 by 1999. In conclusion, the twentieth century ended on a positive note with respect to advances in reducing risks of premature deaths.

1950-2000 • Kinship Implications of Declining Death Rates ~ The declining death rates occurring throughout the twentieth century meant that an ever-increasing proportion of those who were born would survive to any particular age. For example, the proportion who would survive to age 80 under mortality conditions existing in 1900 was only 12 percent, compared to 58 percent under conditions existing in 2000. This remarkable mortality revolution affected the potential for individuals at every stage of life to have connections with various kin. For children and young adults, it became increasingly likely that some of their grandparents would still be alive when they had their own children. Among middle-aged persons, the odds of having parents still alive increased. For older people, there was a continuously increasing possibility that their spouses, siblings, and children would be alive.

In other words, declining death rates have tended to increase the supply of kin over an entire lifetime. Of course the mere existence of particular kin (grandparents, first spouses, etc.) does not inform us regarding the meaning of these relationships. But a substantial amount of research has confirmed that when these basic kin relationships exist, they are highly valued and meaningful for most people. Therefore it seems likely that the progressively declining death rates have altered social relationships in American society in significant ways.

Grandparents ~ Over the twentieth century a steadily increasing proportion of children and young adults in the United States had a surviving grandparent (see Figure 5). Having at least one grandparent alive during early childhood was usual throughout the twentieth century—even in 1900—about 94 percent of all 10-year olds had a living grandparent. But very big changes occurred over time in the prospects of having a grandparent alive as one moved through adolescence and young adulthood. In 1900, only one in five 30-year olds had a living grandparent. This ratio increased to one in two by 1960, and by the end of the century it had

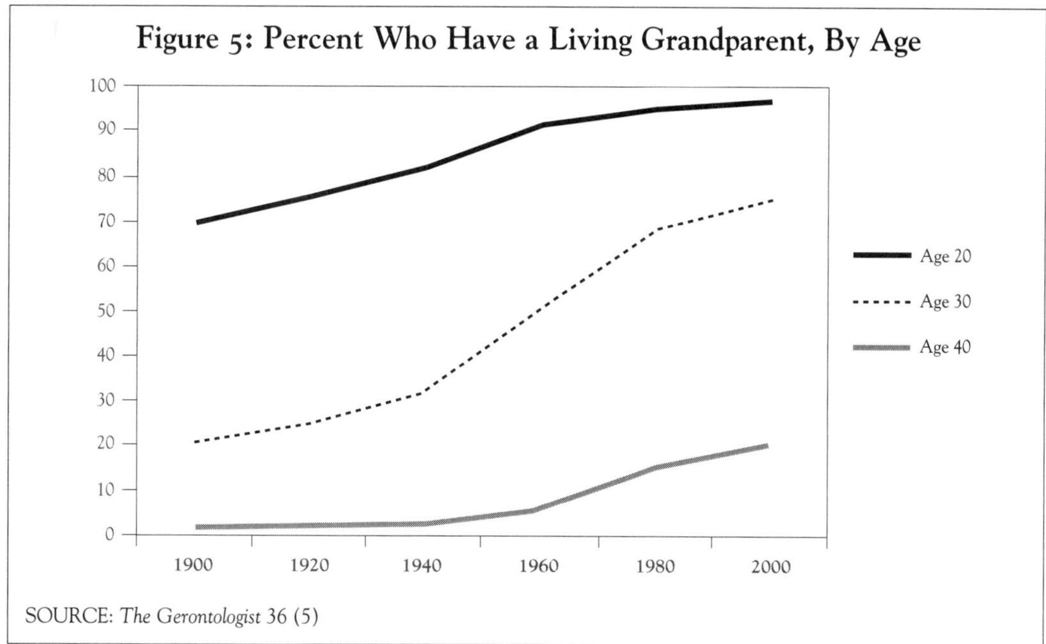

SOURCE: *The Gerontologist* 36 (5)

reached three in four. As it became common for young adults to have grandparents still living, it also became common for young children to have one or more of their great-grandparents still living. In 1900 most children never had a chance of getting to know a great-grandparent; in 2000 most did have this opportunity.

Reflecting the lower death rates for women than men, during each decade more young adults have had surviving grandmothers than grandfathers. As the gender gap in mortality grew larger over most of the century, the imbalance in grandmothers compared to grandfathers increased. The proportion of 30-year olds with a surviving grandmother grew from 15 percent in 1900 to 43 percent in 1960, but the corresponding proportion with a surviving grandfather increased only from six percent to 14 percent. By 2000 about 67 percent of 30-year olds had living grandmothers, compared to 27 percent with a living grandfather. Thus over time, the older relatives in kin networks have increasingly consisted of females, helping to accentuate the matriarchal tilt of American kinship networks.

Old Parents ~ Not surprisingly, as death rates for adults have declined, the typical age at which individuals experience the death of parents has gone up. The trend over the twentieth century in proportion of middle-aged adults who have a mother or father alive is shown in Figure 6. In 1900, only 39 percent of all adults aged 50 had a parent still living, and fewer than eight percent of those aged 60 did. By 1940 a slight majority (52 percent) of the 50-year olds had a surviving parent, but still only 13 percent of the 60-year olds. These percentages continued to grow, however, so that by the end of the century it became relatively common to have a parent alive as one approached his or her own old age. About 80 percent of those aged 50 in 2000 had a living parent, and nearly half (44 percent) of the 60-year olds did.

It has always been more common for adults with just one living parent to have a widowed mother than a widowed father. This contrast grew larger over most of the century. Between 1920 and 1980, the proportion of 50-year-olds with

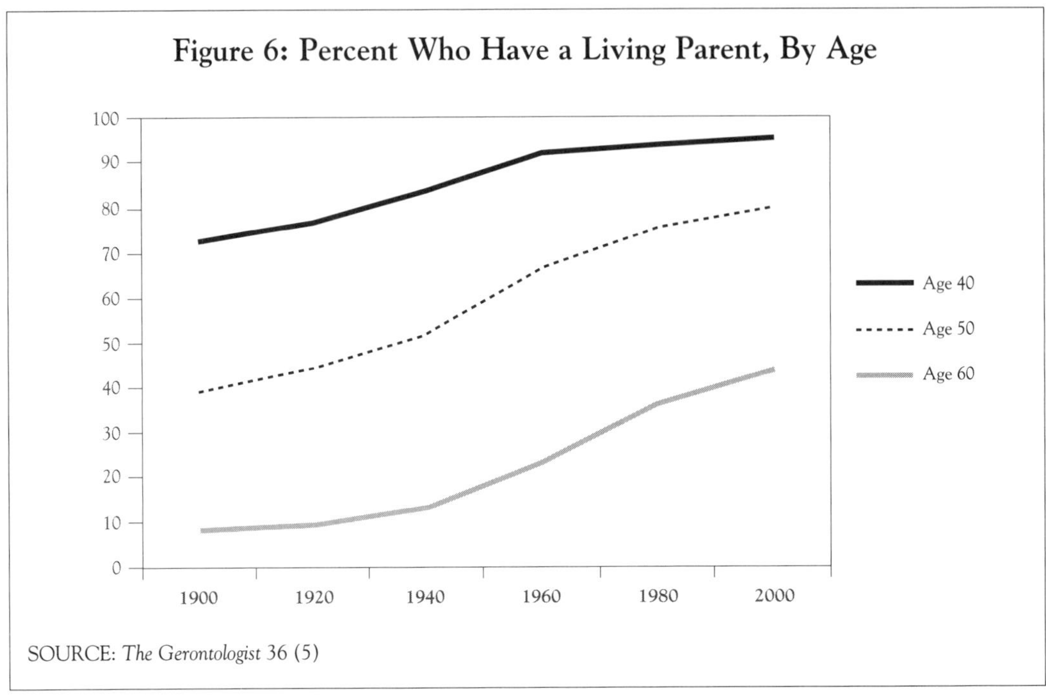

only a mother alive increased from 24 percent to 43 percent, while the proportion with only a father alive actually declined from 14 to 12 percent. The proportion with both parents alive at this stage of life increased over this time period (going from six to 21 percent). By 2000 it was about five times more likely that a person aged 60 had a widowed mother than a widowed father.

SPOUSES ~ Decreasing death rates after 1900 created the potential for large gains in average number of years that men and women could expect to live in uninterrupted marriages. In reality, most of the potential gains in marital duration were not experienced because of the increasing tendency to end marriages by divorce. Nevertheless, it is interesting to see the changes that occurred in men and women

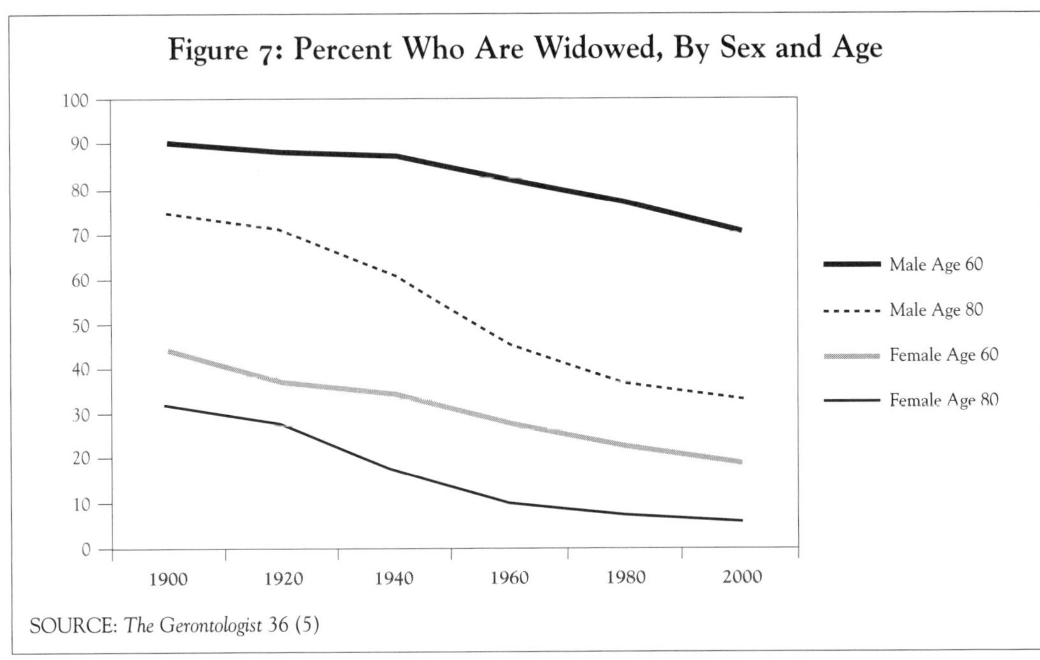

experiencing widowhood before reaching different stages of later life.

Figure 7 shows the historical pattern of men and women who married at fairly typical ages (wife aged 22, husband aged 25) who were widowed before they reached age 60 or 80. Because of gender differences in death rates, it was always more likely that a woman than a man surviving to old age experienced widowhood. But for both men and women, there was a decreasing likelihood that a marriage would be terminated by a spouse's death at any particular age. For example, the proportion of men who could expect their first wife to die before they reached age 70 fell from 50 percent in 1900 to only 15 percent in 2000. The corresponding change for women was from 67 percent in 1900 to 39 percent in 2000. Because about half of all first marriages now end in divorce rather than widowhood, the actual number of long duration marriages has not increased nearly as rapidly as would have been potentially possible.

SIBLINGS ~ Although sibling relationships tend to be less salient than parent-child or husband-wife relationships, many older people report that siblings are an important source of social and instrumental support. Further, sibling relationships are unique in their potential longevity, particularly when mortality is low. Consider the situation of a person aged 80 who had a sibling born two years after he/she was born. In 2000, if that sibling was a sister, there was a 66 percent probability that she would still be living. If the sibling was a brother, there was a 50 percent probability that he was living. In 1900 the chances of a sibling co-surviving were far smaller of course—18 percent if it was a sister—and 15 percent if it was a brother.

CHILDREN ~ Under high mortality conditions it was very common for parents to witness the death of one or more of their children. In 1900 only 85 percent of the women who bore a daughter when they were 25 still had that child living a year later. By contrast, under mortality conditions existing in 2000, 86 percent of these mothers would still have their daughter living 65 years later when the mothers reach age 90. Thus it has become increasingly uncommon for parents to have a child precede them in death. What was commonplace in 1900 is viewed as a great tragedy in 2000.

CHANGING THE PERCEPTION OF DEATH ~ These demographic changes in the distribution of death altered how Americans over the twentieth century perceived death. To understand how the meaning of death changed across the twentieth century, one must appreciate how early Americans viewed death. Historically, death has been a central feature of everyday social life and has held a deeply meaningful place in American society. When the United States was an agrarian nation with limited technological development, it was difficult for people to avoid direct contact with death; survivors were present when loved ones died, typically in their homes or work places. Care for the dying in homes facilitated the mourning process by giving family members a chance to recognize the finality of death.

The experience of death was rarely a lonely event because families were large, neighbors were often close friends, and communities of people knew each other well. Before urbanization, people forged intimate bonds and grew old together in small communities of homogeneous residents. In this context, the death of a

(1943) A mother of three soldiers wears all-black attire while sitting on her porch, Placquemines Parish, Louisiana, during World War II. The front window displays three star signs in support of her three sons, as well as a sign indicating that she donated to the Red Cross.

1800s

community member could not be ignored. It had to be ritually marked by community-wide outpourings of grief in order to assist the survivors in their reintegration back into the community. Thus, early Americans responded to dying and death through ritual, fellowship, and ceremony in the presence of a broader social network.

1800s • Mourning Customs ~ Nineteenth century Americans gave themselves the symbols, rituals, and time in which to work out their response to death. People tried to make death less fearful by beautifying corpses, caskets, hearses, horses, funeral music, cemeteries, and monuments. Funerals were highly meaningful events in rural America, with the community's total attention focused on the survivors. Funerals of the mid-1800s were dark, formal affairs. Families closed curtains and shades and draped black crepe over pictures and mirrors. To indicate mourning, people wrapped themselves in black mourning garb and placed badges over doorknockers.

Women in particular were responsible for carrying out the rituals of mourning. After the funeral, widows were expected to spend a year in deep mourning during which time they wore black clothes and somber accessories. Various forms of memorialization flourished in nineteenth century America, such as embroidered or painted mourning pictures of graveyard scenes and posthumous portraiture that depicted the deceased with conventional symbols of mortality, such as roses or broken shafts that symbolize the end of life. In the 1830s, printed memorials with spaces for names and dates came into vogue. Consolation literature showing mourners the emotional and moral benefits of their pain spread, as did prayer guidebooks, hymns, obituary poems, books about heaven, and mourners' manuals. Such artifacts and symbols magnified the importance of dying and communication with the next world.

These nineteenth century customs reflect the importance of death rituals in societies with high mortality rates throughout the life cycle, as opposed to contemporary societies where death is predominantly confined to the old. Elaborate mourning rituals helped people cope with high mortality rates among children, with modest life expectancy of those who survived childhood, and with the rapid and unpredictable onset of death from infectious disease. They helped survivors continue the lives of family members whose brief lives had been cut unpredictably short.

At the end of the twentieth century, however, when the majority of deaths occurred to older adults and rarely had adverse economic consequences for survivors, death rituals that once reflected the economic and emotional consequences of a death had lost much of their importance. The deaths most Americans experienced at the end of the twentieth century were infrequent, highly impersonal, and viewed as abnormal. The changing meaning of death that took place over the last century was brought about in part by people's collective responses to the changing social distribution of biological death.

~

During the early twentieth century, communal rites surrounding death and disposal of the dead were simplified. Between 1880 and 1920, funeral services became shorter. Solemn music and the sermon gave way to the power of positive thinking. The funeral sermon no longer was a vehicle for ministers to frighten living sinners, but to relieve the sorrow of survivors. Joseph Greene, in *The Funeral,* advised that the aim of the minister in his remarks should be to help: "He is to give hope, consolation, and warning. It is not his aim to move the people to tears, . . . but to bring a peace and comfort to the heart, born of the words of hope falling from the preacher's lips."

~

1900-1920 • Mourning Customs ~ *The Embalmer's Monthly* declared that the undertaker should "relieve the bereaved family of all responsibility. . . of a burden they should, under no circumstances, carry in addition to the one already upon them." This view articulated the declining importance of ritual and the emergence of a therapeutic model of bereavement. By 1920 prolonged mourning was not widely practiced. People generally preferred not to extend the period of death observance beyond the few days devoted to the funeral.

Early twentieth century Americans also tried to make the funeral a place of fond recollection. Funerals which remained in domestic parlors were made more cheerful. Shades were raised and black was replaced by other colors for funeral drapery. Instead of tying black crepe badges to the front door, some people hung baskets of flowers. Flowers also replaced somber black drapery in the parlor as a sign of death. According to Joseph Greene, "Often the placement of the casket in the room, gracefully canopied by an attractive curtain, and banked against flowers artistically arranged, forms a picture so beautiful as to relieve the scene of death of some of its awfulness." Thus, by the second and third decades of the twentieth century a new aesthetic emphasized the absence of death. A 1920 undertaker, for example, advertised the following:

EARLY 1900S

For composing the features: $1
For giving the features a look of quiet resignation: $2
For giving the features a look of Christian hope and contentment: $5

1955-1970s • Denying Death ~ Historian Geoffrey Gorer concluded that by 1955 death had replaced sex as the most taboo topic of modern culture. He argued that after World War I, Americans refused to address personal death and became

(1926) Crowds gathered round the Campbell Funeral Church Inc. trying to get a glimpse of Valentino's body lying in state.

obsessed with the "pornographic" representation of a depersonalized and abstract death in the media. According to Gorer, although Americans tended to ignore the possibility of their own deaths, they were fascinated by the gore of violent, abstract death as filtered through television and movie screens. Various critics in the 1960s concurred with Gorer's assessment of Americans' unreasonable fear of death. Barney Glaser and Anselm Strauss, for example, conducted a study of death and dying in San Francisco Bay area hospitals. They noted how medical personnel rou-

Obituaries

For over two hundred years, American newspapers have memorialized the deceased in obituaries. These death notices inform readers of the accomplishments of individuals, but they also make public statements about our collective values. Early in the 20th century, for example, newspaper obituaries largely omitted the lives and accomplishments of women. In a culture that valued men, money, and industry, women were remembered, if at all, by their associations with male relatives. This obituary, for example, appeared in the *New York Times* on November 5, 1910.

Mrs. Eleanor E. R. Peabody, widow of Arthur J. Peabody, and one of the founders of the Colonial Dames of America, died yesterday at her home, 15 West Tenth Street. Her father, Archibald Russell, was the founder of the Five Points House of Industry, and her grandfather, the late Dr. John Watts, was the first President of the College of Physicians and Surgeons. Mrs. Peabody was a direct descendant of Gen. William Alexander, (Lord Stirling) a member of Gen. Washington's staff, and on her maternal side she was descended from Lewis Morris of Morrisania, signer of the Declaration of Independence.

tinely kept dying patients unaware of their terminal condition. By documenting the various ways Americans attempted to deny the reality of death, medical sociologist David Sudnow and other researchers depicted the alienation of death and dying in U.S. hospitals in the 1960s. Americans banished the old and infirm to isolated institutions, then refused to discuss death with the dying. They relegated burial to funeral homes and memorial parks. They used embalming and cosmetics to gloss over the effects of death, then compensated for the emotional void with expensive and elaborate funeral displays.

The writings of Philippe Aries resonated with the emerging death awareness movement that critiqued the impoverishment and unnaturalness of modern dying. In his classics *Western Attitudes Towards Death and Dying* (1976) and *The Hour of Death* (1977), Aries showed that the general attitude of late twentieth century westerners toward death was characterized by fear and shame. People hid death from public view through a bureaucratic and technological system of care of the dying. In contrast to the elaborate death rites and customs of past centuries, Aries argued, funeral and dying rituals almost disappeared after the 1950s.

1960s-Present • Privatizing Death ~ Although death-related rituals were still widely performed during the last decades of the twentieth century, they were, by and large, removed from the community and relocated in the private world of individuals who had been bereaved. Impersonal bonds linked heterogeneous and interdependent strangers within large urban areas. The scope of grief was limited to the deceased's family and friends who were given only a few days off from work before being expected to return to a social system usually unaffected by the death. This transformation from communal to individual death reflected changing conceptions of selfhood. The twentieth century conception of self that faced death was considerably different from the selves of the past. In the nineteenth century, as in the past generally and even today in many cultures, there was a collectivist orientation toward life. Personal extinction did not hold the terror it currently does because the ultimate social unit—namely, one's tribe, clan, or community—continued to survive despite the singular deaths of its members. As individualism and value-relativism increased over the twentieth century, however, the quest for identity and self-knowledge became people's primary source of life's meaning.

In various ways, funeral directors historically supported this privatization of grief. They proposed a private room for the family during the funeral service and a reduction of the number of people accompanying the family to the cemetery. As people turned away from traditional religious rituals of death from the 1960s through the 1990s, they tended to favor more personal expressions designed to reflect the individuality of the deceased. The family of a teenager who died in 1999, for example, recreated the boy's bedroom in the funeral home, complete with black lights, and played loud rock music by the band Nine Inch Nails. Such growing individuality in death rituals reflected the American tendency to turn every institution into a form of personal expression.

1950s-1970s • Fear of the Atomic Bomb ~ The second half of the twentieth century was labeled "the resurrection of death." The use of the atomic bomb and the ensuing nuclear arms race began to change Americans' mode of thinking about death. The bomb revealed the dreadful and all-encompassing contingency of human experience. In the late 1970s, one-third of high school seniors believed that "nuclear or biological annihilation will probably be the fate of all humankind in my lifetime." The apocalyptic possibility of nuclear megadeath reminded people of the fragility of life and the uncertainty of existence. Numerous writers theorized about death of the person, death of humanity, death of the university, and the death of the divine. Over the past twenty years, fascination with dying and death was evidenced in much of the U.S. population. Fueled by print and electronic media, Americans were bombarded with death and death-related matters: the AIDS crisis, nuclear weapons, fetal transplants, terrorist bombings, ecological disasters, abortion, murder, prolongation of dying from cancer, and physician-assisted suicide. Furthermore, death and dying became legitimate issues for scientific and social discussion in recent years. Thus, at the end of the twentieth century, Americans both avoided and embraced death.

Bureaucratization of Death

Death over the twentieth century increasingly came under the control of institutions and experts with specialized knowledge who tried to make death as routine, predictable, and systematic as possible. As a culture of professionalism conditioned the American public to defer to the decisions of specialists in many areas of life and death, death moved away from ritual and community to bureaucratic management. In the early and mid-nineteenth century numerous full-time mortuary roles were introduced, such as professional casket makers, tombstone carvers, funeral directors, florists, and mausoleum companies. Over the twentieth century, these service providers became an entrenched institutional and bureaucratic response to death. Hospitals, nursing homes, and the funeral industry routinized the handling of death as they treated the terminally ill and deceased. As discussed below, these efforts to rationalize, depersonalize, and medicalize death dramatically altered how people die and what happens to their bodies after death.

Late-1800s-mid-1900s • Medicalization of Death ~ Removing the dying from the home and placing them in hospitals and nursing homes under the supervision of a professional medical staff is one example of the bureaucratization of death. In pre-twentieth century America, families were primarily responsible for caring for the sick and dying in their own homes, considered the best environments for recuperation. In fact, 85 percent of deaths in 1900 occurred in the home, with relatives surrounding the dying person. By 1949 half of all deaths occurred in hospitals and long-term-care institutions. By the close of the twentieth century, over 80 percent of all deaths occurred in institutions, generally in hospitals or nursing homes, with only a few relatives and friends present. This trend occurred despite Americans' expressed preference to die at home surrounded by friends and family.

In the first half of the twentieth century, hospitals ceased to be poorhouses and became instead places for caring, curing, and dying. Figure 8 shows the dramatic expansion of hospitals in the

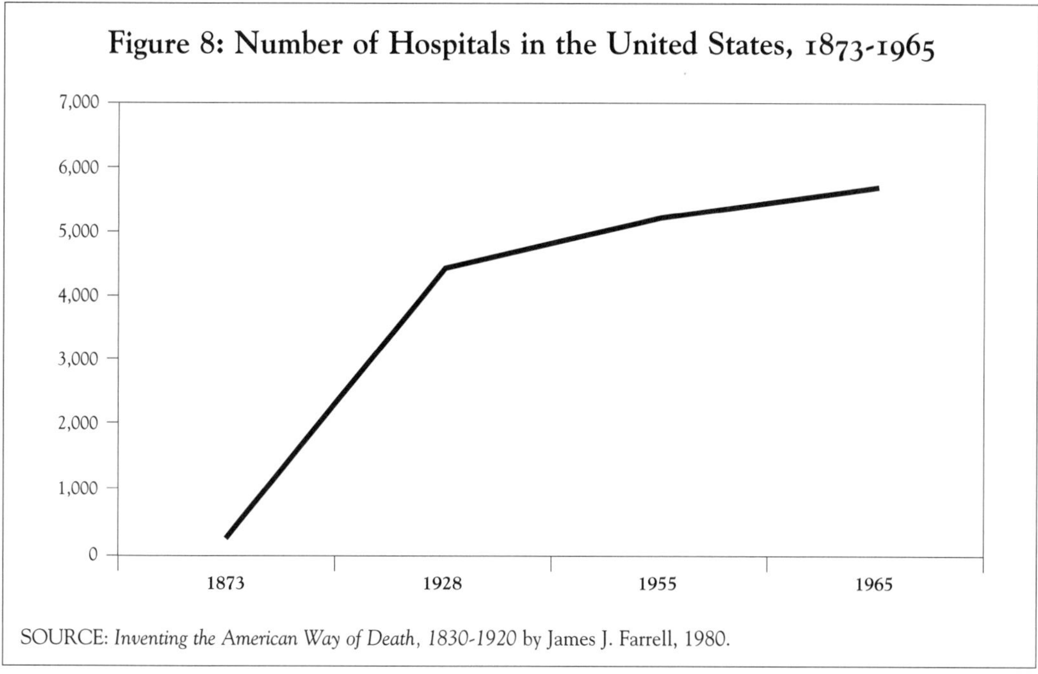

SOURCE: *Inventing the American Way of Death, 1830-1920* by James J. Farrell, 1980.

United States from 1873 to 1965. This figure attests to Americans' changing preference for professional treatment and access to the latest medical technology over being cared for lovingly in the home. Doctors' expertise became unquestionably established as they and they alone diagnosed medical problems and administered appropriate treatments. Nineteenth century doctors complained about the presence of friends and neighbors at the dying hour, so death became reserved for close family members.

1945-1970 • Medicalization of Death ~ The increased usage of invasive medical procedures required the dying to be relocated to the hospital. The Hill-Burton Act of 1946 also played a key role in the emergence of hospitals as the place where people administer modern medicine and cure ailments. The Act provided federal money to build hospitals and equip them with advanced medical technology. Medicare and Medicaid laws in the 1960s also contributed to Americans' acceptance of hospitals and nursing homes as the acceptable places for elderly people with long-term chronic problems to live out their final days. In addition to control of dying resting in the hands of medical professionals, grieving also became medicalized. Erich Lindermann in 1944 and George Engel in 1961 wrote highly influential papers in which they considered grief in terms similar to that of a disease. Based on this premise, they argued that medical professions should manage the grieving process.

As death became medicalized, it was no longer seen as a natural event but an end point of untreatable or inadequately treated disease or injury. The resuscitation pioneer Claude Beck, for example, pushed for the dissemination of one of his inventions, the electrical defibrillator, to reverse the dying process. In 1962 Beck wrote, "some hearts are too good to die" and "death can be reversed in these good hearts." Ignoring the psychosocial dimensions of dying, the medical perspective understood death as something the body did to the person and viewed the goal of medicine as preventing death.

In fact, various studies showed that physicians at the end of the twentieth century frequently saw death as a sign of their failure to treat patients properly. The American view that death should be fought off as long as medically possible was reflected in the societal commitment to sophisticated medical technologies and the use of extraordinary medical techniques becoming commonplace.

The medicalization of death created a culture in which most Americans did not directly observe the death of another. Instead, white-coated professionals behind closed doors were assigned the task of keeping death at bay. For many Americans, this resulted in an isolated, private, anonymous death in a hospital room where the dying person was surrounded by strangers. When a person died, many hospitals went to great lengths to hide this fact. Hospitals protected the public and other patients by moving the dying to another room or not removing the body during visiting hours. Hospital morgues were usually on the ground floor with a private loading platform so the public would not see the departure of the deceased.

Rise of the Death Industry

1800s • Home Burial ~ While dying was removed from the home and placed under the supervision of qualified personnel in systematically organized settings, professional experts, rather than family, also prepared and handled the body for death rituals. In pre-twentieth century America, families were typically responsible for cleaning, dressing, and disposing of the body. They would place a board between two chairs, drape it with a sheet, and then lay the deceased on the covered board. Family members would wash the corpse, sometimes preparing the features for presentation. They would close the mouth by placing a forked stick between the breastbone and chin and closed the eyes by placing coins on the eyelids. They dressed the body for burial with either a shroud or winding sheet. In warm weather, they put a large block of ice in a tub beneath the board, with smaller chunks around the body. These "corpse coolers" surrounded the body with cold air that delayed the onset of putrefaction.

Family and friends would then visit the home of the deceased. While family members prepared the body, a neighbor notified the cabinetmaker or furniture dealer to make a coffin or provide one from his limited stock. Early nineteenth century coffins were simple six-sided boxes with hinges. After 1850, coffins were lined with cloth. On the day of the funeral, the undertaker carted the coffin to the house in a wagon. He placed the corpse in the coffin for the funeral. After the religious ceremony, survivors viewed the body, closed the coffin, and then set it back on the wagon for its journey to the graveyard. At the graveyard, friends committed the body to the earth, placed it in the grave, and then scooped dirt back into the hole. Thus, bodies were usually buried as soon as the women could prepare the corpse and the men could dig the grave.

1870-1920 • The Beginning of the Funeral Industry ~ The funeral industry began in the late 1800s when an increasing sense of domestic privacy led to the decline in customs of communal layout and corpse-visiting in the home. Privatization of the family pushed the public funeral out of the home and funeral directors began offering "parlors" in their "homes" for the funeral. In 1885 Harry Samson of Pittsburgh, Pennsylvania, built the first chapel in the United States connected to the business of funeral director. People could bring bodies to this one location, which was equipped with an embalming laboratory, corpse viewing room, and chapel for funeral services. Such comprehensive funeral homes appeared throughout the country after 1885. A speaker at the 1910 National Funeral Directors Association convention estimated that 90 percent of all funerals in Southern California proceeded from undertakers' chapels.

In the early twentieth century, a more transient society required that someone other than the deceased's family or neighbors handle the body. Families began calling on undertakers to perform more of the services of the funeral, such as preparing the body. Undertakers began as carpenters who built rough coffins on the side, but moved to the position of cabinetmakers, furnishing ready-made polished coffins for four to ten dollars. Then they became furniture dealers, with a small stock of ready-made coffins with trimmings. Eventually, they added boxes to their wagons to make them hearses and went out as undertakers on service calls.

1870s-1925 • Improvements in Caskets ~ The invention and marketing of various death products after the Civil War allowed undertakers to switch from selling commodities to selling services. The Stein Manufacturing Company of Rochester, New York, for example began mass producing caskets in many styles, colors, and grades in the early 1870s. The Stein Company published *The Casket*, a trade journal for the industry that kept undertakers aware of new styles of funeral goods and encouraged them to offer new forms of funeral service. W. P. Hohenschuh advised readers of *The Casket* to "change the style of caskets, trimmings, linings, and robes as often as possible . . . Occasionally introduce novelties because there are people who will take fancy to them and will pay a price for them."

(1851) A child's casket carved in ivory and exhibited by Matifat at the Great Exhibition of 1851.

1870-1925

Rich and ostentatious caskets appealed to the new middle class who tried to distinguish themselves from common people, even in death, through opulent displays of wealth. A 1912 advertisement described the "Montross Sanitary Casket"

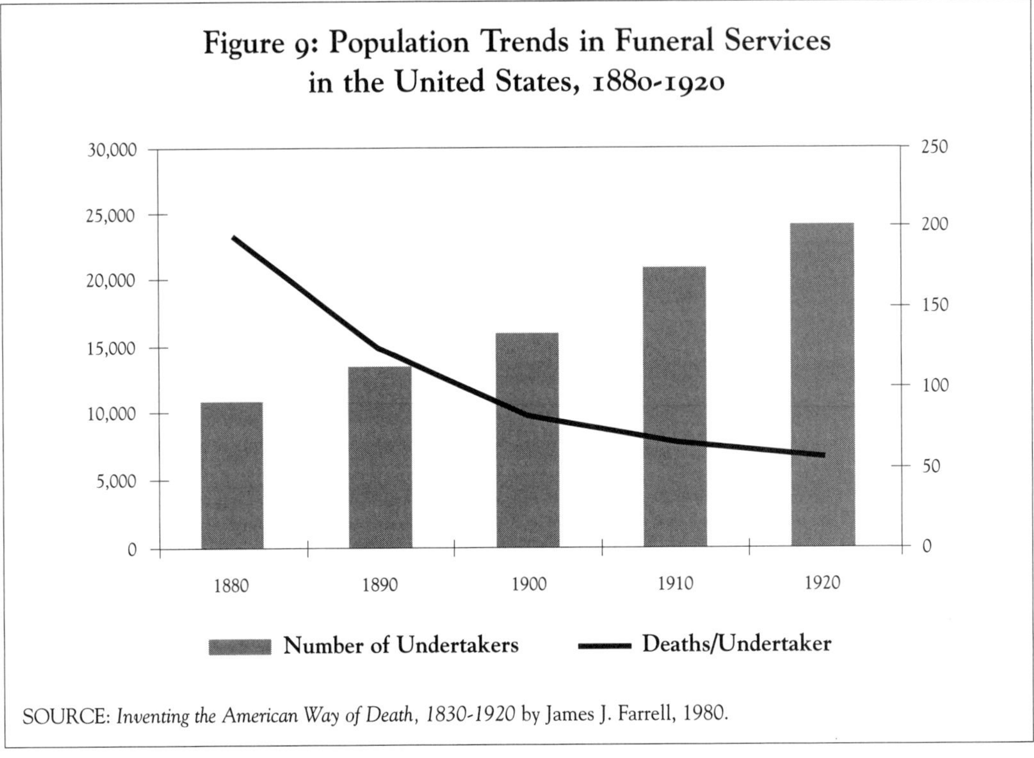

SOURCE: *Inventing the American Way of Death, 1830-1920* by James J. Farrell, 1980.

as "indestructible, and impervious to the ravages of the earth. Hermetically sealed, air-tight, water, vermin, and germ-proof," the casket insured, "a lasting, humane tribute to the dead." By 1927 the wedge-shaped coffin that was shaped to the form of the human body was obsolete and manufacturers of embalming fluids promoted their products as a means of making the corpse look as good as its silk-lined container.

1880-1920 • THE PROFESSION OF UNDERTAKING ~ The number of undertakers in the United States increased as the death rate dropped. As shown in Figure 9, the average American undertaker could expect to supply almost two hundred funerals in 1880; by 1920 this number dropped to fifty-seven. In order to maintain a constant income, funeral directors had to realize a greater profit per funeral. Funeral costs increased by as much as 250 percent between 1880 and 1920. Undertakers banded together to control the prices of the goods they purchased and services they sold and to ensure the professionalization of their services. The National Funeral Directors Association (NFDA), founded in 1882, was the spearhead to control rising costs of coffins and guarantee professionalism. Membership in the NFDA increased from less than 4,000 members in 1900 to almost 10,000 in 1920.

Undertakers wanted to secure their profession by convincing the public to defer to the decisions of an educated elite in matters of death. In *The Modern Funeral: Its Management*, a 1907 undertaker wrote that he hoped "that what is here offered may be found by the funeral director enough of an authority to enable him to convince his clients, without offense, that there are better methods than have been prescribed by custom." In 1887 the United States College of Embalming opened and by 1900, funeral directors had secured legislation in twenty-five states to license embalmers. Illinois embalmers in the 1920s were required to study six months at embalming school and one year with an experienced embalmer before passing a state licensing test.

The burgeoning funeral industry also used semantic changes in their quest for professional credentials, such as substituting the word "funeral director" for "undertaker" to symbolize a new sense of professional identity. Funeral directors tried to protect themselves financially by preventing unskilled undertakers from underselling the quality services of a funeral director. They made good use of judicious advertising and public relations to ensure the profit at the core of their profession. Over the twentieth century, professional funeral directors increasingly handled funerals, serving as counselors, advisors, and business consultants to bereaved families.

Funeral institutions were designed to keep death out of sight and mind, relieving families of many of the burdens of death-related tasks. Death rituals occurred in special facilities and special areas were set aside to segregate the remains of the dead from the living. When someone died at the end of the twentieth century, survivors typically called in a medical professional. A funeral director took the body of the deceased directly to the

(circa 1955) Prior to a burial service at Arlington National Cemetery, a mat of sward is laid over the turned up earth.

funeral home, where it remained until it was moved to the burial ground. At the funeral home, the body was prepared for public visitation and last rites. Survivors did not see the body until it was ready for viewing, which meant the funeral director made the person look as alive as possible through the use of cosmetics. The casket was not lowered into the ground until after friends and family left the cemetery because of a desire to avoid any emotional scene in which observers saw the finality of death.

1960-1980 • Fraud and Funeral Expenses ~ Since its early history, the funeral industry has become a lucrative business—$16 billion dollars a year in 1996 alone. Because of consumers' highly emotional state and sparse public knowledge of funeral practices, funeral homes have many opportunities to take advantage of consumers. In the 1960s, investigative journalist Jessica Mitford critically analyzed the practices of the funeral industry in her widely read book, *The American Way of Death.* Mitford argued that the funeral industry was excessively commercial and took advantage of grieving survivors. She charged that American funeral practices were overly lavish and expensive. Mitford's book and the movie version of Evelyn Waugh's 1948 satire of the funeral industry, *The Loved One*, spurred a wave of funeral reform efforts in the 1960s. Memorial societies and non-profit organizations sprang up, primarily in California, to assist people in obtaining low-cost death services. In 1978 concerns over the high costs of funerals prompted a Federal Trade Commission investigation of the funeral industry. The FTC's report found that although most funeral directors were ethical, practices of some reflected poorly on the industry. Unethical practices they found included the unauthorized removal of remains from hospitals, nursing homes and morgues; embalming without consent; requiring a casket for cremation; interference with releasing the remains; overcharging or kickbacks, and inappropriate merchandising.

1980s • Funeral Surcharge ~ Before 1984 the cost of a funeral mainly depended on the price of a casket. The basic necessities for a funeral service—transportation of the deceased, embalming, and staffing the services—were included in the price of a coffin. In 1984, however, the Federal Trade Commission ruled that a funeral director had to agree to use caskets that consumers could buy from independent casket dealers, but they could bill customers for allowing it into their mortuary. In order to protect the consumer from additional costs, the FTC banned these fees in 1994. This resulted, however, in increased costs to the consumer because now, even though all costs are itemized, the funeral directors can charge a "non-declinable fee" covering the cost of overhead, which can be however much the funeral home decides to charge.

In the 1980's, funeral homes also started assessing an extra "handling fee" for people who were HIV positive. When civil rights groups protested, the funeral industry renamed it a "contagious-disease fee." Then both the Centers for Disease Control and the Occupational Safety and Health Administration (OSHA) showed that the additional fee was unnecessary because the protective gear worn to protect against HIV was the same required gear that must be worn at every embalming. California was the first state to enact legislation that prohibited such discriminatory fees.

Betting on Death

~

The AIDS epidemic generated a great deal of interest in a new type of investment strategy for speculators in the 1980s, the viatical settlement industry. A viatical investment company would purchase the life insurance policy of someone with AIDS (or other terminal illness) who was expected to die in the near future. For example, the original policyholder might be offered $50,000 for his $100,000 insurance policy. The person with AIDS would then have money to spend on health care or other things while he was living, and the purchaser of the policy would collect $100,000 upon his death. This typically was a win-win situation for both the sick person and the investor in the early stages of the AIDS epidemic when death tended to occur rapidly after the onset of AIDS. As new drugs extended the life expectancy of AIDS patients, however, investors were not able to turn a quick profit and interest in viatical investments has waned since the mid-1990s.

1990s • Consolidation of Funeral Homes ~ Another trend in the death industry of the 1990s was the increasing consolidation of the funeral industry. Independent local funeral homes confronted a competitive landscape as a handful of large funeral home conglomerates purchased almost twenty percent of the nation's funeral homes as well as a growing number of its cemeteries and crematoriums. In fact, one in nine American funerals was performed by one company, Houston-based Service Corporation International. The conglomerates frequently purchased multiple funeral homes in the same city or town, giving them a cost advantage over smaller homes. Analysts say the consolidation of the funeral industry was driven in part by economics and the aging of the U.S. population. One conglomerate noted in its 1995 annual report that baby boomers turning fifty represented "a most receptive audience." With potential profits growing, conglomerates reportedly paid on average one million dollars for each funeral home they acquired.

1850-1920

1850-1920 • Embalming ~ Disposal of the dead, like the process of dying, has become rationally organized and bureaucratically medicalized. Americans across the twentieth century increasingly advocated human activity in the face of death and decay. Through embalming, cremation, and cryogenics they attempted to control the dying process. Embalming aims to deter decay of the body, cremation prevents putrefaction, and cryogenics seeks to make future revitalization possible by freezing the deceased either in whole or in part.

Between 1850 and 1920, Americans experimented with embalming and cremation, two new treatments of the body in funeral service. Before 1880 most people viewed embalming as a historical phenomenon, unnatural and irreligious. They concurred with Henry Tuckerman who found "something revolting in the artificial conservation of what by the law of nature should undergo chemical dissolution." Tuckerman considered it "senseless homage to cling to the shattered chrysalis when the winged embryo has soared away." By 1920, however, almost all dead bodies were embalmed.

1850-1920

Acceptance for embalming was brought about by a strong and widely publicized sanitary movement, an increased concern for appearance in a consumer culture, privatization of the home, and Americans' increasing respect for medicine. The main reason embalming became a common practice among Americans was for preservation of the corpse for shipment, appearance, or protection from long-term decay. Embalming became popular during the Civil War when battleship casualties needed to be shipped home over several days. Americans wanted to delay the spoiling of the body.

After the Civil War, embalmers continued to prepare the bodies of geographically mobile kin to their family and friends and by 1890 embalming replaced ice as the main method of preserving the appearance of dead bodies. The NFDA also promoted embalming as a means to preserve the living by disinfecting the dead. In a 1907 NFDA speech, Dr. Charles H. McCully exhorted the funeral directors that "it was a sacrilege that those we love should become a thing of horror; a distorted, loathsome stench; food for the worms; and for this reason alone you sought out a more perfect tissue preservation. . . . Today, you do not preserve the bodies alone for the sake of sentiment."

McCully encouraged funeral directors to work closely with physicians for sanitation and disease prevention. Embalming also assisted funeral directors who wanted to hide the sorrows of human existence behind a façade of life and disguise the reality of death. Funeral director Hohenschuh advised funeral directors to "lay out the body so that there will be as little suggestion of death as possible." Early embalmers traveled the country selling embalming fluids and demonstrating how to beautify corpses. Representing funeral supply companies, these itinerant teachers taught undertakers in hundreds of towns how to preserve bodies. They aimed for a natural lifelike appearance, applying theatrical cosmetics to attain the desired look. They began dressing corpses in clothes worn in life rather than in a funeral shroud.

1876-1913 • Cremation ~ Although embalming was a widely accepted practice in early twentieth century America, cremation was not. Despite some physicians' advocacy of cremation as a remedy to public health problems, only twenty-eight formally recorded cremations occurred in the United States between 1876 and 1884. Contrasting the effects of ashes in an urn to the effects of a corpse decaying in the ground, advocates of cremation linked incineration and sanitation, highlighting hygiene. Cremationists argued that interment risked the health of the living as germs from decaying bodies infected water supplies and seeped into the air. Although the central argument for cremation was sanitation, cost was another concern. Cremation would reduce the cost of funerals that featured lifelike bodies. There would be no need for a lavish casket, large cemetery lot, or transporting the casket to a cemetery. In 1898 one cremation advocate estimated that the average cost of burial in New York City was one hundred dollars, while an urn burial would cost as little as five dollars. The author of a pamphlet on incineration posed a choice between "incineration which disposes the body in one hour in a beautiful glow of heat, and earth burial which prolongs the process through 14 to 20 years of loathsome decay." State cremation societies and the Cremation Society of America—formed in 1913—tried to change the pub-

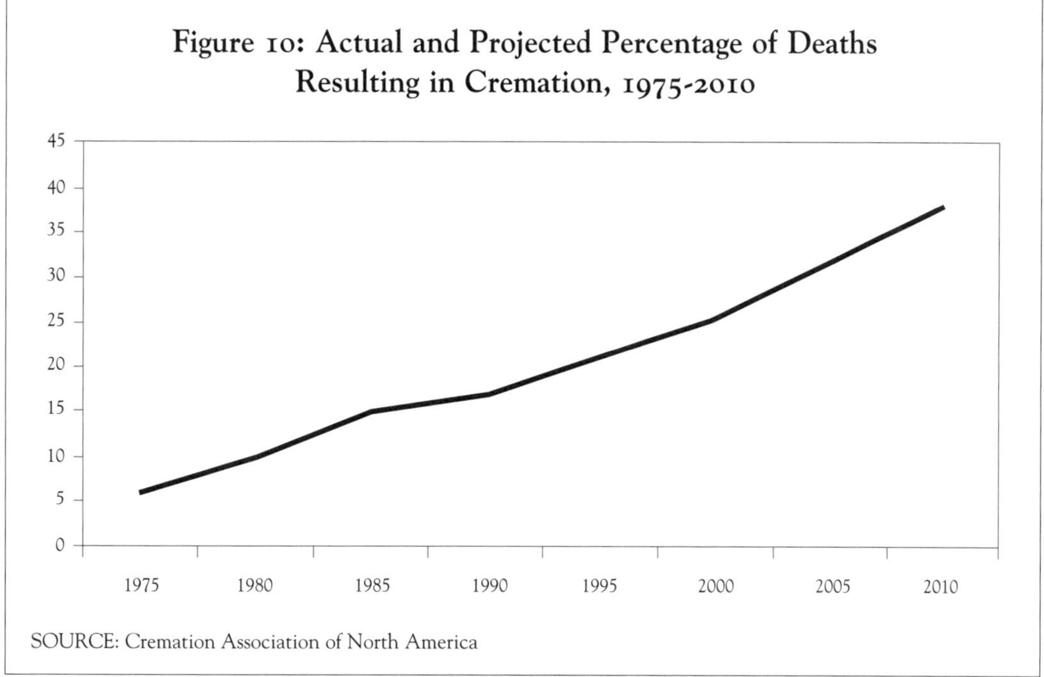

Figure 10: Actual and Projected Percentage of Deaths Resulting in Cremation, 1975-2010

SOURCE: Cremation Association of North America

lic prejudice against cremation, which is still often viewed as a cruel, quick, cheap, easy, and ceremony-less way to solve an uninvited problem.

1960s-Present • Opposition to Cremation ~ Despite cremationists' efforts, only seven percent of all human corpses in the U.S. were disposed of by cremation in 1977. One reason cremation did not catch on quickly was its fierce religious opposition. Some Christians argued that since Jesus was laid in his grave, believers should follow his example. Thus, until the 1960s earth burial was the only method of body disposition supported by most Protestant denominations and Catholicism. Some Protestant clergy, primarily in New England and the Great Lakes region, however, advocated cremation. Interested in burial reform, they promoted cremation as a humanitarian act. Cremationists also believed that opposition to cremation came from religion and custom, but that cremation came from reason, common sense, and scientific knowledge. The funeral industry also advocated earth burial and only reluctantly began to accept cremation in the 1990s. Although lobbying and lawsuits reflect the funeral industry's resistance to reforms that include cremation, between 1975 and 2000 the number of cremations more than quadrupled. Figure 10 shows the significant increase in the percent of all deaths that resulted in cremation over the late twentieth century and forecasters' predictions of a continuation of this trend.

1970s-Present • Cryonics ~ In the last quarter of the twentieth century, the cryonics movement ushered in another aggressive human attempt to conquer death. Through cryonic suspension, a person's dead body or just head (for a reduced price) is frozen in dry ice and liquid nitrogen until such time as a cure for the condition that caused the demise of the cryonically suspended person could be found. At that time, the person would be "reanimated," or thawed out and cured of their previously fatal condition. If only the head was frozen, it would be

Cryonics

When Dr. Richard Marsh, long-time governor of the American Cryonics Society (ACS), died of a heart attack in 1994, his body was cryonically suspended. The procedure that was followed after his death is described on the ACS website (http://www.jps.net/cryonics/): "Dick's brother and sister-in-law, with help from a duty nurse, started CPR and packed him in ice. CPR was continued until about fifteen minutes before he was flown to Southern California by air ambulance. At the BioPreservation facility he was washed out, perfused, cooled down to -79 degrees C. (dry ice temperature) and then flown to the Cryonics Institute where he was cooled down to –196 degrees C. (liquid nitrogen temperature). Mike Darwin of BioPreservation reported that they were able to achieve good washout and to attain a high level of cryoprotective perfusion."

attached to a body created by cloning, using DNA from the frozen head.

The cost of freezing an entire body is approximately $135,000, with frozen heads costing $35,000. Companion animals may also be cryopreserved. At least forty people so far have had their bodies frozen after death in hopes that new technology would someday restore them. Even the American Cryonics Society, however, admits that there are no guarantees that anyone frozen by today's technology will ever be reanimated successfully. They state that, "we cannot demonstrate that our procedures will lead to anything except frozen bodies." As of 1994, cryogenic suspension organizations had only 500 members nationwide. The cryonics movement, however, is the latest human attempt to conquer death.

1850-1920 • Cemeteries ~ Over the twentieth century, cemeteries also underwent a bureaucratic transformation. Rural cemeteries of the mid-nineteenth century were usually on church grounds and were designed to surround bereavement with beauty. They offered a place to bury bodies and ease the grief of survivors by bringing people into communion with their god and nature. These cemeteries were planned with picturesque atmospheres, inefficient but aesthetically pleasing serpentine roadways, and economically impractical wide pathways and natural land reserves. The rural cemeteries took the public by storm in the mid-nineteenth century, with 30,000 people a year touring them.

From the mid-1850s into the 1920s lawn park cemeteries proliferated. Cemetery designers in the mid-1850s became disturbed by the crowding and spatial confusion in the first generation of rural cemeteries. They wanted to streamline the landscape by a more rational and efficient design. New owners also altered the management of the cemetery beginning in the 1850s. Unlike earlier graveyards, most of the new lawn park cemeteries were owned and managed by private, secular associations established solely for the development of a cemetery. Lawn-park cemeteries were more dependent on professionals to develop and maintain the landscape. Further establishing themselves as an entrepreneurial enterprise, cemetery superintendents formed the Association of American Cemetery Superintendents in the late nineteenth century to adopt modern business principles.

Around 1917 there was a trend to rename cemeteries "memorial parks." Founders wished to obscure the morbid connotations they believed the public perceived in the word cemetery. Designers wanted a park-like atmosphere, not a cemetery appearance. American society no longer desired a mysterious relationship with the grave, and customers wanted the area to be comfortable and familiar. Cemetery designers freely used elements of the increasingly popular suburban landscape in developing the look and atmosphere of memorial parks.

Memorial parks were simpler and more accessible than lawn-park cemeteries. Cemeteries underwent decorative changes as Americans mechanized and standardized monument production. They encouraged fewer gravestones and inscriptions. Superintendents banned grave mounds because they reminded people of death and obstructed views and lawn mowers. They wanted uncluttered landscapes that required less upkeep than the enclosures and elaborate monuments of rural cemeteries. Superintendents tried to remove or conceal any uncouth aspects of interment. They carted away dirt from graves or hid it beneath flowers. They lined graves with cloth to make them look like little rooms and escorted mourners away from graves before filling them. Some superintendents zoned cemeteries to permit monuments only in certain areas. This allowed them to charge premium prices for such lots and for prime hillside and lake-front locations. Thus, ambitious dead people could be moved to better "neighborhoods" as survivors saw fit, and social mobility could continue even in death.

1990s

1990s • Burial at the End of the Century ~ At the end of the twentieth century, Americans have become increasingly indifferent to the cemetery as a sacred space or as a community and cultural institution. The cemetery's role as a repository of the history and memories of the local community is fading. Other cultural institutions, such as art galleries, botanical gardens, and local historical societies have assumed the earlier functions of the cemetery. As this happened, Americans replaced community cemeteries with service cemeteries. The institutionalization of the cemetery reflects a greater distance between the residents of the community and the

(circa 1955) Hollywood's cemetery to the stars, Forest Lawn Memorial Park, Los Angeles. At the entrance of the park stands an iron policeman, drawing attention to the 20 mile an hour speed limit.

graves of their ancestors. Reflecting mainstream American practices such as acceptance of the hospital as the place to die and removal of the funeral from the home, the purchase of a cemetery lot is now a simple business transaction. Hospital death is now in the care of strangers, and final disposition of the dead is left to specialists trained to view death as their profession.

1800s • Religious Secularization and Death ~ Throughout most of history, religion has provided explanations for why we die and what happens to us in the afterlife. Religion also has prescribed ritual observances for dealing with remains. By controlling the knowledge and rituals associated with death, religion has been the social institution that helps many people cope with anxieties related to mortality. Its message has generally been the same: life does not conclude with death, but rather one is resurrected, reincarnated, absorbed into a collective soul, or moves on to an afterlife. In the past, most Americans held an unwavering belief in a personal afterlife, where death could mean atonement and salvation. This belief held out hope, thus reducing fear of death.

Such consolations, however, carry a price. By creating and maintaining anxieties related to death—such as the possibility of being consigned to hell—religion developed perhaps the most effective mechanism of social control ever devised. Previous generations of Americans lived their lives in the complete certainty that they would have to face some sort of judgment after death, that their every action was being observed by a grand evaluator.

(1979) Louisiana Mausoleum. The institutionalization of the cemetery reflects a greater distance between the residents of the community and the graves of their ancestors. Seen here is a large tomb in a Louisiana Cemetery.

A common nineteenth century belief, as articulated by Minister Nathaniel Emmons in an 1802 funeral sermon, was:

> God used death to show people that he can do what he pleases, without their aid or instrumentality. He exhibits his own power, wisdom, and sovereignty; and at the same time sets the folly, weakness, and dependence of all human agents, in the most clear and instructive light. God undoubtedly designs, by concealing the order of death, to teach mankind the importance and propriety of being constantly prepared for it.

1900s • More Positive Attitudes about Death ~ In the twentieth century, however, major American religious denominations increasingly stressed a loving and beneficent God, thus easing earlier anxieties emanating from religious teaching. As modern society became more secular and worldly, it saw the waning of the traditional belief in personal immortality. An 1899 author wrote, "The fear of death is being replaced by the joy of life. The flames of hell are sinking low, and even heaven has but poor attraction for the modern man. Full life here and now is the demand; what may come hereafter is left to take care of itself." He cited as reasons for the disappearance of death as an influence on everyday life, the disappearance of hell from popular theology, the secularization of the churches, and the human search for pleasure in the present via the pursuit of wealth.

1850-1920 • Science and Religion ~ The spread of scientific thinking after 1850 also undermined religious interpretations of death and bereavement by substituting scientific explanations for divine ones. The spread of science influenced some Americans to view death as a natural occurrence, not a time of judgment. People accepted scientific assumptions and ideas, and began to see death as a natural phenomenon governed only by laws of nature.

Between 1850 and 1920, some scientific thinkers asserted their authority over facts and tried to relegate religious and sentimental interpretations to secondary status. By 1906 Thorstein Veblen defined the culture of modernity as "peculiarly matter of fact." Some naturalists claimed that "matter and force are the only reality," thus defining the traditional deity out of existence. Scientists' increased knowledge of nature provided them with confidence in their accomplishments and abilities. Naturalists discarded the deist idea of god as "first cause" of the cosmos and ultimate cause of death. Instead they attributed death solely to natural causes. Scientific belief in the early twentieth century stressed immortality and improvement of the species rather than mortality of the individual.

1845-1910 • Body and Soul ~ The reinterpretation of death as a matter of fact is evident by a comparison of the accepted definitions of death in mid-nineteenth and early twentieth century America. The *1845 Encyclopedia Americana* entry for death stated:

> Death, in common language, is opposed to life, and considered as the cessation of it. It is only, however, the organic life of the individual that becomes extinct; for neither the mind nor the matter which constituted the individual can perish. That view of nature which considers the whole as pervaded throughout by the breath of life, admits only of changes from one mode of existence to another.

By 1903, *Encyclopedia Americana* redefined death:

> Death, in common language, is a state opposed to life, and considered as the cessation of it. Strictly speaking, we can trace only the cessation of organic life. The matter of which the body is composed does not perish on the death of an organized being; it undergoes various changes, which are known by the names of decay and putrefaction, and which are the preparation for its being subservient to new forms of life. What becomes of the mind, or thinking principle, whether in man or animal, is a matter of philosophical conjecture or religious faith. The investigations of science do not throw the least light upon it.

Gone from this updated definition is the mention of "breath of life," a reference associated with Biblical imagery and supernaturalism. A doctor speaking at a 1910 convention of the National Funeral Directors Association confirmed this transformation. He said that in the past, people saw death as the expression of divine will. . . . But today we have thrown off the shroud of mystery and mysticism thrown about the uncertainty of man's life and looked the causes of death square in the face.

This redefinition of death reflects similar changing understandings of disease at the time. In 1832, for example, a common belief among Americans was that God caused cholera. By 1866 most Americans accepted cholera as a social problem with sanitary solutions. They played down the arbitrary aspects of divine distribution of death and disease and instead emphasized orderly arrangement in nature. Thus, between 1845 and 1903, scientific interpretations of disease and death drove supernatural assumptions out of the definition.

1900-1912 • Science and Death ~ With Americans' increasing reliance on scientific rather than religious thinking, the belief that death was something to be eradicated spread after 1900. In a 1912 article on "Our New Attitude to Disease," Earl Mazo wrote:

> Today we know that it is not "God's will" that children should die of diphtheria or young men be destroyed in the flower of their manhood by typhoid fever. We are awake to the fact that it is man's ignorance or man's carelessness that is responsible, and we are inspired to work on toward the glorious ideal set before us by Pasteur when he said, "It is within the power of man to cause all infectious diseases to disappear from the earth."

By 1910, many believed that death finally could be conquered. In 1911, Elie Metchnikoff, the 1908 Nobel Prize winner for medicine, argued against the inevitability of death and offered Americans hope that modern medicine might divert the course of death. By defining death as an evasion of the body outside of the organism, Metchnikoff renounced the notion of natural death. Alexis Carrel, a Rockefeller Institute researcher who won the 1912 Nobel Prize in physiology and medicine for his work on organ transplants, was able to preserve life functions of organic tissues in artificial solutions and graft them onto other organisms where they continued to function. Some scientists believed that these results promised the possibility of preserving whole organisms. Because the cells of the human body survived in other forms after death, John H. Girdner denied that death was the cessation of life. He admonished Americans to substitute the word "change" for "death" to make it less fearful. People would say, for example, "John Doe changed at Bellevue Hospital today" or that "Richard Roe is changing." His semantic argument reinforced the conception of death as a disease that could be controlled by humans.

To a considerable degree, death and dying have been taken under human control. Twentieth century Americans rejected the idea of death without order, embracing instead an ideology of political autonomy, moral free agency, and economic independence. With modernization and secularization, religion lost its historic monopoly over death, most notably to the medical and legal institutions. As a result, death was transformed from being something natural and respected into something unnatural and polluting. For some, death no longer represented a transition to an afterlife, but the end of existence.

Death was understood to be an absolute end, rendering life devoid of meaning. Life appeared futile since what one achieved and how one lived did not matter. Without belief systems and rituals to move people through the death process, many Americans searched for practices that reduced their fear of death and made it manageable. Religion's role in shaping death fears, funerary ritual, burial practices, and attitudes toward death-related moral issues remained considerable, however. For instance, the role of religious faith and religiosity still played a key role in shaping Americans' attitudes toward the use of life-extending technologies.

1900-1950s • Prolonging Death ~ Prior to the 1900s, people generally spent only a short period of time dying. Infectious diseases or accidents tended to be resolved quickly, either by death or recovery. Modern medical technology, with its improved diagnostic techniques and early detection, has enabled people to live for longer periods of time with terminal illnesses. In addition to prolonging chronic illnesses, technological advances over the twentieth century have altered Americans' response to sudden deaths, such as those caused by heart attacks, strokes, or accidents. More and more, the timing of death is not an event that happens according to nature, but is a decision made by human beings. Before the 1950s, a person who was unable to breathe without help would typically die in a few minutes. Fifty years later, mechanically assisted respiration coupled with artificial nutrition and hydration can sustain life for years. Below are some medical advances that have forced Americans at the end of the twentieth century to make decisions unforeseen just a few decades ago. The medical technology that is a benefit to some is perceived as a burden by others. Reactions against advanced technology have spurred the right to die and hospice movements, both discussed below.

1920s-1930s • Life-Saving Technology ~ Technological advances over the twentieth century have kept many chronically ill people alive long past the point at which they would have died naturally in the past. In the first decade of the twentieth century, American doctors began using a resuscitation technique called the Schafer method. This procedure of manual ventilation involved intermittent pressure on a recently deceased patient's thorax, with the patient in the face-down position. By 1927 this method had become standardized in the United States. Medical advances in the 1930s included a new and safer way to do blood transfusions, an advance that was to save many soldiers' lives in the upcoming war. In 1937 Chicago's Cook County Hospital opened the first blood bank that stored blood given by live donors. This, with improved anesthesia, greatly enhanced the chances of surviving major surgery on vital organs.

1950s-1960s • Resuscitation Research ~ The Second World War provided a fruitful climate for researching resuscitation technology. For example, many people drowned on sinking ships, offering an opportunity to accumulate resuscitating experience. Into the early 1950s, resuscitation research continued to focus on drowning accidents. An international group of researchers recommended in 1960 that mouth-to-mouth ventilation become the only method to resuscitate people. Also in 1960, researchers at Johns Hopkins University argued that death was not only a matter of respiration, but also of cardiac functions. Thus, they recommended closed-chest cardiac massage, a simple technique in which the rescuer rhythmically compresses the victim's chest to restore circulation. In a 1960 article in the *Journal of the American Medical Association*, researchers wrote that, "Anyone, anywhere, can now initiate cardiac resuscitative procedures. All that is needed are two good hands." For the first time, resuscitation proponents argued that their technology was useful not only for drowning, but for "anyone, anywhere." In the early 1960s, a leading group of medical researchers agreed that cardiopulmonary resuscitation (CPR)—the combination of securing an open airway, mouth-to-mouth ventilation, and chest compressions—was one more step toward clearing the roadblock of sudden death.

1970s • Emergency Medicine ~ With emergency medicine still in its infancy, the scope of CPR was limited in the 1960s and early 1970s. In 1973, however, researchers and national rescue organizers designed and implemented a vast emergency system and embarked on an ambitious CPR-training program. Over the remaining decades of the twentieth century, the sprawling emergency infrastructure became part of the institutionalized American response to death, as more and more Americans came to believe that anyone can aspire to prolonged life. Medical advances from the first modern human organ transplant in 1950 to the approximate 17,000 organ transplants in 1996 have given thousands of people who might have otherwise died an opportunity to live.

1960s • Death and Dignity ~ Such advances have not gone without criticism, however. The 1960s saw an explosion of literature concerning the social organization of death and its psychological consequences. In her best-selling 1969 book, *On Death and Dying*, Elizabeth Kubler-Ross critiqued the contemporary way people died. Kubler-Ross interviewed dying patients and noted that death had become an "unavoidable reality" that people still much avoided. She observed how frequently health care professionals and family members abandon dying patients.

> He may cry for rest, peace, and dignity, but he will get infusions, transfusions, a heart machine. He may want a single person to stop for one single minute so that he can ask one single question, but he will get a dozen people around the clock, all busily preoccupied with his heart rate, pulse, electrocardiogram or pulmonary functions, his secretions and excretions, but not with him as a human being. He may wish to fight it all but it is going to be a useless fight since all this is done in the fight for his life, and if they can save his life they can consider the person afterwards.

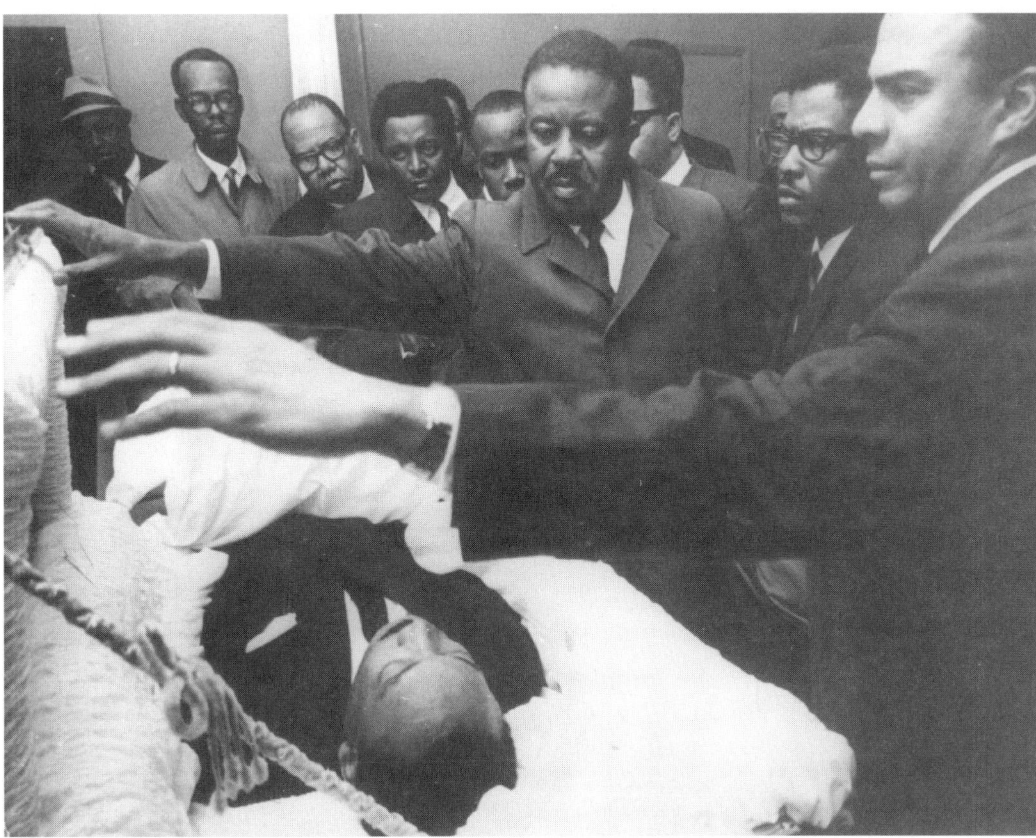

(1968) American civil rights leader Dr. Martin Luther King, Jr. (1929 - 1968) lying in state in Memphis, Tennessee, while his colleagues pay their respects to him (right to left); Andrew Young, Bernard Lee and Reverend Ralph Abernathy (1926 - 1990).

Kubler-Ross criticized American medicine for educating physicians to treat diseases rather than people and to deal with patients impersonally rather than holistically.

The widespread use of advanced medical technologies has created the illusion that every death may be averted and every sudden death is reversible. Although the vast majority of resuscitative efforts prove unsuccessful, Americans increasingly turn to resuscitative efforts to bring the deceased back from the dead. Although the exact number of people resuscitated from sudden death by emergency personnel is not known, it is estimated that no more than one to three percent of victims live to be discharged from the hospital.

As philosopher Daniel Callahan discussed in his books, it is difficult for people to die peacefully due to technology and societal and professional ambivalence about whether to fight or accept death. Clinging relentlessly to life may add misery to family members by creating hopes, then dashing them. Aggressive treatments may only prolong suffering through the use of painful and invasive methods. Medical teams may focus on pointless therapies rather than palliative care. Americans' attempts to prolong life have raised numerous ethical issues and given birth to the right to die movement.

1950s-Present • Right to Die Movement ~ As medical science which could prolong life through high-technology developed, the death awareness movement raised the issues of death with dignity and the right to die. In 1969 the notion of a living will was first proposed. This document is a declaration by a competent adult expressing the desire that if she or he becomes seriously ill and there is no prospect of recovery, any extraordinary means to sustain or prolong life will be withheld or withdrawn. At the end of the twentieth century, all states had legislation authorizing the use of such legal documents.

Also raised in various state legislatures is the issue of euthanasia, or the intentional killing of a mentally competent individual in response to that individual's voluntary request for death. Changes in technology and the practice of medicine to preserve life have heightened the right to die debate. As early as 1906, a bill was introduced in the Ohio state legislature to provide for voluntary euthanasia. In 1938, the Euthanasia Society of America was established to help introduce legislation that gave the terminally ill the right to die with dignity. The right to die controversy has been raging in the United States at least since the 1950s. Before mid-century, the right to die, however, was not a major concern because medical science was unable to extend the lives of terminal patients. Most people died at home without extraordinary medical effort. Today, eighty percent of the population dies in hospitals or nursing homes with almost no end to medical innovations and the power of doctors and machines to prolong life. Busy doctors in impersonal settings focus on treating physical problems, not learning about a patient's outlook on illness, treatment, and quality of life.

The first highly publicized euthanasia case occurred in 1976 when the parents of Karen Quinlan, a woman in vegetative state, sued to have her life supports removed. The New Jersey Supreme Court ruled that neither the parents nor the physicians were legally obligated to sustain the life of a comatose patient with no hope of recovery. After the court's decision, Ms. Quinlan's respirator was unplugged. She continued to breathe on her own and was moved to a nursing home where she eventually died.

The issue reached the U.S. Supreme Court in the 1990 case of Nancy Cruzan. In 1983, 25 year-old Nancy Cruzan was in a car accident. The medical staff inserted a feeding tube, but years passed with Ms. Cruzan remaining in a vegetative state with no hope of improvement. Her medical care cost the state of Missouri $130,000 a day. When Ms. Cruzan's parents tried to remove the artificial feeding tube in 1987, the medical staff refused. After several trials and appeals, the U.S. Supreme Court ruled in 1990 that food and hydration could be withdrawn if the patient requested. Protesters tried to get to Nancy's hospital room to reconnect the feeding tube. She died December 26, 1990, twelve days after the tube was removed.

1990s • Physician-assisted Suicide

~ The battle over euthanasia again reached the U. S. Supreme Court in 1997, when it unanimously decided to uphold states' rights to outlaw physician-assisted suicide. The court's decision did not silence the divisive national debate between advocates and opponents of the right to die. Mass media directed attention to Oregonians voting to allow physician-assisted suicide and juries acquitting Dr. Jack Kevorkian of killing terminally ill patients. In April 1998, an Oregon woman in her eighties suffering from breast cancer became the first known American to die under the nation's only physician-assisted suicide law.

Although Americans hold diverse opinions on the right to die, public opinion has moved steadily in favor of the right to die over the past fifty years. Polls spanning five decades have asked the following question: "When a person has a disease that cannot be cured, do you think doctors should be allowed to end the patient's life by some painless means if the patient and his family request it?" As shown in Figure 11, only thirty-six percent of the national sample said "yes" in 1947. The following decades witnessed growing support for physician-assisted suicide, euthanasia, and right-to-die legislation, with seventy-two percent of the American public supporting physician-assisted suicide in 1991.

1967-1974 • Hospice Movement ~ As the right to die movement articulates, modern hospitals are dominated by medical practitioners with the priority of providing medical cures for the acutely ill rather than caring for those who are incurable. The hospice concept of care, in contrast, specializes in serving patients with life-threatening illnesses. St. Christopher's Hospice of London, England, which opened in 1967, played a key role in the global development of the modern hospice movement to minister to the spiritual and physical needs of dying patients. It disseminated the hospice concept of care and was a model for the first hospice in the United States, which opened in 1974 in New Haven, Connecticut. Now, there are over 2,000 hospices in the United States.

Hospice's primary goal is to promote patient-family autonomy and to assist patients in obtaining pain control and real quality of life before they die. Traditional medical care is often based on a PRN (Latin for *pro re nata*) approach: as

Figure 11: Percent Supporting the Allowance of Incurable Patients to Die

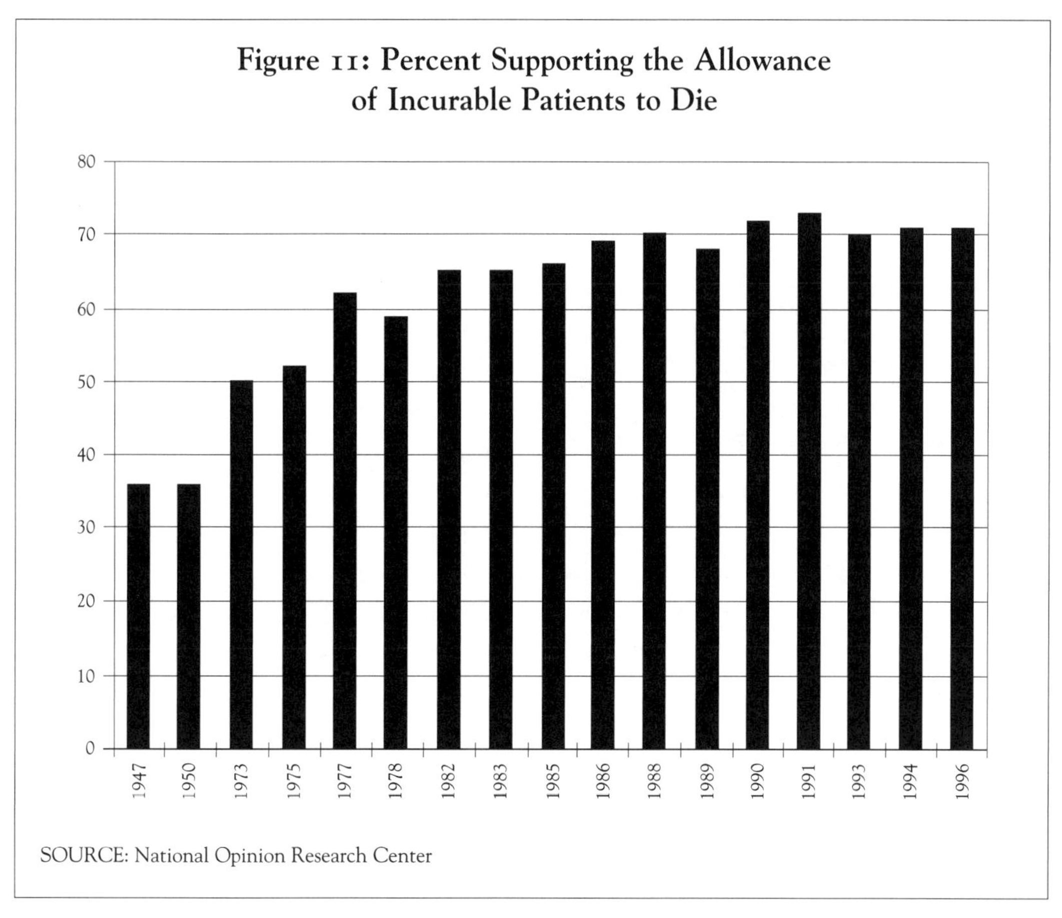

SOURCE: National Opinion Research Center

the situation demands. This means that a person must first hurt and then ask for relief before the pain can be stopped, a procedure that is responsible for much suffering among the terminally ill. In hospices, patients receive drugs to prevent pain from happening.

Unlike a traditional institutionalized death, the majority of hospice services are delivered in the home by an interdisciplinary team of physicians, social workers, chaplains, financial counselors, psychiatrists or psychologists, home health aides, homemakers, physical and occupational therapists, lawyers, funeral directors, artists, and volunteers. In hospice, the patient-family is the unit of care. This means that patients make decisions about how and where they want to live and die. Patients and families have the right to make decisions in their own care, even if it is contrary to the beliefs of their caregivers. Family members are provided with respite support and bereavement counseling. Hospice staff are dedicated to helping patients move beyond the curative power of medicine to remain in familiar environments that can minimize pain and maintain personal dignity and control over the dying process.

Conclusion

For most of human history, death has been an ever-present fact of life and a distinct possibility for people of all ages. Until the twentieth century the highest percentage of deaths occurred within the first ten years of life. Today, however, death in America is highly concentrated among older adults. In this nation's agricultural past, growing up in a rural environment gave people direct exposure to birth and death as everyday events. Most deaths occurred at home where parents socialized their children to view dying as a natural process that all family members should accept.

With less than ten percent of Americans living on farms at the end of the twentieth century, scenes of birth and death have been removed from most people's direct observations. Death over the past hundred years became increasingly segregated from everyday life and sequestered from public space. Death was transformed from a living part of the American experience to an event that most people tried to avoid, shun, and conquer. Biomedical advances that extended life also extended the process of dying, and thus generated a host of complicated ethical questions related to when and where death should occur. The dramatic reduction in death rates over the twentieth century was an amazing accomplishment that radically altered the whole society.

Bibliography

Centers for Disease Control. "Achievements in Public Health, 1900-1999: Decline in Deaths from Heart Disease and Stroke—United States, 1900-1999." *Mortality and Morbidity Weekly Report* 48(30): 649-656, 1999.

Farrell, James J. *Inventing the American Way of Death, 1830-1920*. Philadelphia: Temple University Press, 1980.

Hume, Janice. *Obituaries in American Culture*. Jackson: University Press of Mississippi, 2000.

Leavitt, Judith Walzer and Ronald L. Numbers, eds. *Sickness and Health in America*. 3d Rev. ed. Madison, WI: University of Wisconsin Press, 1997.

Leming, Michael R. and George E. Dickinson. *Understanding Dying, Death, and Bereavement.* New York: Harcourt Brace and Company, 1998.

Moller, David Wendell. *Confronting Death: Values, Institutions, and Human Mortality.* New York: Oxford University Press, 1996.

Uhlenberg, Peter. "Mortality Decline in the Twentieth Century and Supply of Kin Over the Life Course." *The Gerontologist* 36(5): 681-685, 1996.

White, Kevin M. and Samuel H. Preston. "How Many Americans Are Alive Because of Twentieth-century Improvements in Mortality?" *Population and Development Review* 22(3): 415-429, 1996.

Internet Resources

Statistics
Official government source for statistics regarding death in the U.S.
Http://www.cdc.gov/nchs

Death and Dying Site
Comprehensive site linking to many aspects of death.
http://dying.about.com/index.htm

Grief & Bereavement Support Site
Mental Health Counseling and Therapy Grief Counseling
http://www.counselingforloss.com/

Kearl's Guide to Sociological Thanatology
Family Health, Death and Dying, Dying and Terminal Care Guides and Directories
http://www.trinity.edu/~mkearl/death.html

End of Life
Resources on death from National Public Radio
http://www.npr.org/programs/death/

Death of a Child
Coping with the death of an child of any age.
http://dying.about.com/library/weekly/aa092897.htm

Near-Death Experiences and the Afterlife
http://www.near-death.com/

International Association for Near-Death Studies
Provides reliable information about near-death experiences, and giving resources for more information,
http://www.iands.org/

Peter Uhlenberg
Jenifer Hamil-Luker
University of North Carolina, Chapel Hill

ECONOMY, 1865-1900: THE RISE OF CORPORATE CAPITALISM

~

(1893) Uncle Sam rescues the nation's Business Interests from the Silver Flood, in a celebration of the repeal of the Sherman Silver Purchase Act.

TIMELINE

1850-1879 ~ The Beginning of a Modern Economy

Corporations shift from public charters to private enterprises (1850s) / Bessemer steel process invented (1850s) / Transatlantic cable laid from the U.S. to Europe (1857-1866) / First oil well drilled, in Pennsylvania (1859) / First cattle drives begin (1866) / Gold rush in California and Colorado attracts hoards of prospectors (1848-1860) / Proliferation of mining, ranching, and farming on the frontier (1860-1880) / Silver rush in Nevada and the Dakotas (1860-1880) / Patent office issues 440,000 patents between 1860-1890 / Homestead Act provides free land to pioneer settlers (1862) / Railroads improved by dining cars (1868), air brakes (1870), steam heat (1881), and electric lights (1887) / Invention of the typewriter (1868), cash register (1879), adding machine (1891) / Electric arc light system invented (1870s) / Rise of the modern corporation in which the stockholders are not responsible for corporate debt (1870s)

MILESTONES: Census shows great increase in the types of occupations (1850) • Invention of the elevator by Elisha Otis paves the way for skyscrapers (1850s) • Congress makes the first federal land grants for development of U.S. railroads (1850) • Debates rage over restricting slavery in the western territories (1850) • Freed slaves elect sharecropper farming over paid wages (1867-1868) • Seven out of ten working women hold jobs as domestic servants (1870) • Widespread use of child labor (1870) • Barbed wire fencing invented, making cheap fencing available to farmers on the plains (mid-1870s) • American Express establishes the first railroad pension plan (1875) • Alexander Graham Bell with George Watson invent the telephone (1876)

1800-1889 ~ Rise of Corporate Capitalism

F.W. Taylor begins the study of scientific management (1880s) / Dominance of iron, steel, railroad, and oil industries (1880s) / Standardized time imposed by the railroads (1883) / Rockefeller dominates the oil industry (1880s) / Corporate capitalism provides opportunities for small entrepreneurs (1880s) / First of a series of droughts begins in the Great Plains causing the decline the farms (1887)

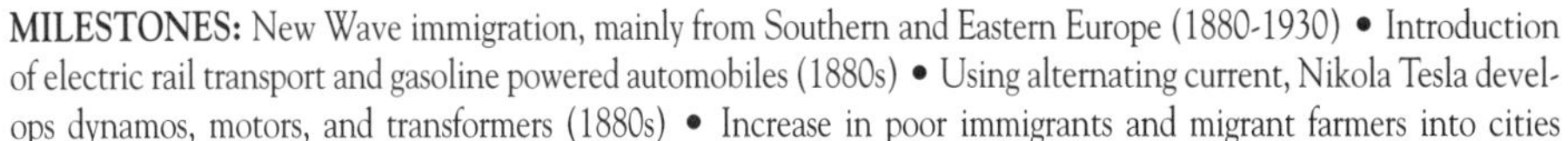

MILESTONES: New Wave immigration, mainly from Southern and Eastern Europe (1880-1930) • Introduction of electric rail transport and gasoline powered automobiles (1880s) • Using alternating current, Nikola Tesla develops dynamos, motors, and transformers (1880s) • Increase in poor immigrants and migrant farmers into cities (1880s) • Railroads create first professional managers (1880s) • Interracial alliances of workers and farmers forge national organization, the Knights of Labor (1880s-1890s) • State courts rule that labor reform laws violate the rights of employers to enjoy the freedom to operate their businesses (1881-1900) • Creation of Coca Cola (1886) • Congress passes the Interstate Commerce Act to control certain economic practices of railroads (1887) • George Eastman invents celluloid rolls of film for use in Kodak cameras (1888) • Modern electric motor opens way for consumer appliances (1888)

1890-1899 ~ Corporate Power and Industrial Might

McKinley Tariff raises duties on imported goods to 50% (1890) / Commercial farming develops international markets (1890s) / American Telephone and Telegraph Co installs 2,000 telephones (1890s) / Sherman anti-trust legislation is passed to control monopolies (1890) / Depression and panic begin when the Philadelphia and Reading Railroad declares bankruptcy (1893) / 20% of the labor force loses their jobs to the panic (1893) / Silver Purchase Act requires the federal government to purchase silver with gold (1893) / Supreme Court rules against a Sherman Anti-trust case, weakening its authority (1895) / Maintaining the gold standard is the central issue in the presidential campaign (1896) / 193,000 miles of railroad track is laid by 1899 / One percent of the nation's families control 88% of the nation's assets (1899)

MILESTONES: First American electric car produced (1891) • Foundation of The National Consumer League (1892) • Free rural postal delivery proliferates mail order catalogs (1896) • Henry Ford begins production of the gas-powered automobile (1896) • U.S. manufacturers produce 35,000 electric cars between 1896 and 1915 • First functional gasoline automobile designed in Germany (1885) • First gasoline driven car produced in the U.S. (1903) • Alaskan gold rush begins after the discovery of gold in the Klondike (1897) • U.S. fleet conquers the Spanish navy in a one-day fight at Manila Bay in the Philippines (1898) • Proliferation of installment credit plans (1898-1925) • Open door trade policy with China initiated (1899)

Introduction

The decline of family farms and small businesses, the growth of labor unrest, the advent of the corporation, the reorganization of business, the invention of new technologies and techniques, the debate over tariffs, monopolies, and money: these developments and others converged to define the economic history of the United States not only during the last thirty-five years of the nineteenth century but throughout much of the twentieth century as well.

At the end of the nineteenth century a new economic order and a new set of cultural attitudes were coming to dominate the United States. This new economy and culture centered on the quest for security, wealth, comfort, pleasure, and satisfaction. Emerging in the decades that followed the Civil War, the new economy and culture were increasingly unconnected to traditional family and community life or to traditional moral and religious values. The emphasis instead was on business, money, and the marketplace.

The focus of American life shifted from the church and the meeting house to such new pleasure palaces as department stores, theaters, restaurants, hotels, dance halls, and amusement parks. By the late nineteenth century, America was no longer a "Land of Opportunity." It had become instead a "Land of Desire" in which the acquisition and consumption of goods was not only the key to happiness in this world, but, for many, to salvation in the next.

The new economic order, and the culture that accompanied and supported it, did not emerge without exciting social and political opposition. Workers and farmers challenged the vision of a corporate America, harkening back to older conceptions of property ownership and civic virtue. Liberty, independence, and democracy, critics argued, rested on independent families owning their own land and producing for themselves most of what they needed to survive. People living in such a society not only worked for their own benefit, but also for the welfare of their neighbors. They argued that the new economic order, by contrast, set every person against every other person in a competitive struggle that bred restlessness, anxiety, envy, resentment, hatred, and could only end in the destruction of society itself. Opponents of the new corporate order were convinced that in a world where every man was for himself alone, the devil would get most of them. Yet, despite opposition and resistance, the new corporate economy in time replaced the old order, fundamentally altering the nature of American society and the meaning of America itself.

1865 • The New Economic Order ~ "The truth is," wrote Senator John Sherman to his brother General William Tecumseh Sherman in 1865, "the close of the war with our resources unimpaired gives an elevation, a scope to the ideas of leading capitalists, far higher than anything ever undertaken before. They talk of millions as confidently as they talked formerly of thousands." Senator Sherman was prescient. Within twenty-five years of the assassination of Abraham Lincoln, the United States had become the leading industrial nation in the world.

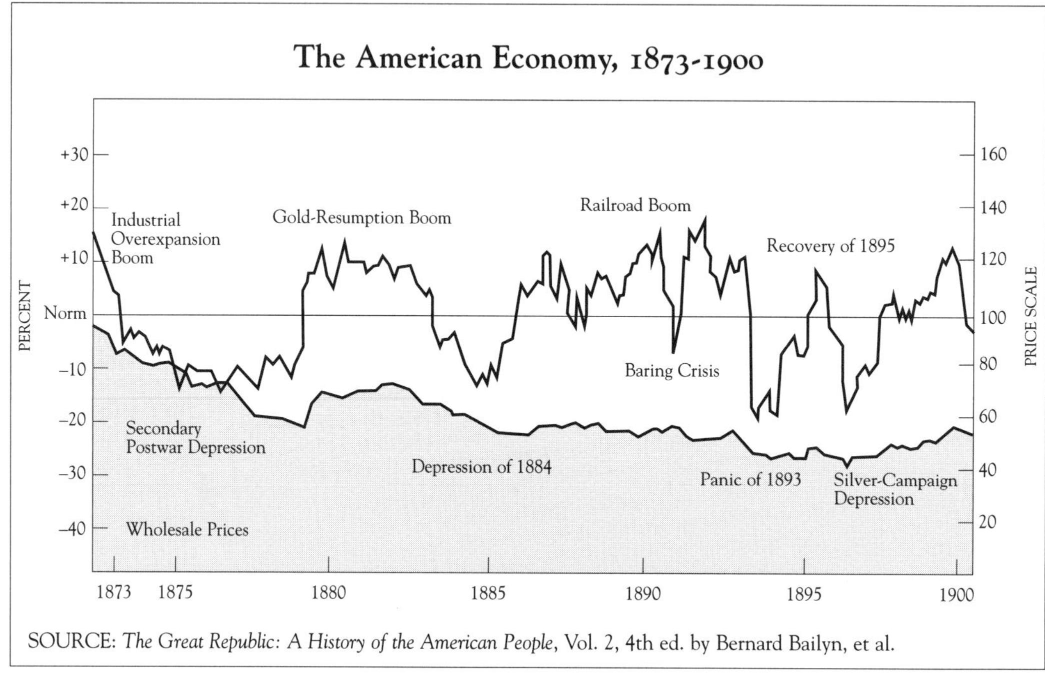

SOURCE: *The Great Republic: A History of the American People*, Vol. 2, 4th ed. by Bernard Bailyn, et al.

1870-1910 • Toward Industrial Supremacy ~ The rise of the United States to industrial supremacy, however, was not as sudden as it seemed. Since the early nineteenth century Americans had been building an industrial economy and, in the northeast at least, industry was well established before the Civil War. Still, the accomplishment of the last three decades of the nineteenth century, from 1870 until 1900, overshadowed all that had come before. Americans during those years witnessed nothing less than a swift and total transformation of the national economy. Manufacturing production, for example, increased more than six fold between 1870 and 1910.

Six basic elements contributed to the achievement of American industrial and economic supremacy. They were, first, the existence of abundant and accessible raw materials; second, a large and growing supply of cheap labor, which rural migrants and foreign immigrants provided; third, a surge of technological innovation; fourth, the emergence of a wealthy, ambitious, talented, and sometimes ruthless group of entrepreneurs; fifth, a national government eager and able to assist business and subsidize industry; sixth, a rising demand and an expanding market for manufactured goods.

1860-1890 • New Technologies and New Industries ~ The development of new technologies, the discovery of new materials, and the evolution of new processes were prerequisites to the industrial and economic growth characteristic of the late nineteenth century. Until 1860, for example, the government of the United States had granted only 36,000 patents. Between 1860 and 1890, by contrast, 440,000 were issued by the patent office.

Some of the first and most important innovations came in communications, a field that continues to flourish today as we have entered the age of cyberspace. Between 1857 and 1866, Cyrus W. Field supervised the laying of the transatlantic cable to Europe, a far cry from the World Wide Web but clearly one of its direct antecedents.

During the next decade, Alexander Graham Bell developed the first commercially useful telephone. By the 1890s, the American Telephone and Telegraph Company (AT&T) had installed more than two thousand telephones across the United States, most of them in government bureaus, business establishments, and the residences of the wealthy. By 1920, over 12 percent of the American population had telephones.

Other inventions that speeded the pace at which business was done and, in important ways, altered its organization, were the typewriter, which Christopher L. Sholes invented in 1868, the cash register, which Joseph Ritty invented in 1879, and the adding machine, which William S. Burroughs invented in 1891. Before these inventions, life was more complicated. For example, before the calculator, one had to either add numbers longhand on a piece of paper or use a instrument called a slide-rule (looking a little like a ruler with many numbers on it). Before the typewriter, one had to hand-write all correspondence.

Among the most revolutionary innovations was the introduction of electricity in the 1870s. Charles F. Brush devised the arc lamp, which provided illumination for businesses and streets. The Brush electric arc light system was installed in Wanamaker's department store in Philadelphia, Pennsylvania, and in the streets of Cleveland, Ohio, in 1879, and throughout New York City in 1880.

Thomas Alva Edison invented the incandescent lamp (commonly known now as the light bulb), which made the illumination of offices and homes by electricity both practical and affordable. Edison also designed improved generators and large power plants that furnished electricity to entire cities. By 1900, electricity was becoming commonplace in large cities to operate street cars, elevators in the new skyscrapers, machinery in factories, and increasingly, lights in offices and homes.

1850s-1860s • Innovations in Industry ~ Three industries formed the basis of the modern industrial economy: iron, steel, and oil. In each of these industries, inventors made important breakthroughs during the second half of the nineteenth and early years of the twentieth century.

In the 1850s an Englishman, Sir Henry Bessemer, and an American, William Kelly, independently and almost simultaneously developed a process by which iron could be transformed into steel, a more flexible, versatile, and durable material. The Bessemer process, as this development came to be known, consisted of blowing air through molten iron to burn off the impurities.

A New Jersey ironmaster named Abram S. Hewitt introduced in 1868 another method for making steel: the open-hearth process. Together the Bessemer and open-hearth processes made possible the production of high-quality, inexpensive steel in great quantities and of large dimensions. Steel became the building block of the industrial economy. It was used in the manufacture of ships, locomotives and railroad cars, train tracks, girders for the construction of skyscrapers, factories, and industrial machinery.

1850s-1880s • Oil ~ The oil industry emerged in the late nineteenth century largely in response to the need to lubricate machines used in the manufacture of steel. For some time Americans had known of the existence of petroleum

Table 1: Value of Selected U.S. Exports, 1870-1910
Value (in millions of dollars)

	1870	1880	1890	1900	1910
Cotton	227	212	251	242	450
Tobacco	21	16	21	29	38
Wheat	47	191	45	73	48
Oil	B	B	54	84	107

SOURCE: *Historical Statistics of the United States*, Part 2, pp. 898-899.

1876-1901

reserves in western Pennsylvania. At first, though, no one was sure what to do with the oil that seeped to the surface of streams and springs. Then, in the 1850s, a Pennsylvania businessman named George H. Bissell commissioned a series of experiments that revealed oil could be burned in lamps and also used as a lubricant.

In 1859, Edwin L. Drake, one of Bissell's employees, constructed the first oil well near Titusville, Pennsylvania. Drake's well soon yielded 500 barrels of oil per month. The demand for petroleum grew quickly, and promoters set about developing other oil fields in Pennsylvania, Ohio, and western Virginia. By the early 1880s, oil and related petroleum products were among the leading American exports, although still trailing such agricultural commodities as raw cotton and unprocessed tobacco and wheat.

1876-1901 • The Impact of the Automobile ~ Twenty years later, in 1900, the demand for oil expanded dramatically, for its value as fuel became apparent. But the available oil reserves in the East had already dissipated. A search began in other parts of the country for oil deposits, or "black gold" as oil was called, recalling the California Gold Rush of 1848–1849. In 1901, explorers discov-

(1901) Texan oil field belonging to Texas Oil Co, at the turn of the century.

ered the Spindletop oil field in Texas, one of the richest and most extensive deposits of oil in the world. A few years later, other discoveries followed elsewhere in Texas as well as in Oklahoma and California.

With the turn of the century came the first sustained demand for petroleum. The internal combustion engine was invented in 1876. In 1885, a German engineer, Gottlieb Daimler, set it on four wheels and obtained a French patent for his innovation. Daimler had produced the first automobile. For many years, however, the automobile remained a novelty that only the wealthy could afford.

Brothers Charles Edgar and James Frank Duryea built the first gasoline-driven motor vehicle in the United States in 1903. Three years later Henry Ford produced his first automobile, the Model-T, which eventually became affordable to large numbers of ordinary consumers. Henry Ford's use of assembly line production reduced manufacturing costs, enabling him to lower prices. By 1910, the automobile industry had become a driving force in the American economy. In 1900, for example, there had been approximately eight thousand automobiles on American roadways. Twenty years later, there were more than eight million.

1890s • The Importance of Petroleum ~ The development of the automobile and the new industrial uses of petroleum greatly expanded demand for it. Before the 1890s Americans had primarily used oil for lighting. Soon, however, it became, and has remained, the basis for transportation, manufacturing, and much of the chemical industry. European nations, then as now, were almost entirely dependent on imported oil. The United States was more fortunate in having its own domestic supply. But since the end of the Second World War the growing dependence on imported oil has embroiled Americans and Europeans alike in deepening political and economic conflicts with the oil-rich Arab nations of the Near East.

Table 2: Automobile Sales and Registrations, 1900-1920

	No. of Automobiles Sold	No. of Automobiles Registered
1900	4,100	8,000
1905	24,200	77,400
1910	181,000	458,300
1915	895,900	2,332,400
1920	1,905,500	8,131,500

SOURCE: *Historical Statistics of the United States*, Part 2, p. 716.

The Science of Production

1880-1911 • Scientific Management ~ Essential to the growth of the industrial economy were changes in the techniques of production and management. By the turn of the twentieth century, many industrialists had adopted and applied the principles of "Scientific Management" or "Taylorism," as they were known after their chief theoretician, Frederick Winslow Taylor. Taylor argued that labor had to be made compatible with the machine age. He believed that scientific management would organize and discipline the labor force so that workers would be more dependent and productive, thereby increasing managers' control of the work place.

During the nineteenth century, first unskilled workers and then machines began to replace skilled craftsmen. Yet, because of their specialized knowledge, highly skilled workers continued, even after the advent of industrialization, to exert considerable control over the pace of work and the level of productivity. While working as a foreman at the Midvale Steel Company in the 1880s, Taylor concluded that to improve efficiency and increase production, managers had to take control of the work process.

To accomplish this task, Taylor began conducting time studies of each factory job. These studies involved observing workers meticulously, analyzing every step in the work process to determine the time spent and the energy expended on it, and using the results to discover the most efficient way of performing not only each job but each separate function within the job. Taylor required all workers to adopt this standard method, with scaled piecework rates providing the incentive for greater efficiency and higher output. Under Taylor's program, workers themselves became interchangeable parts.

Taylor's methods worked. Applying them, he dramatically increased productivity at Midvale Steel. Taylor then became a pioneer management consultant, publicizing his system and advising corporations on how to implement it in his book, *The Principles of Scientific Management*, published in 1911. For workers, Taylorism brought a marked loss of autonomy as managers more closely supervised activities on the shop floor. Many workers asserted that they knew more about production than did the managers, planners, and experts now in charge of the process. Some declared that the gains in incentive pay were not worth the increased pressure and regimentation that came with working in a scientifically-managed factory. But Taylorism fit with the trend toward large-scale, mechanized production, and it appealed to the emerging class of corporate managers who were distrustful of labor and intent on maximizing efficiency, productivity, and profits.

Manufacturers also began placing greater emphasis on industrial research. The phenomenal success of Thomas Edison's celebrated industrial laboratory in Menlo Park, New Jersey, prompted dozens of corporations to establish research laboratories of their own. By 1913, Bell Telephone, Du Pont, General Electric, Eastman Kodak, and approximately fifty other companies budgeted hundreds of thousands of dollars annually for research by their own engineers and scientists.

Early 1900s • Mass Production

~ The most important change in production technology during the industrial era was the emergence of mass production. Two technological developments were especially significant: the evolution of the continuous assembly line and the development of interchangeable parts. Henry Ford introduced both innovations in his automobile factories in 1914. The continuous assembly line had been in use in slaughter houses at least since the middle of the nineteenth century. Ford was the first to apply it systematically to industrial production.

The assembly line cut the time for building a chassis from twelve-and-one-half to one-and-one-half hours. Along with the use of interchangeable parts, which made the manufacture and maintenance of automobiles simpler and cheaper, assembly line production enabled Ford to lower the base price of his Model-T from $950 in 1914 to $290 in 1929. As

(1870) American industrialist Cornelius Vanderbilt (1794 - 1877) standing astride two railroads competing with James Fisk (1835 - 1872) for control of the Erie Railroad

his production costs diminished and his profit margins rose, Ford could reduce the hours and raise the wages of his workers to five dollars per day, an astonishing rate in the 1910s. In a short time, workers in the Ford factory could save enough to put a down payment on the cars that they helped to make.

LATE 1800S • THE RAILROAD ~ The principal agent of industrial development in the late nineteenth century, however, was not the automobile but the railroad. Railroads made possible the creation of a vast national economy and dominated the American technological imagination for a generation. To many Americans, the railroad was the symbol of progress.

Railroads promoted industrial growth in three ways. First, they gave industrialists access to distant markets and sources of raw materials. Second, they were the first big business in the United States and, as such, prompted new forms of corporate organization that served as models for other industries. Third, they stimulated economic growth through investment and through enormous expenditures on construction and equipment.

1865-1900 • INNOVATIONS IN RAILROADS ~ During the late nineteenth century railroads achieved numerous technological advances that greatly improved the efficiency and uniformity of their operation. The use of heavier rails, the construction of bridges, and the introduction of block and interlocking signals all led to better service. In 1886, all railroads in the continental United States at last adopted a standard gauge that eliminated time-consuming and costly transfers of passengers and freight from one line to another. Passenger travel also became safer and more comfortable with the introduction of dining cars in 1868, air brakes in 1870, steam heat in 1881, electric lights in 1887, and all-steel coaches in 1904.

These innovations permitted a decline in average freight rates from about 2.0 cents per ton-mile in 1865 to 0.75 cents per ton-mile in 1900. With such low rates, cattle from Texas, beef from Illinois, Missouri, or Nebraska, shoes from New England, steel from Pennsylvania, Ohio, and West Virginia, corn from Iowa, grain and flour from Minnesota, fruit from California, and lumber from Washington could all be shipped greater distances at lower cost. American industry boomed as local and regional markets became national. The entire economy became more active, more interconnected, and more productive.

1883 • Railroad Time ~ Just how thoroughly the railroads transformed American life is suggested by one further change they brought about. Until the 1880s, every community in the United States had its own local time. People set their clocks according to the rules of astronomy. Noon was the moment when the sun stood highest in the midday sky. When it was noon in Chicago, for example, it was 11:50 A.M. in St. Louis, 11:27 A.M. in Omaha, and 12:18 P.M. in Detroit, with an almost infinite number of variations in between.

For railroad companies, trying to keep track of hundreds of different times in hundreds of different cities and towns along their routes was a logistical nightmare. Such scheduling problems caused not only confusion and delays, but accidents as well. Consequently, on November 18, 1883, without authorization from Congress, the railroad companies imposed four uniform time zones on the nation in order to rationalize train schedules and timetables. Representatives of the railroad companies agreed to ignore all local times. Henceforth, for the railroads, every community within a single time zone would have the same time. The government did not ratify this change until 1918, but most communities were quick to adopt standard "railroad" time. The railroads, it seems, were not only conquering space, but time itself.

1890-1910 • Railroads Triumphant ~ After 1860 the total mileage of railroad track increased every decade through 1900, even though railroad construction declined following the depression of 1893. By 1900, there were 193,000 miles of track in the United States. Subsidies from federal, state, and local governments, to say nothing of investments from abroad, were essential to the completion of these vast undertakings, which required far more capital than private entrepreneurs could accumulate by themselves.

Of equal importance was the emergence of the great railroad combinations that brought most of the railroads under the control of a handful of men. By 1906, approximately 76 percent of the railroad mileage was controlled by seven combinations under the leadership of such financial and industrial magnates as James J. Hill, Edward H. Harriman, J. P. Morgan, Collis P. Huntington, Cornelius Vanderbilt, and later his son, William and his grandson, Cornelius. These men, and others like them, became symbols of great wealth concentrated in a very few hands, and often of the corruption, fraud, chicanery, and scandal that accompanied it.

In the development of the railroads, however, American businessmen recognized a model of ever larger firms practicing economies of scale; that is, economies made possible by doing a volume business and passing the savings on to consumers. Hence, the railroad was ultimately less significant for the individual fortunes that it generated than for its contribution to the growth of a new economic institution: the modern corporation.

1850-1900 • The Western Economy ~ The western economy was as varied and diverse as its eastern counterpart. By the late nineteenth century, three major industries dominated the western economy: mining, ranching, and farming. Each had a distinctive history and distinctive characteristics. Yet, each provided resources essential to industrial development. The western economy thus figured prominently in the industrialization and incorporation of America.

1850s-1870s • Mining ~ The initial economic boom in the West came in mining. It began in earnest about 1860—the California gold rush of 1848-1849 was exceptional—and flourished until the 1890s, when it abruptly declined.

The first substantial mineral strikes, other than the California gold rush, occurred in the late 1850s. In 1858, a prospector discovered gold in the Pike's Peak district of the Colorado territory. The next year, 50,000 prospectors stormed into the region from California, the Mississippi Valley, and the eastern seaboard. Denver and other mining camps blossomed into "cities" overnight. Almost as rapidly as it had developed, though, the mining boom ended. Eventually, corporations revived Colorado gold mining, and the discovery of silver supplied a new source of mineral wealth. Yet, the huge profits of which many miners dreamed remained largely unrealized.

~

The number of railroad tracks increased from 23 miles in 1830 to 208,000 in 1890. The profit that the railroads received increased from $106 million in 1890 to $671 million in 1915.

~

1850-1870

While the Colorado gold rush of 1859 was still in progress, news of another strike drew miners to Nevada. The most valuable ore in Nevada was not gold, but silver. When miners had exhausted the first surface (or placer) deposits, eastern corporations bought the claims and began mining beneath the surface to retrieve silver from deeper veins. For two decades these mining corporations reaped tremendous profits. From 1860 until 1880, the Nevada mines yielded silver worth approximately $306 million. After 1880, though, the mines were largely played out.

The next important discoveries came in 1874. Miners in the Black Hills of the Dakota Territory discovered gold. Once more, prospectors swarmed into the region. As in the earlier booms, however, this one flared for a short time and then faded.

Discoveries of gold and silver generated popular excitement, but in the long run less glamorous minerals proved more important to the development of the West economy. The mining of copper, lead, tin, quartz, and zinc, although less immediately profitable than the mining of gold or silver, actually generated greater profits over a longer period of time and were more useful to the industrial economy of the East.

1860s-1880s

1860s • The Cattle Kingdom ~ A second important component in the western economy was cattle ranching. The vast grasslands of the public domain provided a huge area on the Great Plains where cattle ranchers could graze their herds free of charge and unrestricted by the boundaries of private farms. The railroads spawned the cattle industry and gave it access to markets. Ironically, these same railroads destroyed the open lands by bringing farmers to the plains.

By ancestry, the western cattle industry was Mexican. Long before citizens of the United States settled in the Southwest, Mexican ranchers had raised cattle on the plains of Mexico and Texas. At the end of the Civil War, an estimated 5 million head of cattle already roamed the Texas ranges. They brought attractive prices in eastern markets. The challenge for ranchers was to get the animals from the range to the railroad and from there to market.

1860s-1870s • The Cattle Drives ~ Early in 1866, some Texas cattlemen began driving their herds north to Sedalia, Missouri, located along the route of the Missouri Pacific Railroad. Traveling across the rough country, beset by rustlers, outlaws, and Indians, the caravan suffered heavy losses. Only a fraction of the animals arrived in Sedalia. But the drive was an important experiment with lasting consequences. It proved that cattle could be driven to distant markets and turned out to pasture along the trail. The cattle drive from Texas to Missouri laid the foundation for the cattle kingdom.

With the precedent established, the next step was to find an easier route to market through more accessible country. Joseph G. McCoy, a livestock dealer from Illinois, secured contracts with the Kansas Pacific and the Hannibal & St. Joe railroads and began to transport cattle to slaughter houses in Chicago as early as 1867. McCoy brought cattle from as far south as Corpus Christi, Texas, and established Abilene, Kansas as the terminus of the drive. Abilene became the first of many "cow-towns" so renowned in Western legend and lore.

Between 1867 and 1871, cattlemen drove nearly 1.5 million head up the Chisholm Trail to Abilene. Yet, by 1875, agricultural development in western Kansas was already eating away at the open range land at the same time that the number of animals was increasing. Ranchers, therefore, had to develop other trails and other market outlets. As the railroads began to reach farther west, Dodge City and Wichita, Kansas, Ogallala and Sidney, Nebraska, Cheyenne and Laramie, Wyoming, and Miles City and Glendive, Montana all began to rival Abilene as major cattle marketing centers.

1880s • The Decline of the Cattle Industry ~ Accounts of the lofty profits to be made in the cattle business attracted eastern, English, and Scottish capital to the plains. Increasingly, the cattle industry tied the West more firmly than ever into the emerging corporate economy of the East. In one year, for example, twenty corporations with a combined capital of $12 million were chartered in Wyoming. In addition, numerous slaughterhouses and meatpacking companies acquired direct ownership of the large western herds.

The result of this frenzied, speculative expansion was that the ranges, already diminished by the railroads and the farmers, became overstocked. There was no longer enough grass to support the crowded herds or to sustain the long cattle drives. At last, nature intervened. Two consecutive severe winters in 1885-1886 and 1886-1887, with a blistering summer between them, reduced the herds and scorched the plains. Streams dried up, grass burned, hundreds of thousands of cattle died, and princely ranches and substantial investments disappeared in a season.

The cattle industry never recovered. Railroads displaced the trail as the route to market for livestock. Despite these changes, most of the large, established cattle ranches with fenced in pastures and an inexhaustible supply of hay for winter feed survived, expanded, and eventually produced more beef than ever. But the open range and the romance of the cattle drive were gone, never to return. Cattle ranching, like mining, had become fully integrated into the corporate economy.

1870s • Farming ~ The arrival of the miners and the ranchers and the dispersal of the Indian nations served as a prelude to the decisive phase of white settlement in the West. Even before the Civil War, farmers had begun to move onto the plains, challenging the dominance of the ranchers and the Indians, and occasionally coming into conflict with both. By the 1870s, what began as a trickle became a deluge. Farmers poured into the plains and beyond. They enclosed land that had once been hunting territory for the Indians and pasture for cattle.

1870s • Railroads and Agriculture ~ The construction of the railroads made the settlement of the West possible and thereby stimulated the development of the agricultural economy. Railroad companies actively promoted settlement, both to provide customers for their services and to increase the value of their extensive land holdings. Railroad companies set low rates for settlers so that almost anyone could afford the westward journey. They also sold much of their land at low prices and provided liberal credit to prospective settlers.

In addition to the railroads, a temporary change in climate contributed to the surge of agricultural expansion in the West. For several consecutive years beginning in 1870 rainfall in the plains states was well above average.

Even under the most favorable conditions, though, farming on the plains presented special difficulties. First was the problem of fencing. Farmers had to enclose their land, if for no other reason than to protect crops from the herds of cattle that roamed freely. Traditional wood or stone fences were too expensive and, in any event, proved ineffective barriers against cattle. In the mid-1870s, two Illinois farmers, Joseph H. Glidden and I. L. Ellwood, solved this problem by developing and marketing barbed wire, which provided a cheap and effective fencing.

1887 • Water and Irrigation ~ The second, more intractable, problem was water. Water was scarce even when the amount of rainfall was above average. After 1887, a series of droughts began, and lands that had been fertile now returned to a semi-arid condition. Some farmers dealt with the problem by digging deep wells and pumping out the water with steel windmills. Others turned to dryland farming, a system of tillage designed to conserve moisture in the soil by covering it with a blanket of dust to slow evaporation. Still others planted hardier, drought resistant crops such as soybeans, sugar beets, and certain strains of wheat.

In many areas of the Great Plains only large-scale irrigation could save the endangered farms. Irrigation projects of the necessary magnitude, however, required government assistance, and neither the states nor the federal government were prepared to fund such projects.

During the early 1880s, with land values rising, western farmers had no difficulty obtaining credit and had every reason to believe that they would soon retire their debts. By the late 1880s, though, with crop prices falling and the costs of production increasing, farmers' prospects changed for the worst. Tens of thousands of farmers could not pay their debts and had to abandon their farms. There was, in effect, a reverse migration. Settlers moved back to the East, turning once flourishing agricultural communities into desolate ghost towns. Those who remained continued to endure falling prices and chronic indebtedness.

1880s • The Decline of Western Agriculture ~ For a time during the late 1870s and early 1880s, western farmers prospered once more. By 1887, however, the agricultural boom had ended and farmers in the Midwest, Far West, and especially the South faced worsening economic conditions. The expansive new lands brought under cultivation in the United States during the last three decades of the nineteenth century resulted in an increasing volume of agricultural produce. American farmers were too successful; they were producing far more than the market could absorb. As a result, agricultural

(circa 1870) Cash and Credit. A poster warning of the evils of credit. The one side reads, "Peace and Plenty are the results of cash"; the other side, "Empty pockets and fear are the results of credit."

prices declined and the entire agricultural economy stagnated.

Like most Americans at the time, farmers could not understand how deprivation and poverty arose from productivity and abundance. They shared the confusion that the Populist governor of Kansas, L. D. Lewelling, expressed when he exclaimed:

> There were hungry people . . . because there was too much bread and so many . . . poorly clad . . . because there was too much cloth.

How could economists speak of overproduction, farmers wondered, when so many remained in need? Many farmers concluded that something had gone terribly wrong with the American economic system.

1890s • The Development of Commercial Agriculture ~ By the 1890s American farmers no longer bore much resemblance to the popular myth of the sturdy, rugged, independent yeoman that Americans had long cherished. Commercial farmers had replaced the yeomen and commercial agriculture had supplanted the family farm, much as the corporation was displacing the family business.

Commercial farmers were not self-sufficient and made no effort to become so. They specialized in the production of cash-crops, which they sold on national and world markets. They neither made their own household supplies nor grew their own food. Instead, they purchased all that they needed to live. Commercial farming, when successful, raised the farmers' standard of living. It also rendered farmers vulnerable to banks, mortgages, interest rates, railroad freight charges, and the laws of supply and demand. Moreover, unlike industrial capitalists, commercial farmers could not easily regulate their output or influence the price of the commodities that they produced and sold.

~

The number of western farmers increased from 35,000 in 1860 to 378,000 in 1910.The average value of a farm in 1860 was $2,033, $5,329 in 1900, and $10,271 in 1910.

SOURCE: *Historical Statistics of the United States*, Part 1, pp 457-464.

~

1865-1900

1865-1900 • The Incorporation of Agriculture ~ Between 1865 and 1900 agriculture became an international business. Farm output increased dramatically, not only in the United States but in Canada, Brazil, Argentina, Australia, New Zealand, and Russia. At the same time, modern forms of communication and transportation such as the transatlantic cable, the telegraph, the telephone, and the railroad were creating new markets throughout the country and around the world for agricultural produce.

American commercial farmers, constantly opening new lands to cultivation, relied increasingly on the international market to consume the surplus they produced. Cotton farmers, for example, depended on export sales for 70 percent of their annual income, wheat farmers for between 30 and 40 percent. This development exposed commercial farmers in the United States to the volatility and unpredictability of international markets.

Beginning in the middle 1880s, worldwide over-production led to the general decline of agricultural prices. By the early

1890s, 27 percent of the farms in the United States were mortgaged. By 1910, the figure stood at 35 percent. In 1880, 25 percent of all farms had been operated by tenants who did not own the land that they worked. By 1910, that figure had grown to 37 percent. Commercial farming made some people fabulously wealthy. Yet, the farm economy as a whole suffered a significant decline relative to the rest of the economy.

1880s-1890s • Farmers' Grievances ~ American farmers were painfully aware that something was wrong. Few yet understood the intricacies and implications of worldwide over-production. Instead, they concentrated their attention, frustration, and anger on more immediate, more comprehensible, but no less real problems: inequitable freight rates, high interest rates, and an inadequate currency.

The farmers' first and most serious grievance was against the railroads. In many cases, the railroads charged higher freight rates for farm products than for goods of other types, and higher rates in the South and West than in the Northeast. Railroads also often controlled grain elevator and warehouse facilities and charged exorbitant and arbitrary storage fees.

Farmers also resented banks, mortgage companies, and insurance corporations. Since the sources of credit in the West and South were few, farmers had to accept loans on whatever terms they could get. Commonly, interest rates ran as high as 25 percent and farmers had to repay the loans in years when agricultural prices were dropping and money was becoming scarce.

A third grievance concerned prices—both the prices that farmers received for the goods they sold and the prices they paid for the goods they purchased. Farmers sold their produce on competitive markets over which they had no control. A farmer could plant a large crop at a moment when prices were high and find that by harvest time the price had declined. The fortunes of commercial farmers rose and fell in response to the unpredictable and uncontrollable fluctuations in demand.

Many farmers became convinced that speculators, bankers, merchants, and railroad agents had conspired to fix prices to benefit themselves at farmers' expense. Farmers also came to believe that eastern financiers and manufacturers were contriving to keep the prices of farm produce as low as possible and to raise the prices of manufactured goods as high as possible. Although farmers sold their crops on the competitive world market, they purchased manufactured goods in a domestic market that was protected by tariffs and dominated by the corporations that could manipulate prices to their advantage.

These economic grievances generated a sense of discontent among farmers that helped to create a national political movement in the 1890s. Once farmers had viewed themselves as the backbone of American society. Now they were becoming bitterly aware that their status was declining in relation to the rising urban, industrial, corporate world of the East.

1870-1900 The Major Economic Issues

1870s • The Tariff ~ Tariffs levied against imported goods and materials were the single most discussed and debated issue of Gilded Age politics. The leaders of the Republican party believed that the tariff enabled them to create a national constituency that cut across class lines. Tariff policy was the central tenant of the Republican appeal to workers and capitalists alike, for it seemed to offer the best of all possible worlds: high profits for manufacturers and high wages for workers.

Republicans began with the premise that American industrialists suffered from severe disadvantages in their competition with foreign, especially British, manufacturers, whose costs were considerably lower. They concluded that American businessmen could survive and prosper in the international marketplace only if they also reduced their production costs, primarily by driving down the wages of labor to the level of mere subsistence. This effort, though, presented serious political problems in the United States. For unlike most British workers even after passage of the Reform Bill of 1867, American workers had the vote and might conceivably use their political power to make fundamental changes in the organization of the economy, the government, and the society.

The objectives of the Republican party were thus to ensure both political and social stability and economic prosperity. By assuring American manufacturers control of the home market, a high tariff guaranteed the continuation of comparatively high wages for workers, which gave them an incentive to preserve the existing order. Freed from the need to cut wages to keep up with foreign competition, American industrialists could compete among themselves by making their own enterprises more efficient and more productive. These developments, they believed, would eventually reduce the price of manufactured goods at home and the entire economy would benefit.

1870s • The Debate Over the Tariff ~ During the Civil War, Republicans had doubled the tariff. They justified the large increases because of the need to finance the war effort. After the war, however, high tariffs remained. Despite persistent demands from Democrats to reduce tariff rates, they stayed at between 40 and 50 percent throughout the late nineteenth century. The southern planters and eastern merchants who dominated the Democratic party maintained that high tariffs hurt their economic interests. The tariff compelled planters to pay higher prices for manufactured goods. It forced merchants to pay higher costs for the commodities that they imported, and required them to pass these costs on to their customers in the form of higher prices.

1880s • Democratic Opposition ~ The Democrats insisted that the tariff gave one class of citizens—the industrialists—special privileges and benefits for which other classes of citizens—farmers, merchants, workers, and consumers—had to pay in the form of higher costs and higher prices. Typical of the Democratic position was President Grover Cleveland's denunciation of the tariff in 1887 as a "vicious, inequitable, and illogical source of unnecessary taxation."

Cleveland blasted protectionists for lusting after "immense profits instead of moderately profitable returns." He hinted darkly that they had "organized a combination all along the line to maintain their advantage." By his calculations fewer than one in six American workers was employed in an industry that the tariff protected from foreign competition. Only big capitalists, Cleveland asserted, benefited from high tariffs. The majority of consumers, by contrast, would profit from significant tariff reduction.

According to the political economy of the Democratic party, all producers ought to be equally subjected to the discipline of the market. It was unfair that the law compelled farmers and merchants to subsidize the profits of manufacturers, who alone enjoyed the protection the tariff offered. As for workers, any benefits that they might receive from higher wages were more than offset by the higher prices that they paid for manufactured goods.

Despite his condemnation of the tariff and his defense of American farmers, merchants, workers, and consumers, Cleveland lost the election of 1888 to the Republican candidate Benjamin Harrison, even though Cleveland won the popular vote. Following Harrison's election, the Republican party used the tariff issue to make the first session of the 51st Congress in 1890 the most productive of any during the Gilded Age.

1890-1892 • The Imposition of New Tariffs ~ Picking up the gauntlet that Cleveland had thrown down in 1887, the Republicans fought to raise, not lower, tariff rates. The McKinley Tariff of 1890, introduced by Representative William McKinley of Ohio in the House of Representatives and Senator Nelson W. Aldrich of Rhode Island, raised the average duties on manufactured goods to almost 50 percent.

But Republican leaders had misinterpreted public sentiment, for the party suffered a stunning reversal in the congressional elections of 1890. Their substantial majority in the Senate was reduced to eight. In the House, the Republicans retained only 88 of 323 seats. McKinley himself was among the casualties. Nor did the Republicans recover during the next two years. In the presidential election of 1892, Harrison once more supported the protective tariff and Cleveland, whom the Democrats had renominated, once again opposed it. Cleveland won 277 electoral votes to Harrison's 145, and had a popular margin of 380,000 votes. In 1890 and 1892 American voters apparently punished Republicans for their burst of activism in economic affairs.

1880s-1890s • The Trusts ~ Yet, during Harrison's administration, public opinion also began to force the government to confront some of the pressing social and economic issues of the day. Most notably, sentiment was rising in favor of federal legislation to curb the power of corporations, or the "trusts" as Americans called them at the time.

By 1885, fifteen western and southern states had adopted laws prohibiting combinations that restrained economic competition. For their part, however, corporations found it easy to escape this legislation by incorporation in such states as New Jersey and Delaware, which offered them special privileges. If antitrust legislation were to be effective, it would have to come from the national government.

Responding to growing popular demands, both houses of Congress passed the Sherman Antitrust Act (1890), sponsored by Senator John Sherman of Ohio, almost without dissent. Most members of Congress saw that the law was largely a symbolic measure to help deflect public criticism of corporate monopolies, not likely to have any real effect on corporate power.

They were right. For more than a decade after its passage, the Sherman Antitrust Act had virtually no impact. As of 1901, the Department of Justice had initiated only fourteen law suits under the statute. In fact, the Justice Department used the law with greater frequency against striking labor unions accused of restraint of trade for denying the right to work.

Meanwhile, the courts significantly weakened the law. In *United States v. E. C. Knight Company* (1895) the government alleged that a single corporation controlled 98 percent of sugar manufacturing in the United States. The Supreme Court rejected the government's case. The sugar trust was engaged in manufacturing, the justices argued, not in interstate commerce. Congressional authority extended only to the control of interstate commerce and thus it was beyond the scope of Congress to regulate the corporation. The sugar trust, despite being an obvious monopoly to the American public, was not illegal according to the Supreme Court of the United States.

(1870) Political propaganda issued by the Greenbackers, members of a midwestern and southern movement who endorsed an American national currency based on bimetallism and paper money rather than on gold. They attack both the Republican and Democratic parties for using racial politics to divert attention from the issue of the economy.

1870-1900 • The Money Question

~ The other economic issue that became the focus of national political debate during the late nineteenth century was government monetary policy. The problem for many Americans was that there was not enough money in circulation. After the Civil War, the money supply fell sharply, remained static during the 1870s, and then grew slowly throughout the 1880s and 1890s. In the meantime, because production was growing at a much faster pace than was the money supply, prices fell throughout the period.

Three groups suffered economically from the scarce money supply and falling prices: first, small farmers and businessmen pressed by debt; second, workers who endured stagnating wages; third, entrepreneurs anxious for easier credit and higher profits. All three groups sought relief by calling for an expansion of the money supply. Conversely, creditors in general, who benefited from the deflationary currency, fought to prevent monetary expansion. The so-called money question thus became the source for some of the most dramatic political conflicts of the era.

1870s-1880s • The Gold Standard

~ The debates over the currency issue were complex and confusing. Later generations have often had difficulty understanding the enormous passions that the controversy aroused. The heart of the argument was over what would establish the value of the dollar. In the nineteenth century, a currency was assumed to be worthless if there was not some precious metal, usually gold or silver, to support its value. Those who held paper currency could collect the gold or silver if they presented their paper to a bank or to the Treasury Department.

During most of its history, the United States government had recognized both gold and silver as having monetary value. In the 1870s that situation changed. The official ratio of the value of silver to the value of gold was 16 to 1: that is, the value of sixteen ounces of silver equaled the value of one ounce of gold. Yet, the commercial value of silver remained high. Owners of silver could make more money by selling it for the manufacture of jewelry and other objects than they could by taking it to the United States Mint for conversion into coins. As a consequence, the mint stopped coining silver.

In 1873, Congress had passed a law that seemed simply to recognize the existing situation by officially discontinuing the coinage of silver. Few objected at the time. During the 1880s, however, the commercial value of silver fell below the official ratio of 16 to 1. The value of 16 ounces of silver, in other words, was now less than the value of 1 ounce of gold. It again became profitable to coin silver, but Congress had already foreclosed this potential means of expanding the money supply. Before long, many Americans concluded that a conspiracy of big bankers and financiers had been responsible for the "demonetization" of silver.

1890s • The Politics of Silver and Gold ~ Two groups were especially determined to undo the law that prohibited the coinage of silver. One was the owners of silver mines, now understandably eager to have the government purchase their silver and pay them more than the going market price. The other consisted primarily of discontented farmers, who wanted to increase the amount of money in circulation and thereby lower the value of the dollar as a means of raising the price of agricultural produce and easing the payment of debts. The advocates of an inflated currency demanded that the government immediately resume the coinage of silver.

Meanwhile, the gold reserves of the United States had steadily dwindled. The Panic of 1893 increased the demands on those reserves. President Cleveland believed that the principal cause of the diminishing gold supply was the Sherman Silver Purchase Act of 1893, which required the government to purchase silver and pay for it in gold. Early in his second administration, therefore, Cleveland called a special session of Congress to request the repeal of the Sherman Silver Purchase Act. Cleveland's monetary policy split the Democratic party. It aligned southern and western Democrats, who favored of the coinage of silver, into a solid bloc against the president and his eastern supporters, who did not.

1890s • Coin's Financial School ~ A graphic illustration of the magnitude of the silver issue was the enormous popularity of William H. Harvey's *Coin's Financial School*, published in 1894. The fictional Professor Coin operated an imaginary school of economics and finance. Harvey's book consisted of his lectures and dialogues with students. The professor's brilliant commentary left even his most vehement and unyielding critics dazzled as he persuaded his audience, with simple logic, of the almost miraculous powers of silver. The coinage of silver, he declared "means the reopening of closed factories, the relighting of fires in darkened furnaces;" it means "hope instead of despair; comfort in place of suffering; life instead of death."

1896 • A Cross of Gold ~ By the end of the nineteenth century, both the advocates of a strict gold standard and those favoring a return to the coinage of silver had invested the currency question with great symbolic and emotional importance. The issue aroused passions rarely seen in American politics, culminating in the tumultuous presidential election of 1896. The old guard of the Democratic party rallied to Cleveland's conservative monetary policies and, like their Republican counterparts, endorsed the gold standard.

The defenders of the gold standard dominated the Democratic convention until the final speech when William Jennings Bryan of Nebraska delivered one of the most famous political orations in American history, "The Cross of Gold." Bryan declared that if the Republicans, the conservative Democrats, and their wealthy allies:

> . . . dare to come out in the open and defend the gold standard as a good thing, we will fight them to the uttermost. Having behind us the producing masses of this nation and the world, supported by the commercial interests, the laboring interests and the toilers everywhere, we will answer their demand for a gold standard by saying to them: "You shall not press down upon the brow of labor this crown of thorns; you shall not crucify mankind upon a cross of gold.

Bryan's speech sent the delegates into a frenzy. They voted not only to incorporate the free silver plank into the party platform but to give Bryan the Democratic nomination for president.

1896 • The People's Money ~ The American people must arise in their majesty to smite the moneylenders and drive them from the temple, Bryan intoned repeatedly throughout the presidential campaign. Audiences came to know his argument by heart and gathered to hear a confirmation of their belief in the Protestant ethic of hard work and the earning of a just reward. When Bryan reassured them that "every great economic

(1895) Dragging a Supreme Court Decision from its leg, the mongrel dog Income Tax tries to slink into the US Treasury but is driven away by the force of Public Disapproval and the Press.

question is in reality a moral question," they instinctively understood his meaning. As he preached about the saving grace of free silver, Bryan promised that he would open "the door . . . for a progress which would carry civilization up to higher ground."

Supporters of the gold standard, on the contrary, considered its survival essential to the political integrity and economic stability of the United States. Advocates of silver coinage considered the gold standard an instrument of tyranny. "Free silver" became for them a symbol of political and economic liberation. Silver was the "people's money." It would eliminate the indebtedness of small farmers and small businessmen. Gold, by contrast, was the money of economic oppression and exploitation.

Yet, in the election of 1896, it was hard for the majority of Americans not to vote for Bryan's Republican opponent, William McKinley and, consequently, for the gold standard. The cultural, political, and economic elite of the nation equated both with the continuance of prosperity and civilization.

1895-1900 • The Government and the Economy ~ The controversies about the tariff, the trusts, and money were indications that the dramatic changes taking place in the American economy were creating problems too important and too potentially dangerous to ignore. The response of the federal government to the growing agitation reflected its continued ineffectiveness and weakness. The government still lacked institutions adequate to perform any significant role in American economic life. As much from necessity as from desire, therefore, officials of the federal, state, and local government enabled the moguls who dominated the corporations to operate the economy as they saw fit.

1800-1900 Corporations

1880s • Incorporation and the Changing Nature of Business ~ By the 1880s, many Americans had come to perceive business as a kind of open warfare in which all was fair that succeeded and in which only the strong survived. In fact, however, the wealthiest and most powerful businessmen of the era sought means to control, evade, or eliminate this destructive economic competition. Increasingly, the instrument of success in business proved not to be the traditional virtues of diligence, self-reliance, thrift, and hard work, but rather a superior organization that demanded the restructuring of enterprises into corporations in which finance, production, and sales fell under the control of a single entity. In the age of wealthy, powerful, and flamboyant capitalists who seemed the epitome of individual prowess, another age took shape: the era of the corporation.

1800-1850 • The Rise of the Corporation ~ Traditionally, the granting of a corporate charter required the special act of a sovereign, such as when King James I of England granted corporate charters to the Virginia Company of London and the Virginia Company of Plymouth under whose auspices the first English settlers came to the New World. After the American Revolution, the power to confer corporate charters fell to the state legislatures.

Until the early nineteenth century, the law defined corporations as public bodies entrusted with certain privileges in the pursuit of the public good. The most common sort of corporation in colonial America was a municipality. Most other corporations received charters in return for religious, charitable, or educational services rendered to the public. Justice Spencer Roane of the Virginia Supreme Court set forth the prevailing definition of a corporation in 1809 when he wrote:

> With respect to acts of incorporation, they ought never to be passed, but in consideration of services to be rendered to the public. . . . It may be often convenient for a set of associated individuals, to have the privileges of a corporation bestowed upon them; but if their object is merely private or selfish; if it is detrimental to, or not promotive of the public good, they have no adequate claim upon the legislature for the privileges.

Even as Roane articulated this definition, the nature of the corporation was changing.

1850s-1870s • The Corporate Revolution ~ The corporate revolution of the nineteenth century has been so successful and so complete that it is now easy to forget it ever occurred. Beginning in the 1850s, the corporation gradually lost the public character that Justice Roane ascribed to it and became an almost wholly private enterprise organized to accumulate capital and make money. Older American businesses were typically small, family-owned and operated firms in which a single entrepreneur, or perhaps a few partners, made all the economic decisions. The same persons who owned these businesses also managed them.

Limited life and unlimited liability characterized traditional business. Limited life meant simply that the enterprise or company legally ended when all the owners or partners withdrew from it or died. Unlimited liability meant that each owner or partner was personally responsible for any debts that the business incurred. The financial risk was not limited to an individual's actual contribution to the firm, but extended to personal property as well. Creditors could sue the owner or any partner for the full recovery of company debts. This impermanence and risk severely limited the ability of unincorporated businesses to attract investment capital to finance expansion. Hence, such businesses tended to remain small. For the most part, the personal savings of owners, partners, and their families provided the working capital.

The technological innovations, the rise of mass production, and the creation of mass markets that occurred between 1865 and 1900 worked a fundamental change in the nature of American business. Now the sheer size of a company became a decided economic advantage, and manufacturers with access to large pools of investment capital to finance expansion enjoyed the best chances of survival and prosperity.

As more entrepreneurs began to incorporate their businesses in order to attain and organize the financial resources that they needed to grow, the legal practice of incorporation became simpler and easier. No longer did incorporation require the granting of a special charter by an act of the state legislature. By the 1870s in many states, but especially in New Jersey and Delaware, incorporation had become more of a right than a privilege, a status to be had virtually for the asking.

1870s • The Modern Corporation ~ The definition of a corporation also changed. The modern corporation that emerged after the Civil War, unlike its earlier counterpart, embodied a legally sanctioned fiction. The corporation was an association of persons assumed to constitute and function as a single entity or individual. The corporation had, in essence, a life of its own. Unlike the family business or limited partnership, the corporation was permanent. It did not die with its founders or owners, but, barring bankruptcy, lived on as long as the courts did not revoke its charter.

The modern corporation also had the same legal rights and responsibilities as a person. It could own property, sue and be sued, and enter into contracts with individuals or other corporations. Each of these arrangements, like the corporation itself, would continue to exist beyond the lifetime or membership of any or all original participants.

1870s • Corporate Organization and Operation ~ In the organization and operation of the modern corporation, the ownership of property was separated from its control and management. The modern corporation was run by a board of directors who did not necessarily own it. The stockholders legally owned the corporation, but they handed over control to a board of directors in exchange for limited liability: immunity from individual responsibility for the debts that the corporate entity had incurred. Shareholders, of course, might still lose all or part of their investment if the corporation failed. No creditor, though, could seize their personal assets or private property as compensation for corporate debts.

Incorporation thus permitted entrepreneurs to amass and use huge amounts of capital for investment, bringing it under the control of a single entity. In a period of rapid economic expansion and an inadequate money supply that could not keep pace with the rate of economic growth, the ability to accumulate large sums often meant the difference between the success or failure of an enterprise.

1870 • Standard Oil ~ The railroads may have been the prototypical corporations, revealing all the advantages of corporate organization. John D. Rockefeller's Standard Oil Company of Ohio, however, perhaps most clearly exemplified the motives for the evolution of business toward incorporation, and consequently for the growth of a corporate economy in the United States.

In 1870, when Rockefeller incorporated Standard Oil, competition in the oil industry was so fierce that it bordered on chaos, which Rockefeller and other entrepreneurs regarded as the greatest curse of the modern economy. Like many big businessmen of the time, Rockefeller feared the existence of too many firms competing for limited resources and markets. Such "cutthroat competition" brought not economic prosperity but economic instability. Although neither Rockefeller nor anyone else dared say so in public, they desired to limit or, if possible, to eliminate competition. Determined to bring order out of chaos by eradicating his competitors and, in the process, making a fortune, Rockefeller attempted to take over the entire American oil industry.

He proceeded by utilizing two methods to bring about his desired end. First, he applied "horizontal integration," that is, the combining of a number of firms engaged in the same enterprise, in this case the drilling and refining of oil, into a single corporation. Second, he applied "vertical integration," that is, the takeover of all the different businesses on which a company relied to manufacture and market its product.

1880s • Rockefeller's Dominance ~ Within a few years of forming Standard Oil, Rockefeller had acquired twenty of the twenty-five refineries operating in Cleveland, Ohio, as well as others in Pittsburgh, Philadelphia, New York, and Baltimore. Under the permissive incorporation laws of New Jersey, Rockefeller and his lawyers then chartered the South Improvement Company, which linked Standard Oil and its subsidiaries to a handful of other oil refineries and several railroads. Members of the South Improvement Company agreed to ship oil to market only by the member railroad companies. In turn, member railroad carriers agreed to pay generous rebates to member refineries. Rockefeller's objective was to eliminate all competition and to gain a monopoly over wells, refineries, pipelines, railroads, and marketing organizations.

Rockefeller's scheme worked to perfection. Eventually, he owned his own barrel factories, warehouses, pipelines, railroad cars, and had developed his own marketing and sales association. He had also resorted to fraud, chicanery, threats, coercion, and violence against anyone who refused to accept his methods, his product, or his supremacy. By the 1880s, Standard Oil drilled, refined, shipped, and sold approximately 84 percent of all the oil produced in the United States.

Ultimately, Rockefeller carried the day because of the superior organization, efficiency, and wealth of Standard Oil. He could thus eliminate most rivals and establish a virtual monopoly in the oil industry. A disciple of order and efficiency throughout his life, Rockefeller fully understood the significance of the new corporate order that he had done so much to create. He wrote:

> This movement [toward incorporation] was the origin of the whole system of modern economic administration. It had revolutionized the way of doing business all over the world. The time was ripe for it. It had to come. . . . The day of combination is here to stay. Individualism has gone, never to return.

The Triumph of Corporate Capitalism ~ The shift from the older proprietary capitalism of the early nineteenth century, characterized by small businesses and family farms, to the corporate capitalism of the late nineteenth century fundamentally reshaped the government, society, and economy of the United States. The main political battles between 1890 and 1940 were waged between the workers, small farmers, and businessmen who dominated proprietary enterprises and the partisans of the corporate economy.

Despite the explosive passions that excited both the advocates of proprietary capitalism and the advocates of corporate capitalism, the transition from propriety to corporate capitalism took place in relative peace and within the framework of existing social, political, and economic institutions. There was violence to be sure, but that violence never erupted into the full-scale revolution or civil war that many Americans expected.

After the Civil War, there was no powerful, organized class in the United States whose interests were threatened by the rise and development of corporate capitalism. Workers, farmers, and professionals, each of whom had reason to oppose the advent of corporate capitalism, were so internally divided and in

(1930) A former slave standing by a slave block in Fredericksburg, Virginia, on which slaves stood to be auctioned off to the highest bidder.

1880s

flux that they could not solidly array themselves against its advance. Yet, each class had some power, which, when coupled with divisions among the capitalists themselves, made it impossible for the proponents of corporate capitalism fully to impose their will on the nation. They instead had to proceed by compromise and accommodation.

1880s • The Success of Corporate Capitalism ~ This flexibility actually turned out to be the strength of corporate capitalism. It could offer something to almost everyone, even those who had reason to oppose it. Corporate capitalism could make room for the small entrepreneurs as well as members of the growing working, middle, and professional classes. The rising productivity that the corporations helped to inaugurate and sustain offered small capitalists more stable prices and markets, a chance to merge with larger firms and diversify their operations, and an opportunity to enhance their profits through the ownership of corporate stock.

To middle-class professionals, corporate capitalism offered opportunities for employment, advancement, and higher incomes without the responsibilities, inconveniences, and uncertainties that accompanied the ownership and management of a small business. To workers, corporate capitalism offered greater stability of employment, higher wages, pensions, and even on occasion the possibility of advancement from blue-collar to white-collar jobs. At the same time, corporations offered small businessmen protection from unions. By sustaining the so-called open shop in their own factories, large industrial firms helped to keep unions weak and thereby assisted small manufacturers and entrepreneurs in their battle against them. Corporate capitalism could thus accommodate itself to a vast array of class interests in a way that the older proprietary capitalism could not.

Finally, the conflict between proprietary and corporate capitalism took place in the context of a growing hostility to economic competition. Corporate capitalists seemed not only receptive to, but enraptured by, the managed competition of a regulated market. The critical questions of American political economy between 1890 and 1940 were; By whom was the market to be administered? For what purposes? To whose benefit? These questions went to the heart of the economic controversies that dominated the first half of the twentieth century.

1890-1900
America at a Crossroads

1890s • The Significance of the Corporate Revolution ~ For both the proponents and critics of corporate capitalism the struggles of the late nineteenth century were about the very meaning of America, about who had the political and economic power as well as the cultural authority to define what kind of society America was and ought to be. Few Americans rejected capitalism. Many were concerned, though, about the growing wealth and influence of the corporations and the apparent indifference of big capitalists to the public good.

Adding to the apprehension about corporations was the emergence of a new class of enormously and conspicuously wealthy people. One estimate suggests that in 1900 one percent of the families in the United States controlled 88 percent of the nation's assets. Some, like the industrialist Andrew Carnegie, lived modestly and donated large sums to charity. Others, though, like the Vanderbilts, lived in almost grotesque luxury.

Observing these flagrant displays of wealth were the 8 percent of Americans who lived comfortably but humbly and the approximately 10 million men, women, and children who lived in poverty. The standard of living was improving for almost everyone, but the gap between rich and poor was also widening. Which group would at last define the American way of life became the concern of every thoughtful citizen as the nineteenth century drew to a close.

1890s • The Economic Crisis ~ The last decade of the century was a period of economic, political, and social turmoil in the United States. There was widespread labor unrest and violence, culminating in a series of the tumultuous strikes. There was the continuing failure of either major political party to respond to the growing distress. There was the rigid conservatism of President Cleveland, who took office for the second time at the very moment the American economy collapsed in 1893.

The Panic of 1893 precipitated the most severe depression that the United States had yet to experience. It began in March 1893, when the Philadelphia and Reading Railroad declared bankruptcy. Two months later, in May, the National Cordage Company failed. Together, these two corporate breakdowns triggered a collapse of the stock market. Since a number of major New York banks were big investors in the market, a wave of bank failures ensued, which caused the contraction of credit. Many businesses soon went bankrupt because they could

(1890s) View of pedestrian, trolley car, and horse-drawn carriage traffic in front of the Union Dime Savings Bank at 32nd Street, between Broadway and Sixth Avenue, New York City.

no longer secure the loans they needed to operate or expand.

There were, of course, other, long-range causes of panic and depression. Falling prices of agricultural produce since at least 1887 had weakened the purchasing power of farmers, still the largest single group in the population. Europe was already in the throes of a depression, which resulted, first, in the loss of overseas markets for American goods, and second, in the withdrawal of foreign gold invested in the United States, further inhibiting thc expansion of American business and industry.

The Panic of 1893 also reflected the degree to which the corporate economy was now interconnected; failures in one sector affected all other areas. The depression at last revealed how dependent the whole economy had become on the railroads, which remained the most powerful corporate and financial institutions in the nation. When the railroads suffered, as they did beginning in 1893, the whole economy felt the impact.

Once the panic began, its effects spread with astonishing speed. Within six months, more than 8,000 businesses of all kinds, including 156 railroad corporations and 400 banks, had failed. Declining agricultural prices fell even further. As many as 1 million workers—20 percent of the labor force—lost their jobs. This level of unemployment was the highest in American history until the Great Depression of the 1930s. The leading financial newspaper of the time declared during the summer of 1893 that:

> The month of August will long remain memorable in our industrial history. Never before has there been such a sudden and striking cessation of industrial activity. Nor is any section of the country exempt from the paralysis.

The Panic of 1893 was unprecedented not only in its severity but also in its persistence. Although there was slight improvement beginning in 1895, prosperity did not fully return until 1901.

1890s • The Corporate Revolution and the American Ideal ~ By the 1890s, Americans sensed that they had reached a crossroads in their national history. They were engaged in one of the last great debates about the nature and meaning of the United States. At stake, perhaps, was not the republic itself, but competing visions of the republic.

The cardinal values of the early republic had been liberty and independence. The ownership and control of private property were the means of achieving and sustaining that cherished freedom, and the security that accompanied it. According to republican ideology, no one who relied on another for his livelihood could be truly free. Such persons would be forever beholden to whomever paid their wages and, indirectly at least, put clothes on their back and food on their table. In the minds of the Founding Fathers, therefore, political liberty and economic independence were inseparable. The ownership, control, use, and enjoyment of private property were essential to the survival of a free society.

The farmers and artisans who constituted the overwhelming majority of the free population before 1815 had defined property as tangible and static, designed not to enhance individual wealth but to provide economic independence, stability, and security across the generations. Landed property or its equivalent thus made possible the maintenance of an independent and virtuous citizenry, without which the republic would degenerate into an anarchy that invited despotism. Moreover, an independent citizenry did not mean an isolated citizenry. An ethic of mutual economic, political, and social responsibility bound individuals together in families, neighborhoods, and communities.

1890s • New Definition of Property ~ Throughout the nineteenth century, the meaning of property changed. By the late nineteenth century, more and more Americans came to interpret "property" as an instrument essential to economic growth and development. Self-interest rather than a sense of reciprocal family and social obligations now regulated economic choices and activities. In responding to economic opportunities, so the argument ran, individuals would naturally stabilize society through a competitive balance in which all were free and equal to earn more money and to consume more goods. Any resulting inequalities were obviously natural, dividing the fit from the unfit, and could hardly be criticized as immoral or unjust.

According to the customary definition of property, though, most Americans by the twentieth century were no longer economically independent or politically free. They were, instead, servile, for their property was mortgaged and they depended on a wage or a salary for their livelihood. As greater numbers of Americans lost access to private property, such as farms and workshops, from which they could provide a livelihood for themselves and their families, they became the economic pawns of their employers.

1870s-1890s • A Conflict of Values

~ Almost constant friction arose between these older and newer sets of priorities and values. On one side were industrial workers, family farmers, and small businessmen who felt victimized by an emerging corporate economy that deprived them of their independence. On the other side were salaried middle-class professionals, successful commercial farmers, and wealthy corporate capitalists whose economic opportunities expanded with every increase in the scope of business activity.

The successive traumas of first an agricultural and then an industrial depression transformed this debate into a full-scale cultural war by the 1890s. This collision, however, for all its passion, yielded no structural change in the American economy. Despite sharing a vision of America as a cooperative commonwealth, workers, farmers, and small businessmen never coalesced as a unified political movement. When it came down to a choice, the overwhelming majority of Americans rejected the older proprietary capitalism and embraced the newer corporate capitalism.

1896-1900 • And the Winner Is. . . .

~ Oliver Wendell Holmes, who was poised to become an associate justice of the United States Supreme Court at the time, expressed the fears of many wealthy and middle-class Americans when he identified 1893 as the year in which "a vague terror went over the earth and the word socialism began to be heard." To combat the vague terror of socialism, the American economic elite threw all of their resources behind the presidential campaign of William McKinley. When the campaign of 1896 ended, McKinley and the Republican party had won more than an election. McKinley's victory affirmed the power of the corporation in American life. By the twentieth century, American citizens had come to identify the political, social, and, of course, the economic welfare of the republic with the size of the gross national product—calculated as the sum of all goods and services produced by a country.

The voices of an alternate America, the cooperative vision of workers, farmers, and others were all but silenced by the end of the nineteenth century. The emphases of the new American system were administrative efficiency, political stability, economic growth, and corporate profits. The majority of Americans at last rejected the ethic of the small property holders and embraced the ethic of the corporate capitalists, which they then struggled to reconcile with the individualism, opportunity, independence, and liberty that had long exemplified the essence of the American tradition and the substance of the American dream.

Bibliography

Please see the composite bibliography at the end of Part III.

Mark Malvasi
Randolph-Macon College

Economy, 1900-1945: Managing Corporate Capitalism

(1935) *Exterior view of a pub called Idle Hour that is 'OUT OF BUSINESS' during the Great Depression.*

TIMELINE

1900-1919 ~ Industrial Expansion and War

Proliferation of automobiles (1905-1920) / Rise of the consumer economy (1910s) / Introduction of "Scientific management" replaces union floor bosses (1911) / Personal income tax imposed (1913) / Industrial research pioneered by Bell, DuPont, General Electric, Eastman Kodak / Mass production and assembly lines created (1913)

MILESTONES: Non-whites excluded from union membership (1900) • Mexicans strike against the Pacific Electric Railway company for equal wages and parity (1903) • Blouses mass produced in sweatshops (1910s) • F.W. Woolworth has 600 stores (1912) • Ford perfects assembly line production (1913) • Panama Canal completed (1914) • Railroad (standard) time ratified (1918)

1920-1929 ~ Search for Prosperity

Half of American homes have electricity (1920) / Postwar recession and economic recovery (1920-1923) / Invention of Freon makes widespread home refrigeration feasible (1920s) / Welfare capitalism by businesses reduces the power of unions over workers (1920s) / Low unemployment prevails (1921-1927) / Hostility toward labor unions increases / Introduction of Industrial relations/psychology (1920s) / Beginning of economic crisis (1928) / Slackening capital investment in durable consumer goods / Worsening levels of consumer debt (1928) / Stock market crash (1929) / Workers laid off and production cut back due to over-production and large stocks of unsold inventory (1929)

MILESTONES: First transcontinental airmail route established between New York City and San Francisco (1920) • Tariffs close foreign markets to farmers (1921) • One out of every eight American workers is employed in automobile-related industries, including rubber, steel, and petroleum (1920s) • Over 800,000 workers invest more than a billion dollars in 315 companies (1927) • Total advertising budget for the major newspapers rises to $860 million (1929)

1930-1939 ~ The Great Depression

Labor unions gain foothold among semi-skilled workers (1930s) / Economy Act stipulates that married women be discharged from their jobs (1932) / Unemployment is 24.9%; 9,000 banks fail; 100,000 businesses fail (1932-1933) / Construction falls by 78%, private investment drops by 88%; farm income, already low, falls another 50% (1932-1933) / Establishment of Reconstruction Finance Corporation designed to assist failing banks (1932) / Roosevelt's "New Deal" program begins (1933) / Federal Housing Administration insures long-term mortgages to encourage lending institutions to make loans in a difficult market (1934) / Rate of unemployment for workers over 65 has increased to more than 50% (1935) / Miller-Tydings, known as the Fair Trade Act, compels local retail merchants to sell nationally advertised products at the manufacturers' suggested retail price (1937)

MILESTONES: U.S. provides war material to the Allies (1939-1940) • Nevada legalizes gambling, founding the economic basis for Las Vegas (1931) • Works Progress Administration launches the Federal Theater (1935) • Social Security Act provides social insurance for both the unemployed and the elderly (1935) • American corporations spend $80 million a year spying on their employees (1935) • United Mine Workers of America (UMW), one of the nation's few interracial organizations, provides the organizational foundation for the emergence of industrial unionism (1935-1939)

1940-1945 ~ American Economy and the Second World War

Two Oceans Navy Bill appropriates funds for 1.3 million tons of new warships (1940) / Five million women enter the labor force (1940-1944) / War Production Board coordinates production of war material with industry and labor (1942) / Coal, petroleum, steel, aluminum and rubber production expanded (1942-1944) / Farmers dramatically increase crop production for the war (1942-1945) / Aircraft industry expansion (1943)

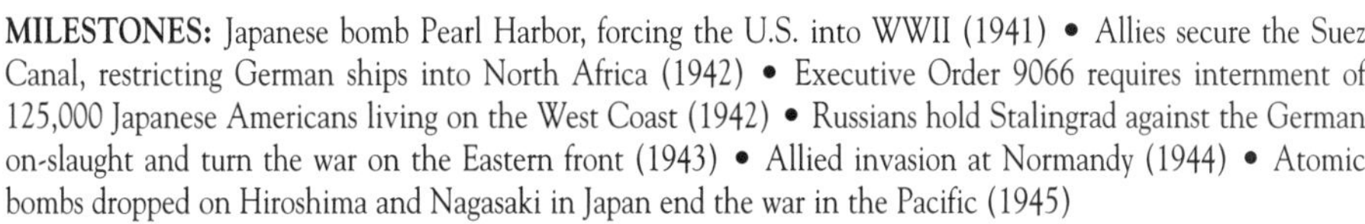

MILESTONES: Japanese bomb Pearl Harbor, forcing the U.S. into WWII (1941) • Allies secure the Suez Canal, restricting German ships into North Africa (1942) • Executive Order 9066 requires internment of 125,000 Japanese Americans living on the West Coast (1942) • Russians hold Stalingrad against the German on-slaught and turn the war on the Eastern front (1943) • Allied invasion at Normandy (1944) • Atomic bombs dropped on Hiroshima and Nagasaki in Japan end the war in the Pacific (1945)

INTRODUCTION

Attempts to regulate the giant corporations engaged a greater variety of reformers and elicited more controversial solutions than any other problem Americans faced at the end of the nineteenth and beginning of the twentieth century. Concerns about the concentration and abuse of economic power took on a new vitality as reformers, politicians, intellectuals, and even businessmen became more receptive to the ideas of an administered market and managed competition. The central questions of national politics and economic policy between 1890 and 1935 were: by whom was the market to be administered? For what purposes? To whose benefit?

The American political ideal promised equal liberty for all citizens and special privileges for none. The supreme purpose of government in the minds of many Americans was to preserve that arrangement by eliminating unearned advantages wherever and whenever they appeared. Government intervention into the economy was necessary, the majority of Americans had once thought, only to remedy or nullify special privilege and monopoly power.

With the rise of corporate capitalism during the late nineteenth and early twentieth century, however, many Americans, such as workers and farmers, maintained that the American political tradition was incompatible with anything but a proprietary capitalism of small producers. If large-scale industry and corporate enterprise represented the outcome of social and economic evolution, they wondered, did it mean that traditional American political principles were incompatible with progress?

Throughout the first half of the twentieth century, reformers, economists, social theorists, and politicians struggled to reconcile economic equality for all with corporate capitalism. "Corporate liberalism" is the name historians have given to the general movement to adapt traditional American values to the new realities of the corporate world. The two principal characteristics of corporate liberalism were, first, the administration of the market place, and second, governmental regulation of the economy. Debates arose during the century about just what agencies ought to administer the market place and to just what extent and for just what purpose the government was to regulate the economy.

Three major variants of corporate liberalism emerged during the early years of the twentieth century. They were associated with the administrations of Theodore Roosevelt, William Howard Taft, and Woodrow Wilson. Each variant became fairly well distinguished between 1909 and 1912. From this three-way division emerged the most important controversies of twentieth-century American economic policy.

THE FEDERAL GOVERNMENT AND THE AMERICAN ECONOMY

1901-1909 • THEODORE ROOSEVELT'S ECONOMIC POLICIES ~ "Presidents in general are not lovable," wrote political journalist Walter Lippmann, who had known many. "They've had to do too much to get where they are. But there was one President who was lovable—Teddy Roosevelt—and I loved him."

Lippmann was not alone. To a generation of reformers, Theodore Roosevelt was more than an admired public figure. He was an idol. No president before, and few since, attracted such attention and won such devotion. Yet, for all his popularity among reformers, Roosevelt as president was decidedly conservative. He earned his extraordinary reputation less because he actually championed economic reform and more because be brought to office a broad conception of the powers of the presidency.

As president, Roosevelt advocated a program of moderate, cautious change. Reform, he believed, was less a vehicle for remaking American society than for protecting it against more radical challenges. These attitudes found expression nowhere more fully than in Roosevelt's policies toward the American economy in general and the giant industrial corporations in particular. Roosevelt did not oppose in principle the concentration of economic power. He acknowledged, though, that such consolidation could produce dangerous abuses. He therefore allied himself with those reformers who urged the regulation, but not the destruction, of the corporations.

Central to Roosevelt's economic program was his desire to win for government the authority to investigate the activities of corporations and to publicize the results. Like most Americans of the time, Roosevelt both respected and feared corporations. He believed there were good and bad trusts. Gentlemen who were often Roosevelt's personal friends and generous patrons of the Republican Party operated the good trusts. The products that these corporations manufactured and introduced into the market promised a better, richer, more bountiful life for all.

Bad trusts were those under the control of ruthless and greedy entrepreneurs interested in private profit at any cost, even if it meant undermining the public sense of decency and morality. The pressure of informed public opinion, Roosevelt thought, would by itself eliminate most of the abuses of bad corporations. Government could legislate solutions for those that remained. Although he filed forty-four antitrust suits during his presidency, Roosevelt made no serious commitment to reverse the prevailing trend toward economic concentration. Even his narrow victory in the case against the Northern Securities Company, a railroad trust, in 1904 was more a reprimand than a condemnation. "This is the age of combination," Roosevelt wrote, "and any effort to prevent all combination will be not only useless, but in the end vicious."

1910-1912 • THE NEW NATIONALISM

~ Not until Roosevelt had been out of office for almost four years and sought to return to the presidency in 1912 did he articulate the principles of the "New Nationalism," in which he called for more exacting government regulation of the market place and the economy, including the corporations. In a speech delivered in Osawatomie, Kansas on September 1, 1910, Roosevelt first outlined the principles of the "New Nationalism." He made it clear that he had moved a considerable way from the conservatism that characterized the first years of his previous administration.

Social justice, Roosevelt argued, was possible only through the vigorous efforts of a strong federal government whose executive acted as the "steward of public welfare." To those who thought primarily in terms of private property rights and personal wealth, Roosevelt declared:

Corporations must now give way to the advocate of human welfare, who rightly maintains that every man holds his property subject to the general right of the community to regulate its use to whatever degree the public welfare may require it.

Roosevelt did not wish to get rid of private property and foster state ownership. Such an arrangement would have constituted socialism, which he abhorred. Instead, he wished to maintain property in private hands, but to place it under the strict regulation of the government. His objective was to create what he called a "public-service capitalism," which, under the direction of the government, would ensure greater social justice and, at the same time, protect individual property rights. "The essence of any struggle for liberty," Roosevelt told his audience at Osawatomie, "has always been, and must always be to take from some one man or class of men the right to enjoy power, or wealth, or position or immunity, which has not been earned by service to his or their fellows."

1909 • Roosevelt and Taft ~ Roosevelt, in essence, shared two sentiments with other reformers. First, he believed that government should be efficiently run by competent people. Second, he was convinced that industrialization and incorporation had created the need for expanding the scope of governmental activity. "A simple and poor society," Roosevelt observed, "can exist as a democracy on the basis of sheer individualism. But a rich and complex society cannot so exist."

Roosevelt's critics charged that state-directed corporate capitalism would generate powerful tendencies toward socialism. One of the most powerful and influential critics of Roosevelt's economic programs was William Howard Taft, who in 1909 had followed Roosevelt as president of the United States. Taft had been Roosevelt's choice to succeed him. After the election, however, Roosevelt disavowed Taft for his refusal to continue Roosevelt's policies. In a fury, Roosevelt denounced Taft in 1910, saying that he had "completely twisted around the policies I advocated and acted upon."

Taft was more conservative than Roosevelt in his view of governmental power. "The lesson must be learned," Taft stated, "that there is only a limited zone within which legislation and governments can accomplish good." The power of government could, and frequently was, misapplied, to the detriment of all. Taft pointed out, for example, that "We can, by passing laws which cannot be enforced, destroy the respect for laws. . . which has been the strength of people of English descent everywhere." Taft fundamentally disagreed with Roosevelt about the role that government should play in regulating corporations, the market place, and the economy.

1909-1912 • Taft's Economic Policies ~ Taft believed that the free market would operate on its own, without interference from the government, to ensure both economic prosperity and social justice. He was sympathetic to the reform of various abuses, but was also certain that the market, if left to operate according to its own rules, was self-regulating and that it still rewarded individual virtue and ability and punished individual vice and incompetence. Like Roosevelt, Taft affirmed the efficacy of corporate capitalism. He insisted, however, on minimal government regulation of the corporations, the market, and the economy as a whole. The government,

(1914) The barrier of big business in the way of small business on the highway of competition, the Federal Trade Commission is an attempt to regulate the monopolistic trusts.

Taft declared, should merely act as a watchdog to police the market against unfair privileges and monopolistic practices that, in fact, disrupted the performance of the truly free market.

1911-1912 • TAFT THE "TRUST-BUSTER" ~ The rift between Roosevelt and Taft split the Republican party. Although Roosevelt steadfastly denied that he had any presidential ambitions, his political allies clamored for him to challenge Taft for the Republican nomination in 1912. Roosevelt demurred, and insisted that his only purpose was to compel Taft to return to his original agenda. Two events, though, changed Roosevelt's mind about running for president.

The first was Taft's attack on the United States Steel Corporation. On October 27, 1911, the Taft administration announced that it had filed an antitrust suit against U.S. Steel, alleging among other things that its acquisition of the Tennessee Coal and Iron Company in 1907 had been illegal. Roosevelt himself had approved the sale of Tennessee Iron and Coal to U. S. Steel, and was enraged by the implication that he had acted improperly.

Although growing angrier by the minute, Roosevelt was still reluctant to become a candidate for president. Senator Robert La Follette of Wisconsin had been working since 1911 to secure the Republican nomination for himself. In February 1912, La Follette's campaign faltered. Exhausted and distraught about his daughter's serious illness, La Follette suffered a nervous breakdown during a speech in Philadelphia. With indecent haste, many of his supporters abandoned him and turned to Roosevelt, who at last formally announced his candidacy on February 22, 1912.

1912 • Roosevelt and Wilson ~ The program of Democratic presidential nominee Woodrow Wilson came to be identified as the New Freedom, which differed most clearly from Roosevelt's New Nationalism in its policy toward the corporations. The campaign for the presidency in 1912 was thus marked by an unusually provocative debate about the proper role of government in a modern, industrial, corporate economy. Wilson declared that "What this country needs above everything else is a body of laws which will look after the men who are on the make rather than the men who are already made." His objective was to restore economic competition; his tool was to destroy the power of monopolies, which he believed to be both inefficient and unjust.

Roosevelt, by contrast, thought that big business was not necessarily bad. He responded to Wilson's proposal, saying that "Somehow or other we shall have to work out methods of controlling the big corporations without paralyzing the energies of the business community." For Roosevelt, the power of big government would counter the power of big business.

1914 • Wilson and the Problem of Monopoly ~ The cornerstone of Woodrow Wilson's campaign for the presidency in 1912 was his promise to attack the concentrated economic power of the corporations, most notably to dismantle monopolies. By 1914, two years into his first term in office, Wilson's approach to the problem of corporate monopoly had changed. He moved away from his earlier insistence that government tear down corporate monopolies and toward a commitment to regulating them. On this issue, at least, Wilson's New Freedom came to resemble Roosevelt's New Nationalism.

In 1914, Wilson proposed two measures to deal with the problem of monopoly. First, he sought to create a federal agency through which the government would help business to police itself, in other words, a regulatory commission of the type that Roosevelt had advocated in 1912. Second, he proposed measures to enhance the power of the federal government to prosecute and dismantle corporate monopolies. These two measures took legislative shape as the Federal Trade Commission Act and the Clayton Antitrust Act.

1914 • The Federal Trade Commission Act ~ The Federal Trade Commission Act (1914) created an independent regulatory agency, the Federal Trade Commission (FTC), designed to provide information to businessmen in an effort to help them determine whether their activities were acceptable to the government. The purpose of the act and the agency was to ensure free and fair competition among American businesses and corporations. The Federal Trade

Commission also had broad authority to monitor, investigate, discipline, and prosecute companies engaged in "unfair trade practices." The act, in short, significantly increased the regulatory power of the federal government.

1914 • The Clayton Antitrust Act ~ The Clayton Antitrust Act (1914) was designed to outlaw any corporate practice that tended to create a monopoly or inhibit economic competition. This legislation specifically prohibited price-fixing agreements, outlawed interlocking directorates whereby the members of the board of directors of one corporation also sat on the boards of their competitors, and made it illegal for a firm to acquire stock in a rival company.

Wilson happily signed the Clayton Anti-Trust Bill into law. Then he lost interest in it, and permitted the courts to weaken it. The vigorous legal assault on corporate monopoly that Wilson had promised during the presidential campaign of 1912 never materialized. In the end, the Clayton Act was more a triumph of public relations than a substantive reform of monopoly practices.

1914 • Wilson's Economic Policies ~ Wilson, however, never abandoned his conviction that some agency had to regulate the corporations, the market, and the economy. Yet, he came to think that perhaps the corporations themselves, with advice and assistance from the government, were in the best position to do so. Consequently, Wilson rejected both Roosevelt's vision of strict state regulation and Taft's vision of a free market operating with minimal regulation. Instead, he granted to the corporations themselves the primary responsibility for regulating the market, and assigned to government a secondary role of supervising the corporations. By the end of 1914, Wilson began a conspicuous retreat from economic activism and reform.

Wilson had sought to strike a balance between Roosevelt's and Taft's policies. Like Taft, he wanted to enhance economic prosperity and social progress. Like Roosevelt, he also wanted to control corporations so that in their pursuit of wealth, they did not injure the public welfare or impede the quest for social justice. The principles and programs of the New Freedom marked Wilson's attempt to solve the economic problems that had troubled the Gilded Age.

1914-1916 • The New Freedom ~ Woodrow Wilson sought to achieve economic expansion and yet to maintain social peace, to provide for steady but orderly social progress uninterrupted by economic stagnation and depression or by social unrest and political revolution. He believed that the present and future welfare of the United States depended on the continued health of the American economic and political system. Hence the continued but regulated evolution of corporate capitalism in the United States would forestall a revolution of any kind, whether a socialist revolution that sought to eradicate private property or a conservative revolution that sought to restore proprietary capitalism.

In the final analysis, Wilson believed that only corporate capitalism could ensure continued economic progress at home and, at the same time, sustain the expansion of American political and economic influence around the world. Wilson got an opportunity to put his theory to the test in a way he neither expected nor desired with the American entry into the First World War in April 1917.

1917

The American Economy and the First World War

The American Economy in 1917 ~ By 1917 the United States had already passed through an era of remarkable economic change. On the eve of American participation in "the Great War," the United States was predominantly an industrial nation; only 28.2 percent of Americans continued to work in agriculture.

Even more revealing of the economic transformation the country had experienced, the Gross National Product (GNP) in 1917 was more than eight times larger than it had been in 1870 and the output per individual worker was more than twice as great.

Contrary to the expectations of some, American economic growth had continued despite periodic depressions, the closing of the frontier, and the end of railroad construction. In the twentieth century, the United States had taken the lead in worldwide industrial production for a mass market. The size of the American domestic market certainly aided this development. Even more important, however, were the ideas, activities, and policies of American industrialists.

1917 • Continuing Economic Growth ~ Americans in 1917 inherited an economy that was still growing, that was, in fact, entering a new stage of development, becoming more productive and promising a richer material life for greater numbers, but most people did not understand its vast potential. In the nearly two-and-one-half decades before American entry into the war, the period between 1893 and 1917, the performance of the American economy had not been impressive. The industrial economy seemed at times to falter badly.

Even when it did operate, the economy did not seem to allocate resources and benefits efficiently and equitably through an autonomous and apolitical market system. Some groups, such as the wealthy industrialists and financiers, had apparently seized control of the economy and used it for their private benefit at the expense of the commonwealth. Yet, these concerns initially overshadowed another development of at least equal importance: the rise of the consumer economy.

1917 • The Rise of the Consumer Economy ~ It was not only innovations and improvements in machine tools and new systems of manufacturing such as the continuous assembly line that, by the 1910s, had laid the foundation for the stunning advances in American industrial productivity. It was also the advent of a consumer economy devoted to providing goods, services, and entertainment to the masses.

Already by 1917, the motion picture industry, for example, was beginning to generate huge profits. Professional athletics, especially baseball, were also well on their way to becoming big business. At the same time, the health care profession, education, the media, and the hospitality trades were undergoing a rapid expansion.

Not only a new economy but a new culture was coming to dominate the United States. At its heart was not the

> ~
>
> In 1910, 32.6 percent of the American civilian force worked on farms. By 1920, that number had dropped to 26.6 percent.
>
> ~

traditional emphasis on hard work, self-sacrifice, frugality, and delayed gratification, but the quest for leisure, self-indulgence, wealth, comfort, and pleasure. The cardinal values of this new culture were acquisition and consumption.

According to the principles governing the culture of consumption, the diffusion of money, goods, and services that brought personal satisfaction became the promise of American life. All Americans now had the right to desire whatever quantity and variety of things they pleased and to entertain expectations that the industrial economy would fulfill those desires. What formerly they considered the most extravagant luxuries, many Americans now thought of as everyday necessities.

1917 • The Organizational Revolution ~ American entry into the First World War disrupted the smooth operation of this emerging consumer economy and subjected it to new and more extensive forms of organization and management. An "organizational revolution" had been reshaping the American economy since at least the 1880s. The "social chaos," "destructive competition," and "defective coordination" that threatened liberty, prosperity, and progress had become the targets of politicians and businessmen alike.

By the turn of the century, three distinct, and at times competing, elites—financial, managerial, and business—had emerged to dominate the economic life of the nation. The financial elite, composed primarily of investment bankers, such as those who operated the House of Morgan and Kuhn, and Loeb and Company, controlled the money supply, credit, and investment capital.

The managerial elite enjoyed growing influence within the corporate hierarchy. They addressed the wish for continued economic development and the simultaneous desire to maintain social order. By the early twentieth century, these technical specialists argued convincingly that they could transform an exploitative and wasteful economic system into one that was productive, profitable, efficient, and humane.

The business elite fostered the immense growth of business organizations that took place toward the end of the nineteenth century. Businessmen began to organize in part to protect themselves from rival organizations, such as socialist parties, labor unions, and reform movements. But they also hoped to master the economic environment and thereby enhance their ability to predict, rationalize, and control the behavior of the economy.

By 1917 these impulses toward organization and cooperation in business had led to the creation of hundreds of industrial and trade organizations and cooperative business councils. Of particular importance was the formation of the Chamber of Commerce in 1912. Designed as an association of associations, the Chamber of Commerce sought to enable the business community to serve the cause of national economic progress.

For good and ill, the land of the yeoman farmer and the rugged individual had, by 1917, become the land of the "organization man." Nevertheless, the emergence of these various organizational elites and the economic model that they helped to create proved indispensable to the operation of the American economy during the First World War.

1917-1918 • Fashioning the War Economy ~ The American war experience of 1917 and 1918 accelerated the process of organizational change and

1917-1918

established the pattern for future economic development and management. As old economic institutions and methods failed under the pressure of wartime exigencies, the war brought a new reliance on the private organizational elites that had taken shape in the prewar years.

Even while the United States remained officially neutral in the conflict between European belligerents, the Americans were already at war economically with the Central Powers (Germany, Austria-Hungary, Bulgaria, and the Ottoman Empire). In September 1915, for example, President Wilson signed legislation that made it possible for American bankers to extend long-term credit to the Allied Powers (Great Britain, France, Portugal, Italy, Greece, Romania, Serbia, and Japan). American lenders had advanced more than $2 billion to the Allies even before the United States entered the war in 1917.

Early in the conflict, official declarations of impartiality notwithstanding, American political leaders decided that they had substantially to increase the supply of war material moving across the Atlantic. The United States must determine to meet the Allies' urgent requests for credit, weapons, ammunition, and foodstuffs. This decision, which Wilson and his advisors made in the first year of the war, shaped the way in which they sought to manage the American economy at least for the duration of the conflict. From the outset, Wilson conceded that efforts to meet these demands through existing institutions were likely to result in economic, and perhaps social, chaos.

1917-1918 • Coordinating the War Economy ~ Officials of the federal government thus sought new mechanisms to reduce or eliminate economic competition for scare resources and to bring production into line with wartime standards. Instead of building a state bureaucracy to manage the economy, the Wilson administration fostered voluntary cooperation between public agencies and private organizations. Economic mobilization for war in the United States differed from that of Great Britain, France, and Germany, for it relied less on compulsion and coercion and more on persuasion and collaboration. Nevertheless, the war brought a substantial and in many ways unprecedented expansion of government power to intervene in the economy.

1917-1918 • The War Industries Board ~ By the summer of 1917 administrative and legislative action had brought several public-private associations into being. Chief among them was the War Industries Board (WIB), which the Council of National Defense had created in July 1917. The WIB was responsible for supervising the procurement of crucial raw materials and the operation of key defense industries. The WIB struggled to fulfill its mission until March 4, 1918, when Wilson appointed Bernard M. Baruch as chairman. Baruch did more than any other single individual to effect the shift from a peacetime to a wartime economy.

Wilson charged Baruch, an urbane Wall Street speculator and a generous contributor to the Democratic Party, with bringing a semblance of order to wartime industrial production and distribution. The organization that Baruch inherited was in near chaos. The WIB coordinated the various committees that the government had established in 1917 to oversee the economy. By the end of 1917, the proliferation of these committees (there were 150 of them by then), the lack of authority to enforce their decisions, and the suspicious War Department made the work of the WIB nearly impossible. As a result, economic mobilization almost came to a halt, especially the delivery of essential material to the army.

Through personal charm, meticulously cultivated relations with the press, and a seemingly encyclopedic command of information, Baruch created the impression, and thereby something of the reality, that he was an economic tsar with the power to dictate policy to business and industry: to award contracts, allocate resources, set prices for all government purchases, fix quotas and standards of production, demand compliance, and punish violations. One major struggle, which confirmed Baruch's image as an economic tyrant, involved getting automobile manufacturers to convert their factories to meet the needs of wartime production. When, during the summer of 1918, automakers balked at Baruch's requirements, he simply announced: "You won't get your steel; that is all." American automakers soon came to recognize and accept Baruch's authority and modified their production accordingly, changing from cars to trucks and tanks for the army.

Actually, "Dr. Facts," as Wilson and reporters had nicknamed Baruch, resorted less frequently to confrontation and force and rather more often to stratagems and compromise to get his way than his reputation suggests. Baruch understood the WIB was only one member of the business-government partnership that had formed to win the war. He and his subordinates, therefore, most of whom were not government bureaucrats but businessmen on leave from their companies, usually made their decisions regarding the economy in consultation with leading members of the business community.

With anti-trust legislation suspended for the duration of the conflict, Baruch encouraged businessmen and industrialists to work together to meet production quotas and conserve valuable resources. He offered incentives rather than imposed penalties to invite voluntary compliance with the regulations and directives of the WIB. On military contracts, for example, the WIB guaranteed payment of all costs in addition to ensuring a predetermined profit. Far from declining, corporate profits soared during the war, tripling between 1914 and 1917 and then leveling off at an annual increase of approximately 30 percent. Net corporate earnings grew from $4 billion in 1913 to $7 billion in 1917. Even after the wartime increase in taxes corporate profits totaled $4.5 billion in 1918.

1917-1918 • The Dollar-a-Year Men ~ To attain maximum efficiency in the acquisition and use of national resources for the war effort, Wilson enlisted the help of other academic and business experts besides Bernard Baruch. The businessmen, most of whom continued on the payrolls of their companies, received one dollar per year as compensation for their services, hence becoming known as dollar-a-year men. To administer the indispensable coal and oil supply, Wilson appointed his friend Harry A. Garfield, the son of former president James A. Garfield. To manage the production, distribution, and price of food used to feed American and Allied troops fighting in France as well as the civilian population, Wilson selected Herbert Hoover, who had resigned the directorship of the Commission for Relief in German-occupied Belgium when the United States entered the war.

1917-1918 • The Fuel Administration ~ The initial performance of the American economy under the direction of these agencies, however, fell far below everyone's expectations. During the winter of 1917-1918, the economy lurched from one crisis to another. The Fuel Administration, for instance, faced difficulties in getting mine owners to agree on prices and deliveries. In the wake of the worst blizzard to hit the east coast in forty-one years, Garfield had to ration coal and to close eastern factories for five days in January 1918, and for nine subsequent Mondays.

To combat shortages, the Fuel Administration attempted to increase the domestic production of coal by raising coal prices to artificially high levels. As a wartime measure, the federal government also mandated the adoption of daylight savings time to extend the workday and to save on the consumption of fuel.

1918-1919 • The Food Administration ~ Similar problems notwithstanding, the Food Administration became the most successful government regulatory agency and Herbert Hoover the most prominent and respected of the wartime managers. Rather than resorting primarily to price controls and rationing, Hoover encouraged increased production and decreased consumption. Operating under the auspices of the Lever Food and Fuel Control Act (1918), which granted the Wilson administration extraordinary authority over the production, distribution, and price of fertilizers, farm implements, and foodstuffs, the Food Administration helped to increase agricultural production. By 1919, the value of agricultural exports, and especially of food, had tripled over prewar levels, growing from $869 million in 1910 to nearly $3.4 billion in 1919.

The income of farmers also soared during the war, as the wholesale price of agricultural commodities more than doubled between 1913 and 1918. The wholesale price of raw cotton, which a Congress dominated by southern Democrats protected from price controls, increased almost three-fold by 1920; that of finished cotton more than tripled. The wholesale price of agricultural products combined more than doubled between 1913 and 1920.

In conjunction with one of his assistants, Harriot Stanton Blatch, the daughter of nineteenth-century feminist Elizabeth Cady Stanton, Hoover sponsored an extensive economic education program aimed at women who did the grocery shopping and the cooking. Maintaining that "Food Will Win the War," Blatch and Hoover promoted economy and conservation. Among other strategies, the Food Administration solicited pledges from individual households to abide by Wheatless Mondays, Meatless Tuesdays, and Porkless Thursdays and Saturdays. They published lists of companies engaged in unfair pricing and persuaded large numbers of Americans to grow vegetables for their own consumption in "Victory Gardens."

1918 • Ongoing Problems with the War Economy: Transportation, Production, and Finance ~ Although some sectors of the economy performed admirably during the war, others faltered. Despite passage of the Overman Act (1918), which gave President Wilson virtually unlimited power to organize national resources, the economic system that had emerged by the summer of 1918 was far from satisfactory.

1917-1918 • TRANSPORTATION ~ The inability or unwillingness of railroad managers to cooperate or comply with government demands and regulations had delayed the movement of troops, slowed the shipment of arms and munitions, and interrupted the transport of food. The situation had already become intolerable by the autumn of 1917, even before the United States entered the war. Efficient transportation was so obviously crucial to the war effort, and the companies that operated the railroads proved so inept or recalcitrant in providing it, that the federal government had taken them over as of January 1, 1918.

To assume control of the railroads and untangle the transportation snarl, Wilson appointed William Gibbs McAdoo, his able but frustrated secretary of the treasury. As head of the Railroad War Board, McAdoo guaranteed profits for owners and wage increases for workers in exchange for the complete government management of the railroads. McAdoo's efforts succeeded. By the end of the war, the efficiency of rail transportation had dramatically improved. Yet, after the war, the railroads quickly reverted to private ownership, a symbol of the determination of most big businessmen to ensure that government control of the economy during wartime remained a temporary phenomenon.

1918 • PRODUCTION ~ Although McAdoo eventually resolved most of the problems with rail transportation, neither he nor anyone else could overcome the failure to meet production quotas. The War Shipping Board, for example, failed to build a merchant fleet. The Aircraft Production Board did not deliver even one of the 20,000 proposed airplanes before the war ended on November 11, 1918. As a consequence of these production shortfalls, the United States contributed almost no merchant vessels, heavy artillery, tanks, or airplanes to the Allied war effort.

(1918) On a Government poster a naked child clasps the hand of the Statue of Liberty bearing a torch. The message reads, 'Save your Child from Autocracy and Poverty Buy War Savings Stamps'.

1917-1918

Nevertheless, war production, which had made up one percent of the GNP between 1914 and 1916, grew to 9 percent in 1917 and 23 percent in 1918. The overall output of war material, measured in 1914 dollars, rose from $4.1 billion in 1917 to $9.7 billion in 1918.

1917-1919 • FINANCING THE WAR ~ Along with the increase in the value of wartime production, the costs of war also soared, eventually reaching $32 billion. President Wilson and then-Secretary of the Treasury McAdoo had at first opted to raise half of the revenue they needed to cover the costs of the war through loans and the other half through taxes. They hoped that the combination of these methods would curtail the inflation that widespread borrowing was sure to provoke.

Many business leaders and other fiscal conservatives agreed with Wilson and McAdoo. They supported financing a large portion of the costs of war through a federal sales taxes and the extension of the income tax to the working- and middle-class families. This approach, they maintained, had the dual advantages of raising revenue while reducing inflationary pressures on the economy. Others determined, though, to make the wealthy and the corporations underwrite the costs of war. Senator Robert La Follette of Wisconsin and Representative Claude Kitchin of North Carolina fought tirelessly to impose stiff taxes on big corporations and steeply graduated income and inheritance taxes on the wealthy.

The Revenue Acts of 1917 and 1918

If the conscription of men into military service had met with little serious resistance in the United States, the government "conscription" of money was entirely another matter. After furious debate, Congress passed the Revenue Acts of 1917 and 1918, which raised both the income tax and the excise tax on goods, services, estates, and corporate profits in excess of ordinary earnings. The Revenue Act permitted the government to pay approximately 31 percent of the costs of war from tax revenues. It ultimately raised $10 billion.

1918-1919 • Inflation ~ Inflation rather than taxation, however, proved the more politically attractive and expedient way of paying the costs of war. Instead of financing half the cost of war through loans, as Wilson and McAdoo had proposed, the federal government had to borrow approximately 69 percent of the money it needed, a sum that eventually totaled almost $23 billion. (European nations, incidentally, relied almost entirely on loans to finance their war efforts).

To restrain private demands for capital and thus to curb inflation as much as possible, the Federal Reserve Board, established in 1913, created the Capital Issues Committee, which was empowered to prevent the investment of capital in enterprises deemed nonessential to the war effort. At the same time, however, the Federal Reserve expanded the money supply, making credit in general easier to obtain. Federal expenditures skyrocketed to $14 billion for the fiscal year 1918 and to $19 billion for the fiscal year 1919. In the meantime, the federal debt grew from $1 billion in 1915 to $20 billion in 1920 and never returned to prewar levels.

Massive government borrowing and the expansion of the money supply also contributed to rising prices between 1914 and 1918 when the Wholesale Price Index climbed almost 50 percent. Although wholesale prices increased at a comparatively low 10.5 percent between 1917 and 1918, and at an even lower 5.3 percent for 1919, they had risen by a total of 54.8 percent between 1913 and 1920. Moreover, the Consumer Price Index also rose by more than 50 percent between 1913 and 1920, with the cost of food climbing almost 53 percent. The Great War brought Americans their first real experience with sustained, large-scale government spending and its inflationary consequences.

1917 • Short and Long-term Financing ~ Having to borrow most of the money the government needed to finance the war placed Woodrow Wilson in an awkward and difficult position. He could either borrow large amounts from wealthy financiers or small amounts from average citizens. In the end, he opted to do both. He depended on Wall Street brokerage and investment firms to make large, short-term loans to the government through the purchase of Treasury bills.

This approach had the benefit of raising large amounts of capital quickly and efficiently and of enlisting the financial community in support of the war. But it was also expensive. Since the market determined interest rates, such immense and repeated borrowing could only worsen the already severe inflationary pressures buffeting the American economy. Moreover, relying on Wall Street to finance the war mortgaged the federal government to the financial interests. The *quid pro quo* required the Wilson administration to alter its tax policies to appease the financiers.

To ensure the long-term financing of the war, Wilson turned directly to the American people. The government raised $21.4 billion through a series of popular bond drives. The first four were called Liberty Loans and the last, launched in 1919, was renamed the Victory Loan.

Table 1: Consumer Price Index, 1913-1920

Year	All Commodities	% Increase	Food	% Increase
1913	29.7	—	29.2	—
1914	30.1	1.3	29.8	2.0
1915	30.4	0.99	29.4	-1.4
1916	32.7	8.0	33.1	11.2
1917	38.4	14.8	42.6	22.3
1918	45.1	14.9	49.0	13.1
1919	51.8	12.9	54.6	10.3
1920	60.0	13.7	61.5	11.2

SOURCE: *Historical Statistics of the United States*, Part 1, p. 211. Base Year 1967.

1917-1918 • Liberty Loans ~ The proposal of William Gibbs McAdoo,

Liberty Loans presented a less inflationary means of paying for the war. The Department of the Treasury fixed successive interest rates of Liberty Bonds at 3.5, 4, and 4.5 percent, with a thirty-year maturity and partial redemption possible after fifteen years. Those terms, together with the work of the Price-Fixing Committee under the leadership of Robert S. Brookings, enabled the Wilson administration to enjoy greater success controlling inflation in 1917 and 1918 than at any time since the outbreak of war.

From Wilson's perspective, though, Liberty Loans had some disadvantages. To make the bonds attractive, the earnings they generated had to be exempt from federal taxation. The tax exemption induced wealthy individuals and big corporations to buy bonds in large numbers, costing the government millions in lost tax revenues. In addition, the Federal Reserve Board ruled that banks could include Liberty Bonds as assets against which to issue bank notes. The decision of the Federal Reserve further increased the money supply and partially countered the anti-inflationary exertions of the government.

1917 • Selling the War ~ Whatever their economic defects, Liberty Loans conferred an inestimable psychological benefit. They offered the Wilson administration an opportunity literally and figuratively to sell the war to American citizens. Not only did the Liberty Loan campaigns get ordinary Americans to contribute financially to the war effort, they also furnished a splendid instrument to build morale on the home front.

McAdoo employed the latest advertising techniques to sell bonds. Posters and newspaper and magazine advertisements promoted the bond drives with visually arresting images that were sometimes shockingly violent or, alternately, luridly sexual. Businesses, private clubs, and patriotic organizations staged competitions to boost sales. Liberty Bond assemblies served as occasions to stage huge public rallies at which sports figures such as Ty Cobb and Babe Ruth, matinee idols such as Douglas Fairbanks, Mary Pickford, Charlie Chaplin, and Al Jolson either spoke or performed.

Their efforts, and those of others, were a resounding success. The four Liberty Loan drives and the one Victory Loan campaign elicited more than 60 million subscriptions, representing a broad segment of the American people. They also went a considerable way toward establishing and sustaining Americans' patriotic sentiment toward the conflict.

1919 • The Economic Consequences of the War ~ The First War World hastened the development of the American economy. Intervention in the war accelerated the growth of industry, the expansion of agriculture, the advancement of technology, especially in the electrical and chemical industries, and the progress of economic organization and management. As had been the case during the Civil War, the military needs of the First World War further encouraged the standardization of products, particularly clothing and shoes. Less cumbersome and expensive equipment for radio transmission was among the other technological innovations of the war, as were improvements in aviation. Finally, the requirement for additional sources of power and energy stimulated the construction of hydroelectric plants at such locations as Muscle Shoals, Alabama along the Tennessee River.

1920 • Agriculture ~ No group profited more directly from the war than American farmers. Even before the United States entered the conflict, the overseas demand for corn, wheat, pork, beef, and cotton brought unrivaled prosperity to American agriculture. Herbert Hoover's incentives for greater output through more extensive and efficient cultivation raised farm income even further.

Yet, this stimulation revived the chronic problem of American agriculture: overproduction. By 1920, when the government withdrew orders for foodstuffs and European farmers again put their land under cultivation, the price of agricultural commodities precipitously declined. Depression haunted American farmers for the next two decades.

1920-1924 • Organized Labor ~ Organized labor reaped a comparable economic bonanza during the war. Samuel Gompers, the head of the American Federation of Labor (AFL), traded wage restraints and no-strike pledges for government approval of AFL organizing activities. As a result, membership in the

(1920) A family of Berliners living in temporary Nissen Huts tend to their gardens during the hardships of the post-war era.

AFL rose from approximately 2.4 million in 1917 to more than 4 million in 1920, but began to decline as early as 1921.

Organized labor also received direct support from the War Labor Board, under the leadership of former president William Howard Taft. Taft proved surprisingly sympathetic to workers. He affirmed the employees' right to collective bargaining, outlined minimum-wage and maximum-hour standards, and required equal pay for female workers.

War and American Prosperity

Although the United States had suffered more than 300,000 casualties (killed and wounded) during the First World War, these losses were minuscule compared to those that the European belligerents had endured. Moreover, no American civilians had died in combat, and the war had destroyed no American bridges, roads, farms, factories, towns, or cities. The war, by contrast, had laid waste to vast areas of France, Belgium, Italy, Poland, and Russia.

As a consequence, the United States profited economically from the war. The Gross National Product (GNP) had risen from $48.3 billion in 1916 to $84.0 billion in 1919. By 1919, too, the $7 billion of private investment abroad was more than double the amount of foreign investment in the United States, almost exactly the reverse of the situation that had existed at the outbreak of war in Europe in 1914.

Table 2: U. S. & Foreign Investment, 1908, 1914, 1919, 1924

Invest. in U.S. in billions of dollars

Year	Total Invest.	Private	Gov't	Foreign
1908	$2.5	$2.5	$0	$6.4
1914	$5.0	$3.5	$1.5	$6.7
1919	$9.7	$7.0	$2.7	$2.5
1924	$15.1	$10.9	$4.2	$2.9

SOURCE: *Historical Statistics of the United States*, Part 2, p. 869.

1921-1923

In addition, the Allied governments owed the United States Treasury more than $10 billion. Not only had the balance of debt shifted, making the United States a creditor nation for the first time in its history, but the United States had become the leading creditor nation in the world.

The Search for Prosperity

1921-1923 • The Debate Over Economic Policy ~ Long considered the haven of corrupt public officials and rapacious special interests, the administration of President Warren G. Harding also brought rising standards of living, stable prices, and nearly full employment. Despite the scandals that have justly tarnished his reputation, Harding presided over a series of developments that made the American economy the envy of the world.

When Harding took office in 1921, he inherited a deepening postwar recession and an increasingly shrill debate about how best to resolve it. Some members of Harding's cabinet, such as Secretary of the Treasury Andrew Mellon, advocated a cautious, even passive, approach on the part of the government, permitting the economy to recover in its own time and its own way. Mellon argued for a reduction in federal spending and for extensive tax cuts, which he secured in 1921 and again in 1924, to stimulate capital investment and economic growth.

At Mellon's urging, however, the administration was far from inert when dealing with organized labor. Mellon feared that labor unrest would disrupt, delay, and perhaps even prevent economic recovery. He therefore encouraged President Harding to take every action within his authority to suppress the labor movement and, if possible, to destroy labor unions themselves. In 1921, for example, Harding ordered federal troops to restore order in the coal fields of West Virginia. The next year he encouraged state action to break a nationwide coal miners' strike. When the government supported wage reductions for railroad workers thereby precipitating a national railroad strike in 1922, Attorney General Harry M. Daugherty obtained a court injunction that prevented the striking workers from assembling or demonstrating.

In opposition to Mellon's proposals, Secretary of Agriculture Henry A. Wallace and Secretary of Commerce Herbert Hoover advocated more extensive government intervention into the economy. Hoover, in particular, promoted the reestablishment of the partnership that had existed between business and government during the war years. He asserted that such an understanding would improve economic efficiency, reduce production costs, and stimulate capital investment without forcing companies to cut wages or layoff employees. Economic planning, Hoover and Wallace were convinced, would bring economic stability.

1921-1923 • Resistance to Planning ~ Hoover's and Wallace's recommendations encountered resistance both inside and outside of the Harding administration. Mellon, of course, criticized all government efforts at economic management. Similarly, conservatives such as prominent biologist Raymond Pearl complained that an administration elected to prevent government interference with business was now "doing more interfering with business than any other administration that we have had in peace times."

The enemies of monopoly feared that the partnership between business and government violated antitrust legislation. Hoover, in fact, became involved in a long feud with both the Justice Department and the Federal Trade Commission, which charged that the exchange of information among businesses and trade associations that his programs invited facilitated price fixing.

Had economic distress persisted, the ideas of Hoover, Wallace, and their cohorts might well have been discredited. With the exception of agriculture, however, most sectors of the American economy experienced a significant recovery during 1922 and 1923. Unemployment, which had reached approximately 12 percent in 1921, dwindled to less than 3 percent by 1923.

From 1923 on Americans enjoyed the auspicious combination of growing productivity, rising income, stable prices, and nearly full employment. They regarded Hoover as the principal architect of the resurgent economy, and many wondered aloud whether he had not inaugurated an era of permanent economic prosperity.

Table 3: Unemployment, 1920-1929
(in thousands of persons 14 years of age and older)

Year	No. Unemployed	% of Work Force
1920	2,132	5.2
1921	4,918	11.7
1922	2,859	6.7
1923	1,049	2.4
1924	2,190	5.0
1925	1,453	3.2
1926	801	1.8
1927	1,519	3.3
1928	1,982	4.2
1929	1,550	3.2

SOURCE: *Historical Statistics of the United States*, Part 1, p. 135.

Toward a New Economy

1924-1928 • A "People's Capitalism" ~ During the 1920s, the American economy became oriented toward producing goods, services, and entertainment for the masses. Widely hailed as a new kind of economy, a "people's capitalism," the American economy prospered through volume production and by creating a material abundance that benefited virtually all citizens. Peoples around the world marveled at the American accomplishment, concluding that the Americans had miraculously built an industrial economy that was technologically sophisticated, productively efficient, and yet attuned to popular needs. In the United States, economic development had apparently linked manufacturers, businessmen, financiers, workers, and consumers into an interdependent community. Even more incredible, the government had accomplished this task without seizing control of the economy or destroying private property.

This vision of the American economy, of course, was too good to be true, or at least too good to last. American arrangements and institutions did no better than their European counterparts in reversing the severe economic contraction that occurred after 1929. The later failures of the America economy, however, ought not to obscure the achievements of the 1920s. Nor should those failures conceal the extent to which the organization and structure of the American economy in the 1920s anticipated and spawned the economic growth and prosperity that characterized the 1950s and much of the 1960s.

1922-1928 • Mass Affluence ~ Cumulatively, the economic statistics for the 1920s tell a story of extraordinary success. Between 1922 and 1928 the index of industrial production increased 70 percent. The Gross National Product (GNP) rose from $85.1 billion to $103.1 billion, an increase of nearly 18 percent, while per capita income climbed approximately 30 percent and real wages by an average of 22 percent. During these same years, unemployment virtually disappeared (See Table 3) and both wholesale and consumer prices remained stable.

In large measure, increased productivity explained the virtuoso performance of the American economy. Output per factory worker-hour grew by nearly 75 percent. During the 1920s, the Americans made the first excursion into mass affluence in the history of the world.

Mid-1920s • Technology and Management ~ Behind these unprecedented advancements lay the new capaci-

(circa 1925) Traders on the floor of a stock exchange while a man posts updated figures for commodities such as wheat, cotton oil, corn, oats, and flax for markets like Chicago, New York City, Duluth, Winnipeg, Minneapolis, Toledo, St. Louis, and Kansas City.

ty to produce standardized goods at low per-unit costs. Many of the technological and managerial innovations pioneered during the late nineteenth and early twentieth century reached their culmination in the 1920s, such as the use of interchangeable parts and continuous assembly line production, the scientific management of shops and factories, and the systematic application of industrial research and development. In addition, during the 1920s more manufacturers introduced electric motors and internal combustion engines to operate machinery.

Mid-1920s • Managing Workers ~ Many government officials and businessmen regarded organized labor as potentially the most serious threat to continued economic development. They acknowledged that a recalcitrant work force could disrupt and perhaps destroy economic prosperity. It was imperative, therefore, to restrain or eliminate volatile labor organizations. Contented and secure workers, labor relations experts had come to believe, were not merely socially desirable but absolutely essential to the successful operation of a modern industrial economy.

The specialists who staffed corporate personnel departments thus set out to engineer a new kind of worker. They organized their programs to fashion a motivated and disciplined labor force by instilling in workers both a sense of responsibility for and participation in the welfare of the company.

1920s • Hostility Toward Labor Union ~ Corporate administrators targeted labor unions for destruction. They, of course, failed to do away with unions entirely, but throughout the 1920s union membership declined from approximately 5 million to fewer than 3.5 million. Company officials replaced the independent labor union with a variety of employee representation plans. By 1929 more than 500 "company unions" were operating at such firms as Standard Oil, International Harvester, American Telephone and Telegraph, and the Goodyear Tire and Rubber Company.

1920s • Industrial Psychology ~ Also instrumental in the management of labor was the work of Elton Mayo in industrial psychology. The Dean of the Harvard Business School, Mayo carried out a series of influential experiments at the Western Electric Company in Hawthorne, Illinois during the early 1920s. Finding that complaints about working conditions were vague and abstract, Mayo concluded that to increase workers' happiness and productivity companies had first to improve communication between labor and management. He thus set out to dissolve the tension, anxiety, and antagonism that characterized industrial relations.

Mayo believed that if workers had an opportunity to express their grievances and to feel that company executives were sympathetic to them, they would come to realize that their interests were not in conflict with those of management. This process of identification would occur, Mayo reassured company officials, even should the grievances of workers remain unresolved.

Mayo sought to create a social environment in the factory that fostered workers' sense of loyalty and thereby enhanced their output. He advised that workers participate in, or at least consent to, every aspect of company operations in order to associate themselves more fully with the product that they helped to manufacture. In his book, *Human Problems of Industrial Civilization*, Mayo made it clear that he idolized the communal relations of preindustrial America. The age of industry and bureaucracy, and the zest for material acquisition that accompanied it, had destroyed community and produced fragmented, isolated individuals. Through industrial psychology, Mayo hoped to restore the equivalent of this cooperative, communal ethos in a modern, industrial, corporate setting. He argued that companies would be wise to nurture this renewed sense of community, as long as management also controlled it by enlisting workers in a common enterprise.

At Western Electric, the application of Mayo's theories proved a resounding success. They stopped workers' complaints, increased productivity, and prevented the formation of a militant labor union. The only substantive change that the company made was to install brighter lights throughout the factory and in the workers' dining room.

1920s • Consumerism ~ The new economy of the 1920s depended on consumers who were ready, willing, and able to buy. Another group of business specialists, advertising agents, sought to engineer willing consumers by altering old attitudes toward spending and indebtedness and by exciting a new demand for fashionable goods. The rapid evolution of consumer credit supplemented purchasing power and enabled Americans to mortgage future earnings to purchase expensive products they could never have otherwise afforded. In the hope that continuing economic growth would ease the burden of debt into which they had fallen, middle-class Americans during the 1920s abandoned traditional warnings to buy with caution, to fear debt, and to save money, and instead embraced the consumer economy as a national imperative.

The ethic of consumption that reached its apex in the 1920s fomented a subtle cultural as well as economic revolution. The new ideals of consumption undermined the old ideals of production and the Protestant work ethic. According to the values of a consumer culture, Americans no longer found satisfaction and meaning primarily in work and self-denial but in habitual consumption and immediate gratification. Freedom for Americans had come to mean the freedom to consume without hesitation or restraint.

1920s • The New Managerial Elite ~ Not only did Americans' attitudes toward work, spending, saving, and consumption change during the 1920s, so too did the kind of persons who directed corporate enterprise and made business policy. As the ownership of corporations became increasingly diluted, the accountability of management to stockholders became more a myth than a reality. Once managers found ways to generate new capital internally by withholding and reinvesting corporate profits, they could also reduce the dependence of their companies on the great investment banks that had dominated an earlier period of American economic history.

Corporate managers thus became accountable to no one but themselves. They no longer had to answer to stockholders or financiers in deciding how best to use corporate property. This arrangement led the managers of some corporations to behave irresponsibly, plundering company treasuries to enrich themselves and misrepresenting the value of company stock to potential investors and creditors. These financial and speculative abuses contributed to the onset of the Great Depression.

1920-1929 • Mergers and Consolidations ~ The potential of the new managerial elite for corruption did little to diminish its popularity in the government or the academy. The image of the "new manager" directing the great corporation to sustain economic prosperity, to augment national wealth, and to ensure the welfare of the American people remained appealing and powerful. Modern managerial corporations seemed eminently capable of administering orderly economic progress. If such organizations were truly a benefit to both the society and the economy, then neither the courts nor the legislature ought to oppose the mergers and consolidations that would create larger, more productive, more efficient, and more responsive corporations.

According to statistics compiled by the Federal Trade Commission (FTC), between 1920 and 1929, 6,818 manufacturing and mining firms combined. In the utilities industry, similar amalgamations reduced the number of companies by more than 4,000. Vertical integration also created manufacturing concerns that controlled every aspect of their business, from producing raw materials to managing distribution and sales. To administer these diverse operations the new managers developed elaborate bureaucracies that supervised production, marketing, hiring, public relations, and research and development.

Business promotional literature emphasized that corporate bureaucracies functioned only in the public interest. Americans, contended the apologists for business, owed their prosperity to a corporate system that had ensured efficiency and profits while avoiding the perils of state economic control that would have imperiled or eliminated private property. These claims have some merit. Without significant state intervention, the private sector had generated material abundance for a large segment of the American population.

At the same time, however, corporate bureaucracies masked gross inefficiencies in production and distribution, sustained high profit margins by resorting to illegal price fixing, and defrauded investors by overestimating or inflating the value of company stock. Economic conditions in the United States were much less balanced and stable than they at first appeared.

The Roots of Economic Crisis

1928-1929 • The Tools of Macroeconomic Management ~ In order to avoid the depression that troubled the United States during the immediate postwar years (1918-1921), economists, businessmen, and politicians sought ways to manage the economy. One proposal, which never came completely to fruition, was the establishment of a national economic advisory council to enable the leaders of business and government to coordinate their activities, identify developing problems, and organize remedial action much as they had done during the war.

A less formal advisory system did come into being during the 1920s with the principal intention of steadying the business cycle. In 1923, the Business Cycle Committee, chaired by Owen D. Young of General Electric, recommended a variety of measures designed to minimize or avoid economic fluctuations. A voluminous report entitled *Recent Economic Changes in the United States*, published in 1927 under the direction of the economist Wesley Clare Mitchell, codified many of these proposals. Chief among them were: first, the adoption of a cooperative system of unemployment insurance to prevent unpredictable swings in consumer spending; second, a regular, uniform, and constant supply of currency to avert both an irrational speculative enthusiasm and an equally irrational retrenchment hysteria; third, the careful management of exports to avoid glutting the international market with American products and thereby driving down the price; fourth, the accumulation of reserve investment capital to sustain construction through brief periods of economic adversity.

Few companies implemented these suggestions; most corporate managers did not think them necessary. American businessmen felt certain that the economic system they were devising was less susceptible to recession and depression, more sensitive to the danger signals of approaching economic crisis, and more amendable, should the occasion arise, to corrective adjustment. They could not have been more wrong.

1928 • Early Signs of Trouble ~ Beneath the superficial indications of stability, the American economy was already showing signs of trouble by 1928. Markets for automobiles, appliances, radios, and other durable consumer goods were becoming saturated. Meanwhile, capital investment in these industries and their ancillaries, such as steel, petroleum, glass, and rubber, was slackening. Individual and corporate investors did not develop new growth industries because worsening levels of consumer debt contracted potential markets even further. Exports declined because European capitalists had little disposable income with which to buy American goods.

Nor could financiers and bankers offer much help. The banking system could not protect weak or overextended banks from collapse, and could not prevent the ruin of these feeble banks from spreading to their more solvent counterparts and causing a general contraction of money and credit.

As the 1920s drew to a close, the movement toward a new economy was about to encounter impediments that made a mockery of efforts to establish a people's capitalism. The approaching economic crisis idled at least 25 percent of the work force and temporarily arrested the productive capacity and development of American industry. In October 1929 Americans left behind the era of quiet economic efficiency and prosperity and entered a new, clamorous, and impoverished age that few understood.

Table 4: Average Stock Prices Per Share, 1927-1935

Year	Total	Industrial	Railroad	Utilities
1927	15.34	12.53	38.17	27.63
1928	19.95	16.92	40.40	36.86
1929	26.02	21.35	46.15	59.33
1930	$21.03	$16.42	$39.82	$53.24
1931	13.66	10.51	23.72	37.18
1932	6.93	5.37	8.75	20.65
1933	8.96	7.61	12.75	19.72
1934	9.84	9.00	14.05	15.79
1935	10.60	10.13	11.78	15.15

SOURCE: *Standard and Poor's Index of Common Stock and Historical Statistics of the United States*, Part 2, p. 1004.

1928-1929 • The Stock Market Crash and the Onset of Depression ~ The Great Depression was a worldwide economic crisis into which the United States was drawn as much a victim as a responsible agent. The stock market crash of October 29, 1929 did not cause the depression. Rather, the crash was one of the more dramatic symptoms of structural weaknesses in the national and international economies.

Between February 1928 and September 1929 prices on the New York Stock Exchange steadily rose. For eighteen months, Americans enjoyed a "Bull" market in which most investors made money. The cumulative market value of stocks in 1929 reached an estimated $67.5 billion with 1 billion shares traded. The price of stock, however, had in many cases long ceased to bear any relation to the earning power of the corporations issuing it. The ratio of corporate earnings to the market price of stocks climbed to 16 to 1; a 10 to 1 ratio was the standard. In the autumn of 1929, the stock market began to fall apart.

On October 19, 1929, stock prices dropped sharply, alarming Wall Street financiers, stockbrokers, and investors. Big bankers tried to avert a crisis by conspicuously buying stock in an attempt to restore public confidence in its value. Ten days later, on October 29, "Black Tuesday," all efforts to save the market failed.

By November 13, the crash had wiped out $30 billion in stock value. Most knowledgeable Americans, including Herbert Hoover who had been elected president in November 1928, viewed the crash of the stock market as a necessary and healthy adjustment provoked by inflated stock and undisciplined speculation. Only paper empires had toppled, Americans reassured themselves.

The crash, though, had brought down the economies of a number of European countries. The American economy shortly followed. The Great Depression had begun.

Causes of the Great Depression

Perhaps the most remarkable aspect of the Great Depression was not that it occurred, but that it was so severe and that it lasted so long. There are five underlying causes that explain the onset of the crisis as well as its severity and longevity.

(1929) Investors rushing to withdraw their savings during the stock market crash.

1928-1929

The Lack of Economic Diversification

The American economy of the 1920s lacked diversification. Although not readily apparent at the time, prosperity rested on a few basic industries, primarily construction and the manufacture of automobiles. When these two industries faltered toward the end of the decade, the rest of the economy fell into stagnation. Moreover, by 1929, the 200 largest corporations in the United States (out of a total of 400,000 corporations) controlled 49 percent of all corporate assets and received 43 percent of all corporate income. The 1,350 largest corporations secured 80 percent of all corporate profits. These corporations failed to adjust to changing economic conditions. For instance, in a period of slowing economic activity and declining purchasing power, corporations maintained artificially inflated prices.

The generally unsound structure of some large corporations introduced a further element of instability into the American economy. When a large firm encountered financial difficulties, those problems often spread quickly to smaller corporate subsidiaries leading to the collapse of the entire conglomerate, which, in turn aggravated unemployment.

The Lack of Disposable Income

The indebtedness and consequent lack of disposable income among growing numbers of Americans strictly limited their purchasing power and their ability to consume the products that industry made available to them. Consumer demand could not keep pace with supply. This situation created a dual crisis of over-production and under-consumption. Even in 1929, before the worst years of depression, more than 60 percent of American families earned annual incomes below $2,000, then considered the minimum for economic self-sufficiency. These Americans were too poor to afford to buy houses, cars, and in some instances, adequate supplies of food. The laying off of workers that began after 1929 further depleted the purchasing power of American consumers.

One percent of the population, by contrast, received 19 percent of the national income by 1929, compared to only 12 percent in 1919. The 10 percent who earned the highest wages garnered 40 percent of the national income. Unfortunately, these wealthy individuals provided a limited market for consumer goods. Had income been more equitably distributed among a larger segment of the American population, the number of potential consumers would have been vastly increased.

The Lack of an Adequate Credit Structure

By 1929 Americans in general, and especially American farmers, were trapped in a deepening spiral of debt. Farmers had gone into debt to buy more land and equipment during the profitable war years, then had faced steadily declining crop prices throughout the 1920s that made it impossible for them to pay what they owed. American agriculture had suffered from depressed conditions since 1921, following a period of about seven years in which farmers had prospered as the result of the First World War. During the 1920s, many of the small banks that served the rural community and the agricultural economy had failed at an alarming rate as their customers defaulted on loan payments.

The Decline of Overseas Commerce

Although the United States was far less dependent on overseas trade than it is today, exports had accounted for a significant proportion of American economic prosperity in the 1920s. By the late 1920s, however, European demand for American goods had begun to decline for two reasons. First, the increasing productivity of European industry and agriculture, having at last recovered from the war, made it possible to reduce the volume of American imports. Second, toward the end of the decade, most European capitalists could no longer afford to buy American goods.

The International Debt Structure

The international debt structure devastated the European economies. The crushing system of reparations that the Allies had imposed on Germany, in addition to the huge debt that the Allies owed to the United States to pay the costs of war and reconstruction, seriously hampered economic recovery. Almost all the profits that European economies managed to generate were devoured by debt. Throughout the 1920s, the leaders of European nations, especially in Great Britain, repeatedly called on American leaders to cancel the debts owed to the United States. The Americans always refused, but did agree to restructure the debt payments as long as the Allies also extended the same courtesy to Germany.

In the early 1920s, the German economy was in shambles. Increasing taxation, a huge national debt, a trade deficit, reparation payments, and runaway inflation combined to wipe out the value of savings, war bonds, and pensions that represented years of toil and thrift. To meet its financial obligations, the German government continued to print more paper money, which only made inflation worse and destroyed the value of the Deutschmark, the basic unit of German currency.

Before the outbreak of the First World War, the value of the mark stood at a ratio of 4.2 marks to 1 U.S. dollar. In 1919 the ratio was 8.9 marks to a dollar. By early 1923, however, the ratio was 18,000 marks to the dollar. By August 1923, inflation in Germany had reached absurd levels when a single U.S. dollar could be exchanged for 4.6 million marks; by November the ratio was 1 dollar to 4 billion marks. At this point it had become impossible for the German government any longer to meet its financial obligations. Germany defaulted on its debts, including the reparation payments made to the Allies.

In August 1923, Gustav Stresemann (Chancellor of Germany, August-November, 1923) became chancellor of Germany. Although Stresemann's government survived only until November, during his one hundred days in office Stresemann skillfully placed Germany on the path to economic recovery. He declared his willingness to resume reparation payments and issued a new currency backed by a mortgage on German real estate, the one commodity that had held its value. To protect the value of the new currency, Stresemann ordered the government not print another issue. Inflation receded. Stresemann had restored national and international confidence in the German economy.

Recognizing that Germany could not meet its obligations, the United States and Great Britain pressured France to permit a restructuring of the reparation payments. In 1924, all the Allies accepted the Dawes Plan, named for Charles Gates Dawes, the American financier, politician, and diplomat, who presided over the commission that devised it. The Dawes Plan reduced reparations according to the German capacity to pay.

Between 1924 and 1929 economic conditions in Germany improved. Foreign investment, particularly from American capitalists and the United States government, stimulated German economic recovery. By 1929, iron, steel, coal, and chemical production exceeded pre-World War I levels. The value of German exports also surpassed that of 1913. Real wages for German workers were higher than they had been before the war, and improved unemployment compensation helped to maintain the standard of living even for those out of work.

Germany at last appeared to have achieved economic stability, but on the eve of the Great Depression, Germany still owed the Allies $33 billion; the Allies still owed the United States $22 billion. The Allies had relied on prompt German payment to meet their obligations. If Germany did not pay the Allies, then the Allies could not pay the United States. To make payments, Germany borrowed funds from private banks around the world, and especially from Americans. When international credit suddenly contracted in 1929, it became more difficult to borrow money. Without ready sources of foreign capital, first Germany and then the other nations of Western Europe defaulted on their loans, drawing the United States after them into the Great Depression.

(circa 1960) The hands of American industry and Uncle Sam are joined in this promotional poster encouraging investment in the American economy through the Pay Roll Savings Purchase Plan.

1931 • The Response to Economic Crisis ~ Most Americans, including President Hoover, did not initially interpret the crash and depression as catastrophic events. Economic panics and depressions had occurred throughout American history, in 1819, 1837, 1857, 1873, 1893, 1907, and as recently as 1921. Leading economists and businessmen explained these economic downturns as part of the cyclical nature of capitalism. Although they had sought ways to minimize and regulate these troubling economic fluctuations, experts believed that depressions often purified the economy, purging it of weaker, less efficient, and less profitable businesses. Not only would the economic system eventually recover, it would be stronger than before. There was thus no need for alarm and no rush to embrace revolutionary solutions to problems that in time would take care of themselves.

Hoover believed that the depression had not arisen from internal defects in the American economy. In his opinion, the depression had resulted from weaknesses in the world economy, such as the instability of international banking, currency, and credit. Restructuring the debt, he argued, was the key to ending the depression. Hoover reasoned that the United States might, from a combination of generosity and self-interest, attempt to salvage the world economic system.

Yet, Hoover does not seem to have understood how deeply enmeshed in the international economy the United States had become by 1929. He concentrated his efforts on reviving the American economy, but refused to do more than propose in 1931 a one-year moratorium on the payment of all war debts and reparations, a measure that he later expanded to include all private debts. Hoover's proposals were economically sound, but they offered too little and came too late to end the crisis.

1932 • The Reconstruction Finance Corporation ~ The most important action that the Hoover administration took to end the depression in the United States was establishing the Reconstruction Finance Corporation (RFC) in 1932. An agency of the federal government, the RFC was designed to provide federal loans to troubled banks and business and to make funds available to local and state governments to support public works projects. Although endowed with a huge operating budget, the RFC failed to deal forcefully enough with the problems of the economy to generate significant recovery. Under the direction of conservative Texas banker Jesse Jones, the RFC lent money only to businesses and banks with sufficient collateral, those likely to weather the economic storm of their own accord. The RFC, in effect, remained solvent by refusing to make loans to the institutions most desperately in need. Even Hoover's most vigorous and expansive program was crippled by the fiscal conservatism of his administration.

1932 • Changing Attitudes Toward the Depression ~ By the fall of 1932, most Americans had come to perceive the depression differently than they had at its beginning. They now saw that it affected not only one or two but all sectors of the economy from agriculture to industry and from commerce to banking. Americans had also come to fear that the depression would not go away by itself, as economists, businessmen, and politicians had at first predicted. Growing numbers began to worry that depression, rather than being a temporary and purgative event, marked a permanent condition of material scarcity and economic stagnation.

The response of the government proved inadequate. Hoover called for an expansion of local, voluntary relief efforts of the sort that had proliferated during the 1920s. Yet, Hoover's insistence on local management to alleviate the crisis reflected attitudes common among the American people. Most Americans were not inclined to see the federal government as the cause of their problems or the source of their rescue.

There were no loud or sustained outcries from the American people for massive federal intervention into the ailing economy. Even as thousands stood in bread lines or sifted through garbage cans in search of food, they blamed themselves for their plight. Unemployed Americans walked the streets day after day looking for jobs that did not exist. When they at last gave up in despair, many stayed out of sight to hide their shame.

Americans had elected Herbert Hoover to manage a functioning, prosperous economy, not to fix what did not appear to be broken. The drama of New Deal legislation, particularly in its early days, distorts the image of the years that preceded it. The advent of the New Deal implies that Congress enacted a multitude of laws in response to a public that demanded extensive federal intervention into the economy after enduring Hoover's inactivity. Such was simply not the case.

1932 • Hoover's Contribution to Recovery ~ Throughout 1931 and 1932, Hoover had employed an army of social scientists to gather an astonishing quantity of information on every aspect of the economic crisis. From the accumulation of this data Hoover and his advisors had begun to formulate plans and strategies to solve the most pressing economic problems. Hoover, though, was slow to act and, after he lost the election, reluctant to do so without Roosevelt's approval. When Roosevelt took office, therefore, he inherited a wealth of evidence about the state of the economy that Hoover's researchers had collected. Roosevelt did not hesitate to put these findings to use in an effort to propel the United States out of the depression.

1933 • Roosevelt Comes to Power ~ Franklin Delano Roosevelt became president of the United States on March 4, 1933, after winning a landslide victory that was more a repudiation of Hoover than an endorsement of Roosevelt. Confidence in Hoover had gradually ebbed since 1928 but had never completely disappeared, as evidenced by the more than 15 million Americans who voted for him in 1932.

From the outset of his administration, Roosevelt soothed Americans' fears about the economy. He exuded confidence and hope that the crisis would soon end and conveyed those sentiments to the American people.

On March 5, 1933, Roosevelt declared a four-day national bank holiday, closing all banks in the country. He reassured the American people that when the banks reopened on March 9, they would again be solvent. Roosevelt's action did little to restructure and stabilize the banking system, but went a long way toward restoring public confidence. When the banks reopened, Americans stood in line to put their money in, not to withdraw it. Within a month, $1 billion in gold and currency flowed back into American banks and the immediate banking crisis was over.

The New Deal

1933 • The "Hundred Days" ~ Historians have labeled the initial legislative program of the New Deal the "Hundred Days." The three pieces of legislation most characteristic of the Hundred Days were the Emergency Banking Act (March 9, 1933), the Agricultural Adjustment Act (May 12, 1933), and the National Industrial Recovery Act (June 16, 1933). The Roosevelt administration designed each measure to restore prosperity to an important sector of the economy (banking, agriculture, and industry) in an effort to promote total economic recovery.

The Emergency Banking Act protected big banks from being ruined by smaller, weaker banks. The bill provided for officials of the Treasury Department to inspect all banks before permitting them to reopen. The federal government also offered direct assistance to some troubled institutions and required a thorough reorganization of those in the greatest financial difficulty. "I can assure you," Roosevelt told the public in his first "Fireside Chat" broadcast on March 12, 1933, "that it is safer to keep your money in a reopened bank than under the mattress."

The Agricultural Adjustment Act raised crop prices by paying farmers not to plant, thereby introducing artificial scarcities. The Agricultural Adjustment Administration (AAA) set production quotas for seven basic commodities: corn, wheat, rice, cotton, tobacco, dairy products, and hogs.

The administrators of the AAA told farmers how much of a particular crop they could plant and paid them subsidies for their cooperation. A tax on food processing and the milling of wheat provided a fund from which to make the subsidy payments that compensated farmers for their lost income.

1933-1935 • The Accomplishments and Limitations of the AAA ~ The initial efforts of the AAA were heartening. Farm prices rose after 1933, and the agricultural economy as a whole emerged from the 1930s much more stable and prosperous than it had been during the 1920s. The terrible droughts and dust storms that struck the Great Plains in 1934 substantially aided the AAA in its efforts to reduce agricultural production. Conditions displaced hundreds of thousands from the land and diminished the wheat crop from 850 million bushels in 1932 to 550 million bushels in 1935. This decline naturally led to a rise in prices.

The curtailment of agricultural output benefited many farmers. Their share of the national income had increased from 11 percent to 15 percent by 1936. At the same time, their total indebtedness fell by more than $1 billion. The AAA, however,

(1930) Red Cross workers give boxes of seed to crowds of drought victims gathered around a small Red Cross outpost, Mississippi.

favored large farmers over small, and even unintentionally dispossessed some struggling farmers, notably sharecroppers and tenants, whom planters evicted from the land in a move to reduce the amount of acreage under cultivation.

Moreover, as the AAA began operations in 1933, the Secretary of Agriculture, Henry A. Wallace, ordered the slaughter of 6 million hogs and 220,000 sows to reduce surpluses and maintain prices (see Farming). Cotton farmers plowed under 100 million acres, a quarter of their crop, for the same reasons. Did it make sense, many Americans wondered, to create artificial scarcities and to raise the price of agricultural commodities in a period of high unemployment, unrelenting poverty, and widespread hunger?

In January 1936, the Supreme Court of the United States declared the Agricultural Adjustment Act unconstitutional in *U.S. v. Butler*. Arguing that the federal government had no constitutional authority to require farmers to limit production or to tax food processors, the Supreme Court dismantled the AAA.

The essence of the AAA programs survived, however, for within weeks the Roosevelt administration had secured passage of the Soil Conservation and Domestic Allotment Act. This new piece of legislation enabled the government to pay farmers not to plant in an effort to prevent erosion. Since the avowed purpose of the Conservation and Domestic Allotment Act was soil conservation, the new law met the constitutional objections of the court.

1932-1935 • The National Industrial Recovery Act ~ Proponents hailed the National Industrial Recovery Act (NIRA) as the first major step toward a permanent government-supported system of industrial planning and economic administration. The principal objective of the National Recovery Administration (NRA) established under the act was to bring production and consumption back into balance. To achieve this goal, the NRA gave the leading companies in each industry the opportunity to establish production quotas and standards of quality; to fix prices; to set wages and hours; to determine the appropriate number of employees that each member of a given industry could hire; and to decide other appropriate details of production and distribution.

1933 • NRA Codes ~ Having suspended operation of the anti-trust laws for two years, the NIRA made it possible for the NRA to install these code-making bodies in each industry. The code-making bodies consisted of representatives not only from management but from labor and consumers' groups as well. Once President Roosevelt had approved the industrial codes, they were to have the same binding effect as laws passed by Congress.

Business participation in the NRA remained voluntary, although the government urged citizens to boycott businesses refusing to take part. Those businessmen who abided by the NRA codes governing their industries could display the symbol of the NRA: the Blue Eagle with its wings spread above a slogan that read "We Do Our Part." Failure to comply with the codes once adopted exposed malefactors to federal prosecution.

1933 • The Problems of the NRA ~ Under the direction of the flamboyant and energetic Hugh S. Johnson, a retired general and businessman, the NRA garnered extraordinary public support. From the beginning, though, the

NRA encountered serious difficulties that at last caused the entire enterprise to dissolve in failure.

The codes governing industry were hastily and ambiguously written. Representatives of large corporations dominated the code-writing process to ensure that the new regulations worked to the advantage of their companies. Section 7a of the National Industrial Recovery Act, for example, gave legal protection to labor unions and guaranteed the right of workers to engage in collective bargaining. Large corporations, nevertheless, continued to deny unions the recognition that they sought, and thus kept wages low while actively and artificially raising prices. The actions of many large corporations actually hampered the purchasing power of American consumers, thus inhibiting one of the crucial mechanisms, consumer spending, that economists thought might pull the economy out of the depression.

By the end of 1933, corporate violation of the industrial codes was rampant. The task of supervising and enforcing NRA regulations was beyond the bureaucratic competence of the agency. Furthermore, since many officials at the NRA and the Department of Justice had serious doubts about the constitutionality of the NIRA, no one was prepared to use sanctions to obtain compliance. By 1934, opposition to the NRA was widespread and growing.

1933 • The Civilian Conservation Corps and the Public Works Administration ~ One of the main initiatives of the Roosevelt administration was putting people back to work and otherwise easing the plight of the unemployed. Under the auspices of the NIRA, Congress authorized $3.3 million to fund a federal public works program. Roosevelt had earlier asked Congress to enact a law creating the Civilian Conservation Corps (CCC). On March 31, 1933, he announced that the CCC would recruit 250,000 men between the ages of 18 and 25 to begin work by the summer.

Although the CCC provided work-relief to some 300,000 young men by June 1933 (in 1935 the number employed in CCC projects approached 2.5 million), Roosevelt was acutely aware that it accommodated only a minuscule fraction of the 13 million unemployed. The Public Works Administration (PWA), he hoped, would do more. In this prospect, Roosevelt was disappointed. He had entrusted the PWA to the Secretary of the Interior Harold L. Ickes. A miserly if scrupulously honest man, Ickes personally scrutinized every significant request for PWA funds to satisfy himself that it would not result either in waste or fraud.

During the first year of its existence, the PWA disbursed slightly more than $100 million. But Ickes spent money so slowly and cautiously that his agency exercised little impact in creating jobs or generating sufficient consumer spending to rouse the national economy.

1935 • Legal Challenges ~ The NRA did not bring the industrial revival that Americans expected. After two years, production indexes still lagged behind the levels of 1920, and more than 12 million Americans remained unemployed. In 1935, the Supreme Court intervened to end the troubled experiment. As with the AAA, the Supreme Court, in a rare unanimous decision, declared the NIRA unconstitutional.

In the case of *Schechter Poultry Corporation v. U. S.*, two bureaucracies, one ancient and religious, the other modern and secular, reached an impasse. The A.L.A. Schechter Poultry Company engaged in the ritual slaughter of chickens according to the requirements of orthodox Jewish dietary laws, a process not easily compatible with the bureaucratic restrictions that officials of the NRA had devised to regulate the poultry industry. According the Kosher rules, butchers had to reject any birds suffering from conditions that Talmudic law deemed unwholesome and unhealthy. The NRA codes, however, forbade butchers from making such a careful selection. In order to protect commodity prices and to prevent less desirable chickens from being sold at reduced rates, the NRA required Jewish butchers to accept the first available birds.

Religious law, the Supreme Court Justices concluded, superseded the secular codes governing the poultry industry. They also found constitutionally unacceptable the provision of the NIRA granting unelected code-making bodies the authority to formulate rules that, when signed by the president, had the power of laws enforceable in federal court. The Justices opposed what they interpreted as an unconstitutional delegation of legislative authority.

1933-1935 • The Failure of Economic Recovery and the Rise of Government Regulation ~ The legislation of the Hundred Days was supposed to put Americans back to work and to promote economic recovery. Even before the Supreme Court invalidated the AAA and the NIRA, it was clear that these measures had failed. Although approximately 7 million Americans had received some form of federal assistance since 1933, between 12 and 15 million were still not regularly employed; official unemployment figures remained above 20 percent. Unemployment had risen from 3.2 percent in 1929 to 24.9 percent in 1933. The depression persisted.

In response to record high unemployment, early in 1935 Roosevelt altered his strategy in two ways. Rather than aspiring to revitalize the economy through a partnership of business and government, Roosevelt now sought to expand and strengthen federal regulatory authority over the economy. At the same time, he began calling for legislation to alleviate the worst suffering the depression had caused.

1935-1937 • The Expansion of Federal Authority ~ In a series of acts passed between 1935 and 1937, Congress and the administration moved to enhance the role of the federal government in managing critical sectors of the economy. The Banking Act of 1935 authorized the Federal Reserve Board to regulate interest rates, to determine the reserve requirements of member banks, and to issue federal bank notes, thus giving the federal government more direct control over credit and the monetary system.

In an effort to create orderly, regulated, and efficient competition primarily among public utility companies, Congress passed the Holding Company Act of 1935. This legislation required the integration of utility companies and their subsidiaries; Section 11a of the act effected the dissolution of most utility holding companies. In the opinion of many economists, the holding companies were largely responsible for the waste, inefficiency, and instability that characterized the industry.

The Federal Power Act of 1935 instituted the Federal Power Commission, which had the authority to establish rates charged by utility companies engaged in interstate commerce. In a supplementary act, passed in 1938, Congress granted the Federal Power Commission the right to regulate the price of natural gas flowing between states.

The Miller-Tydings Act of 1937 also augmented federal supervision of competitive practices in business. Sometimes known as the Fair Trade Act, this law compelled local retail merchants to sell nationally advertised products at the manufacturers' suggested retail price. This effort to avoid destructive competition and to establish and maintain a uniform and stable price structure represented another attempt to eliminate the economic chaos that Roosevelt now believed had arisen in the absence of federal planning and regulation.

By 1935 Roosevelt and his advisors had also concluded that federal supervision of the transportation system would bring greater order and efficiency. The railroads already operated under the regulation of the Interstate Commerce Commission, but other forms of transportation remained free of federal control. Acting in part on the recommendations of Joseph B. Eastman, the Federal Coordinator of Transportation, and in part on his own desire to bring order out of apparent disarray, Roosevelt persuaded Congress to approve three measures: the Motor Carrier Act of 1935, which placed the trucking industry and inland waterways under the authority of the Interstate Commerce Commission; the Merchant Marine Act, which provided the maritime industry with federal subsidies and loans, administered by the U. S. Maritime Commission; and the Civil Aeronautics Act of 1938, which established the Civil Aeronautics Board empowered to regulate the rates, routes, and services of the fledgling airline companies. Together, these three acts reorganized the transportation system of the United States.

1935-1937 • The New Deal and the Problem of Monopoly ~ The main focus of the New Deal in 1935 became the reorganization of the American economy. Believing that unrestrained competition had contributed to the onset of the depression, Roosevelt and his advisors sought ways to increase federal administration of the economy in an effort to bring about economic stability and managed competition. This initiative required a confrontation with the problem of monopoly.

When he became president of the United States in 1933, Roosevelt had set himself an important task: to reform and salvage, not to dismantle and discard, the capitalist system. How best to accomplish this mission, however, excited bitter disputes and rivalries among his closest economic advisors.

The divisions within the New Deal coalition broke down into three factions that to a remarkable extent duplicated the economic policies of Woodrow Wilson, Theodore Roosevelt, and William Howard Taft. There was a group that advocated self-government in industry and the creation of a planned economy under the control of business. A second group distrusted the motives and capabilities of businessmen and recommended government planning and supervision of the economy. The third group promoted economic competition in a free market, believing that monopoly had caused the depression.

Roosevelt's own preferences remained unclear, and even shifted back and forth from one position to another. By 1935, though, Roosevelt denounced what he

(circa 1930) President Herbert Hoover (1874 - 1964) explaining his 'farm relief program' to a farmer. The relief program is shown as a straw scarecrow scaring off hard times depicted as birds.

characterized as an unjustifiable concentration of economic power in the hands of big business. Disillusioned with the business community, a disenchantment that only deepened with the recession of 1937, Roosevelt, in April of 1938, called on Congress to establish a commission to investigate the problem of monopoly and to propose major reforms in anti-trust legislation.

Congress responded with the creation of the Temporary National Economic Committee (TNEC). At about the same time, Roosevelt appointed Thurman Arnold the new director of the antitrust division of the Justice Department. A professor at Yale Law School, Arnold soon proved a vigorous enemy of monopoly. Using unprecedented applications of the Sherman and Clayton anti-trust laws, Arnold filed and won almost as many anti-trust cases between 1938 and 1941 as the Justice Department had filed in its entire history.

Despite the apparent triumph of the principle of free competition, the policies of the late New Deal did not represent a frontal assault on corporate monopoly or economic concentration. Neither the TNEC nor the crusade of Thurman Arnold enjoyed much lasting impact on economy policy. The investigations of the TNEC continued for nearly three years and generated volumes of testimony. In the end, the committee made no important recommendations for economic planning or reform. Arnold's spirited campaign against monopoly came to a halt when wartime economic pressures convinced Roosevelt that the fight against economic concentration was over.

Even at its height, the New Deal attack on monopoly did not represent an attempt to restore the small-scale, decentralized economy of proprietary capitalism. The paramount commitment of the New Deal by the late 1930s was not to break up the huge and powerful economic combinations but to regulate their conduct. Roosevelt was not interested in destroying monopolies. He was, instead, intent on increasing the regulatory authority of the federal government, which, he believed, under the influence of an energetic and enlightened chief executive, could reconfigure and direct the economy to ensure the attainment of stability, prosperity, and justice.

1935-1939 The Origins of the Welfare State

1935-1937 • The Resettlement Administration, the Farm Security Administration, and the Rural Electrification Administration ~ To ease the plight of farmers, Roosevelt launched the Resettlement Administration (RA), also established by the Emergency Relief Appropriation Act of 1935. The Resettlement Administration, under the leadership of Rexford G. Tugwell, gathered impoverished small farmers in rural communities and gave them the opportunity to farm better land. The Farm Security Administration (FSA), which succeeded the Resettlement Administration, attempted through short- and long-term government loans to assist farmers cultivating marginal land to relocate onto more fertile land.

In comparison to expectations, the accomplishments of both the RA and the FSA were disappointing. Neither agency moved more than a few thousand farmers. Of greater practical importance was the Rural Electrification Administration (REA) also created in 1935, which made low-interest federal loans available to farmers who sought access to electrical power. Within a few years of its inception, the REA had brought electricity to more than 90 percent of American farms.

The agricultural programs of the New Deal had typically benefited rich or middle-class farmers, ignoring the impoverished sharecroppers, tenants, and farm laborers who constituted 33 percent of agricultural workers in the United States. In response to their pleas, Roosevelt supported the Bankhead-Jones Farm Tenancy Act of 1937. This measure offered federal loans to tenants who wished to buy land of their own, and provided for the limited resettlement of farmers currently working exhausted or unproductive land. The act also extended federal aid to the growing numbers of migrant workers.

1935-1943 • The Works Progress Administration ~ The Emergency Relief Appropriation Act of April 8, 1935 created the Works Progress Administration (WPA). The chief objective of the WPA was not to revive the economy, but to create jobs for persons who might otherwise have remained unemployed.

Under the direction of Harry Hopkins, WPA workers, between 1935 and 1943, built 650,000 miles of highways, streets, and roads, 110,000 public buildings, 100,000 bridges, 8,000 parks, and 500 airports. All tolled, the WPA completed more than 1,410,000 projects, employed 8,500,000 workers, and spent $11 billion, 85 percent of which paid wages and salaries.

The WPA also sponsored the Federal Writers Project, the Federal Theater Project, the Federal Dance Project, the Federal Music Project, and the Federal Art Project, ambitious programs designed to provide work relief for struggling writers, artists, actors, musicians, and teachers. These programs not only tendered employment to men and women engaged in the arts, but inaugurated significant federal support for cultural activities.

1935 • The National Labor Relations Act ~ During this second phase of the New Deal, Senator Robert F. Wagner of New York and others cajoled Roosevelt to take more seriously the problems of organized labor. Reluctantly, Roosevelt signed into law in 1935 the National Labor Relations Act (NLRA), which shifted the balance of power in the relations between management and labor by enabling workers to organize into unions and bargain collectively for contracts.

The so-called Wagner Act reestablished and strengthened the rights labor had gained under Section 7a of the NIRA. The National Labor Relations Board (NLRB), which the Wagner Act instituted, could, first, supervise the election of union representatives; second, certify duly elected union leaders as the sole bargaining agents for labor; and third, collect data on the unfair labor practices in which management engaged, including the refusal to bargain in good faith.

The Fair Labor Standards Act of 1938 further expanded federal guidelines concerning labor-management relations. This law stipulated a minimum wage of 25 cents per hour and a maximum work week of 44 hours applicable throughout the United States.

1934 • Labor and the New Deal ~ Perhaps the most serious and persistent challenge that the New Deal had faced came from organized labor. Labor leaders condemned the orientation of the New Deal toward business and demanded a federal policy that addressed the problems of an industrial economy. Foremost among the concerns of labor had been to gather all workers, both skilled and unskilled, into a single union.

As early as 1934 a split had developed in the ranks of organized labor over the nature of industrial unionism. By 1936, John L. Lewis, president of the United Mine Workers (UMW), led advocates of industrial unions out of the American Federation of Labor to a new, more militant labor organization: the Congress of Industrial Organizations (CIO). The CIO staged a series of strikes primarily against the automobile and steel industries that won it recognition as the legitimate representative for its members.

By the late 1930s, it appeared to many observers that a radicalized labor movement had positioned itself to defy the federal government and challenge the corporations. Such a confrontation, however, never materialized. After passage of the National Labor Relations Act and the Fair Labor Standards Act, the rise of organized labor, although still marred by violence and bloodshed and still subject to legal challenge in the courts, proceeded without serious interruption. The unions soon linked their own welfare to that of the corporations and became an essential component of the New Deal coalition, an acknowledged, if not yet fully accepted, part of American economic life.

(1936) Unemployed mine workers crowd around a table, preparing to collect relief checks during the Great Depression, Jere Scotts Run, West Virginia.

1935-1938

1935 • The Social Security Act ~ Indicative of the shift in New Deal legislation away from economic recovery and toward economic relief after 1935 was the Social Security Act. The Social Security Act established a vast welfare system that provided modest compensation for most Americans against unemployment, illness, old age, or other forms of dependency. Coverage was limited. The law excluded domestics, agricultural workers, and employees in businesses of fewer than eight persons.

Yet, the Social Security Act marked a fundamental change in the character of the New Deal and the direction of American social and economic policy. With the adoption of social welfare measures of the sort already in place in the industrialized nations of Europe, officials of the United States government at last abandoned private and voluntary efforts to solve the problems of a modern industrial economy. They now routinely came to assume the administration of the economy among the many other responsibilities of government.

1936-1938 • The End of the New Deal ~ After winning a monumental (60.8 to 36.5 percent) victory over Alfred Landon, the progressive Republican governor of Kansas, in the presidential election of 1936, Roosevelt faced serious economic problems. A severe downturn in the economy during the winter of 1937 and 1938 darkened the morale of the American people and raised new questions about the efficacy of the New Deal programs. Along with the deteriorating economy, Roosevelt's failed attempt to reorganize the Supreme Court and the growing threat of another war in Europe effectively brought the New Deal to an end by 1938.

Although the New Deal did not effect economy recovery, its relief and welfare programs did mitigate some of the worst hardships that the depression had caused. The government purchase of military equipment and supplies before and during the Second World War at last restored economic prosperity. The war put farms, factories, and shops to work once more.

To Roosevelt's conservative critics, the New Deal was a dangerous and radical break with the past. Roosevelt had thwarted the Constitution and sought to establish a dictatorship in which the government controlled society and the economy. To liberal and radical critics, the New Deal amounted to little more than a timid defense of capitalism, a bulwark of economic conservatism that resisted demands for fundamental structural change in the American economic order. There are elements of truth in both these interpretations, but neither captures the essence of the New Deal experiment in economic reform.

Although the New Deal did not end the depression or redistribute wealth or power within the United States, it gave to the federal government the primary authority not only to protect citizens from economic hardship but to stimulate economic recovery and to prevent future depressions. As a consequence of the New Deal, the federal government, guided by the president, acquired the authority to regulate the stock market and the banks, even to the extent of insuring the deposits of individual investors; to protect labor unions and guarantee their right to organize and bargain collectively; to secure full employment or provide unemployment compensation and retirement pensions; and to create the rudiments of the welfare state through relief programs such as the Social Security system.

1938 • The New Deal and the American Economy ~ Since monopoly had proven an ineradicable component of American economic life, the architects of the New Deal tried to organize farmers, workers, consumers, and even the poor to nullify the power of corporations. In 1933, they pointed out, corporations had enjoyed an unrivaled dominance over the national economy. By 1938, corporations found themselves competing with increasingly influential farmer, labor, and consumer groups.

One of the enduring economic (and social) legacies of the New Deal was the creation of "interest-group liberalism," in which the federal government protected and aided some groups within the economy (farmers, workers, consumers, and the poor), while restraining and disciplining others (corporations). By instituting this balance of economic power, the New Dealers hoped to vindicate capitalism, maintain social justice, and preserve democracy. Their enterprise may have exaggerated the proficiency of government, but their innovations also formed the basis of the economic and social reforms carried out in the decades to come.

1939-1945 The American Economy and the Second World War

1938-1939 • Mobilizing American Resources ~ President Roosevelt began preparing the American economy for war as early as 1938, after Bernard Baruch, the former director of the War Industries Board, reported that Germany was the strongest military power in the world. Despite the prevalence of isolationist sentiment, Roosevelt induced Congress to appropriate $525 million to cover military expenditures. The Stockpile Act of 1939 allocated $125 million to enable Roosevelt to stockpile essential materials. The Educational Orders Act of 1939 authorized an annual expenditure of $2 billion to acquaint industrialists, contractors, and suppliers with the needs of the military. Finally, in August 1939, Roosevelt created a new agency, the War Resources Board, to investigate the industrial potential of the United States in the event of war and to formulate a comprehensive plan of economic mobilization.

1939-1941 • The Limits of Economic Mobilization ~ Despite this legislation, and despite the establishment of the Office of Emergency Management, which enabled him to maintain direct supervision of all military preparations, Roosevelt was reluctant to implement a complete program of industrial and economic mobilization. Throughout 1939 and 1940, Bernard Baruch urged Roosevelt to accept a detailed blueprint for centralized economic planning such as the one Baruch had devised during the First World War. Although Roosevelt approved in principal of Baruch's recommendations, he did not wish to bind his administration to a single economic policy. Nor did he wish to offend isolationists before the presidential election of November 1940 by seeming too eager for American intervention into a European conflict.

Between 1939 and 1941, Roosevelt's economic plan remained uncoordinated and experimental, much as the New Deal had been. The flexibility of Roosevelt's economic policy enabled the government to respond quickly to unforeseen problems. It also unfortunately resulted in waste, inefficiency, and duplication that seriously impaired the economic mobilization for war.

1940 • The War Economy ~ Industrial production, especially of military supplies, increased slightly in the United States during 1939. American factories delivered 2,300 airplanes to the Allies, as well as smaller quantities of tanks, weapons, and ammunition. The fall of France in June 1940, however, administered the shock that accelerated American wartime productivity.

During the first six months of 1940 key defense industries had been woefully slow to adapt to the manufacture of military supplies. A haphazard government economic policy was part of the problem. More serious, though, were the continuing shortages of such essentials as aviation fuel, electric power, and railroad freight cars.

To remedy these and others difficulties, Roosevelt created the Council of National Defense (CND) in May 1940 and appointed William S. Knudsen, the president of General Motors, as its chairman. Roosevelt's instructions to Knudsen were to produce 50,000 airplanes. He left the means whereby the CND fulfilled this mandate entirely to Knudsen's discretion.

Knudsen immediately began awarding large defense contracts, averaging about $1.5 million per month, to leading American manufactures. Meanwhile, Congress authorized the Reconstruction Finance Corporation to fund the construction of new factories and to stockpile supplies such as rubber and various metals.

These measures worked, although not as efficiently as Roosevelt had hoped. To improve industrial productivity further, he established a priorities board that was attached to the Council of National Defense. This board had the authority to compel manufacturers to fill military orders before they attended to civilian orders. An independent Office of Production Management (OPM), under the direction of Knudsen and Sidney Hillman, a prominent official in the Congress of Industrial Organizations (CIO), shared leadership of the bureau. The OPM allocated scarce goods, materials, and resources to those industries most in need and most critical to the war economy.

1942 • The War Production Board ~ In January 1942, after the United States had formally entered the Second World War, Roosevelt created the War Production Board (WPB) to provide more comprehensive federal direction of the national economy. As chief of the WPB, Roosevelt appointed Donald Nelson, the executive vice president of Sears, Roebuck and Company. The WPB supervised the production and distribution of a wide range of manufactured goods. Because of its extensive responsibilities, confusion became one of the hallmarks of its operation. Critics charged that the large corporations received preferential treatment, while Nelson believed that he had gone out of his way to allow the military to determine industrial priorities at the expense of the consumer economy.

1942 • The Office of Price Administration ~ Since the War Production Board had no authority to fix prices, Nelson had to cooperate with other federal agencies, a chore often easier said than done. To control inflation, ration scarce commodities, and protect consumers, Roosevelt instituted the Office of Price Administration (OPA). Under the direction of former journalist and advertising executive Chester Bowles, the principal function of the OPA was to set prices for thousands of nonagricultural goods.

The WPB sought to placate manufacturers in an effort to stimulate maximum productivity. Nelson thus recommended keeping prices high. The OPA, by contrast, sought to reduce inflationary pressures on the economy, so Bowles determined to keep prices as low as possible. As a consequence, Bowles and Nelson frequently came into conflict; their dissension did not encourage industrial proficiency.

1942 • The Office of Economic Stabilization ~ On October 3, 1942, Roosevelt instituted yet another federal agency to oversee the operation of the wartime economy: the Office of Economic Stabilization (OES), directed by James F. Byrnes. A former governor of South Carolina, a U.S. Senator, and a U.S. Supreme Court Justice, Byrnes cut an imposing figure. In an effort to unravel production snarls and to resolve disputes between the OPA, the WPB, and the War Department, Byrnes concentrated on establishing rigid controls over the production and allocation of such essential raw materials and industrial products as aluminum, copper, and steel. Byrnes surmounted many of the early obstacles that had hampered wartime industrial productivity, while continuing to keep inflation to a minimum.

Soon Byrnes was second only to Roosevelt himself in authority over the wartime economy. Late in 1944, as quarrels within the WPB rendered it ineffective, Byrnes gained even more influence. He became head of the Office of War Mobilization and Reconversion (OWMR). His responsibilities now not only included managing the wartime economy, but planning the economic transition from war to peace in a concerted effort to avoid a return of the depression when fighting ended.

As a result of these reforms, the American economy by the second half of 1940 entered a period of productivity unlike any other that had occurred in more than a decade. By 1941, 17,000 airplanes, 9,000 tanks, and 17,000 pieces of heavy artillery had rolled off the assembly lines of American factories. Such increases were only the beginning. The production of aircraft in 1943 was twice what it had been in 1942 and more than four times greater than in 1941. By the end of the war, the aviation, automobile, and shipbuilding industries had manufactured more than 300,000 airplanes, 88,140 tanks, and 3,000 merchant vessels.

1941-1945 • The Aircraft Industry ~ The aircraft industry expanded rapidly between 1941 and 1945. Before 1940, aircraft manufacturers had produced fewer than 500 airplanes annually. When, in 1940, Roosevelt had called for the production of 50,000 planes, few Americans believed that manufacturers could meet the quota. The federal government, however, provided funds for the construction of new factories and offered attractive incentives to private manufacturers such as the Boeing Company, Douglas, Ryan, and Lockheed, and Consolidated Vultee. Utilizing the continuous assembly line and other techniques of mass production, these three companies built half of the 300,000 airplanes manufactured in the United States between 1941 and 1945. They also laid the foundations for a vast aerospace and missile industry that developed after the war.

1942-1944 • Shipbuilding ~ The war created an unprecedented boom in shipbuilding as well. Henry J. Kaiser, a former contractor and builder who went into ship building when the United States entered the war, along with his son, Edgar, reduced the average time it took to construct a merchant vessel from 300 days in 1940 to 80 days by 1942. Kaiser achieved these extraordinary results by using prefabricated materials, coordinating diverse manufacturing processes, and motivating his employees with high wages and attractive benefits, such as daycare centers and generous medical insurance. In 1944 workers at the Alabama Dry Dock and Shipbuilding Company in Mobile, Alabama completed a merchant ship, the Tule Canyon, in a record seventy-nine days. At his shipyards in Norfolk, Virginia and New Orleans, Louisiana, Andrew Jackson Higgins produced PT boats in about two weeks.

1941-1945 • Coal and Petroleum ~ Rearmament stimulated a demand for coal and oil that was nearly insatiable. Coal mining had been mired in a depression since the end of the First World War. With the outbreak of the Second World War, coal mines operated at full capacity for the first time in a generation, creating thousands of new jobs.

Even more spectacular growth took place in the petroleum industry, which had suffered depressed conditions since 1929. The demand for lubricants and fuel prompted desperate operators to reopen old wells. Intensive new drilling made Texas and Louisiana the leading oil pro-

(circa 1948) The Louisiana Story. Standard Oil Company attempted to document oil discoveries in Louisiana for marketing purposes. Seen here, Robert Flaherty, (1884-1951) the American documentary pioneer, directs 'Louisiana Story' about an oil strike.

ducing states in the nation. These developments, in turn, led to a vast increase in the construction of oil refining facilities and provided the basis for an extensive petrochemical industry that was essential for the manufacture of plastics.

1940-1945 • Steel and Aluminum ~ A new steel industry developed in the United States as the result of war. The federal government subsidized the construction of new steel mills in Provo, Utah, operated by the United States Steel Corporation, and federal funds also made it possible for Henry J. Kaiser to build a steel mill in Fontana, California. Older mills, like those in Birmingham, Alabama, operated at full capacity for the first time in more than a decade.

Similarly, the aluminum industry increased its output during the war. Before 1940 the Aluminum Company of America (Alcoa) had enjoyed a virtual monopoly in the industry. The demands of war, however, and especially the needs of aircraft manufacturers, made its production inadequacies so painfully obvious that Roosevelt persuaded Congress to authorize more than $300 million for the construction of seven new aluminum manufacturing plants in the Columbia River Valley, where the Bonneville and Grand Coulee federal power projects furnished inexpensive electricity.

1941-1944 • The Rubber Industry ~ Of the major industries stimulated by the war, the manufacture of synthetic rubber was the most prominent. When Japanese forces captured the Dutch East Indies in 1941, they cut off the principal American source of natural rubber. President Roosevelt immediately ordered the development of an artificial substitute. The Reconstruction Finance Corporation contributed more than $400 million to the effort to underwrite research and construct new manufacturing facilities. As a result of these efforts, American factories by 1944 were producing more than 800,000 tons of synthetic rubber.

1940-1945 • Agriculture ~ American farmers also increased productivity during the war by almost 33.3 percent. They provided food not only for domestic consumption and American troops, but for the Allies as well, especially Great Britain and the Soviet Union. Expansion of the armed forces indirectly benefited cotton and tobacco farmers as the demand for uniforms and cigarettes grew exponentially.

The achievement of American farmers was all the more remarkable because the farm population declined by 17 percent between 1940 and 1945, as agricultural workers moved to the cities in search of lucrative jobs in the defense industry or joined the armed services. Farmers sometimes employed German and Italian prisoners of war or migrant workers from Jamaica and the Bahamas as an alternative, or turned to the production of fruits, vegetables, and other less labor-intensive crops. Increased mechanization, such as the use of tractors, the invention of a mechanical cotton picker, and the development of chemical fertilizers and insecticides, also helped farmers to overcome the shortage of agricultural labor and meet the high production quotas the federal government had set.

The war at last effected the consolidation of farms, with larger units absorbing smaller ones. As a result of the war, American agriculture became a large-scale operation dependent on mechanization and diversified production.

1942-1944 • Labor ~ By 1942, the American economy had attained the once elusive goal of full employment. At the end of the war, more than 53 million Americans were at work, including teenagers, women, the elderly, and minorities previously excluded by discrimination.

Women in particular made indispensable contributions to the wartime economy. Mobilization accelerated the movement of women into the work force. Between 1940 and 1945, the number of working women increased from 12 million to 18.6 million, a rise of 55 percent. At the end of the war, women constituted more than 33.3 percent of the American work force, up from just 27 percent in 1940.

Most women worked in shipyards, aircraft factories, and ordnance depots. In 1939, only 36 women were employed in ship construction. By 1942 that number had grown to 200,000 and increased to 800,000 by 1945. When investigators for the Women's Bureau of the Labor Department surveyed seven aircraft plants in April 1941, they found only 143

(1943) Servicewomen look at a design of artificial silk-plated stocking, called 731, specially designed for servicewomen at a fashion show at Kennards of Croydon.

women employed. Within eighteen months, by October 1942, that number had risen to 65,000. Women did every conceivable kind of work. In shipyards and factories they welded, assembled parts, riveted, operated cranes, and performed clerical duties.

Between 1941 and 1944 the federal government itself hired almost 1 million women. The number of women employed in the civil service increased from 200,000 in 1939 to 1 million in 1944, constituting 38 percent of civil service workers.

1940-1945 • Unions ~ The need to keep workers on the job during the war greatly enhanced the influence and leverage of labor unions. The number of workers belonging to an independent union rose appreciably, from 8.9 million in 1940 to 14.8 million by 1945. Yet, the generally cooperative spirit that characterized the United States during the war for the most part averted damaging strikes.

American workers, however, like their counterparts in business and agriculture, discovered that large organizations had become vital to achieving their twin objectives of full employment and economic security.

1939-1945 • Income and Debt ~ The rapid increase in wartime productivity brought a corresponding rise in the national income, from $72.6 billion in 1939 to $181.5 billion in 1945. The Gross National Product (GNP) also soared from $90.5 billion in 1939 to $211.9 billion in 1945. Unfortunately, so did the national debt. Nevertheless, by the end of the war, the performance of the economy enabled most Americans to think of the Great Depression, which the New Deal could not reverse, as nothing more than a bad dream.

The Economic Legacy of the Second World War

Mobilization for war rejuvenated the American economy. If the productivity of American industry and agriculture became the envy of the world, it demonstrated to Americans themselves the enormous economic potential of the United States that had languished during the 1930s. Before 1929, the majority of Americans considered the economy to be the domain of private enterprise. The hardships of the depression and the affluence of wartime persuaded them instead that management of the economy was among the most important responsibilities of government. Only government intervention, it seemed, could sustain full employment, maximum productivity, and economic prosperity.

During the depression and the war the federal government had gained tremendous control over the national economy. Through such mechanisms as deficit spending, unbalanced budgets, and the manipulation of interest rates to adjust the pace of growth, the government sought to ensure economic stability. Government supervision of the economy in cooperation with business had produced extraordinary results during the war; Americans hoped this partnership would continue to work its magic in the post-war era.

Between the Great Depression and the Second World War Americans embraced a mixed economy dominated by big corporations operating in conjunction with an intricate network of federal, state, and local regulatory agencies. For good or ill, Americans put their economic faith in the efficacy of the regulatory state, which, during the second half of the twentieth century, accorded to government a primary role in directing the economic life of the nation.

Bibliography

Please see the composite bibliography at the end of Part III.

Mark Malvasi
Randolph Macon College

ECONOMY SINCE 1945: AFFLUENCE AND ANXIETY

~

(1978) A sign reading 'Sorry No Petrol' outside a service station during a gas shortage, a common sight in the mid 1970s.

TIMELINE

1945-1959 ~ Post-war Prosperity

Farmers Home Administration makes loans available for farmers to buy or modernize their houses (1946) / Full Employment Act is passed to promote increased employment but does not specify how the government will accomplish this (1946) / Taft-Hartley Act limits unions' political activities and prohibits a long list of labor practices, as well as empowering the president to postpone major strikes for an eighty-day "cooling off" period (1947) / Truman's Fair Deal extends Social Security and the minimum wage to more workers (1948) / General Agreement on Tariffs and Trade expands trade opportunities (1947-1948) / Diner's Club introduces the first general-purpose credit card (1950) / The Keynesian Revolution proposes lowering interest rates, sponsoring public works projects, and undertaking massive government spending in order to increase employment (1948-1952) / Consumer debt rises 800% (1945-1957)

MILESTONES: Marshall Plan to restore Europe is implemented (1946) • President Truman ends workers' strikes (1946) • First electronic computer, ENIAC, is developed (1946) • Truman Doctrine aligns U.S. with Western Hemisphere nations (1947) • House Un-American Activities Committee's investigation of communism in Hollywood (1947) • NATO established (1949) • Korean War (1950-1953) • End of "separate but equal" school segregation (1954) • Federal troops intervene in Little Rock to enforce integration orders (1956) • Soviet satellite Sputnik is launched (1957) • Alaska, Hawaii become states (1959)

1960-1969 ~ The New Frontier and The Great Society

Housing Act includes mortgage interest subsidies for low- and moderate-income rental housing and condominiums, and a subsidy for apartments for the elderly in public housing projects (1961) / President Kennedy signs bills designed to provide investment tax credits, greater depreciation allowances, and increased government spending to increase the number of jobs (1961) / Kennedy initiates the first deliberate use of fiscal policy to ignite and sustain economic expansion (1962) / Multi-billion dollar tax cut prompt greater consumer spending and capital investment (1964) / Gross National Product, driven by increased military expenditures to fund American involvement in Vietnam, nearly doubles during the 1960s

MILESTONES: U.S. adopts a policy to "contain" the Soviet Union to its current borders (1960s) • Introduction of Civil Rights legislation (1962) • Kennedy vows support to West Germany (1962) • Bay of Pigs (1961), Cuban Missile crisis (1962) • 200,000 Civil Rights supporters march on Washington with Dr. Martin Luther King, Jr. (1963) • President Kennedy assassinated (1963) • Civil Rights Act declares that American citizens cannot be segregated in public accommodations or discriminated against in employment (1964) • Gulf of Tonkin Resolution begins official U.S. involvement in Vietnam (1964) • Clean Air Act sets pollution guidelines (1967) • Soviets send a man into space (1967) • Martin Luther King, Jr. and Robert Kennedy assassinated (1968) • Blacks riot across the U.S. after MLK's assassination (1968) • Americans land on the moon (1969)

1970-1979 ~ A Faltering Economy

Decline of industrial productivity after the Vietnam War materials production ceases (1973) / President Nixon's wage and price controls attempt to control inflation (1973) / Arab Oil Embargo causes fuel shortages worldwide (1973) / President Carter deregulates airlines and trucking industries (1976) / Rising interest rates and soaring inflation fuel a deep recession (1973-1980) / Congress approves tax cut totaling $34 billion, raises the minimum wage by 50 percent, increases farm price supports, and eases environmental restrictions on industries (1977)

MILESTONES: U.S. escalates war into Cambodia (1970) • National Guard combats riots at Kent State (1970) • First Earth Day (1970) • Easing of trade restrictions on China (1972) • Minimum voting age lowered to 18 (1972) • Oil exploration in Alaska authorized (1972) • Nixon becomes the first U.S. president to visit China (1972) • Courts uphold right to abortion in *Roe v. Wade* (1973) • Watergate incident forces government to investigate presidential crimes (1973) • Nixon resigns (1974) • U.S. withdraws last troops from Saigon (1975) • Hostages taken from the U.S. embassy in Teheran (1979)

1981-1990 ~ The Reagan Revolution

Congress cuts federal spending on domestic social programs by $41 billion, severely curtailing or abolishing welfare payments, food stamps, Medicaid, medical care for the indigent, and public housing programs (1981) / Congress approves $1.6 trillion expansion of the military budget designed to enhance national security and stimulate the domestic economy (1981) / Congress passes the Economic Recovery Tax Act, decreasing personal income taxes by 25 percent and lowering the maximum tax rate from 70 to 50 percent (1981) / Unemployment climbs to 10.8%, the highest level it had attained since the 1930s (1982) / Depository Institutions Act allows thrifts to offer federally-insured money market accounts to invest in residential and commercial real estate loans (1982) / Gramm-Rudman Act mandates automatic deficit reductions (1986) / Stock market loses more than 500 points and nearly 20% of its value in a single day (1987) / Savings-and-loan institutions begin collapsing, causing the worst banking crisis since the Depression (1988)

MILESTONES: Establishment of state lotteries in Arizona, California, Colorado, Florida, Idaho, Indiana, Iowa, Kansas, Kentucky, Missouri, Montana, Oregon, South Dakota, Virginia, West Virginia and Wisconsin (1980s) • Rise in 'contingent workforce' of temporary, leased, independently contracted, seasonal, and non-permanent part-time workers (1980s-1990s) • President Reagan disbands the Air Traffic Controllers union (1981) • *Challenger* space shuttle explodes killing six astronauts and the first private citizen, teacher Christa McAuliffe (1986) • AIDS becomes the second leading cause of death (following accidents) among American men aged 25-34 (1989)

1990-2000 ~ The Cyber Economy

GM introduces the first mass-marketed electric car, the Saturn EV1 (1990) / Travel and tourism is the second largest industry in the U.S. after health (1992) / Value of all corporate mergers increase nearly ten-fold (1992-1998) / North American Free Trade Agreement opens trade borders to Mexico and Canada (1993) / 27,600 corporations merge, more than in the entire decade of the 1980s (1995-1997) / One million households apply for personal bankruptcy (1998) / E-commerce companies vie for Internet consumers (1998-2000)

MILESTONES: Clean Air Act requires automobile manufacturers to begin developing alternative fuel vehicles (1991) • Family and Medical Leave Act provides worker security during family emergencies (1993) • Bombing of World Trade Center in New York City (1993) • ATF assaults the Branch Davidian Compound in Waco, TX leading to a 51 day stand off (1993) • Louis Farrakhan, the spiritual leader of The Nation of Islam, organizes the Million Man March – the call for black men to take more of a role with their families (1995) • Unionized workers earn nearly one-third more than nonunion workers and receive health and pension benefits (1998) • For the first time, the Hispanic population equals the African American population (2000)

INTRODUCTION

Not until prosperity evaporated during the tumultuous 1970s and the chaotic 1980s did Americans fully realize that, in the thirty years following the end of the Second World War, they had passed through an exceptional, and perhaps a unique, period in the economic history of their nation. They may have taken so long to recognize the uncommon character of the age because the economic developments that took place during the 1950s and 1960s did not seem all that revolutionary. The phenomenal expansion of the economy initially appeared to be a continuation of what had happened during the war, from which the United States emerged controlling nearly 67 percent of world industrial production.

Moreover, during the 1950s and 1960s, the performance of the U.S. economy was not as impressive as was that of other countries, for the simple reason that the American economic behemoth had much less room to grow. Between 1950 and 1973, the U.S. economy grew at a rate slower than that of any other industrialized nation except Great Britain. The gap in productivity per man-hour between the United States and other countries steadily narrowed, and by the 1970s and 1980s France, Germany, Japan, and even Britain approximated the national wealth of the United States.

Comparison of Industrial Growth Rates, 1956-65

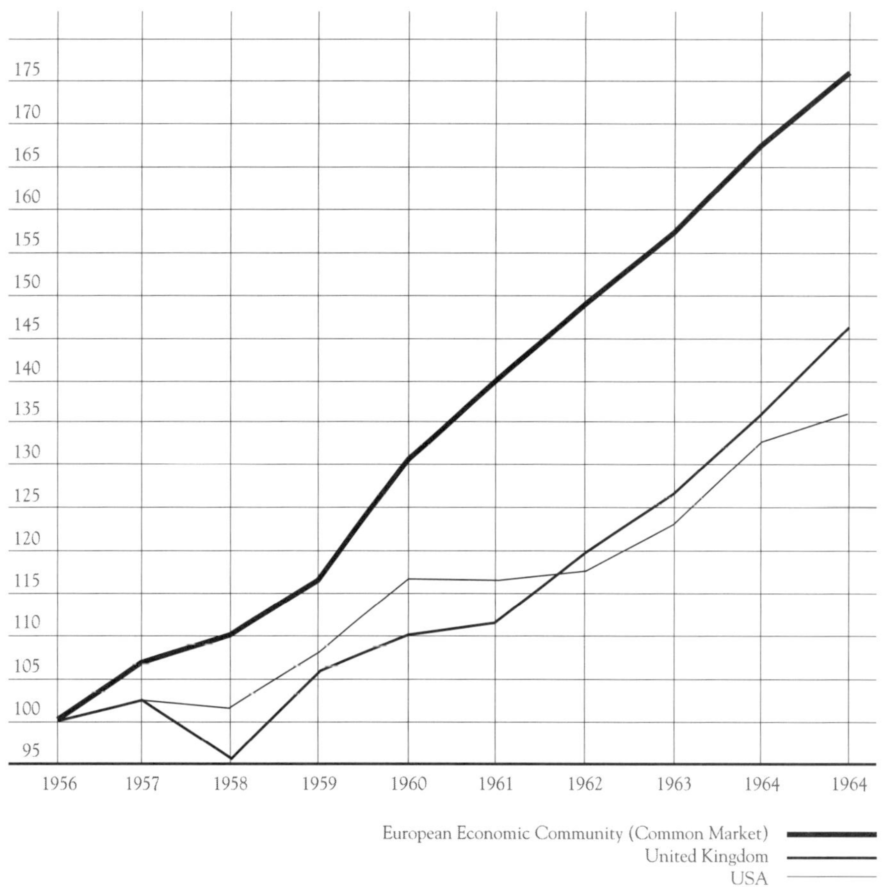

SOURCE: J.H. Hexter and Richard Pipes. *Europe Since 1500*. New York: Harper & Row, 1968.

Yet, the United States did prosper during the 1950s and 1960s as it had at no other time in its history. Toward the end of the Second World War, American political leaders, uncertain about the real strength and vitality of the wartime economy, determined to prevent the reappearance of depression. Along with many American businessmen, they now believed that the unrestrained free market was no longer viable. To ensure uninterrupted prosperity, they resolved to subject the economy to careful government planning and management, as had been the case during the two world wars. "People in this country," proclaimed the American statesman Averell Harriman in 1946, "are no longer scared of such words as 'planning'. . .people have accepted the fact that government has got to plan as well as individuals."

Although the economic system never worked as its architects predicted or intended, it still generated unprecedented affluence for the majority of American citizens, to say nothing of its sustaining international capitalism for twenty-five years. The economic crises that assailed the United States beginning in 1973 brought this affluence to an end. At the same time, they put into sharper focus the extraordinary accomplishments of the era, as politicians and businessmen struggled to coax its return.

1945-1961
The Road to Prosperity

1945-1946 • Postwar Problems ~ Without a clear blueprint to follow, President Harry S. Truman soon became lost in a maze of complex problems as he struggled to guide the American economy out of war. Even before the Japanese surrendered in August 1945, for example, Truman found it impossible to resist pressure from both Congress and the American people to dismantle wartime economic regulations. As he did so, freeing business once again to manage its own affairs, corporate profits soared by 20 percent throughout 1946.

At the same time, however, labor discontent spread. By January 1946, three percent of the labor force, including workers in such key industries as auto and steel manufacturing and meat packing, were simultaneously on strike. When a new round of strikes occurred in the spring of 1946, particularly one involving the railroads, an angry Truman threatened railroad workers with a military draft even after the union agreed to cancel the walkout. Of the wartime economic controls, only those governing prices remained. A feud between Congress and the president allowed these to lapse suddenly in June 1946, producing the worst inflation in American history. The price of agricultural commodities, for instance, rose by nearly 14 percent in one month and by almost 30 percent before the end of the year. A popular Republican campaign slogan informed the American people that "To err is Truman."

1947 • The Taft-Hartley Act ~ Apparently most Americans agreed, for in the off-year elections of 1946, the Democratic party lost eleven seats in the Senate and fifty-four in the House of Representatives. For the first time since the administration of Herbert Hoover, the Republicans were the majority party when the 80th Congress convened in 1947. Yet, the Republicans offered few alternatives to Truman's erratic and faltering economic policies.

Their most important contribution was the Taft-Hartley Act of 1947, an expression of congressional hostility toward organized labor that had been simmering for a decade. A complicated law, the Taft-Hartley Act required financial statements from unions, limited their political activities, and prohibited a long list of so-called unfair labor practices. It also empowered the president to intercede to postpone a major strike for an eighty-day "cooling off" period and permitted state governments to pass "right-to-work" laws that protected workers from being forced to join unions. The Taft-Hartley Act may have slowed the growth and diminished the influence of unions after the Second World War, but it did nothing to disrupt the cordial relations that prevailed between corporate management and organized labor.

1946 • The Fair Deal ~ Amid the welter of demobilization and the maneuvering of various economic interest groups that took place in 1946, Truman had demanded that Congress make the preservation of full employment a national priority. Congress responded by passing the Full Employment Act of 1946 "to promote maximum employment, production, and purchasing power." Although the law made full employment the responsibility of the federal government, Congress neglected to specify how that goal might be met.

Truman had ideas of his own. After winning the presidential election of 1948, Truman announced a comprehensive program of domestic and economic reform, which he called the "Fair Deal." Intended the reach "every segment of the population and every individual," the Fair Deal extended such measures as Social Security and the minimum wage. Congress, though, rejected substantial portions of Truman's economic program, turning aside proposals to establish national health insurance, a Fair Employment Practices Commission (FEPC), a new system of crop subsidies, and a planned regional economy for the Missouri and the Columbia river valleys similar in conception to the Tennessee Valley Authority (TVA) established during the Great Depression.

1946-1952 • The Government and the Economy ~ Despite resistance to expanding government supervision of the economy, nothing could relieve the government of the responsibility it had assumed under Franklin Roosevelt for the economic welfare of the United States. The Full Employment Act had made the bond between business and government explicit by establishing the Council of Economic Advisors. The law enjoined these experts to study economic trends and to suggest ways of avoiding or controlling fluctuations in the business cycle.

During the late 1940s and early 1950s, few politicians and businessmen could have failed to recognize the intimate connection between government economic policy and economic growth. The Gross National Product (GNP) had risen 67 percent during the Second World War. More astonishing, government expenditures accounted for 40 percent of the GNP by 1945. Although government expenditures declined after the war, they remained seven times greater than in the 1930s and double the percentage of the GNP during the New Deal.

The federal government also dominated the credit system simply by virtue of funding the huge national debt and regulated credit and the money supply through the policies of the Federal Reserve Board.

Table 1: The Gross National Product, 1946-1961

Year	Total GNP in billions of dollars*
1946	$312.6
1947	309.9
1948	323.7
1949	324.1
1950	355.3
1951	383.4
1952	395.1
1953	412.8
1954	407.0
1955	438.0
1956	446.1
1957	452.5
1958	447.3
1959	475.9
1960	487.7
1961	497.2

* 1958 prices

SOURCE: *Historical Statistics of the United States*, Part 1, p. 224.

Table 2: Summary of Federal Government Finances, 1946-1961

Year	Receipts	Outlays	Surplus Deficit	Total Gross Federal Debt in billions of dollars
1946	$43.5	$61.7	-$18.2	$271
1947	43.5	36.9	6.6	257.1
1948	45.4	36.5	8.9	252.0
1949	41.6	40.6	1.0	252.6
1950	40.9	43.1	-2.2	256.9
1951	53.4	45.8	7.6	255.3
1952	68.0	68.0	0.0	259.1
1953	71.5	76.8	-5.3	266.0
1954	69.7	70.9	-1.2	270.8
1955	65.5	68.5	-3.0	274.4
1956	74.5	70.5	4.1	272.8
1957	80.0	76.7	3.2	272.4
1958	79.6	82.8	-2.9	279.7
1959	79.2	92.1	-12.9	287.8
1960	92.5	92.2	0.3	290.9
1961	94.4	97.8	-3.4	292.9

SOURCE: *Historical Statistics of the United States*, Part 2, p. 1105.

1946-1952 • Fiscal and Monetary Policy ~ Instead of wholesale economic planning, the most promising formula for managing the American economy after the Second World War seemed to be fiscal and monetary policy, conducted largely through manipulation of tax and interest rates. If the economy faltered, the government could lower interest rates and taxes, thereby expanding the money supply, easing access to credit, increasing its own expenditures, and elevating the deficit. If an economic boom threatened inflation, the government could raise interest rates and taxes, thereby contracting the money supply, restricting access to credit, reducing its own expenditures, and lowering the deficit. This concept became the model for managing the economy through the end of the century.

1946-1952

1948-1952 • The Keynesian "Revolution" ~ This general economic policy reflected the ideas and influence of the English political economist John Maynard Keynes. During the Great Depression of the 1930s, Keynes had urged governments to intervene into the economy to promote full employment whenever the free market failed to do so. He proposed lowering interest rates, sponsoring public works projects, and undertaking massive government spending. Keynes's advice contradicted the accepted methods of battling recession and depression: retrenchment and thrift. Governments, he asserted, ought to spend their way out of economic hardship. Although Keynes's theories had helped to shape the New Deal, it was not until after the Second World War, with the publication of the first edition of Paul Samuelson's now classic undergraduate economics textbook in 1947, that they began to gain widespread currency in the United States.

Like the majority of American politicians, President Truman did not adequately appreciate the principles of Keynesian economics. Even had he mastered them, Truman was ill disposed to recast the fiscal powers of federal government into public policy. He shared Americans' aversion to budget deficits and periodically attacked what he considered irresponsible government spending. John W. Snyder, Truman's secretary of the treasury, regarded the national debt as an unfortunate government burden, not as an instrument with which to direct the economy. Only in the 1960s did American officials at last begin to apply Keynes's precepts in the way he had envisioned.

(1952) A cartoon criticizing President Truman's Fair Deal program, which was an attempt to move beyond the New Deal established by his predecessor, President Roosevelt. The cartoon shows the Fair Deal as a facade built on bad foundations of war spending and inflation.

1952 • Eisenhower's Economic Policy ~ Even after the partisan bickering of the late 1940s and early 1950s had subsided, the new president, Dwight D. Eisenhower, remained as reluctant as Truman had been to apply Keynesian methods or to constrain the federal government to oversee the economy. From the outset, Eisenhower made it clear that his was a pro-business administration dominated by a commitment to free enterprise. Yet, eager to sustain and advance economic prosperity, Eisenhower also introduced legislative measures that built on the economic programs of the New Deal and the Fair Deal.

During his first months in office, Eisenhower seemed determined to reduce federal controls on business and to reverse the economic laws and policies adopted over the previous twenty years. Secretary of Defense Charles E. Wilson, a former president of the General Motors Corporation, summarized Eisenhower's economic policy declaring that "what was good for our country was good for General Motors, and vice versa." In cooperation with the Secretary of the Treasury, George Humphrey, Eisenhower created the impression that he would cut the national budget and minimize the role of government in economic affairs. During the two recessions that took place in the 1950s, Eisenhower resisted the Keynesian mechanisms of deficit spending, unbalanced budgets, and intervention into the private sector that many economists advised him were necessary to revive the economy. Instead, Eisenhower remained steadfastly opposed "to going too far with trying to fool with our economy." Opposition to government regulation of the economy, for example, led to the dismantling of the Reconstruction Finance Corporation (RFC), which Herbert Hoover had established to combat the Great Depression. Eisenhower objected to creating "huge federal bureaucracies of the PWA or WPA type."

1953-1954 • Eisenhower's Economic Reality ~ Eisenhower's opinion notwithstanding, the federal government continued of necessity to mediate the operation of the economy. His evident determination to balance the federal budget and avoid amassing huge deficits gave way to pragmatic attempts to end recession. Only three times in eight years did Eisenhower balance the federal budget (See Table 2), and he ended his presidency with a budget nearly double that of Truman's administration before the outbreak of the Korean War required an enormous increase in government spending.

When Eisenhower responded to the recession of 1953-1954 with the firm assurance that he would not rekindle the New Deal and was content simply to wait for a market adjustment to restore prosperity, he endured a deafening outcry from the American people. Union leaders, workers, farmers, professionals, and consumers demanded more, not less, protection, support, assistance, and money from the government. Under pressure from a variety of constituencies, the Eisenhower administration revealed that its devotion to free enterprise was more talk than action.

A political and economic realist, Eisenhower engineered a quick reversal of policy and adopted measures to counter the downturn in the economy. The federal government continued and, in some instances, expanded subsidies to agriculture, industry, and business. The Department of the Treasury and the Federal Reserve agreed that they ought to monitor the national debt and regulate interest rates so that credit could expand in a weak economy and contract during periods of inflation. Congress agreed to support the economy and aid recovery by adjusting tax rates and federal spending. Near the end of his second term in 1961, Eisenhower acknowledged that federal assistance to ensure economic prosperity was no longer an undertaking to be avoided at all costs. It was now unavoidably the responsibility of the government, he conceded, to preserve the economic welfare of the nation.

1950s • The Economics of Peace ~ Despite Eisenhower's somewhat uncertain policies and the onset of two recessions during the 1950s, the Gross National Product (GNP) rose to more than $476 billion (See Table 1) by the end of the decade and the peacetime economy spread out an unrivaled and apparently limitless feast of goods and services. A combination of government expenditures, private investment, consumer borrowing, and population growth enabled the United States, with only six percent of the world's people, to produce and consume approximately 33 percent of the world's

(circa 1955) A woman standing in front of a pawn shop's advertisement painted on a wall in Louisville, Kentucky.

1950s

economic output. After the Second World War, the standard of living for the majority of Americans improved dramatically, even though 20 percent of the population continued to live in poverty.

The other key element in the postwar economic surge was the increased productivity of American agriculture and industry. Between 1945 and 1970, the yield per acre of wheat doubled, and the yield per acre of corn tripled. As a result, food in the United States became abundant and inexpensive. While the number of farm laborers continued to decrease, falling by approximately 30 percent during the 1950s, total agricultural production increased by a similar percentage. Technological innovations that revolutionized cultivation made American farms the most productive in the world.

At the same time, American factories turned out an unprecedented quantity and variety of goods. By investing an average of $10 billion annually in capital equipment, by introducing automation into the manufacturing process, by relying on electrical energy, and by funding research in such applied sciences as chemistry and electronics, American industrialists exceeded all previous expectations for productivity.

In addition, the increased use of plastics and aluminum in manufacturing marked the end of the old "smokestack industries," which had been the mainstay of the American economy since the 1870s, and the emergence of new "light industries" based on sophisticated technology. The changes in manufacturing that occurred during the 1950s proved immensely profitable to American business. The largest corporations averaged $500 million in sales, ten times the volume of the 1920s.

1945-1957 • The Postwar Consumer Economy ~ The principal beneficiaries of the postwar agricultural and industrial boom were American consumers, who took full advantage of easy credit to borrow and buy at a dizzying pace. Between 1945 and 1957, consumer debt in the United States rose 800 percent as Americans purchased everything from household appliances and television sets to sporting equipment and swimming pools, all unimaginable luxuries only a generation earlier.

Entertainment also consumed a major share of the family budget. Expenditures on leisure activities more than doubled between 1950 and 1960, increasing from 7 to 15 percent of the GNP. By 1960, it cost approximately $85 billion a year to satisfy the American demand for pleasure. Working fewer hours and earning higher wages than ever before, and profiting from a minuscule inflation rate of between one and two percent, Americans spent twice as much on travel, liquor, movies, and sports than they once had on rent. Expendable (extra) income rose from $57 in 1950 to $80 in 1959, providing Americans the opportunity to "splurge" on items that were once considered luxuries. And, while expendable income rose, inflation generally decreased, making goods and services less expensive to purchase.

Inflation Rate, 1947-1969

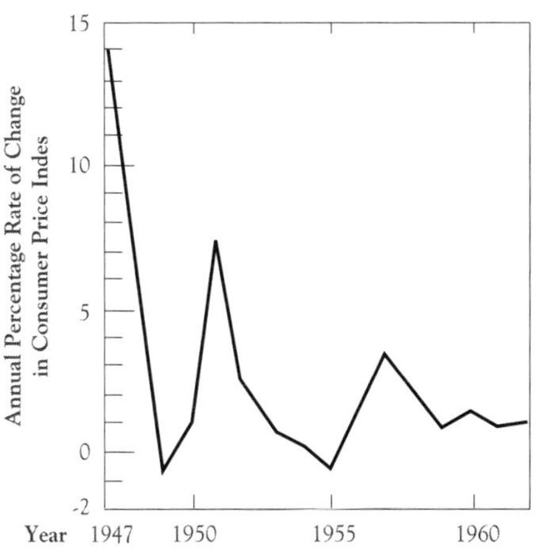

Table 3: Distribution of Durable Consumer Goods in American Families, 1946-1956

Percentage of Families Owning:

	Automobiles	Televisions	Refrigerators	Freezers
1946	N/A	—	69.1	—
1947	N/A	—	71.2	—
1948	54	2.9	76.6	4.3
1949	56	10.1	79.2	5.2
1950	60	26.4	86.4	7.2
1951	65	38.5	86.7	9.3
1952	65	50.2	89.2	11.5
1953	65	63.5	90.4	13.4
1954	70	74.1	92.5	15.1
1955	71	76.1	94.1	16.8
1956	73	81.0	96.0	18.0

	Vacuum Cleaners	Electric Washers	Dryers	Air Conditioners
	48.8	50.5	—	0.2
	49.5	63.0	—	0.2
	51.7	67.4	0.4	0.3
	52.8	68.6	0.7	0.4
	56.5	71.9	1.4	0.6
	57.7	73.5	2.4	0.8
	59.4	76.2	3.7	1.4
	60.5	78.5	5.1	2.6
	62.2	81.3	6.6	4.0
	64.3	84.1	9.2	5.6
	66.7	86.8	11.9	7.6

SOURCES: Ralph Freeman, ed. *Post-War Economic Trends in the United States* (New York: Harper & Row, Publishers, Inc.); John Patrick Diggins, *The Proud Decades: America in War and Peace, 1941-1960* (New York: W.W. Norton & Company, 1989), p. 186.

1950s

1950s • The Military-Industrial Complex ~ The booming consumer economy did not by itself account for post-war American prosperity. During the 1950s military expenditures came to dominate the national budget and were crucial to maintaining economic health. Defense spending rose from $13 billion in 1949 to $22 billion in 1951, and topped the $50 billion mark in 1953. By 1960, the federal government was annually devoting between five and six percent of the GNP to military expenses.

Table 4: Defense Spending, 1950-1990

Year	Total Expenditures in billions of dollars
1950	$13,119
1960	45,908
1970	80,295
1980	134,000
1990	293,600

SOURCES: *Historical Statistics of the United States, Part 2*, p. 1116. U.S. Department of Management and Budget, *Budget of the United States, Fiscal Year 2000*. John W. Wright, ed., *New York Times Almanac 2000* (New York: Penguin Reference Books, 1999), p. 161.

Directly or indirectly, defense spending financed the research that led to the most important technological developments of the postwar era. In addition, giant corporations such as General Electric, General Motors, and Douglas Aircraft began subcontracting portions of their military work to smaller companies. Were the government to cancel a huge defense contract, the jolt would have reverberated throughout the entire economy and disrupted efforts to sustain prosperity.

The deepening attachment between government and industry worried President Eisenhower. In his "Farewell Address," delivered only days before the inauguration of John F. Kennedy, Eisenhower cautioned Americans about "the acquisition of unwarranted influence, whether sought or unsought, by the military-industrial complex." Despite a long and distinguished military career, Eisenhower was an old-fashioned American troubled by large military budgets and a burgeoning defense industry. He saw in both of these developments a threat to traditional democratic practices, individual rights, and limited government.

1950s • Multinational Corporations ~ Multinational corporations also strengthened the connection between the national and global economies. Before the Second World War, nearly all foreign subdivisions of American corporations had been small, dependent outposts of the parent companies. After the war, American businessmen gravitated to poorer nations in which costs were low, governments accommodating, and markets inviting. By the 1950s, corporate offshoots of American companies were thriving throughout Europe, Asia, Africa, and the Near East. Still tied to the United States and yet assimilated into foreign nations, the subsidiaries gave an increasingly international focus to American economic life.

1950s • The Expansion of Business Abroad ~ Yet, multinational corporations were only the most evident aspect of business expansion that took place after the Second World War. In 1946, American private investment in overseas enterprises approximated what it had been in 1929. Within a dozen years it had more than tripled, while total U.S. investment more than doubled.

By 1970, private investment abroad ($120.2 billion) was nearly nine times greater than it had been in 1946.

Investors expended the bulk of this capital to fund the search for minerals and other raw materials that American industry either lacked or used up at a rate faster than it could replenish; the drilling for and refining of oil alone accounted for 33 percent of all overseas investment. American economic prosperity was thus coming more fully to depend on foreign resources and foreign markets, to say nothing of the policies of foreign governments.

Historically, the United States government had regarded its vital interests as confined primarily to the Western Hemisphere. In the years following the Second World War, American politicians and businessmen came to view events in distant lands as potentially jeopardizing national economic interests, which they were bound to protect and defend by negotiation if possible and by force if necessary. Such were the fruits of the emergence of the United States as the greatest economic power on earth.

Table 5: U.S. Investment Abroad, 1946-1958
in billions of dollars

Year	Total Investment	Private	Government
1946	$39.4	$13.5	$25.9
1947	48.3	14.9	33.4
1948	52.5	16.3	36.2
1949	53.9	16.9	37.0
1950	54.4	19.0	35.4
1951	56.4	20.8	35.6
1952	59.1	22.7	36.4
1953	60.2	23.8	36.4
1954	62.4	26.6	35.8
1955	65.1	29.1	35.9
1956	70.8	33.4	37.4
1957	76.4	36.9	39.5
1958	79.2	41.1	38.1

SOURCE: *Historical Statistics of the United States, Part 2*, p. 869.

1950s • The Other America ~ For all the wealth that the United States accumulated during the 1950s, there still remained the "invisible poor," which Michael Harrington poignantly described in *The Other America* (1962). Harrington wrote of a "culture of poverty," the inhabitants of which "did not suffer the extreme privation of the peasants of Asia or the tribesmen of Africa, yet the mechanism of the misery is similar. They are beyond history, beyond progress, sunk in a paralyzing, maiming routine." Perhaps as many as 50 million Americans, Harrington estimated, were the victims of this culture of poverty, living "on the outskirts of hope."

1950s

More than half of all Native Americans and nearly half of all African Americans made up a vast segment of the poor. In addition, approximately 2.5 million itinerant agricultural workers had an annual income of less than $1,000. Men and women who worked at menial jobs that paid less than $1 per hour, the unemployed who scraped by on welfare, and the eight million elderly who lived on a monthly Social Security payment of $70 constituted other impoverished groups. Single women, who routinely earned 60 percent of what men received and often worked at jobs not covered by minimum wage laws or Social Security, were also counted disproportionately among the poor. Finally, the Appalachian region, which extended from western Pennsylvania to northern Alabama, was a breeding ground for mass poverty.

(1952) Marchers protesting the cost of meat during a May Day Parade in New York.

1961-1968 Between 20 and 25 percent of the American population during the affluent 1950s earned less than $4,000 a year. The bottom 20 percent of American families earned only 4.7 percent of total personal income, while the highest 20 percent earned 45.5 percent. Perhaps the most serious problem facing poor Americans was the inability and unwillingness of the federal government or prosperous citizens to take systematic action to end their plight. In *The Other America*, Harrington lamented that "at precisely that moment in history where for the first time a people have the material ability to end poverty, they lack the will to do so. They cannot see; they cannot act. The consciences of the well-off are the victims of affluence."

1961-1968 • The New Frontier and the Great Society ~ In 1960 the United States was at the summit of its power and influence throughout the world. Europeans worried about "the American challenge" to their economic independence. The Japanese had yet fully to reconstruct an economy despoiled by war and so they, too, could not keep pace with the United States. Meanwhile, American fears about Soviet economic competition proved to be groundless. The United States enjoyed a decade of prosperity after recovering from the recession of 1958.

An economic upsurge roused by increased productivity made it possible to finance a massive program of social reform while simultaneously cutting taxes and holding inflation to a rate of about 3 percent a year until 1969. As the generation of baby boomers reached adolescence and young adulthood, they expanded the domestic market for goods and services ranging from automobiles to college educations. Increasingly, manufacturers, entrepreneurs, and advertisers sought to make money by appealing to the young.

1960-1962 • Kennedy's Economic Policy ~ By the 1960s, most Americans had developed a faith in government management of the economy that earlier generations had lacked or, perhaps more accurately, would have found inconceivable. Both Presidents John F. Kennedy and Lyndon B. Johnson embodied such expectations by seeking to enlarge the responsibilities of the federal government to administer the economy.

Kennedy represented a clear and hopeful alternative to Eisenhower who, by the end of his second term, had come to symbolize for many Americans economic lethargy and stagnation. Although Kennedy's record in domestic affairs is uneven at best, perhaps his most impressive and unambiguous successes came in his management of the economy. To overcome the small recession and an unemployment rate of seven percent that he had inherited from Eisenhower, Kennedy signed into law bills designed to provide investment tax credits, greater depreciation allowances, and increased government spending, all aimed at increasing the number of jobs. He also struggled to hold down prices, issuing federal wage and price guidelines to which labor and management generally adhered. When they did not, Kennedy intervened. After the United States Steel Corporation raised prices in April 1962, for example, Kennedy pressured the company until it bought prices back into line with federal regulations.

1964 • Kennedy's Policy in Action ~ Kennedy's economic policies generated an average annual growth rate for the GNP of 5.6 percent, an inflation rate of 1.3 percent, and a reduction in the unemployment rate from 7 to 5 percent. These accomplishments largely resulted from a multi-billion dollar tax cut implemented in 1964, which prompted greater consumer spending and capital investment. Increased spending and investment, in turn, led to greater productivity, economic expansion, more jobs, low inflation, and widespread prosperity.

Like Roosevelt, Truman, and Eisenhower, however, Kennedy loathed unbalanced budgets and deficit spending, and initially recoiled from adopting Keynesian mechanisms to simulate the economy. It was Walter Heller, the chief of Kennedy's Council of Economic Advisors, who convinced Kennedy to initiate the first deliberate use of fiscal policy to ignite and sustain economic expansion. The experiment worked. The tax cut combined with government spending fueled an economic boom that lasted until the end of the decade.

1964 • Johnson's "War on Poverty" ~ The five years that President Johnson spent in the White House are among the most important and divisive in American history. Johnson, who had been Kennedy's vice president, took office following Kennedy's assassination on November 22, 1963. More powerful and persuasive than every president except Franklin Roosevelt, Johnson pressed Congress to support his agenda for extensive economic and social reform. Johnson fought a "war on poverty" that he intended to win by creating the "Great Society." The Great Society, according to Johnson, rested on "abundance and liberty for all." It demanded "an end to poverty and racial injustice, to which we are totally committed in our time."

More explicitly than Kennedy, Johnson linked his economic program to his domestic and foreign policies. To carry out his initiatives at home and abroad, Johnson needed a strong and stable economic foundation. The combination of a tax cut and government spending in 1964 had produced dramatic results. The Gross National Product, also driven by increased military expenditures to fund American involvement in Vietnam, nearly doubled during the 1960s. The economy added 10 million new jobs and increased the median family income by 50 percent. At the same time, the number of Americans living below the poverty line also diminished by half, to approximately 11 percent of the total population.

1965-1969 • The Economic Limits of the Great Society ~ Yet, Johnson's economic program was never as revolutionary as some feared and others hoped. Liberals, who had argued for years that federal programs could bring the poor into the mainstream of national economic life, saw in Johnson's economic policies a realization of their hopes. Many complained, though, that Johnson's efforts remained inadequate. The annual budget for the War on Poverty never exceeded $2 billion, which amounted to less than one-quarter of 1 percent of the GNP. The Great Society programs did little to redistribute income and nothing to guarantee jobs. "For a mere $11 billion," declared liberal economist Robert Lekachman, "we could raise every poor American above the poverty line."

Johnson had no intention of transforming the War on Poverty into a welfare program. He relied instead on traditional American assumptions about self-sufficiency, hard work, education, opportunity, success, and progress. Nevertheless, Johnson's economic programs unmistakably committed the federal government to the direct and vigorous administration of the economy.

1969-1980 A Faltering Economy

1970s • A Decade of Decline ~ Government supervision of the economy produced only mixed results. Beginning in 1969, the United States along with most other industrialized nations endured a frustrating decade of rising inflation, soaring costs, diminishing resources, and contracting prosperity. The economic reforms that Johnson had carried out earlier in the 1960s did not end poverty. In some instances, such as with Medicare and Medicaid, they burdened the American people with increased federal deficits that further inhibited economic growth. Keynesian practice could not reverse, nor Keynesian theory explain, the declining productivity coupled with rampant inflation to which pundits gave the inelegant name "stagflation."

Twentieth-century liberals such as Kennedy and Johnson had regarded continuous economic growth as essential to carrying out a more just distribution of the social benefits of industrial capitalism. By the 1970s, economic realities made that assumption impossible to sustain. The performance of the American economy during the 1970s was generally dismal, precluding the extensive redistribution of wealth that the liberal supporters of Kennedy and Johnson had once envisioned.

1970s • What Went Wrong ~ Between 1969 and 1980 the economies of industrial nations, including, and perhaps especially, the United States, might profitably be compared to powerful but sputtering engines. The rising costs of oil combined with declining industrial productivity brought an end to the prosperity of the 1960s. Double digit inflation wreaked havoc on the American economy. Government deficits largely to fund expanded social welfare programs added to spiraling prices. The so-called peace dividend, which might have accrued with the end of the Vietnam War in 1972, disappeared into the entitlement payments made to various interest groups that no politician could afford to anger or alienate without risking electoral defeat. Finally, the continuing decline of older heavy industries such as steel manufacturing and their replacement by high-tech and financial-service enterprises caused painful economic and social dislocations, particularly in the industrial cities of the Northeast and Midwest.

1970s • Population and the Economy ~ Demographic change also influenced the economic stagnation of the 1970s. During the 1960s the baby boomers had constituted a large pool of cheap, entry-level workers. Entering the national market, they had helped to stimulate rising consumer demand for goods and services. By the 1970s, however, the American population had begun to age. Increasing numbers of Americans were reaching the end of their economically productive lives.

Despite this demographic shift, many young men and women who had been college students during the 1960s, and who may have taken entry-level positions upon graduation, now found their professional advancement blocked by a stagnant economy. Those who had majored in the humanities, the arts, or the social sciences often faced the worst economic prospects of all. For they were least prepared to take jobs in the high-tech and financial service industries that offered the best opportunities for employment during the 1970s and 1980s.

1970-1973 • Remedies for a Sick Economy ~ Johnson's unwillingness to raise taxes to finance his social programs and to pay for the war in Vietnam confronted his successor, Richard M. Nixon, with serious economic problems. At first, Nixon applied standard remedies to cure the economic ills. He reduced federal spending and slowed the growth of the money supply to curb inflation. These efforts only produced a sharp economic decline without a corresponding drop in

Unemployment in the U.S., 1947-1970

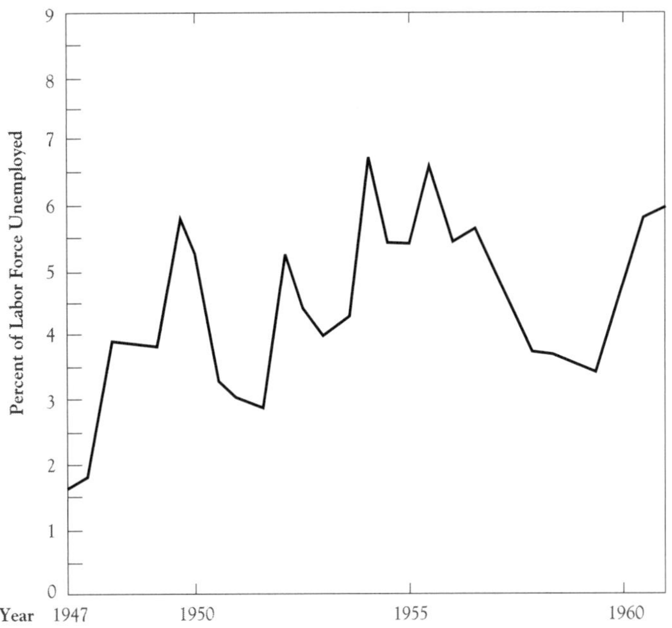

1970-1973

prices. Between 1969 and 1971 interest rates reached their highest levels in a century, the Dow Jones Industrial Index lost 30 percent of its value, unemployment swelled to 4.9 percent, and inflation accelerated to 5 percent, the worst it had been since the Korean War. For the first time since 1893 the United States also recorded a trade deficit, paying more for imports than it earned from exports. In 1970, the Gross National Product declined for the first time since the recession of 1958. Walter Heller, a former economic advisor to John F. Kennedy, derisively characterized falling productivity and rising prices as "Nixonomics."

1971-1973 • The Revival of Keynesian Policies ~ To solve these economic problems, Nixon effected a surprising reversal of policy. He embraced Keynesian doctrines that had formerly been the almost exclusive province of the Democrats and that Republicans had traditionally mistrusted if not scorned. Declaring that "I am now

1973

a Keynesian," Nixon adopted a strategy of deficit spending to stimulate economic growth. He also devalued the dollar to make American exports more attractive on the world market, and abandoned his promise never to cope with inflation by repeating the policies that the Office of Price Administration had imposed during the Second World War. Such "controls," he had maintained, "mean rationing, black markets, [and] inequitable administration."

Yet, when he could not bring inflation below 4 percent, Nixon, beginning in the summer of 1971, introduced wage and price controls. In December he attacked the trade deficit by devaluing the dollar. These departures from strict free market practices reduced inflation and produced the largest increase in the GNP since 1965. Economic recovery was short-lived, however, and Nixon's policies offered no permanent relief from the unprecedented "stagflation" that persisted throughout his first term in office. Price controls had temporarily kept prices from rising as fast as they otherwise would have, but they also resulted in shortages. Moreover, when Nixon removed the controls in 1973, inflation quickly became worse than it had previously been.

(1910) At the turn of the Century people knew that oil was a valuable commodity. Seen here is an oil boom town with battling figures over oil claims.

1973 • The Energy Crisis ~ Compounding Nixon's economic woes, shortly to be overshadowed by the Watergate scandal, was the Arab oil embargo of 1973. The embargo revealed the growing dependence of the United States and other Western industrialized nations on oil from the Near East and their vulnerability to the policies and practices of the Organization of Petroleum Exporting Countries (OPEC). In 1974, OPEC unilaterally increased the price of crude oil. The rising cost of oil caused inflation in the United States to climb to 11 percent.

The energy crisis was one of the defining economic and political events of the postwar era. It signaled the loss of American control over a vital resource that had for decades sustained national prosperity. The American people reacted with disbelief, as their leaders pondered the end of economic growth and the coming age of scarcity. Consumers, meanwhile, had to reconcile themselves to skyrocketing gasoline prices, shortages at the gas pumps, and continuing stagflation.

1974-1975 • The Government Response ~ Gerald R. Ford, who ascended to the presidency when Nixon resigned on August 9, 1974, responded unimaginatively to the economic crisis. Preoccupied with controlling inflation and lowering prices, the Ford administration cut government spending, contracted the money supply, which raised interest rates, urged Congress to pass a tax increase to reduce the federal deficit, and attempted to garner public support with WIN (Whip Inflation Now) buttons distributed to the American people. These actions further depressed an already sluggish economy.

Instead of adopting a flexible policy to revive the economy, as Nixon had done in 1971, Ford persisted in trying to halt inflation by slowing economic growth. The results were predictable. By the spring of 1975 unemployment had reached 9 percent, where it remained for the rest of the year. A precipitous decline in stock prices and the GNP made it plain that the nation was mired in the worst economic slump since the Great Depression.

1975-1979 • Managing the Unmanageable Economy ~ By the mid-1970s, the problems of recession and inflation had come to seem intractable. Upon entering office in 1977, the first concern of new president Jimmy Carter was to stimulate economic recovery and reduce an unemployment rate that had been hovering between eight and nine percent since 1975. Since inflation had plunged to 5.5 percent, half of what it had been in 1974, Carter thought he could concentrate exclusively on reviving the economy and getting Americans back to work.

Believing that deregulation would lower production and operating costs and thereby further reduce inflation and quicken recovery, Carter undertook to free American business from federal supervision. He began by deregulating the trucking and the airline industries. Because controlling the cost of fuel had become central to restoring economic health and stability, Carter hoped that his policy would be especially effective in holding down the price of oil and gasoline.

Carter's policies brought temporary and partial relief. During his first year in office (1977-1978), he maneuvered a number of bills through Congress that were designed to promote economic expansion. In 1977, Carter sponsored and Congress approved a tax cut totaling $34 billion and enacted public works and public service measures costing $14 billion. Congress also raised the minimum wage by nearly 50 percent, increased farm price supports, and eased environmental restrictions on industries struggling to make a profit. The economy responded to these stimuli. Unemployment fell to 5.8 percent by 1979.

1978-1979 • The Return of Economic Stagnation ~ Unemployment, though, proved to be only one among many stubborn problems, most of which Carter could not solve. Carter's attempt to control energy costs, for example, largely failed. In April 1977 he asked Congress to pass a bill that reduced energy consumption by increasing taxes on gasoline and inefficient, "gas-guzzling" automobiles. He also encouraged heavy industries to substitute coal for oil and pressured utility companies to switch to nuclear power. In March 1979, however, the near catastrophic melt down at the Three Mile Island nuclear power plant diluted Americans' confidence in the safety of nuclear energy.

Even before the Three Mile Island disaster, much of Carter's energy policy was in shambles. Although Congress created the Department of Energy in 1977, it took no action on the rest of Carter's program until 1978. Then Congress passed the ineffective National Energy Act, which promised little in the way of energy conservation and imposed no meaningful restraints on rising energy costs. The rest of Carter's energy plan became entangled in a web of competing business and government interests and, as a consequence, made no advance.

Without the means of controlling energy costs and consumption, Carter stood helplessly by as the economy once more began to flounder. Inflation, which Carter thought he had overcome, soared to 9.6 percent by the end of 1978 and kept rising. Shifting his attention to this development, Carter reduced the second of his three tax cuts by 20 percent and vetoed congressional appropriations for defense and public works that he feared would augment inflationary pressures. He also put forth voluntary guidelines to limit wage and price increases and tried to curtail government expenditures. These gestures were futile. The economy continued to struggle.

When the Federal Reserve Board raised interest rates in 1979, the economy experienced another abrupt decline. A second series of oil shortages that occurred the same year, induced in part by a political revolution in Iran, made a bad situation worse, increasing the price of crude oil by 50 percent. In the United States, a gallon of gasoline now cost more than $1. At the end of 1980 the unemployment rate rose to 7.4 percent, the inflation rate was 13 percent, the federal deficit projected at $56 billion, and the prime interest rate, the rate that banks charge other banks and financial institutions to borrow money, stood at an astonishing 20 percent. The American economy was in deep trouble and nothing the government did seemed capable of ending the crisis.

(1895) A cartoon satirizing the Supreme Court's decision to declare the income tax unconstitutional while Democratic politician Benton McMillin (1845 - 1933), a major supporter of the tax, looks on in dismay.

1981-1991 "THE REAGAN REVOLUTION"

1981 • "Supply-Side" Economics ~ The entrance of Ronald Reagan into the White House in 1981 gave the Republican party another opportunity to direct the national economy. To rejuvenate American economic life, Reagan proposed to lower taxes, balance the budget, and limit federal interference with business. "In this present crisis," he said in his inaugural address,

> government is not the solution to our problem; government is the problem.... It is no coincidence that our present troubles parallel and are proportionate to the intervention and excessive growth of government.... It is time to reawaken this industrial giant, to get government back within its means and to lighten our punitive tax burden.

Reagan immediately asked Congress to enact a series of measures that together constituted what became known as supply-side economics. He proposed, first, a 30 percent tax cut implemented over three years and accompanied by reductions in domestic social programs. The tax cut, Reagan and his economic advisors concluded, would enable the economy to expand, which, in turn, would boost employment and increase federal revenue. The government could then easily spend more money on building up the military and paying down the deficit.

1980 • Skeptics and Critics ~ George Bush, one of Reagan's adversaries for the Republican nomination and later his vice-presidential running mate, initially derided Reagan's plan as "voodoo economics." Although they may have disagreed with Bush's flamboyant characterization, most professional economists, whether Keynesians, monetarists, or opponents of government intervention in general, were dubious that Reagan's proposal could at once ease inflation and decrease unemployment. In truth, much of Reagan's economic thinking marked a return to Republican policy of the 1920s. Like his predecessors, Reagan suggested that tax cuts principally for the affluent would stimulate capital investment and a "trickle-down effect" would eventually extend prosperity to the mass of Americans.

Economists were not alone in criticizing Reagan's economic policies. They generated considerable incredulity and opposition in Congress as well. An old-fashioned fiscal conservative such as Republican Senator Robert Dole of Kansas called Reagan's entire scheme "a riverboat gamble." Yet, even skeptics like Dole were prepared to try any experiment that promised to end inflation, eliminate unemployment, and lower interest rates. Communicating in simple concepts and straightforward language, Reagan ultimately made his economic programs irresistible to Congress and the American people.

1981 • Reaganomics in Action ~ During the spring and summer of 1981, Congress agreed to cut federal spending on domestic social programs by $41 billion. The reductions either severely curtailed or completely abolished welfare payments, food stamps, Medicaid, medical care for the indigent, and public housing programs. At the same time, Congress acquiesced in a $1.6 trillion expansion of the military budget that, Reagan asserted, would not only enhance national security but also stimulate the domestic economy. Finally, Congress passed the Economic Recovery Tax Act, decreasing personal income taxes by 25 percent over a period of three years. Lowering the maximum tax rate from 70 to 50 percent, the Economic Recovery Tax Act clearly benefited the wealthiest Americans.

David Stockman, Reagan's budget director, confirmed that the tax package was merely a revision of the "trickle-down" theory. Reagan's economic advisors had thrown the program together quickly and haphazardly, with considerable legerdemain and without a genuine understanding of the probable economic consequences. Stockman later confessed that:

> None of us really understands what's going on or all these numbers. You've got. . . such complexity now in the interactive parts of the budget between policy actions and the economic environment and all the internal mysteries of the budget, and there are a lot of them. People are getting from A to B and it's not clear how they are getting there. It's not clear how we got there.

Reagan also attacked economic stagnation by accelerating the deregulation of business begun during the Carter administration. He limited government controls

1981-1984

on banks, savings-and-loan corporations, hospitals, and any other companies he thought likely to benefit from a restoration of free enterprise. Similarly, Reagan assailed organizations, such as labor unions, that he considered a threat to the smooth operation of the economy. He broke a strike of air traffic controllers by firing many of them for breach of contract, thereby encouraging corporations to intensify their resistance to union demands for higher wages, better benefits, and shorter hours. As a result of Reagan's anti-union sentiment and activity, the political influence of organized labor dwindled during his first years in office.

1981-1984 • The Economic Decline and Recovery ~ Not since Franklin Roosevelt had a president done so much to alter the direction of the economy. Yet, the so-called Reagan Revolution initially produced unsettling results. Stock prices tumbled and, between 1981 and 1983, the economy as a whole went into a sharp decline. Unemployment climbed to 10.8 percent, the highest level it had attained since the 1930s. Capital investment, which supply-side economics was supposed to expand, instead contracted. The federal deficit reached $195 billion.

These disappointing consequences induced Reagan to abandon his supply-side dogma in the summer of 1982. He persuaded the Federal Reserve to expand the money supply and lower interest rates to 10.5 percent, half of what the prime rate had been in 1981. In response, the economy mounted an impressive rally. Stock values began to soar in August 1982, and the surge lasted for the rest of the decade. At the same time, unemployment fell to 8.2 percent and during 1983 the GNP grew at 3.3 percent, the highest rate since 1978. The systematic effort to conserve energy at last began to pay dividends as well, lowering energy costs and helping to reduce inflation to less than four percent. By the summer of 1984, with the national economy prospering, unemployment dropped to 7.1 percent while inflation still remained at less than 5 percent.

1983 • Criticism of the Reagan Revolution ~ The recovery, Reagan declared, proved that "our economic game plan is working." Many economists still disagreed. They acknowledged that Reagan's policies had achieved an immediate improvement, but they were pessimistic about long-term prospects and reluctant to credit "Reaganomics" with reviving the economy. Economists worried in particular about the deficit, pointing out that cuts in entitlement programs had not matched tax cuts. Confronted by elderly middle-class voters who threatened the political career of any senator or representative assenting to reduce Social Security or Medicare, Congress had refused to tamper with either. The costs of entitlements combined with the increase in military expenditures meant deficits of at least $200 billion for the next five years.

In 1983, the consensus among economists was that competition for loans between business and government would eventually raise interest rates, rekindle double-digit inflation, and stall the brief and fragile recovery. They noted, too, that business investment in new factories and equipment had not grown in three years. Since supply-side economics aimed ultimately at expanding the productive capacity of industry, most economists remained unconvinced that Reagan's program was working.

The recuperation of the economy, they argued instead, had originated from activating various Keynesian mechanisms: lowering interest rates, expanding the money supply, easing access to credit, cutting taxes, and deficit spending. At the same time, slackened international demand for oil had created an oil glut that undercut the leverage of OPEC and stabilized energy prices on the world market. These developments had given American consumers additional spending power to create a "demand-side" recovery through the purchase of homes, automobiles, and other durable goods.

Even the critics of Reaganomics had not anticipated the extent to which foreign investors, particularly the Japanese, were willing to finance American deficits by purchasing corporate and government bonds. The infusion of vast sums of foreign capital into the American economy had also stimulated and sustained economic recovery and kept inflation rates under five percent until 1990.

1983-1988 • The Social Consequences of the Reagan Revolution ~ The poor and the young bore the brunt of the Reagan Revolution. More Americans fell below the poverty level than at any other time since Lyndon Johnson had launched the War on Poverty in 1965. During Reagan's presidency the neediest Americans had to subsist on reduced government benefits. There were fewer food stamps, public service jobs, student loans, child nutrition programs, and housing subsidies. There were lower unemployment compensation and welfare payments to mothers with dependent children.

Reagan's critics characterized his fiscal and economic policies as "welfare for the rich." The tax cuts that Reagan guided through Congress gave only 8.5 percent of the overall reduction to the 31.7 million American taxpayers earning an annual income of $15,000 or less. By comparison, the 5.6 percent of Americans with annual incomes of $50,000 or more pocketed 35 percent of the revenue. Corporations, meanwhile, made windfall profits by reducing their share of each federal tax dollar from 13 to 8 cents.

1983-1988 • A Troubled Economy ~ Despite the hardships that Reagan's economic policies caused among some classes of American society, the economy as a whole continued to flourish. Deficit spending and foreign investment to finance the debt helped to create 14.5 million new jobs between 1983 and 1988. With inflation fixed at less than 5 percent annually and the stock market soaring to record heights, unemployment had dropped to 5.4 percent by 1987, the lowest level of the decade. The administration, with some justice, extolled the wonders of Reaganomics.

Behind the facade of prosperity, however, severe structural problems had developed in the American economy. "Many Americans have had the uncomfortable feeling, deep in their minds, that there is something hollow about the Reagan economic policies," declared the Nobel Prize-winning economist Robert M. Solow. "They are right: We have been selling out the future of the American economy."

Corporations did not significantly increase their productivity during the 1980s. Most of the new jobs that the economy generated were in the service sector, not in manufacturing. The combination of tax cuts, defense expenditures of more than $1.6 trillion, and entitlement programs made for annual budget deficits of more than $200 billion.

Reagan had slowed the increase in spending on social programs, but he had

1980s

not abolished them as he promised to do. As a consequence, in four years he tripled the national debt, incurring greater financial obligations than the combined deficits accumulated by all previous administrations. By the end of Reagan's second term in office, the government owed $2.7 trillion and was paying nearly $200 billion a year in interest on the debt. Lamenting the consequences of this surging national debt, economist Benjamin M. Friedman wrote in *Day of Reckoning: The Consequences of American Economic Policy Under Reagan and After* (1988) that since 1980 Americans have lived well:

> ...by running up our debt and selling off our assets. America has thrown itself a party and billed the tab to the future. The costs, which are only beginning to come due, will include a lower standard of living for individual Americans and reduced American influence and importance in world affairs.

Table 6: Federal Surplus/Deficit and Federal Debt, 1950-1980

Year	Federal Surplus/ Deficit	Federal Debt in billions of dollars
1950	-2.2	257.4
1960	+0.3	286.3
1970	+2.8	371.0
1980	-59.5	914.3

SOURCE: Brinkley, *American History: A Survey*, p. A40.

1986 • THE INTERNATIONAL DEBT CRISIS ~ To restore a measure of fiscal sanity to government, Congress passed the Gramm-Rudman Act mandating automatic deficit reductions, which were supposed to balance the budget by 1993. The Gramm-Rudman Act forced Congress to cut social programs that Reagan had failed to circumscribe or eliminate. Should Congress and the president fail to act, the cutbacks were to be involuntarily imposed.

If the severe budget deficit were not enough, the economic vulnerability of the United States became apparent in other ways as well. Since the First World War the United States had been a creditor nation. Under Reagan's leadership, the United States became the largest debtor nation in the world. Running a massive trade imbalance, especially with Japan and the oil-exporting countries of the Near East—imbalances that reached almost $170 billion by 1986—American businessmen had to borrow ever larger sums to meet their financial obligations.

Such extensive credit elevated American interest rates and drew foreign capital to the United States and away from Third World nations, making it harder for Third World countries to service their own debt. By 1988, various Third World countries owed $1.2 trillion to the banks and governments of their industrialized counterparts. Although reluctant to default on their loans, Third World nations found it impossible to pay their interest without diverting funds reserved for capital investment and domestic spending. The Reagan administration and the American financial community saw no escape from this crisis except temporarily to suspend payments and to restructure the debt.

LATE-1980s • THE BANKING CRISIS ~ Increasingly, however, American bankers and financiers had problems of their own with which to contend. By the late 1980s many savings-and-loan institutions, emancipated from government regulation at the beginning of the decade, were collapsing. Dogmatically convinced that regulation equaled inefficiency and that only the operation of the free market could save the economy, Reagan had unleashed the savings-and-loans to govern themselves through the Federal Home Loan Bank Board. Representatives and senators, who collected handsome stipends and contributions from savings-and-loan officials, saw to it that Congress made no attempt to monitor, investigate, or control unwise financial practices.

The savings-and-loans lost billions of dollars to bad debts and unprincipled investments. By 1990 the crisis had spread from the savings-and-loans to banks with hitherto unblemished reputations. As the government began repaying customers for losses sustained in their federally insured accounts, estimates suggested that the financial bailout of the savings-and-loans would cost American taxpayers as much as $500 billion over a period of thirty years.

1986-1988 • Paper Empires ~ A frenzied, undisciplined, greedy outlook also prevailed in the arcane world of corporate finance. The Reagan administration virtually abandoned any semblance of an antitrust policy, and corporate consolidations proceeded at a pace that recalled the 1880s or the 1920s. Billions of dollars circulated in "junk bonds," a new financial instrument that offered high-interest returns on suspect loans floated to finance the buy-outs and takeovers (often hostile) of vulnerable companies by such corporate raiders as T. Boone Pickens, Carl Icahn, and Frank Lorenzo. Having bought up a controlling share of stock in a company, these corporate raiders sold off part of the new acquisition to reduce their financial obligations and streamlined operations in what they kept, usually by eliminating jobs and contracting the labor force.

The fear of hostile takeovers prompted formerly conservative corporate executives recklessly to accumulate debts in an effort to make the companies they managed look less attractive to raiders. Alternately, they, too, began to devour smaller, weaker companies. Some economists defended the corporate consolidations of the 1980s, arguing that the risk of a hostile buy-out or takeover imposed a salutary discipline on corporate management. Most, however, worried that the resulting conglomerate would be inefficient and that the feverish atmosphere of speculation that characterized the junk-bond market would lead to economic crisis.

1987 • The Stock Market Crash ~ Their concerns seemed to have been entirely justified when the stock market crashed on October 19, 1987, losing more than 500 points and nearly 20 percent of its value in a single day. Many economists predicted a general economic collapse, but nothing of the sort took place. The drop in stock values was apparently more the consequence of technical factors, notably the unregulated buying and selling of shares by computers, than of structural problems with the economy. In addition, the Federal Reserve moved quickly to forestall a crisis by expanding the money supply and easing access to credit, exactly opposite the course it had taken in 1929. The stock market soon regained its equilibrium, but investors, their confidence badly shaken, became skittish and cautious in the months ahead.

(1873) The rush from the New York Stock Exchange as banks began to fail and close, leading to a ten-day closure of the Stock Exchange.

1987

More than the stock market crash of 1987, it was the arrest and conviction of prominent Wall Street stockbrokers Ivan Boesky and Michael Milken, the young tycoon who almost single handedly invented the junk-bond market, that signaled the onset of economic turmoil and the end to the economic boom of the 1980s. Despite the federal prosecution of Boesky and Milken, the speculation in junk bonds, the hostile take-over of corporations, and the economic tumult they engendered were symptomatic of the encouragement that the Reagan administration had given to deregulated, unrestrained capitalist enterprise.

1984-1988: The Legacy of Reaganomics on Working People

The Working Class • The benefits of economic growth during the 1980s were not evenly distributed. As wealth became concentrated in fewer hands, more Americans edged closer to poverty. High-paying jobs in manufacturing disappeared, while many of the new jobs that the economy created were low-paying service positions in fast-food restaurants and retail department stores or data-entry jobs in high-tech computer firms. There was also the increasing prevalence of involuntary part-time work, which during the decade grew at a rate of more than one-and-one-half times that of full-time work. These jobs were not only low-paying, but they lacked prospects for long-term employment and career advancement. For many working-class Americans, the prospect of economic opportunity and upward social mobility had simply evaporated.

The Middle Class • Middle-class Americans fared little better. They endured only a slight drop in income during the 1980s, but however affluent they may have felt, middle-class Americans struggled to keep pace with rising costs. While many working-class Americans could find only part-time work, growing numbers of middle-class families earned two incomes. By 1983, 50.5 percent of women worked outside the home, the highest percentage ever in American history. In 1988, 57 percent of married women with children under six years of age entered the labor force.

Personal indebtedness also offered another way to maintain a middle-class standard of living. Between 1982 and

Women in the Work Force, 1940-1992

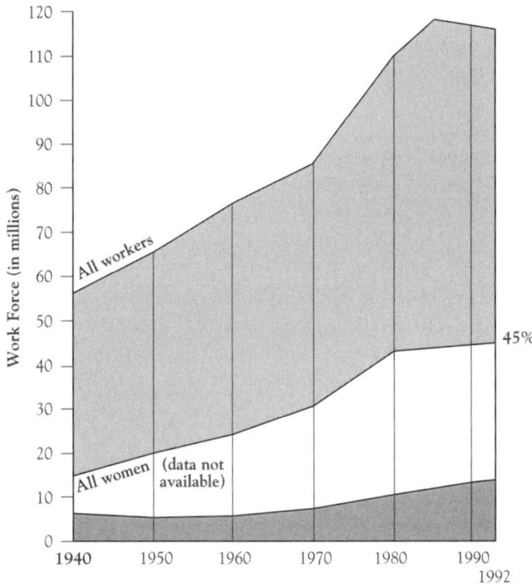

1986 consumer debt rose at an annual rate of 9.5 percent, twice the rate of the 1970s and considerably higher than the yearly increase in income that most middle-class families received. Auto loans, mortgages, home equity loans, and, of course, credit cards, all contributed to the expansion of debt that left many middle-class families defenseless against the recession that began in 1990.

THE POOR • The numbers of poor Americans merely trying to subsist increased substantially during the 1980s, rising from approximately 12 percent at the beginning of the decade to 15 percent at its end. But the demographics of poverty also changed. In the first half of the twentieth century poverty had been concentrated principally among the aged. By the 1980s, those trapped in the worst poverty were commonly children and households headed by single women. Forty percent of the poor were children, although they made up only 27 percent of the population. In 1986, according to economist Benjamin M. Friedman, 20 percent of all American children lived in poverty. At the same time, 12 percent of whites and nearly 36 percent of blacks were impoverished, as were 10.9 percent of American families. All tolled, more than 32 million Americans lived below the poverty line in the 1980s. This figure includes not only those who were retired, disabled, or unemployed, but almost three million Americans who worked full time.

Cuts in federal housing subsidies and escalating rents drove many of these men, women, and children into homelessness. Estimates of this virtually uncountable population varied wildly throughout the decade, ranging from as few as 350,000 to as many as four million. Most of the victims of poverty and homelessness were working people who had previously supported themselves and their families. Crowded into temporary shelters that recalled scenes from the Great Depression, they strove to maintain their dignity and recover their economic independence against overwhelming odds.

"After you're living here a while you begin to lose hold of your dream," explained a middle-class mother forced into homelessness by her husband's chronic unemployment. "You start to tell yourself that it's forever. 'This is it. It isn't going to change. It can't get worse. It isn't going to get better.' So you start to lose the courage to fight back."

1990 • THE END OF THE '80S BOOM ~ By July 1990, the economic boom of the 1980s had run its course. The economy began gradually to sink into recession. Inflation rose to five percent. Unemployment stood at seven percent. The national debt exceeded $3 trillion and the budget deficit was $220 billion. The United States also endured the largest trade imbalance of any nation in the world. In June 1991, the federal deficit exceeded $300 billion, and Americans from all walks of life began to wonder where the money would come from to pay for rescuing insolvent banks and savings-and-loans, cleaning up the polluted environment, rebuilding the battered infrastructure, fighting the war on illegal drugs, and funding the medical, educational, and welfare programs needed by the old, the young, and the indigent. Neither the Republicans nor the Democrats seemed to have an answer.

The American Economy in the 1990s

Given the lethargic and tenuous performance of the American economy during the early 1990s, few could have predicted the remarkable economic developments of late 1990s, which called into question formerly immutable assumptions, methods, practices, values, and truths. Suddenly, and in many instances quite unexpectedly, the old rules governing economic life no longer applied, and no one knew for sure what the new rules were going to be. As volatile and unpredictable a decade as any the American economy has ever experienced, the 1990s were as full of opportunity and promise as they were of peril and apprehension, and whoever could divine the future stood to profit beyond the dreams of avarice.

1995-2000 • The New Economy ~ The second half of the 1990s marked the most sustained period of economic growth in American history. Unlike other periods of long-term economic expansion that were reversed by rising inflation, during the 1990s economic growth continued and even accelerated while inflation receded. The combination of rapid technological change, the rise of the service sector, and the emergence of the global marketplace had experts convinced that the United States was in the midst of "a second industrial revolution." Despite the historical inaccuracy of the label (the second industrial revolution took place during the late nineteenth century), there could be no denying that during the 1990s a new American economy had begun to take shape—an economy that defied many economic axioms of long-standing.

Since 1980, the American economy had lost approximately 43 million jobs through restructuring and downsizing. Economists called them "sunset jobs." At the same time, as analyst Horace W. Brock has pointed out, the economy created 71 million new jobs, a net gain of 28 million jobs. More important, economists regarded these as "sunrise jobs" in industries that had a future. The majority of economists attributed this development to a restructuring of companies and the economy abetted by such governmental policies as the North American Free Trade Agreement (NAFTA), enacted in 1994. The NAFTA created a continental economy, so the argument ran, that helped to initiate and sustain economic growth in the United States. In addition, many economists pointed to the break up of AT&T and the deregulation of the telecommunications industry as enhancing opportunities for competition, innovation, and growth.

1990s • The Decline of Organized Labor ~ Most surprising was that the economic expansion of the 1990s occurred without the traditional stimulus of increased deficit spending. On the contrary, deficit spending decreased from

$290 billion in 1992 to just $67 billion by 1997. At the same time, the decline in the influence of organized labor enabled companies to exercise greater flexibility. During the 1990s companies began with increasing ease and frequency to relocate facilities and jobs to places inside and outside the United States where wages were lower than those paid to unionized workers. Companies also began to hire growing numbers of temporary workers to whom they often paid no health or retirement benefits. Finally, companies began to "outsource" many operations such as book keeping. Taken together, these procedures helped to lower costs and elevate profit margins.

The most unexpected aspect of economic growth during the 1990s was that it challenged two basic assumptions: that a growth rate of more than 2.5 percent and an unemployment rate below five percent, however desirable in theory, were unrealistic because they generated inflation. After 1993, the American economy grew at an annual rate of about four percent, and by the second half of the decade unemployment had fallen below five percent for the first time since the 1970s. Yet, no inflationary pressures appeared to retard or reverse these economic advances.

1990s • The Federal Reserve and the New Economy ~ For years the Federal Reserve Board struggled mightily to fit what happened to the American economy during the 1990s into a traditional framework. Growth was robust, stock values soared, unemployment declined, and yet inflation was virtually nonexistent. Eventually, Chairman Alan Greenspan admitted that he could not explain these extraordinary developments according to the old rules and simply gave up trying to do so. By the middle of 1999, officials at the Federal Reserve agreed that the economy was in the midst of a "productivity boom" fueled by technological innovation that facilitated economic expansion at a rate faster than anyone had once thought possible without initiating the price and wage increases that ordinarily extinguished such growth. By the late 1990s, Greenspan's task had become to adjust fiscal and monetary policy to the new economic reality. "The Fed is moving in a very different direction," acknowledged former Vice-Chairman Manuel H. Johnson in 1999. "You'll probably see less tightening in the future."

Central to Greenspan's thinking was his belief—a belief that eventually gained a consensus among other officials at the Federal Reserve—that productivity growth, which had languished at about 1 percent a year through much of the 1970s and 1980s, had made a long-term and perhaps permanent increase to two percent or higher during the 1990s. Even skeptics such as Roger W. Ferguson, the Governor of the Federal Reserve, became convinced. "Is this rise in productivity cyclical because the economy is strong, or is this a change in the trend?" Ferguson asked. "The evidence is mounting that it's a change in the trend." William Poole, President of the Federal Reserve Bank in St. Louis, initially echoed Ferguson's conclusions. "My earlier position was that the evidence for a convincing breakout of productivity wasn't there." In a speech delivered on April 16, 1999, however, Poole conceded that "it is increasingly reasonable to believe that the U.S. has indeed turned the corner on productivity growth."

To be sure, Greenspan and his colleagues at the Federal Reserve maintained a healthy degree of skepticism about the duration of the "productivity boom." Yet, by the end of the decade, they had come to see it as the only explanation for sustained economic growth without the specter of inflation.

1995-2000 • The Stock Market and the New Economy ~ It is an understatement to say that during the 1990s the stock market was erratic. On April 17, 1991, the Dow Jones Industrial Average closed above 3,000 points for the first time in history. By 1995, the Dow had gained 33.5 percent in value and passed the 4,000 mark. In 1997 the Dow reached a high of 8,000, but began to fluctuate more wildly and unpredictably. In late October 1997, for instance, the stock market came as close to crashing as it had in a decade when the Dow plummeted a record 554 points in a single day, equaling 7.2 percent of its total value, only to rebound with a record 337-point rise the following day. At the end of the week, the market had ebbed and flowed its way to a mark of 7,442.08, the loss of a mere four percent in value.

Even as the market declined, however, the value of stocks remained far greater than it had been at the beginning of the decade. By 1998, the Dow had reached 9,000; it closed the century near 11,000 points with no apparent limits on its ascent. The problem was that no one really knew how the market would perform over the short- or the long-term. Although the market continued to rise steadily and sometimes dramatically after 1997, at decade's end many experts still feared that its volatility suggested the bottom could drop out at any moment without giving much advanced warning of trouble. After the decline of 1997, David Dreman of Dreman Value Management, a New York investment firm, declared "this was a market waiting for a trigger. When all is said and done, this market is still overvalued."

1998-2000 • Riding the Bull ~ Throughout the 1990s, there were consistently more signs of economic strength than weakness, at least insofar as investors were concerned. In the midst of the collapse of stock values in 1997, the federal budget deficit fell to $22.6 billion, the lowest it had been since 1974. At the same time, wages rose only 0.9 percent, relieving fears about inflation. Cheaper imports from Asia helped to keep prices low in the United States. Finally, when market values tumbled, numerous companies bought back shares of their own stock, which helped to stabilize and even to rally the market. Bert Whitehead, a financial consultant in Franklin, Michigan, referred to the 1997 downturn as the "Dow October Clearance Sale," and urged clients to buy while the price per share was low. Market analyst James Bianco of Arbor Trading in Barrington, Illinois estimated that the Dow would have had to fall below 5,000 points before portfolios began to experience any irrecoverable loss in value.

The stock market rallied in 1998, rising during the spring and summer but losing nearly 17 percent of its value by the fall. Such analysts as Robert Samuelson predicted a recession when the market tumbled on April 19, 1999, with such high-tech stocks as America on Line (AOL), Microsoft, Cisco, and other companies in the Dow Jones Internet Commerce Index losing a record 17 percent of their value in a single day's trading. By April 21, however, the Dow had climbed to a record 10,581 points. The rally was driven by investors who abandoned tech stocks and put their money into industrial companies. To experts, this long-awaited shift marked a welcome broadening of the market, which many thought had been too concentrated. "The shift is healthy," said John S. Tilson, a managing director at Roger Engermann & Associates, Inc., an investment firm in Pasadena, California. "The narrow bias that the market had before could have led to something bad happening." Alfred Goldman, chief market strategist at A.G. Edwards & Sons, Inc., added, "the bears have had another arrow taken out of their quiver." Suddenly, many experts were wondering whether the market, despite its volatility, might not after all be entering a stronger phase that would continue for a long time to come.

1990-2000 • The "Long Boom" ~ Would the stock market continue to rise, and if so how far and for how long? Those were the questions market analysts were asking as the 1990s drew to a close. Many apparently looked forward to an endlessly prosperous future, believing that the American economy had undergone a fundamental structural change. Edward Yardeni, chief economist for Deutsche Morgan Grenfell, was lyrical in predicting a "new-era economy" driven by information technology, global markets, and world peace that promised to generate unprecedented corporate earnings and continually rising stock prices. Yardeni and others who shared his perspective posited a "long boom," which would carry the American economy past all the difficulties and limitations that had formerly hampered it.

In an essay entitled "The Long Boom" published in *Barron's* in 1997, Peter Schwartz and Peter Leyden took readers on a journey through a twenty-first century economy so affluent that the problems of poverty and war had simply disappeared. "We are watching the beginnings of a global economic boom on a scale never experienced before," Schwartz and Leyden intoned.

2000 • Permanent Prosperity? ~ Yardeni, Schwartz, and Leyden provided flamboyant visions. But more sedate and mainstream economic and market analysts were also asking whether the economic successes of the 1990s could be sustained. Everyone agreed that, given previous assumptions, the performance of the economy during the second half of the decade was remarkable, unprecedented, and nothing short of incredible. They disagreed, though, about whether the economic accomplishments of the 1990s were a portent of things to come or a temporary phase destined to run its course.

Critical questions remained. Could Americans in the future safely assume that stock prices would continue to soar, that unemployment would continue to decline, and that inflation would continue to recede? No one was certain. Those who argued for the "long boom" based their projections on the extraordinary performance of the American economy since 1994, which had exceeded nearly all predictions and expectations. The optimistic advocates of the "long boom" thus insisted that the American economy had at last solved its persistent structural problems. Sustained economic growth, they believed, would no longer create shortages in labor and raw materials and would no longer tax the productive capacity of industry. It would thus not bring the higher wages, higher costs, and higher prices that have traditionally slowed economic growth.

2000 • Demographics and the "Long Boom" ~ Critics, however, suggest that the changing demographics of the United States would frustrate the "long boom" prosperity. Between 1945 and 1973 the American economy grew at a rate of 3.5 percent a year. Much of that growth resulted from an unusual surge in population: the arrival of the "baby boomer" generation. In 1963, only 38 percent of the population of the United States was in the work force. By 1998, however, more than 50 percent of the population worked. In 2010, when the oldest members of the baby boomer generation begin to retire, there will be fewer young workers to replace them.

Recent low birthrates project that the labor force will grow at a rate of about 0.9 percent per year between 1999 and 2010. After 2020, the projections of the Social Security Administration show the annual growth rate of the labor force falling to 0.2 percent. Even if all the other calculations of the "long boom" theorists prove correct, their critics maintain that the shortage of workers will eventually reverse the sustained economic growth model they anticipate.

1990s • Technology, Productivity, and the "Long Boom" ~ The proponents of the "long boom" respond that if the United States can no longer count on favorable demographics, it can, because of technological innovations and advancements, still anticipate increased productivity. In the coming decades management must therefore make it a priority to coax maximum productivity from each worker. The "long boom" theorists recommend the example of such companies as General Electric and Chrysler, both of which have increased productivity through the judicious use of new technology. There is little evidence, though, that the majority of American companies are following the lead of G.E. and Chrysler.

Since 1975, the productivity growth rate of the economy has been slightly more than 1 percent a year, with virtually no upward trend apparent by the end of the 1990s. Incredible as it may seem considering the massive changes that took place in the American economy during the decade, most economists agree that the overall rate of productivity growth has experienced no substantial transformation. Individual success stories notwithstanding, studies show that companies that downsized or turned to computer technology during the 1990s often did not realize any lasting increase in productivity. There also seems to be no definitive statistical evidence to suggest an aggregate increase in productivity.

Ironically, the greatest gains in productivity during the 1990s came in the manufacturing sector. But because it had become less extensive and more efficient, manufacturing employed an ever-diminishing percentage of the American work force. The proportion of American workers employed in manufacturing declined from 31 percent in 1960 to 15.8 percent by 1995. According to statistics compiled by the Bureau of Labor Statistics and the International Monetary Fund, only 10 percent of the American work force will be employed in manufacturing by 2017.

Given the continual exodus of American workers from highly productive manufacturing jobs to less productive jobs in the service sector (economists measure "productivity" by calculating output per labor hour), many economists believe it unwarranted to expect the phenomenal economic growth and prosperity of the 1990s to continue indefinitely.

Mergers, Monopolies, and the New Economy

1996-1999 • Merger Mania ~ A "merger mania" gripped the new economy. For three consecutive years, between 1995 and 1997, the value of mergers and acquisitions in the United States increased at record levels. Some 27,600 companies joined forces during that period, more than in the entire decade of the 1980s. The trend continues. In 1999, even more companies hastened to unite with the behemoth corporations.

1998 • Rockefeller's Revenge ~ When in December 1998 Exxon and Mobil agreed to merge, pundits immediately labeled the $86.355 billion deal "Rockefeller's Revenge." Both Exxon and Mobil originated as part of John D. Rockefeller Sr.'s Standard Oil monopoly, together accounting for more than half of the Standard Oil Trust until the Supreme Court disbanded it on May 15, 1911.

In 1998 as well, Amoco, also a scion of Standard Oil, agreed to be purchased by British Petroleum (BP) for $55 billion. The following year, BP acquired the Atlantic Richfield Company (ARCO), another successor of Standard Oil, for $33.7 billion. Initially, the U.S. assets of BP derived in large measure from the absorption of another offspring of Standard Oil, Sohio. What the judiciary put asunder at the beginning of the twentieth century entrepreneurs have been busy putting back together at its end.

Historical analogies, however, only go so far. At the zenith of its power, Standard Oil controlled 84 percent of the petroleum market in the United States. Exxon-Mobil, by contrast, although the largest oil company in the world, controls approximately 22 percent.

1998 • The Big Bank Theory ~ One week in April 1998 rocked the financial world. On April 6, the huge insurance and brokerage firm Travelers Group announced plans to merge with Citicorp, then the second largest bank in the United States. The new company was capitalized with assets of $76 billion. If the nonbank assets of Citicorp were calculated into the equation, Citicorp-Travelers could have posted total assets of $697.5 billion, making it the largest financial services compa-

(1864) "Don't let anyone hand you any two dollar bills" is a famous phrase to beware of people trying to cheat you. However, there really was a two dollar bill produced in 1864 – as seen here.

ny in the world. Its nearest competitor, the Bank of Tokyo-Mitsubishi, was as capitalized at $648.2 billion as of 1998.

One week later, on April 13, the chairman of Banc One, John B. McCoy, announced the merger of his company, valued at $116 billion, with First Chicago NBD Corporation, valued at $115 billion. McCoy mused that in the future there would be only five or six banking conglomerates in the world. On the same day, Hugh McColl of NationsBank engineered the $61.663 billion merger with BankAmerica to establish a huge financial conglomerate with deposits totaling $346 billion, the second largest bank in the United States and the fifth largest in the world. These mergers were part of a complex, ongoing revolution that by the 1990s had already begun to transform banking, finance, and investment.

1990s • The Revolution in Banking, Finance, and Investment ~ At the center of this revolution was a conflict between what bankers call "consolidation" and "disintermediation," the latter term meaning the removal of intermediaries, i.e. banks, from financial transactions. The advocates of "disintermediation," such as computer software giants Microsoft and Intuit, believe that the future belongs to the companies that can master computer technology and give customers and investors almost total control over their finances. Investment banker David Shaw stated in 1998 that "the whole financial industry will likely be turned upside down, with shrinkage in some areas and perhaps some outright failures among those firms that are unable to use technology effectively."

Hugh McColl disagreed. The future, McColl has argued, belongs to the mammoth financial institutions that will package investments and provide individual customers and corporate clients with a myriad of services from insurance to investments, from car loans to airline tickets. He acknowledges, of course, that size alone will not be enough to ensure success. Financial institutions, large and small, will have to stay informed about the technological innovations that now govern the banking and financial industry, and be nimble and smart enough to take advantage of them. Those that will not, cannot, or do not will be among the casualties.

The gigantic banks of the sort McColl and McCoy helped to assemble during the 1990s were, McColl asserted, "too large to fail." In the end, the "superbanks" may or may not serve customers and investors well, but by offering a vast array of financial services, they intend to make themselves indispensable to the operation of a modern economy.

1990s • Consolidation, Profits, and Costs ~ During the 1990s "superbankers" like McColl and McCoy went a long way toward accomplishing their objectives. According to statistics compiled by the Federal Deposit Insurance Corporation (FDIC) 599 bank mergers took place in 1997 alone, reducing the number of banks in the United States from nearly 14,000 to 9,143. Consolidation sent bank stocks soaring during the decade. From their low point in 1990, bank stocks rose nearly twice as fast as average stocks, which themselves increased in value at a rate nearly twice as fast as the historical standard. In 1997, the income of the banking industry was $59.2 billion, an increase of thirteen percent ($51.5 billion) over 1996.

Consolidation also saved money for the banks. Several studies showed, however, that despite increased profits banks

Table 7: Fifteen Largest Mergers and Acquisitions of the 1990s

Acquiring Company	Acquired Company	Date Effective	Value in millions
Exxon Corp.	Mobil Corp.	Dec. 1, 1998*	$86,335.1
Travelers Corp.	Citicorp	Oct. 8, 1998*	72,558.2
SBC Communications	Ameritech Corp.	May 11, 1998	72,356.5
Bell Atlantic Corp.	GTE Corp.	July 28, 1998*	71,323.6
AT&T Corp	Tele-Com. Inc	Aug. 9, 1999	69,896.5
Vodafone Group Inc.	AirTouch	June 30, 1999	65,901.9
AT&T Corp.	MediaOne Inc.	Apr. 22, 1999*	63,115.3
NationsBank Corp.	BankAmerica Corp.	Sept. 30, 1998	61,633.4
Elf Aquitaine	Total Fina SA	July 19, 1999*	56,209.9
British Petroleum	Amoco Corp.	Dec. 31, 1998	55,040.1
Qwest Communications	US West Inc.	June 14, 1999*	48,439.8
WorldCom Inc.	MCI Communications	Sept. 14, 1998	43,351.9
Daimler-Benz-AG	Chrysler Corp.	Nov. 12, 1998	40,466.5
Viacom Inc.	CBS Corp.	Sept. 7, 1999*	37,300.0
Olivetti	Telecom Italia	May 21, 1999	34,757.7

* Date merger announced.

SOURCE: *New York Times Almanac 2000*, p. 359.

imposed higher costs on consumers, with the banks themselves the chief beneficiaries of these transactions. In 1998, for instance, non-interest service fees accounted for 33 percent of banking profits, totaling $18.5 billion. A report issued by the U.S. Public Interest Group disclosed that consumers paid 15 percent more to maintain regular checking accounts at big rather than at small banks. The report of the Federal Reserve to Congress in June 1997 confirmed these findings. "Merger mania is making the fee-gouging big banks even bigger," complained Ed Mierzwinski, consumer program director for the Public Interest Group. "Fewer and bigger banks mean consumers face fewer choices, less competition and . . . higher fees."

1996-2000 • Regulating the Revolution ~ Governmental regulation of the emerging system of banking and finance had already become virtually impossible before the end of the 1990s. Alan Greenspan, Chairman of the Federal Reserve, announced the Fed's abandonment of all efforts at regulation. The burden, he conceded, had come to rest on the banking and financial corporations themselves. "To continue to be effective," Greenspan wrote in 1996, "government's regulatory role must increasingly assure the effective risk-management systems are in place in the private sector. As financial systems become more complex, detailed rules and standards have become both burdensome and ineffective."

1998-2000

1998-2000 • Media Moguls ~ A merger, announced on July 28, 1998 and approved by the Federal Communications Commission (FCC) in June 2000, brought together two prominent media and telecommunications firms, Bell Atlantic and GTE. The $70.9 billion deal created the largest local telephone company in the nation and unleashed a telecommunications colossus in an already rapidly consolidating market. The new company, known as Verizon Communications, sells communications packages ranging from long-distance and local telephone service to wireless and high-speed Internet access. Industry analysts also expect Verizon to expand into video entertainment and interactive gaming.

The merger brought 63 million local telephone lines, or 33 percent of all lines in the United States, under the control of Verizon. In addition, Verizon has approximately 25 million wireless telephone customers, more than twice the number of AT&T, making Verizon the largest wireless operation in the country. Company officials reported that Verizon had a market worth of nearly $150 billion with annual revenues of $60 billion. As such, the deal dwarfs the $15.1 billion merger of Time-Warner in 1990 and even the $18.3 billion acquisition of Capital Cities/ABC by the Walt Disney Corporation in 1996.

The Internet and the New Economy

1995-Present • Net Impact ~ During the 1990s, the Internet became a force that transformed life like few before it. Anyone with a computer, a telephone, and a modem literally had at their fingertips a staggering quantity and variety of information. As the decade drew to a close, the possibilities of the new technology seemed endless. Certainly the initial impact of the Internet has been profound, especially for the economy. Upstart online companies humbled corporations that once seemed unassailable. Financial markets became more accessible and efficient for those who wished to raise or invest money. Accessibility and efficiency, in fact, may be the lodestone and the pole star of the Internet.

The Net has broken down bureaucracies, challenged corporate, governmental, and intellectual orthodoxies, and, as some argued, encouraged a stronger sense of democracy and community. For good or ill, such developments have led to revolutions in the past. Is there any reason to expect they will not do so again?

1994-Present • The Internet Revolution ~ Out of the primordial ooze of the Internet there evolved during the 1990s a host of new species: new companies, new business models, new corporate structures, even new industries. The 1990s were a time of such tumult and confusion as far as the Internet was concerned that no one could agree on what was happening at the moment, let alone about what the future was likely to bring. Since 1994, when the World Wide Web made the Internet more generally accessible, all the formerly immutable truths about business and the economy have been called into question. In 1997, for instance, Yahoo! Inc. was nothing more than a Web search index. By 1999, it had become a major media company commanding a $40 billion market capitalization. How did this transformation take place? Experts scratched their heads and shrugged their shoulders in wonder at advertisers and investors who jumped on the Yahoo! bandwagon. They know only that enough did so to make Yahoo! a multibillion dollar corporation.

Equally astonishing, the staid executives at venerable Hewlett-Packard seriously discussed giving away multimillion-dollar computer systems to Internet start-up companies in exchange for a share of the "e-revenues." Finally, and perhaps most fantastic, companies such as Amazon.com and eToys Inc., which have never turned a profit, continued to command multibillion-dollar market caps that attracted untold numbers of investors to their stocks. During the 1990s, the world, at least the world of cyber-business, seemed to have gone mad. It certainly perplexed traditional executives who had spent their working lives trying to build companies with real offices, real factories, real assets, and real profits.

1998-Present • E-Commerce ~ The Center for Research in Electronic Commerce at the University of Texas at Austin estimated that as of 1999 the Internet economy totaled $301 billion if online sales of industrial and consumer goods and services was combined with the equipment and software needed to operate and support e-commerce. The American automobile industry, by comparison, was worth $350 billion in 1999. If the level of growth experienced since 1994 continues, commerce on the Internet will become as perilous to some businesses, and perhaps even to entire industries, as it will be profitable to others. Hardly a company or an industry did not undergo some upheaval, and perhaps changed the way in which it organized and defined itself, because of the Internet. Mark T. Hogan, vice president of the e-GM Internet unit for the General Motors Corporation, admitted, "we've come to realize that if we don't move with Internet speed, we could become extinct." These consequences were the result of one inescapable fact of doing business in the 1990s: the Internet put customers in charge as never before.

In 1999, Gary Hamel, chairman of the management consultancy firm Strategos and a research fellow at the Harvard Business School, explained: "For many companies, customer ignorance was a profit center." With access to the wealth of information that the Internet provides, however, customers pointed and clicked their way to the best goods and services at the best prices. The Internet offered new advantages to merchants as well, who could now identify individual customers and collect unprecedented quantities of data about the character and pattern of their purchases.

1996-2000 • Business Management and the Internet ~ The rise of the Internet also compelled executives to rethink the very nature of the companies they managed. Suddenly, factories, stores, trucks, warehouses, and even employees, once regarded as competitive assets, came to be liabilities. Savvy companies began to jettison, or to avoid altogether, building costly facilities or hiring legions of sales representatives. They concentrated instead on expanding their capacity to use the Internet, which even provided opportunities to access resources outside the company.

It became common corporate practice during the 1990s for one company to form a temporary partnership with another—a partnership that coalesced and dissolved with each new project. The research firm Forrester Research, Inc. has labeled this process "dynamic trade." To reinvent

1995-PRESENT

themselves, many companies moved from being manufacturers into becoming "service providers." Hewlett-Packard, for example, began using the Internet to remake itself from a manufacturer of computers into an "e-services" company. Instead of making and selling computers, HP marketed computing network services via the Internet for a monthly fee, or in the case of an e-commerce site, for a percentage of the transaction revenues. Ann Livermore, CEO of the $14 billion Enterprise Computing Solutions for HP, estimated in 1999 that such fees alone could eventually account for 80 percent of the division's annual revenues.

1995-PRESENT • THE INTERNET AND ECONOMIC GROWTH ~ Throughout the fifteenth century, estimates economist J. Bradford DeLong of the University of California at Berkeley, global per capita income rose at a rate of 0.1 percent a year. During the next five hundred years, the annual rate of growth gradually increased until it reached approximately 3 percent in the second half of the twentieth century. By the 1990s, it appeared as if the growth rate of the economy was poised to expand again, this time exponentially. Experts agreed that the single most important reason for this dramatic worldwide explosion in economic productivity and value was the advent of the Internet.

The Internet altered the dynamics of the economy at least as much as did the introduction of railroads and electricity. Among other considerations, the evolution of the Internet has meant that the traditional requirements of economic growth and development, access to and control of capital and labor, may no longer be the principal determinants of economic strength. During the 1990s, economic power became increasingly and inextricably linked to the control and manipulation of information.

The initial manifestation of the potential the Internet offers was the performance of the American economy during the second half of 1990s. Since the Second World War, Western Europe and Japan had gradually eroded American economic supremacy. In 1970, per capita income in the United States was 31 percent higher than that in other major industrialized countries. By 1991, the difference had narrowed to just 10 percent. With the coming of the Internet, however, the distance had again widened to 22 percent by 1999. "This is historically unique," declared Luc Soete, an economist at Maastricht University in the Netherlands and the leading European expert on the new economy. "For the first time in the postwar period, you have growth divergence—the pulling away of the leading technological country."

1997 • REGULATING THE INTERNET ~ As e-commerce grew into a trillion dollar business by the late 1990s, only one force seemed capable of slowing down or stopping its evolution: politics. Concerned about the potential of the Internet to invade people's privacy, take people's money, and generally to wreak havoc, politicians in the United States and around the world began to contemplate new laws to prevent the revolutionary potential of the Internet from being abused. The impulse to regulate the Net, in turn, distressed entrepreneurs, lest their vision of a global electronic marketplace foundered on the shoals of inconsistent, uncoordinated local and national rules ranging from decency standards to privacy laws to sales taxes.

As a consequence, e-businesses pleaded with government to allow them to police themselves. The Clinton administration complied. In 1997, longtime Clinton aide, Ira C. Magaziner, now a private consultant, wrote "Framework for Global Electronic Commerce," a blueprint for the governance of the Internet. Magaziner argued that regulation ought to be kept to a minimum. Overregulation, he concluded, would inhibit the global reach and the evolving technology of the Net. Magaziner went so far as to suggest that governments recuse themselves from making policy for the Internet and turn the process over to such international groups as the World Intellectual Property Organization (WIPO) or the Organization for Economic Cooperation & Development (OECD).

The problem with Magaziner's proposal, already apparent by the end of the 1990s, was the lack of accountability. Neither of the regulatory boards of the WIPO nor the OECD are composed of elected officials with responsibility toward a constituency. Both organizations, therefore, have tended to operate in relative secrecy, without the obligation even to follow due process. This arrangement has made it easier for corporations to dominate regulatory procedures and harder for governments or consumers to protest their decisions.

Harvard Law School Professor Lawrence Lessing criticized the regulatory process, saying that "You've had interested parties in closed meetings for the past three years making this code for Internet commerce tilted in their favor." Similarly, Professor A. Michael Froomkin of the University of Miami law school complained that "business has figured out that you can get what you want from [private] regulatory processes. Democracy is a messy way of making decisions, but one of the reasons is that we try to ensure that different groups are heard."

One organization that has made some progress toward regulatory democracy is the Internet Corporation for Assigned Names and Numbers (ICANN), the group that monitors the Internet address system. Since its inception in the summer of 1998, ICANN has established conflict of interest rules, opened some of its board meetings to the media and the general public, and worked to develop a mechanism to elect board members. To many, ICANN has come to represent the most viable alternative to cumbersome government regulation on the one hand and self-serving corporate tyranny on the other.

Work and the New Economy

1990s • Me First! ~ In the wide open, free-wheeling job market of the 1990s the mantra became "Me First!" Employers across the country may have welcomed or lamented the newly emboldened American work force, but all accepted it as a fact of life, at least for the foreseeable future. As the American economy prospered throughout the decade, the unemployment rate fell to less than five percent, which is considered by economists to be "full employment." With fewer workers entering the job market and competing for more jobs, perspective employees had greater leverage than they had enjoyed at any time since the 1960s.

Although few experts believe the hiring bonanza of the 1990s will last forever, virtually all agreed that it has already brought revolutionary changes to the work place that will redefine work (and Americans' attitudes toward it) well into the twenty-first century. If the Great Depression of the 1930s produced a cautious and frugal generation, modest in its desires and expectations, the "long boom" of the 1990s created a demanding and impatient generation, brazen in its pursuit of the main chance.

Certainly the job market supported taking bold action. During the second half of the 1990s, employers worried lest a labor shortage force them to close a division or postpone the launch of a new product. They were thus more likely than in years past to accommodate a current or prospective employee who requested a promotion, a substantial raise or signing bonus, stock options, a flexible work schedule, additional vacation time, or special training at company expense. If one company was unwilling to meet an employee's or a candidate's demands, they easily marketed themselves elsewhere.

The establishment of such job-finding mechanisms as career databases on the Internet, job fairs, and internships gave those looking for work more opportunities and more ways to access and explore them. Former Secretary of Labor Robert Reich saw the changing nature of, and attitudes toward, work reflected in the growing numbers of self-employed, which totaled 10.5 million in 1997 compared to 7 million in 1970. In 1997, Reich calculated that the self-employed would soon make up as much as 20 percent of the work force. The self-employed work first for themselves, Reich declared, and are willing "to hopscotch" among jobs. "Loyalty is dead."

MID-1990S • HIDDEN ANXIETIES ~ In part fear drove this new audacity. Despite the remarkable prosperity of the 1990s, to remain competitive companies such as AT&T, Sears, Roebuck, IBM, Boeing, and others faced constant pressure to cut costs. Wall Street analysts punished them for falling short of earnings projections and overseas rivals benefiting from cheaper labor enjoyed a distinct competitive advantage. The easiest, quickest, and surest way to cut costs remained trimming the size of the work force.

In 1996, for example, AT&T announced it would lay off 40,000 workers by 1999. In 1998 alone, in the midst of unprecedented affluence, American corporations laid off 103,000 workers, the most since 1993. Economists at the Federal Reserve Bank of Chicago estimated that in 1995, the most recent year for which complete data exists, workers had a 3.4 percent chance of being laid off. That risk, although comparatively small, increased workers' anxieties and prompted them continually to reevaluate their options.

If workers could not count on their present employer to continue providing them with a paycheck, why not consider the offer from a rival? Increasing numbers of workers opted out entirely and incorporated themselves, selling their services to companies eager to give people work without giving them jobs or paying the costs of insurance and pensions.

1990S • FREE AGENTS, NOMADS, & GLOBALISTS ~ The good news about work in the 1990s was that the economy had created 71 million new jobs. The booming economy combined with changing ideas about work have made older methods of career planning at least temporarily obsolete. During the decade, more Americans created entirely new styles of employment.

There emerged the "Free Agents," who joined the expanding ranks of the self-employed and tried freelancing their way to professional and, they hoped, financial independence.

There were the "Nomads" who went to work for a company but who never stopped looking for another job that brought them higher pay, better benefits, and additional perquisites. When they found what they were looking for, they changed jobs and began the process anew. The "Globalists," who have laptop will travel, also surfaced, vaulting from time zone to time zone in the modern, borderless, international economy.

The most arresting, and often most frightening, aspect of the new style of employment in the 1990s was the enormous demands it made on workers. Even those who remained in corporate jobs had to acquire skills and experience that were transferable to other companies and even to other industries. "Free Agents," "Nomads," and "Globalists" had constantly to stay informed about current developments in an array of fields, from marketing to finance to technology, simply to remain employable.

As a consequence, concluded Joanne B. Ciulla, the Coston Family Chair of Leadership and Ethics at the Jepson School of Leadership Studies, University of Richmond, Americans in the 1990s worked too hard and enjoyed life too little. Part of the problem, in Ciulla's view, was that corporations sought to squeeze maximum profits from their employees, whether they worked full-time, part-time, or freelanced. For their part, workers reflected the growing unwillingness of Americans in the 1990s to live with less in the way of material possessions, and so readily acquiesced in company demands as long as the pay and compensation were to their liking. They purchased their "independence" at a high price.

1990s • Blue-Collar Workers ~ Blue-collar workers had a different problem, and the new 1990s styles of employment provided them fewer opportunities and little solace. For skilled workers, especially electricians, carpenters, and pipe fitters, there was work aplenty. According to the National Center for Construction Education and Research, builders and contractors complained of labor shortages of skilled workers throughout the decade.

Bureau of Labor Statistics projections suggest, however, that between 1996 and 2006 the five fastest growing occupations will be database manager (+118 percent), computer engineer (+109 percent), systems analyst (+103 percent), personal aide (+85 percent), and physical therapy assistant (+79 percent). The growth of such occupations in the 1990s and beyond suggested the development of a high-tech and skilled service economy.

But those who did not aspire, or who lacked the education and skills, to enter this new job market faced rather bleak prospects. For such unskilled workers, wages rose only slightly during the 1990s, an average of approximately 3.8 percent although complete statistics were unavailable as of 1999. Starting salaries for corporate attorneys, by contrast, rose 12 percent in 1997. M.B.A.'s recruited by major Wall Street investment banks did even better. Their starting salaries, including bonuses, increased 33 percent. There was no evidence that the economic prosperity of the 1990s did anything to ease the widening gap in income distribution.

In addition, many blue-collar jobs, especially in manufacturing, continued to evaporate during the 1990s. Estimates suggest that by 2006 manufacturing jobs will account for a mere 12 percent of the work force. Between 1994 and 2005 the Bureau of Labor Statistics calculates that the five fastest growing jobs in real numbers will be

Table 10: The Thirty-Five Largest Economic Entities, 1999

Entity	Market Value	Percentage Increase Over 1998 in U.S. Dollars
1. USA	$15,013 trillion	12
2. Japan	4,244	75
3. UK	2,775	27
4. France	1,304	32
5. Germany	$ 1,229	12
6. Canada	695 billion	27
7. Switzerland	662	-4
8. Holland	618	7
9. Italy	610	7
10. Microsoft (US)	546	50
11. Hong Kong	536	56
12. General Electric (US)	498	71
13. Australia	424	22
14. Spain	390	-3
15. Cisco Systems(US)	355	149
16. Taiwan	339	30
17. Sweden	318	14
18. Intel (US)	305	141
19. Exxon-Mobil(US)	295	merger
20. Wal-Mart (US)	289	68
21. South Korea	285	148
22. Finland	276	79
23. Nippon TT(Jap.)	274	126
24. AOL Time-Warner(US)	244	merger
25. South Africa	232	38
26. Nokia (Eur.)	218	48
27. Greece	217	166
28. Deutsche Tel(Eur.)	215	142
29. IBM (US)	213	14
30. Brazil	194	18
31. BP Amoco (Eur.)	192	45
32. RoyalDutch(Eur.)	190	merger
33. Citigroup (US)	186	62
34. Toyota (Jap.)	181	72
35. Belgium	179	-28

SOURCE: *World Press Review* Vol. 47/No. 4 (April 2000), p. 7.

cashiers (+562,000,) janitors (+559,000), retail sales clerks (+532,000), waiters and waitresses (+479,000), and registered nurses (+473,000). Although all require some skills, only one requires a college education.

Meanwhile, the five jobs expected to undergo the most severe decline are farmers (-273,000), typists (-212,000), bookkeepers, accountants, and auditors (-178,000), bank tellers (-152,000), and garment workers (-140,000), each the victims, not only of a changing economy, but to some extent of technological obsolescence. If they did not learn a new set of skills, many unemployed and unskilled workers, were virtually unemployable in any but the most low-paying service sector jobs. The new economy of the 1990s was leaving them behind.

The Global Economy

1990s • Globalizing the Economy

~ Many economists in the United States and abroad believe that the accelerated growth of the American economy in the 1990s was only the first act in the drama of sustained global economic expansion. For all the efforts by governments to direct and regulate their national economies, however, it was multinational corporations and such international institutions as the European Union (EU), the World Trade Organization (WTO), and the International Monetary Fund (IMF) that became the driving forces of economic globalization during the 1990s. These entities gained substantial control over the national economics of sovereign nation-states.

Critics of this development, such as Ralph Nader and Patrick Buchanan, raised the specter of world government, sensing an alarming concentration of power in multinational and international hands. The triumph of the WTO, Nader complained, "means foreign regulation of America. . . It means secret tribunals can rule against our laws."

1990s • In Defense of Globalization ~ Defenders of economic globalization, on the contrary, believe that it is inevitable, and the only question remaining to be settled is what sort of world economy and world government ought to be established. Nations have always traded with one another for their mutual benefit, argued Robert Wright in *The New Republic*. They will doubtless continue to do so. When the leaders of these nations at last recognize that it is to everyone's advantage to eliminate grievances and animosity they will submit to common governance and adjudication of the sort that the World Trade Organization attempts to provide. The benefits of this arrangement, Wright has speculated, will far outweigh the costs, preserving economic order, dispensing justice, eliminating inequitable advantages, and inhibiting destructive competition.

Globalization, however, has already caused serious problems, especially in the so-called developing countries with transitional economies. Advocates of globalization such as Wright insist that the environmental problems, the exodus of low-skill jobs from high-wage nations, and human rights violations, which have led many to oppose globalization, "are just about impossible to solve without . . . the power of sanction that the WTO, more than any other world body, has to offer." "Globalization is great," Wright concluded. "On balance, it makes the world's poor people less poor. . . . And it fosters a fine-grained economic interdependence that makes war among nations less thinkable."

1994 • Globalization in Action ~ Thanks largely to the North American Free Trade Agreement (NAFTA), many advocates of the global economy cite Mexico as the model to persuade developing countries to pin their markets and their hopes to free trade and economic competition. Since the NAFTA went into effect in 1994, proponents of globalization point out that impoverished Mexican cities such as Ciudad Juarez, located directly across the Rio Grande from El Paso, Texas, have reaped the benefits. Ciudad Juarez has gained more than $4 billion (U.S.) in foreign investment and 150,000 manufacturing jobs.

Yet, a study conducted by the Labor University of Mexico found that the purchasing power of Mexican workers has declined considerably since 1994, and has eroded by 86 percent since the 1970s. In 1995, for example, the average daily minimum wage of Mexican workers was enough to purchase 44.9 pounds (20.36 kilograms) of tortillas or 2.24 gallons (8.5 liters) of milk. In 1999, after operating under the NAFTA for five years, the average daily minimum wage of Mexican workers purchased only 16.9 pounds (7.65 kilograms) of tortillas or 1.4 gallons (5.3 liters) of milk. The Labor University study also indicated a large increase in unemployment in agriculture and small business, sectors of the Mexican economy that cannot compete with the subsidized American imports entering the country as a result of the NAFTA.

Many Mexicans, nevertheless, are happy for the opportunity to work in the *maquiladoras*, the foreign-owned factories in which imported parts are assembled for export. Despite low pay and poor working conditions, factory work represents a vast improvement from the sugar cane and corn fields in which they previously labored. The former president of Mexico, Ernesto Zedillo, has argued that "most people fail to realize. . . that the low salaries and poor conditions to which most workers are subject is their only alternative to extreme rural poverty." Alternately, Bob Jeffcott of the Maquila Solidarity Network located in Toronto maintained that "there's always a place that will have lower wages. There's always a place that will have lower economic standards. It's leading to 'de-development.'"

1999 • The Internet and the Global Economy ~ The global economy, however, is no longer solely or even primarily dependent on commerce in goods, the mechanism that has propelled all previous surges in economic growth. With the advent of the Internet

(circa 1975) The days of European countries being separated from each other by strict borders and many passport checks, like the one here, are gone. With the E.E.O.C., European residents are free to move about Europe as they please without border controls.

it has become easier to import and export services as well: banking, education, consulting, retailing, and even gambling. Not surprisingly, the United States, the first nation to develop and implement Internet technology, has thus far enjoyed a lion's share of the economic benefits. By 1999, the United States accounted for more than 50 percent of all individuals online and 75 percent of all Internet commerce.

Most predict that American advantages will decline over time. A study conducted by Juniper Communications, Inc. in 1999 anticipated that the number of European households with access to the Internet will triple between 1999 and 2004. In Asia, especially in China and Japan, the study projected that the number of persons regularly using the Internet will at least double by 2001. As a consequence, by 2003, the Juniper research calculates, the United States will account for only 50 percent of Internet commerce instead of the current 75 percent. Already Iceland, Finland, and Sweden have more Internet use per capita than the United States.

Late-1990s • Impediments to Globalization ~ Yet, as the 1990s ended, four important impediments remained to the Internet achieving the full impact in Europe that many believe to be its destiny.

First, the United States had the largest home market. Despite movement toward a more economically unified Europe, the multitude of languages, cultures, and governments in Europe and Asia slowed the advance of the Internet compared with the large, consolidated, and still comparatively homogeneous United States.

Second, economists have suggested that the introduction of the euro, the common European currency, also diverted the Internet Revolution. "The Internet is making the world global," economist Luc Soete stated. "But [with the euro] we made Europe more European."

Third, in most European countries local telephone calls are still charged by the minute, a practice that discouraged extensive use of the Internet.

Fourth, despite the increasing availability of venture capital in the last years of the 1990s, Europe still lagged far behind the United States in access to this indispensable component of economic growth and development. Asia was even further behind, and having more difficulty attracting investors. But with its immense markets, Asia may have a better chance of thriving in the Internet Age than Europe.

Economists agree that the key to the next stage of Internet development will be whether financial innovation can keep pace with technological innovation. American financiers were prepared to invest in new Internet companies; Japanese and European investors, by contrast, were not, remaining bound to more traditional corporations. If these differences persist, the locus of technological and economic innovation will likely remain the United States, no matter how many Web sites and Internet users there are in Europe and Asia.

THE PERILS OF GLOBALIZATION

The advocacy of the international free market generally favors developed countries and powerful multinational corporations. Already the wealthiest nation in the world, the United States has gained the most from economic globalization, the progress of which has thus far failed to eliminate, and in some respects has enhanced, the divergence in economic growth and development between rich and poor countries as well as the economic, social, and political inequalities within countries.

Nor have the advocates of globalization adequately addressed the crucial problems of environmental standards and workers' rights. Environmentalists, union organizers, and human rights activists brought many of these issues and concerns to worldwide attention with the violent demonstrations that disrupted the meeting of the World Trade Organization held in Seattle, Washington during December 1999. Becoming ever more mindful of the problems that globalization has created, members of the economic, political, and corporate elite have at last begun to speak out against them, even if they have not yet found the means of solving them.

Michael Camdessus, the former head of the International Monetary Fund (Camdessus stepped down on February 14, 2000) declared in the keynote address delivered at the Tenth United Nations Conference on Trade and Development in Bangkok, Thailand that "the greatest concern of our time is poverty.... It is the ultimate systematic threat facing humanity.... The widening gaps between rich and poor within nations," Camdessus continued, "is morally outrageous, economically wasteful, and potentially socially explosive. If the poor are left hopeless, poverty will undermine the fabric of our societies through confrontation, violence, and civil disorder."

Similarly, Klaus Schwab, the founder and chairman of the World Economic Forum, has called for "responsible globalization," "leadership based on values," and "common ethical and moral standards" that will include in the movement toward economic globalization all those currently being left out. To do so, Schwab acknowledged, will require the reform of the leading international economic and financial organizations. This task will not be completed easily or soon, but it obviously must be high on the global agenda for the twenty-first century.

Whether in favor of or opposed to globalization, economic and political leaders in the 1990s had to begin paying closer attention not only to the distribution of goods, money, and services in the global marketplace, but also to the distribution of the costs and benefits of globalization among various countries and peoples. They could no longer afford to be unaware of who was thriving and who was suffering as a result of this monumental economic transformation.

(circa 1955) Depressed real estate values often follow a downturn in the economy, an increase in interest rates, or social conditions such as "white flight" to segregated neighborhoods in the 1950s.

WILL PROSPERITY LAST?

Predictions abound regarding the course the American economy will take as the United States moves into the twenty-first century. Will the economy continue to expand, or will the inflation of wages and prices and a consequent rise in interest rates bring an end to the spectacular prosperity it has generated?

Some economists worry that the greatest challenge to sustained economic growth might not be traditional concerns about rising wages, inflation, interest rates, and fluctuations in the business cycle, but instead a vast and growing disparity in education and skills between what employers need and what potential employees now have to offer. According to Timothy Parks, president of the Pittsburgh Regional Alliance, 60 percent of all jobs in the United States in 1950 required unskilled labor. That figure contracted to 25 percent by 1997 and will shrink to an estimated 15 percent by 2001. Meanwhile, the quest to find "knowledge workers" goes on unabated and frequently unfulfilled. Many experts fear the inadequate education and training that large segments of the American work force have received may prevent the United States from taking full advantage of the opportunities that the new economy has created.

CONCLUSION: THE END OF THE NEW ECONOMY?

By the end of 2000 additional and unexpected concerns had surfaced about the future of the new economy. A series of government reports that disclosed surprising weaknesses in the economy gave rise to speculation that the eight-year

Stock Market Performance in 2000

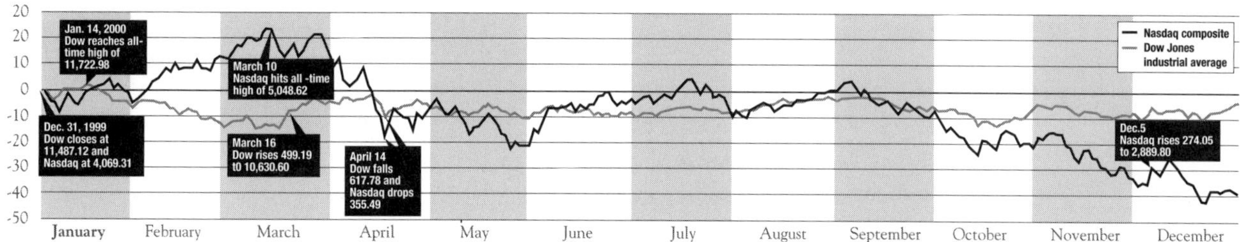

period of uninterrupted growth was about to come to an abrupt end. Until November, the prevailing view among economists suggested that the U.S. was headed for a soft landing, with judicious increases in interest rates gradually slowing growth and keeping inflation at bay without propelling the economy into a severe recession. Reports of a third-quarter growth rate of 2.4 percent, the lowest in four years, drastically altered this thinking and had the Federal Reserve Board considering a reduction in interest rates should the sluggish economy imperil the prospects for long-term expansion.

In response to rumors of a general economic slowdown, the stock market stumbled. By December 21, 2000, the Nasdaq Index, which is dominated by high-tech stocks, had lost nearly half of its value since March, falling to a low of 2,332.78. The Dow Jones Industrial Average held steadier, closing above 10,600 points, but by the end of the year optimism on Wall Street had faded amid apprehension over corporate earnings that were lower than projected; stocks fell, losing approximately $1 trillion in just a few months. Economists remain concerned that the continuing decline in stock values will trigger a cut in capital investment and consumer spending, the two forces that for so long sustained the new economy.

Although the American economy is far from a recession, president-elect George W. Bush, sensing an economic downturn approaching, proposed a $1.3 trillion tax cut to be implemented over a period of ten years. A tax cut, however considerable, will exercise no immediate effect on the economy. "By the time [a] tax cut or spending increase typically has an impact," wrote Stanley Collender, a budget expert at Fleishman-Hillard, "the problem it [sic] was intended to deal with very likely no longer exists." Yet, Bush and his economic advisors hope a tax cut, even one in which the benefits are spread out over a decade, will restore waning public confidence in the economy, a clear indication of mounting concern that the extraordinary prosperity of the 1990s may soon be a thing of the past.

Composite Bibliography for Parts I, II, and III

Albrecht, Karl A., et al. *Service America!: Doing Business in the New Economy.* Homewood, IL: Dow Jones-Irwin, 1985.

Alchon, Guy. *The Invisible Hand of Planning: Capitalism, Social Science, and the State in the 1920s.* Princeton: Princeton University Press, 1985.

Baker, Stephen. "Taming the Wild, Wild Web," *Business Week.* October 4, 1999: 154-160.

Barber, William J. *From New Era to New Deal: Herbert Hoover, The Economists, and American Economic Policy, 1921-1933.* New York: Cambridge University Press, 1985.

Bellush, Bernard. *The Failure of the NRA.* New York: W.W. Norton & Company, 1975.

Bernstein, Michael A. *The Great Depression: Delayed Recovery and Economic Change in America, 1929-1939.* New York: Cambridge University Press, 1987.

Bernstein and David E. Adler. *Understanding American Economic Decline.* New York: Cambridge University Press, 1994.

"Big, Big Banks," *The Economist* 354/8162. March 18, 2000: 5.

Bluestone, Barry and Bennett Harrison. *The Deindustrializing of America.* New York: Basic Books, 1982.

Blum, John Morton. *Years of Discord: American Politics and Society, 1961-1974.* New York: W.W. Norton & Company, 1991.

Bogomolov, Oleg. "A Challenge to the World Order," *Nezavisimaya Gazeta.* Moscow, January 27, 2000. Reprinted in *World Press Review* 47/4. April 2000: 7-8.

Brinkley, Alan. *The End of Reform: New Deal Liberalism in Recession and War.* New York: Alfred A. Knopf, 1995.

Bruchey, Stuart. *The Wealth of a Nation: An Economic History of the United States.* New York: Harper & Row, 1988.

Bruck, Connie. *Predator's Ball: The Inside Story of Drexel Burnham and the Rise of the Junk Bond Raiders.* New York: Penguin Books, 1989.

Calleo, David P. *The Imperious Economy.* Cambridge: Harvard University Press, 1982.

Carnoy, Martin, et al. *The New Global Economy in the Information Age: Reflections on Our Changing World.* University Park, PA: Pennsylvania State University Press, 1993.

Carter, Paul. *The Twenties in America,* 2nd ed. New York: Crowell, 1975.

Chambers, John Whiteclay II. *The Tyranny of Change: America in the Progressive Era, 1890-1920,* 2nd ed. New York: St. Martin's Press, 1992.

Chandler, Alfred D. Jr. *Strategy and Structure: Chapters in the History of American Industrial Enterprise.* Cambridge: MIT Press, 1966, 1990.

———. *The Visible Hand: The Managerial Revolution in American Business.* Cambridge: Harvard University Press, 1980.

———. *Scale and Scope: The Dynamics of Industrial Capitalism.* Cambridge: Harvard University Press, 1990.

Chandler, Lester V. *Inflation in the United States, 1940-1948.* New York: Harper, 1951.

Chernow, Ron. *The House of Morgan: An American Banking Dynasty and the Rise of Modern Finance.* New York: Simon & Schuster, 1991.

———. *Titan: The Life of John D. Rockefeller, Sr..* New York: Alfred A. Knopf, 1999.

Ciulla, Joanne B. *The Working Life: The Promise and Betrayal of Modern Work.* New York: Times Books, 2000.

Clark, Kim, "Why it Pays to Quit," *U.S. News & World Report* 127/17. November 1, 1999: 47-86.

———, "Gimme, Gimme, Gimme," *U.S. News & World Report* 127/17. November 1, 1999: 88-92.

Cochran, Thomas and William Miller. *The Age of Enterprise.* New York: The MacMillan Company, 1942.

Conkin, Paul K. *The New Deal,* 3rd ed. Arlington Heights, IL: Harlan Davidson, 1987.

Conner, Valerie Jean. *The National War Labor Board.* Chapel Hill: University of North Carolina Press, 1983.

Cooper, John Milton Jr. *Pivotal Decades: The United States, 1900-1920*. New York: W.W. Norton & Company, 1990.

Cortese, Amy, "The Battle for the Cyber Future," *Business Week*. June 1, 1998: 38-41.

Crainer, Stuart. *The Management Century: A Critical Review of 20th Century Thought and Practice*. San Francisco: Jossey-Bass, 2000.

Cuff, Robert D. *The War Industries Board: Business-Government Relations During World War I*. Baltimore: Johns Hopkins University Press, 1973.

Dale, Edward. *The Range Cattle Industry: Ranching on the Great Plains*, rev. ed. Norman: University of Oklahoma Press, 1969.

Davidson, Paul. [Microsoft] "Appeal Could Go Directly to Supreme Court," *USA Today*. June 8, 2000: 1A.

———. "Microsoft Awaits a New Hand," *USA Today*. June 8, 2000: 1B-2B.

Dawley, Alan. *Struggles for Justice: Social Responsibility and the Liberal State*. Cambridge: Belknap Press of Harvard University Press, 1991.

Degler, Carl. *Affluence and Anxiety*. Glenview, IL: Scott, Foresman, 1968.

———, ed. *The Age of Economic Revolution, 1876-1900*, 2nd ed. Glenview, IL: Scott, Foresman, 1977.

De Santis, Vincent P. *The Gilded Age, 1877-1890*. Northbrook, IL: AHM Publishing Corporation, 1973.

______. *The Shaping of Modern America, 1877-1920*, 3rd ed. Arlington Heights, IL: Forum, 2000.

Diggins, John Patrick. *The Proud Decades: America In War and Peace, 1941-1961*. New York: W.W. Norton & Company, 1989.

Dowd, Ann Reily, "The Panic of '98," *Kiplinger's Personal Finance Magazine* 52/7. July 1998: 24-25.

Dubofsky, Melvyn. *Industrialism and the American Worker, 1865-1920*, 3rd ed. Arlington Heights: Harlan Davidson, 1996.

Faulkner, Harold U. *Politics, Reform, and Expansion, 1890-1900*. New York: Harper & Row, 1959.

Fine, Sidney. *Laissez Faire and the General Welfare States*. Ann Arbor: University of Michigan Press, 1956.

Fite, Gilbert C. *American Farmers: The New Minority*. Bloomington: Indiana University Press, 1981.

Flink, James J. *America Adopts the Automobile, 1895-1910*. Cambridge: MIT Press, 1970.

———. *The Automobile Age*. Cambridge: MIT Press, 1988.

———. *The Car Culture*. Cambridge: MIT Press, 1975.

Foer, Franklin, "Protest Too Much," *The New Republic* 222/18. May 1, 2000: 21-23.

Fogel, Robert. *Railroads and American Economic Growth*. Baltimore: Johns Hopkins University Press, 1964.

Fox, Stephen. *The Mirror Makers: American Advertising and Its Creators*. New York: William Morrow, 1984.

France, Mike, "What Penalties for Microsoft?," *Business Week*. February 22, 1999: 76, 80.

———, "The Net: How to Head Off Big-Time Regulation," *Business Week*. May 10, 1999: 89-90.

Fraser, Steve and Gary Gerstle, eds. *The Rise and Fall of the New Deal Order, 1930-1980*. Princeton: Princeton University Press, 1988.

Friedman, Benjamin M. *Day of Reckoning: The Consequences of American Economic Policy Under Reagan and After*. New York: Random House, 1988.

Friedman, Milton and Anna Schwartz. *A Monetary History of the United States*.

Princeton: Princeton University Press, 1963: Chapter 7

______. *The Great Contraction, 1929-1933*. Princeton: Princeton University Press, 1965.

Galambos, Louis. *The Public Image of Big Business in America, 1880-1940*. Baltimore: Johns Hopkins University Press, 1975.

Galambos and Joseph Pratt. *The Rise of the Corporate Commonwealth: U.S. Business and Public Policy in the Twentieth Century*. New York: Basic Books, 1988.

Galbraith, John Kenneth. *The Affluent Society*. Boston: Houghton Mifflin, 1958, 1984.

Garraty, John A. *The New Commonwealth*. New Yorker: Harper & Row, 1968.

Garten, John E. *World View: Global Strategies for the New Economy*. Cambridge: Harvard Business School Publishing, 2000.

Gilbert, Charles. *American Financing of World War I*. Westport, CT: Greenwood Publishing Corp, 1970.

Goodwyn, Lawrence. *Democratic Promise: The Populist Moment in America*. New York: Oxford University Press, 1976.

Greever, William S. *Bonanza West: The Story of the Western Mining Rushes, 1848-1900*. Moscow, ID: University of Idaho Press, 1963.

Gutman, Herbert. *Work, Culture, and Society in Industrializing America*. New York: Vintage Books, 1977.

Hamilton, David E. *From New Day to New Deal: American Farm Policy from Hoover to Roosevelt, 1928-1933*. Chapel Hill: University of North Carolina Press, 1991.

Hamm, Steve. "Microsoft: How Vulnerable?," *Business Week*. February 22, 1999: 60-64.

Haski, Pierre. "The Bosses Grow Rich on Vocabulary," *Liberation*. Paris, January 31, 2000. Reprinted in *World Press Review* 47/4. April 2000: 9.

Hawley, Ellis W. *The New Deal and the Problem of Monopoly*. Princeton: Princeton University Press, 1966.

———. *The Great War and the Search for a Modern Order: A History of the American People and their Institutions, 1917-1933*, 2nd ed. New York: St. Martin's Press, 1992.

Hays, Samuel P. *The Response to Industrialism, 1885-1914*. Chicago: University of Chicago Press, 1990.

Heilbroner, Robert L. *The Limits of American Capitalism*. New York: Harper & Row, 1965.

———, and Aaron Singer. *The Economic Transformation of America*. New York: Harcourt, Brace, Jovanovich, 1977.

Higgs, Robert. *The Transformation of the American Economy, 1865-1914*. New York: Wiley, 1971.

Himelstein, Linda. "Yahoo!: The Company, the Strategy, the Stock," *Business Week*. September 7, 1999: 66-76.

Hobsbawm, Eric. *The Age of Extremes: A History of the World, 1914-1991*. New York, Vintage Books, 1996.

Hof, Robert D. "The Click Here Economy," *Business Week*. June 22, 1998: 122-130.

———. "A New Era of Bright Hopes and Terrible Fears," *Business Week*. October 4, 1999: 84-98.

Hofstader, Richard. *The Age of Reform: From Bryan to F.D.R.* New York: Alfred A. Knopf, 1955.

Holmes, William F., ed. *American Populism*. Lexington, MA: D.C. Heath & Company, 1994.

Holstein, William J., Steven D. Kaye, and

Fred Vogelstein. "One World, One Market," *U.S. News and World Report* 123/18. November 10, 1997: 40-43.

Holstein, William J., "The New Economy," *U.S. News and World Report* 122/20. May 26, 1997: 42-48.

Hoover, Herbert. *American Ideals Versus the New Deal.* St. Clair Shores, MI: Scholarly Press, 1972.

Horowitz, Daniel. *The Morality of Spending: Attitudes Toward the Consumer Society in America, 1875-1940.* Baltimore: Johns Hopkins University Press, 1985.

"Invasion of the Superbanks," *Business Week.* November 1, 1999: 175.

Josephson, Matthew. *The Robber Barons.* New York: Harcourt, Brace, & Company, 1934, 1976.

Karl, Barry. *The Uneasy State: The United States from 1915 to 1945.* Chicago: University of Chicago Press, 1983.

Kelly, Kevin. *New Rules for the New Economy: 10 Radical Strategies for a Connected World.* New York: Viking, 1999.

Keynes, John Maynard. *The End of Laissez-Faire.* London: L. & Virginia Woolf, 1927.

———. *The General Theory of Employment, Interest, and Money.* New York: Harcourt Brace, 1936.

Kirkland, Edward C. *Dream and Thought in the Business Community, 1860-1900.* Ithaca: Cornell University Press, 1956.

———. *Industry Comes of Age: Business, Labor, and Public Policy, 1869-1897.* New York: Holt, Rinehart, & Winston, 1961.

Klein, Maury. *The Life and Legend of Jay Gould.* Baltimore: Johns Hopkins University Press, 1997.

Kuttner, Robert. *The End of Laissez-Faire: National Purpose and the Global Economy After the Cold War.* New York: Alfred A. Knopf, 1991.

Laderman, Jeffery M. and Marci Vickers, "A Wiser Bull?," *Business Week.* May 3, 1999: 38-41.

Lamoreaux, Naomi R. *The Great Merger Movement in American Business, 1895-1904.* New York: Cambridge University Press, 1999.

Leuchtenburg, William E. *A Troubled Feast.* Boston: Little, Brown, 1973.

———. *Franklin D. Roosevelt and the New Deal.* New York: Harper & Row, 1963.

———. *The Perils of Prosperity 1914-1932*, rev. ed. Chicago: University of Chicago Press, 1993.

Lief, Louise, "An End to the Dead-End Job?," *U.S. News & World Report* 123/16. October 27, 1997: 86-87.

Livesay, Harold C. *Andrew Carnegie and the Rise of Big Business.* Boston: Little, Brown, 1975.

Longman, Philip J., "Is Prosperity Permanent?," *U.S. News & World Report*, 123/18. November 10, 1997: 36-39.

———, and Jack Egan, "Why Big Oil is Getting a Lot Bigger," *U.S. News & World Report* 125/23. December 14, 1998: 26-28.

Magretta, Joan, ed. *Managing in the New Economy.* Cambridge: Harvard Business School Publishing, 1999.

Mandel, Michael J., "The Internet Economy," *Business Week.* February 22, 1999: 30-32.

———, "The Internet Economy," *Business Week.* October 4, 1999: 72-77.

"March Madness," *The New Republic* 222/18. May 1, 2000: 9.

Marchand, Roland. *Advertising and the American Dream: Making Way for Modernity, 1920-1940.* Berkeley: University of California Press, 1985.

McSeveney, Samuel. *The Politics of Depression.* New York: Oxford University Press, 1972.

Martin, Albro. *Railroads Triumphant: The Growth, Rejection, and Rebirth of a Vital American Force*. New York: Oxford University Press, 1991.

Montgomery, David. *Workers' Control in America: Studies in the History of Work, Technology, and Labor Struggles*. New York: Cambridge University Press, 1990.

———. *The Fall of the House of Labor: The Workplace, the State, and American Labor Activism, 1865-1920*. New York: Cambridge University Press, 1990.

Mowry, George. *Theodore Roosevelt and the Progressive Era*. Madison: University of Wisconsin Press, 1946.

Nash, Gerald D. *The Crucial Era: The Great Depression and World War II, 1929-1945*, 2nd ed. New York: St. Martin's Press, 1992.

Nau, Henry R. *The Myth of America's Decline: Leading the World Economy in the 1990s*. New York: Oxford University Press, 1990.

Nelson, Daniel. *Managers and Workers: Origins of the New Factory System in the United States, 1880-1920*. Madison: University of Wisconsin Press, 1995.

Nevins, Allan. *Study in Power: John D. Rockefeller*, 3 vols. New York: Scribners, 1954-1962.

Noble, David F. *America By Design: Science, Technology, and the Rise of Corporate Capitalism*. New York: Oxford University Press, 1977.

Olson, James S. *Herbert Hoover and the Reconstruction Finance Corporation*. Ames: Iowa State University Press, 1977.

———. *Saving Capitalism: The Reconstruction Finance Corporation and the New Deal, 1933-1940*. Princeton: Princeton University Press, 1988.

Painter, Nell. *Standing at Armageddon: The United States, 1877-1919*. New York: W.W. Norton & Company, 1987.

Palmer, Bruce. *"Man Over Money": The Southern Populist Critique of American Capitalism*. Chapel Hill: University of North Carolina Press, 1980.

Patterson, James T. *Grand Expectations: The United States, 1945-1974*. New York: Oxford University Press, 1996.

Paul, Rodman W. *Mining Frontiers of the Far West, 1848-1880*. Albuquerque: University of New Mexico Press, 2001.

———. *The Far West and the Great Plains in Transition, 1859-1900*. New York: HarperCollins, 1989.

Polenberg, Richard. *The Era of Franklin D. Roosevelt, 1933-1945: A Brief History with Documents*. Boston: Beford/St. Martin's Press, 2000.

Port, Otis. "Customers Move into the Driver's Seat," *Business Week*. October 4, 1999: 103-106.

Potter, Jim. *The American Economy Between the World Wars*. London: MacMillan, 1974.

Ramo, Joshua Cooper. "The Big Bank Theory," *Time*. April 27, 1998: 46-58.

Reich, Leonard S. *The Making of Industrial Research: Science and Business at GE and Bell, 1876-1926*. New York: Cambridge University Press, 1985.

Rifkin, Jeremy. *The End of Work: The Decline of the Global Labor Force and the Dawn of the Post-Market Era*. New York: G.P. Putnam's Sons, 1995.

Rivlin, Gary. *The Plot to Get Bill Gates*. New York: Times Books, 1999.

Rodrik, Dani. "The Global Fix," *The New Republic* 219/18. November 2, 1998: 17-19.

Rogers, Daniel T. *The Work Ethic in Industrial America, 1850-1920*. Chicago: University of Chicago Press, 1979.

Roosevelt, Phil. "Hunting Season: Get Ready for Another Round of Bank Mergers," *Barron's* 79/49. December 6, 1999: 20-21.

Rosenberg, Nathan. *Technology and American Economic Growth*. White Plains, NY: M.E. Sharpe, 1972, 1977.

Salmond, John. *The Civilian Conservation Corps*. Durham, NC: Duke University Press, 1967.

Samuelson, Robert J., "The Crash of '99?," *Newsweek* 132/15. October 12, 1998: 26-31.

———. "Global Boom or Bust?," *Newsweek* 130/19. November 10, 1997: 35.

Schaffer, Ronald. *America in the Great War: The Rise of the Welfare State*. New York: Oxford University Press, 1991.

Schwartz, Peter and Peter Leyden. "The Long Boom," *Barron's* 77/35. September 1997: 17-19.

Siklos, Richard and Amy Barrett. "The Net-Phone-TV-Cable Monster," *Business Week*. May 10, 1999: 30-32.

Sklar, Martin J. *The Corporate Reconstruction of American Capitalism, 1890-1916: The Market, the Law, and Politics*. New York: Cambridge University Press, 1988.

Smith, Anne Kates and James M. Pethokoukis, "The Bucking Bull." *U.S. News and World Report* 123/18. November 10, 1997: 26-32.

Soule, George. *Prosperity Decade: From War to Depression*. New York: Rinehart, 1947.

Stackhouse, John, "Happy to Be Exploited," *The Globe and Mail*. Toronto, December 2, 1999. Reprinted in *World Press Review* 47/4. April 2000: 10.

Stilglitz, Joseph. "The Insider: What I Learned at the World Economic Crisis," *The New Republic* 222/16 & 17. April 17 & 24, 2000: 56-60.

Strasser, Susan. *Satisfaction Guaranteed: The Making of the American Mass Market*. New York: Pantheon Books, 1989.

Swartz, Jon. "Microsoft Split Ordered," *USA Today*. June 8, 2000: 1A-2A.

Taylor, Frederick W. *The Principles of Scientific Management*. New York: Harper, 1911.

"Telephone Giants Cleared to Merge." *Richmond Times-Dispatch*. June 15, 2000: A1, A7.

Thurow, Lester C. *Building Wealth: The New Rules for Individuals, Companies, and Nations in a Knowledge-Based Economy*. New York: HarperCollins, 1999.

Trachtenberg, Alan. *The Incorporation of America: Culture and Society in the Gilded Age*. New York: Hill & Wang, 1982.

Ullmann, Owen, Laura Cohn, and Michael J. Mandel. "The Fed's New Rule Book." *Business Week*. May 3, 1999: 46-48.

Vatter, Harold G. *The U.S. Economy in the 1950s*. New York: W.W. Norton & Company, 1963.

Wallace, Anthony. F.C. *St. Clair: A Nineteenth-Century Coal Town's Experience with a Disaster-Prone Industry*. New York, Alfred A. Knopf, 1987.

Weinstein, James. *The Corporate Ideal in the Liberal State, 1900-1918*. Westport, CT: Greenwood Press, 1969, 1981.

West, Robert Craig. *Banking Reform and the Federal Reserve, 1863-1923*. Ithaca: Cornell University Press, 1977.

Wiebe, Robert. *Businessmen and Reform: A Study of the Progressive Movement*. Cambridge: Harvard University Press, 1962.

———. *The Search for Order, 1877-1920*. New York: Hill & Wang, 1968.

Wilkins, Mira. *The Maturing of Multinational Enterprise: American Business Abroad from 1914 to 1970*. Cambridge: Harvard University Press, 1974.

Williams, William Appleman. *The Contours of American History*. Chicago: Quadrangle Books, 1966.

Worcester, Donald E. *The Chisholm Trail: High Road to the Cattle Kingdom*. Lincoln: University of Nebraska Press, 1980.

Wright, Robert. "Continental Drift." *The New Republic* 222/3. January 17, 2000: 18-23.

Zahavi, Gerald. *Workers, Managers, and Welfare Capitalism, 1890-1950*. Urbana: University of Illinois Press, 1988.

Internet Resources

U.S. Department of Commerce Home Page
http://www.commerce.gov/

United States Economy
Economic research, analysis and data
http://woodrow.mpls.frb.fed.us/economy/usindex.html

US Economy: Business Cycle Indicators
Provides the U.S. Business Cycle Indicators
http://www.concentric.net/~netlink/bci/bci.html*

U.S. Economy at a Glance
http://stats.bls.gov/eag/eag.us.htm

Prosperity and Thrift
The Coolidge Era and the Consumer Economy, 1921-1929. Assembles a wide array of Library of Congress source materials from the 1920s that document the widespread prosperity of the Coolidge years.
http://memory.loc.gov/ammem/coolhtml/

Glossary of Some Economic Terms

Balance of Trade: The balance of trade is the ratio between goods and services exported and imported. When the goods and services that a country imports are worth more than the value of its exports, the country has a *trade deficit*. The balance of trade indicates the strength of the economy relative to those of other nations. Between 1995 and 2000, as the American economy grew more robust, the U.S. trade deficit actually widened. During that period the export of American goods and services did not kept pace with imports in part because the strength of the dollar made American goods more expensive abroad and made imported goods cheaper, and thus more attractive, to American consumers.

Consumer Price Index: Also referred to as the "cost of living index," the consumer price index is the most commonly used measure of inflation. The index traces the average change in the price of a wide variety of goods and services relative to an arbitrary base year.

Debt and Deficit: The federal government raises most of its revenue through taxes, but it can also raise money through borrowing. The government borrows money by selling bonds, such as treasury bonds or savings bonds. The bonds raise money now but the government must repay them with interest in the future. The *budget deficit* indicates the difference between the amount the government takes in through taxes and other forms of revenue and government expenditures. The deficit reflects the amount the government must borrow to make up that difference. The total amount borrowed and owed, including interest, constitutes the *national debt*. *Deficit spending* is the spending of public funds raised by borrowing rather than through taxation.

Some economists worry that debt damages the economy in two ways. First, when the government borrows large sums of money, it is competing with private borrowers for limited investment dollars. This competition for credit makes it both more difficult and more expensive to borrow money and thus harder to accumulate capital to fund economic growth. Second, the future taxes required to pay off the government debt also drain the economy of valuable investment capital. In addition to higher taxes, paying off the debt may require a reduction of government spending in other areas, such as defense or entitlement programs.

Although the government posted a one year surplus of $69.2 billion in 1998, the total national debt remains at $5.4 trillion with interest payments alone constituting 14 percent of the federal budget.

Dow Jones Industrial Average: Dating from 1893, the Dow Jones Industrial Average is an index of thirty blue-chip stocks in industry traded on the New York Stock Exchange (see below). The Dow Jones Industrial Average is the most widely accepted indicator of how the stock market is doing. (A blue-chip stock is considered the safest kind of stock investment. Issued by companies renowned for their good management and consistent performance over a long period of time, blue chips are generally higher in price per share and offer lower but steadier profits than more volatile stocks).

Federal Reserve System: The Federal Reserve Act of 1913 created the Federal Reserve System, or the "Fed" as it has become popularly known. The principal operations of the Federal Reserve System are to monitor the banking industry and manage the money supply, functions carried out through policies set by its Board of Governors.

There are twelve regional Federal Reserve banks located in major cities throughout the United States: Boston, New York, Philadelphia, Richmond, Atlanta, Cleveland, Chicago, Minneapolis, St. Louis, Kansas City, Dallas, and San Francisco. Commercial bankers in each region select the majority of directors who oversee the regional Federal Reserve banks. The president of the United States appoints the board of governors for the entire system.

The Federal Reserve controls the *reserve requirements* at all institutions of deposit. These requirements determine the percentage of a bank's assets that must be held in reserve either as deposits in a Federal Reserve bank or as cash in the bank's own vault. Raising the reserve requirements reduces the amount of capital available for credit and thus helps to slow down economic growth and curtail inflation.

The Federal Reserve also adjusts the *discount rate*, the interest rate that the Federal Reserve banks charge commercial banks to borrow money. Raising the discount rate generally leads commercial banks to raise both the *prime rate*, the interest rate that banks charge each other to borrow, and the interest rate that banks charge to private customers. A hike in the discount rate thus raises the cost of borrowing money and also serves to slow economic growth. Ideally, a cut in the discount rate has the opposite effect of stimulating the economy.

Finally, the Federal Reserve controls the money supply. The most common mechanism for doing so is through *open market operation*. Open market operation is the direct sale or purchase of government debt instruments. When the Federal Reserve sells government bonds and securities, it removes money from circulation and holds it in reserve, thereby reducing the money supply. When the Federal Reserve buys government bonds and securities it pays for them by taking money from its reserves, thereby increasing the money supply. Adjusting the money supply through open market operation is the most common and, many economists argue, the most important function of the Federal Reserve.

Fiscal Policy: the policies of a government relating to taxation, public revenues and finances, and public debt.

Gross National Product: The Gross National Product is the most common measure of economic productivity and consumption. The GNP constitutes both the total output and the total value in market prices, before deduction of depreciation and other charges, of the goods and services produced and consumed by the residents of the United States during a specified period of time.

Inflation: Inflation is the sustained, general, and sometimes rapid increase in the price consumers must pay to purchase goods and services. Inflation may result from what economists call "cost-push factors" or "demand-pull factors." Cost-push factors, such as a rise in the cost of labor or raw materials, will raise the costs of production and lead to higher prices for consumer goods as manufacturers strive to sustain their profit margins. Demand-pull factors, such as the increasing demand for limited goods and services or a rise in wages as employers compete for workers, may also lead to higher prices.

Income: The federal government has several different categories of income. Some of the most common include:

Disposable Personal Income: The income available to persons after taxes for spending and saving.

Family Income: The combined income of a group of two or more persons living together and related by birth, marriage, or adoption.

Household Income: The combined income of family members and all unrelated persons, such as lodgers, foster children, wards, or employees, who share a single dwelling.

Mean and Median Income: Mean (or average) income refers to the sum of all incomes in a group divided by the number of incomes in that group. Median income is the middle income in the group when they are arranged in order of size; there are the same number of incomes above and below the median income. Consider the following illustration. In a group of five annual incomes of $20,000, $32,000, $40,000, $57,000, and $72,000 the mean, or average, income is $44,200 (the sum of all incomes in the group divided by 5). The median, or middle, income is $40,000.

National Income: The sum of employee compensation (wages, salaries, and benefits), proprietors' income, rental income, corporate profits, and net interest. The government calculates national income before the deduction of taxes.

Personal Income: The income received by persons from all sources minus personal contributions for social insurance.

Junk Bonds: Junk bonds are unrated bonds or bonds with a rating below investment grade. Small companies that have been limited to borrowing from banks to raise capital to finance growth often issue junk bonds. Despite being considered risky investments (investors stand to lose their entire investment if the company issuing the junk bonds fails to grow), junk bonds have had a historically low default rate of 1.5 percent. In the 1980s, however, the junk bond market grew exponentially, until, by 1987, junk bonds constituted more than 25 percent of the value of all outstanding corporate bonds.

Laissez Faire: Literally meaning "to let do," laissez faire is a doctrine opposing government intervention into the economy beyond the minimum necessary to maintain peace and property rights.

Stock Exchange: The stock exchange is a market in which securities issued by central and local government bodies and public companies are traded. Only members may deal on a stock exchange, and membership and requirements for trading are strictly regulated.

Stock Market: The stock market is an institution in which government bonds and shares of stock are traded. Stock markets enable governments and companies more easily to raise capital by selling bonds or shares of stock to investors who expect to make a profit either from receiving a dividend from the company or selling off shares when the price rises. (A dividend is a payment made to stockholders from the profits of a company either in the form of cash or additional shares of stock).

Established in the nineteenth century, the U.S. stock market began as a merchant-organized public auction in company stocks and government bonds for the purpose of financing government, business, and commerce. Although the form in which business is transacted on the stock market has changed dramatically since then, the purpose remains the same.

There are three principal stock and bond markets in the United States, all located in New York City. The *New York Stock Exchange (NYSE)*, founded in 1817, is the oldest and most prestigious. By 1998, more than 169.7 billion shares of stock valued at $10.9 trillion were traded on the NYSE. The *American Stock Exchange (AMEX)* is known as the stock market for small companies and small investors. Seven hundred seventy companies were listed on the AMEX by the end of the 1990s, with more than 7.3 billion shares traded. In 1998, the AMEX merged with the *National Association of Securities Dealers Automated Quotations (NASDAQ)*. Founded in 1971, NASDAQ was the first exchange to use computers and high-tech telecommunications to trade, and to monitor the trading of, stock. The NASDAQ is the largest stock exchange in the world, with a record 202 billion shares of stock changing hands in 1998. In total market value, however, NASDAQ, at $2.6 trillion, still lags significantly behind the NYSE.

Mark Malvasi
Randolph Macon College

EDUCATION AND LITERACY

~

(1953) Students at Brooklyn High School in New York learn to handle the controls of a car and experience simulated traffic conditions flashed onto a screen by means of projected film.

TIMELINE

1850-1900 ~ The Beginning of Public Education

Massachusetts passes first compulsory education law (1852) / Office of Education created (1867) / Comstock Law prohibits possessing any book, pamphlet, paper, writing, advertisement, circular, print, picture or drawing of an immoral nature, including educational materials (1873) / Committee of Ten favors uniform, liberal curriculum (1892-93) / *Plessy v Ferguson* solidifies segregation in American schools by confirming a "separate but equal" policy in public schools (1896)

MILESTONES: Old Immigration from England, Ireland, Scandinavia, and Germany (1830-1870) • Darwin's *Origins of the Species* theorizes that man is descended from apes (1859) • Fourteenth Amendment declares that all persons born or naturalized in America are citizens (1866) • Widespread use of child labor (1870) • Massachusetts is the first state to collect unemployment statistics (1878) • Russell Conwell becomes famous for his sermons on the virtues of wealth, which he preaches 6,000 times (1880-1900)

1900-1929 ~ Diversifying Educational Paths

College entrance examination board established (1900) / Women enrolled in college rises from 20 percent in 1870 to 40 percent in 1910 / Albert A. Michelson becomes the first American scientist to win a Nobel Prize for his invention of the interferometer to measure stellar spaces (1907) / Standardized tests developed to determine racial intelligence (1910s) / U.S. Army develops multiple-choice testing (1917) / Smith-Hughes Act provides federal matching funds for vocational education (1917) / Mississippi is the last state to pass compulsory education laws (1918) / John T. Scopes, a school teacher in Tennessee, is arrested for teaching evolution to his students (1925)

MILESTONES: Andrew Carnegie endows a foundation for the retirement of college teachers (1905) • Formation of Intercollegiate Athlete Association and reformulation of its football rules (1905) • Einstein theorizes that light is composed of particles that he calls photons (1905) • Flexner Report questions the inadequacy of American medical schools and poor training of physicians (1910) • Margaret Sanger risks arrest by opening up birth control clinics and importing and distributing contraceptives illegally (1914) • Harlem Renaissance produces renowned African American writers, artists, and musicians (1920s) • Supreme Court decision, *Buck v. Bell,* rules that involuntary sterilization for eugenic purposes is constitutional (1927)

1930-1944 ~ Depression and War-time Opportunities

One-third of college professors are women (1930) / School attendance rises as jobs decrease (1930-1933) / Civilian Conservation Corps provides some Depression era education (1933-35) / School bus standardization (1937-39) / G.I. Bill provides educational opportunities for thousands of World War II veterans (1944) / Supreme Court strikes down religious instruction in public schools (1948)

MILESTONES: First psychoanalytic institute for training analysts opens in Boston (1930) • Under pressure, the movie industry enacts the Production Code, addressing crime, sex, vulgarity, obscenity, profanity, costumes, dancing, and religion (1930) • Supreme Court rules that "malicious, scandalous, and defamatory" journalism can be suppressed (1931) • Henry R. Luce begins *Fortune* for businessmen and *Life* for family readers (1936) • Westinghouse Science Talent Search (later sponsored by Intel) is organized to identify high school students who have extraordinary scientific potential (1941)

1945-1959 ~ Opening Education to Minorities

Mendez v. Westminister desegregates Mexican American education rights (1946) / *Brown v. Board of Education* ends school desegregation (1954) / Massive resistance to integration at Little Rock High School in Arkansas (1957) / National Defense Education Act encourages scientific curriculum (1958)

MILESTONES: *Lamp Unto My Feet*, a Sunday morning religious show originally aimed at children premieres, and broadcasts for more than thirty years, making it one of TV's longest-running shows (1948) • Asian intellectual immigration permitted (1950-1980) • Edward R. Murrow's exposé of Joseph McCarthy begins investigative reporting (1954) • Supreme Court rules that a literary work containing explicit materials must be judged as a whole and not by its parts (1957)

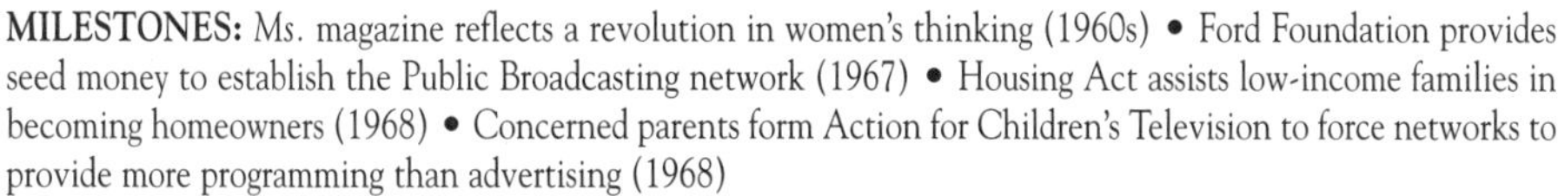

1960-1969 ~ Federal Intervention in Public Education

Supreme Court prohibits school prayer (1962) / Civil Rights Act declares that American citizens cannot be segregated in public accommodations or discriminated against in employment (1964) / The Elementary and Secondary Education Act (ESEA) provides federal funds for disadvantaged students (1965) / Bilingual Education Act provides funds for classes taught in Spanish (1968) / Supreme Court rules in favor of free speech for students (1969)

MILESTONES: Ms. magazine reflects a revolution in women's thinking (1960s) • Ford Foundation provides seed money to establish the Public Broadcasting network (1967) • Housing Act assists low-income families in becoming homeowners (1968) • Concerned parents form Action for Children's Television to force networks to provide more programming than advertising (1968)

1970-1989 ~ School Choice and Home Schooling Movements

Ethnic studies curriculum inaugurated in colleges (1970s) / Federal funds granted for educating handicapped students (1975) / Proliferation of home schooling (1980s) / *Plyer v. Doe* grants free public education to illegal immigrants (1982) / School choice movement begins (1984) / Civil Rights Restoration Act prohibits sexual discrimination in public schools (1988)

MILESTONES: Women make up 40 percent of the overall labor force and represent a substantial increase in married women who work (1970) • Watergate hearings become the top rated program on television (1973) • Jerry Falwell founds Moral Majority, Inc. and pledges to use its political influence to re-establish traditional values in American society (1979) • World Health Organization announces worldwide eradication of smallpox (1980) • Barbara McClintock becomes the first woman to win a Nobel Prize, not shared by other scientists, for her work in gene behavior (1983) • *Challenger* space shuttle explodes killing six astronauts and the first private citizen, teacher Christa McAuliffe (1986)

1990-2000 ~ Debate and Dissent over Public Education

First charter schools established (1991) / Rampant violence in public schools (1997-present) / Supreme Court prohibits prayers before public school athletic events (2001)

MILESTONES: Dissolution of the Soviet Union ends the Cold War (1991) • Rodney King is videotaped being clubbed and kicked by Los Angeles police (1991) • North American Free Trade Agreement opens trade borders to Mexico and Canada (1993) • The federal government withdraws funding for the Superconducting Super Collider, which scientists had used for highenergy physics research (1993) • Louis Farakhan, the spiritual leader of The Nation of Islam, organizes the Million Man March – the call for black men to take more of a role with their families (1995) • U.S. scientists clone a male calf (1997)

Introduction: Schooling the Nation

Modern nations mark their well-being and progress in terms of education. A literate, well-educated citizenry connotes a prosperous and enlightened nation, one that can afford to school its youth for their own individual self-improvement and for the common good. A national system of education is capable of a variety of tasks: it should unify individuals from diverse backgrounds, drive the economy, and give young people and adults the skills and knowledge to function in a complex society.

None of these tasks is possible without access to schooling, and this leitmotiv has dominated United States educational developments in the twentieth century. Decisions surrounding who should go to school and what should be taught have spurred passionate national debates since the late nineteenth century and the rise of universal public schooling. These questions have focused on basic concepts of inclusion, such as offering equal access to education regardless of race, class, gender, physical ability, or language. But they have also addressed issues of competency: What role should religious organizations play in public education? To what degree should the federal government be involved in determining curriculum? And finally, how public should public education be—are parents or state agencies ultimately responsible for the education of children? The search for answers to these questions by twentieth-century educators, policymakers, the public, and students has guided a century of national self-definition, accompanied by a myriad of successes and failures.

1850-1900

1850-1900
The State Enters the Classroom

The history of American education in the twentieth century actually began in the mid-nineteenth century. In 1852, Massachusetts passed the first state law for compulsory school attendance at the elementary level, a measure resulting from the work of the "father" of common, or public education in the United States, Horace Mann. This law resulted from Mann's almost twelve-year term as secretary of the state's board of education from 1837 to 1848, when he set out to reform public schooling by creating state institutions of teacher training, establishing a municipal system of taxation to fund schools, and providing pupils with free libraries.

By the beginning of the twentieth century, approximately two-thirds of the forty-eight states and territories had gradually adopted some sort of school attendance law for elementary pupils, and this trend continued into the first two decades of the twentieth century. Mississippi was the last continental state, in 1918, to pass a compulsory attendance law. (All new states to the Union had to legislate provisions for public schooling after the Civil War.) Still, the push to require children to attend school did not occur without debate, and states enforced their laws haphazardly, if at all.

Opponents of compulsory attendance saw it as an encroachment upon their rights to determine how children should be educated or otherwise spend their days, and claimed that literacy and other educational skills could be just as well or better

Estimated Elementary and Secondary Public School Enrollment, Kindergarten – Twelfth Grade, 1900-1994

School year ending	Total pupils enrolled, in thousands	% of total population 5-17 years old	Total pupils enrolled in 9-12 grade, in thousands
1900	15,503	71.9	519
1910	17,814	74.2	915
1920	21,578	78.3	2,200
1930	25,678	81.7	4,399
1940	25,434	84.4	6,601
1950	25,112	83.1	5,725
1960	36,087	82.2	8,485
1970	45,550	87.0	13,037
1980	45,651	86.7	13,616
1990	40,543	90.2	11,390
1994	43,465	91.7	11,961

SOURCE: See page 440, "Notes to Tables."

learned elsewhere. Advocates of religious freedom feared that Protestant teachings and ethics would dominate the curriculum. Many churches as well felt threatened by the possibility of state-sponsored education that was increasingly non-sectarian, even secular. Moreover, the claim that public education would benefit individuals and societies in the long term did not convince those working families who, in the short term, saw schools robbing the household of their children's contribution to the family income.

Nevertheless, large portions of the American public increasingly agreed that young people belonged in school at the elementary level, a development brought about by many factors. First, the passing of compulsory school attendance laws tended to occur initially in those regions that already had high voluntary attendance rates. Generally, those regions were relatively wealthy ones, with low immigrant and non-Protestant populations, and little industry. Such communities had a tax base that could support public schools, and, influenced by the high value placed on literacy by Protestant denominations for reading the Bible, agreed to finance education for the common public and moral good. The absence of industry in those areas meant that there was a low opportunity cost for young people to attend school, since they did not have the possibility of earning money in jobs elsewhere.

Second, the passing of child labor laws helped pull young people out of the workplace and into the classroom. Thus, even in industrial regions, young people no longer saw short-term economic advantages in working instead of attending school.

Third, at the same time, waves of immigrant children worried those Americans who perceived different cultures as a threat to the dominant national culture. Some immigrants provided private schooling for their children, often in their native languages, such as the German communities in the Midwest. With the First World War, however, these schools became the target of anti-German sentiment and largely closed down under public pressure. In 1900, whereas white individuals who were born in the United States self-reported an illiteracy rate of 4.6 percent, white immigrants self-reported a higher rate of illiteracy, 12.9 percent (self-reporting was the only instrument used by the U.S. census at this time). Non-whites self-reported an illiteracy rate of 44.5 percent, and these two latter figures were beginning to concern educators and politicians. The socialization function of public schooling, including the education of pupils in the values, language, and mores of the nation, thus took on a specific "Americanization" task towards recent arrivals and minority groups.

(circa 1900) A native American boy returns to his reservation from the Carlisle Indian Industrial School in Pennsylvania, a boarding school dedicated to 'kill the Indian and save the man' by helping Native Americans to integrate into modern society.

Fourth, political reforms in this era focused on increasing the power of the citizenry over their politicians. Aside from passing reform measures that checked the corruption of those in political office, the women's suffrage movement fought for women's right to vote. This development not only resulted in a larger electorate with more power over the political machinery, it also focused attention on the need to teach all members of the nation equally how to fulfill their civic duties, which necessitated a modicum of rudimentary literacy. Finally, the U.S. economy was expanding as the nineteenth century came to a close, and arguments in favor of making schools efficient garnered tremendous support. Although three-quarters of the population still lived in the countryside, America was moving away from an agricultural economy to an industrialized one, and its residents were moving from rural centers to urban ones. Public education, as educational reformers were beginning to claim, offered the possibility of better training for these new jobs, including the possibility of advancement up the social ladder.

1870s • Expanding Public Education: From Schoolroom to Schoolhouse ~ The move towards standardized education, motivated at both the state and the federal level, had been made definitively, but further steps came only slowly. A new national office of education, founded in 1867, took on prima-

Estimated Public and Private High School Graduates

Graduation Year	Number	% of 17-yr olds	M	F
1900	94,883	6.4	38,075	56,808
1910	156,000	8.6	64,000	93,000
1920	31,266	16.8	123,685	187,582
1930	667,000	28.8	300,000	367,000
1940	1,221,475	50.8	578,718	642,757
1950	1,199,700	59.0	570,700	629,000
1960	1,864,000	65.1	898,000	966,000
1970	2,906,000	75.6	1,439,000	1,467,000
1980	3,043,000	71.4	1,491,000	1,552,000
1990	2,586,000	72.4	—	—
2001	2,875,000	—	—	—

SOURCE: See page 440, "Notes to Tables."

rily an information-gathering function. This work provided the groundwork for later educational policy arguments based upon national statistics, although the office was not inclined to direct changes at the local level. The consolidation of school districts happened under local and state auspices, with one and two-room schoolhouses and entire small districts being dissolved in favor of centralized, multi-grade schools and larger districts for an expanding school population. Municipalities were still responsible for organizing and financing their own schools, a situation that would not change significantly until the mid-twentieth century.

As school systems began to take on clear structures, and jobs began to necessitate more education, high schools began to appear in greater numbers than before. To some extent, they began to replace or absorb other forms of post-elementary education, such as private academies. Whereas high schools had primarily been located in urban, middle-class areas in the late 1880s, by the turn of the century, they were widespread throughout the country. At the beginning of the twentieth century, less than 10 percent of pupils continued school beyond eighth grade, and less than 7 percent earned a high school diploma. These numbers increased steadily over the next decades, with more than three quarters of young people attending secondary school in 1940 and over half of them receiving high school diplomas.

1890s • The Changing Curriculum ~ The purpose of all this education became a concern for policymakers and parents alike. With more and more young people in school, the question of what they should be learning took on a new importance. Faced with an expanding patchwork of public schools throughout the nation, educational experts began to identify common problems in the nation's schools. High school curriculum became the focal point of efforts to improve schools. With additional pupils, not all of whom would continue to college, the schools' function as college preparatory institutions was called into question. In 1892, the National Education Association, a professional organization of teachers and administrators, created a so-called Committee of Ten and instructed the members, all college presidents, to make recommendations for better coordination between the nation's schools and colleges.

The result was a report, published in 1893, that set the tone for educational debates for the next several years. The Committee of Ten came out in favor of a uniform, liberal education for all pupils, separated only according to the course of study: Classical, Latin-Scientific, Modern Languages, and English. All pupils, regardless of later career plans, could select any of these course paths according to their interests, argued the Committee, insisting that a high school should prepare young people for whatever life they chose in or out of the university. It also supported the introduction of modern educational subjects, such as modern foreign languages, history, and the non-physical sciences, to the classical curriculum of Latin, Greek, and mathematics.

Many schools implemented the Committee's curriculum suggestions and colleges began accepting high school graduates with modern subject training. Yet the division between college preparatory courses and standard courses did not disappear, and a legacy of subject and career "tracking" is still evident today. In fact, the report has most often been remembered as a conservative refusal to expand the high school curriculum to include practical and vocational courses.

1900 • The College Entrance Examination Board ~ Perhaps the Committee's most lasting contribution to education was its creation in 1900 of the College Entrance Examination Board, an organization that offered a single examination for admission to all universities. This Examination Board brought about a significant standardization of school curricula, since high schools began to prepare their college-bound graduates for the same test. Nonetheless, the overwhelming majority of American high school pupils at the beginning of the twentieth century did not attend college, and the evolving high school curriculum reflected a variety of courses necessary for their many career paths, from teacher training, to music, to vocational education. With the appearance of junior high schools in the early twentieth century and their widespread popularity by the 1920s, vocational and career tracking then moved down into the seventh and eighth grades, which previously had been part of the common curriculum elementary school.

1896 • "Separate but Equal:" Policy Decisions about Black Students ~ The beginning of the twentieth century also saw the emergence of debates about how to treat African Americans. In 1896, the Supreme Court ruled in *Plessy* v. *Ferguson* to uphold the "separate but equal" division of society, here focusing on separate train cars for blacks and whites. Schools began to point to the contradictions in this ruling. Especially in the South, where almost 90 percent of blacks lived until World War I, separate schools for blacks were far from equal in terms of financial or material resources. By the end of the First World War, schools for black pupils received only a third of the per capita spending of schools for white pupils. Black pupils in southern states even had less schooling than their white counterparts, attending school 101 days a year in comparison to 118 days for white pupils. Given these conditions, the claim of near-universal education for all pupils for this period must be viewed with caution. Access to education in terms of quantity had certainly increased overall, but access to quality was an issue only just beginning to be considered.

1890-1920 • From Progressive to Vocational Education ~ Debates about the role of the school in society reached their height with the "progressive education" movement at the turn of the century. This pedagogical approach, which remained most popular in the United States from the last decade of the nineteenth century until the 1920s, was part of a larger international educational reform movement. Although progressive education involved a wide variety of reform attempts that were often contradictory, some general trends can be identified. Two key competing themes were "individualism" and "institutionalism:" should schools assign equal social value to each individual, and be organized accordingly; or should the school as an institution take on the role of judging how much social value a child's abilities carried? Within this debate, progressive education supporters generally believed that education should reflect life experiences, and they promoted a constellation of educational reforms that included vocational training, social education, and critical thinking. Progressive educators interested in pedagogical reforms worked for a new pedagogy that centered on the individual child rather than a homologous group, and that was supported by a more democratic sharing of power between teachers and administrators. Administrative progressives looked to professional and "scientific" organizational and administrative reforms to address the expanding role of the school and its administrators in society.

Early • 1900s John Dewey and Edward Thorndike ~ The leading American philosopher of progressive education was John Dewey (1859-1952), also known for his philosophy of pragmatism, or instrumentalism. A pioneer of pedagogical progressivism, his key works on the subject were published between 1899 and 1916 and included *The School and Society* (1899), and *Democracy and Education* (1916). Dewey favored a school reform that permitted individualized education, without attention to a hierarchy of ability. He also believed that schools should be seen as part of society, rather than a preparation for it. To this end, Dewey's pedagogical theories supported a curriculum that both responded to the individual child as well as society. Reforming the classroom experience meant enabling societal reforms, since the school was an integral part of society and not separate from it.

Progressive education faced attacks from its opponents, led by a growing group of psychologists such as Edward L. Thorndike (1874-1949) who challenged ideas about uniform education and ability. Thorndike, the "father of the measurement movement," focused on children's individual intelligence, which he believed could be measured and used to determine appropriate subject tracks according to ability. No longer were children to be seen as having different but equally valued abilities that the school should help foster. Thorndike and his followers proposed a hierarchy of abilities, and the school's curriculum was to institutionalize these differences by preparing children to follow different vocational paths. Thus pupils with strong language or mathematics skills were to attend advanced courses that would prepare them for college, whereas average-scoring pupils would enroll in courses aimed at technical or vocational careers.

1917 • Screening Abilities through Multiple-choice Testing ~ This approach to measuring ability was mirrored and supported by developments in other sectors, resulting especially from the outbreak of World War I. In an attempt to render the U.S. Army's use of troops more efficient, in 1917 the Harvard psychologist Robert Yerkes developed the Army Alpha, the first multiple-choice intelligence test. The age of mass screening and placement according to easily administered intelligence tests thus began, and schools were among the first and most enthusiastic subscribers to this practice. Tracking young people for career paths received a "scientific" basis, and pedagogical progressivism largely died out by the end of the First World War. Schools continued to accept more and more pupils, but young people no longer received an identical education upon entering the building.

World War I and America's continuing growth as an industrial power also gave rise to new concerns about how well public schools were serving the nation's needs. In response to the military's complaints that recruits were in poor shape, military-style physical education courses became part of the school curriculum. Likewise, the war fueled existing expectations that schools should teach civic duty and national pride, in part a result of the growing anti-communism that crystallized with the Soviet Union's Bolshevik revolution in 1917. Many U.S. states mandated the teaching of state and the federal constitutions, and patriotic practices became more common in classrooms, such as singing the national anthem. On the other hand, anti-German sentiment led to a decrease in foreign language instruction in all languages and at all levels, a move with consequences still evident today.

1917 • The Beginning of Vocational Education ~ Many of these reforms had been under discussion since the beginning of the century; World War I simply provided extra momentum to legislation and curriculum reform. The Smith-Hughes Act of 1917, for instance, was a $7.2 million annual appropriation offering federal matching-funds to states for vocational education, specifically in agriculture, home economics, and industrial training. Although the act responded to labor shortages brought on by the war, a decrease in the number of highly skilled immigrants from Europe, and a drain on the workforce due to the draft, Smith-Hughes also continued a clear trend towards vocational education programs in schools.

Smith-Hughes profoundly changed the nature of American high schools on two levels. First, it crystallized the division between academic and vocational education within schools. It kept vocational teachers' salaries distinct from the budget for academic teachers, and gave vocational pupils a different curricular track that included shop time and reduced coursework in academic subjects. Vocational education took on a parallel nature in the educational system, one whose objective was seen as directly related to society's larger needs. Although the government and the public saw the provision of workplace skills and training as a response to workforce needs, vocational education's separate character made it easy to cast as a national defense strategy in the 1920s, as a solution to unemployment then in the 1930s, again as a national defense contribution in the 1940s, and then as integral to rebuilding the postwar economy after World War II.

Second, Smith-Hughes was the first major step by the federal government toward federal involvement in education nationwide. By attaching certain requirements to its financial packages and providing funding for analysis of its programs, the government forced states and local schools to meet uniform, national standards. The act also established a federal-state-local partnership for categorical funding. By opening up some of the educational system to direct contact with the workplace, the Smith-Hughes Act gave the federal government as well as the business community access to a section of the schools. It also significantly restricted vocational pupils' access to the academic offerings of the schools.

1925 • The Monkey Trial ~ Increasing government interest in education mirrored increasing public interest in what pupils were being taught in schools. In 1925, the Tennessee legislature made it illegal to teach evolution in public schools, and the American Civil Liberties Union offered to defend any teacher in the state who was charged for teaching evolution. John T. Scopes, a twenty-four-year-old high school science teacher and football coach from the rural town of Dayton, agreed to be involved in

(1925) Attorney Clarence Darrow (1857 - 1938) (L) defense lawyer, with politician William Jennings Bryan (1860 - 1925), director of the prosecution, in the courtroom during the Scopes 'monkey trial', South Dayton, Tennessee. Bryan died of a cerebral hemorrhage a few days after the trial.

a case to test the constitutionality of Tennessee's new law. Local leaders hoped in the process to gain some attention for their small community.

The fiery orator William Jennings Bryan, "The Great Commoner," headed the prosecution against the famous defense lawyer Clarence Darrow. Darrow had long openly supported the evolutionary theories popularized by Charles Darwin in his *1859 On the Origin of Species by Means of Natural Selection, or the Preservation of Favored Races in the Struggle for Life*. Soon identified as the Scopes Monkey Trial, in reference to the evolutionary postulation that human beings had descended from apes, the trial was more about academic and state freedom than it was about science versus religion. The nation watched anxiously as Bryan argued in favor of a state's right to determine the content of its schools' instruction, and Darrow attempted to show the scientific flaws in creationism. In the end, neither side achieved its goal. The jury fined Scopes one hundred dollars, Bryan died five days later in his sleep, and the national debate over evolution versus creationism fizzled out. Yet the topic of science in the classroom has continued to surface sporadically throughout the country in various forms.

1930s • The Depression and Education ~ Within just a few years, however, the American public had more immediate worries. The stock market crash of October 24, 1929, signaled the beginning of the Great Depression, which lasted a decade. Industries fired workers, and unemployment reached record heights, although the effects on school funding were not felt until the early 1930s. Schools thus realized only slowly that the Depression would affect pupils and their families, and educational institutions were not ready with solutions when the economic crisis began to make itself felt among the younger generation. At a time when young people found themselves faced with no possibility of employment, many adolescents stayed in or returned to school or college, deciding to continue their education until jobs became available again. Meanwhile, school budgets were cut drastically. The combination of increased school enrollment and curtailed funding resulted in overfilled classrooms and the elimination of many non-academic programs.

Throughout the Depression, many young people dropped out of school and university to support families in which both parents had become unemployed. This situation worried policymakers, who feared the negative moral effects of unemployment on idle teenagers and young. In 1932, Franklin D. Roosevelt was elected President, and he announced the "New Deal," a program designed to administer temporary economic and work relief. In 1935 he created the Works Progress (later Projects) Administration (WPA), which provided funds for massive public-works programs, including constructing school buildings and federal aid to hard-hit schools. Another New Deal program, the Civilian Conservation Corps (CCC), was a pseudo-military program. Designed in 1933, it provided over 2.5 million young men with some skilled training and limited education, while they worked as preservationists and resided in over 2,000 forest camps. The women's version of the CCC offered neither wages nor training, although they did receive meals and medical care. Educators viewed the CCC with suspicion, complaining that it lacked an academic component; but the program enjoyed both

Congressional and public support. In contrast, the women's camps were eliminated without discussion in 1937.

The New Deal also saw the creation of the National Youth Administration, a program that encouraged young people to stay in school and college by offering them part-time employment and providing on-the-job training for young people who were out of school. With these measures, the government clearly expanded its role in overseeing educational opportunity for young people, deciding to intervene with financial and legislative measures in order to equalize access to education. The educational system itself, though, underwent almost no reform, in spite of the financial crises that plagued most schools.

The Great Depression created an increasing awareness of civil rights. Under the leadership of Thurgood Marshall, who eventually became the first black justice of the U.S. Supreme Court, the National Association for the Advancement of Colored People (NAACP), founded in 1909, began to challenge the constitutionality of some discriminatory educational policies. The NAACP directed its energies primarily towards black students' lack of access to graduate and professional schools and towards the lower salary scales for black teachers. Although the NAACP did not achieve major results in this time period, it laid the groundwork for major tests of the "separate but equal" philosophy in American society, particularly at the level of educational access.

1930s • The Big Yellow School Bus ~ Another significant but frequently overlooked development of the late 1930s was the adoption of the yellow school bus as the standard means of transportation to and from school. Until that time, pupils walked long routes to school, rode in horse-drawn carts, hitched rides, or, if their school districts provided them, rode in a motley variety of school buses. In 1937, Frank Cyr, a professor of rural education at Teachers College-Columbia University, conducted the first survey on how pupils in the United States attended school, and the results worried him. In 1939, he organized a national conference on school transportation, inviting school and political officials as well as bus engineers.

The result of the conference was a set of manufacturing and safety standards for school buses. Although school buses have undergone significant developments since the first models, they have retained one important legacy: their bright yellow color, known as National School Bus Chrome. Thus visible at night and in bad weather, school buses have remained a clear sign of cooperation among states, educational reformers, and industry to improving pupils' access, at least physically, to schools.

1945-1955 • Soldiers Returning from War ~ If the turn of the nineteenth to the twentieth century was the era of the common elementary school, and the first half of the twentieth century marked the rise of the high school, World War II permanently reshaped the landscape of higher education. In 1944, Congress passed the "G.I. Bill," part of the 1944 Servicemen's Readjustment Act. The bill, by providing veterans with financial support for continuing education, aimed to prevent an unemployment crisis that would likely have occurred if all returning servicemen had sought employment at the same time. Approximately 7.8 million young men

(1955) Vacation For Students. Spring Break becomes popular before high school graduation. Here seen are "spring breakers" picnicking on the beach at Bonita Springs, Florida.

who fought in World War II received higher education that would otherwise have been impossible due to financial considerations. As a result, the number of college students nearly doubled in the years immediately following the war. No one had expected so many veterans to take advantage of the G.I. Bill, and the resulting influx of individuals from different social and economic backgrounds changed college campuses forever. The college degree lost its elitist character, permanently becoming a goal for a wider variety of young people with numerous career plans.

1946-1962 • Expanding Educational Opportunities ~ After the war, the federal government continued to expand its role in education in certain areas, beginning with the federal school lunch program in 1946 and the school milk program in 1954. Disabled children, too, were gaining access to classrooms with federal help: the 1958 passage of the Education of Mentally Retarded Children Act provided funding for the training of teachers for mentally retarded pupils. The government moreover clearly confirmed the school as an extension of the state in the 1948 Supreme Court decision *McCollum* v. *Board of Education*, which struck down religious instruction in public schools definitively. And in 1954, the Supreme Court refused to review a 1953 lower court ruling in *Tudor* v. *Board of Education*, which prohibited the distribution of religious literature on school property as a violation of the separation of church and state. Finally, in 1962, the Supreme Court ruled in *Engel* v. *Vitale* against allowing a government-composed, nondenominational "Regents" prayer to be recited by pupils, with the explanation that such moments coerced individuals to participate in religious activities. In the face of the 1954 Congressional addition of the words "under God" after the word "nation" in the United States *Pledge of Allegiance*—which had previously read "I pledge allegiance to the flag of the United States of America and to the republic for which it stands, one nation indivisible, with liberty and justice for all"—such moves to keep religious organizations out of the classroom were a significant statement by the federal government of its right to control the content of classroom instruction.

Additionally, curriculum reform again became a topic of contentious debate in the postwar years. On the eve of World War II, high schools had come under attack as not responding to the needs of the 60 percent of pupils on neither a vocational nor college-preparatory track. Thus began the postwar "life-adjustment education" movement, which advocated giving schools a more functional purpose in preparing young people for adult life. De-emphasizing traditional academic subjects, life-adjustment courses covered a range of practical topics, from dating to social etiquette.

1958 • Renewed Emphasis on the Sciences ~ Dovetailing the life-adjustment curriculum was a renewed emphasis on academic subjects, especially science and mathematics. In 1957, the United States lost its first battle in the "race to space" against the Soviet Union, when that country launched the world's first satellite, "Sputnik," to orbit Earth. The American public and politicians alike blamed the nation's schools for inadequately preparing young people to enter scientific careers. In 1958, Congress passed the National Defense Education Act (NDEA) to respond to this perceived national emergency. This legislation asked the eight-year old National Science Foundation (NSF) to develop new curricula in the mathematics and sciences. NSF then provided funding to academic groups and individuals to analyze fields of study and to supply new curricular and instructional directions. Once educational shortcomings had been conceptualized as a national crisis, traditional opponents to federal involvement in education retreated into silence. Even though the overall increased federal contribution to education was still very small, an important precedent had been set.

The results of the NDEA represented a significant change in the curricular focus in American schools over the next two decades. Whereas mathematics courses had traditionally taught necessary, basic skills for accounting and consumer transactions, elementary pupils now began to learn about sets and number theories. High school pupils were exposed to the basic theoretical principles of arithmetic, geometry, and trigonometry. Much of this approach, identified as "new math," did not take hold. Parents complained of not understanding the basic concepts, and the textbooks did not explain adequately the objectives that motivated the new method of learning about mathematics. Similarly, as NDEA funding spread to the social sciences, a course of study was developed to encourage pupils to think critically about their world, using an anthropological framework as the starting point. Called "Man: A Course of Study" (MACOS), this program also succumbed to criticism and fell by the wayside by the mid-1970s, under pressure from conservative groups who raised questions about the cultural relativism and apparent amorality of the course.

Estimated Percentage of Finance Sources for Public Elementary and Secondary Schools

School year ending:	Estimated revenue in millions of dollars	Federal	State	Local
1920	$970	0.2%	16.5%	83.3%
1930	2,089	0.35%	17%	83%
1940	2,261	1.8%	30.3%	67.9%
1950	5,437	2.9%	40%	57%
1960	14,747	4%	39%	56%
1970	40,267	8%	40%	52%
1980	97,635	9%	49%	42%
1990	208,656	7%	48%	45%
1996	289,230	6.4%	48.1%	45.5%

SOURCE: See page 440, "Notes to Tables."

1960s • The United States' Changing Global Role ~ As John F. Kennedy entered the White House in 1961, a combination of social forces were lining up to alter American attitudes towards their society, and the role that schools had in shaping it. The youngest man elected president, and the first Catholic, Kennedy symbolized a new era of possibilities. His challenge to Americans, "Ask not what your country can do for you—ask what you can do for your country," encouraged his compatriots to become active in the shaping of their world. During a stop on his campaign tour at the University of Michigan, he introduced the possibility of an international volunteer organization. The resulting Peace Corps represented his determination to put the United States in a leading global role of educator and reformer.

(1941) One-teacher School. African American pupils at a school with only one teacher, in Veazy, Georgia, clearly not equal but separate from their white counterparts.

In 1962, more than 70 million American households owned television sets. The problems of the world appeared nightly, increasingly in color, in living rooms throughout the nation. A decade and a half after the Second World War, young Americans coming of age in front of television sets in the 1960s—a generation typically referred to as the baby boomers—were claiming that postwar optimism about the state of the world was not warranted. This generation's concerns about the threat of nuclear war, or the unavoidable realization that the majority of the world lived in abject poverty, combined with their heretofore unparalleled level of education, providing them with the analytical skills to "question authority," a new watchword. Their activism on college campuses both mirrored and structured new social concerns about America's commitment to defending individual and group rights.

1950s-1960s • Civil Rights, Equal Rights, Same Rights ~ The first solution towards resolving the emerging concern for equal rights came about with the NAACP's new approach to fighting educational discrimination. Whereas the goal of the pre-World War II years had been to win better segregated facilities for black pupils and university students, the NAACP now demanded the elimination of the parallel system for blacks. In June 1950, the NAACP saw its first significant gain in this regard when the Supreme Court ruled that separate institutions for blacks did not, in fact, provide equal educational opportunities at the graduate school level. Although not yet a reversal of the *Plessy* doctrine, it was a major step towards ending segregation.

The famous case of *Brown* v. *Board of Education* actually came out of several separate cases. Of these, none of the plaintiffs won from the 1951 lawsuits *Bolling* v. *Sharpe* in Washington, D.C., *Briggs* v. *Elliot* in South Carolina, and *Brown* v. *Board of Education* in Kansas; or in the March 1952 *David* v. *School Board of Prince Edward County* in Virginia. The next month, however, a Delaware judge in the companion suits *Belton* v. *Gebhart* and *Bulah* v. *Gebhart* ordered white schools to accept black pupils, even though he did not rule against segregation as a principle. He left this decision to the Supreme Court. Later that year, the Supreme Court agreed to hear appeals. The four state cases became known collectively as *Brown* v. *Board of Education*; the District of Columbia case was treated separately. The court was locked in indecision until the death of Chief Justice Fred Vinson, Jr. and President Dwight D. Eisenhower's naming of Earl Warren as his successor had a catalytic effect. It was Warren who announced the justices' unanimous opinion in *Brown* v. *Board of Education* on May 17, 1954. The Supreme Court ruled that separate education violated the Fourteenth Amendment of the U.S. Constitution, which guaranteed equal protection to black citizens. Since the Washington D.C. case did not fall under the equal-protection clause, the justices ruled that segregated schools violated pupils' right to liberty as guaranteed by the due-process clause of the Fifth Amendment. "We conclude that in the field of public education the doctrine of 'separate but equal' has no place," stated the justices. "Separate educational facilities are inherently unequal," read the court's opinion.

This milestone in civil rights did not provide directions for how to go about the practical and messy task of desegregating the nation's schools. The court asked to hear more arguments on this subject, and a year later made its decision in what has come to be known as *Brown II*. Rejecting the NAACP's plea to set a one-year deadline for desegregation, the justices turned to the lower courts with instructions that schools should desegregate "with all deliberate speed." The lower courts were to take into account communities' good faith attempts to enact desegregation, but to intervene if desegregation was proceeding slowly because of disagreements about the ruling.

Many states did disagree. Of the twenty-one states that either allowed or required segregated schools, the states bordering northern states were quickest to comply. Other southern states subscribed to the "Southern Manifesto," signed by a majority of congressional leaders there in 1956, which pledged "to resist enforced integration by any lawful means." Arkansas provided the most blatant display of resistance in 1957, when its governor, Orval Faubus, dispatched the National Guard to prevent nine black pupils from enrolling at Little Rock Central High School. After the threat of violence became too great to ignore, President Eisenhower federalized the Arkansas National Guard and sent in additional troops, showing the federal government's determination to enforce the Supreme Court's order by force, if necessary. Even so, the war against discrimination was far from over at Central High or elsewhere. Tensions at the school remained high that year, and one of the nine black pupils left the school.

Almost a decade later, Congress tried a different approach. In 1964, the Civil Rights Act prevented any program with discriminatory practices from receiving federal funds. In the same year, the former public school teacher Lyndon B. Johnson was elected president on his Great Society platform, in which federal aid to education played a key role. In 1965, Johnson signed the Elementary and Secondary Education Act of 1965 (ESEA), the first federal aid program for local school districts. The cornerstone of

(1957) A view of National Guardsmen standing outside Little Rock Central High School and a large group of white students standing with them to prevent any African-American students from entering, during the first year of the desegregation of public schools in Arkansas. Nine black students were escorted into the school under federal protection later in the month.

the act was Title I, which directed funding to regions with disadvantaged children, including those with disabilities. This act was part of Johnson's War on Poverty program, and it cemented the federal government's commitment to eradicating educational inequality. The number of seventeen-year-olds with a high school diploma peaked during 1968-1969 at 77.1 percent.

The stage had been set for a domestic revolution. By the mid-1960s, the number of students graduating from high school and attending college—approximately six million—far exceeded the housing available for them at most state universities. They thus lived in small student communities near the campus, often bordering the poor inner-cities that were beginning to erupt violently. Middle-class students began to compare their privileged family backgrounds to the poverty and racial exclusion suffered by their neighbors. Donning distinctive clothing, including blue jeans and colorful embroidered shirts, and beginning a new mass level of experimentation with drugs like marijuana, these representatives of a new youth culture set out to protest the socio-economic stratification that they saw in their society. From 1964-1966, a series of student protests and riots at the University of California-Berkeley symbolized growing student activism. By 1968, public debates about civil rights and America's role in the Vietnam War peaked in a wave of student revolts that rocked schools and universities. In August 1968, students protesting the injustice of the Vietnam War bombed the Army Math Research Center at the University of Wisconsin-Madison, killing five people. Also that year, the assassinations of Martin Luther King, Jr. and Robert Kennedy fueled a national sense of uncertainty, and students continued their campaigns against societal injustices. In November 1970, violent protests by students at Kent State University in Ohio led the governor to call in the National Guard, which fired shots at protesters, killing four students and wounding nine.

Although student protests centered primarily on college campuses, some high school pupils began to express discontent as well. One important incident occurred in an Iowa high school, where school board officials banned the wearing of black armbands to protest the war, claiming that the practice was disruptive to the school's function. In a 1969 landmark decision in *Tinker* v. *Des Moines*, the Supreme Court ruled that the armbands belonged to pupils' rights to free speech. This decision departed from previous court opinions that had severely curtailed pupils' free-speech rights, and paved the way for future activism in such significant areas as school newspapers.

In this atmosphere of criticism towards America's international and domestic policies, many groups began to question assumptions about the role of Americanization in schools. Issues about equal access to education thus came to rest on concerns about immigrant and non-English speaking children, particularly in the Spanish-speaking community, whose members were termed LEP, or Limited English Proficient. The resulting Bilingual Education Act of 1968 legislated bilingual education and funded it through Title VII of the ESEA. Bilingual programs varied from school to school, ranging from parallel courses in non-English languages to tutorial assistance for LEP pupils. However, some school districts opposed bilingual programs.

In 1974, the Supreme Court heard *Lau* v. *Nichols*, a case involving Chinese-American children in the San Francisco school district. The court ruled that schools there had to offer special programs for LEP pupils so that they might take full advantage of the education being offered. A few years later, in 1982, the Supreme Court extended the rights of free public education to illegal immigrant children in the case of *Plyer* v. *Doe*. These decisions continue to be hotly contested, especially in states such as California, where the immigrant population is high. Nevertheless, the court's rulings have forced schools to adapt at least somewhat to non-traditional pupils, instead of requiring all pupils to adapt to the schools' traditional programs.

1960-1970s • The "Education for All Handicapped Children Act" and "Title IX" ~ The 1960s and 1970s saw new attention directed towards equal rights for everyone. The passage of the Education for All Handicapped Children Act in 1975 initiated a new era in the education of disabled individuals. No longer forced to attend separate schools or to pay for special education services, disabled pupils became involved in schools' experimentation with "mainstreaming" (placing disabled pupils in classes with non-disabled pupils) and "inclusion" (providing the means for disabled pupils to participate fully in all the educational activities of a classroom). This act, like the Bilingual Education Act, elicited criticism from school administrators, who complained of unwanted federal intrusion in regulating the classroom. They criticized especially the burden of fulfilling non-funded mandates.

The extent of access for girls and women to educational programs, including activities such as school sports, also gained ground in the 1970s. In 1972, Congress passed the Higher Education Act, whose Title IX prohibited discrimination based upon gender at educational institutions receiving federal funding. One of the most immediate ramifications of the act was to allow girls' and women's participation in sports. In 1984, however, the Supreme Court ruled in *Grove City* v. *Bell* that Title IX did not cover entire educational institutions, but rather only those specific programs receiving federal funding. This decision was subsequently nullified in 1988 when Congress, overriding President Ronald Reagan's veto, passed the Civil Rights Restoration Act, outlawing sex discrimination throughout an entire educational institution if any part of the institution received federal funding. In 1992, *Franklin* v. *Gwinnett County Public Schools* allowed compensatory and punitive damages to be awarded under Title IX in cases of sexual discrimination or harassment, thereby changing the act from a pure legislative measure to one with enforcement power.

1980s • Rising Concern for Educational Quality ~ In the midst of concern about providing all individuals with the same educational opportunities, regardless of race, gender, or physical ability, the topic of academic standards reemerged as a public issue in the 1980s. Self-reported total illiteracy rates among individuals fourteen years of age and older had dropped to 0.4 percent for whites, and 1.6 percent for blacks. These numbers were even lower for the younger generation, which had attended more schooling than their elders. White fourteen to twenty-four-year-olds reported 0.18 percent illiteracy, and their black age cohort reported 0.23 percent. Still, these impressive numbers only spoke to rudimentary literacy, not to higher order functions or advanced mathematics skills. Reports of a "massive decline" in pupils' test scores during the 1960s and 1970s captured the nation's attention, although the extent and reasons of the drop in academic performance remains disputed. In 1981, the federal government mandated the creation of the National Committee for Excellence in Education, giving it eighteen months to evaluate and propose reforms for pre-college education. The document to come out of this work, *A Nation at Risk: The Imperative for Educational Reform*, released in 1983, made headlines with its criticisms of the educational system. "If an unfriendly foreign power had attempted to impose on America the mediocre performance that exists today," the eighteen-member committee wrote, "we might well have viewed it as an act of war. As it stands, we have allowed this to happen to ourselves."

1980s • The Failure of Previous Programs ~ The report criticized the "unilateral educational disarmament" that had dismantled the sorts of programs created by the NSF in the 1960s and 1970s. Citing poor educational performance in comparison to earlier and international standards, the authors claimed that as many as thirteen percent of all seventeen-year-olds in the United States could be considered functionally illiterate, with as many as forty percent of minority youth being functionally illiterate. They stated further that scores for the College Board's Scholastic Aptitude Tests (SAT) showed a steady decline from 1963 to 1980, with average verbal scores falling over fifty points and average mathematics scores dropping nearly forty points.

Critics of the report insisted that the analysis of these numbers was inaccurate, because the apparent drops in educational testing performance actually represented a more accurate sampling of the population. Even if the dire conclusions of the report were overstated, it is clear that the strong public reaction in favor of improving education represented an overwhelming national fear that the United States was failing in its role of world leader, and that the schools were to blame. From this discussion, two important outcomes resulted from the report's publication. First, *A Nation at Risk* established a new direction in educational reform discussions: the increased collection of reliable educational statistics. Second, the report increased pressure on the federal government to fund public schools—a development that ran counter to President Ronald Reagan's plans to dismantle the Department of Education, which had gained cabinet status under his predecessor Jimmy Carter.

1970-1990s • Home Schooling ~ An interesting phenomenon of the latter twentieth century in America is the rise in popularity of home schooling. Home schooling is usually defined as the full time teaching of your own children at home instead of sending your child to a public or private school to be taught by someone else. One reason given for this new popularity in home schooling is the dissatisfaction of parents with their child's education through traditional methods. Other reasons may be religious, emotional, psychological or physiological. For whatever reason, the movement away from public or private schools toward home schooling is clear. In 1996 the Department of Education reported that one percent of the entire American youth population — 500,000 students — are taught at home. This figure has dramatically increased thirty percent over the past five years and according to some researchers home schooling is increasing at the rate of about twenty five percent every five years.

A policy that the United States prides itself on is the opportunity for all citizens to receive a free education, but this was not always so. Public schools only became pervasive in the United States during the 1830's but by 1852 compulsory education was mandatory in most states — all children must attend school of some kind. By the turn of the century, most children were schooled until the eighth grade either publically or privately and home schooling was virtually extinct. This remained the case until the counter culture movement of the late 1960s and early 1970s. During this time a slow resurgence of home schooling had begun. By the 1980s the number of families' home schooling rose enormously. The majority of this group of home educators were fundamentalist Christians who did not approve of the liberal curriculum taught in many public schools.

The new rise of home schooling during the 1980s led to many legal battles for these parents who wished to educate at home. For example, how was the state to regulate standards or set guidelines for these children? Ultimately, the parents of home schooled students won many precedent setting cases so that home schooling is now legal in every state. Each state sets its own guidelines on how it is to regulate home schooling. Some states are very strenuous while others are more lenient. For example, some states have specific testing requirements and certain curriculum that has to be taught every year or the parents who teach their children at home must have teacher's certificates and college degrees. Other states have school officials monitor the home school programs, while others just require that you let them know that your child will be home schooled.

Though the debate may be settled legally on home schooling, the American community is still deciding whether they approve of educational the value of home schooling. Some of the public's perceptions of home schooling are that parents cannot teach their children as well as professional educators can. Other critics claim that children do not become properly socialized with their peers. After all there are no school dances or football pep rallies to attend at home. However, proponents of home schooling argue that neither of these criticisms is valid. A University of Michigan study conducted in the late 1990s found that most home school children were well adjusted to their peers and adapted socially. Another study on home schooling by the Home School Legal Defense Association (HSLDA) in the spring of 2000 showed that students were doing remarkably well at every grade level. The study also established that young home school children tested one grade higher than public school students of the same grade and that by the eighth grade, home schoolers tested four grade levels higher than the national average.

According to the National Home Education Research Institute, home

Percentile Ranking on National Achievement Tests

	Reading	Language	Math
Conventional Schools	50	50	50
Home Education	87	80	82

National Home Education Research Institute, 1990

schooling is growing at the rate of 7 percent to 15 percent per year; 1,300,000 to 1,700,000 students (grades K-12) were home educated during 1999-2000 in the United States. The institute's survey collected on 5,402 students from 1,657 families found that home school students' academic achievement was very high. In addition, the home educated did well even if their parents were not certified teachers and if the state did not highly regulate home schooling.

Researchers compared the critical thinking skills of four groups of college students who were graduates of two types of private schools, of public schools, and of home schools. There were no statistically significant differences in various critical thinking skills; the home educated students did as well as the others.

1990s • Approaching the New Millennium: States and School Choice ~ In the last decades of the twentieth century, American schooling found itself faced with a radically different international order. The Cold War had ended, and national prosperity had reached unprecedented levels. President Bill Clinton signed the *Goals 2000: Educate America Act* into law in 1994, which generally reflected President George Bush's program of *America 2000* except that it opposed school prayer and tuition tax credits for private schools. *Goals 2000* provided incentives for states to set minimum competency standards for their pupils, and it continued the trend towards measuring success with standardized tests. Tying federal resources to state accountability for setting and achieving standards, *Goals 2000* signaled a readiness by federal and state governments to cooperate in new strategies to improve educational outcomes for the nation's youth. Yet, at the same time, parents and other community groups, suspicious of the federal government's effectiveness in educational realms, began to demand a "choice" in the way their children were educated. "Choice" began a catchword in the 1980s for a variety of new school organizational models.

In 1991, communities began establishing "charter schools" in many states. These public schools, which numbered over 1,800 by the end of the century, are deregulated and autonomous. Some are entirely new schools, while others are reformed, existing schools. Generally run by parents or other concerned community members, the holders of the charter are free to experiment with instructional and other educational techniques. Their charter can be revoked if the pupils do not demonstrate adequate results.

Another type of public school innovation has been the "magnet," or theme, school. Magnet schools are public schools that offer specialized programs, such as advanced foreign language instruction, or a focus on mathematics. The programs have sometimes been used as a voluntary method to achieve racial balance when school districts are seeking to desegregate, since the magnet schools that pupils attend are not necessarily the same schools that they would normally attend according to districting boundaries. Similarly, "open enrollment" allows parents to send their children to any school within the state. A variation on open enrollment is the "post-secondary enrollment option," a program that allows advanced high school pupils to enroll in courses at state universities, typically advanced mathematics, sciences, or foreign language courses, and receive normal high school credit for them.

Because this program redirects funding for the courses from the high school to the university, high schools are forced to compete with universities for pupils, and thus funding.

Finally, the "voucher" system, a frequently discussed program in the 2000 presidential elections, provides a voucher, or a certificate, with an assigned dollar value to parents, who can then use it for tuition purposes at the school of their choice. Depending on the extent of a state's voucher program, the money value could be used at a public or a private

School Data per State, Including School Choice, by State, Kindergarten through Twelfth Grade, as of 1998

States	# of public schools	# of pupils enrolled	# of teachers, public	$ Exp. 1999-2000	% from federal govt.	Per pupil$ exp.	# of private schools	# private school pupils	Choice
AL	1,345	739, 956	46,177	3,581,430,000	9.1	4,832	333	72,486	L
AK	497	135,373	7,696	1,217,365,000	12.6	8,834	70	6,253	N/a; ch
AZ	1,384	823,040	43,219	3,869,440,000	7.6	4,634	283	44,991	S; ch; pr
AR	1,112	456,710	28,108	2,548,001,000	8.1	5,566	196	26,645	S; ch
CA	8,178	5,844,111	260,539	31,959,025,000	8.9	5,531	3,332	609,506	L; ch
CO	1,497	699,135	38,089	3,739,880,000	5.4	5,336	353	52,563	S; ch
CT	1,058	545,663	39,209	5,225,466,000	4.3	9,476	339	69,293	S; ch
DE	185	113,082	7,073	911,261,000	7.3	8,037	103	24,193	S; ch
DC	146	79,434	5,462	563,537,000	15.2	7,105	87	16,671	C; ch
FL	2,877	2,333,570	129,731	13,014,924,000	7.6	5,436	1,481	273,628	L; ch
GA	88,654	1,823	1,401,291	8,471,318,000	6.6	6,046	588	107,065	N/a; ch
HI	250	187,395	11,019	1,149,798,000	8.5	6,075	126	33,300	N/a; ch
ID	636	244,623	13,399	1,296,873,000	6.9	5,275	82	9,635	S; ch
IL	4,228	2,011,530	122,122	11,807,233,000	6.6	5,856	1,408	298,620	N/a; ch; pr
IN	1,859	988,094	57,840	6,594,280,000	4.5	6,658	768	105,358	L; ch
IA	1,548	502,570	33,415	2,947,320,000	4.0	5,919	277	50,138	S; pr
KS	1,453	469,758	31,899	2,875,217,000	5.9	6,112	241	40,573	N/a; ch
KY	1,352	638,830	39,000	3,791,098,000	8.9	5,876	370	70,731	N/a
LA	1,476	764,939	48,721	4,178,023,000	11.4	5,441	452	141,633	L; ch
ME	697	210,927	15,086	1,540,000,000	6.3	7,365	135	17,187	L; ch; pr
MD	1,298	841,671	49,249	5,935,581,000	5.1	6,991	655	129,898	N/a
MA	1,858	948,313	64,985	7,058,413,000	5.1	7,387	657	127,165	L; ch
MI	3,625	1,696,475	91,233	12,672,855,000	6.6	7,483	1,096	187,740	S; ch
MN	2,012	856,421	54,035	6,311,575,000	4.5	7,326	580	90,400	S; ch; pr
MS	874	502,379	29.939	2,220,349,000	13.8	4,410	212	54,529	L; ch
MO	2,194	895,304	62,281	4,761,505 ,000	6.1	5,298	602	119,534	L; ch
MT	889	159,988	10,221	978,286,000	10.2	6,213	94	8,341	N/a
NE	1,353	289,981	20,100	1,711,982,000	4.9	5,870	236	40,943	S

institution. In some cases, the funds for the vouchers are taken from the school that the children would otherwise have attended. Voucher proponents argue that the system allows middle- and lower-income families to send their children to better schools. Critics, however, accuse vouchers of draining funds away from public schools, leaving the poorest schools with even fewer resources. Also, underprivileged pupils usually receive less guidance to attend better schools, thus further institutionalizing inequalities among pupils and schools.

States	# of public schools	# of pupils enrolled	# of teachers, public	$ Exp. 1999-2000	% from federal govt.	Per pupil$ exp.	# of private schools	# private school pupils	Choice
NV	448	311,063	16,653	1,684,435,000	4.4	5,406	71	12,847	L; ch
NH	513	203,127	13,290	1,282,467,000	3.7	6,306	148	21,143	L; ch
NJ	2,313	1,240,874	93,090	12,217,147,000	3.2	9,775	901	205,126	L; ch
NM	744	328,753	19,897	1,700,366,000	13.2	5,172	182	19,251	L; ch
NY	4,204	2,838,554	201,168	25,440,055,000	6.3	8,924	1,924	467,520	L; ch
NC	2,048	1,245,608	78,627	7,636,976,000	7.6	6,042	550	88,127	N/a; ch
ND	565	114,597	7,955	498,832,000	11.6	4,428	60	7,332	S
OH	3,841	1,842,067	111,452	12,040,000,000	5.8	6,554	991	251,543	L; ch; pr
OK	1,818	628,510	40,559	3,311,591,000	8.9	5,266	177	27,675	S; ch
OR	1,252	542,809	29,317	3,626,160,000	6.7	6,641	327	44,290	L; ch
PA	3,115	1,816,566	111,065	13,159,359,000	5.5	7,240	1,989	343,191	N/a; ch
RI	314	153,710	11,859	1,196,133,000	5.6	7,754	130	25,597	N/a; ch
SC	1,055	654,993	42,202	3,932,824,000	8.1	6,015	316	56,169	N/a; ch
SD	814	131,764	9,070	670,454,000	9.8	5,061	91	9,794	S
TN	1,522	903,319	53,593	4,771,068,000	8.0	5,255	513	84,651	s
TX	7,053	3,971,267	261,275	23,706,640,000	8.4	5,970	1,329	223,294	L; ch
UT	759	477,061	21,585	1,863,753,000	6.6	3,889	139	14,543	s; ch
VT	355	106,691	8,084	729,877,000	4.9	6,836	101	10,823	n/a; pr
VA	1,811	1,124,022	79,803	6,927,452,000	5.3	6,153	591	98,307	n/a; ch
WA	2,016	999,616	49,500	6,152,966,000	6.7	6,126	468	81,057	s
WV	819	296,562	20,623	2,042,531,000	10.8	6,878	159	14,640	L
WI	2,112	879,535	56,592	6,708,569,000	4.4	7,588	1,073	143,577	s; ch; pr
WY	412	94,420	6,646	650,000,000	6.2	6,913	43	2,593	L; ch

Permitted Choice: ch = charter schools; pr = private school choice; s = statewide (for Washington, D.C., c = citywide); v = voucher; l = limited; n/a = not applicable

SOURCE: See page 440, "Notes to Tables."

1997-2000

1997-2000 • School Violence ~ The end of the twentieth century has also witnessed disturbing violence in American high schools. Although juvenile violence as a whole decreased the last decade of the century, the scope of violence dramatically increased, as epitomized by the April 20, 1999, shooting spree at Columbine High School. On that morning, two male pupils, eighteen and nineteen years old, opened fire in their school, located in a suburb outside of Denver, Colorado. They had planted two twenty-pound propane bombs in the cafeteria the night before. Fifteen people died, including the gunmen, and more than twenty were seriously wounded; the bombs did not detonate. The young men were members of a loosely organized, local affiliation called the "Trench Coat Mafia" (TCM), which some observers claimed encouraged such behavior; but the shooters' motives were not clear. Although the incident was unprecedented in the extent of its violence, it was not unique. The 1990s were dotted with school murders throughout the country, from a Mississippi youth who killed his mother and two classmates in 1997, to an eleven- and a thirteen-year old who killed five pupils in their school in 1998, to an Oregon fifteen-year old who killed both his parents at home and then fatally shot two classmates in his school's cafeteria and wounded eighteen others. The Columbine incident, though, had reached suburbia, until then believed to be relatively safe from gun-toting pupils.

But it was not only the bitterly-disputed topic of gun ownership that took on new dimensions as upper-middle-class communities faced the question of their children's physical safety on school grounds. The role of the school community itself in such acts of desperation has become a feature in discussions of the purposes of education. In spite of the U.S. Supreme Court's rulings not to allow prayer in organized school settings, including before or after sports games (*Jager* v. *Douglas County School District*, 1989, and *Duncanville Independent School District* v. *John Doe*, 1993), many school districts have looked to an increase in spirituality or religion in school to reorient pupils' values. For instance, in the fall of 2000 a U.S. district court upheld a Virginia law requiring all pupils to observe a sixty-second moment of silence, a ruling that many observers believed violated the 1962 *Engels* v. *Vitale* ruling against government-mandated non-sectarian prayers. The court did not find that the moment of silence was a promotion of religion. Virginia school board officials instructed teachers not to use the word "prayer" in any context, fearing that encouraging or discouraging prayer during the moment of silence would be grounds for a constitutionality lawsuit. Clearly, the issue of school prayer and its variations is far from settled. As perceived moments of educational or societal crises demonstrate, many individuals and groups point to bringing religion into the classroom as a solution. Thus far, the Supreme Court has ruled such scenarios unconstitutional.

Bloodshed in schools permanently altered educational reform discussions. Reports by federal and private centers for the study of youth violence pointed to the statistically insignificant numbers involved in school murders and blamed the media for creating a false sense of crisis, but it is clear that pupils, their families, and the public were not comfortable with even a small number of violent crimes in the schools. The Justice Policy Institute published a report in 1998, stating that children had a one in two million chance of being killed in school, but that 71 percent of Americans feared the possibility of a shooting in their own schools. Aside from the actual issue of safety, school violence affects levels of attendance, as pupils stay away from school due to concerns about their personal safety. The installation of metal detectors deflects funding away from other programs. And anti-violence programs and curricula raise the issue of the academic versus socializing role of public schools. In many instances, young people have pointed to their own responsibility in preventing their peers' feelings of alienation and despair, in contrast to adults, who generally point to parents as the key source of blame. Pupils are still safer in school than out of it; less than 1 percent of youth homicides occur on school grounds or on the way to or from school.

Corporal Punishment

The images of a teacher rapping a student's knuckles with a ruler or standing a student in a corner for punishment are an enduring legacy of American education from Huck Finn to Holden Caulfield. As educational philosophy changed from teacher-centered to student-centered in the 1960s, the wisdom of physically punishing or embarrassing a child was challenged, and as American society became more litigious and teachers became increasing vulnerable to sexual harassment charges, incidents of corporal punishment declined. However, corporal punishment remains legal in 23 states, and the Department of Education's most recent data shows that there are records of 365,000 children being paddled in the 1997-1998 school year. Ten states (Texas, Mississippi, Alabama, Arkansas, Tennessee, Georgia, Louisiana, Oklahoma, Missouri, and New Mexico) accounted for more than 90 percent of the incidents reported in 1997-98.

Psychologists, pediatricians, and many parents are adamantly opposed to physical discipline, while school officials and teachers insist that they must include a hands-on approach to reduce student

Corporal Punishment for Students

The number of paddlings nationwide, according to the Education Department's figures, has dropped from 1.4 million in 1979-80 to 613,000 in 1989-90 to 470,000 in 1993-94. Black students are 2.5 times as likely to be struck as white students, which reflects both cultural practices within black communities and pejorative attitudes whites have against minorities.

The first state to ban corporal punishment was New Jersey in 1867. Massachusetts did not ban it until a century later, in 1971. The last state to ban corporal punishment was West Virginia in 1994.

(circa 1955) A naughty child sits in the corner and wears the dunce's cap, in a reconstruction of the old teaching methods and conditions at a one-room school in York, Maine, that has stood since 1745.

misbehavior in an era when grammar school children bring guns to school. The education package presented by President George W. Bush in 2001 gave principals and teachers broad protection from liability for disciplinary actions.

Challenges for the School of the Twenty-first Century

In 1997, the "Little Rock Nine" returned to school. Nine black men and women, kept out of the white school forty years earlier by Arkansas state governor Orval Faubus and the National Guard, marched up the same school steps to shake hands with President Clinton. A historic moment, it was also a time for reflection. Black pupils now outnumber white pupils at Central High School, but black pupils are in the minority in honors classes—a situation that mirrors national conditions. Public criticism of how much pupils really learn abounds.

During his campaign for the U.S. Presidency, George W. Bush referred to an "educational recession" in American education, claiming that poor academic performance jeopardizes the nation's healthy economy. Other educational observers have different concerns. The idea of "multiculturalism," which indicates a commitment to teaching about all cultures represented in the American population, has aroused fears of further social and cultural fragmentation. A related discussion has centered on bilingual education. The United States Office of Bilingual Education and Minority Languages Affairs estimates that over 150 languages are spoken by pupils in American schools, and this number reflects a steady increase in Limited English Proficient classes. With nearly all children now in school, not all of whom come from homogenous backgrounds, it is clear that new challenges will continue to face the American educational system in the twenty-first century.

As for literacy skills in English, an area that would seem to be a clear indicator of effective schooling, the picture is blurry. In sharp contrast to the self-reported total illiteracy rates in the 1980s, according to the 1992 National Literacy Assessment, over 20 percent of American adults over the age of sixteen have nothing more than rudimentary literacy skills, "Level I literacy." They thus have enough skills to perform only basic reading tasks in English that are part of daily routines in modern society. About 2.5 percent of adults do not even have this skill, a figure still higher than the 1980s self-reported rates. Different literacy studies vary widely in their testing methods and conclusions, so it is difficult both to estimate with certainty the numbers of illiterate adults and to identify the causes of illiteracy; but multiple factors explain this high number, including race, economic status, school dropouts, non-native English speaking abilities, and even visual impairment.

Education obviously plays a central role in curbing illiteracy numbers, but it is not the only factor. Individuals who complete high school are more likely to be found in higher-ranking literacy groups. Race is also another factor. Of the number of adults who stopped their education before receiving a high school diploma (dropouts), only 4 percent of white pupils dropped out, in comparison to 7.8 percent of Hispanic pupils, and 6.5 percent of black pupils. Overall dropout rates were slightly higher for women than for men, at 5.3 percent versus 4.5 percent. Whites achieved overall the highest literacy scores, followed by blacks, and then Hispanics, whose overall average years of schooling is less than whites, at over eleven and a half and ten years, respectively. Gender, though, plays less of a role in literacy rates than it did in the past. Men and women have demonstrated the same average prose literacy testing scores, with men testing somewhat higher for quantitative skills—a difference that has usually been attributed to men being socialized earlier to work mathematically. For more advanced literacy rates, the gap between whites and minority groups is significantly wider. Some of the lower scores by minority populations can be attributed to underprivileged economic and social backgrounds, which have been demonstrated to affect educational performance negatively. Other causes, such as prejudice and discouragement, are less quantifiable, and thus do not lend themselves to easy solutions in curriculum adjustment or increases in school financing.

Against the background of high national limited literacy rates and obvious discrepancies between whites and minority cultures in school completion, data on a new type of literacy must also be considered: information technology (IT) literacy. In 1994, the total number of schools with Internet access was only 3 percent. Just four years later, 89 percent of public schools had Internet access, and the number is growing rapidly. Even 80 percent of poor districts reported Internet connections that pupils could use. The public's expectations for a literate population have quickly expanded to include IT literacy, and schools have been assigned the instructional role. Although the educational attainment gap between races and genders is narrowing, differences persist in terms of years of schooling and performance that will be reproduced among these populations in larger society. Schools risk contributing to the "digital divide" between Internet users and non-users that falls along economic and racial lines.

Conclusion

The end of the twentieth century marked a level of school attendance, literacy, and graduation unthinkable at the beginning of the century. Elementary and secondary school official enrollment averaged 70 percent of all school-aged children at the beginning of the twentieth century, with actual attendance probably closer to 50 percent, and heavily weighted toward the lower grades. At the dawn of the twenty-first century, over 70 percent of seventeen-year olds are graduating from high school. Literacy rates are high at the basic skills level, although not as high as many politicians and educators believe they should be—of course, the desire to bring all pupils up to a higher literacy and education level is a significant phenomenon in and of itself, compared to resistance to universal education a century earlier. The persistent education and literacy gap between races increases with higher level of education and skills, a phenomenon that will likely continue with regards to IT skills.

The role of the federal government has grown significantly over the decades, but this is a development that does not satisfy all Americans. Although the federal budget comprises a minute portion of actual education expenditures, many parents and politicians throughout the nation insist that the government's involvement in educational policy should be less than it now is. These individuals want more direct control of how their tax dollars are spent on education, insisting that offering parents and their children a choice in the best school for local situations is the only way to guarantee improved education.

Americans believe now more than ever that their educational system reflects the progress made by their society. This interpretation offers a mixed conclusion for the state of United States schools. On the one hand, more children are in school, more young people graduate from school, and more young adults—almost a quarter of the population between twenty-five and twenty-nine years of age—complete four or more years of college, compared to 7 percent in 1950. Educational institutions at all levels continue to reflect more accurately the demographic make-up of the population. On the other hand, schools and classrooms have unquestionably become microcosms of the communities that support them, and this development has not only been positive. The bulging school buildings, more accessible to more of American society, must also now find solutions to the same social ills that plague the rest of the nation. School violence, racism, uneven distribution of resources, arguments about the role of the government, and linguistic diversity represent but a handful of the concerns faced by today's schools. Almost a half-century after the *Brown* v. *Board of Education* ruling, and over a century and a half after Horace Mann's insistence that all children should attend school, achieving truly equal education for all Americans remains a distant goal.

Notes to Tables

— = data unavailable.

Data collected before 1960 does not include Alaska and Hawaii.

Data for tables and information compiled from the following sources: U.S. Department of Education, National Center for Education Statistics, Statistics of Public High Schools; Biennial Survey of Education in the United States; Statistics of State School Systems; Statistics of Nonpublic Elementary and Secondary Schools; Common Core of Data surveys; U.S. Department of Commerce, Bureau of the Census, Current Population Reports; Nina Shokraii Rees, *School Choice 2000: What's Happening in the States* (The Heritage Foundation: Washington, D.C., 2000); and my own calculations. Data is based upon schools' reports and estimates, state reports and estimates, and census reports, and is subject to sampling and statistical error. In the case of differing reports for numbers, I selected the figures that most closely corresponded to other documentation. In all cases, overall trends corresponded across the sources.

Bibliography

Altenbaugh, Richard, ed. *Historical Dictionary of American Education*. Westport, CT: Greenwood Press, 1999.

Brooks, Kim, Vincent Schiraldi, and Jason Ziedenberg. "School House Hype: Two Years Later." San Francisco, CA: Justice Policy Institute/Children's Law Center, 1999. http://www.cjcj.org/schoolhousehype.

Dow, Peter B. *Schoolhouse Politics: Lessons from the Sputnik Era*. Cambridge: Harvard University Press, 1991.

Grant, Gerald. *The World We Created at Hamilton High*. Cambridge: Harvard University Press, 1988.

Harlan, Louis. *Separate and Unequal: Public School Campaigns and Racism in the Southern Seaboard States, 1901-1915*. Chapel Hill: University of North Carolina Press, 1958.

Kliebard, Herbert. *The Struggle for the American Curriculum: 1893-1958*. Boston: Routledge and Kegan Paul, 1986.

Kruger, Richard. *Simple Justice*. New York: Alfred A. Knopf, 1976.

Lynd, Robert S. and Helen Merrell Lynd. *Middletown: A Study in American Culture*. 1929. Reprint. New York: Harcourt, Brace, 1956.

National Commission on Excellence in Education. *A Nation at Risk: The Imperative for Educational Reform*. Washington, D.C., 1983.
http://www.ed.gov/pubs/NatAtRisk/

Ravitch, Diane. *Left Back: A Century Of Failed School Reforms*. New York: Simon & Schuster, 2000.

Reese, William J. *The Origins of the American High School*. New Haven: Yale University Press, 1995.

Urban, Wayne and Jennings Wagoner, Jr. *American Education: A History*. New York: McGraw-Hill, 1996.

Westbrook, Robert. *John Dewey and American Democracy*. Ithaca, NY: Cornell University Press, 1991.

Internet Resources

American Educational Research Association
http://www.aera.net/

U.S. Department of Education
http://www.ed.gov

National Education Association
http://www.nea.org

National Home Education Research Institute
http://www.nheri.org
Conducts on-going studies about all aspects of home schooling.

Benita Blessing
Fellow, Institute of European History, Mainz

EMOTIONAL CHANGE

(circa 1950s) The socially acceptable way to express emotions changed dramatically during the twentieth century.

TIMELINE

1830-1919 ~ Tentative Expression of Emotions

Emotions are gender specific / Reason, not love, should determine marriages / Dolls' wardrobes include mourning clothes and caskets (1870) / Women begin to express favorable opinions about sex but in moderation (1890s) / Sibling rivalry recognized as unhealthy (early 1900s) / Public display of grief is attacked (early 1900s) / Much death caused by WWI and the flu epidemic desensitizes people to death (1918-1919)

MILESTONES: Thousands of Indians die during forced relocation on the "trail of tears" (1831-1838) • First use of anesthetic (ether) on humans in the U.S. (1842) • Michigan abolishes capital punishment (1847) • Female moral reformers attack prostitution as product of male lust (1850s) • Queen Victoria dies, ending the Victorian era; Edwardian era begins (1901) • Mammography developed to detect breast cancer (1913) • Child labor abuse made a federal crime (1916)

1920-1929 ~ Milestones for Emotional Change

Ninety-two percent of college coeds engage in petting, and one third in sexual intercourse (1920s) / Gender bias is reduced / Jealousy in children is regarded as unhealthy (1925) / Dying people are moved out of the home into hospitals / *Parents' Magazine* established for child-rearing advice (1927) / Mother-love is questioned / Controlling anger is regarded positively / Casting guilt on children falls out of favor / Boxing is regarded as a healthy sport for boys / Love and sex are considered mutual emotions / Consumer culture accepts envy / Open sexuality increases jealousy / Psychoanalysis becomes popular

MILESTONES: Flappers frequent speakeasies, smoke cigarettes and engage in promiscuous sexual activity • Welfare capitalism by businesses reduces the power of unions over workers • Hays Code restricts filmmakers from expressing violence and sexuality • First year women have the right to vote (1920) • Infant death rates fall by 20 percent (1920) • Mail order catalogues and magazines bring fashion awareness to every household (1925-1929) • Insulin shock is used to treat schizophrenia (1929) • 23,000 registered movie houses estimate100 million admissions each week (1929)

1930-1945 ~ Extreme Emotional Responses Discouraged

Righteous jealousy struck down as a defense for murder (1930s) / Superman emerges as the super cool hero (1930s) / Synthetic hormone diethylstilbestrol treats menopause symptoms (1939) / Expressions of anger discouraged in the workplace (1940s) / Violence is prevalent in films and literature (1940s) / Once considered inappropriate, swing dancing becomes an acceptable method of releasing wartime tension (1942-1945)

MILESTONES: Conservatives lash out against non-Protestants (1930s) • First psychoanalytic institute for training analysts opens in Boston (1930) • Under pressure, the movie industry enacts the Production Code, addressing crime, sex, vulgarity, obscenity, profanity, costumes, dancing, and religion (1930) • 1.5 million latex condoms are produced in the U.S. each day (1935) • Alcoholics Anonymous is founded in New York City (1935)

1946-1979 ~ Gender Differences in Emotions Diminished

Expression of excessive grief is considered a sign of psychological flaw (1950s) / Emotional intensity is systematically discouraged (1950s) / Politicians are expected to be polite (1960s) / Anger is revived in the Vietnam protest and women's movement (early 1970s) / Emotional restraint is again valued (late 1970s)

MILESTONES: Kinsey report on sexual behavior of the human male published (1948) • Beat generation considers itself pilgrims on a spiritual quest (1950s) • Kinsey reports that more than half of the nation's women are not virgins when they marry (1953) • Women's liberation movement encourages smaller families and free access to the birth control pill (1960s) • Medicare provides health care coverage for people over 65 (1966) • Political rebellion causes anti-establishment dress codes (1968-1975) • California is the first state to permit "irreconcilable differences" divorce, leading the way to no-fault divorce (1969) • First test-tube baby is born in England (1978) • Jerry Falwell founds Moral Majority, Inc. and pledges to use its political influence to re-establish traditional values in American society (1979)

1980-2000 ~ Era of Emotional Self-Interest

Assertiveness training for women develops empowerment strategies (1980s) / Male bonding becomes fashionable (1980s) / Punk rock, rap music, and road rage express social anger (1990s)

MILESTONES: Hate crime legislation is passed in every state (1980-1997) • First baby is born from a donated embryo to an infertile mother (1984) • 400,000 Americans die of AIDS (1987-1999) • Family and Medical Leave Act provides worker security during family emergencies (1993)

INTRODUCTION

The twentieth century has been a time of considerable change and debate over emotional standards and, to some extent the actual emotions many Americans experience. The changes relate to wider shifts in work and family life, in health and mental health, and in consumerism. They also pick up other large shifts, such as the dramatic alteration in patterns of death. The *impact* of emotional change also requires consideration as it vividly affects family life and leisure. It helps explain the unusual popularity of psychology and psychological therapy in twentieth-century America. It affects the way different groups of Americans are judged, and it continues to color the relations between men and women. Even political standards pick up the shifting emphases in American emotional life.

Emotions change profoundly the way Americans behave, and how they evaluate important aspect of their society. For example, a century ago, even fifty years ago, it was common for American teachers to display scorn and anger against badly performing students in their classes. They publicly pointed out who had done badly on tests, a routine still common in societies such as Russia. During the later twentieth century, displays of anger against students began to be reined in, viewed as damaging to young people's self-esteem. Only a few special circumstances, such as athletics, maintained older patterns: it was all right for coaches to shout. In other educational situations, teachers had to learn to become much more circumspect.

1900-1930s • Public Displays of Emotions ~ A century ago, a person's grief at a family member's death was a public event. The grieving party wore mourning clothes, and a considerable etiquette described how others should react. From the 1920s onward, however, this grief process was attacked. People were expected to handle their grief quickly and, largely, privately. Special mourning badges and procedures were eliminated.

(circa 1945) In the nineteenth century it was sometimes possible for a man to successfully argue in court that his murder of his wife and/or his wife's lover was motivated by such intense and righteous jealousy that violence was the unavoidable outcome.

During the nineteenth century, American politicians often became visibly angry at their opponents, and crowds responded enthusiastically. During the twentieth century, however, new rules gradually developed. Harry Truman was the last presidential candidate encouraged to "give'em hell". By the 1960s, a new debating format was developed for candidates for major offices that involved reporters asking provocative questions,

Emotion	Nineteenth Century	Twentieth Century	Date Change Begins
Anger	Wrong for women; desirable for men as a spur to vigorous public behavior, though inappropriate in family settings.	Greater gender equality; considerable sense that anger was never useful	1920s
Envy	Regarded as petty and undesirable	Accepted as a normal emotion that might spur desirable interest in higher consumer standards	1920s
Grief	Desirable expression of loss; public trappings	Viewed as awkward, possible requiring psychological help; public trappings withdrawn	1910s
Jealousy	Not approved but noted as an emotion women might show in defense of family; occasionally accepted as motive for male violence	Strongly disapproved for both gender, sign of immature possessiveness	1920s
Guilt	Recommended as a desirable emotional preventative of bad behavior	Widely acknowledged but no longer seem as desirable, but rather uncomfortable and intrusive	1920s
Fear	All right for women; bad for men, who must learn courage	Viewed as a problem for all, should not be imposed on children: expressions of fear understandable	1920s
Love	Widely praised; intense love between mother and child, men and women in courtship urged; not primarily focused on sexuality	Still praised, but cautions introduced; too much mother-love bad; too much soaring passion distrusted; same-sex love discouraged; heterosexual love increasingly associated with sexuality	1920s

with candidates implicitly tested on their capacity to react without anger. The public had come to believe that open displays of anger denoted weakness in a candidate. "Never show anger to the media" became standard political advice.

Laws also changed. In the nineteenth century it was sometimes possible for a man to successfully argue in court that his murder of his wife and/or his wife's lover was motivated by such intense and righteous jealousy that violence was the unavoidable outcome. By the 1930s this legal defense was explicitly eliminated, even in southern states where it had long retained greatest validity. Now, courts ruled, civilized standards required that men (as well as women, who had never been granted this legal option, since violence was not regarded as appropriately feminine) must keep their jealously in check even under extreme provocation.

The twentieth century saw a number of key changes in emotional standards, by which individuals responded and through which they judged the behavior of others. The previous chart suggests patterns of change in key emotions, which sets the basis for the more extensive assessments of emotional change in the balance of this article.

1920s • Changing Attitudes about Emotions ~ Historians who have worked on twentieth century emotional change in the United States have generally pinpointed the 1920s as the point at which significant redefinitions began, though there were a few earlier hints, as with grief. The consequences of emotional change sometimes followed initial shifts in standards by several decades. For example, new concerns about anger began to surface in the 1920s, but it was only by the 1950s that the impact showed up clearly in political behaviors.

(1920s) A woman implores her jealous husband not to be angry with her.

Some observers have wondered if, by the final decades of the twentieth century, another set of changes was beginning to intrude, which would modify the basic directions of the twentieth century change. But the main focus of historical attention has been on the fundamental shift that began to take root in the 1920s, with consequences extending into subsequent decades.

1920s-1970s • Jealousy ~ "Few emotions are experienced by man which from a social point of view are more important than jealousy . . . The jealous person becomes an object of dislike. Often he develops the idea that he is unjustly treated or persecuted, and all too frequently this idea causes uncontrolled resentment and disastrous results." So wrote child psychology expert D.H. Thom in 1925, and the sentiment was echoed in a host of parenting manuals issued between 1925 and 1930 by the Children's Bureau and the Child Study Association of America.

The advice went further: jealousy first manifested itself in very young children, typically directed against the arrival of a new sibling. Sibling rivalry was dangerous in itself: the jealous child might well harm, even kill, a new baby. And it was such a breeding ground for the inculcation of lifelong jealousy that parents much be vigilant against it. Appropriate tactics, including providing an older child with his own possessions and lots of attention, could reduce jealousy. As the Children's Bureau put it, "Nobody likes a jealous person. A jealous person is never happy. . . But with the vigilant tactics, Tony was happy again. Now he loves his

(1946) Young girls on their visit to the sea, argue and fight over whose turn it is to dig to Australia.

baby brother. He is not jealous anymore." True to form, well into the 1950s, parents reported that sibling rivalry was one of the most difficult personality problems they had to cope with, and their concern created an ample market for one new childrearing manual after another.

All this may seem quite unexceptional, even a constant in human affairs, except that acknowledging jealousy and sibling rivalry was new in the study of human behavior. Nineteenth-century childrearing manuals and parental comment had almost never mentioned jealousy among young children, and the specific term, "sibling rivalry", had not been coined. Jealousy in general had received little attention, particularly where men were concerned. And there was even a maverick line of thought that argued that male jealousy might be a good thing, as it could motivate intense achievement in business rivalries (this thought lingered in a few statements in the 1920s, at which point it died).

Some major changes in attitudes toward jealousy had occurred, making the issue a vexing one for parents. A host of experts, many of them trained in psychology, had much to say on the subject of jealousy. It was new expertise, like Thom's, that introduced new concepts like sibling rivalry.

The campaign to control sibling jealousy altered family life, at least to some degree. It was a bonanza for toy makers, who could sell more toys to parents eager to distract a potentially jealous child. (It was at this point that the idea of bringing gifts for older children at a baby's birthday was introduced.) It led children, as they grew, to control their own jealousy in order to seem more mature. By the 1930s, college students were telling observers of their eagerness not to seem jealous, while teenagers termed jealousy as "immature".

Comparative studies by the 1970s indicated that most Americans wished to conceal jealousy. The argument that a crime could legitimately be committed in a fit of jealousy, which could get some murderers off in the nineteenth century, was now explicitly discounted by the courts, on grounds that any mature person should be able to control jealousy. By the 1980s, as the new emotional style continued to do its work, it became illegal for teachers to post grades publicly, lest they occasion jealous embarrassment. After the sexual revolution of the 1970s, society tended to be more critical of the jealous partner than the unfaithful partner in an adulterous relationship. This is a key emotional component of the twentieth-century sexual revolution and the ideal youth behavior. This was no trivial change in emotional culture.

History of Emotions

The history of emotions is a relatively new historical field and is predicated on two assumptions. First, while key emotions have a biological component, in bodily changes associated with feelings such as anger, they also have a strong cultural component that affects the way people define, evaluate and even experience emotions. This cultural factor accounts for different emotional patterns among different emotional groups. A recent study, for example, shows that when experiencing jealousy, French people are likely to become angry, Dutch to become sad, while Americans carefully check with others to see if their emotional reactions have been appropriate. Culture provides what sociologist Arlie Hochschield calls "feeling rules," which tell us how to define and rate our own emotions relative to those of others. These rules can vary widely, from one culture to another, but also from one time period to another.

The second assumption builds on the first: if emotions are partly culturally constructed, they can change. Middle-class Americans had developed some fairly clear emotional definitions in the nineteenth century. These did not totally shift in the twentieth century, but the alterations were considerable, as the previous chart suggests. The development of a new emotional style in twentieth-century America relates to a number of efforts to grasp changes in the larger national character. Sociologist David Riesman, for example, argues that in the nineteenth century the way in which people chose to display emotion was "conscience driven" but in the twentieth century was directed by the opinion of others. Changes in emotional standards help explain the widespread sense of altered behavior. Some of the changes in American emotional style seem to be shared by other Western countries, but others, as the jealousy example suggests, may be more distinctively national.

Studies of twentieth-century developments from several vantage points, both sociological and historical, have reached roughly similar conclusions, though they disagree about causes of change. The United States has many subcultures, and their relationship to mainstream emotional culture—the emotional culture preached, for example, in middle-class child-rearing manuals—is only beginning to be sketched. African-American child-rearing advice picked up the larger cautions about anger by the 1970s, but also indicated that anger against racism was fully justified.

Another important area of research involves the relationship between emotional change and other aspects of the social experience. In psychology, emotions studies are often self-contained, for emotion is the central topic. In history, however, emotions relate to other behaviors and institutions. Some links are obvious.

The shifts in twentieth-century emotional standards help explain the rise of psychology, as well as the recurrent discussion between men and women, in what was often called the "battle of the sexes." Divorce law, and particularly the rise of the no-fault divorce concept from the 1960s onward, picked up another aspect of emotional change, including the growing aversion to guilt and the pride in avoiding intense anger. But researchers are just beginning to untangle the ramifications of the shifts in emotional culture.

When historical work on twentieth-century emotional culture had yet to be created, there was a "modernization" model of twentieth-century emotional change, posited by some sociologists, that had some echoes in popular belief. The argument ran as follows: traditional emotional standards in the United States were fairly rigorous, involving all sorts of repression, but in the twentieth century the slogan increasingly became "anything goes." Emotional liberation was the watchword, even before the cultural challenges of the 1960s. This liberation model has been entirely abandoned by historians and sociologists, even though the concept is still trumpeted periodically by popularizers. Actual twentieth-century patterns are far more complex, and in some ways require more nuanced self-control than nineteenth-century emotional culture had involved.

1830-1900 • Gender Specific Emotions ~ Nineteenth-century advice manuals, directed at parents and young people alike, presented a fairly clear emotional culture. It focused heavily on the family, and it was quite gender-specific, urging different emotional styles for men and women appropriate to their different functions in life. Men, for example, were urged to display courage in face of fear. Boys' stories were filled with imagined episodes in which boys or men were confronted with danger and overcame their fears. This virtue was not relevant for girls, the term courage was never applied to women until the twentieth century, and a certain fearfulness was even attractive as part of blushing femininity.

Anger standards varied as well. Both men and women were urged to avoid anger in family settings. Marriage advice, for example, devoted great attention to the importance of avoiding quarrels. Women were supposed to be anger-free in all circumstances. Temper was simply unfeminine. One of women's great qualities as parents was their ability to present children with an anger-free environment. But the expectation for men concerning anger was more complex. Restrained in family life, men should nevertheless be capable of summoning up anger as a motivation in business competition and protests against social injustice. Boys were supposed to retain their capacity for channeled anger, through boxing lessons, for example, even as they learned to discipline it at home.

Some emotions, however, cut across gender. Guilt was the great emotional anchor of middle-class morality. It replaced the emphasis on shame that had predominated in the eighteenth century. Great effort was devoted to instilling guilt in wayward children, for example, by sending them to their rooms to consider their wrongdoing.

Love was an even more important emotional unifier, bringing men and women together in family life despite their diverse roles and temperaments. To be sure, women had some capacities for love that men lacked; the nineteenth century saw the apotheosis of the idea that women had special loving qualities as mothers. But the family should be a loving site for all parties. Marriage should be founded on love, defined as an essentially spiritual passion that could make a man and a woman emotionally one.

Following from love came an important emphasis also on grief. Nineteenth-century guides celebrated the validity of intense grief on the death of a family member. Etiquette books provided elaborate statements on how to acknowledge grief in others. People should respect grief in others, and allow a long time for its expression.

1830-1900 • Following the Rules ~ Emotional rules, of course, were not always followed. But there was considerable enforcement for Victorian emotional culture amid the middle classes, and ample indications that it was taken seriously. Boys, for example, altered the meaning of the word "sissy" (which initially was simply short for sister), to attack peers who did not display courage or the capacity for righteous anger. Girls spent time role-playing in grief. By the 1870s, dolls' outfits were available that included mourning clothes and coffins. Both men and women, in courtship and also in same-sex friendships, wrote ardently of love. Women worked hard on the tempers, both in fiction, as in Louisa May Alcott's *Little Women*, and in fact. Diary entries reveal sincere efforts to live up to this standard of femininity, and mothers might indeed appear to their children to be anger-free.

Some of the characteristic illnesses of nineteenth-century women, such as hysterical paralysis, probably resulted from the absence of legitimate outlets for anger, though some women, in crusades such as temperance, found indirect ways to express anger against sinful behaviors. Whole institutions, such as men's sports, revolved around the dominant emotional culture, in the case of sports, providing opportunities for courage and the controlled expression of anger.

1890s • Social Expectations about Emotions ~ Finally, there was no particular dispute about the emotional culture, despite the obvious fact that in practice, many people, men as well as women, must have found it complex. Psychologists like G. Stanley Hall, in studies of adolescence, largely confirmed the culture, urging young men, for example, to show courage and aggressiveness. Into the 1890s, child-rearing manuals repeated the standard advice about selfless love, male-female differences concerning anger, and the importance of guilt as the emotional protection against bad behavior.

To be sure, this nineteenth-century emotional culture was not for everyone. Middle-class writers made it clear that they did not expect the lower classes, including minorities and immigrants, to be able to live up to their standards. Discussions of courage, for example, often suggested that ordinary soldiers could not be expected to show the manly virtues of courage. Even courts of law recognized distinctions concerning love. While, by the 1890s, middle-class couples in some states could use absence of proper affection as a sign of mental cruelty in divorce cases, working-class couples could not because they were supposed to lack this refined capacity. And a great deal of criticism was directed against immigrant parents who did not show proper love to their children or who treated them angrily. These class- and race-based distinctions showed the limits of the dominant nineteenth-century emotional culture, but they were also serviceable as the basis for class distinctions in a theoretically democratic society.

1900-1920 • Signs of Change ~ Between 1900 and 1920, there were a number of signs that Victorian emotional culture was beginning to be questioned. The idea of intense love as part of friendship between two women or between two men was certainly reversed, given new fears about homosexuality.

It was at this point that the idea of sibling rivalry began to emerge, and with it the sense that jealousy was a standard problem for children. Parents must help children rid themselves of jealousy, lest immaturity bedevil their adult personality.

Fear was also hauled out for reexamination. Psychological studies in the late nineteenth century began to demonstrate that children, boys and girls alike, often suffered from intense, irrational fears. In this setting, simply urging courage might not be adequate, and indeed might be counterproductive. The stage began to be set for a different approach to dealing with fear in children. Parents were urged to avoid settings in which fear might be encountered and to provide anxious support, rather than injunctions of manly courage, when a boy did express fear. In the process, the idea of gender distinctions softened. Boys still experienced pressures in sports to demonstrate courage in ways girls did not, but in the child-rearing literature the gender distinctions faded in favor of recognizing problems shared by children regardless of sex.

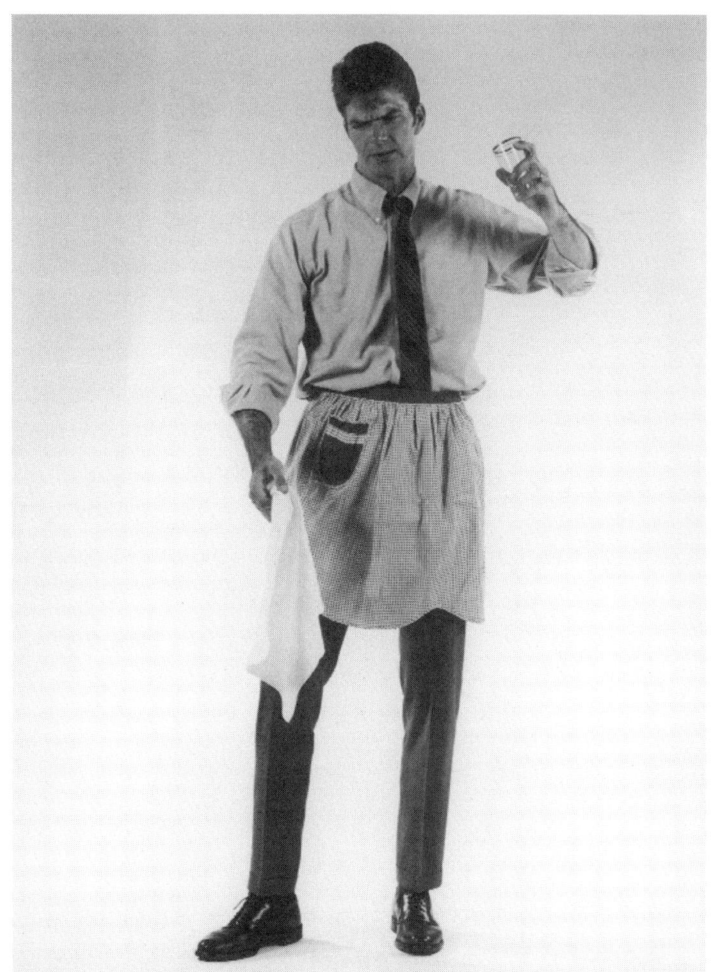

(circa 1955) As the roles that men and women played in society became more alike, the gender bias related to emotions declined.

1920s • Reducing the Gender Bias ~ In general, the new emotional formulation that was beginning to emerge was much less gender-based than its nineteenth century predecessor had been. The nineteenth century emotional culture had assumed that men and women were very different emotionally, by nature, which was a good thing given their different functions in life. Women were suited to domesticity, men to public action. Only in love would they share enough common emotion to bridge their differences in other respects. In the twen-

1900-1920s

tieth century, while gender roles and stereotypes strongly persisted, attention shifted to emotional issues that both males and females shared. Thus jealousy was a problem for children, not either gender particularly; the same held for childish fear. Maternal love began to be criticized, rather than held up as a badge of honor for women. A new breed of marriage counselors began to urge men and women alike to be careful about basing marriage choices on intense love. In all this, the main purpose of emotion was no longer to highlight distinctive natures or roles for men and women.

1900-1920s • Recasting Grief ~
But there was more than gender change involved. The whole current that began to emerge by the 1920s urged respectable Americans to beware of undue emotional intensity in general. We can see this force at play by turning to another specific example, grief, in which the consequences for behavior and self-perception were particularly great.

Grief served as one of the earliest targets for emotional redefinition. Here was not only a classic Victorian emotional outlet, but also the basis for substantial ritual. Elaborate mourning clothes and household decorations, and expensive funerals and cemetery markers symbolized the Victorian reaction to death. In the grief apparatus, people were supposed to express their great love for family members and also their complex reactions to death itself. On the one hand, death was inappropriate in a progressive world, particularly the deaths of children. There was a growing feeling that death should be controlled. On the other hand, death did occur, and feelings of inappropriateness and outright guilt that somehow death should have been prevented, showed up in grief and ritual. Finally, new beliefs, such as the idea the family members would be reunited in heaven (a distinctly nineteenth-century addition to Christian theology), were meant to make grief endurable and in a certain sense an even pleasurable expression of love.

This whole complex of emotion and ritual began to be attacked in the first decades of the twentieth century. Grief began to seem ghoulish and unhealthy. Elaborate funerals were now criticized: as one magazine put it, "Nothing less than ghoulish are some of the stories of the pressure put upon grief-distracted people to honor their dead at excessive expense." *The Independent* noted in 1908:

> Probably nothing is sadder in life than the thought of all the hours that are spent in grieving over what is past and irretrievable. Modern people should be able to live to the fullest and accept death without fuss. When grief persisted, some kind of therapy was clearly called for. When a woman cannot rouse herself from her grief there is need of the care of the physician.

1920s • De-emphasizing Death ~
Here began a campaign that did, however gradually, change the twentieth-century approach to death in the United States (also see the entry on Death). By the 1950s up-to-date etiquette books, far from urging respect for grief, emphasized the responsibility of a grieving person not to impose his or her emotions on others. "Grief work" on the part of doctors and psychologists characteristically involved an assumption that grief was a problem, a sign of psychological flaw, and needed to be dampened as quickly as possible as part of mental health and a smooth social life.

Signs of mourning began to be curtailed, though the process was gradual depending on social class, personality, and religion. Employers no longer allowed much time away from work, even for sensitive middle-class people. Public displays of mourning, such as wearing black or at least black armbands, began to recede. Americans still indulged in more elaborate funerals than their European counterparts (in part because a vast country offered more space for expanding cemeteries), but the practice of cremation gained ground after World War II.

Many observers noted that death itself began to become a taboo subject. Physicians, trained in fighting death, not people more expert in grief such as religious leaders, began to take the lead in dealing with death, and this both reflected and caused new attitudes in the general public. They moved the act of dying.

By the 1920s an increasing number of people were moved to hospitals to die, rather than dying at home. Again, this both reflected and caused new emotional reactions, for grief became more complex in a hospital setting. Many people used their emotional energy to urge on a fight against death, with heroic (and costly) medical procedures in hospital, rather than grappling more directly with grief at the inevitable.

1918-PRESENT • WAR AND GRIEF ~ Generally, mainstream advice during both World Wars urged a stiff upper lip toward military casualties. Grief should not be unduly explored, though of course due credit should go to the mothers of fallen servicemen. Too much emotion might jeopardize the war effort. To some extent, it was noble to sacrifice life for democracy and love of country.

But this formulation began to shift during the Korean war, partly because the war became increasingly unpopular. After the first few months, when casualties were not reported in depth in the media, accounts of war deaths began to become much more emotional than in World War II. The public became fixated on individual examples of suffering and the tragic loss of life. This shift was part of the growing American revulsion against the war, and resentment that the nation should not have to experience grief of this sort. The new attitude carried over strongly to the Vietnam War, when media coverage was intense. From that point onward, it became axiomatic that American life should not be threatened in war, for the emotions involved were unacceptably painful. Bombing raids and intimidation, as in the Gulf War, replaced extensive combat.

The general twentieth-century hostility to grief persisted, but there were two successive interpretations in military affairs, the first to downplay the emotion, the second to recognize grief and use its unacceptability as an argument against the military engagement itself.

1920s-1930s • A NEW EMOTIONAL CULTURE ~ The evolution of grief was paralleled by further changes in emotional rules more generally. The 1920s saw the clearer enunciation of a new emotional approach, signaled by a huge increase in the number of child-rearing manuals and the popularity of their purchase. In large part because of the need to learn new emotional rules, parents eagerly sought guidance. (In 1927 this reeducation process would be furthered by the foundation of *Parents' Magazine*.) And a host of new experts collaborated in the process. Whereas in the nineteenth century, emotional advice characteristically emanated from ministers and authors claiming moral authority, in the twentieth century the quintessential advisor was a doctor or psychologist, or a popularizer who interpreted scientific studies. Many of the new experts sincerely believed that nineteenth-century standards were inappropriate, and they certainly had great self-interest in persuading Americans that both natural instincts and traditional standards might be wrong, and that outside authority was essential.

1920s-1930s • Motherly Love ~ The list of shifting emotional cues became considerable. Jealousy, as we have seen, became a vital problem for the first time, and gradually not only advice manuals but the law itself picked up this change. Mother-love came into question. A new breed of behaviorist psychologists argued that mother-love could be extremely dangerous, robbing children of their capacity for independence and emotional maturity. Mothers should rein in excessive love. A new set of experts coined the term, "smother-love." By the 1930s, this hostility to mothers had been reduced, but the nineteenth-century emphasis on innate maternal virtue was never fully restored.

1920s-1930s • Guilt ~ Excessive guilt was another target. Children were now seen as fragile (a theme reechoed in the concern about childhood fear), and guilt might damage them excessively. Here was the basis for later developments that emphasized the importance of positive signals to bolster children's self-esteem, as opposed to guilt-inducing criticisms. Causing guilt was now judged offensive. "Are you trying to make me feel guilty?" The move to no-fault legislation in divorce was predicated in part in the need to avoid specific guilt.

1920s-1930s • Anger ~ Anger became a new kind of problem. Attacks on women's anger actually eased somewhat, as here, too, emotional culture became less strictly gendered. But men were urged to develop new restraint. The movement began in the workplace. Nineteenth-century comment on emotional rules had not specifically embraced workplace interactions, save for the vague injunctions that anger might usefully motivate competitive zeal. In fact, depending of course on personality, employers frequently became angry in dealing with the labor force. But from the 1920s onward, the importance of curtailing anger became quite explicit. Retraining programs for foremen and middle managers emphasized anger restraint, along with devices to reduce anger among employees as well.

From its origins on the job, the idea of anger restraint spread more broadly. Child-rearing manuals began to label anger as aggression, an obvious sign that this was no longer a neutral, much less potentially useful emotional category. By the 1940s, in standard advice literature, such as Dr. Spock's famous manual, anger had joined jealousy as one of those emotions that could fester in children without explicit parental guidance in teaching children how to vent harmlessly.

A key manifestation of nineteenth century views on anger for boys had been the recommendation of training in boxing. Give a middle-class boy a set of boxing gloves to teach him that anger was a valid motivation (he should not be a sissy), but one that should be channeled to sports, business or public life. But by the 1950s boxing gloves were no longer a common gift to middle-class boys, who were no longer encouraged to be so overtly aggressive. Anger, now seen as aggression, was too dangerous to unleash.

1920s • Jealousy ~ Special factors were involved in the turn against jealousy. Growing interaction among men and women, including the new practice of dating that developed during the 1920s, the availability of the automobile for sexual liaisons, and women's liberation greatly increased opportunities for jealousy, and it took new attention to keep the emotion in bounds. Emotional control resulting from peer pressure replaced some of the structural constraints of the nineteenth century, which had kept middle-class men and women physically apart except in a ritualized, chaperoned courtship that led to marriage.

Also important in the campaign against sibling rivalry were changes in family structure. With increasingly low birth rates, and with the decline in domestic service and live-in grandparents, young children had increasingly direct contact with parents, which in turn increased the opportunities for jealousy concerning parental affection. In several senses, then, jealousy became a greater problem, which in turn produced the new rules for a jealousy-free definition of emotional maturity.

(1954) By the 1950s boxing gloves were no longer a common gift to middle-class boys, who were no longer encouraged to be so overtly aggressive.

1920s • Love and Sex ~ There was also some rethinking of love, even aside from changes in standards for friendship and maternal affection. The specific nineteenth-century ideal of an ethereal, spiritual love progressively diminished. It was explicitly attacked in some quarters, such as the new marriage guidance movement that spawned hundreds of college courses from the 1920s to the 1950s. Love could be dangerous as the basis for marriage choice. A young couple should use reason, and tests of mutual compatibility, instead of strong emotions. More commonly still, love began to be increasingly associated with sexuality, in contrast to nineteenth-century formulations that urged sexual expression as a lesser and not always essential part of love. By the 1920s, references to the word "lover" involved sexual expectations, which had not been the case a half-century before.

1920s

The various changes in emotional categories, such as love or anger, did not develop quickly, and they did not win uniform acceptance. Many people were caught between the old and new concepts. Many women in the 1920s, for example, continued to look for love according to nineteenth-century formulas, enhanced a bit by the new Hollywood ideals of romance; but their search was complicated by their simultaneous sense that this kind of love might be too old-fashioned, and by encountering men who no longer maintained the older love

A United Autoworkers booklet in the 1940s advised "A lost temper usually means a lost argument."

1920s

ideals. Restraining anger was urged on men and women alike, but women were still more likely to cry and feel ashamed when they experienced anger.

In various ways, then, older standards complicated and delayed new reactions. A new kind of gender division opened that both men and women found troubling. In dealing with the new emotional culture, men typically pulled away from wanting to discuss emotions much at all, while women sought to live up to the new restraints by talking about emotional reactions freely. As early as the late 1930s, men were listing women's insistence on emotional discussions, and women men's taciturnity, as key problems in marriage.

But changes in direction were nevertheless quite real. Even the gender split was novel, compared to mutual outpourings in the nineteenth century. Men, for example, might feel less constrained in anger than women, but they knew they had to keep the lid on at work. The United Autoworkers, in a 1940s booklet, advised that "a lost temper usually means a lost argument." By the 1970s middle managers routinely reported on interviews their sense that "you always have to be pleasant, no matter how bad you feel."

1880-1920 • Causes of Change ~ Cultural rules for specific emotions shifted in response to some fundamental changes in American life. The new antipathy to death and its attendant grief, for example, corresponded to a period when dying people were moved out of the home to hospitals, and the reliance on medical support increased. The death rate was also decreasing, especially among children and expectant mothers. Rates of infant and child death plummeted between 1880 and 1920—in 1880, upward of 30 percent of all children died before reaching age five, which meant that most American families faced at least one death of a child. By 1920 the rate was down to five percent and falling fast, and maternal mortality was also dropping.

On another front, the influenza epidemic of 1918-1919 was the last great epidemic of the twentieth century, in terms of mortality rates. Inoculations and new drugs combated diseases, and death increasingly occurred from internal degeneration (cancer, heart problems) or accident (especially automobile deaths) rather than the traditional infectious killers like respiratory disease. Increasingly, high death rates became confined to older age, and while sympathy for death among the elderly grew, it did not reach the intense proportions associated with the untimely death of young people. The huge changes in the nature and incidence of death supported a social shift to fighting death rather than grieving over it.

1950s-1960s • New Rules for Expressing Emotions ~ In addition to changes in specific emotion categories, historians have discussed more general shifts in emotional culture that to some degree sum up the larger changes in tone. Democratization was one key trend. Whereas nineteenth-century emotional guides assumed wide differences among social groups, twentieth-century literature, though still emanating from middle-class sources, sought to be more encompassing. Everyone should be expected to live up to basic emotional standards, but some groups dissented. For example, as part of the Civil Rights movement of the 1950s and 1960s, many black men came to believe that more open expressions of anger were appropriate. But they ran up against the larger cultural expectation, in ways that complicated their ability, for example, to get jobs where self-controlled customer service was a prerequisite. The new democratic assumptions could be complex and demanding.

Another term that has been applied to the new emotional style is "informalization." Emotional rules in some contexts became less rigid, just as manners generally became more informal. But the rules were established, and depended on detailed and subtle knowledge for effective personal operation. Cursing offers a specific example. It was permissible in many settings to use swear words, and in some men's circles it was required to use off-color language to be considered "one of the boys." But while language became more informal, people also had to know that the intent was not very serious. A swear word no longer conveyed intense anger, which is why greater informality was possible. A person could call someone a "son of a bitch" without expecting physical assault in return, unless that person was a foreigner who took personal offense that his mother had been slandered.

Another example of greater informality and its emotional corollaries: men and women had far more informal, mutual contacts than had been the case for the nineteenth-century middle class. Their association extended through coeducational high schools and colleges and, increasingly, into the workplace. Informal contact, however, was not expected to generate jealousy, and casual dress and behavior were not supposed to generate intense emotional reactions or sexual expectations. A habit of "social kissing" developed as a greeting between men and woman, and participants had to know how to do this and keep it apart from any hint of sexualized love, and therefore any potential for jealousy. Knowing the rules could prove a demanding task, when informality depended on a general need to keep intensity low.

The increasing aversion to emotional intensity characterized the new emotional culture. Nineteenth-century emotional rules had insisted on great emotional restraint for some emotions or in some circumstances, but they had also encouraged great intensity in other cases. Male anger against wrongdoing was a case in point, as was intense maternal love. Now, emotional intensity was fairly systematically discouraged. This was particularly true for emotions regarded as "bad" because of adverse social or personal consequences, like anger, fear and grief. But it also applied even to good emotions, like love. People were supposed to present a pleasing demeanor, while keeping deeper emotions in check. As one employment manual suggested for managers and salesmen, "impersonal but friendly" was the new watchword, and it was not readily compatible with profound feelings.

The only emotion that clearly received new stimulus during the period was envy. Older moral objections to envy relaxed by the 1920s, as people were encouraged to see envy as a useful motivation for up-to-date consumer behavior. It was all right to envy your neighbor's car, if this stimulated you to get a better one yourself. But envy was not a very profound emotion (it is typically much less intense than jealousy), so this exception did not seriously counter the more general trend.

1920s-Present • The Influence of Business, Media, and Health Awareness ~ In addition to the specific new contexts for jealousy or grief, there were several general factors that pushed toward the larger changes in emotional style. These influences began to take shape in the 1920s and gained momentum for the next half-century. They explain both the timing and the acceleration of change. Historians debate the precise combination, but agree on four of the components involved:

The organizational changes that shifted the U.S. from a production to a service and managerial economy. Many of the new emotional rules, beginning with anger, related to new economic goals that put a premium on smooth interpersonal relations. People had to get along within the growing corporate hierarchy. Salesmen were urged to keep intense emotions in check, in favor of the customer-is-always-right strategy; this was the approach recommended by the champion salesman trainer, Dale Carnegie, from the 1920s onward. Business management fads, extending all the way to Total Quality Management around 1990, encouraged emotional control, arguing that strong emotions disrupted proper organizational behavior.

The rise of consumerism. This fundamental change in the American economy beginning around 1900 affected emotional life in two ways. First, it promoted a sense that pleasant emotions should be emphasized. Here was another source of the attack on grief, which was not an emotion that could be manipulated to sell many goods. Second, people were urged, from childhood onward, to invest emotions in things. Infants were encouraged to love dolls; siblings were asked to accept gifts in lieu of expressing jealousy. Many people turned to shopping as a direct emotional outlet. In the process, emotional intensity in interpersonal relations was discouraged.

New concerns about health. From the 1920s onward, Americans became increasingly conscious of the unseen, internal bodily processes that could veer out of control. Regular blood pressure checks were accompanied by articles warning people to avoid emotional excess that might lead to strokes or coronary disease.

The importance of media. Americans increasingly patterned themselves on movie stars, whose cool, restrained behavior provided models for emotional restraint. More broadly, the idea that one was "on camera" encouraged a different sense of self-presentation among Americans. Many historians have commented that twentieth-century Americans emphasized personality over character (though character concerns persisted as well). The idea that one should have a malleable emotional arsenal, and the increasing sense of evaluating one's own emotions in light of the perceptions of others, entered into the changes in emotional culture.

1920s • Emotions on the Couch: Psychology in American Life ~ The rise of psychology played a crucial role in causing emotional change, but the results of change also fed into the success of the profession as well. Psychological ideas, such as Freudianism, devised in Europe, turned out to gain a particularly warm welcome in the United States, with an interest in therapy to match. The emphasis on emotionally intense family life, derived from the nineteenth century, already opened the door to the acceptance of therapy when emotional expectations were not realized.

Psychological research and popularization of psychology contributed greatly to the new child-rearing manuals that in turn codified some of the new emotional rules from the 1920s onward. Psychologists also contributed to the goals and strategies of anger control at work. Testing experts claimed that they could identify angry personalities who would be unsuitable for management or sales jobs. Other experts devised tactics that could defuse anger in the workplace, such as asking a disgruntled employee to repeat a grievance three times, by the end of which process the anger would melt into embarrassment. Training programs for flight attendants used experts to teach how to mask emotional reactions to difficult passengers, replacing spontaneity with a constant smile.

The results of the new emotional rules fed psychology in turn. Undue grief or problems controlling anger was an invitation to therapy. Many Americans found it increasingly difficult to sort out authentic emotions from the pleasant demeanor they were supposed to display in public, and they turned to psychological self-help books and to actual therapists in the process. Comparative studies showed Americans particularly willing to accept therapeutic psychology. This was an important occurrence in twentieth-century American history, closely associated with the larger changes in emotional rules and emotional life.

The tremendous surge of psychology was one of the great developments in twentieth century American life, as millions sought therapy and millions more accepted psychological expertise through self-help books, newspaper columns, or training sessions in schools and places of work. The surge was also unexpected. Sigmund Freud, the most important single figure in the rise of therapeutic psychology, had assumed that his ideas would not find much audience in the United States, whose culture he judged to be self-confident and not introspective. In fact, the theories and practices of the great Viennese psychiatrist won more attention in the United States than in Europe. Historians have tried to explain this anomaly. John Demos argues that by the late nineteenth century Americans had developed a very intense family, rather isolated from the broader community; this promoted a "hothouse" emotional environment which, he argues, made Americans ripe for imported psychological ideas.

But the changes in emotional standards also played a role in sustaining and accelerating psychological models. Change itself caused Americans to look for expert guidance, for they could not rely on inherited rules or parental guidelines. Twentieth-century American emotional culture involved a curbing of emotional spontaneity in many ways, which caused people to doubt their emotional authenticity or to seek outlets for powerful emotions, such as intense grief or anger, that they could not legitimately express in daily life.

1920s-1930s • Keep It Cool ~ The Jazz Age evolved an interesting relationship between the dominant emotional rules and leisure life. As many more leisure activities became available, the correct emotional response to them was expected; most leisure activities involved passive spectatorship as people watched movies, sports events, and listened to the radio in groups. Many of these activities reinforced the idea of cool, restrained emotional behavior. The *Superman* comics of the 1930s proffered a new type of hero who was notable for his lack of emotional expression, his calmness under extreme pressure, and his lack of interest in bonding with humans. Athletes and movie stars could be equally cool, but they were also permitted to engage in emotional displays that differed from ordinary life. Male athletes hugged each other. Baseball coaches stood toe-to-toe with umpires in angry exchanges. Some sports, like hockey, gained popularity and growing violence at the same time. Soap operas and movies showed deep love, jealousy, and anger. A whole genre of movies exploited fear.

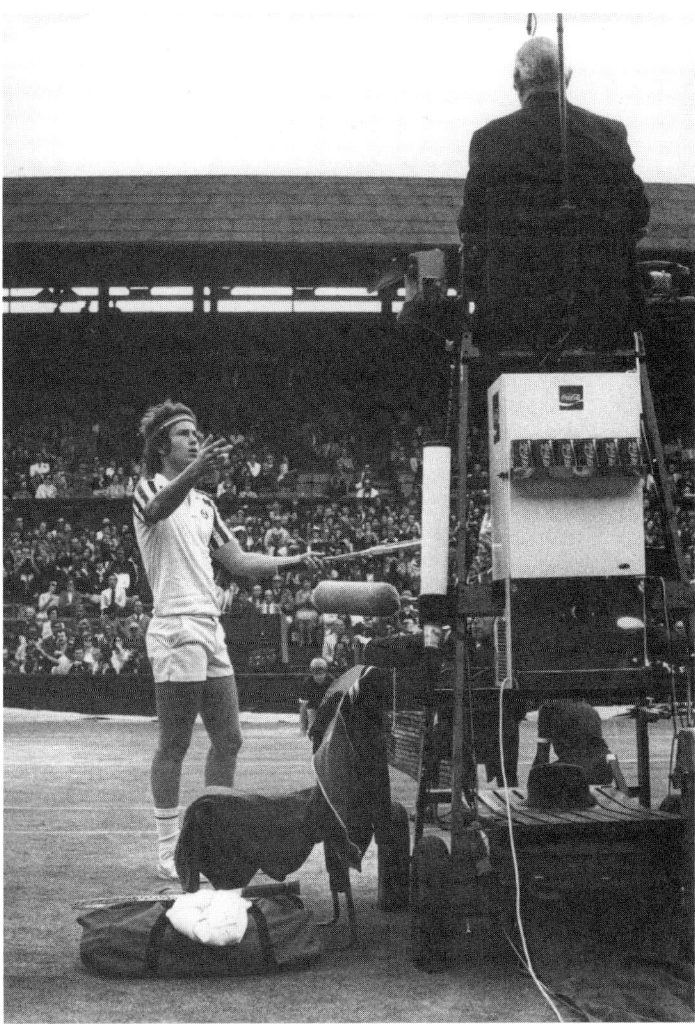

(1980) John McEnroe of the USA argues with the umpire on the Centre Court after disputing a line-call at the Wimbledon Tennis Championships.

Clearly, spectators found outlets for emotions they had to restrain in ordinary life through their leisure activities. In sports stadiums, they could participate in crowd frenzy as they watched athletes act out anger and aggression. In movie theaters the rules were more complex. 1920s audiences had learned middle-class standards of decorum, and they sat silently watching emotional intensity on the screen.

1940s-Present • Becoming Desensitized to Death ~ Ironically, and often tragically, people who experienced the death of a child or a young spouse greatly increased the pressure they felt. Deprived of cultural support and treated as nuisances in a society that did not welcome grief, people began to turn to groups of strangers who had experienced a similar event, who alone could provide real sympathy. Thanatoo groups allowed bereaved strangers to meet. There were also special groups for parents who had lost a child. Such support groups spread widely after World War II. Interestingly, the world wars also tended to increase the campaign against grief, which was seen as unpatriotic. When Americans became more aware of military death rates in the Korean and especially the Vietnam wars, they turned against land-based military actions. Still willing to deal death to others, through air strikes, Americans became more systematically death-averse by the end of the twentieth century.

1960s • Social Protest and Political Behavior ~ The ramifications of the changes in twentieth-century emotional culture lead in several directions. A clear relationship exists between new anger norms and shifts in American protest forms and rates. Collective protest declined in the United States after the 1950s, with a brief outburst in the late 1960s to early 1970s followed again by relative calm. Particularly, the number of strikes and union rallies declined. There are several key factors involved in this change, including the rise of white collar work, the greater hesitancy of white collar workers to engage in collective action, and the relocation of centers of economic activity to parts of the country, like the south and southwest, historically less friendly to labor organizations. But changes in emotional rules may have played a role as well, convincing workers, employees, and labor leaders that angry behavior was less valid or at least less likely to win public favor. Even the youth rebels of the 1960s were somewhat hesitant to admit anger, with slogans like "make love not war", suggesting a certain diffidence about pressing protest too far.

Emotional rules clearly altered political behavior, at least on the part of candidates. Displaying undue emotion in public became a political liability. Presidential candidate Edmund Muskie lost favor for crying in public. Showing anger (except against foreign enemies) was decidedly wrong. Politicians were told never to display anger in public, or in front of journalists. Presidential debates from the 1960s onward were structured to present candidates with provocative questions as a means of making sure they could control their tempers under fire. Careful packaging of candidates was designed in part to make sure that spontaneous emotions would not damage their cause. All this was in marked contrast to more aggressive and open campaigning styles in the nineteenth century, in which angry candidates, like Abraham Lincoln, might charge into crowds to berate hecklers. Whether this change affected broader political behaviors, including the declining voter participation rates after the 1950s and the growing aversion to politics and politicians, is a possibility that warrants further exploration.

1940s-Present • Fiction and Reality in Entertainment ~ The disparity between fictional and real-life emotions has created social confusion related to the themes of violence and sexuality. Americans recurrently express concern that fiction might be taken as fact, particularly by vulnerable young people. Critics of comic books in the 1940s and 1950s argued that they were inciting violence. The same theme reemerged concerning films, video games and popular music in the final decades of the century. It was in fact hard to sort out the extent to which intense spectatorship might induce some viewers to act out their fantasies, versus the extent to which it provided them a surrogate experience that helped them achieve self-control in daily life. Whatever the conclusion, it was clear that twentieth-century American culture involved a degree of schizophrenia, in contrast to the greater coherence in nineteenth-century middle-class culture.

(1956) The 'Gill Man' (Don Megowan, 1922-1981) hurls a man to the ground watched by a horrified group of people on a poster advertising 'The Creature Walks Among Us'. The third 'Gill Man' film was directed by John F. Sherwood for Universal Pictures.

1950s • Democracy and Social Class ~ Another key set of issues involves the relationship between subcultures and the new emotional style preached by and for the middle classes, but with growing emphasis on inclusion and widespread applicability. The expansion of white-collar jobs and prosperity after World War II expanded the middle class itself and increased the number of people expected to conform to standard emotional rules. Whereas nineteenth century emotional rules distinguished between respectable and unrespectable people, twentieth century norms were more democratic and inclusive, with everyone expected to conform.

Yet homogenization was certainly incomplete. Different ethnic groups, for example, maintained different grief practices and cultures, even though these might differ from the accepted standards. African Americans, for example, valued a more expressive and intense emotional culture than did the white middle class.

Religious groups provided outlets for divergent emotional experiences and expressions. Evangelical Protestant groups, both African and white American, established their denominational identity with exuberant religious services even as the dominant culture seemed to de-emphasize emotional intensity. Other religious groups, however, drew closer toward mainstream norms, if with some differences in timing. Changes in Catholic emotional culture by the 1950s reflected concerns about the impact of fear on children, as part of a more general accommodation between Catholic and mainstream Protestant culture.

The analyses of emotional variation between subgroups in American society remain important historical tasks. It is clear that dominant emotional standards gained influence beyond their middle-class origins, but it is also clear that some groups such as militant blacks and evangelical Christians, remained apart or even found ways to intensify their commitment to distinctive emotional values.

1960s-Present • Emotional Culture Changing Again ~ Several developments from the 1960s onward suggested that the emotional culture forged during the 1920s was beginning to change again. As part of the culture of the 1960s, for example, a variety of experts urged reconsideration of the neglect of death and grief. Psychologist Elizabeth Kubler Ross gained great attention for her study of the standard reactions to death, which, she argued, were being ignored or distorted by dominant cultural attitudes.

Imported from Britain, a small hospice movement began as an alternative to standard hospital care and the attendant emotional neglect in dealing with terminally ill patients. Some mental health professionals began to take a more tolerant attitude to grief.

Feminists worried about continued gender disparities in emotional expression, though some of these were holdovers from the nineteenth century. As part of women's growing work roles, efforts to provide assertiveness training compensated for some of the more passive qualities associated with older standards of femininity. But while some feminists were proudly angry, the assertiveness movement sought to dissociate itself from outright anger.

By the 1980s and 1990s, in a more conservative cultural and political climate, attention tended to shift toward indications that Americans had become too tolerant of emotional excess. In the early 1990s a campaign against "road rage" began, based on the assumption that acts of aggressive driving were increasing dangerously. Popular articles featured diagnostic tools that would allow Americans to assess whether they had road rage proclivities or not; symptoms included honking in anger and obscene gestures. It was not in fact clear that aggressive driving was increasing faster than the increase of driving generally, or that the milder symptoms predicted actual road rage.

The campaign was intriguing for two reasons. First, it revealed a sense of concern about emotional standards, whether well founded or not. Second, it actually served to provide yet another inducement for emotional conformity around existing condemnations of angry behavior. Continued American tendencies to exaggerate crime rates (based in part on watching crime shows on television) constituted another symptom of a general belief that anger and aggression were getting out of hand, without solid evidence to support that belief.

(1966) A driver vents his anger at fellow motorists by shooting them with a water pistol.

1980s-1990s • Restraining Emotions ~ Worries about the solidity of the American family, particularly among Christian conservatives, created a public debate about the need for tighter emotional bonds among family members. Disparate activities for each member of the family demanded different emotional responses, and there were no uniform expectations about how family members should regard each others' behavior. During simpler times, the church or the community dictated emotional response, but parents became increasingly concerned as more children and teenagers became involved in dangerous and illegal activities. Restrained emotions seem to be channeled into violent or self-destructive emotions, and parents began to challenge how emotions should be expressed.

People concerned about family values initiated some modest movements against the no-fault divorce legislation, which had reflected the new emotional standards against intense guilt, jealousy and anger. Proponents for repealing no-fault laws argued that jealousy was gaining new approval as an emotion that inhibited sexual experimentation and safeguarded marriage ties, and therefore should be encouraged.

The dominant twentieth-century emotional style involved far more self-restraint than was commonly recognized, particularly in work life. Standards of anger control for teachers, for example, continued to expand. On college campuses instructors who displayed angry responses toward student behavior were typically judged to be in the wrong. Surface friendliness won the top ratings in the classroom; the best teachers were usually the ones who seemed to be nice guys. New management theories emphasized the importance of emotional cooperation among workers, as against any sign of anger or impatience at meetings; behavior at funerals continued to relax;

and many people continued to value the importance of presenting a controlled emotional picture in most public settings.

Conclusion

Americans experienced a profound set of changes in emotional standards during the twentieth century, beginning clearly by the 1920s and continuing into the later part of the century. The 1960s trumpeted a host of new signals associated with youth behavior, which extended the pressures toward greater informality and democratization. Anger rose against the Vietnam War, and then in association with the strivings of a new surge of feminism. Jealousy was vigorously attacked as sexual freedoms expanded, and the association between love and sexuality increased.

Observers have noted a growing concern from the 1970s onward, particularly in personal relationships, for "authenticity." People were worried about dealing with others' emotions that might merely be for show. Demonstrating that one really meant an emotion became increasingly important. This was a new twist, but again it followed from the constraints on spontaneous emotion that had developed through much of the century, and that shaped the worries about what sincere emotion meant. Some sociologists argued in fact that many people found their emotions so manipulated by training at work, like flight attendants, schooled to be nice no matter what, that they themselves lost track of their true emotions.

More generally, the generation of baby-boomers, coming to maturity in the 1960s and 1970s, seemed to take more delight in talking about emotions than had previous, more taciturn generations. Though women still led the way in talking about emotional experience, some men joined in. When Gulf War pilots talked openly about their fear, free from an older military culture that had urged the link between silence and courage, they showed how widespread the acceptability of venting emotions had become. Robert Bly and his "Iron John" movement represented one of several recurrent efforts in the 1980s and 1990s to reemphasize manhood, manly emotions, and family roles. His movement emphasized getting in touch with nature and male bonding, based on assumptions that male characteristics depended on some contact with qualities once linked to hunting activities.

But again, the basic trends, such as the recognition of fear's harmful intensity, had been launched many decades before. Different generations developed their own formulations for the emotional culture of their time, but they did not usually introduce profound new directions. Mental and physical health, and fitting into corporate and consumer culture, continued to involve avoiding emotional intensity wherever possible.

Bibliography

Cancian, F. M. *Love in America: Gender and Self Development.* Cambridge, England: Cambridge University Press, 1987.

Demos, J. "Shame and guilt in early New England." In C. Z. Stearns and P.N. Stearns, eds., *Emotion and Social Change: Toward a New Psychohistory.* New York: Holmes & Meier, 1988.

Gay, P. *The Bourgeois Experience: Victoria to Freud.* 2 vols. New York: Oxford University Press, 1984-1986.

Gordon, S. L. "The socialization of children's emotion: Emotional culture, competence, and exposure." In C. Saarni and P. Harris, eds. *Children's Understanding of Emotion*. Cambridge, England: Cambridge University Press, 1989.

Greven, P. J., Jr. *The Protestant Temperament: Patterns of Child-rearing, Religious Experience and the Self in Early America*. New York: Knopf, 1997.

Gross, Martin L. *The Psychological Society: A Critical Analysis of Psychiatry, Psychotherapy, Psychoanalysis & the Psychological Revolution*. New York: Random House, 1978.

Hochschild, Arlie R. *The Managed Heart: Commercialization of Human Feeling*. Berkeley: University of California Press, 1985.

Kasson, J. F. *Rudeness and Civility: Manners in Nineteenth-century Urban America*. New York: Hill & Wang, 1990.

Kelly, T., and J. Kelly. "American Catholics and the discourse of fear." In P. N. Stearns and J. Lewis, eds. *Emotional History of the United States*. New York: New York University Press, 1998.

Lewis, J. "Mother's love: The construction of an emotion in nineteenth-century America." In A. E. Barnes and P. N. Stearns, eds., *Social History and Issues in Human Consciousness*. New York: New York University Press, 1989.

Lystra, K. *Searching the Heart: Women, Men, and Romantic Love in Nineteenth-Century America*. New York: Oxford University Press, 1989.

Matt, S. J. "Frocks, finery, and feelings: Rural and urban women's envy, 1890-1930." In P. N. Stearns and J. Lewis, eds., *Emotional History of the United States*. New York: New York University Press, 1998.

Mintz, S., and S. Kellogg. *Domestic revolutions: A social history of American family life*. New York: Free Press, 1989.

Phillips, K. L. "'Stand by me': Sacred quartet music and the emotionology of African American audiences, 1900-1930." In P. N. Stearns and J. Lewis, eds., *Emotional History of the United States*. New York: New York University Press, 1998.

Pfister, Joel and Nancy Schnog, eds. *Inventing the Psychological: Toward a Cultural History of Emotional Life in America*. New Haven: Yale University Press, 1997.

Rosenbalt, P. C. *Bitter, bitter tears: Nineteenth-century diarists and twentieth-century grief theories*. Minneapolis: University of Minnesota Press, 1983.

Rosenzweig, L. W. "'Another self'?: Middle-class American women and their friends, 1900-1960." In P. N. Stearns and J. Lewis, eds., *Emotional History of the United States*. New York: New York University Press, 1998.

Rotundo, A. "Romantic friendship: Male intimacy and middle-class youth in the northern United States, 1800-1900." *Journal of Social History*, 23, 1-25, 1989.

Salovey, P., ed. *The Psychology of Jealousy and Envy*. New York: Guilford Press, 1991.

Seidman, S. *Romantic Longings: Love in America*, 1830-1980. New York: Routledge, 1991.

Shields, S. A., and Koster, B. A. "Emotional stereotyping of parent in child rearing manuals, 1915-1980." *Social Psychology Quarterly*, 521, 44-55, 1989.

Shumway, D. R. "Something old, something new: Romance and marital advice in the 1920s." In P.N. Stearns & J. Lewis, eds., *Emotional History of the United States* pp. 305-318. New York: New York University Press, 1998.

Stearns, Peter N. *Jealousy: The Evolution of an Emotion in American History*. New York: New York University Press, 1989.

———. *American Cool: Constructing a Twentieth-century Emotional Style*. New York: New York University Press, 1994.

———. "Emotional change and political disengagement in the twentieth-century United States." *Innovation, The European Journal of Social Sciences*, 104, 361-380, 1997.

———. *Battleground of Desire: The Struggle for Emotional Control in Modern America*. New York: New York University Press, 1999.

Veroff, Joseph, Douban, E. and Kulka, R. *Americans View Their Mental Health, 1976*. Ann Arbor, MI. Inter-university Consortium for Political and Social Research, 1982.

White, K. *The First Sexual Revolution: The Emergence of Male Heterosexuality in Modern America*. New York: New York University Press, 1993.

Wouters, C. "On status competition and emotion management." *Journal of Social History*, 244, 690-717, 1991.

———. "On status competition and emotion management: The study of emotions as a new field." *Theory, Culture and Society*, 9, 229-252, 1992.

Zelizer, V. *Pricing the Priceless Child*. New York: Basic Books, 1985.

Internet Resources

Mental Health Resources Site
http://mentalhealth.about.com/index.htm

Emotional Eating
http://weightloss.about.com/cs/emotionaleating/index.htm

Love in Popular Media
All about the psychology of love
http://psychology.about.com/cs/lovemedia/index.htm

Teen love
Answers to common questions about love. How can you tell if you are really in love, and what does it mean.
http://teenadvice.about.com/cs/whatislove/index.htm

Marriage
Links to many sites addressing various aspects of marriage.
http://marriage.about.com/index.htm

Divorce Support Site
Even the most amicable divorce can be difficult. Learn from and talk with others who know what it's like.
http://divorcesupport.about.com/index.htm

Death and Dying Site
Coping with a terminal illness, or mourning the loss of a loved one
http://dying.about.com/index.htm

Death and Dying - MEDLINE Plus
Resources from the National Library of Medicine
http://mentalhealth.about.com/library/mlp/bldeath.htm

Death and Dying
Death and dying resources and information
http://socialwork.about.com/cs/deathanddying/index.htm

Peter N. Stearns
George Mason University

ENVIRONMENT

~

(circa 1915) Salesmen and boosters demonstrating an irrigation pump near Lewiston, Washington.

TIMELINE

1800-1889 ~ Claiming the Wilderness

Thomas Jefferson advocates open land policy / Romantics and transcendentalists find spiritual meaning in nature / Yellowstone, the first national park, is established (1872)

MILESTONES: Louisiana Purchase doubles the size of the U.S. (1803) • Oliver Evans builds the first steam-powered motor vehicle in the U.S. (1805) • Indian Removal Act forces southern Indian tribes to relocate west of the Mississippi (1830) • Electric rail transport and gasoline powered automobiles introduced (1880s)

1890-1929 ~ Rise in Conservation Responsibility

First forest set aside for conservation, the Sierra redwood groves (1890) / Forest Reserve Act gives presidents the authority to proclaim permanent forest reserves (1891) / Women become involved in the conservation movement (early 1900s) / Boy Scouts of America founded (1910) / Boulder Dam proposed (1910s); completed as Hoover dam in 1935 / Hetch Hetchy dam approved (1913) / National Park Service created (1916) / Grand Canyon becomes a national park (1919)

MILESTONES: Subway systems introduced (1890) • First automobile patent granted (1895) • Leo Hendrik Baekeland patents the first completely synthetic plastic, Bakelite (1907) • Garrett Morgan invents the gas mask to keep firefighters from being overcome by smoke (1912) • First diesel engine railroad put into service (1920) • Iron lung developed for patients who cannot breathe on their own (1927) • First public parking garage is built in Detroit (1929)

1930-1949 ~ The Dust Bowl and Environmental Awareness

Dust Bowl catastrophe awakens farmers to environmental problems (1930-1935) / Tennessee Valley Authority created for watershed management (1933) / Civilian Conservation Corps employs young people for conservation projects (1933)

MILESTONES: Ernest O. Lawrence's use of a cyclotron accelerates nuclear particles to smash atoms and release energy from matter laying the groundwork for nuclear energy (1930) • First Freeway, Pennsylvania Turnpike, opens (1940)

1950-1969 ~ Understanding Pollution and Environmental Degradation

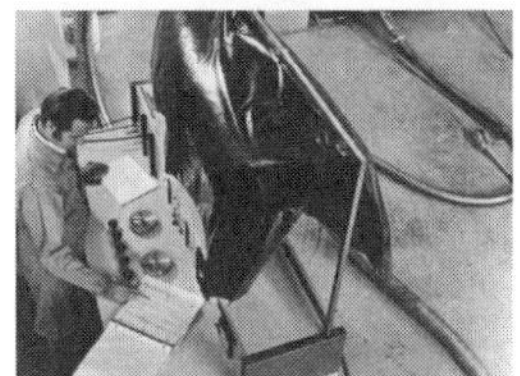

Peaceful uses of atomic energy proposed (1953) / Dinosaur Monument controversy suspends plans to build a dam (1950) / Rachel Carson's *Silent Spring* calls attention to pollution (1962) / Wilderness Act sets aside huge tracts of land for wilderness (1964) / Not in my Backyard protests and evolution of grassroots movement (late-1960s) / Environmental Protection Agency created to control pollution (1969)

MILESTONES: First nuclear submarine, the *Nautilus*, put into service (1950) • Interstate Highway Act passed to fund a vast network of high speed roads (1956) • Hazardous Substances Labeling Act requires warnings on dangerous household products (1960) • Sea World marine theme park opens (1964)

1970-1979 ~ Environmental Crisis

First Earth Day calls attention to environmental problems (1970) / Clean Air Act attempts to minimize vehicle-produced pollution (1970) / Rise of environmental terrorism (1970s) / Arab Oil Embargo creates gas crisis in U.S. (1973) / Development of green culture advocates environmental responsibility (late-1970s) / United Nations sponsors first global environmental conference (1972) / Endangered Species Act protects species from extinction (1970 and 1973) / Alaskan Pipeline constructed (1977) / Three Mile Island meltdown solidifies opposition to atomic reactors (1979) / Residents along the Love Canal re-located because of pollution (late 1970s)

MILESTONES: Supersonic *Concorde* put into service for passenger flight (1972) • Oil exploration in Alaska authorized (1972) • Vegetarian movement advocates eliminating meat products from the diet (1976) • Arno Penzias and Robert W. Wilson win the Nobel Prize for developing the "Big Bang" theory explaining the beginning of the universe (1978) • Realization of the dangers of lead paint, radon gas, asbestos, and fiberglass • Use of wood-burning stoves, fireplaces, and solar energy to conserve oil

1980-2000 ~ Global and Corporate Responsibility

President Carter protects some Alaskan land from oil drilling (1980) / President Reagan's revolution against environmental regulation (1980s) / Exxon *Valdez* oil spill in Alaska wreaks havoc on the environment (1986) / Globalization of environmental concerns, especially global warming (1990) / Clean Air Act requires automobile manufacturers to begin developing alternative fuel vehicles (1991) / Congress approves Everglades National Park restoration (2000)

MILESTONES: Economic sanctions imposed on Iraq after the Gulf War halts the exportation of oil (1991) • EPA labels second-hand smoke a carcinogen (1993) • *e. Coli* bacteria in contaminated hamburgers kills several people (1998) • Fewer men and more women smoke cigarettes (1999)

INTRODUCTION

It may have seemed like an ordinary day, yet instead of the regular television schedule listings, the *New York Times* listed "TV and the Environment." Most impressive, there were a host of programs to delineate. However, many Americans were not taking time to watch TV; instead, they performed clean-up enterprises on behalf of Mother Earth. Internationally, more than 40 million humans marked some kind of celebration on Earth Day 1990.

For American culture, though, April 22, 1990 marked a day of broader recognition. American society celebrated a new relationship with the natural world surrounding it. Polls in 2001 reveal that nearly 70 percent of Americans refer to themselves as "environmentalists." Such developments are simply the latest in a watershed shift in Americans' awareness of the human impact on the natural environment. The 1990s marked a maturing period for the environmental movement, which had been evolving in the U.S. since the nineteenth century.

While the growth of environmentalism is not a uniquely American development, the democratic nature of American politics makes an issue such as the environment a revealing condition of changes in national ideals. During the twentieth century, Americans demanded and received legal mechanisms that empowered branches of the federal government to monitor and regulate American use of natural resources. The middle class roots of the contemporary movement stress environmental health and its connection to personal safety. This is very different from the roots of such ideas in American thought.

American environmental concern traces back to Jeffersonian ideas of a unique American connection to land and the romantic ethos of the nineteenth century. Open land, sometimes viewed as "wilderness," defined the New World for many European settlers. Thomas Jefferson argued that this open land could be transferred into an American strength if development were directed toward an agrarian republic. This played nicely into ideas of individual ownership and Jefferson's confidence in the independent "yeoman" farmer to live by democratic ideals. The connection to the land, in other words, was initially tied to individual rights.

While much of the nation would pursue land-use similar to Jefferson's ideal, some urban Americans remained intrigued by Jefferson's idea of a unique American connection to the natural environment. The argument of Romantics and Transcendentalists found spiritual meaning in nature, but did not necessarily force anyone to live a difficult life off the land. This can be seen in the adoption of European forms such as parks and gardens and in the intellectual tradition of Romanticism and Transcendentalism. By the end of the 1800s, wealthy urbanites pursued "wild" adventures in sites such as the Adirondacks, initiated organizations to conserve animal species or limit pollution, and, finally, set aside areas of nature from development. Federal ownership of such unique sites was debated throughout the twentieth century.

Statistics demonstrate dramatic shifts in overall patterns of land-use and ownership during the previous century. From a preponderance of land in forest or grass in 1900, the 1992 landscape is most remarkable for the growth of "other," which of course denotes places of human habitation (totals in Figure 1 grow as states were admitted to the Union). This trend is also demonstrated by the overall ownership trends seen in Figure 2.

Figure 1: General Land-Use Patterns since 1900 (in million acres)

Year	Cropland	Grassland	Forest	Other	Total
1900	319	1,044	366	175	1,904
1910	347	814	562	181	1,904
1920	402	750	567	185	1,904
1930	413	708	607	176	1,904
1945	451	660	602	193	1,905
1949	478	631	606	189	1,904
1954	465	632	615	191	1,904
1964	444	640	732	450	2,266
1974	465	598	718	483	2,264
1982	469	597	655	544	2,265
1992	460	591	648	564	2,263

SOURCE: U.S. Dept. of Commerce, Bureau of Census.

Land, of course, is where one can best study the evolution of environmental trends. The use of the land can be as revealing as its preservation. Though the first national parks, Yellowstone and Yosemite, proved to be watershed events in environmental history, they were not initially set aside to protect wilderness areas.

1872-1891 • The First National "Mandate" ~ Much of nineteenth century environmentalism occurred without a strict organization or philosophy, and the first national parks are a primary example of this. Some scholars have chosen to view nineteenth century environmentalism as a product of Gilded-Age decadence and not an emerging new consciousness toward natural resource use. For instance, Yellowstone, established as the first national park in 1872, developed closely with railroad interests who hoped it would attract tourists to the American West. Its oddities—geysers, waterfalls—proved more important to observers than its unspoiled wilderness. They also made its utility for settlement questionable, which allowed its sponsors to dub the area "worthless for development." Such a designation made lawmakers more willing to sponsor setting it aside for altruistic reasons.

Figure 2: Land Ownership since 1900 (in percent)

Year	Private and other Public	Federal
1900	52.7	47.3
1910	68.5	31.5
1920	73.8	26.2
1930	74.0	26.0
1959	61.0	39.0
1978	67.2	32.9
1997	75.2	24.8

SOURCE: U.S. Dept. of Commerce, Bureau of Census.

Other parks would be constructed by the end of the nineteenth century. The major development during this era, however, was the institutionalization of national forests. Initially described as "reserved forest lands," the first forests set aside were great Sierra redwood groves in 1890. The Forest Reserve Act of 1891 gave presidents the authority to proclaim permanent forest reserves on the public domain. Motivation for such reserves derived from European shortages of forests. American lawmakers set out to ensure that the U.S. supply of lumber would not be similarly squandered. Unlike National Parks, though, these areas were managed for long-term harvesting under the principles of multiple-use conservation.

1900-1905 • The Era of Progressive Reform ~ The mandate for federal activity in regard to natural resource use took root early in the twentieth century. The Progressive period energized many Americans to identify social ills and use the government to correct them. The impulse to discontinue waste of resources and the pollution, physical and spiritual, of American communities rapidly became an expression for Americans' unique connection to the land.

The earliest interest in environmental policy grew out of wealthy urbanites of the Gilded Age who often combined an interest in hunting and fishing with efforts to maintain recreational sites. This also fueled efforts by women's groups to limit styles of fashion, which included the use of exotic birds and feathers as hat decorations. Efforts to manage the use of certain species and eliminate the practice altogether took root in the 1890s and extended into the early 1900s. Periodicals on topics ranging from gardening to hunting fed Americans' interest. Magazines such as *The Horticulturalist*, *Field and Stream* (then known as *Forest and Stream*), *Godey's Lady's Book*, and *Better Homes and Gardens* helped to merge the women's magazine with practical publications specifically concerned with home design. These popular interests, however, required a leader who could guide them toward concrete expression and policy initiatives.

The leadership of President Theodore Roosevelt and his Chief of Forestry Gifford Pinchot galvanized the upper-class interest with national policies. The aesthetic appreciation of wealthy urbanites grew into Progressive initiatives to create national forests and national parks with a unifying philosophy for each. These policies would deviate in two directions, preservation and conservation. Roosevelt greatly admired the national parks as places where "bits of the old wilderness scenery and the old wilderness life are to be kept unspoiled for the benefit of our children's children." With his spiritual support, preservationists argued that a society that could exhibit the restraint to cordon off entire sections of itself had ascended to the level of great civilizations in world history.

While Roosevelt possessed preservationist convictions, his main advisor on land management, Pinchot, argued otherwise for the good of the nation. Conservationists, such as Pinchot, sought to qualify the preservationist impulse with a dose of utilitarian reality. The mark of an ascendant society, they argued, was the awareness of limits and the use of the government to manage resources in danger of exhaustion. Forest resources would be primary to Pinchot's concern. As the first practicing American forester, Pinchot urged Americans to manage forests differently than had Europe.

Under Pinchot's advice, President Theodore Roosevelt moved the few national forests created in 1891 out of the jurisdiction of the Department of Agriculture and into an independent Forest Service. This, he argued, would allow the forests to be managed by professional foresters. During his administration, Roosevelt added 150 million acres of national forests to transform the U.S. into a global leader in forest management. Under Pinchot's direction, the U.S. Forest Service became one of the most publicly recognized government agencies of the Roosevelt era. Pinchot made forests a national cause with a mailing list of over 100,000 private citizens, frequent public appearances, and penning articles for popular magazines. This public standing, created through forest conservation, further inflamed the approaching altercation that would define the early environmental movement.

1908-1913 • Distinguishing Preservation from Conservation ~ The conflict between preservation and conservation revolved around each side's emerging definitions of themselves. Preservationists such as J. Horace McFarland argued that sites such as Niagara Falls required a hands-off policy so that it would maintain the natural environment that people found so appealing. Conservationists were buoyed by Roosevelt's vociferous and active ideas. In 1908 he stated some of these points in the nation's first Conference of Governors for Conservation:

> The wise use of all of our natural resources, which are our national resources as well, is the great material question of today. I have asked you to come together now because the enormous consumption of these resources, and the threat of imminent exhaustion of some of them, due to reckless and wasteful use, calls for common effort, common action.

So the first lines of disagreement were being drawn: preservationists would not tolerate any intrusion on the natural environment whereas the conservationists believed that a wise use of natural resources would benefit both the environment and humans. This argument continues today under the rubric of "sustainable development."

While the difference between preservation and conservation may not have been clear to Americans at the beginning of the twentieth century, popular culture and the writing of "muckraking" journalists clearly reflected a time of changing sensibilities. After the San Francisco fire, the nation confronted its feelings in order to define national policy. San Francisco, in search of a dependable supply of water, requested that the Hetch Hetchy Valley, located within the boundaries of Yosemite National Park, be flooded in order to create a reservoir to protect against future fires.

Preservationists, rallied by popular magazine articles by naturalist John Muir, boisterously refused to compromise the authenticity of a national park's natural environment. Reviving romantic notions and even transcendental philosophies, Muir used this pulpit to urge, "Thousands of tired, nerve-shaken, over-civilized people are beginning to find out that going to the mountains is going home; that wildness is a necessity; and that mountain parks and reservations are useful not only as fountains of timber and irrigating rivers, but as fountains of life." He called those wishing to develop the site "temple destroyers."

In reaction, Pinchot defined the conservationist philosophy by claiming that

(1906) Theodore Roosevelt (1858 - 1919) (left), the twenty-sixth President of the United States, with the Scottish born American conservationist John Muir (1838 - 1914) on Glacier Point in Yosemite, California.

1902-1935

such a reservoir represented the "greatest good for the greatest number" of people, and therefore should be the nation's priority. The dam and reservoir would be approved in 1913, but the battle had fueled the emergence of the modern environmental movement. The next phase of expression would be the issue of irrigation and reclamation, particularly as it involved the federal government.

1902-1910 • Nature Clubs ~ The image of Roosevelt, the active conservationist, also contributed to the growing appreciation of "rustic" ways of life. His interest in a "vigorous life" and outdoor activity fed the development of organizations such as the Boy Scouts of America, which was founded in 1910, and its predecessors the Boone and Crockett or Izaak Walton Clubs. Each group had an offspring for younger male members, with Sons of Daniel Boone proving the most popular. Neither, however, truly sought to reach young men of all economic classes.

Ernest Thompson Seton, artist and wildlife expert, founded another boys' club, the Woodcraft Indians, in 1902. Interestingly, he chose to unveil the group through articles in *Ladies Home Journal*. Shortly afterwards, Seton became the first Chief Scout of BSA when it was established by Robert Stephenson Smyth Baden-Powell. The concern of BSA was the whole child. For instance, the first Boy Scout manual, *Scouting for Boys*, contained chapters titled "Scoutcraft," "Campaigning," "Camp Life," "Tracking," "Woodcraft," "Endurance for Scouts," "Chivalry," "Saving Lives," and "Our Duties as Citizens." In thirty years the handbook sold an alleged seven million copies in the U.S., second only to the Bible.

1902-1935 • Federalizing Western Water Management ~ Reclamation, better described as the management of scarce water resources, entered into debates about development of the western U.S. in the early 1900s. The Reclamation Act of 1902 recast such planning as the responsibility of the federal government. The Reclamation Service, which would later be renamed the Bureau of Reclamation attracted some of the best engineering talent in the nation. Its greatest demonstration site was the tremendous dam built near the Arizona and Nevada border. Though it was not completed until 1935, Hoover Dam became the symbol of these efforts.

As proposed in the 1910s, the mammoth Boulder Dam (as it was first referred to) served as the linchpin of a western land-use policy designed to "reclaim" dry, barren regions by applying human ingenuity. This ingenuity would be applied to the few existing waterways, including the Colorado River. In 1912, five western states agreed on the Colorado Compact, which parceled up the great river's flow among the signers—including at least two states that never made contact with the river. Most of the flow, including the electricity made at Hoover Dam, would be managed by the Six Companies contractors to power development over 300 miles away in Southern California. By the end of the twentieth century, the majority of Hoover Dam's power is passed over wires to Los Angeles.

The symbolic significance of this immense structure became obvious immediately, which led developers to name it after President Herbert Hoover (an engineer who had been a great supporter of the project). Upon its completion in 1935, Hoover Dam became a symbol of America's technological prowess, firmly placing the U.S. with the great civilizations in world history. More importantly, however, conservationists had adopted a policy format that included scientific management based in ecological understanding. This perspective viewed technology, such as dams, as a tool of conservation.

1930-1935 • The Dust Bowl ~ Ecology only emerged as a bona fide field in the 1930s; however, it quickly became the basis of portions of the New Deal's massive works projects. These policies incorporated the emerging ecology with federal policies to manage watersheds,

(1938) Overfarming. The New Deal brought to light the problems of over-farming land in the United States. Seen here is a dust bowl farmstead in Dallam County, Texas, showing the desolation produced by the dust and wind on the countryside, adding to the problems of the Depression.

maintain forests, teach agriculture, and stabilize the flying soils of the southern plains. The main impetus for federal action derived from a surge in joblessness. The economic collapse of 1929 left millions of Americans incapable of making a living. Nowhere was this more evident than on the American southern plains.

Terrible drought combined with economic difficulty to make many farmers in the rural Midwest incapable of farming. Okies fled westward to California, creating resettlement problems as well. In the southern plains, the loose topsoil was lifted by heavy winds creating dust storms of epic proportions. Press coverage of the "dust bowl" of the 1930s, for instance, presented a natural disaster caused by drought and bad luck. Through government-made documentary films such as *The Plow that Broke the Plains*, the New Deal infused a bit of ecological background to explain desertification and agricultural practices that can be used to combat it. In the process of a natural disaster, the American public learned a great deal about its role within the natural environment. Proper land use could be taught and the federal government installed extension agents to do so.

1933 • The Tennessee Valley Authority ~ This also was apparent in New Deal river projects, particularly the Tennessee Valley Authority (TVA). The entire watershed of the Tennessee River contributed to flooding problems on its banks and along the Mississippi River before 1933. In this year, Franklin Delano Roosevelt created the TVA to manage the entire watershed through a system of dams and other structures. The land management system, based in ecology, would restore lost topsoil, prevent floods, stabilize transportation possibilities, and create the opportunity for recreation. Finally, Roosevelt's pet project, the Civilian Conservation Corps, merged scientific understanding of agriculture and watershed management with Roosevelt's trust in the importance of outdoor work for the development of young Americans.

The emergence of ecology had brought a new utility for science in the everyday life of Americans. Scientific knowledge, however, was still largely controlled by experts—often working for the federal government. During World War II, science would be taken out of the laboratories and placed more in the public eye than ever before. While Americans would soon learn more about their connections to the environment around them, the primary symbol of science and technology was an awesome destructive force.

1945-1960s • Atomic Technology and the "American Century" ~ While technology rapidly became a tool for environmental action, it also presented a downside that inadvertently helped to propel environmental concern. No single technology embodies this development like atomic technology, including the bombs developed to end World War II. The technology to manage atomic reactions did not long remain the sole domain of the military. The influence of nuclear weapons and power generation has defined a great deal of domestic politics since the 1960s.

In the late twentieth century, such attention has come because of nuclear technology's environmental impact. If one considers these broader implications and the related technologies, twentieth century life has obviously been significantly influenced by "the bomb," even though it has been used sparingly—nearly not at all. A broader legacy of atomic technology can be seen on the landscape, from Chernobyl to the Bikini Atoll or from Hiroshima to Hanford, Washington.

During the Cold War era, Americans focused on stabilizing everyday life and improving the quality of living for the growing middle class. Atomic bombs, which were being tested in the American West, were not known to be a threat to the environment. Information about radiation was not released to the American public.

Following the Soviet Union's 1949 test of its first atomic weapon, Eisenhower's "Atoms for Peace" speech, given at the United Nations in 1953, clearly instructed the world on the technological stand-off that confronted it. The "two atomic colossi," he forecasted, could continue to "eye each other indefinitely across a trembling world." But eventually their failure to find peace would result in war and "the probability of civilization destroyed," forcing "mankind to begin all over again the age-old struggle upward from savagery toward decency and right, and justice."

To Eisenhower, "no sane member of the human race" could want this. In his estimation, the only way out was discourse and understanding. With exactly these battle lines, a war—referred to as cold, because it never heats up to direct conflict—unfolded over the coming decades. With ideology as its point of difference—communism versus capitalism—the conflict was fought through economics, diplomacy, and the stockpiling of a military arsenal. With each side possessing a weapon that could annihilate not just the opponent but the entire world, the bomb defined a new philosophy of warfare.

On an individual basis, humans had lived before in a tenuous balance with survival as they struggled for food supplies with little technology. Never before, however, had such a tenuous balance derived only from man's own technological innovation. Everyday human life changed significantly with the realization that extinction could arrive at any moment. Some Americans applied the lesson by striving to live within limits of technology and resource use. Antinuclear activists composed some of the earliest portions of the 1960s counter culture and the modern environmental movement, including "radical" organizations such as the Sea Shepherds and Greenpeace, each of which began by protesting nuclear tests. More mainstream Americans would also eventually question the use of such devices.

1970-1990 • Opposition to Nuclear Reactors ~ At a time when atomic technology was viewed as a destructive force, the Eisenhower administration attempted to "domesticate" it with uses ranging from road construction, powering greenhouses, planes, and cars, and fertilizing agricultural fields with radioactive manure. Americans accepted this argument for a time. As the potential dangers of radiation became more obvious, however, atomic power generation became less and less popular. In fact, the movement against nuclear power that began in the 1970s crystallized into a form of contemporary environmentalism often referred to as "Not in my Backyard" or NIMBY. People fought against the construction of nuclear power plants and nuclear waste storage facilities in their communities.

The most important event in this movement may have been the 1979 nuclear accident at Three Mile Island, Pennsylvania. Located within a working-class neighborhood outside of a major population center, this nuclear power plant experienced a partial core meltdown. As pregnant women and children were evacuated from Pennsylvania's nearby capital, Harrisburg, the American public learned through the media about potential hazards of this technology as well as many other sources. A new grass-roots activism gained steam as people began to expect the federal government to oversee the nation's environmental health. While such a movement effectively squelched further development of nuclear reactors not yet planned in 1979, the data in Figure 3 demonstrate that it could not completely alter the pattern of American energy development.

While the number of nuclear units increased through 1990, most of the contracts had been drawn up many years before. By 1990, most American voters refused to help finance new reactors. Most communities lobbied to remove or shut down reactors too near residential areas. While the dangers of radiation were more widely understood, Americans also had an expectation of physical safety that is unique in human history. In short, Americans expected to live in uncontaminated safety. Responsibility for ensuring this safety would fall to the federal government.

Figure 3: U.S. Nuclear Energy Generation

Year	Nuclear Units	Billed Kilowatt Hours
1958	1	0.2
1962	9	2.3
1967	15	7.7
1973	42	83.5
1978	70	276.4
1979	69	255.2
1984	87	327.6
1988	109	527.0
1990	112	576.9
1998	104	673.7

SOURCE: U.S. Dept. of Energy.

1960s • Counterculture Environmentalists ~ This general change in environmental concerns actually extends back to the 1950s. Historians point to a clear correlation between the 1950s growth in the middle class and the popularity of environmentalism. Samuel P. Hays wrote that out of such public interest this era "displayed demands from the grass-roots, demands that are well charted by the innumerable citizen organizations..." that grew out of such public interest. Within growing suburbanization, middle-class Americans expected health and home safety.

While there was as yet little regulatory authority available, grass-roots environmentalists would demand their government to intercede and insure community safety. The groundswell of interest mobilized with the counter-culture movements of the 1960s. As Americans rethought the ethics of everyday human existence, some explored a more ecologically sustainable way of life. Alternative fuels, natural foods, and communal living are only a few examples. Most importantly, a national stage linked scientific data with environmental concern. National parks, which had begun innocently enough, became a major forum in which this debate would play out.

1913-1917 • Defining National Parks ~ The earliest National parks possessed little if any unifying philosophy or ethic. Increasingly, this lack of a mandate would trouble the development and at times, such as the 1913 effort to con-

(1942) Gasoline shortages in the U.S. are not a new occurrence. Here, cars are waiting in line in Washington, D.C. to buy gasoline a day before strict rationing was to begin to conserve fuel for the war effort.

struct the Hetch Hetchy dam, threaten the existence of some parks. The first bona fide step toward a unifying idea came with passage of the National Park Service Act in 1916. This act created the National Park Service (NPS) as a unit of the Department of the Interior, staffed no longer by military personnel but now specially charged rangers, though this change would not be truly noticeable until later in the century. In his popular 1917 book, *Your National Parks*, Enos Mills stated their mission as: "A national park is an island of safety in this riotous world. Within national parks is room—glorious room—room in which to find ourselves, in which to think and hope, to dream and plan, to rest, and resolve."

Stephan T. Mather, a businessman, was made the first NPS director. In addition to creating a unifying mission based in preservation, Mather also sought to develop national parks as certifiable tourist attractions. By mid-century some critics even criticized overcrowding in the parks. Preservationist organizations such as Muir's Sierra Club and the Land Conservancy would argue for as little use as possible; others argued that National parks were a trust open for the use of any citizen. This, of course, meant Americans had every right to use the sites as they saw fit.

1950s • Mobilizing Public Opinion ~ Environmental policy also continued to move forward from 1950 through the 1960s. The initial interest of the public in the 1940s and 1950s was garnered through an event similar to Hetch

Hetchy. The Bureau of Reclamation, an agency developed by applying Pinchot's idea of conservation to waterways of the American West, set out to construct the Echo Park Dam along the Utah-Colorado border and within little-used Dinosaur National Monument. As Congress neared a vote on the issue in 1950, 78 national and 236 state conservation organizations expressed their belief that National parks and monuments were sacred areas and the dam should not be built.

David Brower, executive director of the Sierra Club and Howard Zahniser of the Wilderness Society used the opportunity to create a model for environmental lobbyists to follow. Direct-mail pamphlets asked: "What is Your Stake in Dinosaur?" and "Will You DAM the Scenic Wildlands of Our National Park System?" Additionally, a color motion picture and a book of lush photos, each depicting the Echo Park Valley's natural splendor, were widely viewed by the public. Such images and sentiments forced Americans to react. With mail to Congress late in 1954 running at eighty to one against the dam, the bill's vote was suspended and the project eventually abandoned. The issues had been packaged by environmentalists to connect concerns with romantic images of the American past. Americans loved this idea and reacted more positively than ever before.

National parks have become the greatest tourist attraction in the nation (see Figure 4). Of the federal lands, the acreage of the national parks in 2000 was a distant fourth in the four major divisions: Bureau of Land Management, 270 million acres; U.S. Forest Service, 191 million acres; Fish and Wildlife Service, 91 million acres; and NPS, with 80.7 million acres.

Figure 4: National Park Visitation

Years	Visitors
1904	122,594
1915	337,214
1920	1,060,375
1930	3,248,586
1940	16,755,251
1950	33,254,539
1960	79,230,960
1970	172,006,570
1980	220,465,179
1990	258,682,828

SOURCE: National Park Service

Figure 4 demonstrates the direct correlation between times of peace and the leisure to enjoy parks. With more freedom and flexibility, Americans flock to national parks. Of course, the irony of such dramatic increases in visitation is their commensurate impact on the natural resources of each site.

1950s-1960s • Basing Policy in Ecology ~ Zahniser identified this moment as the best to press for the environmental movement's greatest goal: a national system of wilderness lands. Based on the idealistic notion of pristine wilderness espoused by Teddy Roosevelt and others, such a system had been called for since Aldo Leopold in the 1910s. With increased recreation in parks and public lands, argued Zahniser, it had become even more crucial that some of the land be set aside completely.

His bill, introduced to Congress in the 1950s, precluded land development and offered recreational opportunities only for a few rather than for the great mass of

Figure 5: Additions to the Wilderness Preservation System

Congress	# of Laws	# of New Areas	Acres
88th (72-73)	1	54	9,139,721
90th (74-75)	5	5	794,550
94th (79-80)	6	35	2,142,486
96th (81-82)	6	70	60,799,111
97th (82-83)	5	7	83,261
98th (83-84)	21	177	8,576,450
99th (84-85)	4	11	97,393
102nd (87-88)	2	6	424,590
103rd (88-89)	2	79	8,272,699
TOTAL	88	630	103,740,989

SOURCE: Congressional Research Service

travelers. Such an ideal goal required great salesmanship, and Zahniser was perfect for the job. As the political climate shifted in the early 1960s, lawmakers became more interested in wilderness. Finally, in 1964, President Lyndon Johnson signed the Wilderness Act into law. The U.S. had taken one of the most idealistic plunges in the history of environmentalism: nearly ten million acres were immediately set aside as "an area where the earth and its community of life are untrammeled by man, where man himself is a visitor who does not remain." Additional lands would be preserved in similar fashion by the end of the decade.

While the concept of wilderness forced the general American public to begin to understand ecosystems and the webs of reliance operating within natural systems, the application of scientific understanding to environmentalism occurred most often in other realms. Defeating the dam at Echo Park and the passage of the Wilderness Act set the stage for a 1960s shift in environmental thought that combined with

Figure 6: Where's the Wilderness?

States	Forest Serv.	National Park Serv	US Fish and Wildlife Serv	Bureau of Land Mgm	Share of Wilderness
Alaska	5,752,899	32,979,370	18,676,320	0	55.33%
California	4,435,889	5,975,052	9,172	3,550,311	13.46%
Washington	2,572,799	1,739,771	839	6,900	4.16%

SOURCE: Congressional Research Service
(These are states with more than four percent wilderness.)

NIMBY culture of the 1970s to create a federal mandate for policy action. From a vague ideal, wilderness became a structuring agent for the administration of federal lands. This is shown in Figures 5 and 6. The massive growth during the 96th Congress, for example, is Jimmy Carter's effort to set much of Alaska aside from development. Figure 6 demonstrates the extreme concentration of wilderness lands in a few states.

Creating a Popular Movement

1960s • Pollution ~ Pollution composed the most frequent environmental complaint, but its nuisance derived more from physical discomfort than a scientific correlation with human health. A government biologist turned nature writer presented the American public with its lesson in science in 1962. Rachel Carson's *Silent Spring* erupted onto the public scene to become a bestseller after first being serialized in the *New Yorker*.

The story of pollution (particularly that from the popular pesticide DDT) and its effect on ecological webs of life linked water runoff to fish health and then to depletion of the bald eagle population. Readers were left to infer the effects of such chemicals on humans. Flexing their increased environmental awareness, the American public scurried to support Carson's parade through television talk shows. The Kennedy administration appointed a commission to study Carson's findings and one year later banned DDT from use in the U.S. Carson became identified with "mother nature" and a maternal impulse to manage the natural environment through federal regulation.

Carson's ideas were welcomed by a general public more interested than ever in understanding its place in the natural environment. Her scientific findings added credibility and meaning to students involved in "back to nature" movements. As students grew willing to question nearly every aspect of their existence, the human role in nature came under increasing scrutiny. Was our lifestyle sustainable? Did we take more than we gave to the environment? Were we good stewards of the world around us? Many Americans started local recycling projects or became active in local politics. Others checked out completely. Such disenfranchised people would become known as hippies.

For many hippies as well as others interested in such ideas, the need to live more simply was largely defined by Stewart Brand's *Whole Earth Catalogue* (TWEC), which introduced Americans to green consumerism in 1968. The book contained philosophical ideas based in science, holistic living, and metaphysics as well as listings of products that functioned within these confines. As many Americans sought to turn their backs on America's culture of consumption, TWEC offered an alternative paradigm based in values extending across the counter-culture. Even if Americans did not choose these values, they garnered a valuable lesson in discerning consumption. As the trend-setting publication of green consumption, TWEC is viewed by many Americans as having started the movement toward whole grains, healthy living, and environmentally-friendly products.

1960s-1970s • The Era of Environmental Protection ~ The cultural change and environmental awareness evolving through the 1960s led to passage of environmental legislation, most notably the National Environmental Protection Act in 1969, which created the Environmental Protection Agency (EPA). The public entrusted the EPA as its environmental regulator to enforce ensuing legislation monitoring air and water purity, limiting noise and other kinds of pollution, and monitoring species in order to discern which ones required federal protection. The public soon realized just how great the stakes were.

During the 1970s, oil spills, river fires, nuclear accidents, and petroleum shortages made it appear as if nature were in open rebellion. In short, nearly every industrial process was seen to have environmental costs associated with it. From chemicals to atomic power, long-believed technological "fixes" came to have long-term impacts in the form of wastes and residue. Synthetic chemicals, for instance, were long thought to be advantageous because they resist biological deterioration. In the 1970s, this inability to deteriorate made chemical and toxic waste the bane of many communities near industrial or dump sites.

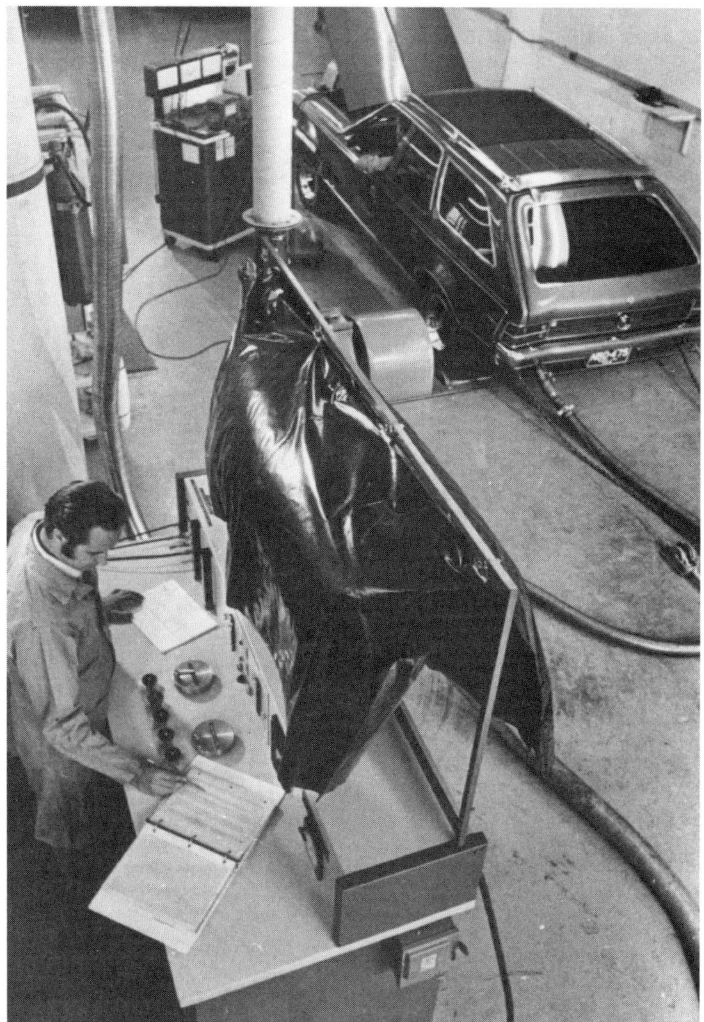

(1971) A newly produced Hornet car undergoes an exhaust test at the American Motors plant at Kenosha, Wisconsin. U.S. car makers are trying to eliminate pollution caused by car exhaust fumes.

Among the assorted catastrophes, Love Canal stood out as a new model for federal action. When community members in this residential area of northern New York state complained about toxic wastes seeping through the topsoil and infecting their children, the federal government declared the site a federal disaster area. By the end of the 1970s, residents of Love Canal had been relocated with the federal government purchasing their property and vowing to clean up the dump.

The connection between health and environmental hazards became obvious throughout the nation. Scientists were able to connect radiation, pollution, and toxic waste to a variety of human ailments. The "smoking gun," of course, contributed to a new stage of litigation in environmentalism. Armed with scientific data and NIMBY convictions, environmental groups legally challenged some of the nation's largest corporations.

Rapidly, this decade instructed Americans, already possessing a growing environmental sensibility, that humans—just as Carson had instructed—needed to live within limits. A watershed shift in human consciousness could be witnessed in the popular culture as green philosophies infiltrated companies wishing to create products that appealed to the public's environmental priority. Recycling, daylight-saving time, car-pooling, and environmental impact statements became part of everyday life after the 1970s

1970s • Creating Mechanisms for Grassroots Action ~ During the late 1900s, environmental special interest groups evolved into major political players through lobbying. Non-government organizations (NGOs) broadened the grassroots influence of environmental thought. It also created a niche for more radical environmentalists, however. While the Nature Conservancy, Sierra Club, and Greenpeace (among others) became mainstream, organizations such as Earth First!, led by Dave Foreman, pursued their goals differently. Beginning in the 1970s, ecoterrorism became standard fare, particularly in the American West. Radical tactics such as tree-spiking, tree-sitting, damaging equipment, and even burning resorts were designed to shock the public into demanding action to stop environmental abuse. Most often, such activists came from the movement's intellectual fringe as well, including the philosophy of Deep Ecology.

Earth Day 1970 suggested to millions of Americans that environmental concern could be expressed locally. Through organized activities, many Americans found that they could actively improve the environment with their own hands. Many communities responded by organizing ongoing efforts to alter wasteful patterns. Recycling, mandated by the first legislation in Oregon in 1972, has proven to be the most persistent of these grassroots efforts. Though the effort is trivialized by extremist environmentalists, trash and waste recycling now stands as the ultimate symbol of the American environmental consciousness.

(1942) A man looks at a poster that tells people how they can conserve rubber by carpooling to work during World War II. In the accompanying illustration, invisible Nazis ride with a motorist and declare, 'Wasting Much Rubber are Very Helpful For We!'

1980-2000 • Recycling ~ The culture of consumption of post-World War II America reinforced carelessness, waste, and a drive for newness. Environmental concerns contributed to a new "ethic" within American culture that began to value restraint, reuse, and living within limits. This ethic of restraint, fed by overused land-fills and excessive litter, gave communities a new mandate in maintaining the waste of their population. Reusing products or creating useful byproducts from waste offered application of this new ethic while also offering new opportunity for economic profit and development. Most often referred to as industrial

Figure 7: Does Recycling Work?

(in millions of tons)	1980	1990	1997
Wastes generated, total	151.5	205.2	217
Materials recovered, total	14.5	33.6	60.8
Percent of generation recovered, total	9.6	16.4	28

SOURCE: U.S. Bureau of the Census

ecology, businesses such as DuPont, 3M, and Dow Chemical have used cost-benefit analysis to restructure their production in order to minimize environmental costs and also waste.

Green, or environmentally conscious, industries have taken form to facilitate and profit from this impulse, creating a significant growth portion of the American economy. Even more impressively, the grassroots desire to express an environmental commitment has compelled middle-class Americans to make recycling part of an everyday effort to reduce and better manage waste. Local institutions, such as hospitals, have also established practices to control waste disposal. By 2000, children and schools were helping to organize community efforts to recycle. It would be understandable if most children born after the 1980s assumed that the "recycle, reduce, and re-use" mantra had always been practiced, but in actuality, it serves as a continuing ripple of the cultural and social impact of Earth Day 1970 and the effort of Americans to begin to live within limits.

1970s • Endangered Species ~ In response to the green culture attitudes of the late 1960s, the U.S. Department of Interior began collecting data on animal species that were in danger of becoming extinct. In 1970 Congress authorized funds for a more formal study of endangered animals and plants. By 1973, about 200 species had been identified as endangered and the problem of imminent extinction for these species raised public awareness and concern. In 1973 Congress passed the Endangered Species Act mandating that the Department of the Interior protect species classified as endangered or threatened by the U.S. Fish and Wildlife Service.

Few Congressmen anticipated the firestorm of controversy that would sweep the nation five years later when environmentalists came head-to-head with economic interests over the 1978 proposal to construct the Tellico Dam under the authority of the Tennessee Valley Authority. Building the dam would destroy the habitat of the snail darter, an endangered fish protected by the Endangered Species Act. Congress would have to amend or reverse the 1973 act so the dam could be built.

In 1979, Congress exempted the Tellico dam project from the Endangered Species Act. The snail darter population was moved to another habitat where it survived, but the precedent was set for Congress to grant exceptions, and a continuing battle was set in motion between wildlife conservationists and developers.

One of the most contentious fights was adding the northern spotted owl to the list of endangered species, which would have restricted logging activities in Oregon.

Since 1951, The Nature Conservancy has attempted to save species from extinction by preserving natural habitat. Through partnerships with business, government, and industry, and through donations from individuals, TNC has purchased and maintained millions of acres of habitat containing rare and endangered species.

1960s-Present • Interpreting Green Culture ~ The dissemination of greener ethics also has greatly impacted popular culture. Most prevalent might be the genre of culture that seeks to give viewers access to the natural world, which lay quite distant from the professional worlds of most viewers. Mutual of Omaha's *Wild Kingdom* began this tradition in the 1970s. In the tradition of *National Geographic*, Marlon Perkins created adventures in far-off locations based in the unknown secrets of the natural world. Breeding an entire genre of television—even an entire network—*Wild Kingdom* continues production and has spawned a great deal of other programming, particularly for young viewers. Finally, Perkins's search for showing animals in their natural surroundings contributed to the interest in "eco tourism" in which the wealthy can travel to various portions of the world to view nature without disturbing it.

Zoos and wildlife parks have also seized on this interest and attempted to create similar experiences for visitors. Sea World, the marine theme park that first opened in 1964, now operates parks in Florida, California, and Ohio. Unlike Disneyland and other amusement parks, Sea World carries a full-blown theme: the effort to bring visitors into closer contact with the marine world. As this agenda has become more routine since 1980, performing mammals have taken center stage. The most famous of these performers is Shamu the killer whale. In the highly competitive amusement industry, Sea World has exploited its niche by focusing since 1990 on environmental themes deriving from threats to marine life.

Such cultural interest in natural history and science is most clearly evident for children. While entire school curricula have been altered to include environmental perspectives, juvenile popular culture has guided such interest. From Disney's the films *Bambi*, released in 1942, and Dr. Seuss's *The Lorax* (1972), artists have identified a sensitivity most common in juveniles. Each of these tales stresses overuse, mismanagement, or cruelty toward the natural world. The typical use of easily recognizable examples of good and evil that support child's media had been radically expanded.

Mixing science with action, environmentalism proved to be excellent fodder for American educators. More importantly, though, the philosophy of fairness and living within limits merged with cultural forms to become mainstays in entertainment for young people, including feature films such as *Lion King* (1994), *Free Willie* (1993), and *Fern Gully* (1992), environmental music, and even clothing styles. Compared to earlier eras, contemporary films, such as *Lion King* bring complex ecological principles of balance between species to the child's level.

Many parents find children acting as environmental regulators within a household. Shaped by green culture, a child's mindset is often entirely utopian, where-

Figure 8: Going Green for a Living

Industry Segment	1980	1990	1997
Analytical Services	6.0	20.2	12.7
Wastewater Treatment	53.9	95.0	104.8
Solid Waste Mgt	83.2	209.5	249.9
Hazardous Waste Mgt	6.8	56.9	49.4
Remediation	6.9	107.2	96.0
Consulting and Engineering	20.5	144.2	174.4
Water Equipment & Chemicals	62.4	97.9	117.0
Water Utilities	76.9	104.7	121.3
Resource Recovery	48.7	118.4	141.2
Environmental Energy	22.4	21.1	26.4
Totals, including occupations not listed	462.5	1,174.3	1,348.0

(employment figures in thousands)

SOURCE: Environmental Business International, Inc., San Diego, CA.

as parents possess more real world stress and knowledge. Even so, many adults long for such simplicity and idealism, and scholars say that children awaken these convictions in many adults. In fact, a growing number of adults began jobs that were involved with the environment. Environmental regulation and green culture created a mandate for a new segment of the workforce: technically trained individuals to carry out new ways of managing waste and consumption.

1970s-1980s • Political Fluctuation ~ By the 1970s and 1980s, environmental concerns had emerged as a major player in local and federal politics. As such, federal regulation and policy

Figure 9: Federal Expenditures on Natural Resources and Environment

Years	Water	Land Mgt	Recreation	Pollution Ctrl	TOTAL
1962	5.673	1.530	0.668	0.308	8.989
1972	6.122	1.398	1.622	2.401	13.328
1982	5.959	1.636	2.166	7.565	19.620
1992	4.964	4.988	2.589	6.628	21.804
1999	9,256.100	5.700	8,848.200	4.200	104.610

(in billions of dollars, 1996)

SOURCE: U.S. Dept. of Commerce, Bureau of Economic Analysis.

(circa 1979) A dead duck washed up on the shores of the polluted Lake Ontario, New York.

initiatives would vary with the political winds. This dynamic was most obvious through issues such as petroleum development and the regulation of industrial development. Figure 9 demonstrates that political difference may be most noticeable in the allocation of the overall spending of funds for environmentalism, not necessarily in the total spending, which has consistently increased.

The early 1970s brought many examples of the limits on human life. The most troubling was the Arab oil embargo carried out by member countries of the Organization of Petroleum Exporting Countries (OPEC). The embargo led to major fuel shortages within the U.S. Long lines at many service stations plagued many Americans and fueled the consideration of new ideas growing out of the conservation ethic. Particularly under the administration of President Jimmy Carter, the nation began turning to alternative fuels, car-pooling, and the use of smaller vehicles (which opened American markets to Japanese vehicles).

Drilling for oil in the pristine Alaskan wilderness was approved by Americans worried about the gas crisis. This drilling required constructing the Trans-Alaska pipeline to transport Alaskan oil overland into the contiguous 48 states. After heated debate over the environmental threat, authorization for pipeline construction squeezed through Congress in 1977. Carter used this threat to pass the Alaska National Interest Lands Conservation Act in 1980. This act set guidelines for the use of 375 million acres in Alaska. However, oil development would continue—even after the 1986 *Valdez* oil spill in Prince William Sound. One of the hotly debated issues of the 2000 presidential election was whether to open the Arctic National Wildlife Refuge to gas and oil drilling.

1980s • Reagan's Pro-Industry Environmental Policy ~ Each president has the ability to alter the intensity with which federal regulation of environmental factors is carried out. The primary example of such fluctuation is the presidency of Ronald Reagan, first elected in 1980. Reagan and his successor George Bush each directed the EPA to cease being an advocate agency—that is, finding offenders to prosecute—but a "neutral broker" who would foster cooperation between industry and government. Reagan advanced his pro-industry and anti-regulation policies by installing James Watt as Secretary of the Interior and Anne Gorsuch as head of the EPA. Watt and Gorsuch had worked together in Colorado to dismantle federal policies controlling the use of federal lands. Personnel in the EPA dropped by 25 percent and its budget was reduced by more than half. Policies and limitations were put in place to limit the number of lawsuits that could be brought and effectively stopped most other legal action.

1972-PRESENT • GLOBAL ENVIRONMENTAL CONCERN ~ Earth Day 1990 continued environmental traditions of the past, but also marked an important change in environmentalism's scope. Worldwide, fourteen nations participated in this celebration. While a global perspective seemed inherent in the web of life put forward by Rachel Carson and others, it would take global issues, such as the Chernobyl nuclear accident in 1986 and shared problems, such as greenhouse gases and global warming, to bind the world into a common perspective. Organizations, including Greenpeace, assisted members from many nations to shape a common stand on issues.

The United Nations presented the leading tool for facilitating global environmental efforts. With its first meeting on the environment in 1972, the global organization created its Environmental Program. This organization would sponsor the historic Rio Conference on the

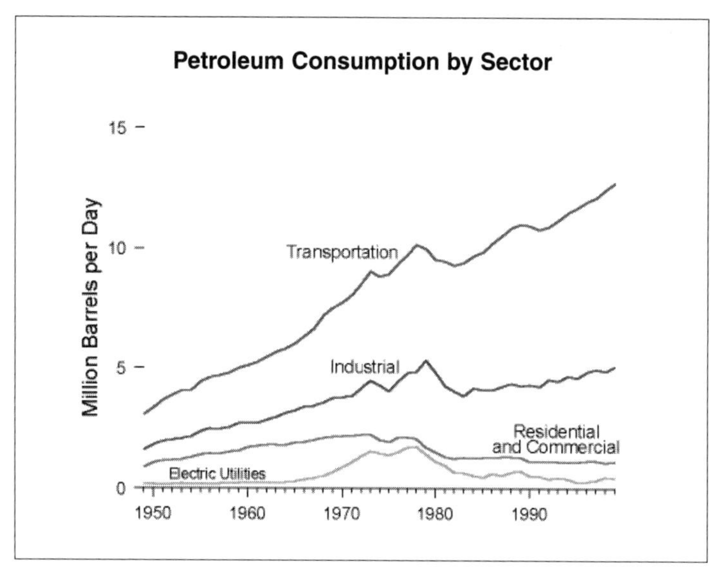

Environment in 1992 and the conference on global warming in 1997. In response to such activities, the U.S. federal government declared the environment a genuine diplomatic risk in global affairs by creating a State Department Undersecretary for the Environment in 1996.

What began as an intellectual philosophy had so impacted the human worldview that it would now influence global relations. Currently, global warming and the emissions of greenhouse gases has fueled international debate over the ratification of the Kyoto Protocol. Such legislation would place caps on emissions from all nations. The reality, though, is that since 1990 the U.S. has increased production of greenhouse damaging emissions, including carbon dioxide, methane, nitrous oxide, hydrofluorocarbons (HFCs), and perfluorocarbons (PFCs). It also appears unlikely that American leaders will accept limitations on emissions that may impact industrial productivity—even in the short term. In April 2001, the new Bush administration issued a statement that it would not honor emissions standards set by the Kyoto Protocol.

The most difficult portion of this global debate may be the fairness of each nation to be allowed to develop economically. Many less-developed nations resent the environmental efforts of nations that have already industrialized, including many European nations and the U.S. Such nations believe they are being denied their own opportunity to develop economically simply because of problems created by industrial nations. This sentiment has been part of major demonstrations in recent meetings of global organizations, such as rioting during the World Trade Organization meeting in Seattle, Washington, in 1999. Any global agreements will need to balance the basic differences of these constituencies.

1990s • A Green Nation ~ In the 2000 presidential election, Ralph Nader ran as a member of the Green Party with a platform against development, large corporations, and in support of environmental causes. Even though 70 percent of Americans call themselves environmentalists, Nader's campaign garnered less than five percent of the national vote. However, genuine pockets of such sentiments were seen in states such as Wisconsin, Florida, Oregon, and California. It seems a growing percentage of Americans are willing to entertain radical political change in the interests of environmental causes.

Under the Clinton administration, many new National Monuments were set aside in western states. The EPA and other agencies monitored industrial effects on air and water pollution. The nation began discussing ways of controlling urban sprawl and maintaining green spaces. Most impressive, designers began modeling communities on "New Urbanism," which required residents to live without a reliance on the automobile. This is made more important because, since 1950, Americans have changed from a nation in which 44 percent lived on farms and 23 percent in suburbs, to a nation in 1998 that reverses these figures.

With suburbanization has come a preponderance of NIMBY concerns. The federal regulations that such public support brings have ushered in a new era for heavy industry. While no industry is untouched by Occupational Safety and Health Administration (OSHA) or EPA regulation, many have now reached beyond these minimal standards to radically change policies. The best example may be the Ford Motor Company. The Clean Air Act requires all auto manufacturers to create a viable mixed-fuel automobile. In addition to working toward this goal, Ford has also implemented plans to radically alter its main plant, the famed River Rouge facility in Michigan. Formerly the symbol of mass production, the facility will be transformed into a model of green production, including a living roof that is covered in plants to help break down pollution as it is released.

Recent years have also seen a growth in the use of ecosystem management to control development around national parks, including Yellowstone. In 2000 Congress approved the largest management plan in its history for the restoration of Everglades National Park, which had been drained over the years to increase land for sugarcane production. Possibly the nation's most threatened national park—if only because wetlands are particularly affected by the living patterns of their surroundings—Everglades National Park has been dammed, diked, and drained to the point in which it can no longer support the web of life that depends on it. Federal initiatives will spend billions attempting to restore the natural hydrologic conditions over the next 10 to 20 years.

In the western U.S., a grassroots movement of the late 1990s made states seriously consider dismantling some of the hydroelectric dams. Environmentalists' most urgent argument against such dams is the restoration of salmon spawning runs. By 2000-2001, however, energy shortages throughout the Northwest made such environmental hopes seem unlikely. For most Americans, maintaining everyday living patterns still outweighs many environmental arguments.

Starting from associations of conservation hunters, including the Audubon Society founded in the 1870s, organizations such as the Sierra Club, Wilderness Society, The Nature Conservancy, World Wildlife Fund, and the American Wildlife Federation have evolved with the environmental movement. Additionally, global emphasis spawned Greenpeace, the world's largest environmental organization. Financial support from membership dues broadens the cultural impact of environmental philosophies while also allowing many Americans to define themselves as supporters even if they possess few of the movement's primary convictions.

Conclusion

The embattled election of 2000 became a referendum on environmental thought and forced a debate as to how serious Americans considered environmental issues. The Green Party and its candidate Ralph Nader offered voters the opportunity to make the environment the priority in selecting a political agenda. Democrat Al Gore, author of the environmental treatise *Earth in the Balance*, argued a moderate environmental line, including an energy policy based on conservation and the development of alternative fuels. Republican George W. Bush wanted to de-federalize environmental regulations and policies developed under the Clinton administration. While Bush's victory did not hinge entirely on his environmental platform, he regarded his election as permission from the people to pursue a new course of environmental policy.

By shifting environmental policy from government regulation of corporate activities to federal cooperation with industry, Bush echoed many sentiments of the Ronald Reagan era. Corporate leaders were placed in control of a variety of government environmental agencies, and efforts were made to reverse some environmental developments of the 1990s. Most important, President Bush confronted energy shortages with a strategy for growth and further development of fossil fuels. This plan called for drilling for natural gas and petroleum in federally-owned areas, including the National Arctic Wildlife Refuge in Alaska. Additionally, Bush rejected the Kyoto Accord designed to control global warming by reducing the emission of greenhouses gases.

The environmental lobby, led by many long-established organizations such as the Sierra Club, began an organized effort to rally public support against such policies. Additionally, groups of scientists presented the public and the administration with statistics demonstrating the existence of global warming and the benefits of a policy of energy conservation. The international community openly criticized Bush's rejection of the Kyoto Accord. With such developments occurring in rapid succession over the first months of his presidency, the administration was forced to reconsider its position on environmental issues.

Environmental groups and industrial interests squared off over many complicated issues during the late 1970s and throughout the 1980s and 1990s. Clean water and clean air became health issues paramount in public opinion, and the opposition of industry and business to achieving acceptable levels of clean air and water dramatically pitted the "good guys" against the bad, as popularized in the Oscar winning film *Erin Brockovich* (2000). But smokestack polluting industries were not the only significant source of gaseous emissions, and if city smog were to be controlled, Americans would have to change their driving habits, refineries would have to improve the quality of gasoline, and automobile producers would have to design more efficient engines and alternative fuel engines, all of which required sacrifice. Were drivers willing to carpool in meaningful numbers? Were automobile workers willing to sacrifice jobs to newer technologies? Were stockholders willing to put more of their companies' assets into research and development and less into dividends? The argument between saving jobs and protecting the environment was vividly illustrated in the battle between saving the habitat of the Northern spotted owl in the Pacific Northwest and allowing logging companies to cut old growth forests.

In a monumental 9-0 decision in 2000, the Supreme Court ruled that only public health issues and not the cost of compliance should govern the federal government's authority to force companies to comply to clean air and water standards. This decision clarified the court's position on health and set a precedent for other public health areas, but a larger question remains: what is the government's authority to regulate the public "good" as distinct from public health? And in the realm of global well being, can individual countries be held accountable for their share of pollution and resource mismanagement? If a healthy U.S. economy is essential to stabilizing the world economy, should the U.S. be forced by other nations to reduce its industrial output in order to reduce pollution? President Bush argues that the Kyoto Accord gives undue and unwarranted power to other nations that could disrupt American industry and the stability of U.S. and world economies.

The power of human beings to inextricably change the Earth did not become apparent to humankind until the invention of the atomic bomb, which had (has) the potential of annihilating the world, perhaps even of blowing the Earth out of its axis. The environmental issues of the turn of the century—preserving our natural heritage—were transformed into protecting the environment for future generations. How quickly and how assiduously that can and should be accomplished will be one of the most hotly debated social issues of the twenty-first century.

Bibliography

Anderson, Terry H. *The Movement and the Sixties*. New York: Oxford University Press, 1995.

Beacham, Walton, ed. *Beacham's Guide to the Endangered Species of North America.* 6 vols. Detroit: The Gale Group, 2001.

———. et al., eds. *Beacham's Guide to Environmental Issues and Sources*. 5 vols. Washington, DC: Beacham Publishing, 1993.

Boyer, Paul. *By The Bomb's Early Light.* Chapel Hill: University of North Carolina Press, 1994.

Fox, Stephen. *The American Conservation Movement*. Madison: University of Wisconsin Press, 1981.

Gottleib, Robert. *Forcing the Spring.* Covelo, CA: Island Press, 1993.

Hayden, Dolores. *Redesigning the American Dream: The Future of Housing, Work, and Family Life.* New York: W.W. Norton and Co., 1984.

Hurley, Andrew. *Environmental Inequalities.* Chapel Hill: UNC Press, 1996.

Jackson, Donald C. *Building the Ultimate Dam.* Lawrence: University of Kansas Press, 1995.

The Millennium Whole Earth Catalog. San Francisco: Harper, 1998.

Merchant, Carolyn. *Major Problems in American Environmental History.* New York: DC Heath, 1993.

Nash, Roderick. *Wilderness and the American Mind.* New Haven: Yale University Press, 1982.

Opie, John. *Nature's Nation.* New York: Harcourt, Brace, 1998.

Peterson, Robert W. *Boy Scouts: An American Adventure.* New York: American Heritage, 1985.

Reisner, Marc. *Cadillac Desert.* New York: Penguin, 1986.

Runte, Alfred. *National Parks: The American Experience.* Lincoln: University of Nebraska Press, 1987.

Sale, Kirkpatrick. *The Green Revolution* New York: Hill and Wang, 1993.

Schuyler, David. *Apostle of Taste: Andrew Jackson Downing, 1815-1852.* Baltimore: Johns Hopkins University Press, 1996.

Shabecoff, Philip. *A Fierce Green Fire.* New York: Hill and Wang, 1993.

Stevens, Joseph E. *Hoover Dam.* Norman: University of Oklahoma Press, 1988.

Worster, Donald. *Nature's Economy.* New York: Cambridge University Press, 1977.

Wright, Gwendolyn. *Building the Dream: A Social History of Housing in America.* Cambridge: MIT Press, 1992.

Internet Resources

A timeline of important people and events in environmental history
http://www.runet.edu/~wkovarik/hist1/
timeline.new.html

American Society for Environmental history: a gateway to information concerning past human interactions with nature
http://www2.h-net.msu.edu/~environ/

A chronology of environmental history by the Gale Group
http://www.gale.com/freresrc/earth
day2000/time.htm

Learn about participating in environmental projects at the national, regional, and local levels
http://www.cnr.berkeley.edu/departments/
espm/env-hist/

A history of environmental ethics
http://www.cep.unt.edu/novice.html

Sierra Club
http://www.sierraclub.org

The Nature Conservancy
http://nature.org

U.S. Fish and Wildlife Service
http://www.fws.gov

World Wildlife Fund
http://www.wwf.org

Brian Black
Pennsylvania State University, Altoona